Measurement and Evaluation for Physical Educators

Measurement and Evaluation for Physical Educators

Don R. Kirkendall
Kansas State University

Joseph J. Gruber
University of Kentucky

Robert E. Johnson
Kansas State University

wcb
Wm. C. Brown Company Publishers
Dubuque, Iowa

wcb

Wm. C. Brown
Chairman of the Board

Larry W. Brown
President, WCB Group

Wm. C. Brown Company Publishers,
College Division

Book Team
John Stout
Editor

William J. Evans
Designer

Patricia L. A. Hendricks
Production Editor

Mary Heller
Visual Research Manager

Lawrence E. Cremer
President

Raymond C. Deveaux
Vice President/Product Development

David Wm. Smith
Assistant Vice President/National Sales Manager

David A. Corona
Director of Production Development and Design

William A. Moss
Production Editorial Manager

Marilyn A. Phelps
Manager of Design

Consulting Editors
Physical Education—Aileene Lockhart
Texas Woman's University

Health—Robert Kaplan
The Ohio State University

Parks and Recreation—
David Gray
California State University,
Long Beach

contents

3 The Metric and English Systems of Measure (Optional)   14

4 Organizing and Analyzing Test Scores   27

preface

The evaluation of students in physical education involves a great deal of decision making on the part of the teacher. In order to make accurate and fair decisions that will be helpful to physical education students, teachers, and programs alike, a thorough knowledge and understanding of measurement and evaluaton is a must for the physical education teacher. The material presented in this text is intended to provide prospective physical educators with the necessary knowledge and understanding to make intelligent decisions about their students and programs.

The introductory chapter of this text presents a decision-making model that is useful in planning programs and providing individualized instruction. This model shows the link between measurement and evaluation and the rest of the instructional program.

The purposes and principles of measurement and evaluation are presented in the next chapter. It is important to know the specific reasons for measuring and evaluating, and we need guidelines for operating an evaluation program. Related to this is a teacher's desire to select or construct the best tests possible. Chapter 5 deals with the criteria to be used in the selection and construction of tests; Chapter 6 gives some guidance in the administration of the evaluation program, including the problem of grade assignment.

Anytime we have test scores, we must represent them compactly and fairly. Additionally, valuable information about a group or class of students can usually be gained through test scores if they are properly analyzed. Chapter 4 presents the statistical tools necessary for gaining such information from scores.

Chapters 7 through 11 present tests that might be used in an evaluation program. Great care was taken to select tests that can be practically administered by the teacher in a typical school setting.

Three chapters in this text are rarely, if ever, found in measurement and evaluation texts. These are Chapters 3, 11, and 12. It is evident that we must soon convert to the metric system of measures, and Chapter 3 describes how to go from the English to the metric system and vice versa. Also, throughout the text both English and metric units are given for each test presented in the hope that you will become familiar with the metric system. Finally, when norms are reported, they too are given in English and metric units.

Elementary physical education is now appropriately receiving a great deal of emphasis. Chapter 11, which deals with the evaluaton of elementary students, presents information that will be of great value to the elementary physical education teacher. Further, most physical education teachers must deal with students who have special problems, either mental or orthopedic. Some guidelines are given for evaluation in adapted physical education programs in Chapter 12.

A number of other unique features in this text are intended to assist the reader in the study of measurement and evaluation for physical educators. An introduction to computer utilization in measurement and evaluation is presented in Chapter 4, for example. Summary review questions, with reference to where the answers are found, are located at the end of each chapter. These questions identify the important concepts that should be acquired. Exercises are also found at the end of most chapters. Answers to the odd-numbered exercises are given so that you will know when you are on the right track. Also, references are provided for each chapter should there be a desire for more in-depth reading on particular topics.

Throughout the text, the emphasis is on practical application. The knowledge available about measurement and evaluation must be applied if it is to be of any real value. The last chapter of this book gives examples of two evaluation programs in physical education.

We hope that you will find this text informative, challenging, and interesting. With serious participation in the learning process, the knowledge you gain about measurement and evaluation will make you a better physical educator.

The authors are especially indebted to a number of individuals for their assistance in making this book possible. Several physical educators reviewed the manuscript through its various stages. We are grateful to Professor Tom Dobbs, Ball State University; Professor Elmo Roundy, Brigham Young University; Professor William Herman, Slippery Rock State College; Professor Owen J. Wilkinson, Ohio University; Professor Mary Jo Campbell, University of New Mexico; and Professor Art Wegner, Arizona State University, who assisted us with their helpful praise, criticisms, and suggestions. We thank the following individuals for allowing us to use photographs of them: Suzanna Folk, George Bell, Judy Logan, Eric Brooks, Pam Baker, Jay Gruber, Diane Beauchamp, Melissa and Randy Kirkendall, Melody Noland, and Paul McGurl. Thanks also to Ms. Sandy Forston, Mrs. Lorane Goin, and Ms. Kim Adams who greatly assisted in the typing of the manuscript. Finally, we are most grateful to our wives, Gloria, Lorene, and Juanita, and our children—Randy, Lissa, Mike, Jay, Kathy, Jody, Steven, and Kris—who provided the encouragement and understanding necessary for completing the manuscript.

introduction to measurement and evaluation

One of the most perplexing problems facing a teacher of physical education today is how to evaluate student performance fairly. Also, in this age of accountability teachers are compelled to justify objectively the existence and/or expansion of physical education programs. It is the intent of this text to provide you with the tools necessary for evaluating students and justifying programs of physical education.

When the term *evaluation* is mentioned, many people immediately think only about administering tests and assigning grades to students. While these are aspects of evaluation and are of major concern, evaluation covers a much broader range than just testing and grading. As will be seen, grading is not even the most important aspect of evaluation.

test, measurement, and evaluation

Before continuing further it is necessary to distinguish among three terms that are used commonly, but often wrongly. These three terms—*test, measurement,* and *evaluation*—are often incorrectly used interchangeably. They each have a definite meaning.

TEST: A test is an instrument used to gain information about individuals or objects. These instruments may be in the form of questions asked on paper or in interviews, requested physical performance, or observation of behavior through checklists or anecdotal records. However, regardless of the form, there are certain characteristics we should require of tests. These will be presented in chapter 5. Much of the rest of this text will be devoted to a presentation of tests useful to the physical education teacher.

MEASUREMENT: Measurement is the process of collecting information. It is through measurement that the present status of students is determined. Administering a test is part of the process of measurement. We usually think of measurement as the objective determination of a numerical score based on performance. The results of measurement need to be quantifiable in terms of time, distance, amount, or number correct. Unfortunately, most "measurements" in physical education are not pure. For example, instead of saying that the time recorded for the 50-yard dash measures speed, it might be better to state that the measurement procedure of administering the 50-yard dash yields a test score indicative of a person's speed.

EVALUATION: Evaluation is the process of determining the value or worth of collected data. Evaluation includes both tests and measurement. It might be thought of as the process that qualitatively appraises the quantitative data made available through measurement. Collected data are usually appraised so that a fair and informed decision can be made. (Is our program accomplishing stated objectives? Has the student made satisfactory progress? And so on.) These may be decisions about individual students, an entire class, course objectives, teaching methods, or a combination of these.

The interrelationship among the terms *test, measurement,* and *evaluation* can now be seen. Evaluation is all-encompassing. It reflects one's philosophies, goals, and objectives; these in turn determine the tests and measurements to be used. Measurement provides the means by which information pertinent to our philosophies, goals, and objectives is collected, and tests are the instruments used to gain the information. Finally, evaluation involves the appraisal of this information against standards. This appraisal tells us how well we have satisfied our philosophies, goals, and objectives.

summative and formative evaluation

As mentioned earlier, grading is one aspect of evaluation carried out by most teachers. (Unfortunately, it is often carried out very poorly.) Grading is an important task required in most school situations and must be conducted seriously and fairly. Material contained in the remainder of this text will aid you in the process of grading fairly. Grading is an example of one type of evaluation. This type of evaluation is called *summative evaluation.* It is usually conducted at the end of a unit, course, semester, or year. Issuing certificates or achievement badges is another example of summative evaluation. Evaluating the worth of a class is also summative evaluation.

Perhaps a more important type of evaluation in the teaching–learning process is *formative evaluation,* which provides information about a student's progress to the student and the teacher throughout a learning unit. In the process of formative evaluation, daily, on-the-spot information about a student's performance is obtained, evaluated, and immediately fed back to the student so that necessary adjustments in performance can be made. Practice with such feedback should enhance skill acquisition. Formative evaluation involves breaking down a learning unit into smaller parts; this allows both the teacher and student to identify precisely the parts of a task or performance that are in error and must be corrected. An example of this type of evaluation is use of videotape devices to learn physical skills.

objectives and evaluation

Whatever the type of evaluation—summative or formative—it must be conducted in terms of program goals and objectives. Goals and objectives determine what is to be measured and evaluated. Even more importantly, program objectives provide the very reasons for measuring and evaluating. In determining instructional objectives, we should move from general goals to specific behavioral and/or performance objectives.

Perhaps the most commonly stated general goals of physical education are the following ones expressed by Jay Nash.[1]

organic development

This goal involves physical fitness and the basic components of fitness, namely, muscular strength, power, and endurance, and cardiovascular endurance.

neuromuscular development. This goal involves sports skill, balance, flexibility, agility, coordination, and speed.

interpretive development. In physical education this goal involves knowing and understanding game rules, strategies, courtesies, and equipment.

emotional development. This goal involves such things as leadership, attitudes, and sportsmanship.

Numerous other sets of general physical education goals have been stated. Most are quite similar to these stated by Nash. Within the relatively recent trend in movement exploration, goals such as the development of creativity and/or individual awareness might also be developed. Regardless, the final selection of general goals and the relative emphasis given to them should depend on the teacher's philosophy, the institutional philosophy, and above all the needs of the students for whom a program is planned.

Once the general goals are decided upon, a teacher must move to teaching unit objectives and then to specific behavioral or performance objectives. These performance objectives state exactly what must be measured. The level of their specificity is a matter to be decided by the teacher. In all cases, performance objectives can be established for individual students as well as for an entire class. To see how one might move from general goals to specific performance objectives, examples involving two general goals are given.

Under the general goal of organic development, we might have for one semester the general objective of improving the physical fitness of the students in our class. Since cardiovascular endurance is a component of physical fitness, one objective would be to improve the students' cardiovascular endurance. Specifically, we may wish to improve our students' scores on a 12-minute run test that purports to measure cardiovascular endurance. Even more specifically, we could state the objective as being to have all students be able to run at least 1 mile in 12 minutes. This last statement is a behavioral or performance objective for the class. Of more value would be a performance objective for each student. For example, the performance objective for a student named Ben might be for him to run 1¾ miles in 12 minutes; for Jim, the objective might be to run 1¼ miles in the same time. The Cooper 12–minute run test should be administered at least at the end of the semester although it is best to administer it first at the beginning of the semester so that specific performance objectives can be realistically determined. That is, realistic improvement expectations can be set. Moving from a general goal to a performance objective can be shown diagrammatically as follows on page 4.

1. Jay B. Nash, *Physical Education: Interpretations and Objectives* (New York: A. S. Barnes, 1948).

Goal of all physical education programs —Organic development

to

General objective for a semester —Physical fitness

to

Identified behavior —Cardiovascular endurance component

to

Class performance objective —Ability to run at least 1 mile in 12 minutes
which requires the

to

What to test —Administration of Cooper's 12–minute run
test

If a unit on basketball is planned in a program, the general goal of neuromuscular development should receive considerable emphasis. A logical unit objective would then be to improve the basketball skill of the students. One basketball skill that needs to be developed is the ability to shoot free throws. If we administer a free-throw test consisting of shooting 20 free throws and find that, on the average, our students hit 60 percent of their free shots, one of our performance objectives might be to improve that shooting accuracy to 70 percent.

Some people feel that there are situations where the use of behavioral and performance objectives are not appropriate—for example, in the area of emotional development, specific behavioral and performance objectives are difficult to determine and express. Other professionals totally oppose any use of behavior and performance objectives. They argue that their use restricts student development since, when numerous performance objectives are identified, students simply practice the required tests until

Goal of most physical education programs —Neuromuscular development

to

General objective for unit —Basketball skill

to

Identified behavior —Free-throw shooting ability

to

Class performance objective —Improve free-throw shooting accuracy
from 60 percent to 70 percent
which requires the

to

What to test —Administration of a 20–free-throw test at
the beginning and end of unit

There would be numerous other behavioral and performance objectives for this unit. Some of these would deal with passing ability, dribbling ability, field-goal shooting ability, and so on. This is true of any objective for any unit.

they can pass them. This is *mastery learning,* which may be desirable in some situations, but is not a substitute for a complete instructional program. Expanded coverage of mastery learning is given in chapter 7.

evaluation in program planning

Evaluation procedures can and should be used by the teacher in making decisions about the appropriate program for individual students and classes. Knowledgeable physical educators approach the problem of program planning with a definite pattern of decision making. They will first establish general goals for their programs; these depend on the teacher's and institution's philosophies. The general goals provide the guidelines for assessing the initial level of students. Initial behavioral and performance objectives also need to be decided on. Then decisions are made about what to test, what tests to employ, and how to use the information derived from the tests. This information, once obtained, helps the teacher establish the priorities and specific objectives for each participant and for the total class.

Once the specific objectives have been set, the teacher must choose activities for the program that should achieve the objectives. Periodically retesting students on the same tests will yield information on their progress during their participation in the program. Then by comparing the test results with previous test results, the teacher will be able to decide if the level of each has improved, leveled, or regressed. Such a comparison will also help the teacher decide whether the program and its objectives are sufficient or should be changed. This process allows for the continuous modification of the program and/or its objectives.

This planning process is student-centered and requires the dynamic interaction of tests, measurements, and evaluations. Figure 1.1 is a diagrammatic model of the process.

Examination of Figure 1.1 reveals the interaction between the teacher or decision maker and the student. Since the planning process is participant-focused, it should be noted that the student is at the top of the planning model and moves through the tests, programs, and retest cycles while the deci-

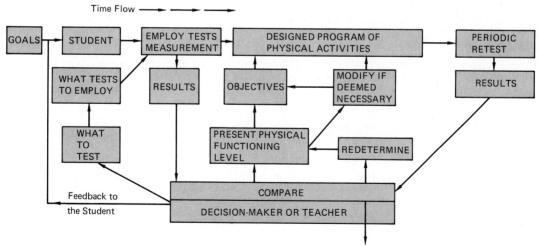

The present test results indicate the present level of each participant. A series of cycles will serve for continuous modification of the program and/or objectives.

Figure 1.1 Planning model in the decision-making process

sion maker or teacher is at the bottom of the planning model and responds as a guide for the participant. The teacher must determine what to test and what tests to employ. The tests are then applied and the results obtained. Evaluation of the test results helps the teacher set objectives and design a program of physical activities that should improve the present level of the student. The program is then applied. After a period of time, decided by the teacher, retests are applied and the results compared to the results of the first test. The teacher decides if the level of the participant has increased, leveled, or decreased. The teacher then gives feedback to the student, may modify the objectives, and, if necessary, may redesign the program of physical education. The new program is then applied and the cycle repeated. In an informal way, the cycle may occur one or more times in a day rather than just once in a unit, semester, or year. However, on a larger scale, the process should be conducted at the end of each unit, semester, and/or year.

Most good teachers have undoubtedly used this approach without ever formalizing it conceptually. This discussion simply puts it in writing so that perhaps others will see its value. It must be pointed out again that this approach is completely student-centered and does allow for individual student differences. Additionally, it provides a sensible means for changing a program instead of allowing it to become stagnant. This model will be used throughout this text. More importantly, the knowledge necessary for implementing it will be presented.

basic terminology

In the study of any subject, terms need to be defined in order to ensure that all concerned are speaking the same language. While the language of measurement and evaluation is not particularly complex, there are nonetheless several terms besides *test, measurement,* and *evaluation* that need to be explicitly defined. Some of these are given below.

Ability: Level of present performance—present status. For example, a student may be able to consistently score 7's on floor exercises in gymnastics.

Achievement: Accomplishment of an individual beyond a defined starting point. For example, a student who had an initial grip strength of 58 pounds and now has a score of 65 pounds has achieved an improvement in strength.

Anthropometric measurements: Body measurements of individuals. Examples are height, weight, and shoulder girth.

Classification: Arrangement of individuals into homogeneous (similar) or heterogeneous (dissimilar) groups on the basis of some common trait or ability. For example, wrestlers are classified for competition according to their weights.

Criterion: Basis for judging the worth of something for a specific purpose at a certain time.

Diagnosis: An analysis of the strengths and weaknesses of an individual in reference to certain traits. After administering a fitness test, a student might be found to have excellent speed, but lack sufficient muscular strength.

Motivation: Force or forces that drive an individual to ultimate achievement. A student may be driven to improve her fitness because she scored very low on a fitness test.

Objectivity: The degree to which different scorers of a test assign the same scores on the test.

Prediction: An estimation of future performance based on available facts. One might predict that on the basis of a skill test in tennis, a particular student should be the best varsity tennis player.

Reliability: The degree to which a test measures whatever it measures consistently. If students take a test more than once and score nearly the same each time, we say the test is highly reliable.

Standard: Minimum acceptable level of excellence an individual should reach in performing an activity at a certain time. Two types of standards are commonly used by teachers: *norm-referenced standards* and *criterion-referenced standards.* With norm-referenced standards, a student's performance is judged or evaluated in relation to the performances of some defined group. For example, one might state that Jane scored in the top third of all eighth graders who took a tennis test. With a criterion-referenced standard, student performance is compared to a level of performance set by the teacher. For example, a teacher may determine that a student must be able to perform at least three chins before being given credit on a fitness test.

Trait or characteristic: A distinguishing feature of an individual or group. For example, a class of students may all be right-handed.

Validity: The degree to which a test measures what it is supposed to measure. For example, if a test that is supposed to measure golfing ability does in fact do that very well, then we say it is a highly valid test.

summary review questions

1. What is a test? (*answer on p. 1*)

2. What is measurement? (*answer on pp. 1–2*)

3. What is evaluation? (*answer on p. 2*)

4. How do test, measurement, and evaluation differ? (*answer on p. 2*)

5. What is the main function of tests and measurements in evaluation? (*answer on pp. 2–3*)

6. Do testing and measuring assure that the physical education teacher will make an accurate and fair decision? (*answer on p. 5*)

7. The decision making model presented in this chapter suggests a definite pattern for making decisions. What is this pattern? (*answer on pp. 5–6*)

bibliography

Barrow, Harold M., and McGee, Rosemary. *A Practical Approach to Measurement in Physical Education.* 2d ed. Philadelphia: Lea & Febiger, 1971.

Baumgartner, Ted A., and Jackson, Andrew S. *Measurement for Evaluation in Physical Education.* Boston: Houghton Mifflin, 1975.

Bloom, B. S. "Toward a Theory of Testing Which Includes Measurement-Evaluation-Assessment." In *The Evaluation of Instruction: Issues and Problems,* edited by M. C. Wittrock and David E. Wiley, pp. 25–50. New York: Holt, Rinehart and Winston, 1970.

Bloom, B. S.,; Englehart, M. D.; Furst, E. J.; Hill, W. H.; and Krathwohl, D. R., eds. *A Taxonomy of Educational Objectives: Handbook 1, The Cognitive Domain.* New York: David McKay, 1956.

Bloom, B. S.; Hastings, J. T.; and Madaus, G. F. *Handbook on Formative and Summative Evaluation of Student Learning.* New York: McGraw-Hill, 1971.

Clarke, H. Harrison. *Application of Measurement to Health and Physical Education.* Englewood Cliffs, N.J.: Prentice-Hall, 1967.

Ebel, Robert L. *Measuring Educational Achievement.* Englewood Cliffs, N.J.: Prentice-Hall, 1973.

Ebel, Robert L. "The Social Consequences of Educational Testing." In *Readings in Educational and Psychological Measurement,* edited by Clinton I. Chase and H. Glenn Ludlow, pp. 26–31. Boston: Houghton Mifflin, 1966.

Harrow, Anita J. *A Taxonomy of the Psychomotor Domain.* New York: David McKay, 1972.

Jewett, A. E. et al. "Educational Change Through a Taxonomy for Writing Physical Education Objectives." *Quest* 16 (1971): 32–38.

Johnson, Barry L., and Nelson, Jack K. *Practical Measurements for Evaluation in Physical Education.* Minneapolis: Burgess, 1969.

Kibler, Robert J.; Baker, Larry L.; and Miles, David T. *Behavioral Objectives and Instruction.* Boston: Allyn and Bacon, 1970.

Krathwohl, D. R.; Bloom, B. S.; and Masia, B. *A Taxonomy of Educational Objectives: Handbook II, The Affective Domain.* New York: David McKay, 1964.

McCloy, Charles H., and Young, Norma D. *Tests and Measurements in Health and Physical Education.* New York: Appleton-Century-Crofts, 1954.

Mager, Robert F. *Preparing Instructional Objectives.* Palo Alto, Calif.: Fearon, 1962.

Mathews, Donald K. *Measurement in Physical Education.* 5th ed. Philadelphia: W. B. Saunders, 1978.

Safrit, Margaret. "Criterion-Referenced Measurement: Applications in Physical Education." *Motor Skills: Theory into Practice* 2, no. 1 (1977): 21–35.

Safrit, Margaret J. *Evaluation in Physical Education, Assessing Motor Behavior.* Englewood Cliffs, N.J.: Prentice-Hall, 1973.

Simon, G. B. "Comments on Implications of Criterion-Referenced Measurement." *Journal of Educational Measurement* 6 (1969):259–60.

There must be a purpose for everything done in a physical education program. This is certainly true of program measurement and evaluation. A measurement and evaluation program without purpose becomes an end in itself and cannot be justified. If a test is given, it must be given for an educationally sound reason and not just because it is a popular thing to do.

purposes of measurement and evaluation

Measurement and evaluation can serve several purposes, some of which are presented here. Not all of these purposes will be appropriate for all situations at all times. It is hoped that the relationship between these purposes and the decision-making process presented in chapter 1 will be evident.

determine status

The most commonly stated purpose of measurement and evaluation is to determine the status, progress, or achievement of students. This determination may be used for the assignment of grades, the promotion from one grade to another, or the elevation of a student to the next level of instruction.

classification

There are times when we need to arrange students into homogeneous or heterogeneous groups on the basis of some trait or ability. Thus, a purpose of measurement and evaluation may be to classify students. Some common types of classification are those made on the basis of a student's grade level or age, medical condition, body structure (height and weight), functional ability (skill), sex, and interest. In general, the goal of classification is to improve the instructional setting.

selection

Measurement and evaluation are useful for selecting a few students from many. We may, for example, select varsity team members, class leaders, or students who need special attention physically, socially, or emotionally.

guidance and diagnosis

This purpose is closely linked with the decision-making process discussed in chapter 1. A need exists to assess continually the strengths and weaknesses of students, so their development can be guided through physical education programs designed to meet their needs. Guidance should be thought of as a way of giving systematic assistance to students.

motivation

If properly administered, evaluation can be a positive motivational process. Likewise, the unwise use of tests and evaluation can result in negative motivation. Students can be motivated to improve their performance by being informed and counseled about their present level as indicated by test performance. In connection with this, it is hoped that through evaluation and counseling, students will become self-motivated to participate in physical activity outside the physical education instructional program.

maintenance of standards

A quality evaluation program helps maintain standards of performance expected of students. We can determine if a program is providing students with instruction that allows and motivates them to achieve at desired levels. In other words, measurement and evaluation allow us to determine if we are meeting our objectives. If we are not,

then the instructional program needs to be revised. Not only what is being taught will be evaluated but also how it is taught will be scrutinized. This evaluation must be an ongoing process and can be effectively done only if it is planned. The decision-making model provides the framework for this purpose.

furnishing educational experiences

The student and teacher should learn from the evaluation process. The student should learn about herself or himself as well as about the activity being evaluated. The teacher should not only learn something about the student, but also learn valuable information about his or her teaching methods, the activity, and its effect on the students.

conduct of research

Research is a means by which a body of knowledge is expanded. Research depends on precise and accurate information being gathered through carefully planned measurement procedures. Data gathered for research purposes must be evaluated for their significance. Thus, another important purpose of measurement and evaluation is to provide the tools for conducting research.

principles of measurement and evaluation

A principle should be thought of as a guiding rule for action. If we are to have a successful evaluation program, we must be cognizant of certain principles. These are presented and discussed as follows.

A measurement and evaluation program must be compatible with one's philosophy of life and education. It is inconceivable to think that one would conduct a program at variance with his or her basic beliefs. Related to this is the principle that *measurement and evaluation must recognize an institutional philosophy.* For example, if a school says grades will be given for all classes, then teachers must make provision for this in their programs. However, if this or some other basic belief or policy of the school is in strong conflict with a teacher's own philosophy, then he or she must either change the philosophy, find a way of resolving the difference, or find another place to teach.

In order to evaluate effectively, all measurement must be conducted with program objectives in mind. We need to know what our objectives are before tests are administered if we plan to evaluate the results of those tests against objectives. In all aspects of evaluation, we must keep our objectives in mind. Otherwise, we will end up with a testing program with no direction or purpose.

Tests are a part of measurement; measurement is but one phase of evaluation. Evaluation includes both tests and measurement. However, as pointed out in chapter 1, evaluation is much broader than just tests and measurement. It is the very essence of decision-making. Data collected through measurement procedures are appraised for their educational worth.

Measurement and evaluation must be conducted and supervised by trained people. That is why you are enrolled in a measurement and evaluation class and why you are studying (we hope) this text. Not just anyone can effectively administer an evaluation program. It is too serious a matter to leave to untrained personnel. After all, decisions are made about perhaps the most important aspect of children's lives, their education. In order to administer an effective physical education evaluation program, a teacher must be proficient both in what is to be taught and in how to evaluate what is taught.

The results of measurement and evaluation must be interpreted in terms of the whole individual: social, mental, physical, and psychological aspects. If a student performs poorly on a test, the conscientious teacher will look beyond the score and try to determine the reasons for such a poor performance. The teacher who cares will attempt to find out the reasons and then provide assistance when necessary and possible. The reasons for poor performance on a physical test may be other than physical. If the reason is physical, however, the good teacher will wish to find out exactly where the difficulty lies in order to improve the student's performance.

Measurement and evaluation are tools of educational activity and have a place in education. Evaluation is not an educational fad. It must be an integral part of the education process, a tool to aid in the accomplishment of educational goals. It should be recognized, however, that there are other things in physical education besides measurement. Some people have operated physical education programs that were nothing more than testing programs. This extreme is just as unsound as having no measurement at all. In general, approximately 10 percent of instructional time spent on measurement can be justified.

Measurement and evaluation rest on the premise that whatever exists, exists in amount and hence can be measured. In other words, anything we include in our physical education program should lend itself to sound definition and thus be measurable. There are, of course, areas in physical education that are not as well defined as we might like. The area of social-personal development, which includes such things as sportsmanship, socialization, and emotional development, is one of those that is not exactly defined. As a result, our measurements in this area are not very precise and caution should be taken when using them. However, this important area should not be ignored—rather the limitations of the measurements should be recognized.

We must never lose sight of the fact that *no test or measurement is perfect.* There are times when people acquire such faith in their tests and measurements that they begin to believe they are infallible. We must always use the best tests possible, but must always realize that errors are likely. Sound judgment must always prevail in the use of tests.

There is no substitute for judgment in measurement and evaluation. This is perhaps the most important principle of measurement and evaluation. As a matter of fact, evaluation is judgment. Sometimes people attempt to substitute objective measures for judgment. We definitely strive for objectivity; however, objective measures can never take the place of professional judgment. If there were no place for judgment in measurement and evaluation, then the teacher could be replaced by a technician or a machine. On the other hand, judgments made without substantiating data are also unacceptable. Measurement provides the data that allow us to make the best judgment or decisions possible.

If students' initial abilities are not measured, then we have no knowledge about their achievement in the physical education program. It is not likely that we will be able to provide the type of program students need if we do not know where they are starting from. Also, we cannot determine what students learn or achieve if we do not know where they started. Measuring students' abilities only at the end of a unit, class, or semester tells only where they are at that point. It tells nothing about the effects the program had on them. In other words, if we do not measure both at the beginning and at the end, the worth of our instructional methods and materials will remain unknown.

People sometimes argue that the use of tests creates a deadly uniformity in teaching and mechanizes teachers and teaching. We hope it is obvious to the reader that *the use of tests need not produce deadly uniformity, or mechanize teachers and teaching.* Should the teacher ignore the principle of there being no substitute for judgment, then perhaps these things could occur. However, just the opposite should occur for the serious-minded, well-prepared teacher. Through tests, measurement, and evaluation the possibility of a program individualized for each student is greatly enhanced. The evaluation model presented in chapter 1 emphasizes continual change and the importance of meeting individual student needs.

Always use the most valid, reliable, and objective tests possible. The terms *validity, reliability,* and *objectivity* are further explained in chapter 5. Here we are simply stating that we must always use tests that are fair. Tests should measure what they claim to measure consistently and should be scored the same regardless of who is doing the scoring. As stated earlier, no test is perfect, so no test will be perfectly valid, reliable, and objective. However, we must use the best available and continually search for improving our tools of measurement.

summary review questions

1. Why should the physical education teacher continually assess the strengths and weaknesses of the students under his or her direction? (*answer on pp. 9–10*)

2. What types of things should a student and teacher learn from the implementation of a quality measurement and evaluation program? (*answer on pp. 1–10*)

3. Why must we have clearly in mind our own philosophy of life and education, our general objectives, and the institutional goals before determining what factors to test? (*answer on pp. 10–11*)

4. Why must measurement and evaluation be conducted and supervised by trained people? (*answer on p. 11*)

5. Some physical educators acquire such faith in their tests and measurements that they begin to believe they are infallible. What have these physical educators lost sight of? (*answer on p. 12*)

6. What is the most important principle presented in this chapter? (*answer on p. 12*)

7. A board of education in a particular school system, due to budget problems, has decided to drop the physical education program. They have taken the position that physical education is a fringe benefit and not essential to the education of the students. As one board member put it, "Physical education seems to be fun and games and all we really need to do is have recess time and allow the students to take a break. We can have our regular classroom teachers organize some physical activities for fun and relaxation and supervise the program. We need not pay full-time physical educators money for the same thing our regular classroom teachers can do." However, before eliminating the physical educa-tion program the board has decided to call the physical educators into a meet-ing to explain why they, the board, are taking this position. You are one of the physical educators in the system. As a professional, how would you defend your profession in front of this board of education?

bibliography

Barrow, Harold M., and McGee, Rosemary. *A Practical Approach to Measurement in Physical Education.* 2d ed. Philadelphia: Lea & Febiger, 1971.

Baumgartner, Ted A., and Jackson, Andrew S. *Measurement for Evaluation in Physical Education.* Boston: Houghton Mifflin, 1975.

Clarke, H. Harrison. *Application of Measurement to Health and Physical Education.* Englewood Cliffs, N.J.: Prentice-Hall, 1967.

Ebel, Robert L. "The Social Consequences of Educational Testing." In *Readings in Educational and Psychological Measurement,* edited by Clinton I. Chase and H. Glenn Ludlow, pp. 26–31. Boston: Houghton Mifflin, 1966.

Johnson, Barry L., and Nelson, Jack K. *Practical Measurements for Evaluation in Physical Education,* 2d ed. Minneapolis: Burgess, 1974.

Larson, Leonard A., and Yocom, Rachael D. *Measurement and Evaluation in Physical, Health, and Recreation Education.* St. Louis: C. V. Mosby, 1951.

Mathews, Donald K. *Measurement in Physical Education.* 5th ed. Philadelphia: W. B. Saunders, 1978.

McCloy, Charles H., and Young, Norma D. *Tests and Measurements in Health and Physical Education.* New York: Appleton-Century-Crofts, 1954.

Safrit, Margaret J. *Evaluation in Physical Education, Assessing Motor Behavior.* Englewood Cliffs, N.J.: Prentice-Hall, 1973.

the metric and english systems of measure (optional)

There are two widely used systems of measure in this world today, the metric system and the English system. Although the metric system is the official international measuring system, the English system is still in use in the United States. However, it is important to begin thinking in metric units since the official U.S. system will soon be the metric system, requiring the physical education teacher to mark court dimensions, weigh students, and measure performance using the metric units of measure. The basic metric units of measure are convenient to use because they are based on unity; all other measures become larger or smaller than unity through multiples of ten.

There are many different units of measure, but we will consider only those the physical education teacher is most likely to use in measuring various physical performances in the physical education class. These are units of distance, time, speed, acceleration, weight, force, area, pressure, and temperature. They are discussed, using both the metric and English systems of measure, along with a method for converting from one system to the other or equating within a single system.

distance

The basic method for converting from one system to the other or within a single system is the same for all units of measure. This being the case, we will introduce the conversion method using units of distance.

The fundamental unit for distance in the metric system is the meter (m); the fundamental unit for distance in the English system is the foot (ft.).

Figure 3.1 is a relative comparison of the distances representing the meter stick and the foot ruler.

Figure 3.1 Relative comparison of the meter (m) and foot (ft.)

Table 3.1 shows metric system distance equivalents.

Table 3.2 shows English system distance equivalents.

Table 3.3 shows conversion factors for distance.

Converting from one system to another or changing units within a system is not as difficult as it may seem. First, determine the unit of measure available. Second, determine what you wish to convert the available unit into, remembering that the conversion must be between like units such as distance to distance, force to force, temperature to temperature, and so on (never between unlike units such as distance to time, force to pressure, speed to acceleration). Third, find the conversion factor value in one system that is applicable to the other system or find the equivalent value within a system, and eliminate what is not wanted (that is, cancel out the unwanted literal values), leaving the literal value that is wanted. For example, 1 m = 100 cm is an important statement because the numbers 1 and 100 are the number values of the equivalence and m and cm are the literal values of the equivalence. The literal value of a unit of measure is the name of the unit of measure while the number value is how many of the literal values were used in a measurement. Saying (a) 1 m = 100 cm is the same as saying (b) 1 m per 100 cm, which in turn is the same as saying (c) 1 m/100 cm. So (a), (b), and (c) are but different ways of writing the same statement. Likewise, 100 cm = 1 m is 100 cm per 1 m, which in turn is 100 cm/1 m. This concept is very important, so get in the habit of writing equivalents or conversions in fraction form. The fraction form of equivalents or conversions shows you what must be done to get the available measure into the unit of measure desired.

Table 3.1   Metric System Distance Equivalents

1 meter (m) = 100 centimeters (cm)
1 meter (m) = 1000 millimeters (mm)
1 kilometer (km) = 1000 meters (m)

Table 3.2   English System Distance Equivalents

1 foot (ft.) = 12 inches (in.)
1 yard (yd.) = 3 feet (ft.)
1 mile (mi.) = 1760 yards (yd.)

Table 3.3   Conversion Factors for Distance

1 meter (m) = 3.28 feet (ft.)
1 inch (in.) = 2.54 centimeters (cm)
1 mile (mi.) = 1.609 kilometers (km)

The Metric and English Systems of Measure (Optional)   15

Following are some example problems using the fraction form of equivalents and conversions. Study these problems carefully. See what is being done because this method of converting from one system to another and finding equivalents within a system is used extensively throughout this chapter. Once you have mastered the method, going from the English system to the metric system, from the metric system to the English system, and finding equivalents within a system will not be a problem.

Example Problem 1: A student being tested in a physical education class did a standing broad jump of 2.430 meters (m). What distance did the student jump in: (a) centimeters, (b) feet, and (c) yards?

Solution: (a) First we place 2.430 m over 1 in the following manner: 2.430 m/1 (note that 2.430 m/1 = 2.430 m). This point may seem of little importance, but it places our literal value, meters (m), in the numerator (that part of a fraction above the line) so we can eliminate (cancel out) the literal value we do not want. Next we find the metric system distance equivalent from Table 3.1: 1 meter = 100 centimeters (cm). We then write this equivalent in fractional form such that we eliminate meters (m) and leave centimeters (cm). By examining the 2.430 m/1 and the equivalent, we can see that the meters (m) of the equivalent should go in the denominator (that part of the fraction that is below the line) and the centimeters (cm) in the numerator. Writing 2.430 m/1 × 100 cm/1 m permits us to cancel out the literal value we do not want (m) and leaves the literal value we do want (cm). Multiplying through our numerical values and carrying through the literal value remaining gives us the solution to the problem:

$$\frac{2.430 \, \cancel{m}}{1} \times \frac{100 \, cm}{1 \, \cancel{m}} = 243.0 \, cm$$

We can carry out this procedure several times within the same problem, eliminating the literal values we don't want until we have only the one literal value we do want. For example, examine solution (c) of this problem where we are asked to convert 2.430 m to yards (yd.).

(b) $\dfrac{2.430 \, \cancel{m}}{1} \times \dfrac{3.28 \, ft.}{1 \, \cancel{m}} = 7.97 \, ft.$

(c) $\dfrac{2.430 \, \cancel{m}}{1} \times \dfrac{3.28 \, \cancel{ft.}}{1 \, \cancel{m}} \times \dfrac{1 \, yd.}{3 \, \cancel{ft.}} = 2.66 \, yd.$

Example Problem 2: A physical education student measured the height of another student and secured a value of 172.7 centimeters (cm). What is the height of the student in: (a) inches, (b) feet and inches, and (c) meters?

Solution:

(a) $\dfrac{172.7 \, \cancel{cm}}{1} \times \dfrac{1 \, in.}{2.54 \, \cancel{cm}} = 67.99 \, in. = 68 \, in.$

(b) $\dfrac{68 \, \cancel{in.}}{1} \times \dfrac{ft.}{12 \, \cancel{in.}} = 5.6666 \, ft. = 5.67 \, ft.$

$\dfrac{0.67 \, \cancel{ft.}}{1} \times \dfrac{12 \, in.}{\cancel{ft.}} = 8.04 \, in. = 8 \, in.$

$5 \, ft. + 8 \, in. = 5 \, ft. \, 8 \, in.$

(c) $\dfrac{172.7 \, \cancel{cm}}{1} \times \dfrac{1 \, m}{100 \, \cancel{cm}} = 1.727 \, m$

As these examples show, solving such problems is a simple matter of determining what measured value you have and what value you want, then setting up the fractional equivalent or conversion to cancel out the literal value you do not want and leave the literal value you do want. This method also tells what operation—that is, multiply or divide—to use with the number values.

time

The fundamental unit for time, the second (sec.), is the same in the metric and

Table 3.4   English and Metric System Time Equivalents

1 hour (hr.) = 60 minutes (min.)
1 minute (min.) = 60 seconds (sec.)
1 kilosecond (ksec) = 1000 seconds (sec.)
1 second (sec.) = 10 deciseconds (dsec)
1 second (sec.) = 100 centiseconds (csec)
1 second (sec.) = 1000 milliseconds (msec)

English systems. The instrument used most often by a physical education teacher to measure time is the hand-controlled stopwatch. This type of stopwatch usually measures time to the nearest tenth of a second. Other time measurements commonly used are the hour (hr.) and minute (min.). Table 3.4 shows English and metric system time equivalents.

Example Problem 3: A particular physical education class went on a 10–mile run-walk. The average time for the class was 1 hr. 39 min. 54.8 sec. What is the average class time in: (a) hours, (b) minutes, and (c) seconds?

Solution:

(a) 1 hr. = 1 hr.

$$\frac{39 \ \text{min.}}{1} \times \frac{\text{hr.}}{60 \ \text{min.}} = 0.65 \ \text{hr.}$$

$$\frac{54.8 \ \text{sec.}}{1} \times \frac{1 \ \text{min.}}{60 \ \text{sec.}} \times \frac{1 \ \text{hr.}}{60 \ \text{min.}} = 0.015 \ \text{hr.}$$

1 hr. + 0.65 hr. + 0.015 hr. = *1.665 hr.*

(b) $\frac{1 \ \text{hr.}}{1} \times \frac{60 \ \text{min.}}{1 \ \text{hr.}} = 60 \ \text{min.}$

39 min. = 39 min.

$$\frac{54.8 \ \text{sec.}}{1} \times \frac{1 \ \text{min.}}{60 \ \text{sec.}} = 0.91 \ \text{min.}$$

60 min. + 39 min. + 0.91 min.
= *99.91 min.*

(c) $\frac{1 \ \text{hr.}}{1} \times \frac{60 \ \text{min.}}{1 \ \text{hr.}} \times \frac{60 \ \text{sec.}}{1 \ \text{min.}} = 3600 \ \text{sec.}$

$$\frac{39 \ \text{min.}}{1} \times \frac{60 \ \text{sec.}}{1 \ \text{min.}} = 2340 \ \text{sec.}$$

54.8 sec. = 54.8 sec.

3600 sec. + 2340 sec. + 54.8 sec.
= *5994.8 sec.*

Example Problem 4: The average response time to a light stimuli of a particular physical education class taking a kinesiology course at the university level was found to be 169 milliseconds (msec). The average response time of the class to a sound stimuli was found to be 147 msec. What is the average response time of the class to sight and sound stimuli in: (a) centiseconds, (b) deciseconds, (c) seconds, and (d) minutes?

Solution: (a) $\frac{169 \ \text{msec}}{1} \times \frac{1 \ \text{sec.}}{1000 \ \text{msec}} \times \frac{100 \ \text{csec}}{1 \ \text{sec.}} = 16.9 \ csec \ (light)$

$$\frac{147 \ \text{msec}}{1} \times \frac{1 \ \text{sec.}}{1000 \ \text{msec}} \times \frac{100 \ \text{csec}}{1 \ \text{sec.}} = 14.7 \ csec \ (sound)$$

(b) $\frac{169 \ \text{msec}}{1} \times \frac{1 \ \text{sec.}}{1000 \ \text{msec}} \times \frac{10 \ \text{dsec}}{1 \ \text{sec.}} = 1.69 \ dsec \ (light)$

$$\frac{147 \ \text{msec}}{1} \times \frac{1 \ \text{sec.}}{1000 \ \text{msec}} \times \frac{10 \ \text{dsec}}{1 \ \text{sec.}} = 1.47 \ dsec \ (sound)$$

(c) $\dfrac{169 \ \cancel{msec}}{1} \times \dfrac{1 \text{ sec.}}{1000 \ \cancel{msec}} = 0.169 \text{ sec. (light)}$

$\dfrac{147 \ \cancel{msec}}{1} \times \dfrac{1 \text{ sec.}}{1000 \ \cancel{msec}} = 0.147 \text{ sec. (sound)}$

(d) $\dfrac{169 \ \cancel{msec}}{1} \times \dfrac{1 \ \cancel{sec.}}{1000 \ \cancel{msec}} \times \dfrac{1 \text{ min.}}{60 \ \cancel{sec.}} = 0.00281 \text{ min. (light)}$

$\dfrac{147 \ \cancel{msec}}{1} \times \dfrac{1 \ \cancel{sec.}}{1000 \ \cancel{msec}} \times \dfrac{1 \text{ min.}}{60 \ \cancel{sec.}} = 0.00245 \text{ min. (sound)}$

Many tests in physical education use the time unit of measure. Some tests determine how much time it takes to do a given physical act. Some tests use a controlled constant amount of time as the period in which to perform a given physical act. Other tests use the time unit of measure to determine the acceleration or speed at which a given physical performance is accomplished.

speed

Speed is defined as distance per time. That is, speed is measured by a unit of distance divided by a unit of time. Most tests by a physical education teacher that involve speed are a measure of average speed. Average speed is defined as the total distance divided by the total time it took to travel that distance. Only rarely if ever will a student being tested run or perform a given physical act at a constant speed over a measured distance. The speed of the student will vary throughout the run or physical act. Therefore, we usually measure average speed.

$$\text{average speed} = \frac{\text{total distance}}{\text{total time}}$$

Example Problem 5: A student in a physical education class ran the 100-yard dash in 11.2 seconds. What is the average speed of this student?

Solution:

$$\text{average speed} = \frac{\text{total distance}}{\text{total time}}$$
$$= \frac{100 \text{ yd.}}{11.2 \text{ sec.}}$$
$$= \frac{8.93 \text{ yd.}}{1 \text{ sec.}}$$

Since the distance and time units of measure are used to calculate average speed, you should refer to Tables 3.1, 3.2, 3.3, and 3.4 to secure the numerical and literal values for equivalence and conversion.

Example Problem 6: Sprinter A ran the 100-yard dash in 9.0 seconds while sprinter B ran the 100-meter dash in 10.0 seconds. Determine: (a) the average speed of sprinter A in miles per hour, (b) the average speed of sprinter B in miles per hour, and (c) which sprinter had the fastest average speed.

Solution:

(a) average speed (sprinter A)
$$= \frac{\text{total distance}}{\text{total time}}$$
$$= \frac{100 \text{ yds.}}{9.0 \text{ sec.}} = \frac{11.11 \text{ yds.}}{1 \text{ sec.}}$$

$$\frac{11.11 \ \cancel{yd.}}{1 \ \cancel{sec.}} \times \frac{1 \text{ mi.}}{1760 \ \cancel{yd.}} \times \frac{60 \ \cancel{sec.}}{1 \ \cancel{min.}} \times \frac{60 \ \cancel{min.}}{1 \text{ hr.}} = \frac{22.73 \text{ mi.}}{1 \text{ hr.}}$$

(b) average speed (sprinter B)
$$= \frac{\text{total distance}}{\text{total time}}$$
$$= \frac{100 \text{ m}}{10 \text{ sec.}} = \frac{10 \text{ m}}{1 \text{ sec.}}$$

$$\frac{10 \ \cancel{m}}{1 \ \cancel{sec.}} \times \frac{3.28 \ \cancel{ft.}}{1 \ \cancel{m}} \times \frac{1 \ \cancel{yd.}}{3 \ \cancel{ft.}} \times \frac{1 \text{ mi.}}{1760 \ \cancel{yd.}}$$
$$\times \frac{60 \ \cancel{sec.}}{1 \ \cancel{min.}} \times \frac{60 \ \cancel{min.}}{1 \text{ hr.}} = \frac{22.36 \text{ mi.}}{1 \text{ hr.}}$$

(c) Sprinter A had an average speed of 22.73 miles per hour while sprinter B had an average speed of 22.36 miles per hour. Sprinter A had the faster average speed.

Since most physical performances do not involve a constant speed but rather a change in speed, we should try to understand acceleration.

acceleration

Unbalanced forces cause a change in speed. Because acceleration is caused by unbalanced forces, it is defined for practical purposes in this text, as a change in speed over a given amount of time.

$$\text{acceleration} = \frac{\text{change in distance per time (speed)}}{\text{time it took to make the speed change}}$$

$$\text{acceleration} = \frac{\text{distance/time}}{\text{time}} = \frac{\text{distance}}{\text{time} \times \text{time}}$$
$$= \frac{\text{distance}}{(\text{time})^2}$$

Suppose a physical education teacher wants to measure the change in speed of one of the students in the class. The student is to start out of starting blocks and sprint as fast as possible for 50 yards. Since the student starts at zero speed in the blocks and will accelerate—that is, continually change the speed at which the sprint is being done, for a period of at least 3 seconds, the physical education instructor decides to determine the distance the student runs in the first second, the distance the student runs in the second second, and finally the distance the student runs in the third second. The physical education teacher knows the student will be changing the speed of the run, and she wants to know what the change in speed is for each second. She finds the student travels 8 feet in the first second, 24 feet in the second second, and 40 feet in the

third second. The average speed of the student in the first second is $\frac{8 \text{ ft.}}{1 \text{ sec.}}$, the average speed in the second second is $\frac{24 \text{ ft.}}{1 \text{ sec.}}$, and the average speed in the third second is $\frac{40 \text{ ft.}}{1 \text{ sec.}}$. The change of speed from the first second to the second second is $\frac{24 \text{ ft.}}{1 \text{ sec.}} - \frac{8 \text{ ft.}}{1 \text{ sec.}} = 16$ ft./sec. for a second of time, which gives an acceleration of $\frac{16 \text{ ft./sec.}}{\text{sec.}} = \frac{16 \text{ ft.}}{\text{sec.}^2}$. The change in speed from the second second to the third second is $\frac{40 \text{ ft.}}{1 \text{ sec.}} - \frac{24 \text{ ft.}}{1 \text{ sec.}} = 16$ ft./sec. for a second of time, which gives an acceleration of $\frac{16 \text{ ft./sec.}}{\text{sec.}} = \frac{16 \text{ ft.}}{\text{sec.}^2}$. The student is changing the speed of the run at 16 ft./sec. for each second of time. Figure 3.2 is a graphic representation of the first 3 seconds of the sprint by the student coming out of the blocks.

The acceleration of the student can also be determined by:

$$\text{acceleration} = \frac{2 \times \text{total distance}}{(\text{total time})^2}$$

$$\text{acceleration} = \frac{2 \times 72 \text{ ft.}}{(3 \text{ sec.})^2} = \frac{144 \text{ ft.}}{9 \text{ sec.}^2} = \frac{16 \text{ ft.}}{1 \text{ sec.}^2}$$
$$= \frac{16 \text{ ft./sec.}}{\text{sec.}}$$

Since we are dealing with the units of distance and time in acceleration, Tables 3.1, 3.2, 3.3, and 3.4 may be used to secure the numerical and literal values for equivalence and conversion.

Example Problem 7: In a physical education class a test was being performed by having each student start in a sitting position and climb a 20-foot rope hand over hand. One particular student did the climb in 3.2 seconds. What is the: (a) acceleration produced in ft./sec.² and (b) acceleration produced in m/sec.²?

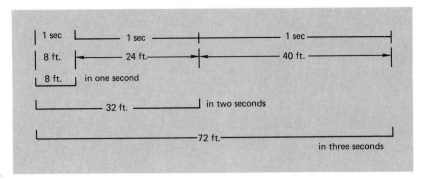

Figure 3.2   Graphic representation of acceleration for three seconds

Solution:

(a)   acceleration $= \dfrac{2 \times \text{total distance}}{(\text{total time})^2}$

$= \dfrac{2 \times 20 \text{ ft.}}{(3.2 \text{ sec.})^2} = \dfrac{40 \text{ ft.}}{10.24 \text{ sec.}^2} = \dfrac{3.9 \text{ ft.}}{1 \text{ sec.}^2}$

(b) $\dfrac{3.9 \text{ ft.}}{1 \text{ sec.}^2} \times \dfrac{1 \text{ m}}{3.28 \text{ ft.}} = \dfrac{1.19 m}{1 \text{ sec.}^2}$

Example Problem 8: A student in a physical education class, using a standing start, accelerated $\dfrac{4 \text{ m}}{1 \text{ sec.}^2}$. What is this acceleration in:

(a)   feet per sec.² and (b) yards per sec.²?
    Solution:

(a) $\dfrac{4 \text{ m}}{1 \text{ sec.}^2} \times \dfrac{3.28 \text{ ft.}}{1 \text{ m}} = \dfrac{13.12 \text{ ft.}}{\text{sec.}^2}$

(b) $\dfrac{13.12 \text{ ft.}}{\text{sec.}^2} \times \dfrac{1 \text{ yd.}}{3 \text{ ft.}} = \dfrac{4.37 \text{ yd.}}{\text{sec.}^2}$

weight

Weight is a force. It is the force the earth puts on objects and is usually measured by an instrument called a "scale." The metric scale is marked in kilogram weight units; the English scale is marked in pounds.
    Table 3.5 shows metric system weight equivalents.

Table 3.6 shows English system weight equivalents.
    Table 3.7 shows conversion factors for weight.

Table 3.5	Metric System Weight Equivalents

1 kilogram weight (kg wt) = 1000 gram weights (gm wt)

1 gram weight (gm wt) = 1000 milligram weights (mg wt)

Table 3.6	English System Weight Equivalents

1 pound (lb.) = 16 ounces (oz.)

1 ton = 2000 pounds (lb.)

Table 3.7	Conversion Factors for Weight

1 kilogram weight (kg wt) = 2.2 pounds (lb.)

1 gram weight (gm wt) = 0.0352 ounce (oz.)

Example Problem 9: A student weighs 90 kg. wt. What is the weight of this student in pounds?

Solution:

$$\frac{90\,\cancel{kg\ wt}}{1} \times \frac{2.2\ \text{lb.}}{1\,\cancel{kg\ wt}} = 198\ lb.$$

Example Problem 10: A high school shot put weighs 12 pounds, and the college shot put weighs 16 pounds. What is the weight of:
(a) the high school shot put in kg wt, and
(b) the college shot put in kg wt?

Solution:

(a) $\dfrac{12\,\cancel{lb.}}{1} \times \dfrac{1\ \text{kg wt}}{2.2\,\cancel{lb.}} = 5.45\,kg\ wt$

(b) $\dfrac{16\,\cancel{lb.}}{1} \times \dfrac{1\ \text{kg wt}}{2.2\,\cancel{lb.}} = 7.27\,kg\ wt$

Weight is a special type of force resulting from the pull of the earth's gravity. There are other forces: the force we apply to lift an object, the force we apply to push or pull an object, and the force we apply to cause or prevent the motion of an object.

force

The force we need to apply to an object to lift it against the pull of gravity must be greater than the weight of the object or the object will not move. The force we need to apply to an object to push or pull it must be greater than the force of friction between the object surface and the surface upon which it rests, or the object will not move. In other words, force causes or prevents the motion of an object.

Most instruments used in physical education to measure force—that is, the force applied to the instruments—are spring scale devices that are calibrated to read directly in kilogram weights or pounds.

Force units of measure are the same units used in measuring weight. Tables 3.5,

3.6, and 3.7 may be used to secure the numerical and literal values for equivalence and conversion.

Example Problem 11: Testing stations were established in the gymnasium of a school. One of the stations tested the grip strength (that force applied to the instrument) of the student's dominant hand by utilizing a hand dynamometer. One particular student registered a 50-pound pull. What is the grip strength of this student in: (a) kg wt and (b) gm wt?

Solution:

(a) $\dfrac{50\,\cancel{lb.}}{1} \times \dfrac{1\ \text{kg wt}}{2.2\,\cancel{lb.}} = 22.72\,kg\ wt$

(b) $\dfrac{22.73\,\cancel{kg\ wt}}{1} \times \dfrac{1000\ \text{gm wt}}{1\,\cancel{kg\ wt}}$
$$= 22,730\,gm\ wt$$

Example Problem 12: A student doing a chin up during a physical education class weighed 74.5 kg wt. It took 75 kg wt force to accomplish the chin up. What was the force applied to the weight of the student in pounds to accomplish the chin up?

Solution:

$$\frac{75\,\cancel{kg\ wt}}{1} \times \frac{2.2\ \text{lb.}}{1\,\cancel{kg\ wt}} = 165\ lbs.$$

Force may cause an object to move or prevent that object from moving. When force is applied to a given surface area we can calculate the resulting force per area.

area

Area is always expressed in terms of some distance squared: meters squared (m^2), centimeters squared (cm^2), feet squared ($ft.^2$), inches squared ($in.^2$), and so on.

Table 3.8 shows metric system area equivalents.

Table 3.9 shows English system area equivalents.

Table 3.8   Metric System Area Equivalents

1 meter squared (m²) = 10,000 centimers squared (cm²)

1 centimeter squared (cm²) = 100 millimeters squared (mm²)

Table 3.9   English System Area Equivalents

1 foot-squared (ft.²) = 144 inches squared (in.²)

1 yard squared (yd.²) = 9 feet squared (ft.²)

Table 3.10   Conversion Factors for Area

1 meter squared (m²) = 10.7584 feet squared (ft.²)

1 inch squared (in.²) = 6.4516 centimeters squared (cm²)

Table 3.10 shows conversion factors for area.

Example Problem 13: The length of a soccer field is 300 ft. and the width is 150 ft. What is the area of a soccer field in: (a) yards squared and (b) meters squared?

Solution:

(a) Area = length × width = 300 ft. × 150 ft. = 45000 ft.²

$$\frac{45000 \ ft.^2}{1} \times \frac{1 \ yd.^2}{9 \ ft.^2} = 5000 \ yd.^2$$

(b) $$\frac{45000 \ ft.^2}{1} \times \frac{1 \ m^2}{10.7584 \ ft.^2} = 4182.78 \ m^2$$

Example Problem 14: The area of a particular hand was calculated to be 136.5 cm². What is the area of the hand in inches squared?

Solution:

$$\frac{136.5 \ cm^2}{1} \times \frac{1 \ in.^2}{6.4516 \ cm^2} = 21.16 \ in.^2$$

When we know the force applied to a given area we can calculate the pressure.

pressure

Pressure is defined as force per area.

$$pressure = \frac{force}{area}$$

Pressure is measured in

$$\frac{kilogram \ weights}{(meter)^2} \left(\frac{kg \ wt}{m^2}\right)$$

$$or \ \frac{gram \ weight}{(centimeter)^2} \left(\frac{gm \ wt}{cm^2}\right)$$

$$or \ \frac{pounds}{(inch)^2} \left(\frac{lb.}{in.^2}\right) or \ \frac{pounds}{(feet)^2} \left(\frac{lb.}{ft.^2}\right)$$

Since the force and area units of measure are used to calculate pressure, you should refer to Tables 3.5, 3.6, 3.7, 3.8, 3.9, and 3.10 to secure the numerical and literal values for equivalence and conversion.

Example Problem 15: 1 atmosphere of pressure equals 14.7 pounds per inch², which is called "standard atmospheric pressure." What is 1 atmosphere equal to in gram weight per centimeter²?

Solution:

$$\frac{14.7 \ lb.}{1 \ in.^2} \times \frac{1 \ in.^2}{6.4516 \ cm^2} \times \frac{1 \ kg \ wt}{2.2 \ lb.}$$
$$\times \frac{1000 \ gm \ wt}{1 \ kg \ wt} = \frac{1035.68 \ gm \ wt}{1 \ cm^2}$$

1 atmosphere = 1035.68 gm wt/cm²

Example Problem 16: Suppose that a gymnast's hand area is 0.01365 m² and he does a one-hand stand. The gymnast weighs 81.8 kg wt. What is the pressure on his hand in: (a) kg wt/m², (b) gm wt./cm², (c) lb./ft.², and (d) lb./in.²?

Solution:

(a) $\dfrac{81.8\,kg\ wt}{0.01365\ m^2} = \dfrac{force}{area} = pressure =$

$$\dfrac{5992.67\,kg\ wt}{1\,m^2}$$

(b) $\dfrac{5992.67\,\cancel{kg\ wt}}{1\,\cancel{m^2}} \times \dfrac{1\,\cancel{m^2}}{10000\ cm^2}$

$\times\ \dfrac{1000\,gm\ wt}{1\,\cancel{kg\ wt}} = \dfrac{599.267\,gm\ wt}{1\ cm^2}$

(c) $\dfrac{5992.67\,\cancel{kg\ wt}}{1\,\cancel{m^2}} \times \dfrac{2.2\,lb.}{1\,\cancel{kg\ wt}} \times \dfrac{1\,\cancel{m^2}}{10.7584\ ft.^2}$

$$= \dfrac{1225.4\,lb.}{1\ ft.^2}$$

(d) $\dfrac{1225.4\,lb.}{1\,\cancel{ft.^2}} \times \dfrac{1\,\cancel{ft.^2}}{144\ in.^2} = \dfrac{8.5\,lb.}{1\ in.^2}$

The standard atmospheric pressure of 1 atmosphere, which is discussed in example problem 15, is used in calibrating a thermometer, an instrument used to measure temperature.

temperature

The Celsius scale is a temperature scale in the metric system that registers the freezing point of water as 0° C, and the boiling point as 100° C at the standard atmospheric pressure of 1 atmosphere. The Fahrenheit scale is a temperature scale in the English system that registers the freezing point of water as 32° F and the boiling point as 212° F at the standard atmospheric pressure of 1 atmosphere.

To calibrate an unmarked vacuum mercury thermometer, the bulb is placed into a mixture of ice and water under standard atmospheric pressure. When the mercury settles to a steady position, the stem is etched as 0° C or 32° F at this position. Then the bulb is placed in steam just above boiling water, and when the mercury settles to a steady position, the stem is etched as 100° C or 212° F at this position. The distance be-

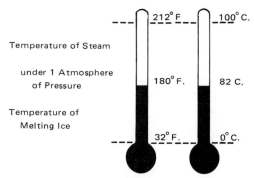

To change Celsius to Fahrenheit, multiply by 9/5 (1.8) and add 32.

Figure 3.3   Comparing Celcius and Fahrenheit scales

tween the two etched positions is then measured and marked off in 100 (100° C − 0° C) equal etchings on the stem for the Celsius scale (with each etched position representing 1° C); the Fahrenheit is marked off in 180 (212° F − 32° F) equal etchings on the stem for the Fahrenheit scale (with each etched position representing 1° F). (See Figure 3.3).

Figure 3.3 should help you see the relationship between the Celsius and Fahrenheit temperature scales.

To convert from Celsius to Fahrenheit we use the formula:

$$F° = 1.8\,(Celsius\ reading) + 32$$

To convert from Fahrenheit to Celsius we use the formula:

$$C° = \dfrac{Fahrenheit\ reading - 32}{1.8}$$

Example Problem 17: A physical education teacher became concerned about one of the students in the class. She thought the student looked flushed so she took the student's temperature and found it to be 37.8° C. What is the temperature of the student in Fahrenheit degrees?

Solution: F° = 1.8 (Celsius reading) + 32 = 1.8 (37.8) + 32 = *100° F*

Example Problem 18: The temperature on the surface of a field just before the start of a football game was 58° F. What is the temperature in Celsius degrees?

Solution:

$$C° = \frac{\text{Fahrenheit reading} - 32}{1.8} = \frac{58 - 32}{1.8}$$
$$= 14.4°C$$

In this chapter we have looked at units of measure in both the metric and English systems. We have also looked at conversion factors and the fractional method of writing conversion factors when going from one system to the other conveniently. And finally, we have discussed equivalent values, by which we can change from one value to another within a single system.

The example problems, it is hoped, will give the practicing physical education teacher who works daily with children and young adults a better grasp of the nature of tests and measurements in physical education, particularly when using the metric system. Now is the time for the practicing physical education teacher to think metric.

summary review questions

1. Which measuring system is more accurate, the metric or English?

2. Which measuring system is more convenient to use, the metric or English? (*answer on p. 14*)

3. What is the literal value and numerical value of a unit of measure? (*answer on p. 15*)

4. Which is the longer measure of distance: (a) 1 kilometer or 1 mile, (b) 1 meter or 1 foot, (c) 1 centimeter or 1 inch? (*answer on p. 15*)

5. What is the fundamental unit of time in: (a) the metric system and (b) the English system? (*answer on p. 16*)

6. What is average speed? (*answer on p. 18*)

7. What is acceleration? (*answer on p. 19*)

8. What is weight? (*answer on p. 20*)

9. Which force unit is greater: (a) 1 kilogram weight or 1 pound, (b) 1 gram weight or 1 ounce, and (c) 1 kilogram weight or 1000 gram weights? (*answer on p. 21*)

10. What is the difference between area and pressure? (*answer on p. 22*)

11. Why does the formula F° = 1.8 (Celsius reading) + 32 give the temperature reading in Fahrenheit degrees? (*answer on p. 23*)

exercises

1. The length of a football field is 100 yd. from goal line to goal line. What is this distance in meters?

   Answer:
   (*91.463 m*)

2. A javelin thrower in the Olympic trials threw the javelin 276 ft. What is this distance in meters?

3. The mean height of a girls' physical education class was found to be 1.625 m. What is the mean height of the class in feet and inches?

Answer:

(5 ft. 4 in. = mean height)

4. A retarded child in the Special Olympics did a standing broad jump of 1.295 m. What is this distance in feet and inches?

5. A physical education teacher found the mean time for a girls' physical education class to run 400 m to be 76.8 sec. What is this time in: (a) minutes, (b) deciseconds, (c) centiseconds, and (d) milliseconds?

Answer:

[(a) 1.28 min., (b) 768 dsec, (c) 7680 csec, and (d) 76,800 msec]

6. A particular long distance runner ran the marathon in 2 hr., 36 min., 6.8 sec. What is the total time in: (a) minutes and (b) seconds?

7. A baseball thrown by a particular pitcher was found to have an average speed of 90 mi./hr. This was calculated by taking the total distance the ball traveled from pitcher to catcher and dividing it by the total time it took the ball to travel that distance. What is this average speed in: (a) feet per second and (b) meters per second?

Answer:

[(a) 132 ft./sec. and (b) 40.243 m/sec.]

8. An average speed of 5.210 m/sec. was calculated for a girl who ran the 400 m in a physical education class. What was the girl's average speed in: (a) feet per second, and (b) miles per hour?

9. Once a diver starts his or her controlled fall toward the water he or she falls with the acceleration due to gravity (ignoring any air resistance). This acceleration is approximately 9.8 m/sec.^{2}. What is this acceleration in ft./sec.^{2}?

Answer:

(32 ft./sec.^{2})

10. A physical education student accelerated from a standing start for 80 ft. He ran this distance for 4.2 sec. What is the acceleration of the student in: (a) ft./sec.^{2} and (b) m/sec.^{2}?

11. A physical education teacher weighed each male student in all of his classes on an English scale. He calculated the mean weight to be 155 lb. What is this weight in kilogram weights?

Answer:

(70.45 kg wt)

12. A physical education teacher weighed each female student in all of her classes on a metric scale. She calculated the mean weight to be 55 kg wt. What is this weight in pounds?

13. A force of 152 lb. was exerted on a 150–lb. barbell and, of course, the student lifted the 150–lb. weight. What is the force exerted on the barbell in kilogram weights?

Answer:

(69.09 kg wt)

14. An adapted physical education teacher found that one of her orthopedically disabled students could produce a 20–kg wt pull on a hand dynamometer. What is this force exerted on the hand dynamometer in: (a) pounds, (b) ounces, and (c) gram weights?

15. The length of a field hockey field was 100 yd. and the width was 60 yd. What is the area of this particular playing field in: (a) yd.², (b) ft.², and (c) m²?

Answer:

[(a) 6000 yd.², (b)54,000 ft.², and (c) 5019. 33 m²]

16. There are 90 ft. between the bases of a baseball diamond. What is the surface area covered by a baseball diamond in: (a) ft.² and (b) m²?

17. A particular swimming pool measured 50 m long by 25 m wide. What is the area covered by this pool in: (a) m², (b) ft.², and (c) yd.²?

Answer:

[(a) 1250 m², (b) 13,448 ft.², and (c) 1494.22 yd.²]

18. At a depth of 10 ft. in a swimming pool on a given day it was found that the pressure was 19.0 lb./in.². What is this pressure in (a) kg wt/m² and (b) atmospheres?

19. If the surface area of a particular swimming pool is 13,448 ft.² and the atmospheric pressure inside the pool area is 14.7 lb./in.², what is the force in pounds that the air is exerting on the water surface?

Answer:

(28,466,726 lb.)

20. The normal body temperature is 98.6°F. What is this temperature in Celcius degrees?

21. A physical education student found the temperature of the gymnasium to be 25°C. What is this temperature in Fahrenheit degrees?

Answer:

(77°F.)

organizing and analyzing test scores

It will not be possible nor would it be desirable to make a complete presentation of statistical techniques in this text. However, in order to administer a measurement and evaluation program successfully, some basic understandings of statistics must be acquired.

reasons for studying statistics

By itself, a score does not have much meaning. For example, if a student answers 70 out of 95 questions on a written test, how good or how poor is this performance? To answer this question, we need to answer some preliminary questions. Is the score above or below the average for the class? For all classes? For the district or state? We might also wish to know how this score of 70 compares to a standing long jump of 75 inches or 191 cm. We might also wish to compare the performance of one class with the performance of another class. A knowledge of statistics helps us answer these questions. Thus, one reason for studying statistics is to *aid in the interpretation of test scores*. The interpretation of test scores helps the physical education teacher make decisions that are an integral part of the planning model.

Closely related to this is the problem of assigning grades in physical education. One must be able to justify the grades given in classes. These grades should be determined fairly and objectively. Usually, when determining grades we combine scores from various activities into one composite score. How does one come up with a total performance score for a student who throws the shot put 36 feet or 11 meters, runs the 440–yard dash in 66 seconds, and scores 70 correct on a written test? With the application of statistics, we can solve this problem and at the same time provide an objective means for assigning a grade to this performance. Statistics then can *aid in making decisions in grading*.

While it is critically important to be able to interpret performance scores, it is equally critical that students and their parents also know the meaning of performance scores. It is necessary to present scores to students and their parents so they understand them. Part of the study in this chapter involves the *presentation of scores or data.*

In order to construct tests to be used in a measurement and evaluation program properly, some knowledge of statistical techniques is necessary. We must apply statistical techniques in order to determine the validity, reliability, and objectivity of a test. Thus, *knowledge of statistics is necessary to construct tests properly.*

If you wish to read professional literature that involves research or if you wish to conduct research, you must have some knowledge of statistics. Although this text will not fully prepare you to do either of these, it will, we hope, be a foundation upon which you can build.

statistics defined

The term *statistics* has unnecessarily struck fear into the hearts and minds of many students. Rumors have been spread that you must be a mathematical whiz to study statistics. Although statistics is a branch of mathematics, the level at which we discuss it in this text requires only the ability to perform basic mathematical manipulations, namely, addition, subtraction, multiplication, and division.

The major goal in statistics is to describe a group or the characteristics possessed by the group concisely and precisely. By describing a group, we can not only better understand it, but we can also understand the individuals making up that group. Sometimes we have information on every individual in a group. When that is the case, the methods used to describe the group are called *descriptive statistics.* Many times, however, it is desirable to make a statement concerning an entire group when there is information on only part of the group. In this case, we use *inferential statistics.*

Although we are mostly concerned with descriptive statistics in this text, the following may give some insight into the use of inferential statistics. Inferential statistics may basically be described by the four terms *population, parameter, sample,* and *statistic* and their relationship to one another. A *population* is any group of people or objects with a common characteristic(s). A population is to be defined. For example we might define a population to be all the seventh-grade girls at Central Junior High School. The characteristics they have in common are that they are girls, they are seventh graders, and they are students at Central Junior High School.

A *parameter* is a measurable characteristic of the population. In our example, the average height of the Central Junior High School girls would be a parameter. The number of girls with blond hair could be another parameter.

A *sample* is any subgroup of a population. In our example, the seventh grade girls in Ms. Jones's physical education class would be a sample from our population of all seventh-grade girls at Central Junior High School. A *statistic* is a measureable characteristic of the sample. The average height of the seventh-grade girls in Ms. Jones's physical education class is an example of a statistic. We can see that a parameter is to a population what a statistic is to a sample.

In inferential statistics, a sample is carefully selected from a population, statistics are determined for that sample and these sample statistics are used to estimate the parameters of the population. In other words, we infer something about the population on the basis of what is known about the sample.

For example, let's suppose there are 300 seventh-grade girls in our defined population. We might carefully select 30 of these girls for our sample and measure their heights in inches. If the average height for these 30 girls is found to be 61 inches (154.9 cm), this would be our sample statistic. If we had carefully selected the sample, we could estimate that the average height for all 300 seventh-grade girls is 61 inches (154.9 cm). We would have used the sample statistic to estimate a population parameter.

When we talk about carefully selecting a sample, we are usually referring to a procedure called *random sampling*. A random sample is one in which each member of the population has an equal chance of being selected for the sample. Drawing names out of a hat is a crude example of a random sample. It should also be mentioned that we usually estimate a population parameter with an interval and an accompanying statement of probability. In our example, we would probably make a statement like the following: We are 95 percent sure that the average height in our population is between 59 (149.9 cm) and 63 inches (160.0 cm). Such intervals and probabilities are precisely deter-

mined by established statistical procedures.

In other instances we may wish to compare the parameters of two or more populations. Again, procedures in inferential statistics allow us to make comparative statements about populations on the basis of information gathered from samples.

For the most part, the study of inferential statistics is beyond the scope of this text. However, it is important for the student of measurement and evaluation to have some knowledge of the procedures involved with it as they are frequently used in the development of the many measurement devices described throughout this text.

organization of scores

When we simply record a group of scores such as the 110 push-up scores for freshmen in Table 4.1, it is difficult to know very much about the class's performance or how good or poor any individual performance is. It would be helpful if these scores were organized into some form that would allow us to note the relative position of particular scores.

Table 4.1   Push-Up Scores for 110 Freshmen

30	31	30	32	36	33	31	26	32	31
34	25	34	37	32	29	28	30	29	30
22	20	26	30	30	29	31	32	34	25
36	29	26	34	26	31	26	36	30	29
28	33	27	29	33	37	32	27	28	30
33	38	32	27	27	28	30	33	31	28
22	29	31	35	29	32	30	29	27	36
30	34	28	33	25	27	31	28	26	30
35	32	35	32	30	34	29	31	23	33
31	28	29	34	28	30	25	33	30	29
38	24	24	37	27	35	40	35	23	25

Any group of scores can be said to be a *distribution.* If we place scores in order and record the frequency with which each occur, we then have a *frequency distribution.* In the first two columns of Table 4.2, this has been done for the 110 push-up scores.

The next column in Table 4.2, relative frequency, is obtained by dividing each frequency by the total number of scores, in this case 110. The frequency percent is obtained by simply multiplying the relative frequency by 100. It should be noted that all calculations were rounded to two decimal places. In our

example, we can now state that 0.14 or 14 percent of our students did 30 push-ups, while 0.11 or 11 percent did 29.

Even with just this much of the table, we begin to get a picture of the distribution of scores. More students, 15 or 14 percent of them, did 30 push-ups than did any other number. Also, more students tended to score in the middle of the distribution than at the extremes. So, we already have a better description than when the scores were in a disorganized array.

The remaining columns in Table 4.2 are

Table 4.2   Frequency Distribution of Push-up Scores

Push-up Score	Frequency	Relative Frequency	Frequency Percent	Cumulative Frequency	Relative Cumulative Frequency	Percentile Rank
40	1	.01	1	110	1.00	100
39	0	0	0	109	.99	99
38	2	.02	2	109	.99	99
37	3	.03	3	107	.97	97
36	4	.04	4	104	.95	95
35	5	.05	5	100	.91	91
34	7	.06	6	95	.86	86
33	8	.07	7	88	.80	80
32	9	.08	8	80	.73	73
31	10	.08	9	71	.65	65
30	15	.14	14	61	.55	55
29	12	.11	11	46	.42	42
28	9	.08	8	34	.31	31
27	7	.06	6	25	.23	23
26	6	.05	5	18	.16	16
25	5	.05	5	12	.11	11
24	2	.02	2	7	.06	6
23	2	.02	2	5	.05	5
22	2	.02	2	3	.03	3
21	0	0	0	1	.01	1
20	1	.01	1	1	.01	1
TOTAL	110					

simple to attain and they provide us with further useful information. The column labeled *cumulative frequency* is an accumulation of frequencies starting at the bottom of the table. That is, one person scored 20 or below, three people scored 22 or below, five people scored 23 or below, and so on. The *relative cumulative frequency* is determined by dividing each cumulative frequency by the total number of scores, 110. The *percentile rank* column is obtained by multiplying the relative cumulative frequencies by 100. This last column, percentile rank, is most useful in presenting students' performances to them or their parents.

The percentile rank of a score represents the percentage of scores that are equal to or less than that score. We usually denote a percentile rank by the letter P, with a subscript representing the rank. For example, a percentile rank of 85 is represented as P_{85}. This allows a student to know his or her relative standing in a class or group. In our example, a student who did 35 push-ups performed as well or better than 91 percent of his classmates while the student who did 23 push-ups fell into the lower 5 percent of the class. Another way of writing these would be: $P_{91} = 35$ and $P_{05} = 23$. This interpretation of a score is easy for the lay public to understand. Norms for tests are frequently presented in percentile ranks. We will see that there is another way to determine percentile ranks later in the chapter.

Certain percentile ranks have special names and are worthy of mention here. Each 10th percentile rank is called a "decile" and is represented by D. In other words, $D_1 = P_{10}$, $D_2 = P_{20}$, $D_3 = P_{30}$, and so on. Each 25th percentile rank is called a "quartile" and is denoted by Q. So, $Q_1 = P_{25}$, $Q_2 = P_{50}$, $Q_3 = P_{75}$, and $Q_4 = P_{100}$.

There may be occasions when we wish to reduce the frequency distribution into a more compact picture. To do this, we group our scores into intervals. If we take the scores from Table 4.2 and group them into seven intervals, each interval containing three scores, we obtain the grouped frequency distribution shown in Table 4.3.

The frequency, relative frequency, frequency percent, cumulative frequency, relative cumulative frequency, and percentile rank are determined in the same manner for the grouped frequency distribution of scores as they were for the original frequency distribution. The midpoint of each interval is the score that represents the interval. All the

Table 4.3   Grouped Frequency Distribution of Push-up Scores

Interval	Mid-Point	Frequency	Relative Frequency	Frequency Percent	Cumulative Frequency	Relative Cumulative Frequency	Percentile Rank
38–40	39	3	.03	3	110	1.00	100
35–37	36	12	.11	11	107	.97	97
32–34	33	24	.22	22	95	.86	86
29–31	30	37	.34	34	71	.65	65
26–28	27	22	.20	20	34	.31	31
23–25	24	9	.08	8	12	.11	11
20–22	21	3	.03	3	3	.03	3

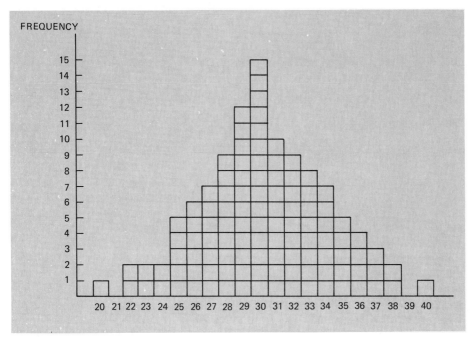

Figure 4.1 Histogram of push-up scores

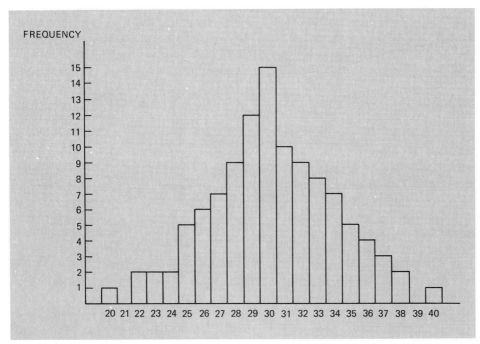

Figure 4.2 Histogram of push-up scores

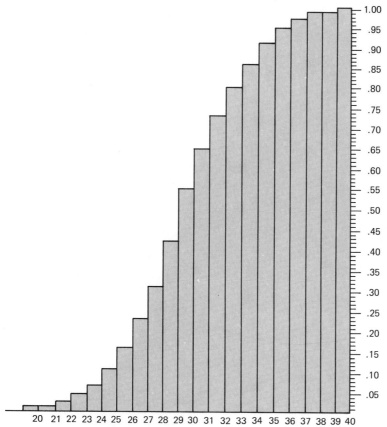

Figure 4.3 Histogram for cumulative frequencies

scores in the interval 38–40, for example, are represented by 39. What we are doing is collapsing our distribution into a more compact array. However, by doing so we lose accuracy in our scores since in Table 4.3 the scores in any interval are considered the same. For example, no distinction can now be made between the scores 26, 27, and 28 as they all are now represented by the score 27.

histograms, polygons, and ogives

We may sometimes wish to present scores by a graphical drawing. When this is the case, we can use a histogram, polygon, or ogive. These show a frequency distribution or grouped frequency distribution pictorially.

In a histogram, each unit of measure is represented by some chosen area. A histogram is shown in Figure 4.1 for our push-up scores.

Usually a histogram is made without the horizontal lines. These were presented here only to emphasize that each unit of measure occupies the same area. Figure 4.2 is our histogram without the horizontal lines.

A histogram can be used to present any of the columns from Table 4.2. In Figure 4.3, the relative cumulative frequency is presented in histogram form.

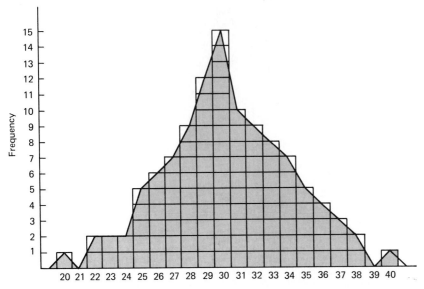

Figure 4.4   Frequency polygon for 110 push-ups

Note the different placement of the scores for the cumulative representation. The scores are placed directly below the vertical lines instead of in between them.

A polygon is another way of representing frequencies and/or cumulative frequencies pictorially. To go from a histogram to a polygon, connect the points on the histogram as illustrated in Figures 4.4 and 4.5. Note that at each end of the frequency polygon a line is drawn back to zero. This is done to avoid having the polygon appear as though it is floating. The polygon is usually presented without being superimposed over the histogram. See Figures 4.6 and 4.7.

The ogive is a smooth curve also used to present a picture of frequencies and/or cumulative frequencies. To make the ogive curve, smooth out the polygon. An ogive for the relative cumulative frequency or the percentile rank is presented in Figure 4.8. This can be a handy graph for quickly estimating percentile ranks.

As mentioned previously, all of these graphic techniques can also be applied to

grouped frequency distributions. We leave that as an exercise for you.

descriptive statistics

The foregoing techniques are useful for presenting a group of scores and for providing some insight into the meaning of individual scores. There is frequently a need, however, to describe a distribution of scores more succinctly. The two characteristics that can represent a distribution of scores are the distribution's central tendency and variability.

measures of central tendency

In almost any group of scores (distribution) there tends to be a greater concentration of scores towards the middle than anywhere else. This "central tendency" was quite evident in the frequency distribution example for push-ups in the previous section. One of

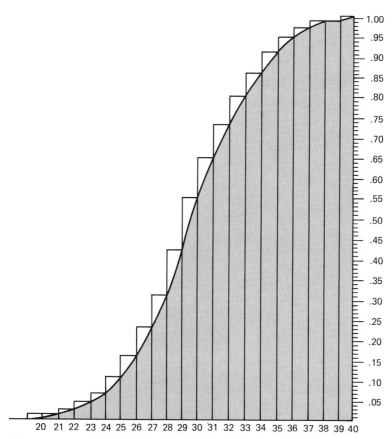

Figure 4.5 Cumulative frequency for 110 push-up scores

the ways to describe a distribution, therefore, is to have a measure of this central tendency. Three such measures are commonly used and will be presented here: the mode, the median, and the mean.

mode

The mode is the most frequently occurring score. If we have pull-up scores for seven students of 9, 7, 6, 6, 6, 4, 4, the mode for this distribution of scores will be 6 since it occurs more times (three) than any other score. The mode is symbolized by M_o. Thus, we write $M_o = 6$. It is possible to have more than one mode for a distribution. For example, if we had the distribution of push-up scores 7, 7, 6, 5, 5, 4, the modes would be 7 and 5. When a distribution has two modes it is said to be bimodal. If it had had three modes it would be trimodal, and so on.

The mode is not a particularly good measure of central tendency in that there may be more than one mode and not every score is involved in its determination. Thus, it may misrepresent the central tendency of the distribution. The mode should be used only to give a quick and approximate estimate of central tendency.

median

Another measure of central tendency is the median. *The median is the middle point in an*

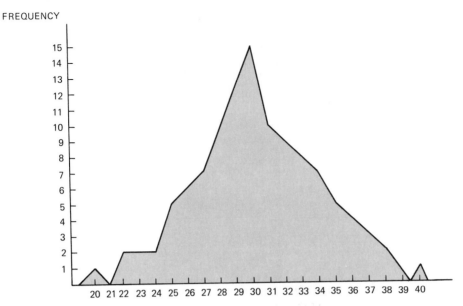

FREQUENCY

Figure 4.6   Frequency polygon for 110 push-up scores

ordered distribution. It is the point in a distribution where an equal number of scores lie on each side of it. In other words, with an ordered array of scores, it is the $(N + 1)$th/2 score from either end of the distribution. From our earlier example of the seven pull-up scores of 9, 7, 6, 6, 6, 4, 4, the median, denoted by *Mdn,* is the $(7 + 1)/2 = 4$th score from either end of the ordered distribution, or Mdn = 6. If our distribution consisted of the push-up scores 7, 7, 6, 5, 5, 4, the Mdn would be the $(6 + 1)/2 = 3.5$th score, or Mdn = 5.5 since it lies halfway between 5 and 6. The median can be a useful measure of central tendency, particularly in distributions with a small number of scores (fewer than 15) or when there are a few extreme scores at one or both ends of the distribution. It does have the drawback of not being mathematically determined, which means that it cannot be used in later calculations. Additionally, only the position and not the size of each score is taken into account.

mean

The most useful and commonly used measure of central tendency is the mean. The *mean of a distribution is simply the arithmetic average of the scores.* For example, for the scores of 9, 7, 6, 6, 6, 4, 4, the mean is equal to

$$\frac{9 + 7 + 6 + 6 + 6 + 4 + 4}{7} = \frac{42}{7} = 6$$

We denote the mean by a capital letter with a bar over it. The most commonly used letter is X, so we can denote the mean as $\overline{X}$, read as "X-bar." (We could call it $\overline{Y}$, $\overline{K}$, or any other letter.) In our example $\overline{X} = 6$.

We need to be able to write our definition for the mean symbolically so that it tells how to find the mean for all situations. If we allow X_1 to represent any score in a distribution and N to represent the number of scores in that distribution and if we have five scores, then $N = 5$ and our scores will be represented by X_1, X_2, X_3, X_4, and X_5, and

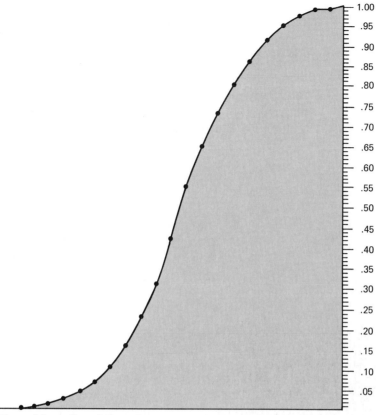

Figure 4.7   Cumulative frequency polygon for 110 push-
up scores

$$\overline{X} = \frac{X_1 + X_2 + X_3 + X_4 + X_5}{5}.$$

In a more general expression for any size distribution,

$$\overline{X} = \frac{X_1 + X_2 + \ldots + X_N}{N}$$

To shorten the expression even further we can write:

$$\overline{X} = \frac{\displaystyle\sum_{i=1}^{N} X_i}{N}$$

where the Greek capital sigma (Σ) tells us to sum. This expression is then read "X-bar equals the sum of the X_i's for $i = 1$ through N divided by N," which gives the definition of the mean for *any* distribution.

The mean is an excellent measure of central tendency in that it takes into account the value and not just the position, of every score in the distribution. This characteristic allows us to use the mean in other mathematical operations that are necessary to determine the variability in a distribution. In most situations, the mean is the measure of central tendency that should be used.

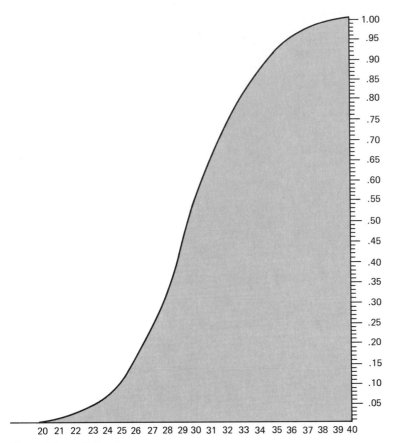

Figure 4.8 Ogive for cumulative frequency for 110 push-up scores

measures of variability

It is possible for two distributions to have equal means, medians, and modes but still be quite different. For example, if we have the following two distributions of scores,

X	Y
1	5
2	6
6	6
6	6
15	7

we see that the mean, median, and mode are equal to 6 for each distribution. However, the Y-scores are less spread out than the X-scores. So, the other characteristic of a distribution that interests us is the variability among the scores, or the extent to which the scores are spread out. The measures of variability to be presented here are the range, semi-interquartile range, variance, and standard deviation.

range and semi-interquartile range

Range is a simple and easy-to-determine measure of variability. It is found by subtracting the smallest score in the distribution from the largest score. For example, if our distribution consists of the sit-up scores of 33, 30, 30, 25, 21, and 18, the range will be $33 - 18 = 15$. The range is not a particularly good estimate of variability in that it is rather unstable, being determined by only the two most extreme scores in the distribution. It is recommended that the range be used only as a quick and *temporary* measure of variability. It is comparable in quality to the mode.

Occasionally in measurement and evaluation literature, the *semi-interquartile range* will be reported as a measure of variability. It is defined as one-half the difference between the 75th and 25th percentiles, or

$$\text{semi-interquartile range} = \frac{P_{75} - P_{25}}{2}$$

Although extreme scores do not affect this measure to the extent they do the range, the semi-interquartile range cannot be used readily in mathematical operations and will thus not be used in this text.

variance and standard deviation

For a measure of variability to be effective, it should be large when the scores are spread out or heterogeneous and smaller when the scores are homogeneous or clustered closely together. Another desirable feature would be that each score in the distribution be included in the determination of the measure. At first thought, the sum of the deviations between each score and the mean seems a good candidate. Symbolically, we would write this:

$$\sum_{i=1}^{N} (X_i - \bar{X})$$

Let's try this measure for the X-scores of 1, 2, 6, 6, and 15, given at the beginning of this section. Since $\bar{X} = 6$,

$$\sum_{i=1}^{N} (X_i - \bar{X}) = (1 - 6) + (2 - 6) + (6 - 6) + (6 - 6) + (15 - 6)$$
$$= -5 + -4 + 0 + 0 + 9$$
$$= -9 + 9 = 0$$

We get a value of zero. For *any* distribution, the sum of the deviations about the mean will always equal zero. Therefore, this measure is eliminated from consideration. However, if we were to square each deviation before summing, we might have a useful measure of variability. This would be written symbolically as:

$$\sum_{i=1}^{N} (X_i - \bar{X})^2$$

For our X-scores:

$$\sum_{i=1}^{N} (X_i - \bar{X})^2 = (1 - 6)^2 + (2 - 6)^2 + (6 - 6)^2 + (6 - 6)^2 + (15 - 6)^2$$
$$= (-5)^2 + (-4)^2 + 0^2 + 0^2 + 9^2$$
$$= 25 + 16 + 0 + 0 + 81$$
$$= 122$$

The only apparent problem now is that in order to have a large variability value, we would only need to have additional scores that are not equal to the mean. So, let's divide this measure of variability by the number of scores that will give us a *mean squared deviation.* We can write:

$$\sigma_x^2 = \frac{\sum_{i=1}^{N} (X_i - \bar{X})^{2*}}{N}$$

This measure is called the "variance of a distribution" and is represented by σ_x^2.

---

* The authors are fully aware that if we have a sample, the variance estimate of the population is $s^2 = \frac{\Sigma(X - \bar{X})^2}{n - 1}$. However, we are assuming that inference to a population is not desired.

Let's see if the variance will distinguish between two distributions that do not have the same homogeneity among scores. The X- and Y-scores previously used should suffice for this purpose in that the Xs are obviously more dispersed than the Ys. Therefore, the variance of the Xs (1, 2, 6, 6, 15) should be larger than that for the Ys (5, 6, 6, 6, 7). For the X-distribution, we had already found that

$$\sum_{i=1}^{N}(X_i - \bar{X})^2 = 122$$

So,

$$\sigma_x^2 = \frac{122}{5} = 24.4$$

In the Y-distribution:

$$\sigma_y^2 = \frac{\sum_{i=1}^{N}(Y_i - \bar{Y})^2}{N} \quad \begin{array}{l}(5-6)^2 + (6-6)^2+ \end{array}$$

$$= \frac{(5-6)^2 + (6-6)^2 + (6-6)^2 + (7-6)^2}{5}$$

$$= \frac{(-1)^2 + 0^2 + 0^2 + 0^2 + 1^2}{5}$$

$$= \frac{1+0+0+0+1}{5}$$

$$= 2/5 = 0.4$$

The variance does in fact work since $\sigma_x^2 = 24.4$ and $\sigma_y^2 = 0.4$.

If the mean were not a round number, as it has been in our examples, and if the variance formula were used in its present form, the calculation of the variance could be a tedious procedure. (Imagine subtracting a mean of 8.64 from every score, squaring it, and then summing.) However, by algebraically manipulating the variance formula, we come up with an equivalent formula that is much easier to use.

$$\sigma^2 = \frac{\sum_{i=1}^{N}(X_i - \bar{X})^2}{N} = \frac{N\left(\sum_{i=1}^{N}X_i^2\right) - \left(\sum_{i=1}^{N}X_i\right)^2}{N^2}$$

The $\sum_{i=1}^{N}X_i^2$ tells us to square each score and then add these squared scores. The $\left(\sum_{i=1}^{N}X_i\right)^2$ tells us to sum all of the scores and then square this sum.

Let's use this new form of the variance formula to calculate the σ_y^2 again and see if it works. The scores were 5, 6, 6, 6, 7. Therefore,

$$\sum_{i=1}^{N}Y_i^2 = 5^2 + 6^2 + 6^2 + 6^2 + 7^2$$
$$= 25 + 36 + 36 + 36 + 49 = 182$$

$$\left(\sum_{i=1}^{N}Y_i\right)^2 = (5 + 6 + 6 + 6 + 7)^2$$
$$= (30)^2 = 900$$

and

$$\sigma_y^2 = \frac{N\left(\sum_{i=1}^{N}Y_i^2\right) - \left(\sum_{i=1}^{N}Y_i\right)^2}{N^2}$$

$$= \frac{(5)(182) - 900}{(5)(5)}$$

$$= \frac{910 - 900}{25} = \frac{10}{25} = 0.4$$

We see that this is an equivalent formula!

The variance is a most useful measure of variability. It meets the criteria we suggested for a measure of variability. The only possible drawback it has is that it is a value presented in squared units. In our examples, if we were working with centimeters, our variances would be 24.4 cm squared and 0.4 cm squared. To get our variability measure back to units with which we can work, we take its square root and have the most useful and commonly used measure of variability, the standard deviation.

The standard deviation is the square root of the variance and is defined as:

$$\sigma_x = \sqrt{\frac{\sum_{i=1}^{N}(X_i - \bar{X})^2}{N}}$$

$$= \sqrt{\frac{N\left(\sum_{i=1}^{N}X_i^2\right) = \left(\sum_{i=1}^{N}X_i\right)^2}{N^2}}$$

In our examples,

$$\sigma_x = \sqrt{24.4} = 4.94$$

and

$$\sigma_y = \sqrt{0.4} = 0.63$$

If our scores were in centimeters, then we would say that our standard deviations are 4.94 cm and 0.63 cm. Unfortunately, there is no exact literal interpretation of the standard deviation. However, in order to have a feel for the meaning of the standard deviation, we can think of it as being a "kind of average" deviation between the mean and the scores in the distribution. We use "kind of average" since it is not exactly the average but is a close approximation.

The mean and standard deviation usually describe a distribution of scores quite sufficiently. They are the descriptive measures to be used throughout the remainder of this text.

standard scores

We often wish to combine or compare scores from performances that have dissimilar units of measure. For example, we might have performance scores from the shot put, the 100–yard dash, and a written test, and wish to combine them into a composite score. Suppose the respective scores from these performances for a particular individual, call

him Jim, are 38 feet, 12.2 seconds, and 79 correct. With these units, it is impossible for us to combine or compare scores. We need a standard means of reporting scores. Three such standardizations are presented here: the standard Z-score scale, the T-score scale, and the 6–σ score scale.

From the example, if we know the mean and standard deviation for each of the activities, we have some basis for knowing the relative position of Jim's performance in each. For example, let's suppose that the mean and standard deviation for the shot put for Jim's class were $\bar{X} = 42$ feet, $\sigma = 8$ feet; for the 100–yard dash, $\bar{X} = 12.0$ seconds, $\sigma = 0.2$ seconds; and for the test $\bar{X} = 75$ correct, $\sigma = 8$ correct. We can immediately see that Jim performed below the mean on the shot put and better than the mean on the written test. On the 100–yard dash his time was greater, therefore it was below average in terms of performance.

More exactly, Jim's score is 0.5 standard deviation unit below the mean for the shot put, 0.5 standard deviation unit above the mean for the written test, and one standard deviation unit below the average on the dash. These standard deviation units are called "Z-scores" and are found by subtracting the mean from an individual score and dividing by the standard deviation.

$$\text{Z-score} = \frac{X - \bar{X}}{\sigma}$$

For Jim's 38-foot shot put performance,

$$Z = \frac{38 - 42}{8} = \frac{-4}{8} = -0.5;$$

for his 100-yard dash score of 12.2,

$$Z = \frac{12.2 - 12.0}{.2} = \frac{.2}{.2} = 1.0;$$

and for his test score of 79,

$$Z = \frac{79 - 75}{8} = \frac{4}{8} = 0.5.$$

When working with activities involving speed and having time as the unit of measure, we must always change the sign of our Z-score if we wish to speak of performance. Thus, in terms of performance, Jim's 100-yard dash Z-score will be − 1.0 instead of + 1.0.

The Z-score not only allows the comparison of an individual's performance in dissimilar activities, but also allows one to combine these performances into an average performance score. The Z-scores for Jim were:

Shot put Z-score   = − 0.5

100-yard dash Z-score = − 1.0

Written test Z-score   = + 0.5

His overall average performance is (−0.5 + −1.0 + 0.5)/3 = −⅓ = −0.33 or 0.33 standard deviation units below the mean. It is advantageous to find Z-scores for all students in an event in order to standardize the reporting of their performances. If we were to average all the Z-scores for any particular event, we would find that the mean $\overline{Z} = 0$. Furthermore, the standard deviation for Z, $\sigma_z = 1$.

All standard scores are based on the Z-score. The maximum range of Z-scores for distributions is usually −3 to +3. Since there is some objection to working with these small numbers and negative numbers, which are prevalent with Z-scores, many people prefer to use standard scores, which are usually positive and larger.

Adding a constant to every score in a distribution will in no way alter its shape or the relative position of the scores in that distribution. Also, multiplying every score in a distribution will not alter the shape of the distribution or the relative position of scores. Multiplying every score in the distribution by a constant simply has the effect of placing a picture of the distribution under a magnifying glass. These two procedures are what we do in order to obtain other standard scores.

If we multiply each Z-score in a distribution by 10 and add 50, we obtain T-scores. In other words,

T-score = 50 + 10Z

or, if we replace the Z with what it equals, we have:,

$$T\text{-score} = 50 + 10 \frac{(X - \overline{X})}{\sigma}$$

The mean of all T-scores in a distribution is equal to 50 and the standard deviation is equal to 10. Therefore, T-scores will usually range from 20 to 80.

Because of the range of T-scores, some teachers and researchers do not prefer it. They prefer a range of 0 to 100. The 6-σ score scale generally achieves this range. In order to obtain 6-σ scores, we multiply each Z-score by 16.67 and add 50, or

6-σ = 50 + 16.67 Z

or

$$= 50 + 16.67 \frac{(X - \overline{X})}{\sigma}$$

The mean for the 6-σ scale is 50 and the standard deviation is 16.67.

The graph in Figure 4.9 should help in seeing the relationship among several standard scores.

It must be emphasized again that all of these are based on standard deviation units above or below the mean. Numerous other standard scores have been and can be utilized. Some of these are also summarized in Figure 4.9.

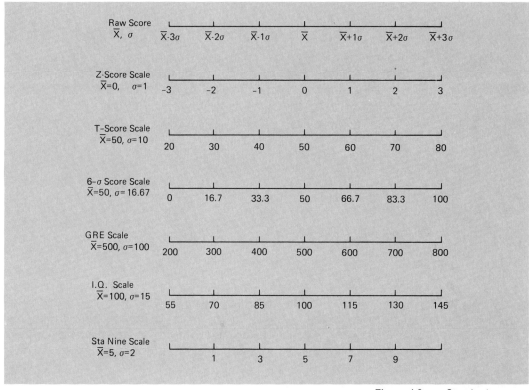

Figure 4.9   Standard scores

normal curve

In the frequency distribution of push-up scores and its graphic representations shown earlier, it was quite noticeable that more scores occur toward the center than at the extremes. This phenomenon is present with most real-life measures. It is certainly true with most performance measures used in physical education. Mathematicians worked with this phenomenon until they were able to define mathematically a curve that closely approximates the distribution of real-life measures. This curve has been labeled the *normal curve.* Its use can be very helpful in working with physical educational measures.

The normal curve is a curve or ogive representing a frequency distribution for a population. The normal curve is presented graphically in Figure 4.10.

It can be seen that this curve is bell-shaped and has a single peak or mode at the same place as the mean. As a matter of fact, in a normal distribution, the mean, median, and mode fall at exactly the same point. The curve is also symmetric, meaning that the left half is a mirror image of the right half. Additionally, the curve is concave downward between the mean and one standard deviation on each side and concave upward outside these points.

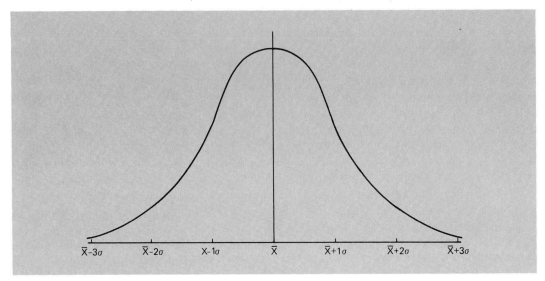

Figure 4.10   Normal curve

Although very few distributions of scores fit the normal curve perfectly, we can expect that most distributions, if they contain at least 30 scores, will approximate the normal curve nearly enough to warrant its use. However, there are examples where scores are not normally distributed. For example, if a test were extremely difficult, a disproportionately large number of scores would fall at the lower end of the distribution. When this occurs, we say the distribution is *skewed to the right or positively skewed.* A distribution that is skewed to the right is illustrated in Figure 4.11.

If a disproportionately large number of scores fall at the high end of the distribution, then we say the distribution is *skewed to the left or negatively skewed.* If an extremely easy test were given, we would expect the scores on it to be skewed to the left. An illustration of a negatively skewed distribution is also shown in Figure 4.11.

The main use of the normal curve in this text is in the determination of percentile ranks. Since the normal curve is mathe-

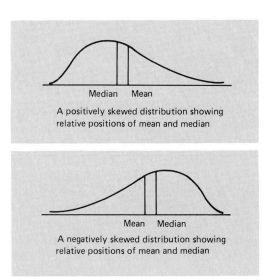

Figure 4.11   Examples of skewed distributions

matically defined, the percentage of scores expected between any two points can be determined. For example, it has been determined that in a normal distribution, between the mean and one standard deviation unit, 0.3413 or 34.13 percent of the scores will occur; between the mean and two standard deviation units, 0.4772 or 47.72 percent of the scores will occur; and between the mean and three deviation units, 0.4987 or 49.87 percent of the scores will occur. Finally, 50 percent of the scores can be expected to be on each side of the mean. This is illustrated in Figure 4.12.

Percentages can and have been figured out mathematically for numerous intervals; these are found in Table 4.4 (p. 46). Our task is to see how we can use this table.

Table 4.4 shows the percentage of scores expected to occur between the mean and a specified number of standard deviation units or Z-scores. For example, by using this table we can see that between the mean and 0.52 standard deviation units, 19.85 percent of the scores will occur. Another example shows us that 46.25 percent of the scores can be expected to fall between the mean and 1.78 standard deviation units.

After working through a few examples, you should be able to see how this table is used.

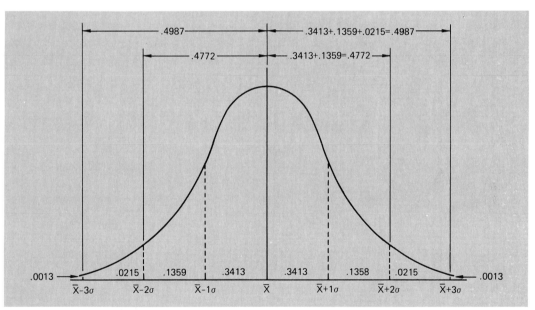

Fig 4.12   Normal curve percentages

Table 4.4   The Normal Distribution*

Percentage area under the standard normal curve from 0 to Z, shown shaded, is the value found in the body of the table.

Z	0.00	0.01	0.02	0.03	0.04	0.05	0.06	0.07	0.08	0.09
0.0	0.0000	0.0040	0.0080	0.0120	0.0160	0.0199	0.0239	0.0279	0.0319	0.0359
0.1	0.0398	0.0438	0.0478	0.0517	0.0557	0.0596	0.0636	0.0675	0.0714	0.0753
0.2	0.0793	0.0832	0.0871	0.0910	0.0948	0.0987	0.1026	0.1064	0.1103	0.1141
0.3	0.1179	0.1217	0.1255	0.1293	0.1331	0.1368	0.1406	0.1443	0.1480	0.1517
0.4	0.1554	0.1591	0.1628	0.1664	0.1700	0.1736	0.1772	0.1808	0.1844	0.1879
0.5	0.1915	0.1950	0.1985	0.2019	0.2054	0.2088	0.2123	0.2157	0.2190	0.2224
0.6	0.2257	0.2291	0.2324	0.2357	0.2389	0.2422	0.2454	0.2486	0.2517	0.2549
0.7	0.2580	0.2611	0.2642	0.2673	0.2704	0.2734	0.2764	0.2794	0.2823	0.2852
0.8	0.2881	0.2910	0.2939	0.2967	0.2995	0.3023	0.3051	0.3078	0.3106	0.3133
0.9	0.3159	0.3186	0.3212	0.3238	0.3264	0.3289	0.3315	0.3340	0.3365	0.3389
1.0	0.3413	0.3438	0.3461	0.3485	0.3508	0.3531	0.3554	0.3577	0.3599	0.3621
1.1	0.3643	0.3665	0.3686	0.3708	0.3729	0.3749	0.3770	0.3790	0.3810	0.3830
1.2	0.3849	0.3869	0.3888	0.3907	0.3925	0.3944	0.3962	0.3980	0.3997	0.4015
1.3	0.4032	0.4049	0.4066	0.4082	0.4099	0.4115	0.4131	0.4147	0.4162	0.4177
1.4	0.4192	0.4207	0.4222	0.4236	0.4251	0.4265	0.4279	0.4292	0.4306	0.4319
1.5	0.4332	0.4345	0.4357	0.4370	0.4382	0.4394	0.4406	0.4418	0.4429	0.4441
1.6	0.4452	0.4463	0.4474	0.4484	0.4495	0.4505	0.4515	0.4525	0.4535	0.4545
1.7	0.4554	0.4564	0.4573	0.4582	0.4591	0.4599	0.4608	0.4616	0.4625	0.4633
1.8	0.4641	0.4649	0.4656	0.4664	0.4671	0.4678	0.4686	0.4693	0.4699	0.4706
1.9	0.4713	0.4719	0.4726	0.4732	0.4738	0.4744	0.4750	0.4756	0.4761	0.4767
2.0	0.4772	0.4778	0.4783	0.4788	0.4793	0.4798	0.4803	0.4808	0.4812	0.4817
2.1	0.4821	0.4826	0.4830	0.4834	0.4838	0.4842	0.4846	0.4850	0.4854	0.4857
2.2	0.4861	0.4864	0.4868	0.4871	0.4875	0.4878	0.4881	0.4884	0.4887	0.4890
2.3	0.4893	0.4896	0.4898	0.4901	0.4904	0.4906	0.4909	0.4911	0.4913	0.4916
2.4	0.4918	0.4920	0.4922	0.4925	0.4927	0.4929	0.4931	0.4932	0.4934	0.4936
2.5	0.4938	0.4940	0.4941	0.4943	0.4945	0.4946	0.4948	0.4949	0.4951	0.4952
2.6	0.4953	0.4955	0.4956	0.4957	0.4959	0.4960	0.4961	0.4962	0.4963	0.4964
2.7	0.4965	0.4966	0.4967	0.4968	0.4969	0.4970	0.4971	0.4972	0.4973	0.4974
2.8	0.4974	0.4975	0.4976	0.4977	0.4977	0.4978	0.4979	0.4979	0.4980	0.4981
2.9	0.4981	0.4982	0.4982	0.4983	0.4984	0.4984	0.4985	0.4985	0.4986	0.4986
3.0	0.4987	0.4987	0.4987	0.4988	0.4988	0.4989	0.4989	0.4989	0.4990	0.4990

* Abridged from Table 9 in *Biometrika Tables for Statisticians,* vol. 1, 3d ed., edited by E. S. Pearson and H. O. Hartley (New York: Cambridge, 1966). Reproduced with kind permission of E. J. Snell for the *Biometrika* trustees.

Example: Given that the mean and standard deviation on a test were $\overline{X} = 65$ and $\sigma = 11$. If Charlene scored a 72 on the test, what was her percentile rank, assuming the scores on the test were normally distributed?

Solution: In order to answer this question we should first diagram Charlene's position on the normal curve.

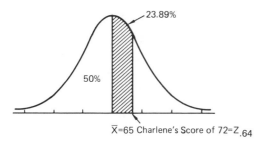

$\overline{X}=65$ Charlene's Score of $72=Z_{.64}$

Next, let's determine her Z-score.

$$Z\text{-score} = \frac{72 - 65}{11} = \frac{7}{11} = 0.64$$

Thus, Charlene's score lies 0.64 standard deviation units above the mean.

From Table 4.4, we learn that between the mean and 0.64 standard deviation units lie 23.89 percent of the scores, but since 50 percent of the scores fall below the mean, this means that 23.89 percent + 50 percent or 73.89 percent of the scores are at 0.64 standard deviations or below. Therefore, Charlene's percentile rank is 73.89 or a score of $72 = P_{74}$.

Example: Given the same $\overline{X}$ and σ as in the previous example, determine Bill's percentile rank if he scored 53 on the test. Let's locate Bill's position on the normal curve.

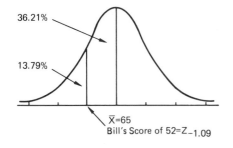

$\overline{X}=65$
Bill's Score of $52=Z_{-1.09}$

Solution: Bill's Z-score $= \dfrac{53 - 65}{11} = \dfrac{-12}{11}$
$$= -1.09$$

From Table 4.4 we find that 36.21 percent of the scores fall between the mean and a Z of 1.09. This is shown on our curve. Since we want to know the percentage of scores at or below Bill's score and since 50 percent of the scores fall below the mean, Bill's percentile rank will be $50 - 36.21$ or 13.79 percent or $P_{14} = 53$. It is highly recommended that you draw a graph for solving each of your problems. These graphs indicate what you need to know and how to find it.

Example: Given the same $\overline{X}$ and σ as in the first example. We wish to find the score corresponding to the 70th and 40th percentile rank. For P_{70}, our graph would be as follows:

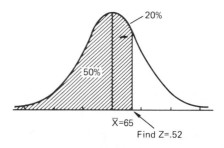

$\overline{X}=65$
Find $Z=.52$

We are looking for the point between which it and the mean lie 20 percent of the scores. By searching in the body of Table 4.4, we find that 20 percent falls between 0.52 and 0.53, but is closer to 0.52. Therefore, a Z-score of 0.52 is equal to P_{70}. To get back to our test score units, we use the following revised Z-score formula, which allows us to go from Z-scores to raw scores:

Since $Z = \dfrac{X - \overline{X}}{\sigma}$

$$X = \overline{X} + Z\sigma$$

In our case, then, $X = 65 + (0.52)\ 11$
$$= 65 + 5.72 = 70.72$$

Therefore, $P_{70} \simeq 71$.

To find P_{40}, we again start with the graph.

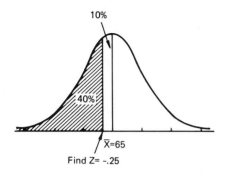

Find Z= -.25

It shows that we are looking for the point between which it and the mean lie 10 percent of the scores. From Table 4.4, we find that to be 0.25. Since this point is below the mean, P_{40} is equal to a -0.25 Z-score. Again, our test score is found using:

$$X = \overline{X} + Z\sigma$$

$$= 65 + (-0.25)\,11$$

$$= 65 - 2.75 = 62.25$$

Therefore, $P_{40} \simeq 62$.

We often hear of instructors grading on the curve. This usually entails the use of the normal curve. An example of this use of the normal curve is given in the following example.

Example: A teacher decides to give 5 percent As, 15 percent Bs, 60 percent Cs, 15 percent Ds, and 5 percent Fs on a test just given. Assume that the $\overline{X} = 60$ and $\sigma = 10$ for this test.

The distribution of grade percentages is shown on the following normal curve.

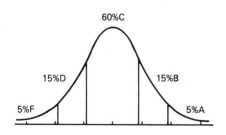

As you can see, this is simply a problem in determining P_{05}, P_{20}, P_{80}, and P_{95}. To find the score needed for an A, we must find P_{95}. For P_{95}, we find from Table 4.4, $Z = 1.64$ and therefore: $X = 60 + 1.64\ (10) = 60 + 16.4 = 76.4$ or 76 and above. For P_{80}, we find from Table 4.4, $Z = 0.84$ and therefore: $X = 60 + 0.84\ (10) = 60 + 8.4 = 68.4$ or 68. For P_{20}, we find from Table 4.4, $Z = -0.84$ and therefore: $X = 60 - 0.84\ (10) = 60 - 8.4 = 51.6$ or 52. For P_{05}, we find $Z = -1.64$ and therefore: $X = 60 - 1.64\ (10) = 60 - 16.4 = 43.6$ or 44. Our grading distribution then turns out to be:

A = upper 5% = 76–above

B = next 15% = 68–76

C = middle 60% = 52–68

D = next 15% = 44–52

F = lowest 5% = 44–below

correlation

We often talk about two or more occurrences or performances being related to one another. For example, we might expect performance on the standing long jump to be related to performance on the jump and reach since both performances rely heavily on leg power. That is, individuals who score high on the one task will also score high on the other, while individuals who score low or average on the one will score the same on the other. Rather than subjectively estimating whether or not performances are related, and if so to what degree, we can use statistical techniques to determine this. These techniques involve the calculation of a correlation coefficient.

A *correlation coefficient* is the mathematically computed degree of relationship or agreement between variables. This coefficient also indicates the direction of a relationship, since in many cases two variables may be negatively related—for example, people who score high on one variable tend to score low on the other variable. The correlation coefficient is universally denoted by the letter *r*.

If there is perfect agreement between two variables, that is, if the person with the highest score on one variable also has the highest score on the other variable and the person with the next highest score on one is also the second highest on the other variable, and so on, there is a perfect positive agreement and $r = 1.00$. If there is perfect agreement but in the opposite direction, that is, the person with the highest score on one variable has the lowest score on the other variable, the person with the second highest score on one has the second lowest score on the other, and so on, there is perfect negative agreement and $r = -1.00$. It is extremely rare to have a perfect correlation. An $r = 0.00$ indicates that no relationship or agreement whatsoever exists between the variables; hence, they are said to be independent of one another. Again, it is extremely rare for variables to have absolutely no relationship. Generally, variables are related in some degree to one another, but not perfectly.

The square of the correlation coefficient (r^2) is often reported in the literature. This r^2 represents the amount of overlap that exists between two variables. More specifically, this r^2 represents the percentage of variance that two variables share. Figure 4.13 shows this in diagrammatic form.

r^2 is called the *coefficient of determination*. Its counterpart ($1 - r^2$) is called the *coefficient of nondetermination*. Their values range from zero to one. The coefficient of determination is a better indicator of relationship than *r* since it can be more easily interpreted. It should also be emphasized that a negative correlation of the same magnitude as a positive correlation indicates the same degree of relationship since the coefficient of determination is the same in each case. For example, a correlation of -0.80

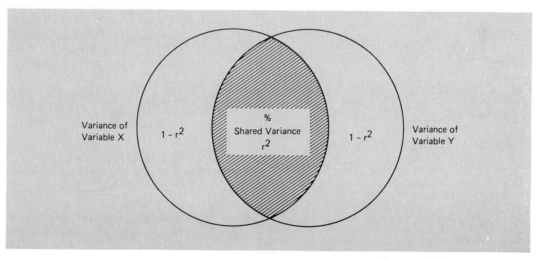

Figure 4.13 Percent of shared variance

indicates just as strong a relationship as a correlation of $+0.80$ since in each case $r^2 = 0.64$.

Two common techniques for determining the correlation between two variables are the Spearman rank-order correlation, which is the agreement between the ranks on two variables and the Pearson product-moment correlation, which indicates the similarity of position on the normal curve for two variables. In each case, there must be a pair of scores or ranks for each person. The Spearman rank-order correlation coefficient is usually denoted by *rho* in order to distinguish it from the Pearsonian *r*. Following are examples of how to determine each of these coefficients.

Example of Applying rho: Suppose that ten students have been ranked 1 through 10, with 1 indicating the best, on their ability to serve in tennis. Further assume that a ladder tournament was conducted for these students and the students' rankings were again recorded from 1 through 10. The results of these two rankings are presented in the first two columns of Table 4.5. It can be seen that student D, for example, was the fifth best on the service rankings, but finished eighth in the ladder tournament. Note that students C and E tied for the third and fourth ranks on serving and were each given the rank of 3.5.

Assume that we want to determine the relationship between these two performances. That is, we want to determine to what degree the rankings on serves are related to the tournament results. Since we have only the performance ranks available, it is appropriate to calculate the Spearman rank-order correlation coefficient.

The formula for determining *rho* is

$$rho = 1 - \frac{6(\Sigma D^2)}{N(N^2 - 1)}$$

Table 4.5   Rank-Order Correlation

Student	Rank on Tennis Serving	Rank in Ladder Tournament	D	D²
A	6	5	1	1
B	9	8	1	1
C	3.5	1	2.5	6.25
D	5	8	−3	9
E	3.5	4	−0.5	0.25
F	8	6	2	4
G	10	9	1	1
H	2	2	0	0
I	7	7	0	0
J	1	3	−2	4
				Sum = 26.5

$\Sigma D^2 = 26.5$ $N = 10$

$$rho = 1 - \frac{6(26.5)}{10(100 - 1)} = 1 - \frac{159}{990} = 1 - 0.16 = 0.84$$

where ΣD^2 is the sum of the differences between the ranks of students on the two tests squared and N is the total number of students.

The column labeled D in Table 4.5 represents the differences between the ranks obtained by the students on the two tests while D^2 simply indicates that each of these differences has been squared.

In this example,

$$rho = 1 - \frac{6(\Sigma D^2)}{N(N^2 - 1)}$$

$$= 1 - \frac{6(26.5)}{10(100 - 1)} = 1 - \frac{159}{990}$$

$$= 1 - 0.16 = 0.84$$

This correlation of 0.84 indicates that a sizeable positive relationship does exist between the two variables, a fact that might have reasonably been expected.

Table 4.6 Correlation Coefficient Calculation

Chins X	X²	Push-ups Y	Y²	XY
5	25	20	400	100
2	4	19	361	38
12	144	35	1225	420
8	64	17	289	136
1	1	12	144	12
7	49	23	529	161
5	25	19	361	95
9	81	29	841	261
3	9	16	256	48
5	25	22	484	110

$\Sigma X = 57$ $\Sigma X^2 = 427$ $\Sigma Y = 212$ $\Sigma Y^2 = 4890$

$\Sigma XY = 1381$

$$\bar{X} = \frac{57}{10} = 5.7 \qquad \bar{Y} = \frac{212}{10} = 21.2$$

$$r = \frac{\Sigma XY - NXY}{\sqrt{(\Sigma \bar{X}^2 - N\bar{X}^2)(\Sigma Y^2 - N\bar{Y}^2)}} =$$

$$\frac{1381 - 10\,(5.7)\,(21.2)}{\sqrt{[427 - 10(5.7)^2]\,[4890 - 10(21.2)^2]}}$$

$$= \frac{1381 - 1208.4}{\sqrt{(427 - 324.9)(4890 - 4494.4)}} =$$

$$\frac{172.6}{\sqrt{(102.1)(395.6)}} = \frac{172.6}{200.9} = 0.86$$

since $r = 0.86$, $r^2 = (.86)^2 = 0.74$

The Spearman rank-order correlation coefficient can also be used when one or both of the variables are quantitative scores and not just ranks. To do this, one simply assigns ranks to individual performances in accordance with the performance. An exercise in doing this is given at the end of the chapter.

Example of Applying Pearson r: In Table 4.6 scores for students on push-ups and chins are presented. Since we have actual scores on both of the variables, the Pearson r should be used to determine the degree of relationship between them. The definitional formula for the Pearson correlation coefficient is:

$$r = \frac{\sum_{i=1}^{N}(X_i - \bar{X})(Y_i - \bar{Y})}{\sqrt{\left[\sum_{i=1}^{N}(X_i - \bar{X})^2\right]\left[\sum_{i=1}^{N}(Y_i - \bar{Y})^2\right]}}$$

An equivalent formula that is convenient for calculation purposes is:

$$r = \frac{\sum_{i=1}^{N}X_i Y_i - N\bar{X}\bar{Y}}{\sqrt{\left(\sum_{i=1}^{N}X_i^2 - N\bar{X}^2\right)\left(\sum_{i=1}^{N}Y_i^2 - N\bar{Y}^2\right)}}$$

All the components in this formula and how they are calculated are shown in Table 4.6, which should be sufficiently self-explanatory.

regression

A correlation coefficient can also be used to predict the performance on one variable when the performance on another variable is known. If you wish to predict performance on one variable from another variable, it is appropriate to use a procedure called *regression*. A regression equation is determined in the form:

$$Y = a + bX$$

which is the equation of a straight line. Y represents the variable scores to be predicted, X represents the variable scores used to predict Y, b represents the amount of change in Y associated with each unit change in *X*, and *a* represents the constant adjustment that must be made in order to put *X* and *Y* on the same scale. In other words, *b* is a weight and indicates the amount that the predicted *Y* score will increase for each corresponding change in *X*. The formula for finding *a* and *b* are:

$$b = \frac{\Sigma(X - \overline{X})(Y - \overline{Y})}{\Sigma(X - \overline{X})^2}$$

$$= \frac{\Sigma XY - [(\Sigma X)(\Sigma Y)/N]}{\Sigma X^2 - [(\Sigma X)^2/N]} \text{ and}$$

$$a = \overline{Y} - b\,\overline{X}$$

Using Table 4.6, if we want to find a regression equation for predicting push-ups from chin scores, we find that:

$$b = \frac{1381 - [(57)(212)/10]}{427 - [(57)^2/10]} = \frac{1381 - 1208.4}{427 - 324.9}$$

$$= \frac{172.6}{102.1} = 1.69$$

and

$$a = 21.1 - (1.69)(5.7) = 21.2 - 9.63 = 11.57$$

Therefore, the regression equation is:

$$Y = 11.57 + 1.69\,X$$

To apply this equation: If a student were to do six chins, we would predict that he could do [11.57 + 1.69(6)] = 11.57 + 10.14 = 21.71 or 22 push-ups.

A graphic presentation of this example is presented in Figure 4.14. Each of the dots

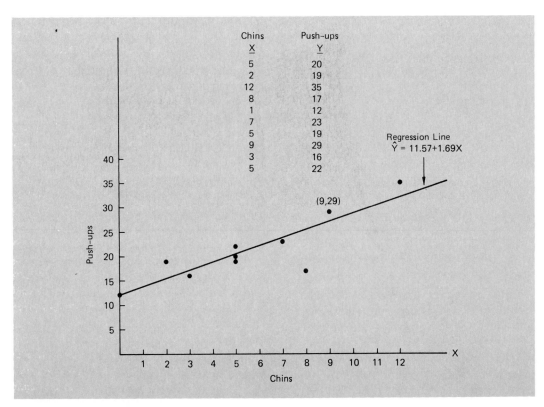

Chins	Push-ups
X	Y
5	20
2	19
12	35
8	17
1	12
7	23
5	19
9	29
3	16
5	22

Regression Line
$\hat{Y} = 11.57 + 1.69X$

(9,29)

Figure 4.14   Graphic presentation of a regression equation

on the graph in Figure 4.14 represents a pair of scores obtained by an individual. For example, the circled dot represents a person who did 9 chins and 29 push-ups. The line represents the determined regression line. This line is called the "best fit" line which means that it is the line that allows the most accurate prediction of Y-scores from X-scores. The correlation coefficient tells us how well this regression line fits the pairs of scores—this is the connection between regression and correlation.

Regression or prediction is important in the development of many tests in physical education. It is often possible to predict a variable that is difficult to measure on the basis of a variable that is not so difficult to measure. For example, max VO_2 has generally been shown to be an excellent indicator of cardiovascular fitness. However, in order to actually measure VO_2 a great deal of expensive lab equipment and time is needed. Therefore, a prediction or regression equation for predicting VO_2 from scores on a 12-minute run for distance or from some other more easily measured variable would be most helpful.

shape of relationships

So far only straight-line regression and/or correlation has been discussed. It is possible, however, to have a relationship between two variables that cannot be represented by a straight line. Such is the case in the relationship between age and speed. We expect people's speed to improve with age until about the age of 25. After the age of 25, we expect speed to decline. Figure 4.15 shows this graphically.

As can be seen in Figure 4.15 a straight line does not fit this relationship very well. Al-

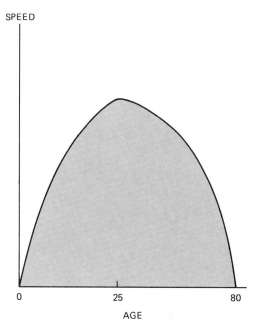

Figure 4.15   Relationship between age and speed

though it is important that you be aware of possible curvilinear relationships, it is well beyond the scope of this text to discuss the procedures for determining curvilinear correlations.

cautions in correlation interpretation

All linear correlations should be viewed with caution. The possible existence of a curvilinear relationship is only one reason for caution. Another reason for caution is that a correlation coefficient represents the relationship for only the range of scores found in the variables. For example, if we relate age with speed, and our subjects range in age from 10 to 25, our correlation can be interpreted only for that age range. To extend it beyond that is obviously dangerous. Also, the size of a correlation coefficient depends greatly on the number of pairs of scores from which it is determined. A small number of score pairs will result in a higher correlation coefficient than a large number of score pairs since it is easier to fit a line to a small number of points than to a large number of points.

A correlation coefficient indicates only the relationship between variables and does not necessarily indicate that a cause-and-effect phenomenon is in effect. For example, the amount of liquor sold in a state and teachers' salaries have been shown to be fairly highly correlated. Hopefully, there is not a direct cause-and-effect relationship present in this example. Finally, the variance for each variable affects the size of a correlation coefficient. If a variable is highly homogeneous, it is extremely difficult to find anything that is highly correlated to it.

other statistical techniques

Numerous other statistical techniques are used in measurement and evaluation. Since this is not a statistics text, only three other commonly used techniques will be very briefly introduced. For a more detailed coverage of these topics, see the references at the end of the chapter.

multiple correlation and regression

We can extend the discussion on regression and correlation by considering the possibility of two or more easily measured variables predicting a variable that is most difficult to measure. This is precisely what is done in multiple regression; namely, two or more variables are used to predict some other variable. The regression equation is written: $y = a + b_1X_1 + b_2X_2 + \ldots b_pX_p$ where b_i represents the weight or importance of that particular predictor. How well the X-variables predict the Y-variable is determined by a multiple correlation coefficient, denoted by R, which ranges from 0 to $+1.00$.

This technique has been applied in physical education in determining the percent lean body mass. The direct methods of determining percent lean body mass (underwater weighing and scintillation counter) are either extremely time-consuming or require very expensive equipment. Exercise scientists have discovered that by taking several skinfold measures and calculating multiple regression equations, the percent lean body mass can be fairly accurately estimated. The exact nature of these equations is given in chapter 10.

factor analysis

Factor analysis is another method of correlation that begins with a set of correlation coefficients between many tests thought to be part of a certain domain. These tests are mathematically arranged into clusters on the basis of a common ingredient(s). That is, tests that are determined to measure something in common are grouped together. This group, cluster, or factor is then usually given a name describing the common ingredient. Usually several (4 to 16) of these factors are identified.

Factor analysis is a valuable statistical tool in measurement and evaluation when we are attempting to determine the underlying ingredients in a complex domain. An example in the application of this tool is in the development of Kenyon's Attitude Toward Physical Activity Questionnaire. Gerald Kenyon identified six dimensions that he and other experts thought were the ingredients in people's attitudes toward physical activity. Questions were written for each of the dimensions and administered to a large number of subjects. The subjects' scores were factor analyzed and five of the six hypothesized dimensions were found to be valid. This questionnaire is presented in chapter 13.

analysis of variance

The term *analysis of variance* actually refers to an entire family of techniques that are extremely useful in the scientific construction of physical performance tests. More specifically, these techniques are particularly useful in establishing the reliability of performance tests and, to a lesser extent, in establishing the validity of tests. No attempt is made in this text to present all the details of these techniques. However, in the appendix an analysis of variance problem in determining reliability is worked out. If further study into this area is desired at this point, we recommend that either the text by Margaret Safrit or the one by Charles Dotson and Don Kirkendall be consulted for excellent coverage of this topic.[2] Let it suffice here to say that in analysis of variance techniques, the total variance in a group of test scores is partitioned into various categories, those categories usually being: within individuals, between individuals, and between trials and/or days.

data processing

Many elementary and secondary schools now either have their own computers or have ready access to a computer. Thus, it is becoming more and more helpful and necessary for the teacher to know something about the use of computers. Such knowledge, when applied, is a great time-saver since the only real purpose of a computer is to perform repetitive tasks rapidly. Computers don't think; they only do very quickly what they are programmed to do.

Certainly, it is not possible, nor is it the intent to give a thorough presentation of computer usage in physical education in this text. Entire courses and texts are devoted to such a goal. Rather, it is the intent here simply to introduce you to some of the possibilities available. Since each computer system operates a little differently only some universal aspects of computers are given. To use a computer system, its unique features need to be learned.

2. Margaret J. Safrit, *Evaluation in Physical Education, Assessing Motor Behavior* (Englewood Cliffs, N.J.: Prentice-Hall, 1973); Charles O. Dotson and Don R. Kirkendall, *Statistics For Physical Education, Health, and Recreation* (New York: Harper & Row, 1974).

optical scanning

One of the most useful devices available with most computer facilities is an optical scanner —a machine that scores written objective tests. To use an optical scanner, students must answer questions by darkening in appropriate boxes on an answer sheet or card. Examples of an answer sheet and card are presented in Figures 4.16 and 4.17.

Students' answer cards are placed in an optical scanner, which scores each one. If a test has more items than those indicated on the card or sheet, additional cards and sheets can be used. Quite frequently systems are set up to handle cards or sheets with item responses on both sides.

The obvious advantage in using optical scanning is the speed with which large numbers of tests can be scored. Also, on most systems individual student scores are automatically fed into a computer program, which computes and prints out a frequency distribution, the median, the mean, standard deviation, standard scores, and other descriptive parameters for the group or class. An example of such a computer printout is given in Figure 4.18. In this example, a 25-item test was given to thirty-six students.

The obvious disadvantage to optical scanning is that only multiple choice or true and false test items can be used. Obviously, optical scanning cannot be used for motor performance tests or for essay and short answer written tests. Nevertheless, computers and computer programs can still be used to one's advantage once scores are obtained by methods other than machine scoring.

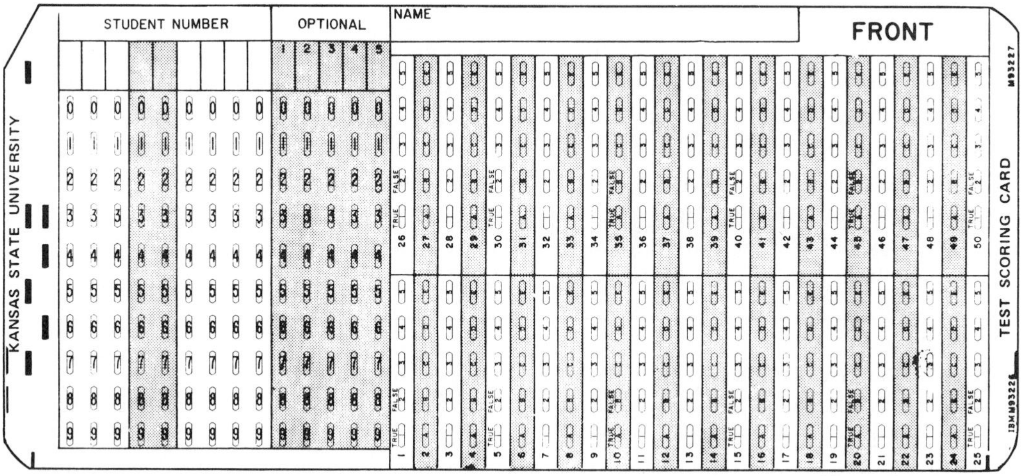

Figure 4.16   Optical scanning card

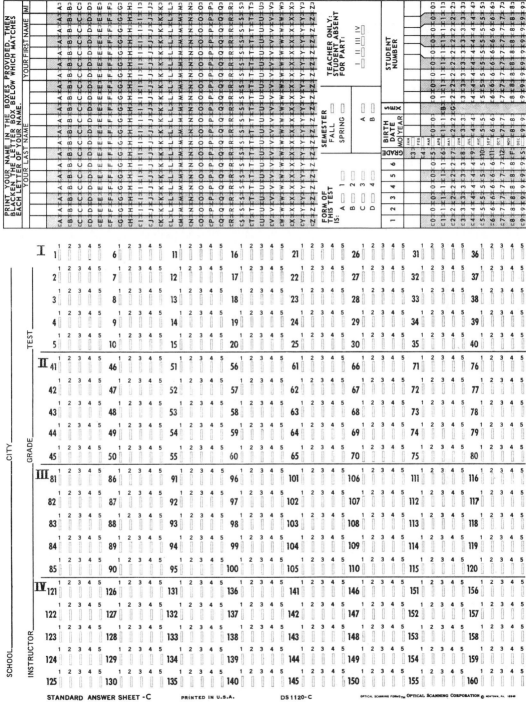

Figure 4.17 Computer scoring sheet

SCORE	FREQUENCY	PERCENTILE RANK	Z-SCORE	T-SCORE	SCALED SCORE
22	4	94	+1.46	65	88
21	4	83	+1.04	60	84
20	5	71	+0.61	56	80
19	7	54	+0.19	52	76
18	5	37	-0.23	48	72
17	5	24	-0.65	43	68
16	2	14	-1.07	39	64
15	1	10	-1.50	35	60
14	2	6	-1.92	31	56
13	1	1	-2.34	26	52

SCORE - LIST OF TOTAL SCORES OBTAINED ON THE TEST, RANKED FROM THE HIGHEST TO THE LOWEST SCORE OBTAINED.

FREQUENCY - NUMBER OF STUDENTS OBTAINING EACH SCORE.

PERCENTILE RANK - THE PERCENT OF STUDENTS IN THE CLASS OBTAINING SCORES EQUAL TO OR LOWER THAN THIS SCORE.

Z-SCORE - A STANDARD SCORE EXPRESSED AS A DEVIATION FROM THE MEAN IN TERMS OF THE STANDARD DEVIATION OF THIS DISTRIBUTION. IT TELLS HOW MANY STANDARD DEVIATIONS A SCORE IS FROM THE MEAN; THE SIGN INDICATES THE DIRECTION.

T-SCORE - A CONVERTED STANDARD SCORE WHICH HAS A MEAN OF 50 AND A STANDARD DEVIATION OF 10. T-SCORE = 50 +10(Z-SCORE)

MEAN - THE ARITHMETIC AVERAGE OF ALL SCORES ON THE TEST.

MEDIAN - THE MIDPOINT OF THE DISTRIBUTION OF SCORES - ABOVE AND BELOW WHICH AN EQUAL NUMBER OF RANKED SCORES LIE.

1ST QUARTILE - THAT POINT BELOW WHICH 1/4 OF THE SCORES LIE.

3RD QUARTILE - THAT POINT ABOVE WHICH 1/4 OF THE SCORES LIE.

STANDARD DEVIATION - A MEASURE OF HOW MUCH THE SCORES ARE SPREAD OUT OR HOW VARIABLE THEY ARE, OR CONVERSELY, THE TENDENCY OF THE SCORES TO CLUSTER ABOUT THE MEAN. IT IS BASED ON THE DEVIATION OF EACH SCORE FROM THE MEAN.

KUDER-RICHARDSON - HOW CONSISTENTLY THE SAME GROUP OF STUDENTS WOULD SCORE IF THEY WERE TO TAKE THE TEST OVER AND OVER. (A MEASURE OF THE RELIABILITY OF THE TEST.)

STANDARD ERROR - AN ESTIMATE OF VARIABILITY EXPECTED IN THE INDIVIDUAL'S SCORES IF HE WERE TO TAKE THE TEST OVER AND OVER. (BASED ON THE STANDARD DEVIATION AND THE KUDER-RICHARDSON RELIABILITY.)

NUMBER OF TESTS	36
POSSIBLE SCORE	25
MEAN	18.56
3RD QUARTILE	20.30
MEDIAN	18.79
1ST QUARTILE	17.10
STANDARD DEVIATION .	2.36
KUDER-RICHARDSON ...	0.40
STANDARD ERROR	1.83

Figure 4.18

data cards

When scores are obtained, regardless of the means, they can be recorded on data cards, which permit the scores/data to be read into the computer. An example of a data card is shown in Figure 4.19.

There are 80 columns on the card, consisting of the digits 0 to 9. The digits that are punched out are what is read into the computer. In the example data card, the numbers to be read into the computer are 3124655-3676. Without a code, these numbers are meaningless; therefore, a code is needed to indicate what each column on the card represents. Let's assume for our example that the first two columns represent a student's number, the next column his class, the next two columns his score on a 50-item test, the next three columns his height in inches to the nearest tenth, and the next three columns his score for the standing broad jump to the nearest tenth of an inch. The remaining columns are not used. Our example card shows then that this is student number 31, who is in the second period class, scored 46 on the 50-item test, stands 55.3 inches in height, and leaped 67.6 inches on the standing broad jump.

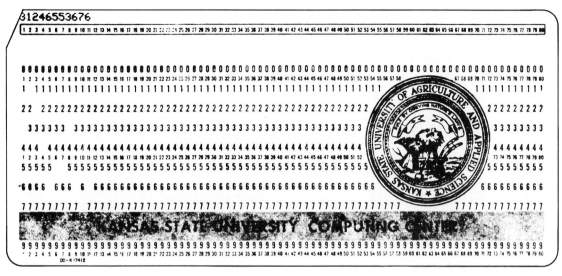

Figure 4.19 Sample data card

Decimal points are not normally punched into data cards. The placement of the decimal point is indicated by a card called a *format card.* The same format is used for each student/subject whose data are to be used in the same analysis. Cards are also needed to tell the computer what to do with these data or scores. These are called *job control* cards, and they will differ for various computer systems.

Rather than attempt to explain further the procedures used for analyzing data with a computer, it is suggested that a visit be made to the computing center at your institution. The best way to learn how to use a computer is to *use it.* You may be surprised how simple it is, and you are certain to be pleased at how easily it does routine calculations for you.

summary review questions

1. What is the basic reason for studying and understanding statistics? (*answer on p. 27*)

2. What is the major goal of statistics? (*answer on p. 28*)

3. When one has information on every individual in a group, what statistical methods are used to describe the group? (*answer on p. 28*)

4. When one has information on only a representative part of a total group, what statistical methods are used to describe the total group? (*answer on p. 28*)

5. Why is it more common for the practicing physical education teacher to use descriptive statistics rather than inferential statistics to describe a group? (*answer on p. 28*)

6. What is a distribution? (*answer on p. 30*)

7. What is a frequency distribution? (*answer on p. 30*)

8. How does one obtain the (a) relative frequency, (b) frequency percent, (c) cumulative frequency, (d) relative cumulative frequency, and (e) percentile rank? (*answer on p. 31*)

9. What does the percentile rank of a score represent? (*answer on p. 31*)

10. Why is the percentile rank of a score a useful representative of that score? (*answer on p. 31*)

11. What are histograms, polygons, and ogives? (*answer on p. 33*)

12. What are the three most common measures of central tendency? Define each of these measures. (*answers on p. 35*))

13. Why is the mean an excellent measure of central tendency? (*answer on p. 37*)

14. What are the four measures of variability presented in this chapter? Define each of these measures of variability. (*answer on pp. 38-41*)

15. What are the three standard scores presented in this chapter? How is each determined? (*answer on pp. 41, 42*)

16. What is the mean and standard deviation of (a) a Z-score distribution, (b) a T-score distribution, and (c) a 6-σ score distribution? (*answer on p. 42*)

17. Why would one wish to change scores to standard scores? (*answer on p. 41*)

18. The normal curve is mathematically defined and may be used to determine the percentage of scores expected between any two points. What is the relative measure usually determined by the practicing physical education teacher in using this concept? (*answer on p. 44*)

19. What is a correlation coefficient? (*answer on p. 49*)

20. What does the square of the correlation coefficient represent? (*answer on p. 49*)

21. Why should all linear correlations be viewed with caution? (*answer on p. 54*)

bibliography

Alder, H. L., and Roessler, E. B. *Introduction to Probability and Statistics.* San Francisco: W. H. Freeman, 1968.

Dixon, Wilfrid J., and Massey, Frank J., Jr. *Introduction to Statistical Analysis.* 3d ed. New York: McGraw-Hill, 1969.

Dotson, Charles O., and Kirkendall, Don R. *Statistics for Physical Education, Health, and Recreation.* New York: Harper & Row, 1974.

Ferguson, G. A. *Statistical Analysis in Psychology and Education.* New York: McGraw-Hill, 1971.

Hall, P. G. *Elementary Statistics.* New York: John Wiley and Sons, 1971.

Hammond, K. R.; Householder, J. E.; and Castellan, N. J., Jr. *Introduction to the Statistical Method.* New York: Knopf, 1970.

Hays, William L. *Statistics.* New York: Holt, Rinehart and Winston, 1963.

Marascuilo, L. A. *Statistical Methods for Behavioral Science Research.* New York: McGraw-Hill, 1971.

Minimum, Edward W. *Statistical Reasoning in Psychology and Education.* New York: John Wiley and Sons, 1970.

Ostle, Bernard. *Statistics in Research.* Ames: The Iowa State University Press, 1963.

Remington, R. D., and Schork, M. A. *Statistics with Applications to the Biological and Health Sciences.* Englewood Cliffs, N.J.: Prentice-Hall, 1970.

Runyon, R. P., and Haber, A. *Fundamentals of Behavioral Statistics.* Reading, Mass.: Addison-Wesley, 1971.

Safrit, Margaret J. *Evaluation in Physical Education, Assessing Motor Behavior.* Englewood Cliffs, N.J.: Prentice-Hall, 1973.

Siegel, Sidney. *Nonparametric Statistics for the Behavioral Sciences.* New York: McGraw-Hill, 1956.

Winer, B. J. *Statistical Principles in Experimental Design.* New York: McGraw-Hill, 1971.

exercises

1. A physical education teacher measured the height of 66 students who were juniors in the local high school. He measured each student's height in centimeters with a stadiometer and obtained the following results:

Student	Height (cm)	Student	Height (cm)	Student	Height (cm)
S1	183.4	S23	185.4	S45	180.1
S2	186.2	S24	172.0	S46	170.4
S3	177.3	S25	170.2	S47	186.4
S4	169.9	S26	175.5	S48	178.8
S5	171.7	S27	177.6	S49	174.5
S6	181.6	S28	180.1	S50	192.5
S7	171.2	S29	188.2	S51	174.8
S8	184.4	S30	176.0	S52	185.9
S9	171.7	S31	174.8	S53	193.6
S10	172.5	S32	174.5	S54	179.6
S11	159.3	S33	175.0	S55	177.0
S12	177.0	S34	173.5	S56	161.0
S13	164.1	S35	172.0	S57	171.7
S14	173.0	S36	172.0	S58	178.8
S15	184.4	S37	179.3	S59	182.9
S16	171.2	S38	176.5	S60	166.4
S17	175.5	S39	165.9	S61	191.3
S18	180.9	S40	171.2	S62	177.6
S19	167.6	S41	174.8	S63	187.7
S20	181.1	S42	174.8	S64	167.9
S21	183.6	S43	168.4	S65	170.4
S22	181.9	S44	179.6	S66	160.0

a. Calculate a mean and standard deviation.
b. Calculate a Z-score for each student.
c. Calculate a T-score for each student.
d. Calculate a 6-σ score for each student.
e. Calculate a range for the distribution.
f. Develop a frequency distribution table. Use an interval of 1 cm change in height from low to high score.
g. Construct an ogive for percentile rank and height.
h. Estimate the percentile rank of students S1, S2, S4, S11, and S53, using the area under a normal curve. Compare this estimated percentile rank with the actual calculated percentile rank from your frequency distribution table.

Answers:
a. $\bar{X} = 176.3\,\text{cm}$ $\sigma = 7.43\,\text{cm}$
b, c, and d.

	(b) Z-score	(c) T-score	(d) 6-σ-score
S1	.96	59.6	66.0
S2	1.33	63.3	72.2
S3	.13	51.3	52.2
S4	− .86	41.4	35.7
S5	− .62	43.8	39.7
S6	.71	57.1	61.9
S7	−. 69	43.1	38.5
S8	1.09	60.9	68.2
S9	− .62	43.8	39.7
S10	− .51	44.9	41.5
S11	− 2.28	27.2	12.0
S12	.09	50.9	51.6
S13	− 1.64	33.6	22.6
S14	− .44	45.6	42.6
S15	1.09	60.9	68.2
S16	− .69	43.1	38.6
S17	− .12	48.8	48.2
S18	.62	56.2	60.3
S19	− 1.17	38.3	30.5
S20	.65	−56.5	60.8
S21	.98	59.8	66.4
S22	.75	57.5	62.6
S23	1.22	62.2	70.4
S24	− .58	44.2	40.4
S25	− .82	41.8	36.3
S26	− .11	48.9	48.2
S27	.17	51.7	52.9
S28	.51	55.1	58.5
S29	1.60	66.0	76.7
S30	− .04	49.6	49.3
S31	− .20	48.0	46.6
S32	− .24	47.6	46.0
S33	− .17	48.3	47.1
S34	− .38	46.2	43.7
S35	− .58	44.2	40.4
S36	− .58	44.2	40.4
S37	.40	54.0	56.7
S38	.03	50.3	50.4
S39	−1.40	36.0	26.7
S40	− .69	43.1	38.6
S41	− .20	48.0	46.6
S42	− .20	48.0	46.6

	(b) Z-score	(c) T-score	(d) 6-σ-score
S43	−1.06	39.4	32.3
S44	.44	54.4	57.4
S45	.51	55.1	58.5
S46	− .79	42.1	36.8
S47	1.36	63.6	72.7
S48	.34	53.4	55.6
S49	− .24	47.6	46.0
S50	2.18	71.8	86.3
S51	− .20	48.0	46.6
S52	1.29	62.9	71.5
S53	2.33	73.3	88.8
S54	.44	54.4	57.4
S55	.09	50.9	51.6
S56	− 2.05	29.5	15.7
S57	− .62	43.8	39.7
S58	.34	53.4	55.6
S59	.89	58.9	64.8
S60	− 1.33	36.7	27.8
S61	2.02	70.2	83.7
S62	.17	51.7	52.9
S63	1.53	65.3	75.6
S64	− 1.13	38.7	31.2
S65	− .79	42.1	36.8
S66	− 2.19	28.1	13.4

e. 34.3 cm

f.

Height (cm.)	f	Rel f	f %	Cum f	Rel Cum f	%tile rank
193–193.9	1	.015	1.5	66	1.00	100
192–192.9	1	.015	1.5	65	.984	98
191–191.9	1	.015	1.5	64	.969	97
190–190.9	0	.000	0.0	63	.954	95
189–189.9	0	.000	0.0	63	.954	95
188–188.9	1	.015	1.5	63	.954	95
187–187.9	1	.015	1.5	62	.939	94
186–186.9	2	.030	3.0	61	.924	92
185–185.9	2	.030	3.0	59	.893	89
184–184.9	2	.030	3.0	57	.863	86
183–183.9	2	.030	3.0	55	.833	83
182–182.9	1	.015	1.5	53	.803	80
181–181.9	3	.045	4.5	52	.787	79

(f—con't.)

Height (cm)	f	Rel f	f %	Cum f	Rel Cum f	%tile Rank
180–180.9	3	.045	4.5	49	.742	74
179–179.9	3	.045	4.5	46	.696	70
178–178.9	2	.030	3.0	43	.651	65
177–177.9	5	.075	7.5	41	.621	62
176–176.9	2	.030	3.0	36	.545	55
175–175.9	3	.045	4.5	34	.515	52
174–174.9	6	.090	9.0	31	.469	47
173–173.9	2	.030	3.0	25	.378	38
172–172.9	4	.060	6.0	23	.348	35
171–171.9	6	.090	9.0	19	.287	29
170–170.9	3	.045	4.5	13	.196	20
169–169.9	1	.015	1.5	10	.151	15
168–168.9	1	.015	1.5	9	.136	14
167–167.9	2	.030	3.0	8	.121	12
166–166.9	1	.015	1.5	6	.090	9
165–165.9	1	.015	1.5	5	.075	8
164–164.9	1	.015	1.5	4	.060	6
163–163.9	0	.000	0.0	3	.045	5
162–162.9	0	.000	0.0	3	.045	5
161–161.9	1	.015	1.5	3	.045	5
160–160.9	1	.015	1.5	2	.030	3
159–159.9	1	.015	1.5	1	.015	2
below 159	0	.000	0.0	0	.000	0

TOTAL 66

g.

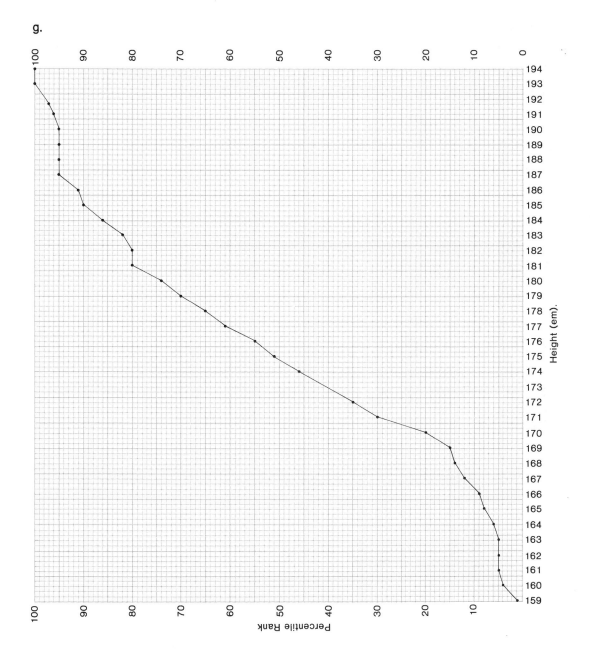

h. S1 Estimated percentile rank   = 83%
  Actual calculated percentile rank   = 83%

  S2 Estimated percentile rank   = 91%
  Actual calculated percentile rank   = 92%

  S4 Estimated percentile rank   = 19%
  Actual calculated percentile rank   = 15%

  S11 Estimated percentile rank   = 1%
  Actual calculated percentile rank   = 2%

  S53 Estimated percentile rank   = 99%
  Actual calculated percentile rank   = 100%

2. The same physical education teacher in problem 1 measured the weight of the same 66 students. He measured each student's weight in kilogram weights, using a metric weighing scale, with the following results:

Student	Weight kg wt	Student	Weight kg wt	Student	Weight kg wt
S1	78.9	S23	78.3	S45	68.6
S2	92.4	S24	69.4	S46	79.4
S3	71.9	S25	69.5	S47	71.4
S4	73.5	S26	63.4	S48	64.5
S5	77.0	S27	74.5	S49	75.6
S6	92.4	S28	86.1	S50	86.6
S7	67.0	S29	68.8	S51	77.2
S8	85.8	S30	71.4	S52	89.9
S9	69.2	S31	79.3	S53	88.0
S10	89.6	S32	69.1	S54	79.4
S11	60.3	S33	79.5	S55	68.2
S12	67.7	S34	68.6	S56	72.7
S13	60.9	S35	76.2	S57	73.4
S14	66.7	S36	74.0	S58	76.6
S15	78.4	S37	80.3	S59	81.4
S16	72.5	S38	72.2	S60	61.1
S17	92.6	S39	70.1	S61	90.7
S18	84.3	S40	77.0	S62	81.3
S19	62.9	S41	68.5	S63	82.4
S20	64.8	S42	76.5	S64	74.4
S21	95.6	S43	74.7	S65	65.0
S22	78.7	S44	94.1	S66	59.0

a. Calculate a mean and standard deviation.
b. Calculate a Z-score for each student.
c. Calculate a T-score for each student.
d. Calculate a $6\text{-}\sigma$ score for each student.

e. Calculate a range for the distribution.

f. Develop a frequency distribution table. Use an interval of 1 kg wt change in weight from low to high score.

g. Construct an ogive for percentile rank and weight.

h. Estimate the percentile rank of students S1, S2, S4, S11, and S53, using the area under a normal curve. Compare this estimated percentile rank with the actual calculated percentile rank from your frequency distribution table.

3. Convert the mean ($\overline{X}$) and the standard deviation (σ) height found in problem 1 to inches.

Answer:
$\overline{X} = 69.4$ *in.* $\sigma = 2.9$ *in.*

4. Convert the mean ($\overline{X}$) and the standard deviation (σ) weight found in problem 2 to pounds.

5. Calculate a Pearsonian *r* for the paired scores of height and weight in problems 1 and 2. Develop a predictive equation for predicting weight from height.

Answer:
$r_{XY} = 0.660$
$\hat{y} = -53.5 + .73X$

6. What is the percentage of shared variance between height and weight of the 66 students in problems 1 and 2?

7. A physical education teacher working with ten early elementary children with problems in motor performance decided to run a Spearman rank-order correlation coefficient between IQ score and strength. The following rankings on the two tests occurred:

Student	Rank on IQ test	Rank on strength test
S1	3	9
S2	8	5
S3	10	10
S4	2	8
S5	7	7
S6	1	3
S7	6	4
S8	9	2
S9	4	6
S10	5	1

What is the *rho* between these paired rankings?

Answer:
rho $= 0.042$

8. The same physical education teacher in problem 7 decided to run a Spearman rank-order correlation coefficient between IQ score and perceptual motor performance with the same ten children. The following rankings on the two tests occurred:

Student	Rank on IQ test	Rank on perceptual motor test
S1	3	4
S2	8	7
S3	10	8
S4	2	5
S5	7	6
S6	1	1
S7	6	3
S8	9	10
S9	4	2
S10	5	9

What is the *rho* between these paired rankings?

criteria for the selection and construction of tests

The selection and/or construction of tests is one of the most important phases of a measurement and evaluation program. If poor tests are selected or constructed, one is doomed to having a poor evaluation program. The purpose of this chapter is to present the criteria used in judging the quality of tests, both those selected and those constructed.

While it is critical that a test possess the characteristics presented, it is also important to emphasize the competence of the test administrator or user. Regardless of how "good" a test may be in terms of the following criteria or characteristics, if it is not administered and interpreted by a competent professional, then it is useless or worse. More is said about this in subsequent chapters.

Without question, the three most important characteristics of a test are its validity, reliability, and objectivity. These criteria are prerequisite to any of the remaining criteria for test selection or construction. *Validity is defined as how well a test measures what it is supposed to measure; reliability is the degree of consistency with which a test measures whatever it measures; and objectivity is the degree of agreement among testers.* A test is never perfectly valid, reliable, and objective. However, it must be reasonably so to be of any value.

validity

A synonym for validity might be relevance. We need to know if a test is relevant for a particular situation. Does it in fact measure what we say it does? Will it tell us who is best, next best, and so on? These are the most important questions we can ask about any test. If a test has poor validity, it is a waste of time to use it. When determining the validity of a test, we are actually determining its fairness and appropriateness.

content or logical validity

One way of determining validity is by using logic. This is usually the first step in constructing a valid test. If a test contains items that will logically measure the skill or ability we wish to measure, then we say it has logical or content validity. For example, if we want to measure baseball ability, we look at the skill components in baseball and try to include test items that will logically measure each of them. The components of the skill might be determined by one teacher or by a panel of experts.

Suppose, for example, that a panel of experts determined that the important skill components in baseball are fielding, throwing, and hitting. We would then, either on our own or through a panel of experts, devise test items that logically measure each component. Perhaps we would have as one item the fielding of ten ground balls on a smooth infield, counting the number of errors made. For the hitting component we might have a batting test where the batter swings at ten machine-pitched balls, scoring a point for each base hit. On the surface, or logically, this test appears to measure a baseball skill.

For written tests we can assume content validity in much the same way we do for physical performance tests, namely, by analyzing what we wish to measure and including items that logically measure it. Processes commonly used to do this include examining course outlines carefully, analyzing textbooks, and/or reviewing other tests in the area.

Establishing content validity is extremely important in test selection or construction. Chapter 7 on test construction has a great amount of detail on how to determine or ensure content validity.

Content validity does not determine the degree to which a test measures what it is supposed to measure. Rather, it is established by assumption or definition. Content validity is essential but not sufficient. We need ways of establishing validity empirically if we are to determine the *degree* of validity. Test items may be determined subjectively, scores may be determined subjectively, but the degree of validity must be determined objectively.

concurrent validity

One empirical means of determining validity is to establish a criterion for the variable we wish to measure and then determine how closely a proposed test relates to this criterion. This form of validity is called *concurrent* or *criterion-related validity*. When establishing concurrent validity, the most important step is determining what criterion will be used.

One commonly used criterion is expert opinion. A panel of judges rates students' abilities in the skill under consideration. Although this rating is subjective in nature, we can provide guidelines to the raters or judges, and have some assurance that they are rating on the same skill components. After obtaining an overall rating from the judges, the proposed test is given to the same students. The correlation between these two sets of scores (ratings and test scores) is the validity coefficient.

Another criterion used in concurrent validity is tournament results. This is a particularly effective method for determining the validity of individual sports skills tests. For a proposed tennis skill test, for example, we might first have a ladder tournament to rank our students' playing abilities. We then give the proposed test to these same students and find the correlation between the test scores and the tournament rankings. This correlation indicates the degree of validity of our proposed test.

Another means of establishing concurrent validity is to use an already established valid test as the criterion. The validity coefficient is then the correlation between the proposed test and the established test. Although this method is commonly used, validity coefficients established in this manner should be viewed with extreme caution. Since the already established test is undoubtedly not completely valid, any relationship between it and the new test may be partially due to the new test's relationship to the invalid portion of the established one. This possibility is even greater if the established test is the third or fourth "generation" or more.

Some guidance should be given as to how large a validity coefficient is considered acceptable. Although acceptable size depends on the particular situation, some guidelines can be given. In general, if the validity coefficient is determined on a group of 100 or more students, the following rating might be used:

Excellent	0.80–1.00
High	0.70–0.79
Average or Fair	0.50–0.69
Unacceptable	0.00–0.49

Again, these coefficients should be viewed with great caution. The acceptability of any validity coefficient depends on the purpose, situation, and intended use of the test, and appropriateness of criterion.

predictive validity

If a test is to be used for predicting future performances of individuals, then predictive validity needs to be determined. For example, if we want a test that will predict playing success in basketball, we administer the proposed test to a group of students, then, at a later date, rate their success at playing the game. The correlation between the test scores and the playing success ratings indicate the test's predictive validity. If the correlation coefficient were satisfactory, we would determine a regression equation for predicting success. This regression equation would then be used with a new group, and if we successfully predicted the relative success of this new group, then we could say that we had truly established predictive validity.

Although we would be interested in the predictive validity of a test used in selecting members of athletic teams, it can only rarely be actually determined. To truly establish predictive validity in the example above, it would be necessary to keep all students on the team so that their performance rating (the predictive criterion) could be established. Then a correlation between the test scores and the playing success rating would be determined. This procedure, of course, is not very realistic.

Universities sometimes use written tests for predictive purposes. Examples are the Scholastic Aptitude Test (SAT), used to predict success in college, and the Graduate Record Exam, used to predict success in graduate school. These tests have many of the same limitations just described, and many universities using them have received considerable criticism because of it.

construct validity

If we want to measure some complex ability we feel may or may not be measured exactly, we might be interested in construct validity. A construct or structure of the ability or phenomenon is proposed, and then a check is made as to whether that construct does in fact exist. We are, therefore, not generally interested in the validity of each item of the test, but are more concerned about whether the test on the whole measures the proposed component parts of the ability or phenomenon. We may want to measure psychological constructs such as anxiety, extroversion, and emotional stability. In physical performance we may want to identify constructs such as reaction time, agility, or balance.

Three techniques commonly used to establish construct validity are factor analysis, multiple regression of test batteries, and testing of differences between extreme groups. Each of these is more appropriate to particular situations. Since these techniques are basically beyond the level of this text, only a brief presentation of each will be made.

In studies using factor analysis to establish construct validity, a theoretical construct or structure of the phenomenon under consideration is established. This is usually done by breaking the phenomenon into various components. Several test items are then prepared for each of the various components, and all are administered to a group of subjects. The statistical technique of factor analysis is applied to the test scores and the *factor*s obtained are compared to the proposed components of the phenomenon. This comparison is subjective, but it does give evidence of the construct validity of the test items. One of the best examples of the use of construct validity in physical education is the development of Kenyon's Attitude Toward Physical Activity Instrument. This instrument, referred to in chapter 4, is presented in part in chapter 13.

Sometimes a battery of test items is proposed as a measure of a complex ability. If an acceptable criterion can be determined, then multiple regression techniques can be used to determine if the proposed battery is the proper construct to measure the phenomenon. In this procedure, the regression weights obtained in the multiple regression are used to indicate the relative degree of importance of each test item. The validity of many of the physical fitness and motor fit-

ness tests found today was established in this way.

The last method for determining construct validity might also be considered as shedding light on concurrent validity. In this method, which tests the differences between extreme groups, it is known in advance that two groups differ greatly in their ability on some variable of interest. A test is proposed to measure this ability; then it is administered to each group, and the average score for each determined. If the average scores are far enough from each other in the direction of known ability difference, the proposed test is deemed as having construct validity.

Some sports tests have established construct validity via the extreme groups comparisons. Usually, the scores on the proposed test by varsity or professional performers are compared with the scores on the proposed test by novice performers. For example, a proposed badminton test could be administered to a group of nationally ranked badminton players and to a group of people who have just learned the game. If the difference between the average scores on the proposed test is large enough, then the test is determined to have some validity. To determine how large a difference between average scores is needed requires the application of inferential statistics, which are not presented in this text. Let it suffice to say that objective means are available, and the reader is directed toward the statistics references in chapter 4 if more detailed information is desired.

factors affecting validity

Numerous factors may affect the validity of a test. A teacher must be aware of these and take them into account when considering test selection or construction.

Any test is valid only for a particular group at a particular time and for a particular purpose. There is no such thing as a generally valid test. A test that is valid for college age students may not be valid for elementary school students. A skill test may be valid when used with beginners, but worthless if used with advanced performers. Also, a test may be valid for middle-class white American girls aged 10 to 13, but not for other groups. Thus, the culture or the unique characteristics of a group will many times be a determining factor of a test's validity.

In written tests, there may unknowingly be response sets present. For example, all of the correct answers on a multiple choice test may be letter *a*. This could affect the responses made by the person taking the test and thus affect the validity of the test. Also, if unclear or complicated directions are given for a test, validity may be adversely affected.

In order for a test to be valid, it must also be reliable. Thus, lack of reliability or low reliability will adversely affect a test's validity. If a test does not measure accurately or consistently, it cannot be expected to measure validly. On the other hand, if a test is valid, it must have some degree of reliability. However, reliability, as we shall see, *does not* ensure validity.

reliability

The second most important criterion to be considered in test construction and selection is reliability. Reliability is the degree to which a test measures whatever it measures consistently. Another way of thinking of reliability is whether a test is measuring the *true* average performance of an individual. We might represent any individual's obtained score as follows:

obtained score = true score + error score

where the *true score* represents the level of performance that is truly indicative of the individual's ability, and the *error score* represents the part of the individual's obtained score that is due to a factor or factors other than the individual's true performance. If a test is perfectly reliable, the obtained scores are equal to the true scores. When a test is measuring true scores, a person taking the test more than once will score the same each time. Most reliability methods are based on this principle. Specifically, the total variance in the obtained scores is found, then the amount of variance due to true performance and the amount due to error performance is estimated.

Using the equation above, we can represent this as:

variance of obtained score = true score variance + error score variance

$$\sigma_{os}^2 = \sigma_t^2 + \sigma_e^2.$$

Theoretically, then, reliability is the percentage of total obtained variance accounted for by the true score variance or

$$\text{reliability} = \frac{\sigma_t^2}{\sigma_{os}^2} = \frac{\sigma_{os}^2 - \sigma_e^2}{\sigma_{os}^2}.$$

As might be expected, these reliabilities are expressed as correlation coefficients.

Two major areas or classifications of error contribute to the error score and error variance. These two classifications are *measurement error* and *systematic error*. Measurement error refers to changes in performance scores due to inaccuracies in equipment, scorer errors, and administrative errors. These will be discussed in more detail later in the chapter. Systematic error is the change in performance or behavior that is biological in nature. Individuals are likely to perform differently on motor skills from day to day or trial to trial since precise consistency of performance is not natural to human beings.

Systematic error is generally more of a concern with motor performance tests than with written tests since many motor performance tests consist of repeating more than one trial of the same task. Sometimes too these trials are repeated on different days. Systematic error is not likely to occur with written tests since, if a test is administered repeatedly, students are likely to remember the questions from previous administrations.

Due to this difference between written tests and motor performance tests, techniques appropriate for determining the reliability of one may not always be appropriate for the other. That is, reliability techniques that do not make a distinction between the two types of error, measurement and systematic, may be appropriate for written tests, but not entirely adequate for use with motor performance tests. The first four methods for determining reliability that are presented below are most appropriately used for determining a reliability coefficient for paper and pencil tests since they make no distinction between or determination of the two types of error. It should be noted, however, that in the literature, one frequently finds these written test techniques applied to motor performance tests; this may not be too serious a problem if the test user realizes its possible limitations.

Unfortunately, the appropriate methods for determining reliability for most motor performance tests require the application of more advanced statistical techniques (such as analysis of variance). Thus, after the presentation of the paper and pencil techniques only a brief introduction to these other techniques is made; it should be sufficient, however, to allow you to select and/or construct motor performance tests intelligently.

test-retest reliability

One means of estimating the reliability or consistency of a written test is to administer it on two different occasions to the same group and determine the correlation between the two sets of scores. This correlation has historically been called the *coefficient of stability*. The time span between the two administrations of the test should be fairly short but not too short. If too short, individuals are likely to repeat error performance, but if too long, they may forget or learn in the interval. In all cases, the conditions for the test administration should be precisely the same both times.

A test-retest reliability can be determined if a test is administered twice on the same day. This method is particularly tempting with physical performance tests. However, since Baumgartner[1] has shown that same day test-retest coefficients consistently overestimate the reliability of a test, it is recommended that test administrations occur on different days.

equivalent forms reliability

If two equivalent forms of a test are available, reliability can be estimated by determining the correlation between scores on the equivalent forms. The correlation coefficient in this case has historically been called the *coefficient of equivalence*. In this method, the two tests must be exactly the same in terms of length, difficulty, content, means, standard deviations, and validities. These equivalencies are difficult to obtain, however, and thus this method is not a particularly practical one, especially in motor performance tests.

split-half reliability

One of the disadvantages of the test-retest method for determining reliability is the difficulty of assuring identical testing conditions during each administration. Also, it is costly

1. Ted A. Baumgartner, "Estimating Reliability When All Test Trials Are Administered on the Same Day," *Research Quarterly* 40 (1969): 222–225.

in terms of time and materials to have two test administrations. In an attempt to overcome this disadvantage, methods for determining reliability through one test administration have been proposed. The most common of these methods is the *split-half* technique. In this method, a test is administered to a group of students and then split into two equal halves for scoring. Separate scores are obtained for each half. Often on objective, written tests, the split is made by scoring all even-numbered items separately from the odd-numbered items. The correlation between the two scores from the two halves of the test is then determined.

This correlation coefficient represents an estimate of reliability for only one-half of the test. However, test reliability is greatly affected by its length—within reason, the longer a test, the more reliable it is likely to be. Thus, a technique has been developed to estimate the reliability of the entire test when the split-half method has been used. The technique for this is a special application of what is called the Spearman-Brown Prophecy formula where:

reliability of the whole test =

$$\frac{2 \text{ (rel. of } \frac{1}{2} \text{ test)}}{1 + \text{(rel. of } \frac{1}{2} \text{ test)}}.$$

It is assumed that the two halves of the test are identical in content and difficulty. (This assumption is often ignored.)

As an example of applying this technique, assume that we had administered a test, scored separately the odd- and even-numbered questions, and found the correlation between the odd and even scores to be .80. The estimated reliability of the whole test would thus be:

reliability of whole test $= \dfrac{2(.80)}{1 + .80} = \dfrac{1.60}{1.80} = .89.$

As you can see, the reliability of the complete test is estimated to be greater than that for half of it.

In general, the longer a test, the more reliable it is apt to be. This fact could, of course, be carried to an extreme if a test were so long that fatigue became a factor. The general Spearman-Brown Prophecy formula can be used to estimate the effects of lengthening a test any amount and not just doubling its length. This formula is:

$$r = \frac{K (r_{xx})}{1 + (k - 1) (r_{xx})},$$

where $r \sqrt{}$ represents the reliability of the lengthened test, r_{xx} represents the reliability determined for the original test, and K represents the number of times the test is lengthened. This formula was used for the split-half reliability example above. In that case, $K = 2$.

As an example of applying this technique, suppose we had a thirty-item test, and had determined its test-retest reliability to be .70. Not being satisfied with this reliability, we write an additional sixty items that cover the same content and are the same in difficulty. The new test thus has ninety items—it is three times longer than the original test. Therefore, the estimated reliability for the new lengthened test would be:

$$r = \frac{3(.70)}{1 + (3 - 1) (.70)}$$

$$= \frac{2.10}{1 + 2(.70)}$$

$$= \frac{2.10}{1 + 1.40} = \frac{2.10}{2.40} = .88.$$

This estimated reliability should be considered the maximum possible reliability, not the actual reliability.

You may sometimes have occasion to determine how many times a test must be lengthened in order for it to have a chance at some specified reliability. In this case our formula is solved for K and we have:

$$K = \frac{r \ (1 - r_{xx})}{r_{xx}(1 - r \ )}$$

For example, if we had a twenty-item test with a test-retest reliability of .60 and we wanted a reliability of .90, how many items would we need to add? To answer this we find:

$$K = \frac{.90 \, (1 - .60) = .90 \, (.40)}{.60 \, (1 - .90) = .60 \, (.10)}$$

$$= \frac{.36}{.06} = 6.$$

We would need a total of $6 \times 20 = 120$ items or 100 additional items.

We emphasize again that the Spearman-Brown Prophecy formula is to be used very cautiously. Reliability coefficients determined by using the split-half and Spearman-Brown Prophecy methods are generally higher than those determined by test-retest methods. It is therefore recommended that in most physical education situations, the split-half method be avoided. Furthermore, reported reliabilities that have been determined by these methods should be viewed with extreme caution. In general, reliabilities determined by test-retest on different days are preferred.

The following rough guidelines are given for possible use in determining the level of acceptable reliability coefficients:

	r
Excellent	.90–1.00
High	.80– .89
Average	.60– .79
Unacceptable	.00– .59

These coefficients should be used cautiously since acceptable reliability depends on the particular testing situation.

reliability of motor performance tests

There are special problems involved in determining the reliability of motor performance tests that may not often occur in written or paper and pencil tests. The problem of sep-arating systematic error from measurement error was already mentioned. Also, the product-moment correlational techniques presented above do not distinguish between the two types of error. Further, the possibility of there being more than one motor performance trial on more than one day is not taken into consideration by these techniques.

On the surface these problems may not seem too serious. However, they can be very significant. To illustrate how much of a problem they might be, assume that a motor skill test consisting of four trials has been administered to five students with the following scores resulting:

Student	Trial 1 Scores	Trial 2 Scores	Trial 3 Scores	Trial 4 Scores
A	2	6	10	10
B	4	8	12	12
C	6	10	14	14
D	8	12	16	16
E	10	14	18	18

The first question that might be asked is, "How do we determine a reliability coefficient for this test?" The answer is that with the methods given so far, we really can't. However, someone might propose that correlations be determined between trial 1 and trial 2, between trials 2 and 3, 3 and 4, 1 and 3, 1 and 4, and 2 and 4. The question then would be, "Which correlation coefficient is the right one?" Hopefully, the difficulties in this procedure are already evident. But, there are more.

If you were to calculate all the correlation coefficients proposed for our illustration, you would find that in every case the correlation coefficient is equal to 1.00 since each student retains his or her same relative position for all trials (calculate them if you doubt it). This indicates the absence of measurement error. Does it indicate perfect reliability? Of course not, since reliability means consistency, and these measures have not remained consistent over all trials. As a check on consistency, one could calculate the mean performance for each trial. In this case, $\overline{X}_1 = 6$, $\overline{X}_2 = 10$, $\overline{X}_3 = 14$, and $\overline{X}_4 = 14$. These results indicate the presence of systematic error. Consistency is not reached until the third and fourth trials. To assess the true performance of the students on this task, then, it might be wise to use only the third and fourth trials.

We still have the problem of tests administered on different days. To deal with this problem, the same number of trials should be administered on more than one day and then the same checks on consistency should be made among trials and between days as indicated.

One additional note about the number of trials needs to be made. In constructing a performance test, a large number of trials should be administered in order to determine at what point the test scores stabilize. This must be done for each sex and age group for whom the test is intended. For example, Baumgartner and Jackson[2] found that in the standing broad jump, performance with senior high school boys did not stabilize until trials 4 through 6, while with junior high boys the first three trials were stabilized and on trials 4 through 6, the boys' performance became unstable. Thus, for senior high boys, six trials need to be administered with only the last three counting; with junior high boys only three trials need to be administered with all of them counting.

Formal solutions to our problems have yet to be presented; however, by utilizing these simple procedures, we can gain some

insight into the problems of motor performance reliability. It is hoped too you will at least be aware of these problems and realize the limitations of the Pearsonian correlation coefficient when selecting and/or constructing motor performance tests.

intraclass correlation coefficient and test for trend

An alternative to the Pearsonian r for determining the reliability of motor performance data, which partially takes care of the problems indicated above, is the *intraclass correlation coefficient*. This coefficient is a measure of how consistent scores remain across performance trials, regardless of the number of trials. Perfect positive correlation is found when scores remain the same for each individual for all trials. In addition, or actually before the intraclass correlation coefficient is calculated, a procedure entitled *test for trend* should be performed to determine the severity of the differences among the trial means. Both of these procedures require the use of analysis of variance procedures, which are not presented in their entirety in this text. For the more advanced reader, who wishes to explore these techniques further, an example problem is presented in the appendix, and some excellent references are given at the end of this chapter. The texts by Margaret Safrit and by Dotson and Kirkendall previously mentioned are particularly recommended.

standard error of measurement

Whether one is working with written or motor performance test scores, it is sometimes desirable to have reliability stated in terms of the variability expected in an individual student's score. The variability may be determined by finding an estimate of the standard deviation of an individual score. This stan-

2. Ted A. Baumgartner and Andrew S. Jackson, "Measurement Schedules for Tests of Motor Performance," *Research Quarterly* 41 (1970): 10–14.

dard deviation is called the *standard error of measurement* and is found as follows:

standard error of measurement =
$$S_e = \sigma \sqrt{1 - r_{xx}}$$

where σ is the standard deviation of the scores with which we are working and r_{xx} is the reliability coefficient, either a Pearsonian or intraclass. For example, if the standard deviation for a grip strength test is 10 pounds and the reliability of this test is $r_{xx} = .84$, then

$$S_e = 10 \sqrt{1 - .84}$$
$$= 10 \sqrt{.16}$$
$$= 10 (.4)$$
$$= 4.0 \text{ pounds.}$$

We may interpret this to mean that if one individual were to take this strength test many times, we would estimate the standard deviation of the scores for this one individual to be 4.0 pounds.

Let's further assume in our example that one person's score on this strength test was 78 pounds. By using the normal curve, we could estimate that this person's performance, if repeated many times, would be between 74 and 82 pounds 68 percent of the time or between 70 and 86 pounds 95 percent of the time. What we did, of course, was find the intervals for ± one standard deviation from the score and ± two standard deviations from the score. Another way of stating what these intervals mean is that we are either 68 percent confident that this person's true score will be between 74 and 82 pounds or 95 percent confident that the true score is between 70 and 86 pounds.

factors affecting reliability

Several factors may affect the reliability of a test. Some of these are the length of the test, nature of the students taking the test, administration of the test, and the testing environment.

The nature of the students taking a test will affect its reliability. In general, the more heterogeneous or variable the group, the greater the possibility for high reliability. If students taking a test are not motivated, the reliability of the test is adversely affected. Related to this is the fact that boredom and fatigue have a negative effect on reliability. The level of skill of the student or the degree of his familiarity with the test will also affect the test's reliability. In general, higher reliability can be expected with higher level performers.

It is critical that a test be administered precisely and exactly as per instructions. Unclear or inconsistent test administration will cause the reliability of a test to be lowered. If such things as cheating occur on a test, reliability will obviously suffer. Also, in physical performance tests, warm-up will tend to help increase a test's reliability. When administering a test, the environment should be as free as possible from distractions. If students are distracted by noise, visual distractions, uncomfortable temperatures, and so on, the reliability of the test performance will decline. A test administrator must try to eliminate as many of these distractions as possible. Finally, the objectivity of a test will affect its reliability.

objectivity

The objectivity of a test is defined as the degree of agreement among testers. In other words, a test that is completely objective is one that will be scored identically by different scorers. Some written tests, such as multiple choice or true and false, have obviously high objectivity. Other written tests and many physical performance tests are not so obviously objective.

A synonym for objectivity could be rater reliability—that is, the consistency with which different raters score or judge a performance. To determine the objecitvity of a test, two individuals score the test or judge the performance of all students and a correlation coefficient is determined. This coefficient indicates the degree of agreement between the two judges' scores or ratings. An alternative sometimes used, but not highly recommended, is to have the same individual score the tests or judge the performances on two different occasions and find the correlation between the two scorings. This latter procedure gives an inflated value for the degree of objectivity.

In physical performance tasks, in order to have an objective test, it is critically important that the criteria for judging the quality of performance be very well defined. Excellent examples of tasks where this has been done are found in gymnastics and diving.

A rough guideline for rating the objectivity of a test follows. Again, remember that these are only rough guidelines and must be viewed with extreme caution. The particular situation will determine the adequacy of an objectivity coefficient.

	r
Excellent	.95–1.00
High	.85– .94
Average	.70– .84
Unacceptable	.00– .69

additional criteria

There is no question that the three most important criteria for selecting and constructing tests are validity, reliability, and objectivity. However, several other criteria must also be met if a test is to be useful. Sometimes a test that is valid, reliable, and objective will be eliminated from consideration because it fails to meet some of these additional criteria.

economy

Is the test economical in terms of time, money, and personnel? The answer to this question may determine the propriety of a test. Regardless of how valid, reliable, and objective a test is, if it is not economically feasible to administer in the setting we have, it is useless to us. An example of this is the max $\dot{V}O_2$ test, which uses gas analysis to determine cardiorespiratory endurance. This test has been shown to be satisfactorily valid, reliable, and objective. However, thousands of dollars worth of equipment is needed to carry it out. Also, only one person at a time can be tested. The test takes about 45 minutes to administer, and requires two or three highly trained individuals to administer it. In a school setting, with 500 students, one physical education teacher, and none of the equipment, it would be impractical to even consider attempting the test. It simply would not be economically feasible.

ease of administration

A test must be relatively easy to administer if we are to use it with large numbers of students. The directions for administering a test must be standardized so that no matter who administers it, the results will be the same. The directions must be explicit, leaving nothing to doubt. (Does a ball on the line, for example, count as a good or poor toss?) By the same token, directions should be simple enough that, with a reasonable explanation, students will understand them.

The test must be reasonable in terms of its demands on the students. If sore muscles and joints are going to result from the test, perhaps it is not appropriate at this time. If the test requires an inordinate amount of preparation time by either the students or the teacher, we may decide its use is not warranted.

developmental value

If at all possible, a test should be a learning experience for the students. Students should learn something about themselves that will be of benefit. Also, it is hoped that they will learn from the test. On a written test, it is possible for a student to learn a fact or concept by missing a question or by getting it correct. In many physical performance tests, if administered properly, test results can motivate students to improve. It is questionable whether the use of a test can be justified if the only function it serves is to assign grades.

interest

In order to get an accurate appraisal of a student's performance, a test should be interesting and challenging. If a test is boringly repetitive, too easy, or too difficult, students may lose interest and not show their true ability. This seems to be particularly so with physical performance tests.

norms

Norms may be thought of as representative values for a particular population. These values are usually the mean, standard deviation, and percentile ranks. If any comparisons between your students and a larger population are to be made for some test, norms are an absolute must. Such comparisons can provide valuable information to the teacher as well as to the students. If your students consistently score well below the national average on most of the items of a physical fitness test, you should consider revising your curriculum.

For norms to be meaningful, they must be based on a population appropriate for comparison with your students. Most physical performance norms should be based on sex, age, height, and weight since these matura-

tional factors generally play an important role in performance. Certainly, norms on the AAHPER physical fitness test for college-aged women would not be appropriate for seventh-grade boys.

There are several other important points to consider about norms before using them. Some of these are: (1) How large a group was used to establish the norms? While numbers of subjects will not cure other problems a test may have, it is critical to have a large enough sampling of a population to assure that the normative values are representative of the total population. Even in the smallest of populations, several hundred scores should be available if norms are to be established and used. (2) What is the nature of the group for which the norms were established? In addition to the factors of sex, age, height, and weight that were mentioned, the geographical region, intelligence of subjects, physical conditioning level of subjects, type of school, and so on, may be relevant information for a particular test. Generally, you will want to compare students to a population that is quite similar to them. (3) Are the test directions explicit enough to ensure that you are administering the test in precisely the same manner as when the normative scores were gathered? (4) How current are the norms? Since society is constantly changing, norms established in 1939 may not be appropriate in 1980.

The most meaningful norms of all may be ones established for a particular school, school system, or region. These are a means for determining the progress made toward the accomplishment of local program objectives. Establishing local norms is simply a matter of keeping records on standardized tests and updating the statistics calculated from the students' scores. Within two to three years, rather reliable norms can be established. However, it is important to keep these norms up to date.

duplicate forms

While this is generally not an important criterion for a test to meet, there may be occasions when it is critical to have available more than one form of a test. This may be particularly true for knowledge, personality, and attitude assessment tests that are to be given before and after a program in order to assess changes in behavior that may occur. Duplicate tests should be carefully scrutinized to be sure that they are in fact duplicates. Similar tests are not adequate in most cases. The tests must be the same in content, length, and difficulty.

The selection and construction of tests is not to be taken lightly. It is a serious task. The quality of tests selected and constructed will help determine the quality of the evaluation program. We know there is no such thing as a perfect test, but if tests are closely scrutinized for the criteria presented in this chapter, we will be using the best tests possible.

summary review questions

1. What are the three most important characteristics of a test? What is the definition of each? (*answer on p. 69*)
2. In what ways does one obtain content or logical validity? (*answer on p. 70*)
3. In what ways does one obtain concurrent or criterion-related validity? (*answer on p. 70*)
4. In what ways does one obtain predictive validity? (*answer on p. 71*)
5. In what ways does one obtain construct validity? (*answer on p. 72*)
6. What factors affect validity? (*answer on p. 73*)
7. In what way does one obtain test-retest reliability? (*answer on p. 74*)
8. What is equivalent form reliability? (*answer on p. 74*)
9. One of the disadvantages of the test-retest method is that it is most difficult to assure identical testing conditions in the two administrations. What method is used to overcome this disadvantage? (*answer on p. 75*)
10. What factors affect reliability? (*answer on p. 78*)
11. How does one determine the objectivity of a test? (*answer on p. 78*)

bibliography

Ahmann, J. Stanley, and Glock, Marvin D. *Evaluating Pupil Growth.* 4th ed. Boston: Allyn and Bacon, 1971.

Alexander, H. W. "The Estimation of Reliability When Several Trials Are Available." *Psychometrika* 12 (1947):79–99.

———. "A General Test for Trend." *Psychological Bulletin* 43 (1946):533–57.

American Psychological Association. *Standards for Educational and Psychological Tests and Manuals.* Washington, D.C.: American Psychological Association, 1966.

Baumgartner, Ted A. "The Application of the Spearman-Brown Prophecy Formula When Applied to Physical Performance Tests." *Research Quarterly* 39 (1968):847–856.

———. "Estimating Reliability When All Test Trials Are Administered on the Same Day." *Research Quarterly* 40 (1969):222–225.

———. "Stability of Physical Performance Test Scores." *Research Quarterly* 40 (1969):257–261.

Baumgartner, Ted. A., and Jackson, Andrew S. *Measurement for Evaluation in Physical Education.* Boston: Houghton Mifflin, 1975.

———. "Measurement Schedules for Tests of Motor Performance." *Research Quarterly* 41 (1970):10–17.

Ebel, R. L. "Estimation of the Reliability of Ratings." *Psychometrika* 16 (1951):407–24.

———. "Measurement and the Teacher." *Educational Leadership* 20 (1962):20–24.

Henry, F. M. "Reliability, Measurement Error, and Intra-Individual Difference." *Research Quarterly* 30, no. 1 (1959):21–24.

———. "Individual Differences in Motor Learning and Performance." In *Psychology of Motor Learning*, ed. L. E. Smith, pp. 243–56. Chicago: The Athletic Institute, 1970.

———. "Influence of Measurement Error and Intra-Individual Variation on the Reliability of Muscle Strength and Vertical Jump Tests." *Research Quarterly* 30, no. 2 (1959):155–159.

Henry, F. M. et al. "Errors in Measurement." In *Research Methods Applied to Health, Physical Education and Recreation*, pp. 459–477. Washington, D.C.: AAHPER, National Education Association, 1949.

Kroll, W. "A Note on the Coefficient of Intraclass Correlation as an Estimate of Reliability." *Research Quarterly* 33 (1962):313–316.

———. "Reliability of a Selected Measure of Human Strength." *Research Quarterly* 33 (1962):410–417.

———. "Reliability Variations of Strength in Test-Retest Situations." *Research Quarterly* 34 (1963): 50–55.

Safrit, Margaret J. "Criterion-Referenced Measurement: Applications In Physical Education." *Motor Skills: Theory into Practice* 2 (1977):21–35.

———. *Evaluation in Physical Education.* Englewood Cliffs, N.J.: Prentice-Hall, 1973.

Safrit, Margaret J. et al. *Reliability Theory Appropriate for Motor Performance Measures.* New York: AAHPER, 1974.

Schmidt, R. A. "Critique of Henry's Paper." In *Psychology of Motor Learning*, ed. L. E. Smith, pp. 256–260. Chicago: The Athletic Institute, 1970.

Symonds, P. M. "Factors Influencing Test Reliability." *Journal of Educational Psychology* 19 (1928):73–87. Reprinted in *Educational and Psychological Measurement*, eds. D. Payne and R. McMorris, pp. 46–54. Waltham, Mass.: Blaisdell Publishing Company, 1967.

Thorndike, R. L. "Reliability." In *Educational Measurement*, ed. E. F. Lindquist, pp. 560–620. Washington, D.C.: American Council on Education, 1951.

Thorndike, R. L., and Hagen, E. *Measurement and Evaluation in Psychology and Education.* New York: John Wiley and Sons, 1955.

exercises

1. A physical education teacher in a large high school developed a new test for measuring service skills in tennis. She wanted to establish the concurrent validity of her test and decided to use an established valid test as the criterion. She measured her 150 students on the known valid test, then measured the same students with her new test. The following results were obtained:

   $X =$ data from established test, $Y =$ data from new test

   $N = 150$

   $\overline{X} = 14.43$ $\qquad$ $\overline{Y} = 5.49$

   $\Sigma X^2 = 32,583.7$ $\qquad$ $\Sigma Y^2 = 4858.5$

   $\qquad$ $\Sigma XY = 12,357.6$

   What is the concurrent validity of this new test? According to the guidelines in this text, is this result excellent, high, average, or unacceptable?

   Answer:

   r = .703 high

2. The same physical education teacher in problem 1 decided to run a test-retest so that she could estimate the reliability of her test. Two days after she measured the students with her test, she administered the same test again with the following results:

   $N = 150$

   $\overline{X} = 5.49$ $\qquad$ $\overline{Y} = 5.58$

   $\Sigma X^2 = 4,858.5$ $\qquad$ $\Sigma Y^2 = 5,156.5$

   $\qquad$ $\Sigma XY = 4,933.3$

   What is the coefficient of stability? According to our text is this excellent, high, average, or unacceptable?

3. A physical education teacher gave a 100-item written test on the techniques of gymnastics. He made the odd and even items identical in content and difficulty. He found a reliability correlation coefficient of one-half the test to be .64. What is the reliability of the whole test?

Answer:
.78

4. A physical education teacher was not satisfied with a test-retest reliability on a test of football rules. The coefficient of stability on the thirty-item test was .75. He wanted a correlation coefficient of .85. How many items have to be added to secure this desired correlation coefficient?

5. The physical education teacher in problem 4 was interested in the correlation coefficient he would secure if he tripled the length of his thirty-item test. What would the reliability coefficient be if he tripled the length of his test?

Answer:
r = .90

6. A test-retest was run on endurance. The number of full-length push-ups done by each student in a ninth-grade physical education class was used. The standard deviation for the class was 6 and the test-retest reliability coefficient was .86. What is the standard error of measurement?

7. A ninth-grade student did 30 push-ups. What would be the estimated performance of this student 68 percent and 95 percent of the time if he repeated the performance many times? Use the standard error of measurement found in problem 6 to determine your answer.

Answer:
It is estimated that 68 percent of the time he would perform between 28 and 32 push-ups, 95 percent of the time between 26 and 34 push-ups.

administration of the measurement and evaluation program

The measurement and evaluation program must be an integral part of the total instructional program. It must contribute to the goals and objectives of physical education. Several critical aspects in the administration of the measurement and evaluation program are presented in this chapter, namely the administration of tests, analyzing test results, follow-up practices, and grading in physical education.

administration of tests

Whenever we administer a test, we must take great care if the testing is to be meaningful to our students and us. Time spent in preparing for the administration of a test will yield great dividends in terms of time saved later and quality of measurements obtained. If certain procedural steps are followed, you will have some assurance that the testing is being conducted smoothly, accurately, and for good reasons.

determine the purpose and use of measurement

The first step in test administration is the most important and a prerequisite to everything else, including the selection of the test(s) we wish to administer. It is unthinkable that anyone would administer a test without knowing why it was being given; but each of us can probably relate an experience where such has apparently occurred. More common is for a test to be selected first and then the purpose of measurement determined. The purpose(s) of measurement, however, must precede test selection. Indeed, the purpose must be the number one determinant in what to test or measure. What we are trying to measure will then guide us in our test selection. Time spent in determining the purpose of measurement should justify the time taken from the rest of the instructional program. Some possible purposes of measurement were discussed in chapter 2. These were classification, achievement, selection, diagnosis, motivation, improved instruction, maintenance of standards, and research. It is recommended that you return to that chapter and review these purposes. Finally, it should again be mentioned that more than one purpose may be served at any one time. For example, we may be testing for purposes of classification and diagnosis at the same time.

select relevant tests

After knowing why and what it is we need to measure, we are ready to select or construct the best test(s) possible. We should employ the criteria for test selection and construction presented in chapter 5. These were validity, reliability, objectivity, economy, ease of administration, developmental value, interest, norms, and duplicate forms.

These criteria must be considered in relation to each unique testing situation: the number of students to be tested, facilities and equipment available, time for testing available, and preparation time of testers. Above all, the unique purpose(s) for a particular situation must be kept in mind.

survey facilities and equipment

It is important to determine what space is required to administer a test or tests. Although this should have been done before the test was selected, it is important to remain aware of space and facility requirements throughout the planning. If sufficient space or facility is not available, it may be necessary to reconsider the test(s) selected or constructed. Also, facilities should be checked for the location of testing stations.

You should also make a list of all the materials and equipment needed for the test(s). In this way, you are not likely to come up embarrassingly short on the day of testing. Further, you should check that all these materials are available and in good working condition. It is difficult to time the 100-meter dash without an accurate, working stopwatch.

outline testing procedures

A determination will first need to be made as to whether the test(s) can be administered to a group or if they must be administered individually. Also, if testing stations are to be used, the number to be tested at each station during a period of time must be determined. You must know too the type of leadership necessary for each test or item. Are testing assistants, recorders, and/or scorers needed?

If different stations are used for each test, the flow of students from one station to the next must be steady. Be sure that in going from station to station students do not interfere with the performance of others. Drawing a diagram to show students the order of testing can be helpful. Also, determine if students are to move to the stations in groups or individually. Finally, the amount of time required for each item or test must be determined.

gather testing materials

All necessary materials should be gathered together before the day of testing. Equipment should be checked again to be sure it is in good working condition. Can you imagine the embarrassment and frustration that would result if students ran a 3000-meter race for time and the teacher discovered that his stopwatch was not working or he had forgotten to wind it? Such disasters are more likely to occur if we don't carefully prepare in advance.

scheduling of students

It is wise to determine in advance which students are to report to a particular testing station. Also, if there is any special preparation students should make before the testing, they will need to be informed in advance. For example, if an exhausting endurance test of some kind is to be given, students should be informed in advance so they can get adequate rest and not overeat beforehand. Provisions must also be made for students who are absent the day of the test.

training of testers

If help is going to be needed, the helpers must be prepared well before the actual testing. Directions and procedures must be standardized, otherwise the same test may be administered differently by different testers. The instructions given should be brief and easily understood, and whenever possible, they should employ demonstrations and/or a preliminary test. Above all, the instructions must be the same for all who take the test.

All testers should be acquainted beforehand with the testing equipment. They should practice using it and should be aware of any peculiarities in it.

The testers should also actually practice administering the items or test(s) for which they will be responsible. They should duplicate exactly what they will do on test day. Questions will arise in these practice sessions that otherwise would not come out until test day.

placement and preparation of testing stations

As suggested before, equipment and testing stations must be placed to result in a smooth flow of traffic. Students taking the test(s) must know where they are to be at all times.

Either a written diagram or simple verbal directions should be planned to allow this. The time required for each item or station should also be determined. More than one station with the same item may be needed.

A few other items, when planned for in advance, will greatly enhance the testing session. All trials for one test item, for instance, should be administered in succession unless the event is too fatiguing. For example, if the standing long jump calls for three trials, one student should perform all three before the next student begins.

Also, a demonstration should be provided for each new group coming to a station. This is better than providing demonstrations for all items to the entire class or group.

Then too an activity should be provided for those students who finish the testing early. This will help prevent potential discipline problems. However, this activity should not be of the type or in a place that will distract those not finished with the testing.

In many tests, special markings need to be made on the walls or floor. These must be determined and done before the actual testing. Usually special tapes or water-soluble paints must be used for marking areas.

scoring plans

Score sheets that are easy to read and understand must be prepared. The arrangement of items on the score sheet or card should reflect a logical sequence in order to minimize recording errors. If possible, the items should appear on the score sheet in the same order as they are to be administered. The general format of the sheet should facilitate accuracy and neatness. For example, sufficient space must be provided for and between recordings if they are to be neatly done.

If possible, the same person should score all students on the same item, particularly when ratings are involved. Also, one recorder for each group of students may be preferred. Finally, in most situations students can carry their own score sheets from station to station. This will be determined in part by their age.

conduct of tests

If close attention has been paid to the details above, the actual testing session should be smooth and trouble-free. The importance of advance planning cannot be overemphasized. Without it, there is a good chance of chaos, embarrassment, and wasted time. With it, there is a good chance of a meaningful educational experience for all concerned.

After the test or tests have been administered, something must be done with the test scores if we are to have an evaluation program instead of just a testing program. Test results must be analyzed and the findings used.

analyzing and utilizing test results

After the scores are obtained for all students, the descriptive parameters presented in chapter 4 should first be determined. Most likely, you will want to find at least the mean and the standard deviation for each test item. This will give a good description of the class's performance. A comparison between a particular class and city, state, or national norms may be made. Is this class above average, below average, or average? Does this result indicate a modification in program is required? Perhaps a comparison can be made between a class's present performance and its earlier performance. The question then becomes, has there been improvement? If not, then why? Finally, decisions need to be made about the accomplishment of instructional objectives. Is the accomplishment sufficient to leave the program as is or does it need to be changed? Were the objectives realistic or do they need to be reexamined and possibly revised? Once again, we are back to the model presented in chapter 1.

We may wish to compare each pupil's performance with his or her peers. This can best be done by determining a standard score (percentile, Z, T, $6-\sigma$, or whatever) for each student. By comparing students with one another, future instruction can be individualized according to students' specific strengths and weaknesses. Along these same lines, students can be counseled into activities most appropriate to their abilities.

Each student should be given his or her results as soon after the test as possible in order to maximize learning and/or motivation. The results should be expressed simply, clearly, and concisely in a manner compatible with the understanding of the group involved and with the purpose served in presenting the results. This implies giving the basic facts in condensed form so that the outstanding points for emphasis will be evident. Individual student profiles can be quite effective. An example of one profile sheet is presented in Figure 6.1. Through the proper presentation of results students should be motivated to improve their performance.

In lieu of a profile chart like this, you may wish to post the norm charts for a test and allow students to make their own comparisons. However, posting individual performances is not suggested. It can lead to the unnecessary embarrassment of the individuals who need the most encouragement.

Students who need special attention must be identified. A good test will help you do this. The attention may be provided by you or it may require the services of professionals in other areas. In any event, it is

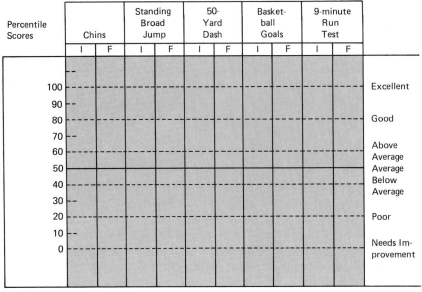

Percentile Scores	Chins		Standing Broad Jump		50-Yard Dash		Basket-ball Goals		9-minute Run Test		
	I	F	I	F	I	F	I	F	I	F	
100											Excellent
90											
80											Good
70											
60											Above Average
50											Average
40											Below Average
30											
20											Poor
10											
0											Needs Improvement

Comments:

Figure 6.1   Individual Profile

the teacher's responsibility to see that these students do in fact receive it.

grading in physical education

A grade given in a class is a summative evaluation representing the achievements of a student during some specified period. Often one of the real problems in teaching is the requirement that grades be given in all classes. There are numerous arguments for and against the policy of assigning grades to students in physical education classes. Some of the arguments usually given for grading are: (a) grades give students and parents a definite idea as to the progress the students are making; (b) grades motivate students to do better; and (c) all other subjects in school give grades so physical education should too. On the other side of the issue are those who argue that: (a) students who receive low grades in physical education will be negatively motivated and perhaps not voluntarily participate in physical activity later in life; (b) the fear of poor grades takes the enjoyment out of participation in physical activity; and (c) there is no really "fair" way to grade in physical education. To grade or not to grade is a decision you may have to make, although in some school systems, the decision will be made for you. Regardless, if the decision is to assign grades, then you must be able to do so fairly in a way that can be logically and educationally justified. Before moving on to some of the ways of doing this it must be reemphasized that grading is not a substitute for the total evaluation program. If the evaluation program involves only grading, there will be great difficulty in justifying its existence.

Teachers of physical education are often perplexed by the problem of how to evaluate the progress of all students fairly since there is usually a great range of ability in almost any class—the very highly skilled will be in the same class as the very poorly skilled. Some people feel that the level of ability at the end of a grading period should be the sole determining factor in the assignment of grades. This approach seems grossly unfair in that a great advantage is given to the student who began the unit or grading period at a high level. Also, this scheme does not make any attempt to evaluate the achievement that took place during the grading period since initial abilities are being ignored. We must in fact be interested in what has been learned or achieved during the grading period.

Since we are most likely interested in achievement, a proposal often suggested is that we grade each student on his or her improvement. However, if we do this without regard to the initial ability level of the students, we greatly penalize the student who began at a high level since this student will not have as much room for improvement as his unskilled classmate. For example, the student who can run the 100-meter dash in 12 seconds will certainly have more difficulty in improving his time by 0.5 second than the student who originally ran it in only 16 seconds.

So what do we do? The authors' suggestion is to classify students at the beginning of a unit or grading period on the basis of their present ability. This classification may involve an objective test, a rating scale, a checklist, or a subjective judgment. At the end of the unit or grading period, each student's performance would then be compared with other students similarly classified. Of course, classifying students does not necessarily mean that they be physically divided into groups. While this may often be advantageous for instructional purposes a classification can also be only a "paper" division for grading purposes.

An extreme position would be allowing each student to represent a classification and making decisions about grades on that basis. This would, of course, make the grading process totally subjective and might leave you, the teacher, open to considerable criticism. One grading system that approaches this scheme is contract grading. A section devoted to this system is presented later in the chapter.

No grading system is foolproof. Whatever the one selected, there will be some problems associated with it. Any grading scheme is, in fact, subjective and must be defended by the teacher using it. Thus, select a grading system on educational bases that are philosophically compatible with your feelings. Then, above all, use good judgment in applying it. Remember, there is no substitute for judgment in measurement and evaluation.

kinds of marks or grades

There are numerous ways in which grades or marks are reported. Some of these are:
1. Actual scores received on tests: usually a numeral such as 85, 55, or 70;
2. Percentages: 65 percent, 90 percent, and so on; often used on written tests; represents the percentage correct;
3. Grades: A, B, C, D, and F—these are most commonly used;
4. Descripters: Excellent, above average, average, below average, poor, and failing;
5. Dichotomies: usually pass-fail, credit-no credit, or satisfactory-unsatisfactory; or
6. Combination: 95–100 = A, 85–94 = B, and so on.

basis for marking or grading

What does an A grade mean? What constitutes a grade of satisfactory? Questions like these are commonly asked. Answers to them can only be given by the person assigning the grade or mark. Assigning grades ultimately means that a teacher decides the standards by which students' performances are to be judged. In chapter 1, two main types of standards were introduced: *norm-referenced* and *criterion-referenced*. Since these standards are relevant to grading systems, we will mention them again briefly. If a teacher assigns grades on the basis of norm-referenced standards, then the criterion for various grades is determined from the performance of some defined group. For example, a teacher might state that for a student to receive an A in fitness he must score on the average at the 90th percentile rank on the AAHPER youth fitness test, for a B at the 70th percentile rank, and so on. When criterion referenced standards are used for grading, the teacher sets the criteria for the determination of the grades.

percentage correct method

A frequently used scale for grades, particularly in colleges, is one that assigns a grade of A when students get 90 percent or more correct on a test, B when they get 80 to 89 percent, C when they get 70 to 79 percent, D when they get 60 to 69 percent, and F if they get less than 60 percent correct. This method may be effective in some cases, but it can be questioned since it is the difficulty of the test(s) that will determine the grades. For example, 60 percent correct may actually represent a better performance on one test than an 85 percent on another test. This method is clearly an example of using criterion referenced standards.

normal curve method

In chapter 4, we suggested using the normal distribution as one way of determining grade assignments. Examples of two different grade distributions using the normal distribution are given in Table 6.2.

Table 6.2 Grade Distributions Using the Normal Curve

			Z-score	T-score
Example 1				
	7% A	=	1.48 and above	64.8 and above
	18% B	=	0.67 to 1.48	56.7 to 64.8
	50% C	=	−0.67 to 0.67	43.3 to 56.7
	18% D	=	−1.48 to −0.67	35.2 to 43.3
	7% F	=	−1.48 and below	35.2 and below
Example 2				
	10% A	=	1.28 and above	62.8 and above
	30% B	=	0.25 to 1.28	52.5 to 62.8
	40% C	=	−0.84 to 0.25	41.6 to 52.5
	15% D	=	−1.65 to −0.84	33.5 to 41.6
	5% F	=	−1.65 and below	33.5 and below

In example 1, the teacher has decided that over the long run, 7 percent of the students will earn As, 18 percent will earn Bs, 50 percent will earn Cs, 18 percent will earn Ds, and 7 percent will earn Fs. In example 2, another teacher has decided on different percentages. This method can be applied to classifications or subgroups of a class that were determined for grading purposes, as was suggested earlier in this chapter. Caution must be used with this method. It should be rigidly applied only if standardized tests are used and the students' grades are based on their performance as compared to normative data compiled by you or from local, state, or national norms. To apply the normal curve to each class independently excludes the possibility of having a class with an unusual number of high or low achievers. In other words, we are assuming that the abilities of the students in each class are normally distributed. We would be forcing the percentages of assigned grades. The normal curve method is a good example of using norm-referenced standards for grade assignment.

contract grading

A method of grading that has been successfully used by some physical education teachers is *contract grading*. In this system, the teacher and each student agree on exactly what the student must do to earn a particular grade. For example, on a fitness unit, a student and his teacher may agree that if the student is able to perform ten chins, do forty sit-ups in a minute, run the mile in less than 6 minutes, read three professional articles on fitness, and write a four-page report on the values of physical activity, then he or she will receive an A. The teacher and student also agree on standards for the other letter grades. The contract is then signed by both the teacher and student. A contract

is "negotiated" for each individual student, although group contracts can be made.

natural gaps in distribution

Usually a distribution of test scores has gaps in it where no scores occur. Some teachers use these gaps to determine the grades for their students. For example, the following distribution of test scores was attained by thirty students:

95	85	77	68	52
95	84	77	67	F 51
A 94	B 83	77	D 67	48
93	83	C 76	66	
92	82	76	66	
		76		
		74		
		74		

A teacher might assign the grades as indicated since there appear to be four natural breaks in the distribution. This is a norm-referenced standard method for determining grades—which is its main criticism. Students' grades are totally dependent on the performance of their peers in the particular class. Thus, performance that is a C this semester, might be an A next semester.

Regardless of the method used to determine a grade, the final decision is subjective. As stated earlier, you should allow reasonableness and good judgment to prevail and be sure that you have a sound justification for what you are doing.

grade reporting

A grade report usually carries only one composite grade. This grade is most frequently a composite of the scores or grades achieved for various instructional objectives or tests. Each part of a grade should be weighted in terms of its importance and the resultant time spent on it in instruction. Examples of how this is done are shown in Table 6.3. In example A, general objectives and their pro-

Table 6.3 **Final Grade Determinations**

Example A: Assume A = 5 points, B = 4 points, C = 3 points, D = 2 points, F = 1 point

Objective	% Importance	Student Grade	Points
Organic development	30%	B (4)	0.3 × 4 = 1.2
Neuromuscular development	30%	A (5)	0.3 × 5 = 1.5
Intellectual development	20%	D (2)	0.2 × 2 = 0.4
Social-emotional development	20%	B (4)	0.2 × 4 = 0.8

Final Grade 3.9 or B

Example B: Assume A = 5 points, B = 4 points, C = 3 points, D = 2 points, F = 1 point

Factor	Weight	Student Grade	Points
Skill achievement	3	B	3 × 4 = 12
Fitness improvement	2	A	2 × 5 = 10
Knowledge	1	C	1 × 3 = 3
Attitude	1	C	1 × 3 = 3
	7	**Final Grade**	28/7 = 4 = B

Example C: Assume we have the following grading scale

Excellent	Good	Fair	Poor	Fail
A+ = 5.3	B+ = 4.3	C+ = 3.3	D+ = 2.3	F+ = 1.3
A = 5.0	B = 4.0	C = 3.0	D = 2.0	F = 1.0
A− = 4.7	B− = 3.7	C− = 2.7	D− = 1.7	F− = 0.7

Objective	Weighting	Grade	Points
Performance, skill	2	4.3	8.6
Knowledge of rules, etc.	1	2.7	2.7
Attitude (personal-social)	1	4.0	4.0
Posture and physique improvement	1	4.0	4.0
	5		19.3

Final Grade $= \dfrac{19.3}{5} = 3.8 =$ Good or B−

portionate importance for a particular grading period are given. The grades earned by some student for each objective and the means for determining this student's composite grade are also given. Examples B and C give similar information.

The means by which grades are reported to students and parents are critically important. Simply placing a composite letter grade on a report card is not sufficient, particularly since many parents do not understand the nature of physical education and may not appreciate the progress made by their children. Thus, it is suggested that a

Wonder City High School

Department of Health and Physical Education

Dear Mr. and Mrs. _____

This letter is intended to acquaint you with our new form for reporting your child's progress in physical education. The school report card will have on it a grade for physical education. Actually, this grade is a summary of progress in the four general goals of our physical education program. We shall describe each of these areas and indicate how your child has progressed in each.

I.   **Organic Development**
     This generally refers to muscular strength, endurance, power, speed, and agility. (30% of the total grade is allotted here.)

                                         Partial grade _____

II. **Neuromuscular Skills**
     This area is concerned with developing a well-coordinated body that can perform complex motor skills such as throwing and catching, pivoting and shooting a basketball, batting in baseball. Finally, these complex skills are put together into recreational game skills such as golf, tennis, swimming, basketball, baseball, etc. (30% of the total grade is allotted here.)

                                         Partial grade _____

III. **Interpretive and Intellectual Development**
     This area evaluates your child's knowledge of rules of games, game strategy, and techniques and also his or her knowledge of the effects and benefits of physical activity to the individual. (20% of the total grade is allotted here.)

                                         Partial grade _____

IV. **Personal Social Development**
     This area deals with the extent to which your child exhibits traits of good sportsmanship, leadership and the extent to which she or he cooperates with fellow students in their assigned class duties. Also included here is an appraisal of conforming to established class procedures, personal cleanliness, health habits, and the knowledge and practice of safety habits in and around the gymnasium. (20% of the total grade is allotted here.)

                                         Partial grade _____
                                         TOTAL GRADE   _____

GENERAL COMMENTS:

                              Sincerely yours,

                              John Doe
                              Physical Education Teacher

PS   Please feel free to discuss your child's progress with me. Call and we can arrange an appointment.

                              Figure 6.2   Suggested Form
                              Letter to Parents

supplemental letter be sent to parents informing them of the marking system used in terms of your objectives and of the progress made by their children. An example of such a letter is presented in Figure 6.2. As the letter suggests, personal interviews with parents should also be encouraged.

cumulative physical education records

Unfortunately, in physical education we typically deal with students for only one to four years and have no knowledge about their prior performance. Nor do we typically pass information on to those who have the students after us. This need not be the case, however, and, hopefully, it is not the case in many schools. A longitudinal account of test scores in areas of physical fitness, skill, and knowledge test scores, record of sports participation, and specific strengths and weaknesses of each student should be kept. These records can be of a great assistance in helping students achieve the objectives of physical education. Programs for classes and individuals can be more soundly planned. One word of caution: Care must be taken not to categorize a student rigidly as "good" or "poor" and assume that he must stay in that category. The "halo" effect and its counterpart, the "devil" effect, must be guarded against.

summary review questions

1. What procedural steps should be considered in the administration of a test? (*answer on pp. 84–86*)

2. What two basic descriptive parameters is one most likely to calculate in order to analyze test results? (*answer on p. 87*)

3. Of what value is a comparison of your class test results with norms? (*answer on p. 87*)

4. What questions can be answered if a comparison is made between your class's present performance and its earlier performance? (*answer on p. 87*)

5. What descriptive tools do we use when comparing students with one another? (*answer on p. 87*)

6. What purposes are served in presenting test results to our students? (*answer on p. 87*)

7. How should test results be fed back to students? (*answer on p. 87*)

8. What arguments are usually given for grading in physical education classes? (*answer on p. 88*)

9. What arguments are usually given for not grading in physical education classes? (*answer on p. 88*)

10. Why not grade on the final ability level of each student at the end of a grading period? (*answer on p. 89*)

11. Why not grade on the improvement of each student during a grading period? (*answer on p. 89*)

12. What methods and thoughts are suggested in this chapter for assigning a grade for each student at the end of a grading period? (*answer on p. 90*)

13. What is contract grading? (*answer on p. 91*)

bibliography

Barrow, Harold M., and McGee, Rosemary. *A Practical Approach to Measurement in Physical Education.* 2d ed. Philadelphia: Lea and Febiger, 1971.

Baumgartner, Ted A., and Jackson, Andrew S. *Measurement for Evaluation in Physical Education.* Boston: Houghton Mifflin, 1975.

Bloom, B. S.; Englehart, M. D.; Furst, E. J.; Hill, W. H.; and Krathwohl, D. R., eds. *A Taxonomy of Educational Objectives: Handbook I, The Cognitive Domain.* New York: David McKay, 1956.

Bloom, B. S.; Hastings, J. T.; and Madaus, G. F. *Handbook on Formative and Summative Evaluation of Student Learning.* New York: McGraw-Hill, 1971.

Hanson, Dale L. "Grading in Physical Education." *Journal of Health, Physical Education and Recreation,* May 1967.

Johnson, Barry L., and Nelson, Jack K. *Practical Measurements for Evaluation in Physical Education.* 2d ed. Minneapolis: Burgess Publishing, 1974.

Larson, Leonard A., and Yocom, Rachael D. *Measurement and Evaluation in Physical, Health, and Recreation Education.* St. Louis: C. V. Mosby, 1951.

Mathews, Donald K. *Measurement in Physical Education.* 5th ed. Philadelphia: W. B. Saunders, 1978.

Safrit, Margaret J. "Criterion-Referenced Measurement: Applications in Physical Education." *Motor Skills: Theory into Practice* 2 (1977):21–35.

―――. *Evaluation in Physical Education, Assessing Motor Behavior.* Englewood Cliffs, N. J.: Prentice-Hall, 1973.

Singer, Robert. "Grading in Physical Education." *Journal of Health, Physical Education and Recreation,* May 1967.

Solley, William H. "Grading in Physical Education." *Journal of Health, Physical Education and Recreation,* May 1967.

exercises

1. A physical education teacher developed the following grading scale for a gymnastics unit:

Excellent	Good	Fair	Poor	Fail
A+ = 10.0	B+ = 8.0	C+ = 6.0	D+ = 4.0	F+ = 2.0
A = 9.5	B = 7.5	C = 5.5	D = 3.5	F = 1.5
A− = 9.0	B− = 7.0	C− = 5.0	D− = 3.0	F− = 1.0

Objective	Weighting
Performance-Skill	4
Knowledge of rules	2
Attitude (personal-social)	1

A student was assigned a subjective grade on performance-skill of 7.5. A test was given on knowledge of rules and the student attained a grade of 4.0. The teacher assigned a subjective grade on attitude of 9.0. What would be the student's final grade for the gymnastics unit?

Answer:
B−

2. An elementary school physical education teacher developed the following grading procedure for determining a final grade for the year: A = 5 points, B = 4, C = 3, D = 2, and F = 1 point. The teacher further decided to test and measure organic development with a weight of 40 percent importance; neuromuscular development, 40 percent importance; intellectual development, 10 percent importance; and social-emotional development, 10 percent importance. The teacher applied standardized tests in each of these areas at the beginning, middle, and end of the year. The teacher also decided to assign a grade of A to any test score that was 1.28 standard Z-scores above the normal, B to any score between .25 to 1.28 standard Z-scores, C to any score between −.84 to .25 standard Z-scores, D to any

score between −1.65 to −.84 standard Z-scores, and F to any score below −1.65 standard Z-scores. The teacher decided to average the Z-scores of each student in each area to get a final grade. One of the students secured the following average standard Z-score in each area:

Objective Area	Average Z-score
Organic development	−.19
Neuromuscular development	0.56
Intellectual development	0.23
Social-emotional development	0.04

What is the student's final grade for the year?

3. A physical education teacher gave a national standardized written test on the basic concepts of physical education. The standardized test had a mean of 40 and a standard deviation of 5. The teacher decided on the following scale for determining a grade:

T-score	Grade
62.8 and above	A
52.5 to 62.8	B
41.6 to 52.5	C
33.5 to 41.6	D
below 33.5	F

The teacher applied the test to twenty students with the following results:

Student	Score	Student	Score
S1	48	S11	31
S2	43	S12	35
S3	47	S13	38
S4	45	S14	41
S5	45	S15	37
S6	48	S16	39
S7	45	S17	43
S8	40	S18	40
S9	41	S19	30
S10	33	S20	49

What grade was assigned to each student?

Answer:

A: S1, S3, S6, S7, and S20
B: S2, S4, S5, and S17
C: S8, S9, S12, S13, S14, S15, S16, and S18
D: S10 and S11
F: S19

4. A physical education teacher gave a local standardized skill test on archery. The test mean was 110 with a standard deviation of 6. The teacher decided on the following scale for determining a grade:

Z-score	Grade
1.48 and above	A
0.67 to 1.48	B
− 0.67 to 0.67	C
− 1.48 to − 0.67	D
below − 1.48	F

The teacher applied the test to twenty students with the following results:

Student	Score	Student	Score
S1	100	S11	114
S2	95	S12	111
S3	100	S13	112
S4	102	S14	109
S5	103	S15	106
S6	118	S16	106
S7	117	S17	105
S8	115	S18	103
S9	114	S19	110
S10	112	S20	102

What grade was assigned to each student?

test construction

Teachers are constantly faced with situations in which they must make decisions about pupils and programs. In previous chapters we learned that the basic substance of good decision making is relevant and reliable information. Testing is a way of securing information. Webster[1] defines a test as "any series of questions or exercises or any other means of determining the skill, knowledge, intelligence, capacities, or aptitudes of an individual or group (noun); to put to the test, to try (verb)." A test, then, can be thought of as a sort of trial to determine the degree of existence of certain qualities or conditions that form the basis for decision making. In reality, in our daily lives as well as in our professional work we are constantly "testing" or collecting information to help us conduct our personal and professional affairs.

The first part of this chapter is a discussion of the various ways one can collect information about pupils. This is followed by descriptions of specific techniques one can use in the construction and evaluation of knowledge tests. At the end of this chapter is a brief bibliography of sources of such tests. The construction of motor performance tests is presented in chapter 8.

preliminary decisions

What is the purpose of the test I wish to construct? How will I use the test data? What decisions will I make about the student and/or program? How crucial are these decisions relative to the educational welfare of the student? These questions must be answered before the teacher either constructs an appraisal instrument or selects an existing standardized test.

1. *Webster's New Collegiate Dictionary*, 2d ed. (Springfield, Mass.: G. and C. Merriam Co., 1953), p. 878.

Tests should be valid and reliable in relation to both our purpose in testing and the characteristics of the people being tested. In the broadest sense, testing should provide for effective *feedback* to pupils, teachers, administrators, and parents so the instructional setting can be continuously improved.

Although the general purposes of measurement and evaluation were covered in greater detail in chapter 2, we will mention them here briefly because the purpose of the test dictates the type of test, difficulty level of items or skills, and how the test is to be administered. The possible purposes of tests are: (1) to determine pupil status, progress made, or achievement level so we can promote from one skill level to another, determine grades, or promote from one grade level to another; (2) to classify pupils into similar-ability groups based on a particular trait; (3) to select a few from among many; (4) to diagnose the strengths and weaknesses of individual pupils so the most appropriate program can be developed for them; (5) to motivate pupils to work hard both in and out of classes; (6) to maintain minimum individual, group, and/or program standards; (7) to appraise teacher effectiveness, teaching methods, and curricular content; (8) to provide an educational experience to both the pupils and teacher through taking and constructing tests; (9) to collect data needed for action research in the schools, such as developing local norms; and (10) to compare local program efforts with acceptable national, regional, or state standards.

A test can serve a number of purposes. An achievement test in basic volleyball can provide some of the information used in arriving at a physical education grade, while at the same time diagnosing weak areas in certain tested skills. These same scores can also be used in the development of local norms for basic volleyball skills. This last point is an example of how a teacher can develop *norm-referenced standards* by which to judge an individual's performance in relation to all those previously tested under similar conditions in the same grade at a particular school. *Criterion-referenced standards* can also be developed. This process involves determining the extent to which pupils have attained a predetermined skill level, such as an ability to swim 50 yards demonstrating two strokes, a front stroke and a back- or sidestroke. The goal here is for the pupil to pass this skill requirement so that he or she may move to the next skill level, not to compare the pupil with others. As Ted Baumgartner and Andrew Jackson suggest, the type of standard selected in this case depends on the teacher.[2] The nature and level of standards to be developed must also be considered when constructing a test.

process or product evaluation

Inherent in testing of motor skills as well as cognitive skills is the concept of process and/or product evaluation. In *product* evaluation we are usually concerned with a summated score (product), such as the number of baskets made in 30 seconds on a basketball skill test. We can also concern ourselves with the *process* of making a basket: proper grip on the ball, mechanics of shot, proper spin on the ball, and so on. In baseball batting, the number of contacts with the ball can be counted *(product)* and/or the mechanics of the swing may be rated *(process).* Other skills, such as gymnastics routines, are primarily concerned with evaluating the *process* or quality of serially ordered sequential movements. Here, the process is the product and both must be jointly evaluated. Before an appraisal instrument is constructed, the teacher must decide what type of evaluation

2. Ted A. Baumgartner and Andrew S. Jackson, *Measurement for Evaluation in Physical Education* (Boston, Mass.: Houghton Mifflin, 1975), pp. 5–7.

will provide the most effective feedback at a particular stage in learning. In arriving at this decision the teacher should consider type of skill, the way it is to be performed, and the skill level of instruction (beginning, intermediate, or advanced).

educational objectives and formative and/or summative evaluation

The steps taken in collecting information for decision making involve defining and appraising our educational objectives, selecting an appropriate test, collecting data through testing, and comparing data against a standard so that we can determine how effectively our objectives have been met. Educational objectives can be of two kinds, and Margaret Safrit indicates that each is related to a type of evaluation made by the teacher.[3] The first type involves the long-term goals of the teacher or school. What are the objectives of this semester's physical education program? When these are stated, appropriate tests can be selected that will provide the teacher with information on how well individual pupils, as well as the class as a whole, met the objectives. This is an example of *summative evaluation,* in which students are compared with other students in the class at the end of the semester for purposes of developing grades in the course of promoting pupils to the next grade level. Such decisions are crucial, hence tests selected and/or constructed must meet high standards of validity and reliability.

The second type of objective, written as a *behavioral objective,* is more specific. Behavioral objectives are used by the teacher in *formative evaluation,* which provides day-to-day feedback to each student. It is an evaluation individualized for each pupil or subgroup, and designed to diagnose weaknesses

in performance so errors can be corrected in the next performance attempt. When the teacher develops each daily lesson plan, defines performance objectives for the day, and lists the processes of movements and/or skill components, she can and should write specific performance behavioral objectives and construct her daily appraisal instrument at the *same* time. The teacher must, of course, be proficient in skill analysis at each skill level. Again, the primary goal of formative evaluation is to provide continuous feedback to the pupil so that future attempts or practices will bring the student closer to the desired standard of performance. The similarities and differences among test purposes, process and product, formative and summative evaluation, criterion- or norm-referenced standards, and type of educational objectives are illustrated in Table 7.1, which is modified from the work of Baumgartner and Jackson.[4]

The teacher must also decide whether to construct a test or select one from existing standardized tests. The decision is made after the teacher knows what use is to be made of the test scores. If the purpose is to determine how well a pupil or class has done in terms of program objectives, the teacher-made test will probably be superior to a standardized test. Using a standardized test may subject the teacher to the charge of "testing for what has not been taught," especially if there is, in fact, a gap between the content of the test and the content of the course. If, however, the teacher wishes to compare class or program data with scores from other regions of the country, she will logically select a standardized test with ap-

3. Margaret J. Safrit, *Evaluation in Physical Education: Assessing Motor Behavior* (Englewood Cliffs, N.J.: Prentice-Hall, 1973), pp. 8–52.

4. Baumgartner and Jackson, *Measurement for Evaluation in Physical Education,* p. 7.

Table 7.1   Objectives, Evaluation, and Standards: Similarities and Differences

Objectives:	Specific Behavioral	General Goals
Evaluation:	Formative (process or product)	Summative (process or product)
Purpose:	Feedback to student and teacher on day-to-day basis throughout an instructional unit	Grading at end of unit or course, promote to next grade, certification examination
Time:	During daily instructional periods	End of unit, semester, or course
Emphasis in evaluation:	Explicitly defined behaviors	Broader categories of behaviors or combinations of several specific behaviors
Standard:	Criterion-referenced	Generally norm-referenced, but can be criterion-referenced

propriate norm data. Statewide competency testing is being adopted in many states. And standardized tests are being used to determine how well local units meet state or national standards in all subject areas. The purpose of this testing is to stimulate local schools to improve their programs when necessary. Standardized tests are probably superior to teacher-made tests from the standpoint of refinement of test construction.

testing for mastery or discrimination

Both knowledge and motor performance tests may be classified as *mastery* or *discrimination* type tests. The classification criteria involve the way test scores are to be used and the method employed in constructing the test. Sometimes it is extremely important for one to "master" a subject. One would expect a certified lifeguard, for example, to have passed all the requirements for the certificate, not merely to have passed some and failed others. In order to determine proficiency we develop a test of mastery. With a test like this, students may be given as much time as needed to master the material, that is, to pass all items at a certain profi-

ciency level. The purpose of instruction and subsequent testing is mastery—it is not to discriminate among levels of student ability.

Discrimination type tests are those one would take after a certain amount of instruction or practice. The purpose of these tests is to determine relative achievement or how pupils differ from one another in terms of achievement. This ranking is important for summative evaluation and may involve norm-referenced standards for purposes of grading on an A, B, C, D, or F scale. Tests of mastery, on the other hand, usually involve criterion-referenced standards for formative evaluation, and one either passes or fails the item or receives a numerical score on the test. Tests of discrimination usually involve norm-referenced standards since the purpose of such tests is to discriminate among individuals, while criterion-referenced standards permit one to determine how well each pupil has mastered important elements of a total body of knowledge or motor performance. Mastery tests usually have a high mean and a small standard deviation since everyone is expected to pass all the items on the test eventually. Thus, not much variability is expected. Discrimination tests, however, should discover the differences in achievement levels among pupils; thus, there should be a suitable standard deviation that reflects student variability.

A test for discrimination purposes has been administered when you take a written examination in a sports officiating class and the teacher compares your score with the scores of your classmates to determine your grade on the test. However, a mastery test has been administered when your state high school officiating standards require a score of 80 out of 100 in order to receive a certificate for officiating a particular sport. This is a mastery test with a stated minimal score standard.

In the area of motor testing, a test for discrimination occurs when a student's scores on a basketball skill test are compared with the scores of others for grading purposes. Examples of motor skill tests for mastery purposes would be the standards of skill proficiency adapted by the American Red Cross for the beginner, intermediate, and advanced levels of swimming. Here each pupil receives instruction, and practices the skill, until he performs it (masters it) with a certain level of proficiency. The pupil then moves on to the next level of skill difficulty. An excellent discussion of testing for mastery and the validity and reliability of criterion-referenced tests is found in Safrit and Safrit and Stamm.[5]

types of testing for evaluation

direct observation

We are continuously evaluating in education. In day-to-day contacts with our pupils, we observe their behavior in many formal and informal school settings. We should note atypical behavior and record it on some form of *anecdotal record*. The entries are brief descriptions of what occurred at a certain time. These records may form the basis

and/or provide content for counseling sessions with the pupil, parents, and school counselors. Much of the observed behavior can form the basis for citizenship, sportsmanship, or social-adjustment grades at the end of a grading period (that is, summative evaluation). Direct observation is also the way in which we secure information about the pupil's attempts to acquire a motor skill. Thus, the basis for formative evaluation of skill learning is the trained eye. The student is then given feedback so adjustments can be made in future performance. The teacher uses the more formal *rating scales* to record frequent observations of motor skill development and personal-social behavior. Rating scales may be used in both process and product evaluation. One danger with them is that they tend to direct the teacher's observations only to those areas covered by the scale, and, unfortunately, other important behaviors may go unrecorded. Thus, teachers should combine both the anecdotal record and rating scale when observing daily pupil behavior.

oral examination

This technique is rarely used in physical education as input to a system of formative or summative evaluation. Does the student understand the motor task? Asking a student to think about and verbally describe the movement sequences in a task may provide us with essential information. We can determine if he understands what is expected but cannot do

5. Margaret J. Safrit, "Criterion-Referenced Measurement: Applications in Physical Education," *Motor Skills: Theory into Practice* 2, no. 1 (1977): 21–35; Margaret J. Safrit and Carol L. Stamm, "The Effect of Varying Performance Standards and Test Length on Reliability Estimates of Criterion-Referenced Measures of Motor Behavior," a paper presented at the NCPEAM-NCPEAW joint meeting in Denver, Colorado, June 2, 1978.

the task; or if he cannot do the motor task because he does not understand what is expected. Oral examinations may be extensive or brief and may occur at any time. As with all examinations, the oral examination must have curricular or content validity. Oral examinations can also be used to assess cognitive ability.

essay testing

An essay examination is one in which the pupil is asked to respond to four or five questions in the normal test period. The student usually must compose an extensive answer by recalling specific information in order to analyze a problem area; propose a meaningful solution to a problem by synthesizing support information; or discuss the pros and cons of issues relevant to a subject. Indeed, these broader, open-ended questions can be designed to assess more complex concepts.

short-answer tests

Short-answer tests are more commonly referred to as objective tests because their responses lend themselves to objectivity and reliability of scoring. Usually, a large number of questions are formulated that require very short responses or require the pupil to mark the correct answer on an answer sheet. Short-answer test questions may be classified into two main types: *recognition* or *selection type* and *recall* or *supply type*. Recognition or selection type items are usually true–false, right–wrong, yes–no, multiple-choice, matching, or rearrangement. The student must recognize and select the correct answer from a set of possible answers provided. Recall or supply type questions require the pupil to recall from memory the correct answer. Listing items, filling in the blanks,

and completion items are examples of recall type questions.

The main advantages of using short-answer tests are: (1) the teacher can touch on a large number of the concepts the students studied; (2) scoring is quick, easy, and reliable since a secretary, teacher's aide, or a scoring machine can be used; and (3) a large number of students can be tested and graded in a short period of time. The main disadvantage of the short-answer test is the length of time and meticulous effort required to construct relevant test questions. Of course, the teacher can profit from this experience as she can review all the material when she writes the test questions.

motor performance tests

Motor performance tests concentrate on the neuromuscular coordinations of an individual, as opposed to knowledge tests, which focus primarily on mental processes. Of course, motor performance tasks beyond the range of innate reflexes, at points in the continuum of skill proficiency, do require degrees of cerebration. Sensory-motor information, for example, must be processed in the cerebral cortex before it can be translated into proficiency in motor skills.[6] Many types of motor tests have been developed. Some assess fine motor skills, others gross motor skills. Fine motor skills such a handwriting, watch repairing, surgical skills, piano playing, and so on can be tested. Indeed, a number of vocational aptitude test batteries include fine motor tests of manual dexterity. Gross motor skills, however, usually involve movement of the limbs and/or the total body. These are the tests most familiar to physical educators. The testing literature in physical

6. Joseph J. Gruber, "Exercise and Mental Performance," *International Journal of Sport Psychology* 6, no. 1 (1975): 28–40.

education is replete with strength and physical fitness tests, motor fitness tests, motor ability tests, perceptual-motor tests, and sports skills tests. Unfortunately, many of these were not subjected to rigorous standards of test construction. Hence, we must be careful in our appraisal of the tests we intend to use. The details involved in constructing motor performance tests are presented in chapter 8.

steps in construction of knowledge tests

It is essential that you become familiar with the steps in constructing and appraising knowledge tests. If you follow these steps, chances are you will develop an adequate test that provides relevant information. When considering a standardized test, carefully examine the test manual to determine if these steps were followed when the authors constructed the test. If they were not followed, the test must be suspect and should be rejected. These basic steps to follow when constructing a test for discrimination purposes are:

1. Plan the examination
   a. Determine the objectives of the examination. How do you intend to use the test scores?
   b. Develop a table of specifications or a test outline
2. Prepare the examination
   a. Establish content or curricular validity
   b. Determine types of items
   c. Prepare or write the items
   d. Arrange items in proper place on the test
   e. Prepare directions for administration and scoring of test
3. Administer the examination

4. Determine the quality of the test
   a. Item analysis-difficulty rating, item discrimination, functioning of responses
   b. Test validity
   c. Test reliability
   d. Test objectivity
5. Revise test items if needed
6. Develop norms

planning the examination

Both test content and difficulty level must conform to the use the teacher is to make of the test scores. Thus, the first consideration is the purpose of the test. Do you want to measure classroom achievement after a lengthy unit of instruction? Do you wish to construct an end-of-the-semester or course-of-study examination? What decisions about pupils must be made on the basis of the test scores? Again, it is possible for a test to satisfy more than one purpose. The primary reason for testing, however, must prevail when we construct a test.

A test is a sample of the information that makes up our instructional unit(s). We may expose pupils to over 300 relevant knowledge facts and/or concepts during classroom lectures, discussions, and assigned outside readings, and we need to determine how well they have both acquired these concepts and can demonstrate an ability to use them in concrete situations. With a 40- or 50-minute testing period, we cannot possibly ask a relevant question covering each concept. Hence, we must construct a shorter version, say a seventy-five-question test designed to sample the total knowledge base adequately. It is important that each question make a contribution toward implementing the purpose of the test. To help sample the information that comprises instructional units, we should develop a *table of test specifications.*

The table of specifications is a blueprint or outline of the intended test content. Its purpose is to ensure that we construct an appropriate test—that we indeed test for what we have taught. The table of specifications guards against concentrating too many questions on some aspects of the instructional material while ignoring others. It should take into consideration the objectives of the instructional unit and the type of mental processes involved in learning material, and it should demonstrate effectively the manner in which knowledge can be used in society. The test outline must also consider the proportion of test items that should be devoted to each of the instructional objectives. This logically would be related to the amount of time, material, and importance attached to each objective. Teachers must exercise their best profesisonal judgment when making this decision.

In knowledge testing we tap some or all of the cognitive behaviors. Benjamin Bloom, in his taxonomy of educational objectives for the cognitive domain, lists six cognitive behaviors in ascending order.[7] Successful demonstration of behavior at any level depends on achieving the levels preceding it. The cognitive behaviors of Bloom and examples or types of mental processes provided by the authors of this text are: (1) knowledge—the recall from memory of specific information, such as a game rule; methods, procedures, or situations; (2) comprehension or the lowest level of understanding—the translation and interpretation of what a rule means; (3) application—the use of a rule, given an appropriate game situation; (4) analysis—the breakdown of an abstraction or a rule into its component parts so that the specific meaning of the parts can be distinguished and applied in a game situation; (5) synthesis—the combining of logical elements of orderly play so that new rules may be developed for future

play; and (6) evaluation—the judging of rules or methods of attacking problems by weighing the values involved in alternate courses of action. How extensively we tap cognitive behaviors depends on the difficulty of instructional material, grade level, intellectual ability of pupils, and their prior background in the subject. All cognitive behaviors can be tested with both short-answer and essay type tests.

An example of a table of specifications for a junior high school physical education class basketball knowledge test appears in Figure 7.1. The instructional objectives appear in the left-hand column and the cognitive abilities across the top. Teachers must determine the percentage of the test content that is relevant for each point on the table. This table might be somewhat different if the test was to be developed to measure the basketball knowledge of the junior high school varsity team. A greater percentage of content would be assigned to rules, strategy, and recognition of various formations. In addition, varsity players would probably be responsible for the higher order cognitive skills of analysis and synthesis. Most highly skilled athletes must analyze and improvise as situations develop while they are performing or during time-outs between performance trials.

A table of specifications for a final examination in a physical education measurement and evaluation course is presented in Figure 7.2. Teachers should try to determine what percentage of items allocated to each objective would tap the various cognitive processes. At this stage in test construction we do not know the type or format of the test items. After we identify the concepts we wish to translate into test items, then we can decide on the multiple-choice, true-false,

7. B. S. Bloom, ed., *Taxonomy of Educational Objectives: Handbook I, Cognitive Domain* (New York: David McKay, 1956).

Objectives of Basketball Test	Percent of Items	Cognitive Behaviors					
		Knowledge	Compre-hension	Applica-tion	Analysis	Syn-thesis	Evalua-tion
1. Basketball Terminology	10	X	X	X			
2. History of Basketball	5	X	X				
3. Knowledge of Basketball Rules	30	X	X	X			
4. Basketball Formations; Offensive and Defensive	30	X	X	X			
5. Basketball Strategy	20	X	X	X			
6. Safety Equipment and Conditioning	5	X	X	X			

Figure 7.1   Specifications for a Junior High School Physi-   cal Education Class Basketball Knowledge Test

matching, or whatever format. The nature of the concept should play a role in deciding the type of item format. Concepts that lack a number of plausible distractors should not be presented as multiple-choice items, but as true–false, matching, or completion items. Paying attention to this detail will help produce items that contribute to the purpose of the test.

preparing the examination

Using our table of specifications as a guide we must now establish the *content* or *curricular validity* of the test. This means developing test items that do indeed sample the fund of information pupils have studied. Content validity can be facilitated by utilizing

some or perhaps all of the following procedures.

1. Analyze the objectives of instruction to make sure they are relevant and are represented on the test by an appropriate number of items.
2. Carefully examine textbooks and other reading materials assigned to the class. Identify relevant concepts and write appropriate test items. Determine what type of mental process may be involved in responding to the item. Write the item with this in mind.
3. Examine state or local courses of study in the subject matter field.
4. Inspect previous examinations on the same subject. Also, authors of textbooks quite often present sample tests in the instructor's manual that cover each chapter.

Objectives of Measurement Final Exam	Percent of Items	Cognitive Behaviors					
		Knowledge	Comprehension	Application	Analysis	Synthesis	Evaluation
1. Scope and Functions of Measurement	5	X	X	X			
2. Statistics and Norm Development	20	X	X	X	X	X	X
3. Program Objectives and Testing Purposes	5	X	X	X			
4. Knowledge of Existing Tests	15	X	X				
5. Criteria for Evaluating and Selecting Tests	20	X	X	X	X	X	X
6. Techniques of Test Construction	20	X	X	X	X	X	X
7. Administration and Scoring Tests	5	X	X	X			
8. Interpretation of Testing Data	10	X	X	X	X	X	X

Figure 7.2 Specifications for a Final Examination in Measurement and Evaluation

You may wish to adopt or revise items suitable to your needs.

5. Ask other experts in the subject field, such as fellow teachers, to rate your test questions. Make necessary revisions when appropriate.

6. Consider the social relevance of the con-cepts. Why is it important for pupils to be tested on these concepts?

The next step is to specifically determine the type of items that will be on the test: essay or short-answer questions? Again, the purpose of the test, the nature of the concepts, and the extensiveness of the material to be sampled must all be considered when deciding on item format.

preparing test items

Once you have identified and listed the concepts you wish to have represented on the test, you are ready to begin item writing. Item writing is an art that can be improved with practice. The first rule to remember is that the nature of the concept should dictate item format—true–false, multiple-choice, matching, or completion type items. The fitness of any form of test item for testing a concept and a mental ability is a function not only of the form of the item but also of its application. H. H. Remmers and N. L. Gage long ago proposed the following general principles to apply when formulating test questions.[8] They still make good sense today.

1. Avoid obvious, trivial, meaningless items.
2. Observe the rules of rhetoric, grammar, and punctuation.
3. Avoid items that have answers that most all experts will accept as correct.
4. Avoid trick or catch items or items so phrased that the correct answer depends on a single obscure word.
5. Avoid items that furnish answers to other items, since one item then becomes useless in evaluation.
6. Avoid items that contain irrelevant cues. These are items phrased in such a way that the correct answer can be easily guessed and does not require knowledge of the concept.
7. Require all students to take the same test, and permit no choice among items if we are to compare pupils with one another.

Two major types of short-answer items are recognition and supply type items. One type of recognition item is the *alternate choice* item. These appear on tests in the true–false, yes–no, right–wrong, or correction of a statement format. Safrit has some suggestions for writing good items:[9]

1. Avoid trivial items. Items should measure meaningful concepts.
2. Avoid using sentences from textbooks as questions.
3. Avoid ambiguity.
4. Include an equal number of true questions and false questions to eliminate the tendency, when guessing, to answer unknown concepts as "true" because the person being tested perceives that most of the items are true statements.
5. Order the items on the test in random fashion to eliminate possible cue carryover from one item to another.
6. Express only a single idea in a statement.
7. Avoid using negative statements unless the concept can only be presented in that manner.
8. Avoid using determiners such as "sometimes," "usually," or "often" in true statements and "always," "never," or "impossible" in false statements.
9. Make false statements plausible. They should appear equally true to the uninformed.
10. Make true statements clearly true.

Use drawings, charts, or diagrams to help test concepts. Test questions can require the student to analyze the material in the diagram before the correct answer can be determined. The following are some example *alternate choice* items.

true–false (type of item)

DIRECTIONS: Encircle T if the statement is true and F if the statement is false.

8. H. H. Remmers and N. L. Gage, *Educational Measurement and Evaluation,* rev. ed. (New York: Harper and Brothers, 1955), pp. 76–77.
9. Safrit, *Evaluation in Physical Education: Assessing Motor Behavior,* p. 180.

1. A primary cause of drowning in boating accidents is not wearing a personal flotation device. (T) F
2. A person with very little body fat has a low specific gravity. T (F)
3. In the competitive butterfly breaststroke, use of the whip kick is illegal. T (F)

(These questions can also appear in yes–no or right–wrong form.)

yes–no (type of item)

DIRECTIONS: If you agree with the statement encircle "yes"; if you disagree encircle "no."

1. Can two people with the same height and weight possess different amounts of lean body weight? (Yes) No
2. Are both the standard deviation and the mean considered to be measures of variability? Yes (No)

correction (type of item)

These can also appear as correctable true–false in order to eliminate guessing. If false, change the underlined words to make a true statement.

1. Proper application of the arms in the backstroke can best be determined by swimming speed. (Correction: analysis of stroke mechanics) T (F)
2. The standard deviation is that measure of central tendency that includes the middle two-thirds of the scores scattered around the mean. (Correction: variability) T (F)

A number of criticisms have been raised concerning the alternate choice type item, most pertaining to the true–false format. One is that these items may be testing only rote memory. This need not be the case if the teacher writes the items carefully so they demand the student to apply information rather than merely remember it. Concern also exists that students will tend to remember false items of information. Studies have revealed that this is not the case since almost all learning material is presented in either a positive or neutral fashion. In addition, the pupil, when responding to true–false items, expects a certain number of the concepts to be presented in such a way as to require a false response as the correct answer. Some are concerned that guessing is encouraged and that alternate choice items are not too reliable. If an equal number of correct true responses and false responses are on the test, we can predict in advance the average number of items a class might get correct due to guessing. Also, scoring procedures that take guessing into account can be used. If we write a large number of clear, meaningful test items, we can enhance test reliability. Certainly thirty such items will add to a greater reliability than only fifteen items.

Another type of recognition item is the *multiple-choice* question. Multiple-choice questions can appear in three forms: *correct answer, best answer,* and *multiple answer.* The multiple-choice question contains an introductory statement known as the *stem* and a set of *alternatives* or suggested answers. The correct alternative is known as the answer and the other alternatives are known as *distractors*. Victor Noll and Dale Scannell, Remmers and Gage, and Julian Stanley and Kenneth Hopkins provide excellent guidelines for use in writing multiple-choice questions.[10] They also present many examples of

10. Victor H. Noll and Dale P. Scannell, *Introduction to Educational Measurement*, 3d ed. (Boston, Mass.: Houghton Mifflin Co., 1972), pp. 221–235; Remmers and Gage, *Educational Measurement and Evaluation*, pp. 95–98; Julian C. Stanley and Kenneth D. Hopkins, *Educational and Psychological Measurement and Evaluation* (Englewood Cliffs, N.J.: Prentice-Hall, 1972), pp. 246–255.

poorly written multiple-choice questions that violate the following rules:

1. The multiple-choice item should cover an important achievement, and the stem should clearly and distinctly identify the task posed by the item.
2. The alternatives should be stated with clarity and be relevant to the stem so that all alternatives or choices appear plausible to the uninformed pupil.
3. A multiple-choice item should not have more than one acceptable answer if possible.
4. The alternatives to the stem should come near the end of the stem.
5. The best or correct answer should appear in each possible position (a, b, c, d, or e) an equal number of times in order to eliminate irrelevant cues and minimize guessing.
6. Alternatives should be listed in parallel form under the stem if possible.
7. Do not use alternatives that can be eliminated on some basis other than the achievement being measured.
8. The length of the stem and alternatives should be determined by the purpose of the item.
9. There should be at least four, preferably five, alternatives. If this is not possible, test the concept with another type of item format.
10. Words that would be repeated in each alternative should be part of the stem.
11. Use "none of the above" and "all of the above" sparingly.

Examples of multiple-choice questions. Select the correct answer.

1. Which of the following is a measure of variability?
    a. average
    b. mode
    *c. range
    d. median

2. What type of approach is *not* recommended when the lifesaver attempts a swimming rescue of a struggling victim?
    *a. front surface approach
    b. front underwater approach
    c. rear surface approach
    d. dive and surface behind victim.

3. In table tennis the receiver returns the serve during a doubles match. Which player is supposed to make the next play on the ball?
    a. the server
    *b. the server's partner
    c. the receiver's partner
    d. the receiver

Multiple-choice questions have been criticized on the grounds that (1) the alternatives are often ambiguous; (2) pupils may select a correct answer for the wrong reason or know the answer but be unable to select it; and (3) not enough relevant distractors can be written. Ambiguity can be eliminated by clearly delineating the idea in the stem and each alternative. Clarity and meaningfulness are again the hallmark. Ambiguity can be detected by asking other teachers in your field to examine your test questions. You can also ask good students to identify ambiguous statements—after all, they are the ones who will eventually take the test. Quite often, ambiguity can be detected through the process of item analysis, which is presented later in this chapter. The fact that pupils may select the correct answer for a wrong reason may apply in any type of test item. Again, clarity should help reduce this fallacy in testing. We never really do know why students respond as they do, or what mental process leads them to select a particular answer. Relevant distractors must be written. The validity of the multiple-choice item depends on relevant alternatives. If they cannot be written, present the concept as a true–false, matching, or completion type question. Even though multiple-choice items are somewhat more reliable than true–false questions due to the greater number of distractors, do not sacrifice item validity for reliability by forcing concepts into a multiple-choice format when it is not appropriate to do so.

Another recognition type item is the *matching question* format. Matching questions usually consist of two columns of words or phrases, with the right-hand column containing the alternatives. The student selects an alternative that goes with the word or phrase in the left-hand column. The following guidelines for preparing matching items are proposed by Noll and Scannell.[11]

1. A matching exercise should usually not contain more than ten or twelve items.
2. Avoid one-to-one matching by allowing the response terms to be used more than once or having a greater number of responses in the right-hand column.
3. If the same response is used more than once, there should be only one correct choice for each phrase in the left-hand column.
4. There should be a high degree of homogeneity in every set of matching questions.
5. The terms in both lists and columns should be arranged alphabetically, or in some other systematic fashion.

Examples of matching questions.

Directions: Place the letter of the phrase in the right-hand column in the space next to the corresponding statement in the left column.

a	1. breaststroke	a.	approach stroke
g	2. heaving line	b.	feet first surface dive
b	3. murky water		
e	4. sidestroke	c.	front surface approach
d	5. struggling victim	d.	front underwater approach
h	6. type II vest		

a	7. victim in constant view	e.	lifesaving stroke
		f.	mask and snorkel
		g.	monkey fist
		h.	PFD
		i.	ring buoy

The second major category of short-answer test items is the recall or supply type. Here the pupil is expected to fill in the blank, complete a statement, list information, or discuss as in an essay type question. Directions for the student must be clear-cut to avoid ambiguous responses. Omit only significant words from completion statements. Some example supply type items follow.

Directions: Place the correct answer in the blank after each question.

1. In what city is the baseball hall of fame located? (Cooperstown, NY)
2. Who was the first Negro player in major league baseball? (J. Robinson)

Directions: Complete the statement by placing the correct answer in the blank provided.

1. In basketball, the person fouled while shooting is awarded (2 free throws).
2. Only the (dolphin) type kick is allowed when swimming the competitive butterfly stroke.

Directions: List the proper sequence for the lifesaver in escaping from the rear head hold.

1. (take bite of air)
2. (tuck chin)
3. (submerge)
4. (place both hands at elbows of victim)
5. (thrust powerfully upward on victim's arms)

11. Noll and Scannell, *Introduction to Educational Measurement*, pp. 216–220.

essay testing

Stanley and Hopkins, in an excellent discussion of the advantages and disadvantages of essay testing, feel that most of the advantages of the essay test can also be attained by a short-answer objective test.[12] However, if you wish to allow a pupil freedom to write novel, relevant responses to controversial or divergent issues, then the essay test is more effective. If language ability is important in a particular setting, then the essay test is best —it can measure the student's ability to express ideas. The primary disadvantage of the essay examination is problems in scoring it. Grading an essay test is very time-consuming. In addition, a good deal of subjectivity enters into the scoring process; this can translate into inadequate test reliability. Answers to a question can vary from pupil to pupil, yet they may all be answering correctly. Student concerns over the reliability of scoring essay questions may be reduced by duplicating and handing out to the class the two or three best student answers to each question. The class then knows the standards applied in grading. Scores on the question can be contaminated by that awarded a previous paper, by the item-to-item carryover effect, by when the papers are graded, and by the "halo effect," that is, the tendency of the grader to award scores partly on the basis of a previous impression of a pupil. Quality of handwriting, as well as grammatical and/or verbal ability, can also unduly influence the scoring of essay questions. Dorothy Wood offers some suggestions for improving the construction and scoring of essay questions.[13] In constructing tests the teacher (1) should devote sufficient time to constructing the essay question; (2) should define precisely the scope and direction of the answers desired in the written question —for example, "Discuss the essay test" may be clearer when written, "Cite the major advantages and disadvantages of the essay test, giving specific suggestions for improving the typical essay test"; (3) may find a larger number of questions requiring shorter answers more desirable than a small number of questions calling for lengthy answers; (4) should consider the time required for thinking and writing when constructing questions; and (5) should give the same examination to all the students if comparisons among student performances are to be made for grading purposes.

General guidelines for scoring essay tests include: (1) prepare a tentative scoring key when constructing the item—formulate extensive possible answers at the same time; (2) apply the tentative scoring key to a random assortment of answers as a preliminary check; (3) grade one question at a time for all pupils in order to reduce the "halo effect," then go to the next question; (4) with a large number of papers, recheck the papers graded earlier to ensure that grading standards have not shifted; and (5) when possible, have other experts score the questions and pool the ratings to increase reliability.

arrangement of items on the test

Test items that are similar in format should appear in the same place on the examination. All true–false questions should cluster together. Similarly, matching, rearrangement, listing, completion items, and essay questions should appear as separate subsections of a test. Also, within each group, items should be presented in order of difficulty—the easier items first, then items of moderate difficulty, and finally the most difficult items. If all the difficult items appeared first, many students would be

12. Stanley and Hopkins, *Educational and Psychological Measurement and Evaluation,* pp. 197–216.
13. Dorothy Adkins Wood, *Test Construction* (Columbus, Ohio: Charles E. Merrill, 1961), pp. 103–107.

discouraged and not motivated to perform well on the remaining items. Since the purpose of achievement testing is to find out how well the students have learned the material, it is important to reinforce them positively in the early stages of testing. Thus, each pupil can be assured that he is being fairly tested and can display his level of achievement. Of course, the first time we administer a test we have no data on item difficulty. In this case, we should randomly assign the order of items within each format category.

prepare directions for administration and scoring of tests

Once the items are written and the general format of the test has been established, the teacher must consider efficient test administration and scoring. If we are to compare a pupil's test score with the scores of other pupils on the same test, it is imperative that all individuals take the test under the same conditions. Classroom achievement tests are usually power tests rather than speed tests, so all students must have sufficient time to respond to all items. Test directions must be clear and specific so that all understand the process they must go through in responding to test items. Selection of the "best" answer rather than the "correct" answer, for example, must be clearly specified and understood. Directions for using special materials such as notes, a textbook, or a calculator during testing must be specified. If special materials are permitted, all students must have equal access to them. Students should be told where their responses are to be recorded. If a separate answer sheet is to be used, directions must be provided for its use. Also, directions for recording scores and/or the procedures for scoring the test should be clearly specified.

All directions should be written in and be part of the test booklet. In this way, the same test can be administered to different classes by different teachers. The real purpose of establishing standardized directions is to increase measurement reliability by controlling measurement error due to faulty testing procedures.

To facilitate the scoring of short-answer (recognition) test items, separate *answer sheets* and a *scoring key* are recommended by Harold Barrow and Rosemary McGee[14] for a number of reasons:

1. They permit the reuse of test papers.
2. They facilitate scoring test papers.
3. They allow for a mark showing the correct answer, so students can study it later.
4. They are economical in time and money.
5. They facilitate performing an item analysis of the test.

Answer sheets can be developed by the teacher. Sufficient space must be provided on the answer sheet to coincide with the number of questions asked on the test. The answer sheet should also provide space for all possible responses to a test question from two responses for true–false items to five responses for multiple-choice items. Answer sheets can be purchased that allow for both electronic scoring by a machine, as well as hand scoring by the teacher by using an overlay scoring stencil. These stencil keys have the correct answers cut out. Electronic machine scoring is a nice luxury when you must score a large number of papers. Some scoring machines in computer centers can be programmed to do an item analysis at the same time. An example of a teacher-

14. Harold M. Barrow and Rosemary McGee, *A Practical Approach to Measurement in Physical Education*, 2d ed. (Philadelphia: Lea and Febiger, 1971), p. 392.

STUDENT NAME _____ COURSE NAME _____ TEST FORM _____

STUDENT NUMBER _____ DATE OF TEST_____ TEST NUMBER _____

ITEM	POSSIBLE RESPONSES *	ITEM	POSSIBLE RESPONSES	ITEM	POSSIBLE RESPONSES
	a b c d e		a b c d e		a b c d e
1.	( ) ( ) (x) ( ) ( )	41.	( ) ( ) ( ) ( ) ( )	81.	( ) ( ) ( ) ( ) ( )
2.	(x) ( ) ( ) ( ) ( )	42.	( ) ( ) ( ) ( ) ( )	82.	( ) ( ) ( ) ( ) ( )
3.	( ) ( ) ( ) (x) ( )	43.	( ) ( ) ( ) ( ) ( )	83.	( ) ( ) ( ) ( ) ( )
4.	( ) ( ) ( ) ( ) ( )	44.	( ) ( ) ( ) ( ) ( )	84.	( ) ( ) ( ) ( ) ( )
5.	( ) ( ) ( ) ( ) ( )	45.	( ) ( ) ( ) ( ) ( )	85.	( ) ( ) ( ) ( ) ( )
.		.		.	
.		.		.	
.		.		.	
40.	( ) ( ) ( ) ( ) ( )	80.	( ) ( ) ( ) ( ) ( )	120.	( ) ( ) ( ) ( ) ( )

* Responses to true-false questions can be placed in columns a or b. Numbers or letters to matching questions can be placed in column a. Responses to completion statements can be identified by item number and written on the back of the answer sheet.

Figure 7.3   Teacher-Made
Answer Sheet

made answer sheet appears in Figure 7.3. A computer score sheet was presented in chapter 4.

administer the examination

Now that the test has been constructed it is ready to be used to collect information about pupil achievement.

The test should be administered to a class in an atmosphere conducive to securing good information. There should be appropriate heating, lighting, and ventilation in the room. There should also be comfortable seating, and seats should be arranged so that possible cheating is inhibited. The teacher should read the test directions to the class and clear up any confusion over them before actual testing begins. The same test can be administered to several classes at the same course and grade level if all students involved have been exposed to the same general fund of information. All classes should take the examination under similar conditions. Reliability of the data to be used in determining the overall quality of the test will be increased if it is possible to have a large number of students take the test. Sufficient time should be allotted so that all pupils can respond to all items.

determining test quality

Was the purpose of the test realized in testing? Did the test provide us with information concerning pupil differences in achievement levels? To answer these questions we must determine the quality of the test. Since a test is composed of test items, it logically follows that every test item should contribute to the discovery of individual differences among pupils. After all, the test score is really a summary of pupil performance on all items. The validity and reliability of a test and its individual items can be determined and improved through internal and external methods. Internal procedures can be implemented by all teachers by conducting an *item analysis*—determining the value of each item in contributing to the purpose of the test. External procedures involve validity strategies such as correlating test scores with an external criterion measure (scores on another known valid test, for example, or experts' rankings of pupil abilities). Such procedures have been described in detail in chapter 5. Most teachers will probably not have sufficient time to engage in external methods. However, since the basis of any good test is still the quality of each item, teachers can and should periodically engage in the internal procedures of item analysis.

item analysis

In conducting an item analysis the teacher essentially determines (1) the difficulty level of each item; (2) the index of item discrimination; and (3) the functioning of all possible responses to a test question. Once this is accomplished the teacher can revise test questions and generally edit the test to improve test quality before it is used again. To conduct an item analysis, the number of correct responses to test questions is recorded at the top of each test paper. This score is the total number of items on the test minus the number of errors (wrong or omitted items). The test papers or answer sheets are then placed in rank order by score, with the paper receiving the highest score on top and then sequentially down to the one with the lowest score on the bottom.

The *item difficulty level* is determined by dividing the number of correct responses to

an item by the total number (N) of people taking the test. This is the proportion of correct responses and is denoted by the letter *p*. Sometimes, if we have a large number of papers, we rank them from high to low on the basis of the total test score and then divide them into two extreme groups—the top 27 percent and the bottom 27 percent.[15] (This is not necessary, however, for doing an item analysis.) The formula for the two procedures described now becomes:

$$p = \frac{\text{no. correct responses}}{N}$$

for small samples; for a larger number of papers the formula becomes:

$$p = \frac{p_{high} + p_{low}}{2}$$

where $p_H = \dfrac{\text{no. correct in top 27\%}}{n}$

and

$$p_L = \frac{\text{no correct in bottom 27\%}}{n},$$

and $p = $ proportion of correct responses in both formulas. It follows that if $p = $ the proportion of people who get the item correct, then $1 - p$ is the proportion of people who get the item incorrect, or q.

Thus, a summary of symbols so far would be:

$p = $ proportion who get the item correct;

$q = 1 - p$ or the proportion who get the item incorrect;

$N = $ total number of test papers;

$n = $ number of people in top or bottom group;

$p_H = \dfrac{\text{number of people in the top 27\% getting the item correct}}{n};$

15. One can split papers into various proportionate groups. With small samples, the split is made in the middle (50 percent). With a larger number of papers the division can be at the top and bottom 10, 27, or 33 percent.

$$p_L = \frac{\text{number of people in the lower 27\% getting the item correct}}{n};$$

$n_H =$ number of people in the high group getting the item correct; and

$n_L =$ number of people in the low group getting the item correct.

Item difficulty is very important in testing. There is an optimal level of item difficulty relative to the purpose of the test and the type of item format. Each test item should produce information concerning the discovery of differences among pupils. An indicator of student differences in test performance is called the "variance of the test" or S^2. If there were no differences, that is, if everyone had the same test score, there would be no variability, hence S^2 would equal zero. It should follow then that if everyone gets an item correct the item variance equals zero. Likewise, if everyone gets an item incorrect the item variance equals zero. These items have the same effect as adding a constant of $+1$ or -1 to everyone's score; the net effect being that variability of the test remains unchanged. In other words, these items contribute nothing to the discovery of individual differences in pupil achievement. David Magnusson[16] has shown that the item variance $= s^2 = p \times q$ and is an indication of the amount of differential information provided by the test item. The greatest amount of differential information is secured when $p = .50$. When this occurs, $q = 1 - p = .50$; thus $pq = .50 \times .50 = .25$. Let us apply this concept to a few items: first to a small number of papers ($N = 32$) and then to a large number of papers ($N = 100$) divided into the top and bottom 27 percent ($n = 27$ in each extreme group).

By examining the variance for each item in Table 7.2, one can readily see that items 1 and 5 in both examples have variances equal to zero. These items make no contribution to

the discovery of individual differences through the testing process. It is also apparent that the most differential information is secured with item 3 in both examples. Teachers should be cautioned at this point that when working with a small number of test papers, the item analysis data can fluctuate from one testing session to another. Thus, do not be too quick to discard items, especially if, in your judgment, the concept being tested is quite appropriate. When items show up to be consistently too hard or too easy and the tested concept is important, then editing the item or changing its format may permit it to operate in discriminating among student abilities. A test composed of very easy items will produce a negatively skewed distribution of scores; a test made up of all difficult items will produce a positively skewed distribution of scores. There are times when a test constructor may want this to occur, that is, when the test has a special purpose. If we want to select the top 75 percent of all who apply to a course or program most of the test items will be fairly easy. If, however, we can admit only 20 percent of the applicants to an honors program, the test items will be quite difficult so only this top group of people can score well. Remember that if a good number of people in our class get all the items correct, we have no information concerning differences among these pupils in achievement levels. The same can be said if some pupils receive zeros on a test. Remember too that at times we may intentionally construct items that test for *mastery* or are to be used as *criterion-referenced standards.* In this special case, all must score the item satisfactorily before being allowed to proceed further in learning. We can see this in certain motor learning situations where the student must learn basic

16. David Magnusson, *Test Theory* (Reading, Mass.: Addison-Wesley, 1966), pp. 21–31.

Table 7.2 Item Difficulty and Item Variances for Different Size Groups

$N = 32$

Item	No. Correct Top 50%	No. Correct Lower 50%
1.	16	16
2.	8	16
3.	16	0
4.	7	1
5.	0	0

$N = 100$; $n = 27$

Item	No. Correct Top 27%	No. Correct Lower 27%
1.	27	27
2.	22	16
3.	14	14
4.	20	6
5.	0	0

Item Difficulty

$$p_1 = \frac{\text{no. correct}}{N} = \frac{32}{32} = 1.00$$

$$p_2 = \frac{\text{no. correct}}{N} = \frac{24}{32} = .75$$

$$p_3 = \frac{\text{no. correct}}{N} = \frac{16}{32} = .50$$

$$p_4 = \frac{\text{no. correct}}{N} = \frac{8}{32} = .25$$

$$p_5 = \frac{\text{no. correct}}{N} = \frac{0}{32} = .00$$

Item Difficulty

$$p_H = \frac{\text{no. correct}}{n}, \quad p_L = \frac{\text{no. correct}}{n}$$

$$p_1 = \frac{p_H + p_L}{2} = \frac{1.00 + 1.00}{2} = \frac{2.00}{2} = 1.00$$

$$p_2 = \frac{p_H + p_L}{2} = \frac{.81 + .59}{2} = \frac{1.40}{2} = .70$$

$$p_3 = \frac{p_H + p_L}{2} = \frac{.518 + .518}{2} = \frac{1.036}{2} = .518$$

$$p_4 = \frac{p_H + p_L}{2} = \frac{.74 + .22}{2} = \frac{.96}{2} = .48$$

$$p_5 = \frac{p_H + p_L}{2} = \frac{0.00 + 0.00}{2} = \frac{0}{2} = 0.00$$

Item Variance

Item	p	q	$pq = s^2$
1.	1.00	.00	.00
2.	.75	.25	.1875
3.	.50	.50	.25
4.	.25	.75	.1875
5.	.00	1.00	.00

Item Variance

Item	p	q	$pq = s^2$
1.	1.00	.00	.00
2.	.70	.30	.21
3.	.518	.482	.2497
4.	.48	.52	.2496
5.	.00	1.00	.00

movements before progressing to a more difficult skill.

Apparently there is an optimal difficulty level for test items. Some people argue that in a routine achievement test, item difficulties should range from 10 to 90 percent. This permits both good and poor students to demonstrate their achievement levels. About two-thirds of the items should have a difficulty rating of 50 percent. Dorothy Adkins argues that the optimal difficulty level for selection type items should be adjusted upward from 50 percent.[17] The number of percentage points between 50 and 100 is multi-

17. Dorothy C. Adkins, *Test Construction*, 2d ed. (Columbus, Ohio: Charles E. Merrill, 1974), p. 98.

plied by the average proportion of items expected to be answered by chance or guessing and added to 50 to arrive at the optimal difficulty level. For true–false questions or two possible choices, the optimal difficulty becomes 50% + ½ (100% − 50%) = 75%; for three choice items, it becomes 50% + ⅓ (100% − 50%) = 67%; for four choice items, it becomes 50% + ¼ (100% − 50%) = 62.5%. In the final analysis, the purpose of the test should dictate optimal difficulty levels for all types of item format.

The *index of item discrimination* tells us how well an item of suitable difficulty actually contributes to the test's effectiveness in discriminating among students of various abilities. Assuming we have established good content or curricular validity, then the total test should have some validity. Likewise, scores on each item should possess validity by agreeing with scores on the entire test. Thus, an item should be answered correctly by a higher proportion of those who make high scores on the test than by those who make low scores on the test. When this occurs, the item is functioning in a manner consistent with the scores on the entire test. This is, in effect, a correlation or relationship between item scores and total test scores. This relationship may be calculated in many different ways. Test papers may be divided according to percentages in the high and low groups, and a variety of correlation coefficients such as the Flanagan procedure, based on the Pearson product-movement correlation, the biserial correlation, the phi correlation, or the tetrachoric correlation could be calculated. Most of these procedures are illustrated in Barrow and McGee, Magnusson, and Adkins.[18]

A simple, time-saving procedure for calculating *D,* the index of item discrimination, is recommended by Stanley and Hopkins, as well as by Noll and Scannell.[19] They indicate that the simplified procedure is highly re-

lated to the biserial correlation procedure and will produce discrimination values of essentially the same magnitude. The simple, recommended procedure for teachers to use in determining the item discrimination index is:

$$D = \frac{n_H - n_L}{n} \text{ or } D = p_H - p_L$$

where D = index of item discrimination; n_H = number in the high group who answered the item correctly; n_L = number in the low group who answered the item correctly; n = the total number in either the high or low group; p_H = the number of correct answers in the high group divided by the number of people in the high group; and p_L = the number of correct answers in the low group divided by the number of people in the low group; or p_H or p_L = proportion getting the item correct in the high or low group. Again, the split into high or low groups can be at any percentage level you choose to establish: for example, with a large number of papers, $N = 100$—split into the upper and lower 27 percent; with a small class, $N = 30$ —split the papers into the top and bottom half. This index of item discrimination has a possible range of +1.00 to −1.00, similar to the possible range for a correlation coefficient. An item answered correctly by all the high group students and missed by all the low group students would have a positive item validity of +1.00. An item missed by all the high students and answered correctly by all the pupils in the low group would have a negative item validity of −1.00. This latter case is an inappropriate situation since we

18. Barrow and McGee, *A Practical Approach to Measurement in Physical Education,* pp. 396–402; Magnusson, *Test Theory,* pp. 197–224; Adkins, *Test Construction,* pp. 100–104.

19. Stanley and Hopkins, *Educational and Psychological Measurement and Evaluation,* pp. 268–270; Noll and Scannell, *Introduction to Educational Measurement,* p. 256.

logically expect good students to respond correctly to items and poor students to respond incorrectly to the same items. Items with a negative index of discrimination must be carefully examined for possible flaws. If such items tap relevant concepts the items must be edited and/or revised before being used again because items with a negative index of discrimination do not contribute to overall test validity. The data in Table 7.3 reveal a number of interesting points. First, items 2, 3, and 4 in the small sample have

adequate item difficulty and allow for a good amount of differential information, but do not always discriminate in the right direction, that is, possess a positive index of item discrimination. Item 2 has negative discrimination, item 3 perfect positive discrimination, and item 4 has quite acceptable positive discrimination. Thus, suitable item difficulty levels do not always guarantee positive discrimination, only discrimination in one direction or the other, or no discrimination, as when an equal number of people in both the

Table 7.3   Examples of Item Discrimination Index (D) for Different Size Groups†

N = 32; split upper and lower 50%					N = 100; split upper and lower 27%				
Item	p	q	pq	D	Item	p	q	pq	D
1.	1.00	0.00	0.00	0.00*	1.	1.00	0.00	0.00	0.00*
2.	.75	.25	.1872	− .50*	2.	.70	.30	.21	.22
3.	.50	.50	.25	+1.00	3.	.518	.482	.2497	0.00*
4.	.25	.75	.1875	.37	4.	.48	.52	.2496	.52
5.	.00	1.00	0.00	0.00*	5.	0.00	1.00	0.00	0.00*

1. $D = \dfrac{n_H - n_L}{n} = \dfrac{16 - 16}{16} = \dfrac{0}{16} = 0.00$; or

$D = p_H - p_L = 1.00 - 1.00 = 0.00$

2. $D = \dfrac{n_H - n_L}{n} = \dfrac{8 - 16}{16} = \dfrac{-8}{16} = -.50$; or

$D = p_H - p_L = .50 - 1.00 = -.50$

3. $D = \dfrac{n_H - n_L}{n} = \dfrac{16 - 0}{16} = \dfrac{16}{16} = +1.00$; or

$D = p_H - p_L = 1.00 - 0.00 = 1.00$

4. $D = \dfrac{n_H - n_L}{n} = \dfrac{7 - 1}{16} = \dfrac{6}{16} = .375$; or

$D = p_H - p_L = .437 - .062 = .375$

5. $D = \dfrac{n_H - n_L}{n} = \dfrac{0 - 0}{16} = \dfrac{0}{16} = 0.00$; or

$D = p_H - p_L = 0 - 0 = 0.00$

1. $D = \dfrac{n_H - n_L}{n} = \dfrac{27 - 27}{27} = \dfrac{0.00}{27} = 0.00$; or

$D = p_H - p_L = 1.00 - 1.00 = 0.00$

2. $D = \dfrac{n_H - n_L}{n} = \dfrac{22 - 16}{27} = \dfrac{6}{27} = .22$; or

$D = p_H - p_L = .81 - .59 = .22$

3. $D = \dfrac{n_H - n_L}{n} = \dfrac{14 - 14}{27} = \dfrac{0}{27} = 0.00$; or

$D = p_H - p_L = .518 - .518 = 0.00$

4. $D = \dfrac{n_H - n_L}{n} = \dfrac{20 - 6}{27} = \dfrac{14}{27} = .52$; or

$D = p_H - p_L = .74 - .22 = .52$

5. $D = \dfrac{n_H - n_L}{n} = \dfrac{0 - 0}{27} = \dfrac{0}{27} = 0.00$; or

$D = p_H - p_L = 0 - 0 = 0.00$

† Data continuation of Table 7.2.
* Items to be discarded or revised.

top and bottom groups get the item correct. Item 3 in the large sample illustrates this last point. Secondly, items 1 and 5 in both groups provide no differential information, thus they do not discriminate in any direction. This is due to the fact that in item 1 everyone got the item correct and in item 5 everyone got the item incorrect.

Generally speaking, items with an index of discrimination of below 0.20 are considered poor items, and as such should be rejected or improved by revision. In addition, Robert Ebel maintains that items with an index of discrimination of 0.40 and up are very good items; those with 0.30 to 0.39 are reasonably good items; and those with 0.20 to 0.29 are marginal and probably need improvement.[20]

There are definite relationships between each item's difficulty and its maximum index of item discrimination (D value), as well as between mean index of item discrimination for all items and the reliability of test scores. First, the potential measurement value of an item is at a maximum when item difficulty is 0.50, that is, when one-half of those tested get the item correct. When this occurs, the maximum amount of differential information is obtained. If the item is too easy or too difficult, it will not assess individual differences very well. Secondly, assuming that we have items of suitable difficulty that discriminate in the positive direction, then Ebel has shown that as the average index of item discrimination increases in a 100-item test from 0.12 to 0.50, there are corresponding increases in the standard deviation of test scores from 5.0 to 20.4, as well as increases in the reliability of test scores from 0.00 to 0.949.[21] In summary, items of a suitable difficulty to produce maximum differential information will produce the higher index of discrimination. When this occurs, we have reliable test scores and can place confidence in the test's ability to discover individual differences in pupil achievement, since with improved reliability we have decreased measurement error. The test now should possess improved validity.

The last thing to check in our item analysis is the *functioning of possible responses* to a test question. In a true–false, yes–no, right–wrong type of item there are two possible responses. In a multiple-choice type format there are usually four or five possible responses. In the ideal situation, the correct response is selected by the better students and the incorrect response(s) by the poorer students. In this situation the various responses are functioning as intended. That is, the correct response has a positive index of item discrimination and the incorrect responses a negative index of item discrimination. In the latter case, each wrong response and/or all wrong responses together should correlate negatively with the test scores since a greater proportion of the poorer students are selecting the wrong response as compared to a small proportion of the better students who are selecting the incorrect response. The incorrect responses are now functioning as intended—they are meaningful alternates to the uninformed students.

Item analysis data consisting of item difficulty, index of discrimination, and functioning of responses should be recorded on a work sheet as shown in Table 7.4. This tally sheet of data (not previously presented in this chapter) contains all the pertinent information needed to determine the quality of test items. Let items 1 and 2 represent true–false item data and the remaining items represent multiple-choice data. A heavy boxed line is drawn around the correct alternative. Item 1 is operating as intended, with a difficulty rating of .60 and an item discrimination

20. Robert L. Ebel, *Measuring Educational Achievement* (Englewood Cliffs, N.J.: Prentice-Hall, 1965), p. 364.

21. *Ibid.,* p. 366.

Table 7.4   Response Pattern Tally Sheet for Item Analysis

Test Swimming   Number of Papers   36   Date   12/12/76   Grade   10, Sec. A & B

Item	(T) a	(F) b	c	d	e	No Answer	No. Correct Answers	Proportion Correct Responses	Item Difficulty $p = \dfrac{p_H + p_L}{2}$	Discrimination $D = p_H - p_L$	Revise or Discard
1. High	17	1					17	17/18 = .94	$\dfrac{.94 + .27}{2} = .60$	.94 − .27 = .67	No
Low	5	13					5	5/18 = .27			
2. High	13	5					5	5/18 = .27	$\dfrac{.27 + .72}{2} = .499$	.27 − .72 = −.45	Yes
Low	5	13					13	13/18 = .72			
3. High	7	2	0	8	1		8	8/18 = .44	$\dfrac{.44 + .27}{2} = .35$	.44 − .27 = .17	Yes
Low	2	6	3	5	2		5	5/18 = .27			
4. High	1	10	3	0	4		10	10/18 = .55	$\dfrac{.55 + .22}{2} = .38$	.55 − .22 = .33	No
Low	0	4	6	1	7		4	4/18 = .22			
5. High	3	4	5	4	2		4	4/18 = .22	$\dfrac{.22 + .33}{2} = .27$	.22 − .33 = −.11	Yes
Low	2	6	3	5	2		6	6/18 = .33			
6. High	1	2	10	3	3		3	3/18 = .16	$\dfrac{.16 + .33}{2} = .24$	.16 − .33 = −.17	Yes
Low	0	4	3	5	6		6	6/18 = .33			
7. High	16	1	1	0	0		16	16/18 = .88	$\dfrac{.88 + .83}{2} = .85$	.88 − .83 = .05	Yes
Low	15	0	1	2	0		15	15/18 = .83			

index of .67. However, item 2 must be revised or discarded since it is discriminating in the wrong direction; the relationship is −.45. Inspection of the other distractors for item 3 reveals that option *a* has a greater positive validity than the distractor keyed as correct. At this point the teacher might count both distractors *a* and *d* as correct responses. One of these distractors should be revised, preferably distractor *d,* before the test item is used again. The other distractors, *b, c,* and *e,* are operating as intended. Item 4 seems to be operating properly with good item difficulty and discriminating power. Distractors *c* and *e* have the desired negative discrimination. Item 5 does not function properly since it possesses a negative index of discrimination. Students seem to be projecting responses equally across all distractors. Since there is no clear-cut pattern for any distractor, the teacher might count this item either correct or incorrect for all students. Item 6 must be carefully examined. It possesses negative validity, yet one other distractor, *c,* clearly seems to be operating as the correct one. Perhaps an error exists in the scoring procedure for the item. In any event, distractor *c* is the correct one and item editing is necessary. In item 7, the item is obviously too easy to provide for any meaningful differential information. The item should be re-

SAMPLE TEST ANALYSIS MAR. 23, 1977

ITEM NO.	NO. CORRECT	% CORRECT	ITEM DISCRIMINATION			RESPONSES (* = KEYED RESPONSE)						
			HI 27%	LO 27%	INDEX	1	2	3	4	5	BLK	OTH
1	33	91.7	10	8	+0.20	1	2	0	33*	0	0	0
2	26	72.2	8	4	+0.40	4	5	1	26*	0	0	0
3	8	22.2	2	2	+0.00	5	8*	16	7	0	0	0
4	29	80.6	9	6	+0.30	1	0	29*	6	0	0	0
5	21	58.3	9	4	+0.50	1	1	13	21*	0	0	0
6	35	97.2	10	9	+0.10	1	35*	0	0	0	0	0
7	29	80.6	9	5	+0.40	29*	3	3	1	0	0	0
8	7	19.4	5	1	+0.40	2	2	7*	25	0	0	0
9	12	33.3	5	1	+0.40	1	0	12*	8	15	0	0
10	34	94.4	9	9	+0.00	1	34*	1	0	0	0	0
11	36	100.0	10	10	+0.00	0	36*	0	0	0	0	0
12	32	88.9	9	7	+0.20	32*	2	2	0	0	0	0
13	26	72.2	7	6	+0.10	1	5	4	26*	0	0	0
14	32	88.9	10	9	+0.10	1	3	32*	0	0	0	0
15	34	94.4	10	8	+0.20	0	34*	2	0	0	0	0
16	27	75.0	8	6	+0.20	0	1	0	27*	8	0	0
17	35	97.2	10	10	+0.00	1	35*	0	0	0	0	0
18	25	69.4	8	6	+0.20	2	9	0	25*	0	0	0
19	18	50.0	7	3	+0.40	18*	7	3	8	0	0	0
20	28	77.8			+0.40	2	5	28*	0	1	0	0
21	34	94.4	10	9	+0.10	1	1	0	34*	0	0	0
22	36	100.0	10	10	+0.00	0	36*	0	0	0	0	0
23	27	75.0	10	5	+0.50	0	4	3	27*	2	0	0
24	18	50.0	8	5	+0.30	6	5	18*	3	4	0	0
25	26	72.2	10	8	+0.20	26*	6	0	0	4	0	0

NUMBER CORRECT - NUMBER OF STUDENTS ANSWERING EACH ITEM CORRECTLY.

% CORRECT - % OF ALL STUDENTS TAKING THE TEST WHO ANSWERED EACH ITEM CORRECTLY.

ITEM DISCRIMINATION:

HI 27% - NUMBER OF CORRECT RESPONSES BY STUDENTS WHO RANKED IN THE UPPER 27% OF THE CLASS ON TOTAL SCORE.

LO 27% - NUMBER OF CORRECT RESPONSES BY STUDENTS WHO RANKED IN THE LOWER 27% OF THE CLASS ON TOTAL SCORE.

INDEX - INDICATES TO WHAT EXTENT SUCCESS ON THE ITEM IS RELATED TO SUCCESS ON THE TEST AS A WHOLE. (MINIMUM ACCEPTABLE INDEX LEVEL SHOULD BE AROUND .20 FOR ALL BUT EXTREMELY EASY OR DIFFICULT ITEMS.)

RESPONSES - NUMBER OF STUDENTS SELECTING EACH OPTION OR ALTERNATIVE FOR EACH ITEM.

KEYED RESPONSES ARE INDICATED BY AN ASTERISK(*).

BLK - NUMBER OF STUDENTS NOT ANSWERING AN ITEM.

OTH - NUMBER OF STUDENTS WHO MARKED MORE THAN ONE ALTERNATIVE. THE ITEM IS SCORED AS WRONG AND CAN RESULT FROM STRAY PENCIL MARKS OR CARELESS ERASURES.

Figure 7.4 Sample Test Analysis Printout

vised or discarded before the test is used again.

computer utilization for item analysis

As suggested in chapter 4, the computer is an extremely useful device for performing routine calculations. Teachers can use the machine scoring answer sheet illustrated in chapter 4. Computer item-analysis programs are available that calculate all the item statistics discussed in this chapter at the same time that machine scoring is taking place. The machine used is called an "optical scanner." An example of a computer analysis printout is provided in Figure 7.4.

technique for a quick item analysis

When the teacher is faced with a shortage of time but still wants to have an indication of item difficulty and discrimination, the following method is suggested.[22]

1. Find the median score on the test.
2. Return test papers to the class, and ask the students with test scores above the median to move to one side of the room and the rest of the students to the other.
3. Announce the correct answer to question 1 and ask those students with correct answers to raise their hands.
   a. On the basis of the approximate percentage of the class who answered cor-

22. Educational Testing Service, *Short-cut Statistics for Teacher Made Tests,* 2d ed. (Princeton, N.J.: Educational Testing Service, 1964).

rectly, classify the question as either easy, of moderate difficulty, or hard.

b. If many more hands are raised in the above-median group than in the below-median group, the question has positive discrimination. If the number of hands is about the same in both groups, item discrimination is zero. If many more hands are showing in the below-median group, the item has negative discrimination.

c. Repeat procedure a and b for each distractor of the multiple-choice question if time permits.

4. Record the test item's difficulty, discrimination, and functioning of response.

5. Repeat steps 3 and 4 for each question.

revise test items

Once the item analysis is complete, the test questions that are not contributing to the purpose of the test can be revised. Then items can be arranged into order of difficulty within type of item format. You are now ready to administer a better test to your next class.

determine test validity, reliability, and objectivity

Once internal validity of the test has been established by item analysis techniques, total test validity, reliability, and objectivity can be determined by using external procedures. These procedures have been described in detail in a previous chapter.

develop norms

The final step is to develop norms. You can do this after you have administered the test to a number of the same type classes under similar conditions. It is desirable to have over 200 cases before developing norms. Norms can be developed based on age,

grade, sex, and subject taught. Norms can be prepared as percentile ranks, standard scores, T-scales, 6-σ scales, and so on. The most appropriate norms with which to compare student performances are local, and as specific as possible as to subject taught and grade level. Methods for constructing norms were presented in chapter 4.

motor skill tests

Specific procedures for constructing tests of motor performance that provide both process and product information are presented in chapter 8.

brief bibliography of knowledge tests

The following bibliography contains examples of sports knowledge tests. Although many are quite old, the student will find a number of example test questions that are still relevant. In addition, the various techniques of establishing content validity and reliability are illustrated in these sources.

general physical education activities

Andrews, Emily R. et al. *Physical Education for Girls and Women*. 2d ed. Englewood Cliffs, N.J.: Prentice-Hall, 1963. Quizzes for twenty different activities.

Brown Physical Education Activities Series. Dubuque, Iowa: Wm. C. Brown. Test manuals for thirty-five different activities.

Fait, Hollis F. et al. *A Manual of Physical Education Activities*. 2d ed. Philadelphia: W. B. Saunders, 1961. Tests for thirty-eight different activities.

Hook, Edgar W., Jr. "Hooks' Comprehensive Knowledge Test in Selected Physical Education Activities for College Men." *Research *Quarterly* 37 (December 1956): 301–309. Tests for badminton, basketball, bowling, field hockey, softball, tennis, and volleyball.

Seaton, Don Cash et al. *Physical Education Handbook—Teachers' Guide.* 6th ed. Englewood Cliffs, N.J.: Prentice-Hall, 1974. Includes written tests on twenty-two activities.

professional student courses

Cowell, Charles C. "Test of Ability to Recognize the Operation of Certain Principles Important to Physical Education." *Research Quarterly* 33 (October 1962): 376–380.

French, Esther. "The Construction of Knowledge Tests in Selected Professional Courses in Physical Education." *Research Quarterly* 14 (December 1943): 406–424. Tests covering twenty-one activities.

badminton

Fox, Katherine. "Beginning Badminton Written Examinations." *Research Quarterly* 24 (May 1953):135–146.

Phillips, Marjorie. "Standardization of a Badminton Knowledge Test for College Women." *Research Quarterly* 17 (March 1946):48–63.

Scott, Gladys M. "Achievement Examination in Badminton." *Research Quarterly* 12 (May 1941):242–253.

baseball

Rodgers, E. G., and Heath, Marjorie L. "An Experiment in the Use of Knowledge and Skill Tests in Playground Baseball." *Research Quarterly* 2 (December 1931): 113–131.

basketball

Schwartz, Helen. "Knowledge and Achievement Tests in Girls' Basketball on the Senior High Level." *Research Quarterly* 8 (March 1937):153–156.

football

Hemphill, Fay. "Information Tests in Health and Physical Education for High School Boys." *Research Quarterly* 3 (December 1932):82.

golf

Waglow, I. F., and Rehling, C. H. "A Golf Knowledge Test." *Research Quarterly* 24 (December 1953):463–470.

gymnastics

Gershon, Ernest. "Apparatus Gymnastics Knowledge Test for College Men in Professional Physical Education." *Research Quarterly* 28 (December 1957):332.

hockey

Dietz, Dorthea, and Trech, Beryl. "Hockey Knowledge Test for Girls." *Journal of Health, Physical Education and Recreation* 11 (1940):366.

Grisier, Gertrude J. "The Construction of an Objective Test of Knowledge and Interpretation of the Rules of Field Hockey for Women." *Research Quarterly Supplement* 5 (March 1943):79–81.

Kelly, Ellen D., and Brown, Jane E. "The Construction of a Field Hockey Test for Women Physical Education Majors." *Research Quarterly* 23 (October 1952):322–329.

physical fitness

Mood, Dale. "Test of Physical Fitness Knowledge: Construction, Administration and Norms." *Research Quarterly* 42 (December 1971):423–430

Stradtman, Alan D., and Cureton, T. K. "A Physical Fitness Knowledge Test for Secondary School Boys and Girls." *Research Quarterly* 21 (March 1950):53–57.

soccer

Heath, Marjorie L., and Rodgers, E. G. "A Study in the Use of Knowledge and Skill Tests in Soccer." *Research Quarterly* 3 (October 1932):33–53.

softball

Waglow, I. F., and Stephens, Roy. "A Softball Knowledge Test." *Research Quarterly* 26 (May 1955):234–237.

sportsmanship

Haskins, Mary J. "Problem-Solving Test of Sportsmanship." *Research Quarterly* 31 (December 1960):601–605.

swimming

Scott, M. Gladys. "Achievement Examinations for Elementary and Intermediate Swimming Classes." *Research Quarterly* 11 (May 1940):104–111.

team-game activities

Rodgers, Elizabeth G. "The Standardization and Use of Objective Type Information Tests in Team Game Activities." *Research Quarterly* 10 (March 1939):103.

tennis

Broer, Marion R., and Miller, Donna M. "Achievement Tests for Beginning and Intermediate Tennis." *Research Quarterly* 21 (October 1950):303–313

Hewitt, Jack E. "Hewitt's Comprehensive Tennis Knowledge Test." *Research Quarterly* 35 (May 1964):149–154.

———. "Comprehensive Tennis Knowledge Test." *Research Quarterly* 8 (October 1937):74–84.

Miller, Wilma K. "Achievement Levels in Tennis Knowledge and Skill for Women Physical Education Major Students." *Research Quarterly* 24 (March 1953):81–89.

Scott, M. Gladys. "Achievement Examination for Elementary and Intermediate Tennis Classes." *Research Quarterly* 12 (March 1941):43–49.

volleyball

Langston, Dewey F. "Standardization of a Volleyball Knowledge Test for College Men Physical Education Majors." *Research Quarterly* 26 (March 1955):60–66.

summary review questions

1. What preliminary decisions should be made before one constructs a test or decides to select an existing standardized test? (*answer on p. 98*)

2. What are the purposes of a test? (*answer on p. 99*)

3. What are process and product evaluation? (*answer on p. 99*)

4. What are the relationships among test purpose, process and product, formative and summative evaluation, criterion- and norm-referenced standards, and

types of educational objectives, as illustrated in Figure 7.1, modified from Baumgartner and Jackson? (*answer on p. 101*)

5. What two types of recording information are suggested in this chapter for direct observation? (*answer on p. 102*)

6. What types of testing and examinations are suggested for use by physical education teachers? (*answer on p. 102–103*)

7. What steps should be considered in constructing a knowledge test? (*answer on p. 104*)

8. What is a table of specifications? (*answer on p. 104–106*)

9. What procedures are suggested in this chapter to facilitate content validity? (*answer on p. 106*)

10. List the general principles of formulating test questions introduced by Remmers and Gage. (*answer on p. 108*)

11. One type of recognition item is the alternate choice item. What are Safrit's suggestions for writing such items? (*answer on p. 108*)

12. What are the guidelines for writing good multiple-choice questions? (*answer on p. 109–110*)

13. What are the advantages of using a separate answer sheet and scoring key in scoring of short-answer test items? (*answer on p. 113*)

14. What factors should be considered in administering a test? (*answer on p. 113*)

15. In conducting an item analysis, what three factors does the physical education teacher essentially determine? (*answer on p. 115*)

16. What should be the range of item difficulty level? What fraction of the items should have a difficulty level of 50 percent? (*answer on p. 116*)

17. What does the index of item discrimination tell us? Generally speaking, what index of discrimination value indicates a poor item? (*answer on p. 117–119*)

18. In an ideal situation, what should the functioning of possible responses indicate? (*answer on p. 120*)

19. What is the desirable number of cases to consider before developing norms? (*answer on p. 123*)

bibliography

Adkins, Dorothy C. *Test Construction*. 2d ed. Columbus, Ohio: Charles E. Merrill, 1974.

Barrow, Harold, and McGee, Rosemary. *A Practical Approach to Measurement in Physical Education*. 2d ed. Philadelphia: Lea and Febiger, 1971.

Baumgartner, Ted, and Jackson, Andrew. *Measurement for Evaluation in Physical Education*. Boston: Houghton Mifflin, 1975.

Bloom, B. S., ed. *Taxonomy of Educational Obectives: Handbook I, Cognitive Domain*. New York: David McKay, 1956.

Ebel, Robert L. *Measuring Educational Achievement*. Englewood Cliffs, N.J.: Prentice-Hall, 1965.

Educational Testing Service. *Short-cut Statistics for Teacher Made Tests*. 2d ed. Princeton, N.J.: Educational Testing Service, 1964.

Gruber, Joseph J. "Exercise and Mental Performance." *International Journal of Sport Psychology* 6, no. 1 (1975): 28–40.

Magnusson, David. *Test Theory*. Reading, Mass.: Addison-Wesley, 1966.

Montoye, Henry J. *An Introduction to Measurement in Physical Education*. Boston: Allyn and Bacon, 1978.

Noll, Victor, and Scannell, Dale. *Introduction to Educational Measurement*. 3d ed. Boston, Mass.: Houghton Mifflin, 1972.

Remmers, H. H., and Gage, N. L. *Educational Measurement and Evaluation*. Rev. ed. New York: Harper and Brothers, 1955.

Safrit, Margaret. "Criterion-Referenced Measurement: Applications in Physical Education." *Motor Skills: Theory into Practice* 2, no. 1 (1977): 21–35.

——. *Evaluation in Physical Education: Assessing Motor Behavior.* Englewood Cliffs, N.J.: Prentice-Hall, 1973.

Safrit, Margaret J., and Stamm, Carol L. "The Effect of Varying Performance Standards and Test Length on Reliability Estimates of Criterion-Referenced Measures of Motor Performance," paper presented at the NCPEAM-NCPEAW joint meeting, Denver, Colorado, June 2, 1978.

Stanley, Julian, and Hopkins, Kenneth. *Educational and Psychological Measurement and Evaluation.* Englewood Cliffs, N.J.: Prentice-Hall, 1972.

Webster's New Collegiate Dictionary. 2d ed. Springfield, Mass.: G. and C. Merriam Co., 1953.

Wood, Dorothy. *Test Construction.* Columbus, Ohio: Charles E. Merrill, 1961.

exercises

1. A physical education teacher gave a 40-item written test on the skills of diving. Thirty-eight students took the test, with the following number of correct responses to each item:

Item	No. Students Getting Item Correct	Item	No. Students Getting Item Correct
1	25	21	21
2	16	22	23
3	10	23	18
4	35	24	15
5	38	25	19
6	20	26	35
7	16	27	14
8	27	28	3
9	8	29	11
10	35	30	17
11	33	31	24
12	21	32	23
13	16	33	16
14	14	34	19
15	12	35	28
16	0	36	35
17	30	37	30
18	24	38	14
19	17	39	6
20	29	40	20

What is the item difficulty level for each item? What is the variance of each item?

Answer:

Item	Item Difficulty Level	$s^2 = pq$	Item	Item Difficulty Level	$s^2 = pq$
1	.66	.22	21	.55	.25
2	.42	.24	22	.61	.24
3	.26	.19	23	.47	.25
4	.92	.07	24	.39	.24
5	1.00	.00	25	.50	.25
6	.53	.25	26	.92	.07
7	.42	.24	27	.37	.23
8	.71	.21	28	.08	.07
9	.21	.17	29	.29	.21
10	.92	.07	30	.45	.25
11	.87	.11	31	.63	.23
12	.55	.25	32	.61	.24
13	.42	.24	33	.42	.24
14	.37	.23	34	.50	.25
15	.32	.22	35	.74	.19
16	.00	.00	36	.92	.07
17	.79	.17	37	.79	.17
18	.63	.23	38	.37	.23
19	.45	.25	39	.16	.13
20	.76	.18	40	.53	.25

2. The physical education teacher in problem 1 divided the students' papers into two groups. In other words, he took the nineteen highest scores on the test and called this the high group and the nineteen lower scores and called this the low group. He then compared the number of correct responses to each item in the high group to the number of correct responses to each item in the low group with the following results:

Item	No. Correct Top 50%	No. Correct Lower 50%	Item	No. Correct Top 50%	No. Correct Lower 50%
1	15	10	13	9	7
2	9	7	14	7	7
3	5	5	15	12	0
4	18	17	16	0	0
5	19	19	17	18	12
6	15	5	18	15	9
7	10	6	19	7	10
8	17	10	20	15	14
9	8	0	21	14	7
10	18	17	22	12	11
11	17	16	23	9	9
12	17	4	24	10	5

Item	No. Correct Top 50%	No. Correct Lower 50%	Item	No. Correct Top 50%	No. Correct Lower 50%
25	9	10	33	14	2
26	17	18	34	18	1
27	10	4	35	15	13
28	3	0	36	18	17
29	11	0	37	18	12
30	7	10	38	12	2
31	12	12	39	6	0
32	16	7	40	15	5

What is the index of item discrimination for each item? If the index of discrimination is:

.40 and up = very good items
.30 to .39 = reasonably good items
.20 to .29 = marginal and probably need improvement
.19 below = eliminate

What items would the physical education teacher retain, rewrite to improve, or eliminate? Has he constructed a fair and reasonable test to measure the knowledge of his students on diving skills?

3. The physical education teacher in problem 1 found that items 1 and 24 were marginal in discrimination and decided to rewrite these two items. He examined the Response Pattern Tally Sheet for Item Analysis and found the following results for items 1 and 24.

Response Pattern Tally Sheet for Item Analysis

Test: Knowledge Diving Skills						No. papers: 38	Date: 1/3/79		Grade: 11

Item	Multiple-Choice No. of Answers a	b	c	d	e	No. Correct Answers	Proportion Correct Answers	Item Difficulty	Discrim- ination	Revise or Discard
1 High	1	15	1	0	1	15	.79	.66	. 26	revise
Low	2	10	4	0	2	10	.53			
24 High	3	0	0	10	5	10	.53	.39	.26	revise
Low	0	2	1	5	5	5	.26			

What changes can he make that will allow items 1 and 24 to become better multiple-choice items?

Answer:

The stem of item 1 might be worded to make it more difficult because the item difficulty indicates that both the high and low group answer the question correctly. Distractor d definitely needs to be rewritten because no one responded to it. Distractor d should be rewritten to pull more low responses toward it.

Item 24 appears to have a fair difficulty rating. Distractor *e* needs to be rewritten because it appears to be confusing—five in the high group and five in the low group responded to this incorrect answer. Likewise, distractor *a* needs to be rewritten because no one in the low group responded while three in the high group responded to this incorrect answer.

4. A physical education supervisor in a large school system developed a physical education concept test for ninth-grade students. She applied her newly constructed twenty-item, multiple choice, concept test to 200 ninth-grade students. She decided to take the top 27 percent and low 27 percent of the scores to run an item analysis. She tabulated the following results:

Item		a	b	c	d	e
			No. Answers Multiple Choice			
1	High	3	48	1	1	1
	Low	15	3	12	15	9
2	High	5	2	1	2	44
	Low	8	10	10	20	6
3	High	2	45	2	2	3
	Low	7	10	17	15	5
4	High	2	5	40	5	2
	Low	4	14	6	28	2
5	High	3	0	1	48	2
	Low	31	9	4	0	10
6	High	40	3	4	3	4
	Low	35	10	4	2	3
7	High	50	1	0	3	0
	Low	2	2	6	40	4
8	High	2	1	1	3	47
	Low	8	2	2	30	12
9	High	2	5	40	5	2
	Low	4	20	7	18	5
10	High	0	54	0	0	0
	Low	25	6	20	3	0

Item		No. Answers Multiple Choice				
		a	b	c	d	e
11	High	0	4	0	50	0
	Low	2	40	2	8	2
12	High	38	3	5	4	4
	Low	2	4	18	15	15
13	High	1	3	3	4	43
	Low	0	1	9	32	12
14	High	4	6	35	6	3
	Low	2	12	16	12	2
15	High	1	1	0	52	0
	Low	8	8	18	12	8
16	High	4	4	2	3	41
	Low	15	16	10	7	6
17	High	2	42	6	2	2
	Low	4	4	34	6	6
18	High	47	1	1	2	3
	Low	8	12	8	16	10
19	High	3	2	47	1	1
	Low	16	12	16	6	4
20	High	0	0	0	3	51
	Low	2	2	2	45	3

a. What is the item difficulty level for each item?
b. What is the variance of each item?
c. What is the index of item discrimination of each item?
d. As a whole, would you say the test is fair and reasonable? What items need to be revised or eliminated?

sport skills and motor ability testing

This chapter deals with constructing a motor performance test that provides the teacher with information about the process and product of motor learning. Both process and product information can be used to meet the summative or formative evaluation needs of the teacher. Thus, information about the number of bat-ball contacts (product) as well as the mechanics of swinging a baseball bat (process) can provide input for both day-to-day (formative) and end-of-unit (summative) evaluation.

The chapter provides a critique of several standardized tests of sports skills and a brief bibliography of sources for locating sport skill tests. It concludes with a brief discussion about the role of classification indices, and tests of general motor abilities.

steps in constructing a motor performance test

The general procedures involved with constructing a test of motor performance are similar to those proposed for constructing a written knowledge test. They include (1) determining the purpose of the test; (2) identifying the abilities to be assessed; (3) selecting or developing motor items that project the abilities of interest according to certain criteria; (4) securing necessary facilities and equipment; (5) conducting a pilot study on a group of pupils; (6) revising items and directions; (7) administering test items to a large number of students; (8) determining internal and external validity where feasible; (9) securing reliability information; (10) developing norms; and (11) making up a test manual.

It may seem as though it would be fairly easy to construct a swimming, baseball, or basketball skill test to use in class. However, since there are many problems and decisions to be made at each stage in constructing motor performance tests, it is not as easy as it appears.

preliminary decisions

The most important decision involves the intended purpose of the test and the way the teacher will use the information gained from testing. Generally speaking, there are two major ways in which motor skills are classified. These concern the nature of the skill and the way the skill is projected in the environment. Richard Schmidt identifies a *discrete* versus a *serial* performance and an *open* versus a *closed* performance environment.[1] If a task has a discrete beginning and end, such as a ball toss or a standing long jump, it is termed a *discrete skill*. On the other hand, if the task involves stringing together a number of the same or different discrete skills to form a continuous performance, we have a *serial skill*. When the shortstop moves in to field a ground ball, straightens up, and throws the runner out at first base, he is performing a serial skill. The hop-step and jump and the pole vault are other examples of serial skills. When serial skills are projected for a long period of time, such as when one plays 40 minutes of basketball or goes bicycling, we have a long-term continuous performance. A motor task in which the environment is not changing and the performer can plan her movement well in advance without fearing any change, as in bowling or archery, is termed a *closed environment task*. A situation in which the environment is constantly changing, such as in a basketball game or a tennis match, is termed an *open environment* performance. Here, each individual's performance is affected by the changing environmental stimuli furnished by teammates, opponents, audience, and so on. Thus, the way the skill will be used by the performer in her everyday physical education class should influence the type of skill test item that is constructed by the teacher. Specificity of testing, or content validity, will thus be assured to some degree.

Both Loretta Stallings and Schmidt[2] provide further insight into the nature of motor skills that teachers must consider when constructing tests. First, skills that are important in early stages of learning often change in complexity and pattern of movement, or they become subordinate at intermediate or advanced skill levels. Cognition and information processing are important in early stages of learning but become less so as skills become more automatic at the advanced levels. Here, cognition may be turned toward strategy instead of toward the correct way to execute a jump shot. Hence, a motor skill test appropriate at the beginning of the semester may be inappropriate at the end when student motor abilities have changed drastically. Discrete skills tests may be more appropriate for beginners, while serial complex skills tests are more suitable for intermediate and advanced students. This is vividly seen in aquatics where beginners are tested on floating, gliding, breath holding, and so on, while intermediate and advanced swimmers are tested on a 25- or 50-yard swim for time in the various strokes.

Age of the learner, grade level, and previous background in skill acquisition must also be taken into consideration. Young children in elementary physical education, or those being tested for prescription in a diagnostic remedial motor skills laboratory, will probably be tested over a large number of simple, discrete motor tasks such as strength, flexibility, jumping, hopping, throwing, catching, turning, twisting, rolling, identification of body parts, balance, eye-hand or eye-foot coordination, speed, and agility. These items are presented in order of difficulty and may become serial in nature as

1. Richard A. Schmidt, *Motor Skills* (New York: Harper and Row, 1975), pp. 24–25.
2. Loretta M. Stallings, *Motor Skills: Development and Learning* (Dubuque, Iowa: Wm. C. Brown, 1973), pp. 103–117; Schmidt, *Motor Skills,* pp. 43–56.

complexity increases. Again, the items selected must satisfy a relevant rationale for testing but must be specific to purpose with the test performance in simulating the performance expected in the game situation at each stage of learning.

Motor skill testing can be used to satisfy the formative or summative evaluation needs of the teacher. Thus, specific skills such as throwing (both distance and mechanics) or shooting a basketball can be identified and used in formative evaluation. These skills usually are the fundamentals that must be practiced daily in our classes. An operational definition of each skill component, that is, the correct *process* of performance, must be known by the teacher and is the model the student attempts to emulate. This definition is also the basis of a rating scale that provides frequent feedback to the student so that performance adjustments can be achieved. If we want to compare a student's performances with the performance of other students for grading purposes at the end of a unit of instruction, we need a test developed for summative evaluation purposes. The test items will probably be more complex serial motor tasks. One important item may be a rating of playing ability. Playing ability is difficult to measure accurately, but one must decide on an accurate definition of it.

motor tests for summative evaluation

This type of test is used as part of the process of arriving at a final grade, promoting from one skill level to another, or selecting varsity squad members. Crucial decisions are made based on these test scores and, to have valid and reliable data, the procedures in test construction must be rigorously adhered to. We must know the motor characteristics of our pupils and, above all, have expert knowledge of motor skills testing. Assume that we wish to construct a basketball skill test to evaluate student achievement after twelve weeks of instruction in a class that met for three fifty-minute periods a week. The first step is to determine the purpose in testing. In this case, our purpose in testing is to measure achievement for grading. Our expert knowledge of the underlying basketball skills that make up beginner, advanced beginner, intermediate, advanced, and varsity level basketball ability must be used in constructing the test. To have good content validity, the test items should reflect the skills in the appropriate ability level. How far along did you get in teaching progressively more complex basketball skills? Always test for what you have taught! A number of different basketball tests can be developed for the various ability levels. If your basketball skill test items are too easy or too hard, they will not differentiate among the abilities of various students at a particular level.

The second step is to identify the skills essential for the basketball ability level you wish to sample with your test. You may wish to consult with other basketball experts to gain a consensus as to which skills belong to various basketball ability levels. Experts in test construction recommend conducting a factor analysis of the many test items on students in known ability groups—beginner, intermediate, or advanced—in order to identify the factors (skills) important to each ability level. We will be unable to conduct a factor analysis, but we can use other methods of establishing content validity in our own school. Using other experts and our own expertise, and thoroughly analyzing basketball skill teaching manuals and coaching texts, should help us identify the relevant skills in each ability level.

Once we have identified the skills we wish to test for, we must develop the motor task that is to produce the test score. In other words, how will we measure dribbling, passing, shooting, rebounding, defense, and so on? We must now develop an operational definition of the skill to be tested. This definition must reflect, if at all possible, the components of the skill as used in a game situation. Skills can be measured in time, distance, accuracy, force, or form. Margaret Safrit, in her book *Evaluation in Physical Education,* has an excellent discussion on the problems inherent in measuring skills in units not related to the way the skill is used in actual practice.[3] The number of baskets made in 30 seconds, for example, is not the way baskets are made in a game. If a time measure is involved, we encourage pupils to rush at the expense of form and accuracy. In distance throws, what is more important, accuracy of throws, force of throw, or the actual distance? In throwing the javelin, distance is primary. However, force and accuracy are essential if the outfielder in baseball is to throw out the base runner after he tags up to run for home. One must carefully think through the movement sequence of the skill and devise the most appropriate way of measuring it, that is, the way the skill is used in actual play.

Next, you need to write detailed directions for the administration and scoring of the basketball skill test items. Use diagrams to illustrate correct procedures if necessary. You must also specify and secure the facilities and equipment needed to administer the test items. Train testers and try out all equipment in advance to make sure everything works properly.

Conduct a pilot study on a small group of pupils. This should enable us to identify any problems in the administration and scoring of items. We should be able to determine if our operational definitions of skill components are relevant to abilities. In addition, our method of scoring can be scrutinized. Do the test items identify students with different abilities? Revise items and procedures if necessary.

To secure an approximation of test validity we must now administer the test items to a large number of students in the same general ability grouping, such as intermediate basketball. A group of experts, all using the same definition of ability, should watch these pupils play basketball and rank them. Other physical education teachers, basketball coaches, and even members of the varsity basketball team may serve as effective judges. The ratings of these experts may now be correlated with each item score, as well as with the total score made by the students on the basketball skill test. In order to compute a total score, all part scores have to be converted to a common scale, such as a T-score. Examine the correlations between each skill item and the criterion of basketball ratings. The higher the correlation, the better the item estimates basketball playing ability. Items should generally have fairly low correlations among themselves. This is to avoid having two items providing the same information—which is a waste of testing time. Retain items that have a high correlation with the criterion and a low correlation with one another. An efficient basketball skill test should probably have no more than four or five items if it is to be economical in terms of testing time. You can compute a multiple correlation between the five items combined and the criterion score. This technique permits the items to combine their contribution uniquely when estimating the criterion. And it permits you to determine the weight or influence (degree of importance) each item has in the multiple relationship. Generally speaking, a multiple correlation (R) of .80 or above is quite acceptable for a skill test.

3. Margaret J. Safrit, *Evaluation in Physical Education: Assessing Motor Behavior* (Englewood Cliffs, N.J.: Prentice-Hall, 1973), pp. 163–169.

Test these students again a few days later. Now you have two sets of scores and can *estimate* the test-retest reliability for each item and for the total test. Again, these reliability coefficients should exceed .80.

In time, you will want to develop local norms. This can be done by testing a number of classes. Thus, pupils can compare their test scores with the scores obtained by all other students tested in the same type class in the school or school district. If other teachers are going to use the test, it is important to develop a test manual containing all the relevant information about testing procedures.

motor tests for formative evaluation

The purpose of a formative evaluation device is to provide immediate daily or weekly feedback to the students so they can benefit as much as possible from daily practice sessions. Once weaknesses in a student's performance are identified, the pupil can practice in class or at home if possible to eliminate them. This type of feedback can be provided on an individual or group basis and at any level of ability: beginner, intermediate, or advanced. The teacher must have expert knowledge of the fundamental skills required at each stage of learning. The teacher must also know how the skill is correctly performed. With this knowledge at hand, teachers can write good operational definitions of the fundamental movements that make up a skill. And their expertise in the area of interest will ensure the content validity of the frequent evaluations. They may also consult some of the excellent teaching manuals that analyze and order skills so they can be taught progressively. Aquatic instructors certainly will want to consult the Water Safety Division of the American National Red Cross and the work of John Torney and

Robert Clayton[4] for assistance in defining skill components and ways to test them at the beginner, advanced beginner, intermediate, and advanced swimming ability levels. Quite often formative evaluation uses criterion-referenced standards when testing for mastery.

Components of skills can be assessed by using checklists and rating scales. The components of skills are identified, listed, and a check mark is made next to the component if the pupil performs correctly. Mary Jane Haskins has developed a golf swing checklist that is illustrated in Figure 8.1.[5] A word description of each component of the swing appears on the scale for ready reference. Teachers should observe the displayed motor behavior on a number of occasions in order to secure a more reliable estimate of the skill components. Checklists can be expanded into a rating scale where the degree of skill is recorded. It is essential that a word definition describe and accompany the degree of skill observed. Haskins presents a golf rating scale for woods and irons that is illustrated in Figure 8.2.[6] The teacher circles the score appropriate to each student.

Teachers can distribute these checklists and/or rating scales so that individual class members can see where their weaknesses lie. Pupils with similar faults can be grouped together for remedial practice. Teachers can also use an individual rating sheet for each student and give it to the student after the rating. An example of this type of rating scale —for the jump shot in basketball—is shown in Figure 8.3. Other basketball skills such as

4. American National Red Cross, *Manual for the Basic Swimming Instructor* (Washington, D.C.: The American National Red Cross, 1974); John A. Torney and Robert D. Clayton, *Aquatic Instruction: Coaching and Management* (Minneapolis, Minn.: Burgess, 1970).

5. Mary Jane Haskins, *Evaluation in Physical Education* (Dubuque, Iowa: Wm. C. Brown, 1971), pp. 181–183.

6. *Ibid.*

GRIP

Left-palm, firm; V to right shoulder
Right-finger, V to right shoulder

STANCE

Club head soled, knees flexed, feet square, left foot turned slightly out, ball off left heel, head down, weight and width of stance appropriate to club.

WRISTS

Slightly cocked at address, cocked at extension of back swing but held firmly, uncocked at low point of swing; work together.

RIGHT ARM AND SHOULDER

Elbow in, shoulder slightly lower, elbow points to ground at top of backswing.

LEFT ARM

Straight until end of follow-through
Slight pronation
Pull on forward swing

BACKSWING

Low until pivot brings it up
Head over ball
Pivot in body, no weight shift
Full pivot

FORWARD SWING

Starts with left arm pull
Weight shifts to left
Head remains over ball
Wrists remain cocked until bottom of swing
Stance as at address on contact

POWER AND TIMING

Clubbed speed at contact
Wrists come to extension at contact
Left hand firm, right hand guides

FOLLOW-THROUGH

Low until pivot brings up in line of intended flight
Head remains in position

Figure 8.1 Golf Swing Checklist and Descriptions

dribbling, passing, defense, rebounding, and so on, can be evaluated with similar rating scales. In the scale in Figure 8.3 the rater indicates the proficiency level observed in each component. The rater can also prescribe in the comment section how to eliminate the error in future practice. Examples of checklists for rating softball batting skills and the sidestroke in swimming are provided by Harold Barrow and Rosemary McGee and Torney and Clayton and are illustrated in Figures 8.4 and 8.5.[7] Use of checklists and rating scales as described in this chapter enhances the process evaluation of skills so important in day-to-day improvement of student performance.

In summary, the steps in constructing a rating scale for formative evaluation purposes include the following:

1. Determine the basic elements or fundamental skills of the sport.

2. Determine the sequential movements of each skill element.
3. Write a definition to accompany each value point on the scale. Define an excellent, above average, good, fair, and poor performance. These definitions will likely vary between beginner, intermediate, and advanced classes.
4. Assign a value (score) to each point on the scale. This will permit you to arrive at an average if desired.

Poor	Fair	Average	Above Average	Excellent
E	D	C	B	A
1	2	3	4	5

7. Harold M. Barrow and Rosemary McGee, *A Practical Approach to Measurement in Physical Education*, 2d ed. (Philadelphia: Lea and Febiger, 1971), p. 323; Torney and Clayton, *Aquatic Instruction: Coaching and Management*, pp. 86–87.

CLASS _____

TIME _____

DATE _____

STUDENTS			COMPONENTS OF SWING							
	GRIP	STANCE	WRISTS	RT. ARM TO SHOULDER	LEFT ARM	BACKSWING	FORWARD SWING	POWER TO TIMING	FOLLOW-THROUGH	
1.										
2.										
3.										
4.										
5.										
6.										
7.										
8.										
.										
.										
.										
.										
25.										

Figure 8.1 *continued*

7. Excellent - Full swing, coordination and timing consistently produces full speed at contact, flight of ball straight, trajectory appropriate to club.

6. Very Good - Does not achieve full swing, timing and coordination consistent.

5. Good - Some inconsistency in swing, contact good most of the time, does not achieve full power.

4. Average - Inconsistent in swing and contact, no major faults.

3. Fair - Inconsistent in swing, some faults in form, does not maintain body relationship to ball, contact erratic.

2. Poor - Several faults in swing, makes contact most of the time but contact seldom produces proper flight.

1. Very Poor - Many faults in swing, frequently misses ball, contact usually poor.

NAME	WOODS AND IRONS						
1.	1	2	3	4	5	6	7
2.	1	2	3	4	5	6	7
3.	1	2	3	4	5	6	7
4.	1	2	3	4	5	6	7
.							
.							
.							
25.	1	2	3	4	5	6	7

Figure 8.2 Golf Rating Scale—Woods and Irons

Name _____ School Attending _____

Date _____ Checked by _____

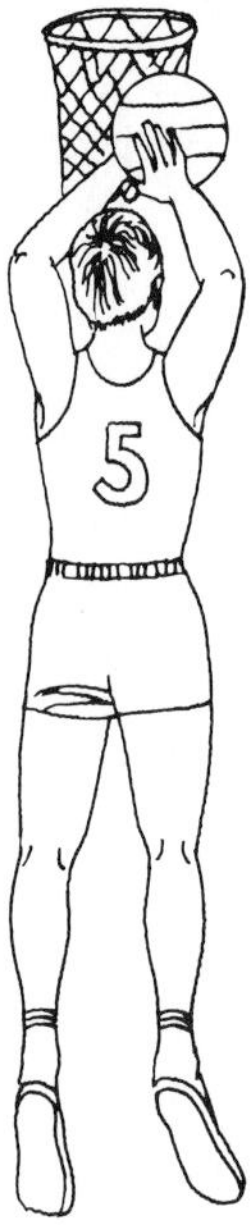

(11 Point Check List)   Excellent   Good   Poor

1. Body Balance and
    Control   _____   _____   _____

2. Stance of Player   _____   _____   _____

3. Grip of Ball   _____   _____   _____

4. Elbow (Position)   _____   _____   _____

5. Proper Position of ball
    just before release   _____   _____   _____

6. Sighting the Basket   _____   _____   _____

7. Proper rotation of
    the ball   _____   _____   _____

8. Strength of the shot   _____   _____   _____

9. Follow-through   _____   _____   _____

10. Arc of the ball   _____   _____   _____

11. Concentration of
    Shooter   _____   _____   _____

COMMENTS: _____

_____

_____

_____

Figure 8.3   Evaluation of the
Jump Shot

Student's Name _____   Date _____

Rated By _____   Score _____

Directions: First check student's performance as good, fair, or poor on each item and then check deviations noted.
Determine the student's score by assigning 1 point for poor, 2 for fair, and 3 for good, and totaling
points.

	Rating	Deviations from Standard Performance
1. Grip	_____ Good	_____ Hands too far apart
	_____ Fair	_____ Wrong hand on top
	_____ Poor	_____ Hands too far from end of bat
2. Preliminary	_____ Good	_____ Stands too near the plate
Stance	_____ Fair	_____ Stands too far from the plate
	_____ Poor	_____ Stands too far forward toward pitcher
		_____ Stands too far backward toward catcher
		Feet not parallel to line from pitcher
		_____ to catcher
		_____ Rests bat on shoulder
		_____ Shoulders not horizontal
3. Stride or	_____ Good	_____ Fails to step forward
Footwork	_____ Fair	_____ Fails to transfer weight
	_____ Poor	_____ Lifts back foot from ground before swing
4. Pivot or	_____ Good	_____ Fails to "wind up"
Body Twist	_____ Fair	_____ Fails to follow-through with body
	_____ Poor	_____ Has less than 90° pivot
5. Arm Movement	_____ Good	_____ Arms held too close to body
or Swing	_____ Fair	_____ Rear elbow held too high
	_____ Poor	_____ Bat not held approximately parallel to ground
		_____ Not enough wrist motion used
		_____ Wrists not uncocked forcefully enough
6. General	_____ Good	_____ Body movements jerky
(Eyes on ball,	_____ Fair	_____ Tries too hard; "presses"
judgment of	_____ Poor	_____ Fails to look at center of ball
pitches, and		_____ Poor judgment of pitches
the like)		_____ Appears to lack confidence
		_____ Bat used not suitable

Figure 8.4   Checklist for
Rating Softball Batting Skills

DIRECTIONS: Check √ all items that apply to the performance
of this skill. Add other noted errors in the spaces provided.

NAME _____

(of performer)

NAME _____

(of analyzer)

ANALYSIS OF PERFORMANCE

BODY POSITION

_____ The form is acceptable.
_____ The form is not acceptable because:
_____ Arms and legs not fully extended.
_____ Legs not together.
_____ Body not stretched and straight.
_____ Body turned toward stomach-down position.
_____ Body turned toward back-down position.
_____ Head not turned toward the upper shoulder to facilitate breathing.
_____ (Other) _____

_____

ARMS

_____ The form is acceptable.
_____ The form is not acceptable because:
_____ Pull of the leading (lower) arm too short.
_____ Pull of leading arm too deep.
_____ Leading arm not recovered with finger tips leading.
_____ Elbow of leading arm not brought to ribs before recovery of that arm.
_____ Trailing (upper) arm does not pull to thigh.
_____ (Other) _____

_____

LEGS

_____ The form is acceptable.
_____ The form is not acceptable because:
_____ Legs separated vertically; resulting

_____ in a breaststroke kick.
_____ Inverted scissors kick used.
_____ Legs do not bend enough at knees during recovery.
_____ Knees brought too far in front of stomach during recovery.
_____ Legs recovered too vigorously.
_____ Legs not straightened before the squeeze.
_____ Too little effort during squeeze.
_____ Ankles not extended to point toes during late part of squeeze.
_____ Legs pass each other at end of squeeze.
_____ (Other) _____

_____

COORDINATION AND BREATHING

_____ The form is acceptable.
_____ The form is not acceptable because:
_____ Both arms pull toward feet at same time.
_____ Leading arm begins pull immediately after recovery.
_____ Leading arm pulls at same time as delivered.
_____ Kick delivered before leading arm ready to recover.
_____ Exhalation is at a time other than during leg kick or during glide.
_____ Inhalation does not follow immediately after exhalation.
_____ The duration of the glide is too brief.
_____ (Other) _____

_____

Figure 8.5 Performance Analysis Sheet for the Sidestroke

critique of sport skill tests

A great number of sport skill tests were developed in the 1930s and 1940s. John Faulkner and Kathryn Luttgens[8] indicate that many of the sports skill tests are twenty to thirty years old. In the last thirty years there have been many improvements in measurement technique, changes in rules and playing procedures, and developments in the identification and classification of skills and skill patterns that make many of the existing tests obsolete. A major flaw is that many of the skill test items and/or the way they are administered to students are not related to actual game play. The validity of such tests, then, is questionable, especially if the test scores are used for grading purposes at the end of a teaching unit. For example, volleying a ball back and forth above a 10-foot line on a wall for 30 seconds is not the way a volley is conducted during a volleyball game. The item may validly be used in grading wall volley ability, but one must question its use in estimating volleyball playing ability. Since a player must return many different types of shots during a game, it seems logical to develop a test that will take this into consideration. The wall volley is a good drill for beginners, though, and may be good for testing them. An item may be relevant for classification but not for other purposes. Indeed, one item may be well suited for classifying pupils into different groups for instructional purposes, but for crucial decisions involving grading students on volleyball playing ability, a number of items and/or ratings that estimate ability must be used. Also, validity, reliability, and norms are situation-specific, and we should not overgeneralize the applicability of tests, items, and norms to purposes and populations for which they are not really intended. Many skill tests and their norms, for example, were developed on college students. As such, they are probably irrelevant for use in junior and senior high schools because of obvious differences in physical and emotional maturation levels of the students.

When evaluating tests, we should employ the criteria of validity, reliability, objectivity, norms, standardized directions, and administrative feasibility to the test and its items. Let us apply them to two sport skill tests: one, a discrete skill performed in a closed environment (archery), and the second, serial skills performed in an open environment (basketball).

archery

In 1967 the American Association for Health, Physical Education and Recreation published the *Skills Test Manual* for archery for boys and girls.[9] The tests are designed to be used as practice rounds or "practice tests" to measure achievement in shooting with a bow and arrow at a 48-inch (1.22 m) target from Distance A = 10 yards (9.15 m); Distance B = 20 yards (18.29 m); and Distance C = 30 yards (27.44 m). The class can be grouped into squads of four with one squad shooting at each target. Each archer shoots two ends of six arrows each for a total of twelve arrows. In addition, each archer can be scored on a pass or fail basis on the following items of form: bracing the bow, stance, nocking the arrow, finger placement, draw, anchor, release, and the follow-through. A more detailed description of actual testing procedures with percentile rank norms established for boys and girls follows.

---

8. John Faulkner and Kathryn Luttgens, "Introduction to Sports Skill Testing," in *An Introduction to Measurement in Physical Education,* ed. Henry J. Montoye (Boston: Allyn and Bacon, 1978), p. 183.
9. American Association for Health, Physical Education and Recreation, *Skills Test Manual: Archery,* David Brace, Consultant (Washington, D.C.: AAHPER, 1967).

Figure 8.6   Archery: drawing the bow

purpose

To measure accuracy in shooting with a bow and arrow at a standard 48-inch (1.22 m) archery target from Distance A—10 yards (9.15 m), Distance B—20 yards (18.29 m), and Distance C—30 yards (27.44 m).

equipment

A shooting range on level ground, of at least 200 feet (60.96 m) in length and 50 feet (15.24 m) in width for each archery target in use. Standard 48-inch (1.22 m) face archery targets placed on suitable stands so that the center of the target is 48 inches (1.22 m) above the ground.

When the test is given indoors, a gymnasium floor at least 96 feet (29.26 m) in length, with appropriate backstops behind the targets will be needed.

Bows of assorted strengths of pull from 15 to 40 pounds should be available depending on the age and ability of archers being tested.

Arrows of 24 (60.96 cm) to 28 (71.12 cm) inches in length to fit the bows and archers will be needed with eight to ten arrows of the same color for each archer. Archers may use their own equipment if it is inspected and found safe.

Each archer should have arm guard, finger tab or glove, and quiver.

Other equipment includes line marker, stakes, measuring tape, whistle, squad scorecards, pencils, and class composite record sheet.

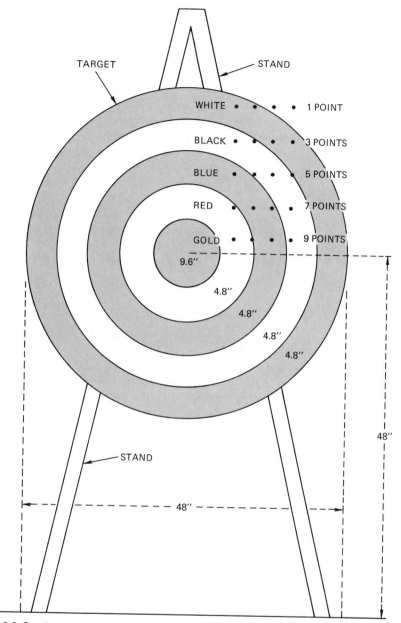

Figure 8.6 *Continued*

description

The standard archery target is made of straw, and is usually mounted on a wooden tripod. The target face may be of oilcloth or heavy paper, with five concentric circles drawn on it, the center being 9.6 inches (24.38 cm) in diameter and the others 4.8 inches (12.12 cm) wide. The center circle is painted gold, the others red, blue, and black respectively, and the outer circle is white (see Figure 8.6).

Squads of four archers only shoot at any one target.

Each archer shoots two ends of six arrows at each distance for which he or she qualifies. Each archer shoots one end and is scored on these, then waits his or her turn to shoot the remaining end.

The scorer withdraws the arrows and announces the score of each arrow as it is withdrawn. The recorder records the score of each arrow on the squad scorecard. After each archer has shot twelve arrows, the total score at the distance is recorded.

After all archers of a squad have completed shooting two ends at Distance A, the squad moves back to Distance B, takes their practice shots, and again shoots two ends. After completing shooting at Distance B, the squad (boys only) moves to Distance C and, after practicing, shoots two ends in rotation as before.

Archers stand astride the shooting line while shooting. Any method of aiming can be used; bow sight, point of aim, or instinctive shooting. The archer may adjust the aim during the practice shots or during testing, but no additional practice shots are allowed for this purpose. Archers who fail to score 10 points at any distance may not be allowed to shoot at the next distance at the tester's discretion.

rules

1. The archer must stand astride the shooting line while shooting.
2. Four practice shots at each distance are allowed.
3. The archer may adjust the point of aim during practice shots or during testing, but no additional practice shots for this purpose will be allowed.
4. Each archer shoots one end at a time, and then waits his or her turn to shoot the other end.

scoring

Arrows hitting in the center or gold circle count 9 points; arrows hitting in the next or red area count 7 points; those in the blue area count 5 points; in the black area, 3 points, and in the outer or white area, 1 point. Arrows striking in two colors count the value of the higher scoring area. Arrows striking the target but falling to the ground count 7 points regardless of where they originally struck. The maximum score at each distance is 108 points; the maximum score at the first two distances (for girls) is 216 points; the maximum score for all three distances (boys) is 324 points.

test critique

Validity is the degree to which a test measures what it is supposed to measure. Although there are a number of different types of validity, any test should have content that is relevant and that enables test scores to correlate highly with the final standing of archers competing in a tournament. In other words, the better archers should score higher on the test, and the archers in the lower tournament rankings should score lower on the skill test. Most information concerning the criteria for evaluating a test should be in a test manual. Careful examination of the AAHPER *Skills Test Manual* for archery indicates that on the surface the test has good content validity as related to purpose: "These skill tests should be regarded as 'practice tests' because they are intended to be used by players as a way of improving abilities in the fundamental skills of archery."[10] Since national norms based on 600 to 900 scores for each sex at each age are presented in the manual, a pupil's score can be compared to the scores of other pupils around the country. Ratings of form, as well as target points, serve as feedback to the

10. *Ibid.*, p. 12.

student. Content validity concerning the fundamental skills of archery as taught in basic courses seems to be well established. However, since the test manual provides no information concerning concurrent or predictive validity, whether or not this archery skill test score can estimate archery ability in actual competition has not been demonstrated. Teachers can and should establish this relationship in their own school if they intend to use the test scores for grading purposes. In all likelihood, this relationship will be quite high since the test items are conducted in a like manner and in fact probably replicate the way a class would shoot in a tournament. This validity should be easy to establish since there is very little variability involved in the nature of the skills and in the environment. The skills are discrete, hence complexity of movement patterns does not exist. Also, targets and archers are stationary in an unchanging terrain. Fundamental archery skills are taught this way and logically are tested this way.

The test manual indicates that shooting from 30 yards (27.44 meters) was too difficult for girls.[11] The manual does not indicate why. Perhaps they did not have sufficient strength to draw the proper bow for that distance. As a general rule, we must be conscious of the fact that students must possess sufficient strength, flexibility, and balance to perform many skill test items. If they lack one of these components, the test becomes one of strength rather than archery skill. Since 65 percent of the girls tested at ages 12 and 13 and 35 percent at ages 17 and 18 were unable to score at 30 yards (27.44 m), it was proper not to include that distance in the norms.

As progression in archery instruction increases through intermediate and advanced levels, skill complexities and environmental conditions change. Jean Barrett briefly describes a variety of archery sports and games, such as field or range shooting, clout shooting, flight shooting, hunting, and novelty shoots.[12] When developing an appropriate test item, the teacher should try to structure the item and its administration to simulate actual performance.

Reliability is reported in the manual to be at least .70 for events scored on the basis of accuracy and form. This standard has been adopted by the AAHPER Skills Test Project Committee for all test items scored in this manner for various sports.[13] Thus, actual reliability coefficients for each distance, each sex, and each age have apparently not been computed. In addition, students are permitted to use any method of aiming, that is, bow sights, point of aim, or instinctive shooting.[14] Thus, one must ask if the reliability coefficient will vary among different sighting methods. Will student scores be just as consistent regardless of sighting method? If within pupil variability is low with a bow sight but high with the point of aim method, then the former is more reliable than the latter, and we can use test data with a greater degree of confidence when students are tested using the bow sight method. In summary then, the *reliability* of archery skill tests discussed here needs to be established. Teachers in local schools can do this, but they must be specific and calculate reliability coefficients for both boys and girls at each age and method of sighting.

Norms for the AAHPER Archery Skill Test appear in Tables 8.1 and 8.2 in percentile ranks that correspond to the test scores in points for boys and girls, ages 12 through 18, at the various distances. Since over 600 pupils of each sex and age were tested, one would assume that these are adequate na-

11. *Ibid.*
12. Jean A. Barrett, *Archery* (Pacific Palisades, Calif.: Goodyear Publishing, 1969), pp. 67–80.
13. AAHPER, *Skills Test Manual: Archery*, p. 9.
14. *Ibid.*, p. 14.

Table 8.1 AAHPER Archery Test (Percentile Scores Based on Age/Test Scores in Points for

	Boys								
Age	12–13				14				15
Yards*	10	20	30	Tot.	10	20	30	Tot.	10
100	91	70	45	195	96	75	50	210	100
95	83	53	28	156	88	61	34	179	97
90	78	44	24	138	80	48	28	160	94
85	73	38	22	128	78	45	24	150	90
80	70	34	18	122	75	41	21	146	88
75	67	31	16	112	72	38	18	143	84
70	64	28	14	103	70	36	16	139	80
65	61	26	12	98	68	33	15	136	78
60	59	24	11	93	67	30	13	130	76
55	57	23	9	87	65	28	11	124	73
50	54	22	8	81	63	26	10	119	69
45	50	20	7	74	60	24	8	114	65
40	48	18	6	67	57	22	7	110	62
35	45	16	4	60	55	20	5	106	59
30	42	14	0	54	52	18	4	98	55
25	38	12	0	47	45	16	0	87	51
20	34	10	0	38	40	14	0	77	48
15	31	8	0	28	36	12	0	69	43
10	26	6	0	21	31	10	0	61	36
5	16	3	0	15	25	6	0	43	25
0	0	0	0	0	0	0	0	0	0

Percentile (vertical label on left side)

* 10 yards = 9.15 meters; 20 yards = 18.29 meters; 30 yards = 27.44 meters.

tional norms. However, one must ask several questions at this point. First, were the data collected in a standardized way in the schools where testing occurred? Secondly, will the norms vary across methods of sighting? As it now stands, everything is pooled in the norms presented. Using the methods recommended in chapter 4 on descriptive statistics, teachers can develop specific local norms that are relevant for grading purposes.

The national norms presented in the AAHPER manual should be used by individual pupils only to see how their performance compares with those of other pupils around the country.

It should be pointed out that the archery test manual is well developed. It includes an explanation of how the tests were selected, testing data collected, the testing environment prepared, the class organized for test administration, and norm tables used. It also

			Boys							
			16				17–18			
20	30	Tot.	10	20	30	Tot.	10	20	30	Tot.
90	81	270	100	100	95	270	100	95	85	270
77	50	215	99	78	56	220	98	78	64	222
70	41	195	97	71	47	205	96	72	53	206
66	35	187	96	67	43	197	93	67	47	197
63	31	177	91	63	40	189	90	63	42	190
58	28	167	90	59	36	181	88	59	39	184
54	25	158	88	56	32	173	86	55	37	176
51	22	149	86	54	30	163	84	52	35	166
47	20	140	84	51	28	160	82	49	31	158
42	17	130	80	48	25	154	79	46	28	151
39	15	120	79	46	23	148	77	43	26	144
36	14	114	77	43	22	142	74	40	24	136
34	13	107	75	41	20	136	71	37	21	130
31	12	100	72	39	18	129	68	34	20	125
28	11	94	70	36	16	123	63	32	17	119
24	10	87	67	33	13	117	59	29	16	112
21	9	79	61	28	11	110	55	25	11	109
18	7	70	51	25	9	103	48	20	9	96
15	6	62	50	20	6	80	40	17	6	86
9	2	43	40	14	2	61	27	11	3	65
0	0	0	0	0	0	0	0	0	0	0

includes a description of facilities and equipment needed, safety precautions, rules for scoring, and sample scoring sheets and class record forms. In addition, the skills tested are well illustrated. Indeed, the criteria of standardized directions and administrative feasibility appear to have been met.

basketball

There are many basketball skill tests for boys and girls, and men and women in the testing literature. Basketball skills are usually serial and continuous in nature when used in an actual game situation. A player may catch a pass, dribble the ball around a screen, and then take a jump shot many times during a game. In addition, the player does this under many varied environmental conditions. Shots are taken from different positions on the floor, against different types of defenses, and with different players acting as defenders. Rarely, however, do we see these serial movement skills, which are actually per-

Table 8.2 AAHPER Archery Test Percentile Scores Based on Age/Test Score in Points for Twelve Arrows

Girls

Percentile Scores	12–13			14			15			16			17–18		
Yards*	10	20	Tot.	10	20	Tot.	10	20	Tot.	10	20	Tot.	10	20	Tot.
100	85	60	129	89	70	159	96	81	160	100	91	161	100	95	180
95	69	40	100	74	47	109	82	55	130	87	58	134	87	71	149
90	60	29	89	68	38	99	75	47	112	80	50	115	80	60	129
85	50	22	81	63	35	89	70	43	103	73	44	107	73	52	123
80	46	19	69	58	32	84	66	39	96	67	40	100	69	47	115
75	41	17	64	54	28	79	63	34	89	64	36	96	66	42	109
70	38	15	60	50	25	75	60	32	85	60	32	91	62	40	104
65	35	13	55	48	23	70	56	29	80	56	29	87	58	36	100
60	34	12	50	46	21	66	53	27	77	53	27	80	55	32	95
55	32	10	46	43	20	62	51	25	73	49	25	76	52	29	91
50	30	9	42	41	18	58	49	23	70	46	22	72	48	26	85
45	27	7	38	38	16	54	46	22	68	43	20	67	46	24	78
40	24	6	35	35	14	50	43	20	62	41	18	63	42	21	73
35	22	1	32	33	12	47	40	18	59	38	16	60	40	19	68
30	19	0	28	30	10	45	37	16	55	33	14	56	38	18	64
25	16	0	25	28	8	42	34	13	51	31	12	52	35	16	60
20	14	0	22	25	7	40	31	11	45	29	10	47	31	14	53
15	12	0	17	22	0	34	27	8	40	25	8	41	28	12	45
10	10	0	12	19	0	28	21	6	33	21	6	36	24	9	38
5	6	0	5	12	0	22	13	0	25	16	0	26	19	0	30
0	0	0	0	0	0	0	0	0	0	0	0	0	0	0	0

* 10 yards = 9.15 meters; 20 yards = 18.29 meters.

formed in a varied, open environment, appear as such on tests purported to estimate basketball skill. Consequently, it is questionable whether we should use current standardized basketball skill tests as a basis for critical decision making. We can ask the same question concerning other sports, such as soccer, volleyball, baseball, football, softball, field hockey, and so on. Beth Kerr and Frank Smoll argue that teachers should teach the performer to decrease her variability in some activities (such as archery) where the advancement in skill level should produce greater consistency in performance; but should construct learning situations to permit skill variability to occur where the nature of the sport demands that a wide range of movement skills be performed under varied conditions.[15] Basketball players should be able to shoot from all over the court, and infielders should be able to throw to first base from different spots in the infield. If teachers structure progressive learning experiences that simulate and transfer into actual game play, it seems logical to expect teachers to sample game play as closely as possible when developing test items. Again, different test items are probably needed for beginners as contrasted with advanced players.

An examination of the test items appearing on basketball skill tests and other sport skill tests reveals that testers want variability in test performance reduced so that everything is standardized. Barry Johnson and Jack Nelson claim that we are confronted with the issue of objectivity of scoring versus realism and validity.[16] The influence of a second person on the performance of the person being tested is eliminated in order to standardize testing conditions that should improve the reliability and objectivity of scoring. Yet, this improvement may be occurring at the expense of the validity of the test. In basketball one dribbles while being guarded by a defender. Yet we do not test for dribbling

skills this way. We usually test by having the pupil dribble around stationary chairs or pylons for time. We usually do not teach dribbling in our classes by having pupils dribble around chairs.

We must all evaluate tests in the literature. If we wish to use a test for grading purposes, we must evaluate the degree to which performance on the skill test reflects the ability to play the game. Skill tests can be used to some advantage for grading at certain ability levels, provided they are combined with careful ratings of the pupils' actual performance in the sport.

Two basketball skill tests found in many measurement texts are the Johnson test for high school boys and the Leilich test for girls and women.[17] Directions for administration and scoring these test items follow.

johnson basketball battery

Johnson's total test battery includes three items of basic skill and four items of potential ability. The Iowa-Brace, footwork, jump and reach, and dodging run tests, which purport to measure potential ability, are not included here since the validity of these test items has not been established.

The validity and reliability coefficients cited in the following sections are based on data obtained from 180 high school boys. The boys were divided into a "good" group, who made the basketball squad, and a "poor" group, who did not. There were 50 boys in

15. Beth Kerr and Frank L. Smoll, "Variability in Individual Student Performance: Implications for Teachers," *Motor Skills: Theory into Practice* 1 (Spring 1977):81.

16. Barry L. Johnson and Jack K. Nelson, *Practical Measurements for Evaluation in Physical Education,* 3d ed. (Minneapolis: Burgess, 1979), p. 317.

17. Johnson Basketball Battery and Girls Basketball Battery in *An Introduction to Measurement in Physical Education,* ed. Henry J. Montoye (Boston: Allyn and Bacon, 1979), pp. 238–42.

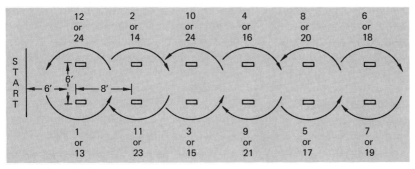

Figure 8.7　Diagram for Basketball Dribble Test

the "good" group and 130 boys in the "poor" group. Johnson used a biserial correlation coefficient to report the validity coefficients between each test item and the total battery, and the criterion of the ability of the boy to make the squad.

Test	Validity	Reliability
Basket shooting	.73	.73
Throw for accuracy	.78	.80
Dribble	.65	.78
Three-item battery	.88	.89

The objectivity has not been reported.

administration: field-goal speed test
The subject may assume any position he desires under the basket. On the signal "Go," he starts making lay-up shots as fast as he can. At the end of 30 seconds, the signal "Stop" is given. One point is scored for each basket made.

dribble
Place the chairs as shown in Figure 8.7. On the signal "Go," the subject starts dribbling from the starting line and continues in the prescribed route for 30 seconds. The number of chairs passed in the time allotted comprise the score. Two trials should be given.

passing test
Hang the target (Figure 8.8) so that the 60-inch (152.4 cm) length of the outer rectangle

is parallel to the floor and the bottom border of this rectangle is 14 inches (35.56 cm) above the floor. Draw a restraining line 40 feet (12.19 m) from the target. The subject is given ten trials with either an overhand or hook pass at the target from behind the restraining line. Three points are granted for hitting the inner rectangle and line; 2 points for the middle one and line; and 1 point for the outer rectangle and line.

girls' basketball battery
administration: half-minute shooting test
The subject may assume any position she desires under the basket. On the signal "Go,"

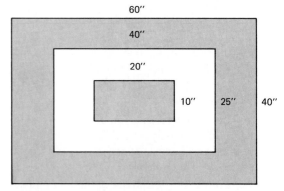

Figure 8.8　Wall Marking for Target in Basketball Passing Test

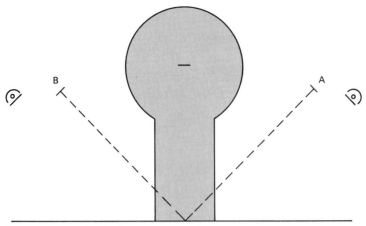

Figure 8.9   Floor Diagram
for the Basketball Bounce and
Shoot Test.

she starts shooting baskets as fast as she can for 30 seconds. If the ball has left her hands before the signal to stop, the basket, if made, counts. Two trials are given and the test score is that of the better trial. This is the same as the boys' test except that two 30-second trials are given.

bounce and shoot test

The equipment includes two chairs, two basketballs, a stopwatch, and a regulation backboard and basket, arranged as indicated in Figure 8.9.

On either side of the basket, at an angle of 45°, an 18-foot (5.48 m) dashed line is drawn from the center of the end line. Perpendicular to the 18-foot (5.48 m) lines, 24-inch (60.96 cm) lines are added. Starting from a point 1 foot (.3048 m) behind and 30 inches (76.2 cm) to the outside of the 18-foot (5.48 m) lines, additional 18-inch (45.72 cm) lines are drawn. On each of these 18-inch (45.72 cm) lines a chair is placed with a ball on it.

The subject starts on line B. On the signal "Go," she picks up the ball from the chair, bounces, shoots, recovers the rebound, and passes it back to a person standing behind

chair B. She then runs to chair A, picks up the ball and repeats the sequence for a total of ten shots (five on each side). Each bounce must start from behind the 24-inch (60.96 cm) line. The timer is responsible for recording the total time (nearest 0.1 second)—that is, until the ball is caught after the tenth trial—and for noting any fouls. The scorer records the points made on the shooting and notifies the timer on the ninth shot. The test score consists of a score for accuracy and a score for time. The accuracy score is as follows: 2 points for each basket and 1 point for hitting the rim but missing the basket. The time score is the total time to the nearest tenth of a second plus one second additional for each foul committed. Fouls include running with the ball and failure to start from behind the 24-inch (60.96 cm) line.

The original source for this test indicates a reliability coefficient of .82 for fifty-one college women. A method of combining the speed and accuracy scores into a composite score is also indicated but no norms are given. A serious criticism of this test is that the time and accuracy elements are both variable. A student taking such a test is apt to ask which is more important, the number of

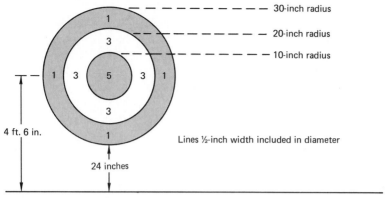

Figure 8.10   Target for the Basketball Push-Pass Test

baskets made or the time it takes to perform ten trials. Attempting to get a very low time score could result in sloppy skill execution and no baskets, whereas total concentration on accuracy could produce a most ungame-like slow pattern of skill execution. The merits of the test are still considerable, however, and it is presented here in hopes that someone might experiment with a revision that would make the time variable constant.

push-pass

The subject stands behind a restraining line 10 feet (3.048 m) from the wall and parallel to it. On the signal "Go," she makes a push-pass (two-hand chest pass) to a target on the wall (Figure 8.10). She recovers the ball and continues to pass to the target from behind the restraining line for 30 seconds. Her score is the total number of target points obtained before the "Stop" signal is called. Points are given according to the area of the target in which the ball lands, as indicated on the diagram. Line hits are awarded the value of the inner circle. No points are recorded for a pass in which the feet are on or over the restraining line. The test score is the best score of two trials. No figures for reliability, validity, or objectivity are given.

critique

Both basketball skill tests have items that test what are thought to be fundamental skills in the game, namely, basket shooting, passing or throwing for accuracy, dribbling, and the bounce and shoot. One would be tempted to say that the tests have content validity. Unfortunately, one performs the test items in a way that these skills would not actually be used in a playing situation. One does not dribble around chairs, throw or pass a ball ten times at a stationary target, or make as many lay-up shots in 30 seconds as possible during game play—although the basic skills should be learned before one can advance to effective game play. The bounce and shoot test comes closer to how one would shoot in a game: receive the ball, dribble, and then shoot. The Johnson test was validated against an extreme group's criterion, namely 50 high school boys who made the basketball squad and 130 boys who did not. The validity coefficients are adequate, thus the test can be used to classify boys into "good" and "poor" groups in performance of these test items. Note that 130 boys are in the poor group; these will probably be the ones in our physical education classes. The relationship between scores on the Johnson test and the basketball ability of these 130 boys is the crucial point in determining if we use these test scores as part of a grading scheme. Teachers can use videotape equipment if available and record games played in class, rating each pupil on basketball game playing ability. Now compute a validity coefficient between these ratings and the scores on the Johnson test. If the coefficient is above .80 you can place confidence in the test scores as part of a pupil's grade.

In an attempt to use game results as a criterion for validating basketball skill tests, Francis Stroup found that the team average skill scores on three items—goal shooting, wall passing, and dribbling around stationary obstacles—were highly related to the ability of teams to win 10-minute games in men's physical education classes.[18] Forty-one games were played, and the average team skill scores allowed for correct predictions of the outcomes of 84 percent of them. Thus, these items can validly be used as a quick, practical way to equate teams for intramural competition. Since each team was composed of players with varied skills in each of the items, these test scores should not be used as an estimate of one pupil's grade in a basketball unit.

The content of the women's basketball test was established by selecting items to represent factors identified in a larger number of basketball skill test items appearing in the literature. Most of these test items represent fundamental components of skills performed in a stationary (closed) environment and do not simulate performance of skills in actual play. Other validity information is unavailable.

Norms developed on junior high school boys in 1960 exist for the Johnson test[19] and norms for college women physical education majors on the Leilich test[20] were developed in 1954. At best, these norms are old and do not apply in most school teaching situations today.

Reliability of testing on the passing, shooting, and dribbling items on the Johnson test seems to be adequate since the coefficients are .80, .73, and .78, respectively. Reliability of the bounce and shoot test is .82 for college women.

Standardized directions for administering and scoring these test items are more than adequate. Administrative feasibility in terms of relatively simple testing procedures and economy of time is also apparent. However, the importance of any sport skill test score depends on how its validity was determined. How do you intend to use the test scores? Has intent been verified by adequate validation study? If not, your professional judgment of skills observed on a daily basis may be the most valid test of all. Do not be afraid to use it. Develop your own tests and rating scales; in doing so, you will be testing for what *you* have taught. Baumgartner and Jackson provide examples of rating scales of a swimming stroke ability and badminton ability that were developed by teachers.[21] These are illustrated in Figures 8.11 and 8.12.

additional sport skill tests

While it is not our intent to present directions for the administration and scoring of tests of skills of all the various sports, we feel that some tests should be presented for teacher reference. Thus, we decided to include tests for a few sports that may be offered in a junior or senior high school curriculum, with

18. Francis Stroup, "Game Results as a Criterion for Validating Basketball Skill Test," *Research Quarterly* 26 (October 1955): pp. 353–357.

19. Barrow and McGee, *A Practical Approach to Measurement in Physical Education,* pp. 264–268.

20. Wilma K. Miller, "Achievement Levels in Basketball Skills for Women Physical Education Majors," *Research Quarterly* 25 (December 1954):450–455.

21. Ted A. Baumgartner and Andrew S. Jackson, *Measurement for Evaluation in Physical Education* (Boston: Houghton Mifflin, 1975), pp. 241–242.

The arm stroke, leg kick, complete stroke, and stroke efficiency are rated on a three-point scale. Complete stroke and stroke efficiency are double-weighted so as to be twice as influential as arm stroke and leg kick in the total rating.

Circle the appropriate score for each area.

A. Arm stroke
   3 points - Arms do not break water or rise above top of head; elbows are kept at sides and fingers move up midline of body; stroke is powerful and smoothly coordinated.
   2 points - Arms do not break water or rise above top of head; elbows are usually kept at sides and fingers move up midline of body; stroke is reasonably powerful and reasonably well coordinated.
   1 point - Arms break water and/or rise above top of head; elbows are not kept at sides and fingers do not move up midline of body; stroke is not powerful and/or poorly coordinated.

B. Leg Kick
   3 points - Legs drop at knees for whip kick; toes are outside of heels as feet spread; kick is powerful and smoothly coordinated.
   2 points - Legs drop at knees for whip kick but some flexation occurs at hips; toes are not outside of heels as feet spread, causing knees to spread; kick is reasonably powerful and reasonably well coordinated.
   1 point - Legs do not drop at knees for whip kick, but are brought toward stomach by flexing at the hips; knees spread too wide; no power in kick; kick is poorly coordinated.

C. Complete Stroke
   6 points - Arms and legs are coordinated during stroke; arms are at sides, trunk and legs straight, and toes pointed during glide position.
   4 points - Minor deviations from the standard for 6 points occur.
   2 points - Arms and legs are not coordinated during stroke; glide position is poor with reference to arm-trunk-leg-toes position.

D. Stroke Efficiency
   6 points - Long distance is covered in glide; body is relaxed in water; swims in straight line; hips on surface.
   4 points - Average distance is covered in glide; body is relaxed in water; does not swim in straight line; hips slightly below surface.
   2 points - Little distance is covered in glide; body is not relaxed in water; does not swim in straight line; hips are well below surface. (Swimmer is sitting in water rather than lying on top of it.)

   Total Score _____

Figure 8.11   Rating Scale
for Elementary Backstroke*

special emphasis on the lifetime sports. You should remember that many of these skill tests were constructed many years ago. Hence, norms will be provided for only the more recent tests. You should critique each test presented in an effort to determine if the test meets your professional needs. Many of these skill tests can also be used as drills to facilitate learning of basic fundamentals. Most of the skill tests involve product evaluation and do not measure actual playing ability.

The four areas of badminton-playing ability may all be rated during competition. However, the first two areas may be rated in the noncompetitive situation, if so desired, by asking the student to demonstrate the various serves and strokes.

Each sub-area is scored on a 3-2-1 basis:

3 points - Above average ability, considerably more skillful than the performance typical of the student's age and sex
2 points - Average ability, typical performance for age and sex
1 point - Below average ability, far inferior to typical performance for age and sex

For each sub-area, circle the appropriate score.

I. Serve
    A.   Position of shuttlecock upon contact—racket head strikes shuttlecock below waist level   3 2 1
    B.   Position of racket at end of serve—if short serve, racket head does not rise above chest; if long serve, racket head stops between shoulders and top of head at end of serve   3 2 1
    C.   Placement of serve—well-placed relative to type of serve and position of opponent   3 2 1
    D.   Height of serve relative to type of serve—short serve is low over net; drive serve is low over net and deep; clear serve is high and deep   3 2 1

II. Strokes (consider placement and quality of each stroke)
    A.   Clear—high and deep   3 2 1
    B.   Smash-hit from position above head and in front of body; path of bird is down   3 2 1
    C.   Drive—sharp and low over net; hit from position about shoulder height; can be deep or midcourt, but not short   3 2 1
    D.   Drop—hit from position waist-to shoulder-height; low over net; a hairpin type shot   3 2 1

III. Strategy
    A.   Places shots all over court   3 2 1
    B.   Executes a variety of shots at the most opportune moments   3 2 1
    C.   Takes advantage of opponent's weaknesses (for example, poor backhand, strength problem in back court, poor net play)   3 2 1
    D.   Uses own best shots   3 2 1

IV. Footwork and Position
    A.   Near center court position so flexible to play any type of shot   3 2 1
    B.   Has control of body at all times during play   3 2 1
    C.   Body is in correct position when making each shot (usually determined by the feet)   3 2 1
    D.   Racket is shoulder-to head-height and ready for use (wrist cocked) at all times; eyes are on the shuttlecock at all times   3 2 1

Total Score _____

*Reprinted from MEASUREMENT FOR EVALUATION IN PHYSICAL EDUCATION by Ted A. Baumgartner and Andrew S. Jackson. Copyright © 1975 by Houghton Mifflin Company. Used by permission.

Figure 8.12   Badminton Ability Rating Scale*

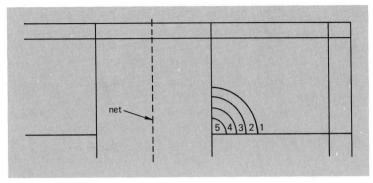

Figure 8.13   French Serve
Target

archery

Test presented and critiqued in the previous section.

badminton

The *Miller Wall Volley Test*[22] was developed upon discovering that men and women consistently use clears more than any other shot in badminton singles play. Test procedures were developed based on movies of the various types of clears. The test requires a wall space of at least 10 feet (3.048 m) in width and 15 feet (4.572 m) in height, with a line marked on the wall at a height of 7 feet 6 inches (2.286 m). A floor line is marked 10 feet (3.048 m) from and parallel to the wall. On the signal, the pupil puts the sponge-end shuttlecock into play with a legal serve from behind the 10 foot (3.048 m) line and continually volleys the rebounds for 30 seconds. Three 30-second trials are given with a rest period of 30 seconds between trials. A practice period of 1 minute is given before the first trial. The final score is the total number of hits made from behind the restraining line that strike the wall on or above the 7-foot-6-inch (2.286 m) line, including "carries" or double hits. The shuttlecock remains in play regardless of faults. A validity coefficient of .83 with a criterion of playing ability in college women is reported. Reliability was estimated to be .94.

The *French Badminton Test*[23] consists of two items: *the short serve and clear*. The serve test involves serving twenty shuttlecocks consecutively, or in two groups of ten, to a target in the opposite service court by directing the bird beneath a rope stretched 20 inches (50.8 cm) above and parallel to the net, as illustrated in Figure 8.13. Illegal serves are repeated. The radii of the target arcs are 22 inches (55.88 cm), 30 inches (76.2 cm), 38 inches (96.42 cm), and 46 inches (116.84 cm), respectively.

The clear test consists of returning twenty serves over a rope stretched across the court 14 feet (4.267 m) from the net and 8 feet (2.438 m) high and onto a target, as illustrated in Figure 8.14. To receive the serve, the student being tested stands on the center line between two 2-inch (5.08 cm) squares marked on the floor 3 feet (0.914 m) on either side of the center line and 11 feet (3.352 m) from the net. An experienced player serves each shuttlecock from the intersection of short service and center lines on the

22. Francis A. Miller, "A Badminton Wall Volley Test," *Research Quarterly* 22 (May 1951):208–213.

23. M. Gladys Scott et al., "Achievement Examinations in Badminton," *Research Quarterly* 12 (May 1941): 242–253.

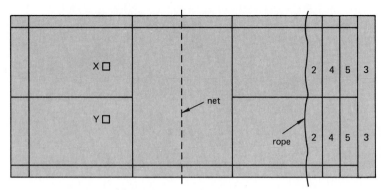

Figure 8.14   French Clear
Target

target side. The serve must reach the testee
and be between the squares, but the testee
may move into desired position once the
serve is made. The target markings consist
of a parallel line 2 feet (0.609m) toward the
net from the doubles rear service line and a
similar line 2 feet (0.609m) further from the
net than the rear singles service line. Illegal
strokes are given another trial. The final
score for each item consists of the total number of points scored by legal hits that passed
either below or above the rope as specified.
A validity coefficient of .85 and reliability coefficients of .77 and .98 are reported on
college women.

basketball (boys and girls)

Tests are in the previous section.

bowling

This activity is a self-testing situation. Have
the pupils bowl three lines and record the
number of pins knocked down in each line.
The teacher can also have certain combinations of pins set up—those that most frequently remain standing after the first ball
and lead to attempts at making a spare. All
class members can practice and be tested
on each combination.

field hockey

Margaret Schmithals and Esther French have
developed a three-item test of field hockey
achievement on college women.[24] The validity of the test was determined by the multiple
correlation of .61 between the three items
and a ratings criterion of playing ability. The
lowest reliability reported was .87. Directions
for administering and scoring each item
follow.

test 1: dribble, dodge, circular tackle, and drive

The player being tested stands behind the
starting line with the hockey ball on the
starting line at any point to the left of the
foul line. At the signal "Ready? Go!" the
player dribbles the ball forward to the left
of and parallel to the foul line. As soon as
the restraining line is reached, the ball is
sent from the left side of the foul line to
the right of the first obstacle (from the
player's point of view), and the player runs
around the left side of the obstacle and recovers it. (This is analogous to a dodge).
Next, the player executes a turn toward her
right around the second obstacle, still keep-

24. Margaret Schmithals and Esther French, "Achieve-
    ment Tests in Field Hockey for College Women,"
    Research Quarterly 11 (October 1940):83–92.

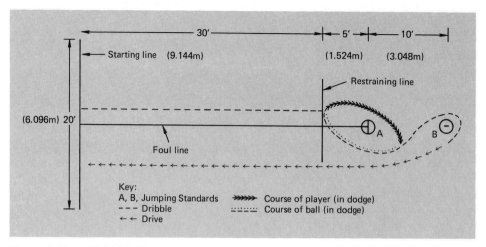

Figure 8.15   Field Markings
for Field Hockey Test 1.

ing control of the ball. (This is analogous to
a circular tackle). As soon as possible after
that, the ball is driven toward the starting
line. If the drive is not hard enough to reach
the starting line, the player may follow it up
and hit the ball again. (See Figure 8.15.)

This procedure is repeated until six
trials have been given, care being taken that
no player is fatigued.

The score for one trial is the time it takes
from the signal "Go" until the player's ball
has again crossed the starting line. The score
for the entire test is the average of the six
trials. It is considered a foul and the trial
does not count if:

a. The ball or player crosses the foul
line before reaching the restraining line.

b. In executing the dodge, the ball is not
sent from the left side of the foul line.

c. The player makes "sticks."

test 2: goal shooting, straight, right, left
A target, 9 inches (22.86 cm) wide, 12 feet
(3.657 m) long, and at least 0.5 inch (1.27 cm)
thick, made of hardwood, is needed. The
board is divided into eleven sections, and
numbers are painted on it in contrasting

backgrounds on alternating spaces, as illustrated in Figure 8.16. The target is placed
directly on the specified target line for the
left, center, and right shots, as depicted in
Figure 8.17.

Drive from the center's position: The
player being tested stands behind the starting line with the hockey ball directly on the
line. At the signal "Ready? Go!" the ball
is dribbled to the rectangle, from *within
which area* it must be driven toward the
board (placed on the center target line). This
procedure is repeated until ten trials have
been given.

Drive from right inner's position: The
same procedure is repeated, except that the
position of the target is changed to the right
inner target line.

Drive from left inner's position: The
same procedure is repeated, except that the
position of the target is changed to the left
inner target line.

The score for one trial is the time elaps-
ing from the timer's signal "Go" until the
ball strikes the board. The score for the
entire test is the sum of the first and second
best odd- and first and second even-num-

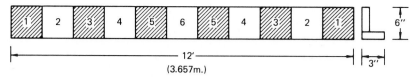

Figure 8.16   Front and Side
Views of Target for Field
Hockey Test 2.

bered trials made on the center drive, the right inner drive, and the left inner drive. The score counts if the ball bounces over the top of the target. In this case, though, the time is taken until the instant the ball clears the target. Player shall receive a score of zero on a trial if:

a. The ball is not driven from within the rectangle.

b. The driven ball fails to reach the board or misses it at either end.

c. "Sticks" are made.

d. Player raises the ball so it doesn't

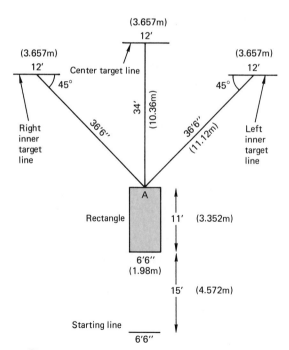

Figure 8.17   Field Markings
for Field Hockey Test 2.

touch the ground before it passes over the target.

test 3: fielding and drive

The player being tested stands behind the goal line. The examiner stands at the edge of the striking circle directly in front of the goal with a hockey ball in one hand and a stopwatch in the other. At the examiner's signal "Ready? Go!" the hockey ball is rolled toward the goal at approximately the speed of 45 feet (13.716m) in 1.7 seconds. Simultaneously, the player runs forward and attempts to field the ball before it reaches the foul line, tap it once, and drive it out of the striking circle from the area between the restraining line and the foul line. This procedure is repeated until sixteen trials have been given (see Figure 8.18).

The score for one trial is the time from the moment the player first touches the hockey ball to the moment the ball reaches the striking circle. The score on the entire test is the sum of the average of the three best even- and three best odd-numbered scores of the sixteen trials.

The attempt does not count as a trial if:

a. The rolled ball does not pass between the two ice picks.

b. The rolled ball is not delivered at approximately the speed designated.

c. The player makes "sticks."

The player receives no score on a particular trial if:

a. The ball is advanced illegally.

b. The ball rolls wholly over the foul

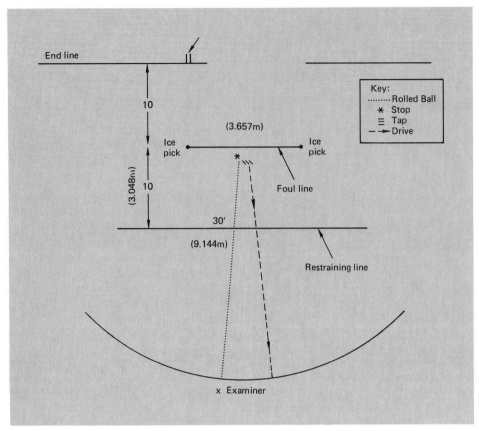

Figure 8.18   Field Markings
for Field Hockey Test 3.

line before or after it is touched by the player's stick.

c. The ball is not driven out of the striking circle from within the area bounded by the restraining line and foul line.

d. The ball is not controlled, that is, stopped, tapped, and driven.

football

The AAHPER has provided a test covering the fundamental skills of football.[25] These ten skill tests should be used as practice tests because they are intended to be used by players as a way of improving their abilities in the fundamental skills of the game. Con-

tent validity is assumed. Minimum reliability of .80 for each item is reported. Percentile rank norms derived on boys ages 10 through 18 are provided in Tables 8.3 through 8.15 (see pages 166–176). Directions for the administering and scoring of each item follow.

1. Forward Pass for Distance. The player throws a forward pass for distance from between two parallel lines 6 feet (1.828 m) apart, taking one or more running steps inside this zone and throwing as far as possible without stepping over the second line. *Scoring:*

25. American Association for Health, Physical Education and Recreation, *Skills Test Manual: Football,* David K. Brace, Consultant (Washington, D.C.: AAHPER, 1965).

The first pass is marked by inserting a stake at the point where the ball first hits the ground. If a succeeding pass is longer, the stake is moved to the further spot. The longest pass is then measured and recorded. Players should warm up and are allowed one practice pass. The test consists of three trials or passes from inside the throwing zone.

2. Fifty-Yard Dash with Football. The subject runs as fast as he can for 50 yards (45.72 m) carrying a football. Two trials are given, with a rest in between. *Scoring:* When the starter shouts "Go" and simultaneously waves a white cloth downward, the timer starts the watch. The time is stopped when the runner crosses the finish line. The score is to the nearest tenth of a second. The better time of the two trials is used as the score.

3. Blocking. On the signal "Go," the subject runs forward and executes a cross-body block against a blocking bag. He immediately recovers and charges toward a second bag placed 15 feet (4.57 m) directly to the right of the first bag. After cross-body blocking that bag to the ground, he scrambles to his feet and races toward the third bag. The third bag is 15 feet (4.57 m) away in the direction of the starting line, but at a 45-degree angle to the line between bags

1 and 2. (This places the bag about 5 feet [1.524 m] from the starting line.) The subject blocks this third bag to the ground with a cross-body block and then runs across the starting line. Two trials are given. The blocking bags must be blocked clear to the ground. (See Figure 8.19 for diagram of bag placement.) *Scoring:* The time is measured to the nearest tenth of a second from the signal "Go" until the subject crosses back over the line. The better of the two trials constitutes the subject's score.

4. Forward Pass for Accuracy. A target is painted on an 8-by-11-foot (2.438 m × 3.352 m) canvas that is hung from the cross-bar of the goal posts. The center circle is 2 feet (0.609 meter) in diameter, the middle circle 4 feet (1.219 m), and the outer circle 6 feet (1.828 m) in diameter. The bottom of the outer circle is 3 feet (0.914 m) from the ground. It is recommended that a wooden or metal bar be inserted in a channel sewn along the bottom of the canvas, and then the channel be tied to the goal posts to keep the canvas stretched taut. A restraining line is drawn 15 yards (13.71 m) from the target. The player takes two or three small running steps along the line, hesitates, then throws at the target. The player may go either to the right or to the left, but he must stay behind the re-

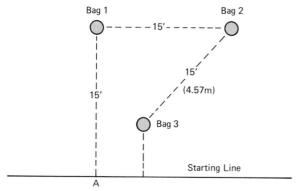

Figure 8.19 Diagram for AAHPER Football Blocking Test

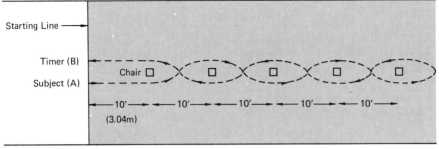

Figure 8.20   Ball Changing Zigzag Run Football Test

straining line. He should pass the ball with good speed. Ten trials are given. *Scoring:* The target circles score three, two, and one for the inner, middle, and outer circles, respectively. Passes hitting on a line are given the higher value. The point total for the ten trials is the score.

5. *Football Punt for Distance.* The player takes one or two steps within the 6-foot (1.828 m) kicking zone and punts the ball as far as possible. The administration and scoring are the same as for the forward pass for distance.

6. *Ball Changing Zigzag Run.* Five chairs are placed in a line 10 feet (3.048 m) apart and facing away from the starting line. (See Figure 8.20.) The first chair is 10 feet (3.048 m) in front of the starting line. Holding a football under his right arm, the subject starts from behind the starting line on the signal "Go." He runs to the right of the first chair, then changes the ball to his left arm as he runs to the left of the second chair. He continues running in and out of the chairs in this manner, changing the position of the ball to the outside arm as he passes each chair. The inside arm should be extended as in stiff-arming. He circles around the end chair and runs in and out of the chairs back to the starting line. He is not allowed to hit the chairs. Two time trials are given. *Scoring:* The time to the nearest tenth of a second is measured from the signal "Go" until the

subject passes back over the starting line. The better of the two trials constitutes the subject's score for this test.

7. *Catching the Forward Pass.* A scrimmage line is drawn with two *end* marks located 9 feet (2.743 m) to the right and left of center. (See Figure 8.21.) At a distance of 30 feet (9.144 m) in front of these marks are *turning points.* The subject lines up on the right end mark facing the turning point 30 feet (9.144 m) directly in front of him. On the signal "Go" he runs straight ahead, cuts around the turning point, and runs to receive the pass 30 feet (9.144 m) away at the *passing point.* On the signal "Go" the center snaps the ball 15 feet (4.572 m) to the passer who takes one step, then passes the ball directly over the passing point above head height. The passer must be able to pass the ball in a mechanical manner to the passing point without paying attention to the receiver. A similar passing point is located 30 feet (9.144 m) to the left of the left turning point. Ten trials are given to the right and ten trials are given to the left. The player need not try for poorly thrown passes, but he must go around the turning point before proceeding to the passing point. *Scoring:* One point is scored for each pass caught. The sum of passes caught from both sides is recorded as the score for this test. *Note:* Considerable practice and skill are needed on the part of the passer to be able to time his pass so as

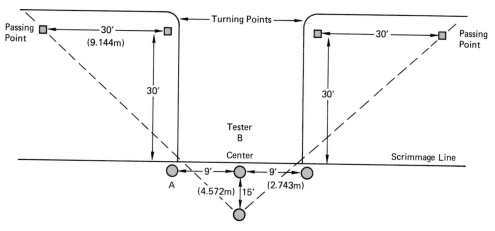

Figure 8.21 Diagram for AAHPER Football Forward Pass Catching Test

to enable the subject to reach the passing point in a controlled manner and get his hands on the ball.

8. Pull-Out. The subject lines up in a set position halfway between two goal posts. On the signal "Go" he pulls out and runs parallel to the imaginary line of scrimmage, cuts around the right-hand goal post and races straight ahead across a finish line 30 feet (9.144m) from, and parallel to, the goal posts. Two time trials are given. *Scoring:* The score is the better of the two trials, measured to the nearest tenth of a second from the signal "Go" until the subject crosses the finish line.

9. Kick-Off. A kicking tee is placed in the center of one of the lines running across the field. The ball is positioned so that it tilts slightly back toward the kicker. The player takes as long a run as he wants and kicks the ball as far as possible. Three trials are given. *Scoring:* Same as for the forward pass and the punt for distance.

10. Dodging Run. The course is laid out as is shown in Figure 8.22. The player starts from behind the line to the right of the first hurdle, which is on the starting line. On the signal "Go" he runs to the left of the second hurdle and follows the course as shown in

the diagram. Two complete round trips constitute a run; two runs are given. The ball does not have to be changed from side to side. *Scoring:* The time is measured to the nearest tenth of a second. The better of the two runs is recorded as the score.

golf

The best test of golf skill is the score an individual makes when playing eighteen or nine holes of golf. Shorter tests may be devised. One may play only four or five holes, and if this short version includes a par 3, 4, and 5 hole, one's golf skill may be adequately sampled.

Ellen Vanderhoff has developed an indoor golf test that involves hitting plastic golf balls with a number 2 wood and a 5 iron.[26] Validity coefficients of .71 and .66 were determined for the drive test and 5-iron test, respectively, with ability ratings and the score on playing six holes of golf for college women as the criteria. Reliability for the drive test was .90 and for the 5-iron test, .84.

26. Ellen R. Vanderhoff, "Beginning Golf Achievement Tests," Master's thesis, State University of Iowa, 1956.

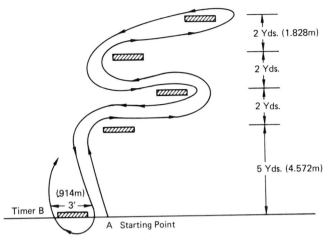

Figure 8.22 Diagram for AAHPER Football Dodging Run Test

Table 8.3   **Forward Pass for Distance**

Percentile Scores Based on Age / Test Scores in Feet									
	A G E								
Percentile	*10*	*11*	*12*	*13*	*14*	*15*	*16*	*17–18*	*Percentile*
100th	96	105	120	150	170	180	180	180	100th
95th	71	83	99	115	126	135	144	152	95th
90th	68	76	92	104	118	127	135	143	90th
85th	64	73	87	98	114	122	129	137	85th
80th	62	70	83	95	109	118	126	133	80th
75th	61	68	79	91	105	115	123	129	75th
70th	59	65	77	88	102	111	120	127	70th
65th	58	64	75	85	99	108	117	124	65th
60th	56	62	73	83	96	105	114	121	60th
55th	55	61	71	80	93	102	111	117	55th
50th	53	59	68	78	91	99	108	114	50th
45th	52	56	66	76	88	97	105	110	45th
40th	51	54	64	73	85	94	103	107	40th
35th	49	51	62	70	83	92	100	104	35th
30th	47	50	60	69	80	89	97	101	30th
25th	45	48	58	65	77	85	93	98	25th
20th	44	45	54	63	73	81	90	94	20th
15th	41	43	51	61	70	76	85	89	15th
10th	38	40	45	55	64	71	79	80	10th
5th	33	36	40	46	53	62	70	67	5th
0	14	25	10	10	10	20	30	20	0

Table 8.4   Forward Pass for Distance

Percentile Scores Based on Age / Test Scores in Meters

| Percentile | AGE | | | | | | | | Percentile |
	10	11	12	13	14	15	16	17–18	
100th	29.26	32.04	36.57	45.72	51.81	54.86	54.86	54.86	100th
95th	21.64	25.29	30.17	35.05	38.40	41.14	43.89	46.32	95th
90th	20.72	32.16	28.04	31.69	35.96	38.70	41.14	43.58	90th
85th	19.50	22.25	26.51	29.87	34.74	47.18	39.31	41.75	85th
80th	18.89	21.36	25.29	28.95	33.22	35.96	38.40	40.53	80th
75th	18.59	20.72	24.07	27.73	32.00	35.05	37.49	39.31	75th
70th	17.98	19.81	23.46	26.82	31.08	33.83	36.56	38.70	70th
65th	17.67	19.50	22.86	25.90	30.17	32.91	35.66	37.79	65th
60th	17.06	18.89	22.25	25.29	29.26	32.00	34.74	36.88	60th
55th	16.76	18.59	21.64	24.38	28.34	31.08	33.83	35.66	55th
50th	16.14	17.98	20.72	23.77	27.73	30.17	32.91	34.74	50th
45th	15.84	17.06	20.11	23.16	26.82	29.56	32.00	33.52	45th
40th	15.54	16.45	19.50	22.25	25.90	28.65	31.39	32.61	40th
35th	14.93	15.54	18.89	21.33	25.29	28.04	30.48	31.69	35th
30th	14.32	15.24	18.28	21.03	24.38	27.12	29.56	30.78	30th
25th	13.71	14.63	17.67	19.81	23.46	25.90	28.34	29.87	25th
20th	13.41	13.71	16.45	19.20	22.25	24.68	27.43	28.65	20th
15th	12.49	13.10	15.54	18.59	21.33	23.16	25.90	27.12	15th
10th	11.58	12.19	13.71	16.76	19.50	21.64	24.07	24.38	10th
5th	10.05	10.97	12.19	14.02	16.15	18.89	21.36	20.42	5th
0	4.26	7.62	3.04	3.04	3.04	6.09	9.14	6.09	0

Table 8.5   50-Yard Dash with Football (45.72m)

Percentile Scores Based on Age / Test Scores in Seconds and Tenths

| Percentile | AGE | | | | | | | | Percentile |
	10	11	12	13	14	15	16	17–18	
100th	7.3	6.8	6.2	5.5	5.5	5.5	5.5	5.0	100th
95th	7.7	7.4	7.0	6.5	6.5	6.2	6.0	6.0	95th
90th	7.9	7.6	7.2	6.8	6.6	6.3	6.1	6.1	90th

Table 8.5—*Continued*

Percentile	10	11	12	13	14	15	16	17–18	Percentile
85th	8.1	7.7	7.4	6.9	6.8	6.4	6.3	6.2	85th
80th	8.2	7.8	7.5	7.0	6.9	6.5	6.4	6.3	80th
75th	8.3	7.9	7.5	7.1	7.0	6.6	6.5	6.3	75th
70th	8.4	8.0	7.6	7.2	7.1	6.7	6.6	6.4	70th
65th	8.5	8.1	7.7	7.3	7.2	6.8	6.6	6.5	65th
60th	8.6	8.2	7.8	7.4	7.2	6.9	6.7	6.6	60th
55th	8.6	8.3	7.9	7.5	7.3	7.0	6.8	6.6	55th
50th	8.7	8.4	8.0	7.5	7.4	7.0	6.8	6.7	50th
45th	8.8	8.5	8.1	7.6	7.5	7.1	6.9	6.8	45th
40th	8.9	8.6	8.1	7.7	7.6	7.2	7.0	6.8	40th
35th	9.0	8.7	8.2	7.8	7.7	7.2	7.1	6.9	35th
30th	9.1	8.8	8.3	8.0	7.8	7.3	7.2	7.0	30th
25th	9.2	8.9	8.4	8.1	7.9	7.4	7.3	7.1	25th
20th	9.3	9.1	8.5	8.2	8.1	7.5	7.4	7.2	20th
15th	9.4	9.2	8.7	8.4	8.3	7.7	7.5	7.3	15th
10th	9.6	9.3	9.0	8.7	8.4	8.1	7.8	7.4	10th
5th	9.8	9.5	9.3	9.0	8.8	8.4	8.0	7.8	5th
0	10.6	11.0	12.0	12.0	12.0	11.0	10.0	10.0	0

Table 8.6   Blocking

Percentile Scores Based on Age / Test Scores in Seconds and Tenths

Percentile	AGE								Percentile
	10	11	12	13	14	15	16	17–18	
100th	6.9	5.0	5.0	5.0	5.0	5.0	5.0	5.0	100th
95th	7.5	6.6	6.6	5.9	5.8	5.8	5.8	5.5	95th
90th	7.7	7.1	7.1	6.5	6.2	6.2	6.1	5.7	90th
85th	7.9	7.5	7.5	6.7	6.6	6.3	6.3	5.8	85th
80th	8.1	8.0	7.7	6.9	6.8	6.5	6.5	6.0	80th
75th	8.3	8.3	7.9	7.2	7.0	6.7	6.7	6.2	75th
70th	8.5	8.6	8.1	7.4	7.1	6.9	7.0	6.3	70th
65th	8.9	9.1	8.4	7.6	7.3	7.0	7.2	6.5	65th
60th	9.3	9.5	8.6	7.7	7.5	7.2	7.4	6.7	60th

Table 8.6—*Continued*

Percentile	10	11	12	13	14	15	16	17–18	Percentile
55th	9.6	9.7	8.8	7.9	7.7	7.4	7.6	7.0	55th
50th	9.8	9.9	9.0	8.1	7.8	7.5	7.8	7.2	50th
45th	10.1	10.2	9.2	8.3	8.0	7.8	8.0	7.4	45th
40th	10.5	10.4	9.4	8.4	8.1	7.9	8.3	7.6	40th
35th	10.7	10.6	9.6	8.6	8.3	8.2	8.6	7.8	35th
30th	11.0	10.9	9.7	8.9	8.5	8.3	8.8	8.0	30th
25th	11.3	11.1	9.9	9.1	8.7	8.5	9.1	8.2	25th
20th	11.6	11.3	10.2	9.4	9.0	8.8	9.5	8.5	20th
15th	12.0	11.6	10.5	9.8	9.2	9.0	9.0	8.9	15th
10th	12.8	12.0	10.9	10.2	9.5	9.4	10.6	9.4	10th
5th	14.4	13.1	11.6	11.2	10.3	10.4	10.7	10.8	5th
0	17.5	18.0	15.0	15.0	15.0	13.0	15.0	14.0	0

Table 8.7   Forward Pass for Accuracy

Percentile Scores Based on Age / Test Scores in Points

Percentile	AGE								Percentile
	10	11	12	13	14	15	16	17–18	
100th	18	26	26	26	26	26	28	28	100th
95th	14	19	20	21	21	21	21	22	95th
90th	11	16	18	19	19	19	20	21	90th
85th	10	15	17	18	18	18	18	19	85th
80th	9	13	16	17	17	17	17	18	80th
75th	8	12	15	16	16	16	16	18	75th
70th	8	11	14	15	15	15	15	17	70th
65th	6	10	13	14	14	14	15	16	65th
60th	5	9	12	13	13	13	14	15	60th
55th	4	8	11	13	13	13	13	15	55th
50th	3	7	11	12	12	12	13	14	50th
45th	2	6	10	11	11	11	12	13	45th
40th	2	5	9	11	10	11	12	12	40th
35th	1	5	8	10	9	9	11	12	35th
30th	0	4	7	9	8	9	10	11	30th

Table 8.7—Continued

Percentile	10	11	12	13	14	15	16	17–18	Percentile
25th	0	3	6	8	8	8	9	10	25th
20th	0	2	5	7	7	7	8	9	20th
15th	0	1	4	5	5	6	7	8	15th
10th	0	0	3	4	4	5	6	7	10th
5th	0	0	1	2	2	3	4	5	5th
0	0	0	0	0	0	0	0	0	0

Table 8.8   Football Punt for Distance

Percentile Scores Based on Age / Test Scores in Feet

Percentile	AGE								Percentile
	10	11	12	13	14	15	16	17–18	
100th	87	100	115	150	160	160	160	180	100th
95th	75	84	93	106	119	126	131	136	95th
90th	64	77	88	98	110	119	126	128	90th
85th	61	75	84	94	106	114	120	124	85th
80th	58	70	79	90	103	109	114	120	80th
75th	56	68	77	87	98	105	109	115	75th
70th	55	66	75	83	96	102	106	110	70th
65th	53	64	72	80	93	99	103	107	65th
60th	51	62	70	78	90	96	100	104	60th
55th	50	60	68	75	87	94	97	101	55th
50th	48	57	66	73	84	91	95	98	50th
45th	46	55	64	70	81	89	92	96	45th
40th	45	53	61	68	78	86	90	93	40th
35th	44	51	59	64	75	83	86	90	35th
30th	42	48	56	63	72	79	83	86	30th
25th	40	45	52	61	70	76	79	81	25th
20th	38	42	50	57	66	73	74	76	20th
15th	32	39	46	52	61	69	70	70	15th
10th	28	34	40	44	55	62	64	64	10th
5th	22	27	35	33	44	54	56	53	5th
0	11	9	10	10	10	10	10	10	0

Table 8.9   Football Punt for Distance

Percentile Scores Based on Age / Test Scores in Meters

| Percentile | AGE | | | | | | | | Percentile |
	10	11	12	13	14	15	16	17–18	
100th	26.51	30.48	35.05	45.72	48.76	48.76	48.76	54.86	100th
95th	22.86	25.60	28.34	32.30	36.27	38.40	39.92	41.45	95th
90th	19.50	23.46	26.82	29.87	33.52	36.27	38.40	39.01	90th
85th	18.59	22.86	25.60	28.65	32.30	34.74	36.57	37.79	85th
80th	17.67	21.33	24.07	27.43	31.39	33.22	34.74	36.57	80th
75th	17.06	20.72	23.46	26.51	29.87	32.00	33.22	35.05	75th
70th	16.76	20.11	22.86	25.29	29.26	31.08	32.30	33.52	70th
65th	16.15	19.50	21.94	24.38	28.34	30.17	31.39	32.61	65th
60th	15.54	18.89	21.33	32.77	27.43	29.26	30.48	31.69	60th
55th	15.24	18.28	20.72	22.86	26.51	28.65	29.56	30.78	55th
50th	14.63	17.37	20.11	22.25	25.60	27.73	28.95	29.87	50th
45th	14.02	16.76	19.50	21.33	24.68	27.12	28.04	29.26	45th
40th	13.71	16.15	18.59	20.72	23.77	26.21	27.43	28.34	40th
35th	13.41	15.54	17.98	19.50	22.86	25.29	26.21	27.43	35th
30th	12.80	14.63	17.06	19.20	21.94	24.07	25.29	26.21	30th
25th	12.19	13.71	15.84	18.59	21.33	23.16	24.07	24.68	25th
20th	11.58	12.80	15.24	17.37	20.11	22.25	22.55	23.16	20th
15th	9.75	11.88	14.02	15.84	18.59	21.03	21.33	21.33	15th
10th	8.53	10.36	12.19	13.41	16.76	18.89	19.50	19.50	10th
5th	6.70	8.22	10.66	10.05	13.41	16.45	17.06	16.15	5th
0	3.35	2.74	3.04	3.04	3.04	3.04	3.04	3.04	0

Table 8.10   Ball Changing Zigzag Run

Percentile Scores Based on Age / Test Scores in Seconds and Tenths

| Percentile | AGE | | | | | | | | Percentile |
	10	11	12	13	14	15	16	17–18	
100th	7.2	7.4	7.0	6.0	6.5	6.0	6.0	6.0	100th
95th	9.9	7.7	7.8	8.0	8.7	7.7	7.7	8.4	95th
90th	10.1	8.1	8.2	8.4	9.0	8.0	8.0	8.7	90th

Table 8.10—Continued

Percentile	10	11	12	13	14	15	16	17–18	Percentile
85th	10.3	8.6	8.5	8.7	9.2	8.3	8.4	8.8	85th
80th	10.5	9.0	8.7	8.8	9.4	8.5	8.6	8.9	80th
75th	10.7	9.3	8.8	9.0	9.5	8.6	8.7	9.0	75th
70th	10.9	9.6	9.0	9.2	9.6	8.7	8.8	9.1	70th
65th	11.1	9.8	9.1	9.3	9.7	8.8	8.9	9.2	65th
60th	11.2	10.0	9.3	9.5	9.8	8.9	9.0	9.3	60th
55th	11.4	10.1	9.5	9.6	9.9	9.0	9.1	9.4	55th
50th	11.5	10.3	9.6	9.7	10.0	9.1	9.3	9.6	50th
45th	11.6	10.5	9.8	9.8	10.1	9.2	9.4	9.7	45th
40th	11.8	10.6	10.0	10.0	10.2	9.4	9.5	9.8	40th
35th	11.9	10.9	10.1	10.2	10.4	9.5	9.7	9.9	35th
30th	12.2	11.1	10.3	10.3	10.5	9.6	9.9	10.1	30th
25th	12.5	11.3	10.5	10.3	10.7	9.9	10.1	10.3	25th
20th	12.8	11.6	10.8	10.8	10.9	10.1	10.3	10.5	20th
15th	13.3	12.1	11.1	11.1	11.2	10.3	10.6	10.9	15th
10th	13.8	12.9	11.5	11.4	11.5	10.6	11.2	11.4	10th
5th	15.8	14.2	12.3	12.1	12.0	11.5	12.2	12.1	5th
0	24.0	15.0	19.0	20.0	14.5	20.0	17.0	15.0	0

Table 8.11   Catching the Forward Pass

Percentile Scores Based on Age / Test Scores in Number Caught

Percentile	AGE								Percentile
	10	11	12	13	14	15	16	17–18	
100th	20	20	20	20	20	20	20	20	100th
95th	19	19	19	20	20	20	20	20	95th
90th	17	18	19	19	19	19	19	19	90th
85th	16	16	18	18	18	19	19	19	85th
80th	14	15	18	17	18	18	18	18	80th
75th	13	14	16	17	17	18	18	18	75th
70th	12	13	16	16	16	17	17	17	70th
65th	11	12	15	15	15	16	16	16	65th
60th	10	12	14	15	15	16	16	16	60th

Table 8.11—*Continued*

Percentile	10	11	12	13	14	15	16	17–18	Percentile
55th	8	11	14	14	14	15	15	15	55th
50th	7	10	13	13	14	15	15	15	50th
45th	7	9	12	13	13	14	14	14	45th
40th	6	8	12	12	12	13	13	13	40th
35th	5	7	11	11	11	12	12	13	35th
30th	5	7	10	10	10	11	11	12	30th
25th	4	6	10	9	9	10	10	11	25th
20th	3	5	8	8	8	9	9	10	20th
15th	2	4	7	7	8	8	8	9	15th
10th	1	3	6	6	6	7	6	8	10th
5th	1	1	5	4	4	6	4	6	5th
0	0	0	0	0	0	0	0	0	0

Table 8.12   Pull-Out

Percentile Scores Based on Age / Test Scores in Seconds and Tenths

Percentile	AGE								Percentile
	10	11	12	13	14	15	16	17–18	
100th	2.5	2.2	2.2	2.2	2.2	2.0	2.0	1.8	100th
95th	2.9	2.8	2.8	2.8	2.7	2.5	2.5	2.5	95th
90th	3.2	3.0	3.0	2.9	2.8	2.6	2.6	2.6	90th
85th	3.3	3.0	3.0	3.0	2.9	2.7	2.7	2.7	85th
80th	3.4	3.1	3.1	3.0	3.0	2.8	2.9	2.8	80th
75th	3.5	3.1	3.1	3.1	3.0	3.0	2.9	2.9	75th
70th	3.5	3.2	3.2	3.1	3.0	3.0	3.0	2.9	70th
65th	3.6	3.3	3.3	3.2	3.1	3.0	3.0	3.0	65th
60th	3.6	3.3	3.3	3.2	3.1	3.1	3.1	3.0	60th
55th	3.7	3.3	3.3	3.3	3.2	3.1	3.1	3.1	55th
50th	3.8	3.4	3.4	3.3	3.2	3.2	3.2	3.1	50th
45th	3.8	3.5	3.5	3.4	3.3	3.2	3.2	3.1	45th
40th	3.9	3.6	3.5	3.4	3.3	3.3	3.3	3.2	40th
35th	3.9	3.7	3.6	3.5	3.4	3.3	3.3	3.2	35th
30th	4.0	3.8	3.7	3.5	3.4	3.4	3.3	3.2	30th

Table 8.12—Continued

Percentile	10	11	12	13	14	15	16	17–18	Percentile
25th	4.0	3.9	3.8	3.6	3.5	3.5	3.4	3.3	25th
20th	4.1	4.0	3.9	3.7	3.5	3.6	3.5	3.4	20th
15th	4.2	4.1	3.9	3.8	3.6	3.7	3.7	3.5	15th
10th	4.3	4.2	4.1	3.9	3.7	3.9	3.9	3.6	10th
5th	4.4	4.4	4.2	4.0	4.0	4.1	4.3	3.9	5th
0	5.5	5.0	5.0	5.0	5.0	5.0	5.0	5.0	0

Table 8.13   Kick-Off

Percentile Scores Based on Age / Test Scores in Feet

| Percentile | AGE | | | | | | | | Percentile |
	10	11	12	13	14	15	16	17–18	
100th	88	110	120	129	140	160	160	180	100th
95th	69	79	98	106	118	128	131	138	95th
90th	64	72	83	97	108	120	125	129	90th
85th	59	68	78	92	102	114	119	124	85th
80th	58	64	74	86	97	108	114	119	80th
75th	55	60	70	81	94	104	108	113	75th
70th	53	58	67	78	90	100	104	108	70th
65th	50	56	65	75	86	96	99	105	65th
60th	47	54	64	72	84	93	97	103	60th
55th	46	52	60	69	81	90	95	98	55th
50th	45	50	57	67	77	87	93	95	50th
45th	43	48	54	64	74	83	90	92	45th
40th	40	46	52	62	71	79	87	88	40th
35th	39	44	48	59	68	76	83	84	35th
30th	37	42	45	56	65	72	79	79	30th
25th	35	40	42	52	62	69	75	74	25th
20th	32	37	38	48	58	64	70	70	20th
15th	30	34	34	42	52	59	65	64	15th
10th	26	30	29	36	45	50	60	57	10th
5th	21	24	22	26	38	40	47	43	5th
0	5	10	0	0	0	10	10	10	0

Table 8.14   Kick-Off

Percentile Scores Based on Age / Test Scores in Meters

| Percentile | AGE | | | | | | | | Percentile |
	10	11	12	13	14	15	16	17–18	
100th	26.82	33.52	36.57	39.31	42.67	48.76	48.76	54.86	100th
95th	21.03	24.07	29.87	32.30	35.96	39.01	39.92	42.06	95th
90th	19.50	21.94	25.29	29.56	32.91	36.57	38.10	39.31	90th
85th	17.98	20.72	23.77	28.04	31.08	34.74	36.27	37.79	85th
80th	17.67	19.50	22.55	26.21	29.56	32.91	34.74	36.27	80th
75th	16.76	18.28	21.36	24.68	28.65	31.69	32.91	34.44	75th
70th	16.15	17.67	20.42	23.77	27.43	30.48	31.69	32.91	70th
65th	15.24	17.06	19.81	22.86	26.21	29.26	30.17	32.00	65th
60th	14.32	16.45	19.50	21.94	25.60	28.34	29.56	31.39	60th
55th	14.02	15.84	18.28	21.03	24.68	27.43	28.95	29.87	55th
50th	13.71	15.24	17.37	20.42	23.46	26.51	28.34	28.95	50th
45th	13.10	14.63	16.45	19.50	22.55	25.29	27.43	28.04	45th
40th	12.19	14.02	15.84	18.89	21.64	24.07	26.51	26.82	40th
35th	11.88	13.41	14.63	17.98	20.72	23.16	25.29	25.60	35th
30th	11.27	12.80	13.71	17.06	19.81	21.94	24.07	24.07	30th
25th	10.66	12.19	12.80	15.84	18.89	21.03	22.86	22.55	25th
20th	9.75	11.27	11.58	14.63	17.67	19.50	21.33	21.33	20th
15th	9.14	10.36	10.36	12.80	15.84	17.98	19.81	19.50	15th
10th	7.92	9.14	8.83	10.97	13.71	15.34	18.28	17.37	10th
5th	6.40	7.31	6.70	7.92	11.58	12.19	14.32	13.10	5th
0	1.52	3.04	0	0	0	3.04	3.04	3.04	0

Table 8.15   Dodging Run

Percentile Scores Based on Age / Test Scores in Seconds and Tenths

| Percentile | AGE | | | | | | | | Percentile |
	10	11	12	13	14	15	16	17–18	
100th	21.0	18.0	18.0	17.0	16.0	16.0	16.0	16.0	100th
95th	24.3	23.8	23.8	23.3	22.6	22.4	22.3	22.2	95th
90th	25.8	24.6	24.6	24.2	23.9	23.5	23.3	23.2	90th

Table 8.15—*Continued*

Percentile	10	11	12	13	14	15	16	17–18	Percentile
85th	26.3	25.0	25.0	24.8	24.6	24.1	23.9	23.7	85th
80th	26.4	25.2	25.2	24.9	24.7	24.6	24.3	24.1	80th
75th	27.5	25.3	25.3	25.3	25.2	24.9	24.7	24.4	75th
70th	27.8	25.8	25.8	25.7	25.2	25.2	25.0	24.7	70th
65th	28.1	26.3	26.3	26.1	26.1	25.5	25.3	25.0	65th
60th	28.4	26.6	26.6	26.5	26.3	25.8	25.5	25.3	60th
55th	28.7	26.9	26.9	26.8	26.6	26.1	25.8	25.6	55th
50th	28.9	27.4	27.3	27.2	26.9	26.4	26.1	26.0	50th
45th	29.3	28.0	27.6	27.5	27.2	26.7	26.3	26.3	45th
40th	29.7	28.3	27.9	27.9	27.5	27.0	26.7	26.6	40th
35th	30.1	28.8	28.4	28.3	27.9	27.4	27.0	26.9	35th
30th	30.5	29.2	28.8	28.7	28.3	27.8	27.3	27.2	30th
25th	30.9	29.8	29.2	29.1	28.7	28.2	27.7	27.6	25th
2Cth	31.3	30.4	29.8	29.5	29.3	28.6	28.1	28.0	20th
15th	31.8	31.1	30.4	30.1	29.9	29.1	28.8	28.7	15th
10th	32.7	32.0	31.3	30.8	30.7	29.8	29.6	29.2	10th
5th	33.6	33.5	33.0	32.3	31.8	31.0	30.6	30.4	5th
0	40.0	40.0	41.0	40.0	36.0	36.0	36.0	36.0	0

For both tests, the pupil is allowed un-limited practice swings, two or three warm-up balls, and fifteen test trials with each club. The fifteen shots or trials are taken at a distance of 14 feet (4.267 m) from the near edge of the target, which is divided, as illustrated in Figure 8.23, into three zones each 20 feet (6.096 m) long and scoring 1, 2, and 3 points, respectively. Score each ball by the value of the area in which it lands. Each shot must go under a rope 8 feet (2.438 m) high, but it must be in the air when it goes under the rope. Total the score for each club for the 15 trials. Two topped balls in succession count as 1 trial. Cocoa or rubber mats should be used. In the drive test, the ball is placed on a plastic tee. No tee is used in the 5-iron test.

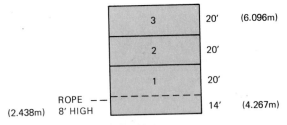

Figure 8.23   Specifications for the Drive and 5-iron Approach Shot Golf Tests

soccer

Two items that appear on a number of soccer skill tests are the soccer ball wall volley and the soccer dribble test. Directions for administering and scoring these two items—

eye-foot coordination and agility—are presented in chapter 9, "Components of Motor Performance." These two items measure the important elements of soccer performance that deal with trapping, dribbling, and overall ball control. Henry Montoye reports validity coefficients ranging from .53 to .94 with a criterion of expert ratings for wall volley and soccer dribble type items.[27] The element of the soccer kick for goal can be included in the soccer dribble test with the following simple modification: The starting line for the dribbling course should be inside the semicircle 20 yards (18.28 m) from the goal line. A regulation goal on a field may be used or the goal dimensions can be painted on a gym wall. When the player crosses the finish line (also the starting line), he or she kicks for goal.

The soccer kick for distance with either foot is another suggested skill test item. The pupil kicks a stationary ball from the end line and within a lane 25 yards (7.62 m) wide. The distance the ball travels in the air is measured. Three trials are allowed with each foot. Record the farthest kick with each foot.

softball

The AAHPER offers a battery of eight items designed to measure the fundamental skills of softball for boys and girls.[28] The eight items are: (1) softball throw for distance, (2) overhand throw for accuracy, (3) underhand pitching, (4) speed throw, (5) fungo hitting, (6) base running, (7) fielding ground balls, and (8) catching fly balls. Content validity of the test items is assumed. Minimum reliabilities of .70 for items of accuracy and form and .80 for items scored on a distance basis are reported. The directions for administering and scoring the items are the same for both boys and girls with the exception of the distances for the throw for accuracy and the underhand pitching, which are shorter

for girls. A diagram locating testing stations is illustrated in Figure 8.24. Percentile rank norms for boys and girls appear in Tables 8.16 through 8.33. Players should go through a suitable warm-up before testing.

1. Softball Throw for Distance. A throwing line is marked off at one end of the field, and a line parallel to and 6 feet (1.82 m) from it is also marked off, thus forming a zone 6 feet (1.82 m) wide from which each of the three throws are made. The player takes a position in the zone, takes one or two steps, and throws the ball as far as possible and as close to a right angle to the throwing line as possible. A stake is inserted in the ground where the ball first lands. The score is the distance of the longest throw in feet or meters.

2. Overhand Throw for Accuracy. The subject throws ten throws from a distance of 65 feet (19.81 m) for boys, 40 feet (12.19 m) for girls, at a target with the following dimensions: three concentric circles with 1-inch (2.54 cm) lines, the center circle measuring 2 feet (0.609 meters) in diameter, the next circle 4 feet (1.21 m), and the outer circle 6 feet (1.82 m) in diameter. The bottom of the outer circle is 3 feet (0.914 m) from the floor. The target may be marked on a wall or, preferably, to conserve softballs, on canvas against a mat hung on the wall. (This target is the same as used in the AAHPER football battery.) The subject is given one or two practice throws prior to the ten trials. The center circle counts three points; the second circle, two points; the outer circle, one point. The total points made on the ten throws is

27. Henry J. Montoye, *An Introduction to Measurement in Physical Education* (Boston: Allyn and Bacon, 1978), pp. 251–252.

28. American Association for Health, Physical Education, and Recreation, *Skills Test Manual: Softball for Boys* and *Skills Test Manual: Softball for Girls*, David K. Brace, Consultant (Washington, D.C.: AAHPER, 1966).

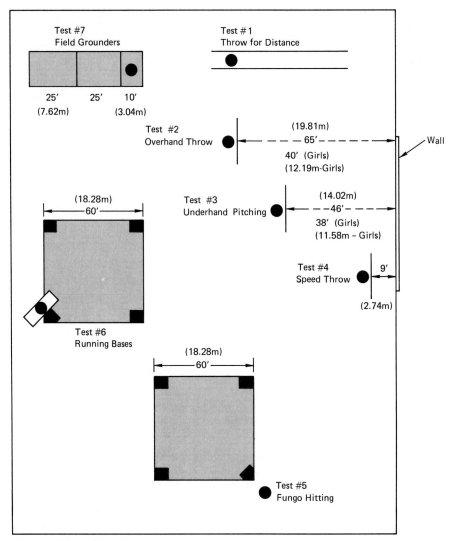

Figure 8.24 Location of Softball Testing Stations

the score. Balls hitting a line are given the higher point value.

3. Underhand Pitching. The target is rectangular in shape, representing the strike zone. The bottom of the target is 18 inches (45.72 cm) from the floor. The outer lines are 42 inches (106.68 cm) and 29 inches (73.66 cm) wide. An inner rectangle is drawn 30 inches (76.2 cm) by 17 inches (43.18 cm). A 24-inch (60.96 cm) pitching line is drawn

46 feet (14.02 m) from the target for boys, 38 feet (11.58 m) for girls. The subject takes one practice pitch, then pitches fifteen underhand trials to the target. He must keep one foot on the pitching line while delivering the ball, but he can take a step forward. Only legal pitches are scored. A mat behind the target helps prevent damage to the softballs. Balls hitting the center area or its boundary line count two points, balls hitting the outer

area count one point. The score is the sum of the points made on fifteen pitches.

4. Speed Throw. The subject stands behind a line drawn on the floor 9 feet (2.74 m) from a smooth wall. On the signal he throws the ball overhand against the wall and catches the rebound, repeating this as rapidly as possible until fifteen hits have been made against the wall. Balls that fall between the wall and the restraining line can be retrieved, but the subject must get back of the line before continuing. If the ball gets entirely away, the subject may be given one new trial. A practice trial is allowed and two trials are then given for time. The watch is started when the first ball hits the wall and is stopped when the fifteenth throw hits the wall. The score is measured in time to the nearest tenth of a second on the better of the two trials.

5. Fungo Hitting. The subject selects a bat and stands behind home plate with a ball in his hand. When ready, he tosses the ball up and tries to hit a fly ball into right field. He then hits the next ball into left field. He alternates hitting to right and left fields until ten balls have been hit in each direction. Every time the ball is touched by the bat it is considered a trial. Regardless of where the ball goes, he must hit the next ball to the opposite (right or left) field. Practice trials are allowed to each side. Hits to a specific side must cross the baseline between second and third, or first and second bases. If a player completely misses two balls in a row, it is considered a trial; otherwise, a complete miss is not counted. A fly ball that goes to the proper field counts 2 points, a ground ball counts 1 point. No score is given for a ball that lands in the wrong field. The point value for each trial is recorded and summed at the end. The maximum is 40 points.

6. Base Running. All subjects stand holding a bat in the right hand batter's box. On the signal to hit, the subject swings at an imaginary ball, then drops the bat and races around the bases. He must not throw or carry the bat, and he must take a complete swing before beginning to run. Each base must be touched in proper sequence. A practice and two timed trials are given. The watch is started on the signal "Hit" and is stopped when the runner touches home plate. The better time of the two trials to the nearest tenth of a second is the score. It is 60 feet (18.28 m) from home plate to first base.

7. Fielding Ground Balls. A rectangular area 17-by-60 feet (5.18 m by 18.28 m) is marked off. Two lines are drawn across the area 25 and 50 feet (7.62 m and 15.24 m) from the front, or throwing, line. This results in three areas being drawn. The subject stands in the 17-by-10-foot (5.18-by-3.04 m) area at the end of the rectangle. The thrower stands behind the throwing line with a basket of ten balls. On the signal to begin, the thrower begins throwing ground balls at exactly 5-second intervals into the first 17-by-25 foot (5.18-by-7.62 m) zone. The throw is made overhand with good speed. Each throw must hit the ground inside the first area for at least one bounce. Some variation in direction is desirable, but the thrower should not try to deliberately make the subject miss. A throw that does not land as specified should be taken over. The subject attempts to field each ball cleanly, holds it momentarily, then tosses it aside. The subject starts back of the 50-foot (15.24 m) line, but thereafter he may field the ball anywhere in back of the 25-foot (7.62 m) line. A practice trial and then twenty trials for score are given. The scoring is on a pass or fail basis. Each throw scores 1 point or 0. The maximum score is 20 points.

8. Catching Fly Balls. The player stands at second base in the center of a 60-foot (18.28 m) square. The thrower stands in a restraining zone 5 feet (1.52 m) behind home plate and throws fly balls to the player as directed. The thrower must throw the ball over an 8-foot (2.43 m) high rope, which is fastened between two standards located 5 feet (1.52 m) in front of home plate. The thrower must throw with regular good speed. The player must catch the ball, toss it aside, and be ready to catch the next throw. Twenty balls are thrown. The tester stands behind the player being tested and indicates to the thrower whether to throw left, right, or straight into the catching zone. At least one-third of the throws should go into each catching zone. Balls not thrown properly into catching zones are not counted. The score is the number of balls successfully caught.

Table 8.16   Softball Throw for Distance (Boys)

Percentile Scores Based on Age / Test Scores in Feet

Percentile	AGE							Percentile
	10–11	*12*	*13*	*14*	*15*	*16*	*17–18*	
100th	200	208	200	230	242	247	255	100th
95th	154	163	185	208	231	229	229	95th
90th	144	152	175	203	205	219	222	90th
85th	127	146	167	191	198	213	216	85th
80th	121	140	160	184	192	208	213	80th
75th	118	135	154	178	187	202	207	75th
70th	114	132	150	173	182	196	204	70th
65th	111	129	145	168	178	193	199	65th
60th	109	125	142	163	174	190	196	60th
55th	106	122	138	159	170	186	192	55th
50th	103	118	135	154	167	183	188	50th
45th	100	115	131	152	165	180	185	45th
40th	98	113	128	148	161	174	182	40th
35th	95	109	125	144	157	171	178	35th
30th	92	106	122	140	154	167	173	30th
25th	91	102	117	137	148	164	169	25th
20th	85	98	113	133	143	159	163	20th
15th	80	93	107	129	138	152	153	15th
10th	72	85	101	123	133	146	147	10th
5th	62	76	97	113	119	140	140	5th
0	24	31	60	105	93	135	90	0

Table 8.17 Softball Throw for Distance (Boys)

Percentile Scores Based on Age / Test Scores in Meters

Percentile		10–11	12	13	14	15	16	17–18		Percentile
					A G E					
100th		60.96	63.39	60.96	70.10	73.76	75.28	77.72		100th
95th		46.93	49.68	56.38	63.39	70.40	69.79	69.79		95th
90th		43.89	46.32	53.34	61.87	62.48	66.75	67.66		90th
85th		38.70	44.50	50.90	58.21	60.35	64.92	65.83		85th
80th		36.88	42.62	48.76	56.08	58.52	63.39	64.92		80th
75th		35.96	41.14	46.93	54.25	56.99	61.56	63.09		75th
70th		34.74	40.23	45.72	52.73	55.47	59.74	62.17		70th
65th		33.83	39.31	44.19	51.20	54.25	58.82	60.65		65th
60th		33.22	38.10	43.68	49.68	53.03	57.91	59.74		60th
55th		32.30	37.18	42.06	48.46	51.81	56.69	58.52		55th
50th		31.39	35.96	41.14	46.93	50.90	55.77	57.30		50th
45th		30.48	35.05	39.92	46.32	50.29	54.86	56.38		45th
40th		29.87	34.42	39.01	45.11	49.07	53.03	55.47		40th
35th		28.95	33.22	38.10	43.89	47.85	52.12	54.25		35th
30th		28.04	32.30	37.18	43.67	46.93	50.90	52.73		30th
25th		27.73	31.08	35.66	41.75	45.11	49.98	51.51		25th
20th		25.90	29.87	34.44	40.53	43.58	48.46	49.68		20th
15th		24.38	28.34	32.61	39.31	42.06	46.32	46.63		15th
10th		21.94	25.90	30.78	37.49	40.53	44.50	44.80		10th
5th		18.89	23.16	29.56	34.44	36.27	42.67	42.67		5th
0		7.31	9.44	18.28	32.00	28.34	41.14	27.43		0

Table 8.18 Overhand Throw for Accuracy (Boys)

Percentile Scores Based on Age / Test Scores in Points

Percentile		10–11	12	13	14	15	16	17–18		Percentile
					A G E					
100th		22	22	23	25	25	27	25		100th
95th		14	17	18	19	20	20	21		95th
90th		12	15	16	17	17	18	19		90th

Table 8.18—*Continued*

Percentile	10–11	12	13	14	15	16	17–18	Percentile
85th	11	13	15	16	16	17	18	85th
80th	9	12	13	15	15	16	17	80th
75th	8	11	12	14	14	15	16	75th
70th	8	11	12	13	13	14	15	70th
65th	7	10	11	12	12	14	15	65th
60th	6	9	10	11	11	13	14	60th
55th	5	9	10	11	11	12	13	55th
50th	5	8	9	10	10	11	13	50th
45th	4	7	8	10	10	11	12	45th
40th	4	6	7	9	9	10	11	40th
35th	3	6	7	8	9	9	11	35th
30th	3	5	6	8	8	8	10	30th
25th	2	4	5	7	7	8	9	25th
20th	1	3	4	6	7	7	8	20th
15th	1	3	3	6	6	6	7	15th
10th	0	2	2	5	5	5	6	10th
5th	0	0	1	3	3	4	4	5th
0	0	0	0	0	0	1	0	0

Table 8.19   Underhand Pitch (Boys)

Percentile Scores Based on Age / Test Scores in Points

Percentile	AGE							Percentile
	10–11	12	13	14	15	16	17–18	
100th	18	23	21	22	24	25	25	100th
95th	12	14	15	16	18	19	19	95th
90th	10	12	13	15	16	17	17	90th
85th	9	11	11	14	15	15	16	85th
80th	8	9	10	12	14	14	15	80th
75th	7	9	10	12	13	13	14	75th
70th	7	8	9	11	12	12	13	70th
65th	6	7	8	10	11	12	12	65th
60th	6	7	8	9	10	11	12	60th

Table 8.19—*Continued*

Percentile	10–11	12	13	14	15	16	17–18	Percentile
55th	5	6	7	9	10	10	11	55th
50th	4	6	7	8	9	9	10	50th
45th	4	5	6	7	8	9	10	45th
40th	3	4	5	7	7	8	9	40th
35th	3	4	5	6	7	8	8	35th
30th	2	3	4	6	6	7	8	30th
25th	2	3	4	5	5	6	7	25th
20th	1	2	3	4	4	5	6	20th
15th	1	2	3	4	4	4	5	15th
10th	1	1	2	3	3	3	4	10th
5th	0	0	1	2	2	2	3	5th
0	0	0	0	0	0	0	0	0

Table 8.20   Speed Throw (Boys)

Percentile Scores Based on Age / Test Scores in Seconds and Tenths

Percentile	AGE							Percentile
	10–11	12	13	14	15	16	17–18	
100th	13.1	11.0	10.0	9.0	13.0	10.0	10.0	100th
95th	16.1	15.3	14.9	13.0	13.5	12.5	12.1	95th
90th	17.1	16.1	14.9	14.0	13.8	13.2	12.8	90th
85th	17.6	16.8	15.7	14.6	14.2	13.7	13.2	85th
80th	18.0	17.3	16.2	15.1	14.5	14.1	13.3	80th
75th	18.6	17.6	16.8	15.6	14.9	14.5	13.9	75th
70th	19.1	18.0	16.9	15.9	15.6	14.8	14.2	70th
65th	19.7	18.4	17.3	16.3	15.9	15.1	14.5	65th
60th	20.2	18.9	17.6	16.6	16.0	15.5	14.8	60th
55th	20.8	19.5	17.9	17.1	16.4	15.8	14.9	55th
50th	21.3	19.8	18.4	17.3	16.7	16.4	15.3	50th
45th	21.8	20.4	19.1	17.7	17.1	16.6	15.6	45th
40th	22.6	21.0	19.3	18.1	17.5	17.1	16.2	40th
35th	23.6	21.5	19.8	18.5	17.9	17.4	16.7	35th
30th	24.6	22.2	20.6	19.0	18.3	18.2	17.2	30th

Table 8.20—_Continued_

Percentile	10–11	12	13	14	15	16	17–18	Percentile
25th	25.7	23.1	21.2	19.5	18.9	18.8	17.6	25th
20th	26.7	23.9	21.9	20.2	19.5	19.4	18.3	20th
15th	28.2	25.4	23.0	21.3	20.2	19.9	18.9	15th
10th	30.1	27.8	24.2	22.5	20.9	20.9	19.9	10th
5th	34.7	29.5	26.4	25.1	22.2	23.0	21.2	5th
0	43.1	36.0	29.3	28.2	24.9	25.5	26.1	0

Table 8.21   Fungo Hitting (Boys)

Percentile Scores Based on Age / Test Scores in Points

Percentile	AGE							Percentile
	10–11	12	13	14	15	16	17–18	
100th	40	40	39	36	40	40	40	100th
95th	35	36	38	35	39	38	39	95th
90th	32	33	34	35	37	36	37	90th
85th	29	31	33	33	34	34	36	85th
80th	27	30	31	31	33	33	35	80th
75th	26	29	30	30	31	33	34	75th
70th	24	28	29	29	30	32	32	70th
65th	22	27	28	28	29	30	31	65th
60th	21	26	27	27	28	29	30	60th
55th	20	25	25	26	26	28	29	55th
50th	19	23	24	24	24	26	28	50th
45th	17	22	23	23	23	25	26	45th
40th	16	20	21	21	21	23	25	40th
35th	14	19	19	19	19	21	23	35th
30th	13	17	18	18	17	19	21	30th
25th	11	15	16	16	16	17	19	25th
20th	10	13	15	15	14	15	17	20th
15th	8	11	14	13	12	13	15	15th
10th	6	10	12	12	11	11	13	10th
5th	3	7	9	11	9	9	11	5th
0	0	0	1	9	1	0	3	0

Table 8.22   Base Running (Boys)

Percentile Scores Based on Age / Test Scores in Seconds and Tenths

| Percentile | AGE | | | | | | | Percentile |
	10–11	12	13	14	15	16	17–18	
100th	10.1	9.6	9.4	9.7	10.0	10.0	10.0	100th
95th	12.9	12.4	11.7	11.5	11.6	11.3	11.1	95th
90th	13.5	12.5	12.2	11.9	11.9	11.6	11.4	90th
85th	13.9	13.3	12.7	12.2	12.2	11.8	11.6	85th
80th	14.1	13.5	12.9	12.5	12.4	12.0	11.8	80th
75th	14.3	13.7	13.2	12.7	12.5	12.1	11.9	75th
70th	14.5	13.9	13.4	12.9	12.7	12.3	12.0	70th
65th	14.8	14.1	13.6	13.0	12.8	12.4	12.2	65th
60th	14.9	14.3	13.8	13.1	13.0	12.5	12.3	60th
55th	15.1	14.5	13.9	13.3	13.1	12.6	12.4	55th
50th	15.2	14.7	14.1	13.4	13.2	12.8	12.6	50th
45th	15.4	14.8	14.3	13.5	13.3	12.9	12.7	45th
40th	15.6	15.0	14.5	13.7	13.5	13.0	12.8	40th
35th	15.8	15.2	14.7	13.9	13.6	13.2	12.9	35th
30th	16.0	15.4	14.9	14.1	13.7	13.3	13.0	30th
25th	16.2	15.7	15.1	14.2	13.9	13.6	13.2	25th
20th	16.5	15.9	15.4	14.5	14.0	13.8	13.4	20th
15th	17.0	16.2	15.7	14.8	14.3	14.1	13.6	15th
10th	17.4	16.5	15.9	15.2	14.5	14.4	13.9	10th
5th	18.2	17.4	16.7	15.8	15.0	15.3	14.9	5th
0	23.0	20.6	17.2	17.2	15.8	18.0	17.8	0

Table 8.23   Fielding Ground Balls (Boys)

Percentile Scores Based on Age / Test Scores in Points

| Percentile | AGE | | | | | | | Percentile |
	10–11	12	13	14	15	16	17–18	
100th	20	20	20	20	20	20	20	100th
95th	19	20	20	20	20	20	20	95th
90th	18	19	19	19	19	20	20	90th

Table 8.23—*Continued*

Percentile	10–11	12	13	14	15	16	17–18	Percentile
85th	18	19	19	19	19	20	20	85th
80th	17	18	18	18	18	19	19	80th
75th	17	18	18	18	18	19	19	75th
70th	16	17	17	17	18	19	19	70th
65th	16	17	17	17	17	18	18	65th
60th	15	16	16	16	16	18	18	60th
55th	15	16	16	16	16	17	17	55th
50th	14	15	15	15	15	17	17	50th
45th	13	15	14	14	15	16	17	45th
40th	13	14	14	14	14	16	16	40th
35th	12	14	13	13	13	15	16	35th
30th	11	13	13	12	12	14	15	30th
25th	10	12	12	10	11	13	14	25th
20th	9	11	11	10	10	10	12	20th
15th	8	9	10	9	9	9	10	15th
10th	6	8	8	8	8	9	9	10th
5th	4	6	6	6	7	8	9	5th
0	0	0	1	1	1	5	6	0

Table 8.24   Catching Fly Balls (Boys)

Percentile Scores Based on Age / Test Scores in Points

Percentile	AGE							Percentile
	10–11	12	13	14	15	16	17–18	
100th	20	20	20	20	20	20	20	100th
95th	20	20	20	20	20	20	20	95th
90th	20	20	20	20	20	20	20	90th
85th	19	19	19	19	20	20	20	85th
80th	19	19	19	19	19	19	19	80th
75th	19	19	19	19	19	19	19	75th
70th	18	19	18	19	19	19	19	70th
65th	18	18	18	18	18	19	19	65th
60th	17	18	17	18	18	18	18	60th

Table 8.24—*Continued*

Percentile	10–11	12	13	14	15	16	17–18	Percentile
55th	17	17	17	18	17	18	18	55th
50th	16	17	16	16	17	17	18	50th
45th	15	16	16	16	16	16	17	45th
40th	14	15	15	15	15	15	16	40th
35th	12	14	14	13	14	13	15	35th
30th	10	12	13	12	12	10	14	30th
25th	9	10	11	10	11	10	11	25th
20th	8	10	10	10	10	10	10	20th
15th	7	8	9	9	9	9	10	15th
10th	6	7	8	8	8	9	9	10th
5th	3	5	6	7	7	8	9	5th
0	0	0	0	0	0	0	0	0

Table 8.25   Softball Throw for Distance (Girls)

Percentile Scores Based on Age / Test Scores in Feet

Percentile	AGE							Percentile
	10–11	12	13	14	15	16	17–18	
100th	120	160	160	160	200	200	200	100th
95th	99	113	133	126	127	121	120	95th
90th	84	104	112	117	116	109	109	90th
85th	76	98	105	109	108	103	102	85th
80th	71	94	98	104	103	98	97	80th
75th	68	89	94	99	97	94	93	75th
70th	66	85	90	95	93	91	89	70th
65th	62	81	86	92	88	87	87	65th
60th	60	77	83	88	85	84	84	60th
55th	57	74	81	85	80	81	82	55th
50th	55	70	76	82	77	79	80	50th
45th	53	67	73	79	75	76	77	45th
40th	50	64	70	76	72	73	74	40th
35th	48	61	68	73	70	70	72	35th
30th	45	58	64	69	67	67	69	30th

Table 8.25—*Continued*

Percentile	*10–11*	*12*	*13*	*14*	*15*	*16*	*17–18*	Percentile
25th	43	55	62	66	64	63	66	25th
20th	41	51	60	61	61	60	63	20th
15th	38	48	56	57	58	56	60	15th
10th	34	43	51	52	54	51	55	10th
5th	31	37	43	43	49	45	50	5th
0	20	20	20	20	20	10	10	0

Table 8.26   Softball Throw for Distance (Girls)

Percentile Scores Based on Age / Test Scores in Meters

| Percentile | AGE | | | | | | | Percentile |
	10–11	*12*	*13*	*14*	*15*	*16*	*17–18*	
100th	36.57	48.76	48.76	48.76	60.96	60.96	60.96	100th
95th	30.17	34.44	40.53	38.40	38.70	36.88	36.57	95th
90th	25.60	31.69	34.13	35.66	35.35	33.22	33.20	90th
85th	23.16	29.87	32.00	33.22	32.91	31.39	31.08	85th
80th	21.64	28.65	29.87	31.69	31.39	29.87	29.56	80th
75th	20.72	27.12	28.65	30.17	29.56	28.65	28.34	75th
70th	20.11	25.90	27.43	28.95	28.34	27.73	27.12	70th
65th	18.89	24.68	26.21	28.04	26.82	26.51	26.51	65th
60th	18.28	23.46	25.29	26.82	25.90	25.60	25.60	60th
55th	17.37	22.55	24.68	25.90	24.38	24.68	24.99	55th
50th	16.76	21.33	23.16	24.99	23.46	24.07	24.38	50th
45th	16.15	20.42	22.25	24.07	22.86	23.16	23.46	45th
40th	15.24	19.50	21.33	23.16	21.94	22.25	22.55	40th
35th	14.63	18.59	20.72	22 25	21.33	21.33	21.94	35th
30th	13.71	17.67	19.50	21.03	20.42	20.42	21.03	30th
25th	13.10	16.76	18.89	20.11	19.50	19.20	20.11	25th
20th	12.49	15.54	18.28	18.59	18.59	18.28	19.20	20th
15th	11.58	14.63	17.06	17.37	17.67	17.06	18.28	15th
10th	10.36	13.10	15.54	15.84	16.45	15.54	16.76	10th
5th	9.44	11.27	13.10	13.10	14.93	13.71	15.24	5th
0	6.09	6.09	6.09	6.09	6.09	3.04	3.04	0

Table 8.27　Overhand Throw for Accuracy (Girls)

Percentile Scores Based on Age / Test Scores in Points

Percentile	10–11	12	13	14	15	16	17–18	Percentile
	A G E							
100th	24	26	26	26	30	30	26	100th
95th	17	17	18	19	19	22	20	95th
90th	14	16	16	17	18	20	18	90th
85th	13	14	15	15	16	18	17	85th
80th	12	13	14	14	15	17	16	80th
75th	11	12	13	13	14	16	15	75th
70th	10	11	12	12	13	15	14	70th
65th	9	10	11	11	12	13	13	65th
60th	8	9	10	11	11	12	12	60th
55th	7	9	9	10	11	12	11	55th
50th	6	8	9	9	10	11	10	50th
45th	5	7	8	9	9	10	9	45th
40th	4	6	7	8	8	9	8	40th
35th	4	5	6	7	8	8	7	35th
30th	3	4	6	6	7	7	6	30th
25th	2	4	5	5	6	6	5	25th
20th	1	3	4	4	5	5	4	20th
15th	1	2	3	3	3	4	3	15th
10th	0	1	1	2	2	2	2	10th
5th	0	0	0	1	1	1	1	5th
0	0	0	0	0	0	0	0	0

Table 8.28　Underhand Pitch (Girls)

Percentile Scores Based on Age / Test Scores in Points

Percentile	10–11	12	13	14	15	16	17–18	Percentile
	A G E							
100th	23	22	24	24	26	27	26	100th
95th	12	14	16	17	16	19	21	95th
90th	10	13	14	15	15	16	18	90th

Table 8.28—*Continued*

Percentile	10–11	12	13	14	15	16	17–18	Percentile
85th	8	11	12	14	13	14	17	85th
80th	7	10	11	13	12	12	15	80th
75th	6	9	10	12	11	12	14	75th
70th	6	8	9	11	10	11	13	70th
65th	5	7	9	10	9	10	12	65th
60th	5	6	8	9	8	10	11	60th
55th	4	6	7	8	7	9	10	55th
50th	4	5	7	8	6	8	9	50th
45th	3	5	6	7	6	8	9	45th
40th	3	4	6	6	5	7	8	40th
35th	2	4	5	5	4	6	7	35th
30th	2	3	4	5	4	5	6	30th
25th	1	2	4	4	3	5	5	25th
20th	1	2	3	3	2	4	5	20th
15th	0	1	2	3	2	3	4	15th
10th	0	0	2	2	1	2	3	10th
5th	0	0	1	1	0	0	2	5th
0	0	0	0	0	0	0	0	0

Table 8.29   Speed Throw (Girls)

Percentile Scores Based on Age / Test Scores in Seconds and Tenths

Percentile	AGE							Percentile
	10–11	12	13	14	15	16	17–18	
100th	10.0	12.0	12.0	12.0	12.0	14.0	14.0	100th
95th	20.1	13.8	13.0	13.0	15.6	15.8	15.0	95th
90th	21.4	15.8	16.3	13.9	16.6	16.9	15.0	90th
85th	22.8	17.7	17.8	15.3	17.6	17.6	15.6	85th
80th	24.1	18.8	18.6	16.5	18.1	18.1	16.1	80th
75th	25.2	19.8	19.4	17.6	18.6	18.5	17.6	75th
70th	26.0	20.8	20.0	18.2	19.1	18.9	18.0	70th
65th	27.0	21.6	20.6	18.7	19.6	19.4	18.5	65th
60th	27.4	22.3	21.3	19.3	20.1	20.0	18.9	60th

Table 8.29—Continued

Percentile	10–11	12	13	14	15	16	17–18	Percentile
55th	28.8	23.1	21.9	19.9	20.6	20.7	19.3	55th
50th	29.8	24.1	22.7	20.7	21.1	21.4	19.8	50th
45th	30.9	25.2	23.4	21.1	21.7	22.2	20.3	45th
40th	31.9	26.2	24.3	21.8	22.6	22.9	20.8	40th
35th	33.0	27.5	25.4	22.5	23.3	23.7	21.4	35th
30th	34.1	28.6	26.4	23.5	24.3	24.8	22.3	30th
25th	35.9	29.8	27.5	24.6	25.4	26.1	23.3	25th
20th	38.0	31.3	28.9	25.8	26.9	27.8	24.1	20th
15th	41.0	33.1	30.9	27.4	28.7	30.4	25.0	15th
10th	46.1	36.7	33.0	30.2	31.5	33.0	26.1	10th
5th	55.2	40.8	38.5	33.5	37.4	36.9	28.9	5th
0	105.0	66.0	52.0	50.0	50.0	52.0	40.0	0

Table 8.30   Fungo Hitting (Girls)

Percentile Scores Based on Age / Test Scores in Points

Percentile	AGE							Percentile
	10–11	12	13	14	15	16	17–18	
100th	30	38	38	38	38	38	38	100th
95th	21	28	30	31	30	30	31	95th
90th	18	24	26	30	27	27	28	90th
85th	15	22	23	26	25	25	26	85th
80th	14	20	22	23	23	24	25	80th
75th	13	18	20	21	22	22	23	75th
70th	12	17	19	20	20	21	22	70th
65th	12	16	18	19	19	19	20	65th
60th	11	15	17	18	18	18	19	60th
55th	9	14	16	17	17	17	18	55th
50th	9	13	14	15	16	16	17	50th
45th	8	12	13	14	15	15	16	45th
40th	7	11	13	13	14	14	15	40th
35th	6	10	12	12	13	13	14	35th
30th	6	9	11	11	12	12	14	30th

Table 8.30—_Continued_

Percentile	10–11	12	13	14	15	16	17–18	Percentile
25th	5	8	10	10	11	11	13	25th
20th	4	7	8	9	10	10	12	20th
15th	3	5	7	8	8	9	10	15th
10th	2	4	6	6	7	8	8	10th
5th	0	2	4	3	4	5	6	5th
0	0	0	0	0	0	0	0	0

Table 8.31   Base Running (Girls)

Percentile Scores Based on Age / Test Scores in Seconds and Tenths

Percentile	AGE							Percentile
	10–11	12	13	14	15	16	17–18	
100th	11.0	11.0	12.0	12.0	12.0	12.0	12.0	100th
95th	13.1	13.4	12.6	12.7	12.9	13.2	13.6	95th
90th	13.8	13.7	13.1	13.1	13.5	13.7	13.9	90th
85th	14.3	14.0	13.5	13.5	13.7	14.0	14.3	85th
80th	14.7	14.3	13.7	13.7	13.9	14.4	14.6	80th
75th	14.9	14.5	13.9	13.8	14.1	14.6	14.8	75th
70th	15.2	14.7	14.1	14.0	14.3	14.8	14.9	70th
65th	15.4	14.9	14.3	14.2	14.5	14.9	15.1	65th
60th	15.6	15.0	14.5	14.4	14.7	15.1	15.3	60th
55th	15.8	15.2	14.7	14.5	14.9	15.3	15.5	55th
50th	16.0	15.3	14.8	14.8	15.0	15.5	15.7	50th
45th	16.2	15.5	15.0	14.9	15.2	15.6	15.9	45th
40th	16.4	15.7	15.2	15.1	15.4	15.8	16.1	40th
35th	16.7	15.8	15.4	15.3	15.5	15.9	16.3	35th
30th	17.0	16.0	15.6	15.5	15.8	16.0	16.5	30th
25th	17.3	16.2	16.0	15.7	16.1	16.2	16.9	25th
20th	17.7	16.5	16.3	16.0	16.3	16.3	17.1	20th
15th	18.2	16.9	16.6	16.4	16.7	16.4	17.6	15th
10th	18.8	17.4	17.2	16.9	17.3	17.8	18.2	10th
5th	19.9	18.2	18.0	17.8	18.1	18.4	19.2	5th
0	27.0	20.0	22.0	23.0	28.0	31.0	32.0	0

Table 8.32   Fielding Ground Balls (Girls)

Percentile Scores Based on Age / Test Scores in Points

Percentile	10–11	12	13	14	15	16	17–18	Percentile
				AGE				
100th	20	20	20	20	20	20	20	100th
95th	18	20	20	20	20	20	20	95th
90th	17	19	19	19	20	20	20	90th
85th	16	19	19	19	19	19	19	85th
80th	15	18	19	19	19	19	19	80th
75th	15	18	18	18	18	19	19	75th
70th	14	17	18	18	18	18	18	70th
65th	13	16	17	17	18	18	18	65th
60th	13	15	17	17	17	18	18	60th
55th	12	15	16	17	17	17	17	55th
50th	11	14	16	16	16	17	17	50th
45th	10	13	15	15	16	17	17	45th
40th	10	12	15	15	15	16	16	40th
35th	9	10	14	14	15	16	16	35th
30th	8	10	13	13	14	15	15	30th
25th	8	9	12	12	13	14	14	25th
20th	7	9	11	10	12	13	14	20th
15th	6	8	10	10	11	12	13	15th
10th	5	7	9	9	10	10	11	10th
5th	3	5	8	8	9	8	9	5th
0	0	0	0	0	0	0	0	0

Table 8.33   Catching Fly Balls (Girls)

Percentile Scores Based on Age / Test Scores in Points

Percentile	10–11	12	13	14	15	16	17–18	Percentile
				AGE				
100th	15	17	19	19	20	20	20	100th
95th	13	15	17	17	19	19	19	95th
90th	10	13	15	16	18	19	19	90th

Table 8.33—*Continued*

Percentile	10–11	12	13	14	15	16	17–18	Percentile
85th	9	11	13	15	18	18	18	85th
80th	9	10	12	14	17	17	17	80th
75th	8	9	11	13	16	16	16	75th
70th	7	8	10	12	15	15	16	70th
65th	7	7	9	11	14	14	15	65th
60th	6	7	8	10	13	13	15	60th
55th	6	6	7	9	12	13	14	55th
50th	5	6	6	9	11	12	13	50th
45th	4	5	5	8	10	11	12	45th
40th	4	5	5	8	9	10	11	40th
35th	3	4	4	7	8	9	10	35th
30th	3	3	3	6	7	8	9	30th
25th	2	3	3	5	6	7	8	25th
20th	2	2	2	4	5	6	7	20th
15th	1	2	2	3	4	5	6	15th
10th	1	1	1	2	3	4	5	10th
5th	0	0	0	1	2	3	4	5th
0	0	0	0	0	0	0	0	0

swimming

red cross progressive swimming skills

The American Red Cross has developed a series of progressive swimming courses that are used in many instructional programs. A series of skills, arranged hierarchically, for the beginner, advanced beginner, intermediate swimmer, advanced swimmer, basic survival, and advanced survival levels are proposed as instructional guides and are listed in Figure 8.25. These skills are also the basis for formative or summative evaluation. Generally, mastery learning techniques using the criterion-referenced standards listed are employed by the teacher.

university of kentucky swimming proficiency test

This test was developed to measure swimming proficiency at the intermediate and advanced swimmer levels.[29] It is proposed for summative evaluation and uses norm-referenced standards. The test consists of the following six items: (1) the 20-yard or 18.28-meter underwater swim, (2) the 25-yard or 22.86-meter crawl sprint, (3) the five-minute swim for distance, and three 25-yard or 22.86-meter swims of each of the following strokes:

29. Department of Health, Physical Education and Recreation, University of Kentucky. Test directions and norms used with permission of the department and Dr. Alfred M. Reece.

BEGINNER SKILLS

1. Breath-holding-10 sec.
2. Rhythmic breathing 10 times
3. Prone float
4. Prone glide-10 ft.
5. Back float
6. Back glide-6 ft.
7. Prone glide with kick-20 ft.
8. Back glide with kick-20 ft.
9. Arm stroke-20 ft.
10. Finning or sculling-20 ft.
11. Crawl stroke-20 yd.
12. Combined stroke (back)-10 yd.
13. Changing direction
14. Turning over
15. Leveling off
16. Jump (chest-deep water)
17. Jump (deep water)
18. Front dive
19. Safety skills
20. Combined skills

ADVANCED BEGINNER SKILLS

1. Rhythmic breathing
2. Survival floating-2 min.
3. Treading water-30 sec.-changing positions
4. Elementary backstroke-25 yd.
5. Crawl stroke-25 yd.
6. Diving and underwater swimming-15 ft.
7. Use of personal flotation device (PFD)
8. Safety and rescue
9. First combined skills
10. Second combined skills

INTERMEDIATE SKILLS

1. Leg   Scissors-20 yd.
   Kicks   Crawl-20 yd.
           Breaststroke-20 yd.

2. Arm   Sidestroke-10 yd.
   Strokes Crawl stroke-10 yd.
           Breaststroke-10 yd.
3. Elementary backstroke-50 yd.
4. Selected stroke-100 yd.
5. Turns (front and back)
6. Survival floating-5 min.
7. Sculling-10 yd.
8. Treading water-1 min.
9. Floating-1 min.
10. Underwater swimming-15 ft.
11. Standing front dive
12. Rescue skills
13. 5-minute swim

SWIMMER SKILLS

1. Breaststroke-100 yd.
2. Sidestroke-100 yd.
3. Crawl stroke-100 yd.
4. Back crawl-50 yd.
5. Swimming on back (legs only)-50 yd.
6. Turns (front, back, side)
7. Surface dive-underwater swimming-20 ft.
8. Disrobing, floating with clothes-5 min.
9. Long shallow dive
10. Running front dive
11. 10-minute swim

ADVANCED SWIMMER SKILLS
(Jr. or Sr. Lifesaving Prerequisite)

1. Elementary backstroke-100 yd.
2. Breaststroke-100 yd.
3. Inverted breaststroke-50 yd.
4. Sidestroke-100 yd.
5. Overarm sidestroke-100 yd.
6. Trudgen crawl or Trudgen-100 yd.
7. Back crawl-100 yd.

8. Crawl stroke-100 yd.
9. 5-minute float
10. Survival float clothed-10 min.
11. Surface dive feetfirst-underwater swimming-10 yd.
12. Running front dive
13. 30-minute swim

BASIC SURVIVAL SKILLS

1. Breath control - rhythmic breathing
2. Survival floating-2 min.
3. Human stroke-40 yd.
4. Elementary backstroke-40 yd.
5. Feetfirst surface dive
6. Underwater swimming
7. Jumping and remaining afloat
8. Lifesaving skills
9. Use of improvised flotation devices
10. Artificial respiration
11. First combined test
12. Second combined test

ADVANCED SURVIVAL SKILLS

1. Sidestroke-100 yd.
2. Breaststroke-100 yd.
3. Crawl stroke-100 yd.
4. Elementary backstroke-100 yd.
5. Breaststroke modifications
6. Sidestroke modifications
7. Jumping and remaining afloat-10 min.
8. Use of improvised flotation devices
9. Lifesaving skills
10. Artificial respiration
11. First combined test
12. Second combined test

Figure 8.25   Testing Swimming Skills

(4) elementary backstroke, (5) sidestroke, and (6) the conventional breaststroke. Six-σ scale scores for both sexes are available for each performance. The mean of a 6-σ scale = 50, and the standard deviation = 16.67. (See Tables 8.34, 8.35, 8.36, 8.37, and 8.38.) These scales were derived from past performances obtained from students enrolled in intermediate swimming sections in the service program at the University of Kentucky.

standardized directions

1. The 20-yard or 18.28-meter underwater swim. Swimmer starts at the deep end of the pool. Use regulation starting commands, namely (a) "Take your marks," (b) "Go." Swimmer dives into the water and attempts to swim entire distance of 20 yards or 18.28 meters under the water. Any style of swimming is permitted. A rubber brick or other type marker is placed on the bottom approximately 20 yards (18.28 m) from the starting end. This enables swimmer to determine the finish line quickly while underwater. *Scoring:* Record the time to the tenth of a second. No score is given if any part of the body breaks the surface before the distance of 20 yards (18.28 m) is accomplished. Consult Table 8.34, locate scale score for the effort.

2. *The 25-yard or 22.86-meter crawl sprint.* Swimmer starts at the shallow end of pool, using starting box. Regulation start is used, as indicated in the first test. Racing dive is permitted, although some few who cannot execute a header are permitted to use feetfirst jump. The student is encouraged to swim as fast as he can and in a straight line. *Scoring:* Record the time to the tenth of a second. No score is granted if the distance is not completed. Locate scale score for this effort in Table 8.35.

3. *The Five-Minute Swim for Distance.* Student is encouraged to swim as far as he can in the five-minute period allotted. Any number of strokes are allowed. Rests are permitted at intervals, although the student is penalized thusly for lowering his distance score. Walking on the bottom of the pool is not permitted. Swimmer or his partner counts the number of lengths swum. Conventional start is used. Swimmer swims until whistle blows to indicate the end of the five-minute period. *Scoring:* Convert the lengths to the nearest yard or meter. No score is given if the swimmer climbs out of the pool before the five-minute period is completed or if the swimmer walks on the bottom in shallow water. Locate the scale score for this effort in Table 8.36 or 8.37.

The gliding strokes—elementary back, side, and breast—are administered in essentially the same manner. Each swimmer negotiates 25 yards (22.86 m), or one pool length, for each stroke. The swimmer's strokes are counted by a buddy, with the push-off necessary to start each length counting as a stroke. The idea is to swim the distance in as few strokes as possible. The student fails in his effort if he uses additional sculling or kicking movements, improper arm or leg movements, or demonstrates none of the coordination necessary for proper execution of the stroke.

4. *The 25-yard or 22.86-meter elementary backstroke.* Swimmer starts at the shallow end, pushing off the wall in the gliding position of the stroke with arms at the side of the body and legs together. Swimmer may use whip or squeeze kick (both versions of the frog kick), but no other kick is permitted. Arms may be raised above the shoulders in the recovery, but not above the water surface. No arm or leg motion is allowed on the push-off. The goal is to swim this stroke the pool's length in as few strokes as possible. *Scoring:* Record the number of push-offs, plus the number of strokes, required to make the distance. A half or split stroke performed at the end of the length is counted as a whole stroke. Consult Table 8.38 to locate the scale score for this effort in the elementary backstroke.

5. *The 25-yard or 22.86-meter sidestroke.* Swimmer starts in the water at the shallow end of the pool with a push-off from the wall. This glide is the normal glide for the stroke, with the lower arm extended forward in line with the body and the upper arm along the side of the body. The legs are together, straight, and in line with the body. No arm or leg movement is permitted in the push-off. Only one leg action, the regular scissors with top leg recovering forward, is allowed for each stroke. Inverted scissors or frog kick is forbidden. Both arms recover under the water. *Scoring:* Record the number of push-offs, plus the number of strokes, required to make the distance. No score is granted for improper strokes. Table 8.38 is used also to locate the scale score for this effort in the sidestroke.

Last Name	First	Init.	Sex	Instructor	Code

Event	Trial I	Points	Trial II	Points
20 Yd. Under- water Swim ( )	_____	_____	_____	_____
25 Yd. Elementary Back	_____	_____	_____	_____
25 Yd. Crawl Sprint	_____	_____	_____	_____
25 Yd. Sidestroke	_____	_____	_____	_____
25 Yd. Breaststroke	_____	_____	_____	_____
Five-Minute Swim	_____	_____	_____	_____
TOTALS		_____		_____

Figure 8.26   Student's Record Card for Indicating Progress in Swimming Achievement

6. The 25-yard or 22.86-meter conventional breaststroke. Swimmer starts in the water at the shallow end with a push-off and glide. The glide must be executed on the surface with the body fully extended, arms extended over the head and the head between the arms. The face is submerged during the extended glide. The same kicking movements are employed here as in the elementary backstroke except that the stroke is swum on the front. No scissors or flutter kick is accepted. Breath must be taken on each stroke cycle at the end of the glide. One paired kick movement and one paired arm movement—a surface stroke with the arms recovering under the water—is correct for each stroke cycle. *Scoring:* Record the number of push-offs and the number of strokes required to swim the distance. Partial strokes are counted as whole strokes. No score is granted for improper movements or improper coordination. Locate the scale score for the effort in this stroke performance in Table 8.38.

There is a scale score for each performance. The average performance for an event approximates 50 scale score points. Any performance exceeding 50 points is above average, any less than 50 points is below average. The standard deviation is 16.67.

The scale scores can be summed to locate a composite score for all six test items. This composite, or criterion, is a total measurement encompassing all events. Thus, a student's record of performances can be recorded. A card such as that in Figure 8.26 is

Table 8.34   **Conversion of Raw Scores, Earned on a 20-Yard or 18.28-Meter Underwater Swim Test, Measured to the Tenth of a Second, to Six-σ (Sigma) Scores**

Seconds	Men	Women	Seconds	Men	Women	Seconds	Men	Women
11.0	80	95	19.0	42	63	27.0	4	31
11.2	79	94	19.2	41	62	27.2	3	30
11.4	78	93	19.4	40	61	27.4	2	30
11.6	77	92	19.6	39	61	27.6	1	29
11.8	76	92	19.8	38	60	27.8	1	28
12.0	76	92	20.0	37	60	28.0	0	27
12.2	74	90	20.2	36	58	28.2	0	26
12.4	73	89	20.4	35	57	28.4	0	26
12.6	72	88	20.6	34	57	28.6	0	25
12.8	71	88	20.8	34	56	28.8	0	24
13.0	70	87	21.0	33	55	29.0	0	23
13.2	69	86	21.2	32	54	29.2	0	22
13.4	68	85	21.4	31	53	29.4	0	21
13.6	67	84	21.6	30	52	29.6	0	21
13.8	66	84	21.8	29	52	29.8	0	20
14.0	66	83	22.0	28	51	30.0	0	19
14.2	65	82	22.2	27	50	30.2	0	18
14.4	64	81	22.4	26	49	30.4	0	18
14.6	63	80	22.6	25	49	30.6	0	17
14.8	62	80	22.8	24	48	30.8	0	16
15.0	61	79	23.0	23	47	31.0	0	15
15.2	60	78	23.2	22	46	31.2	0	14
15.4	59	77	23.4	21	46	31.4	0	14
15.6	58	77	23.6	20	45	31.6	0	13
15.8	57	76	23.8	19	44	31.8	0	12
16.0	56	75	24.0	18	43	32.0	0	11
16.2	55	74	24.2	18	42	32.2	0	10
16.4	54	73	24.4	16	42	32.4	0	10
16.6	53	72	24.6	16	41	32.6	0	9
16.8	52	72	24.8	15	39	32.8	0	8
17.0	51	71	25.0	14	39	33.0	0	7
17.2	50	70	25.2	13	38	33.2	0	6
17.4	50	69	25.4	12	38	33.4	0	6
17.6	48	68	25.6	11	37	33.6	0	5
17.8	48	68	25.8	10	36	33.8	0	4
18.0	47	67	26.0	9	35	34.0	0	3
18.2	46	66	26.2	8	35	34.2	0	2
18.4	45	65	26.4	7	34	34.4	0	2
18.6	44	65	26.6	6	33	34.6	0	1
18.8	43	64	26.8	5	32	34.8	0	0

Table 8.35 **Conversion of Raw Scores Made on the 25-Yard or 22.86-Meter Crawl Sprint to Six-σ (Sigma) Scale Scores**

Seconds	Men	Women	Seconds	Men	Women	Seconds	Men	Women
10.0	88		19.0	44	66	28.0	1	33
10.2	87		19.2	44	65	28.2	0	33
10.4	86		19.4	43	65	28.4	0	32
10.6	85		19.6	42	64	28.6	0	31
10.8	84		19.8	41	63	28.8	0	30
11.0	83	95	20.0	40	62	29.0	0	30
11.2	82	94	20.2	39	62	29.2	0	29
11.4	81	94	20.4	38	61	29.4	0	28
11.6	80	93	20.6	37	60	29.6	0	28
11.8	80	92	20.8	36	60	29.8	0	27
12.0	78	92	21.0	35	59	30.0	0	26
12.2	77	91	21.2	34	58	30.2	0	25
12.4	76	90	21.4	33	57	30.4	0	25
12.6	76	89	21.6	32	57	30.6	0	24
12.8	74	89	21.8	31	56	30.8	0	23
13.0	74	88	22.0	30	55	31.0	0	22
13.2	73	87	22.2	29	54	31.2	0	22
13.4	72	86	22.4	28	54	31.4	0	21
13.6	71	86	22.6	27	53	31.6	0	20
13.8	70	85	22.8	26	52	31.8	0	20
14.0	69	84	23.0	25	52	32.0	0	19
14.2	68	84	23.2	24	51	32.2	0	18
14.4	67	83	23.4	23	50	32.4	0	17
14.6	66	82	23.6	22	49	32.6	0	17
14.8	65	81	23.8	21	49	32.8	0	16
15.0	64	81	24.0	20	48	33.0	0	15
15.2	63	80	24.2	19	47	33.2	0	14
15.4	62	79	24.4	18	46	33.4	0	14
15.6	61	78	24.6	18	46	33.6	0	13
15.8	60	78	24.8	16	45	33.8	0	12
16.0	59	77	25.0	16	44	34.0	0	12
16.2	58	76	25.2	15	44	34.2	0	11
16.4	57	76	25.4	14	42	34.4	0	10
16.6	56	75	25.6	13	42	34.6	0	9
16.8	55	74	25.8	12	41	34.8	0	9
17.0	54	73	26.0	11	41	35.0	0	8
17.2	53	73	26.2	10	40	35.2	0	7
17.4	53	72	26.4	9	39	35.4	0	6
17.6	51	72	26.6	8	38	35.6	0	6
17.8	50	70	26.8	7	38	35.8	0	5
18.0	49	70	27.0	6	37	36.0	0	4
18.2	48	69	27.2	5	36	36.2	0	4
18.4	47	68	27.4	4	36	36.4	0	3
18.6	46	68	27.6	3	35	36.6	0	2
18.8	46	67	27.8	2	34	36.8	0	1

Table 8.36 Conversion of Raw Scores in Yards on Five-Minute Distance Swim Test to 6-σ (Sigma) Scores

Yards	Men	Women	Yards	Men	Women	Yards	Men	Women
330	99	128	250	65	85	170	31	42
328	98	126	248	64	84	168	30	41
326	98	125	246	63	83	166	29	40
324	97	125	244	62	82	164	28	39
322	96	123	242	62	81	162	27	38
320	95	122	240	61	80	160	26	37
318	94	121	238	60	79	158	26	36
316	93	120	236	59	78	156	25	35
314	92	119	234	58	76	154	24	34
312	92	118	232	57	75	152	23	33
310	91	117	230	56	74	150	22	32
308	90	116	228	56	73	148	21	31
306	89	115	226	55	72	146	20	30
304	88	114	224	54	71	144	20	29
302	87	113	222	53	70	142	19	28
300	86	112	220	52	69	140	18	26
298	86	110	218	51	68	138	17	25
296	85	110	216	50	67	136	16	24
294	84	108	214	50	66	134	15	23
292	83	107	212	49	65	132	14	22
290	82	106	210	48	64	130	14	21
288	81	105	208	47	63	128	13	20
286	80	104	206	46	62	126	12	19
284	80	103	204	45	60	124	11	18
282	79	102	202	44	60	122	10	17
280	78	101	200	44	58	120	9	16
278	77	100	198	43	58	118	8	15
276	76	99	196	42	56	116	8	14
274	75	98	194	41	55	114	7	13
272	74	97	192	40	54	112	6	12
270	74	96	190	39	53	110	5	10
268	73	95	188	38	52	108	4	10
266	72	94	186	38	51	106	3	8
264	71	92	184	37	50	104	2	7
262	70	91	182	36	49	102	2	6
260	69	90	180	35	48	100	1	5
258	68	89	178	34	47	98	0	4
256	68	88	176	33	46	96	0	3
254	67	87	174	32	45	94	0	2
252	66	86	172	32	44	92	0	1

Table 8.37 Conversion of Raw Scores in Meters on Five-Minute Distance Swim Test to 6-σ (Sigma) Scores

Meters	Men	Women	Meters	Men	Women	Meters	Men	Women
301.7	99	128	228.6	65	85	155.4	31	42
299.9	98	126	226.7	64	84	153.6	30	41
298.1	98	125	224.9	63	83	151.7	29	40
296.2	97	125	223.1	62	82	149.9	28	39
294.4	96	123	221.2	62	81	148.1	27	38
292.6	95	122	219.4	61	80	146.3	26	37
290.7	94	121	217.6	60	79	144.4	26	36
288.9	93	120	215.7	59	78	142.6	25	35
287.1	92	119	213.9	58	76	140.8	24	34
285.2	92	118	212.1	57	75	138.9	23	33
283.4	91	117	210.3	56	74	137.1	22	32
281.6	90	116	208.4	56	73	135.3	21	31
279.8	89	115	206.6	55	72	133.5	20	30
277.9	88	114	204.8	54	71	131.6	20	29
276.1	87	113	202.9	53	70	129.8	19	28
274.3	86	112	201.1	52	69	128.0	18	26
272.4	86	110	199.3	51	68	126.1	17	25
270.6	85	110	197.5	50	67	124.3	16	24
268.8	84	108	195.6	50	66	122.5	15	23
267.0	83	107	193.8	49	65	120.7	14	22
265.1	82	106	192.0	48	64	118.8	14	21
263.3	81	105	190.1	47	63	117.0	13	20
261.5	80	104	188.3	46	62	115.2	12	19
259.6	80	103	186.5	45	60	113.3	11	18
257.8	79	102	184.7	44	60	111.5	10	17
256.0	78	101	182.8	44	58	109.7	9	16
254.2	77	100	181.0	43	58	107.8	8	15
252.3	76	99	179.2	42	56	106.0	8	14
250.5	75	98	177.3	41	55	104.2	7	13
248.7	74	97	175.5	40	54	102.4	6	12
246.8	74	96	173.7	39	53	100.5	5	10
245.0	73	95	171.9	38	52	98.7	4	10
243.2	72	94	170.0	38	51	96.9	3	8
241.4	71	92	168.2	37	50	95.1	2	7
239.5	70	91	166.4	36	49	93.2	2	6
237.7	69	90	164.5	35	48	91.4	1	5
235.9	68	89	162.7	34	47	86.6	0	4
234.0	68	88	163.3	33	46	87.7	0	3
232.2	67	87	159.1	32	45	85.9	0	2
230.4	66	86	157.2	32	44	84.1	0	1

Table 8.38 Converting Raw Scores to 6-σ Scores Performed on Three Gliding Strokes for 25 Yards or Distance

Number of Strokes	Elementary Back-Stroke		Side-Stroke		Breast-Stroke	
	Men	Women	Men	Women	Men	Women
3	100	94	100	91	84	85
4	93	87	94	86	79	80
5	85	80	88	80	73	74
6	78	73	82	75	68	69
7	71	66	75	70	62	63
8	64	59	69	64	56	58
9	56	52	63	58	51	52
10	49	44	57	53	45	46
11	42	37	50	48	40	41
12	35	30	44	42	34	35
13	28	33	38	37	29	30
14	20	16	32	31	23	24
15	13	9	25	26	18	18
16	6	2	19	20	12	13
17	0	0	13	15	6	7
18			6	10	1	2
19			0	4	0	0
20				0		

available for this purpose. This card is arranged to contain the raw score performances as well as their appropriate scale scores. These were obtained from Tables 8.34, 8.35, 8.36, 8.37, and 8.38. While raw scores cannot be summed, the scale scores can. The total of all six scale scores is the student's total, or criterion, score.

T-scores, percentage grade, and letter-grade equivalents for the total score are available for physical education majors. Students can determine their expected total score performances by consulting Table 8.39, which gives the performance grade.

tennis

Three items are proposed to measure elements of tennis skill, namely the Scott-French version of the Dyer Wallboard Test and the Broer-Miller Forehand-Backhand Drive Test.[30] The validity of the wallboard test was determined to be .61 with criteria of ratings of stroke form and footwork in college women. Reliability was estimated to be .80. Validity of the forehand-backhand tests with a criterion of ratings of ability in college

30. M. Gladys Scott and Esther French, *Measurement and Evaluation in Physical Education* (Dubuque, Iowa: Wm. C. Brown, 1959), pp. 222–225; Marion R. Broer and Donna Mae Miller, "Achievement Tests for Beginning and Intermediate Tennis," *Research Quarterly* 21 (October 1950):303–321.

Table 8.39 Conversion of Total Score to Percentage Grades and T-scores Earned by Physical Education Majors on a Six-item Swim Test

"A" T-Score	Grade		"B" T-Score	Grade		"C" T-Score	Grade		"D" T-Score	Grade		"F" T-Score	Grade	
77.6	98	518–525	67	89	448–462	55	79	370–379	43	69	294–301	31	59	218–223
76	97	510–517	66	88	440–447	54	78	364–369	42	68	286–293	30	58	210–217
75	96	502–509	64	87	432–439	52	77	356–363	40	67	278–285	28	57	202–209
74	95	494–501	63	86	424–431	51	76	348–353	39	66	270–277	27	56	194–201
73	94	486–493	62	85	418–423	50	75	340–347	38	65	264–269	26	55	186–193
72	93	478–485	61	84	410–417	49	74	332–339	37	64	256–263	25	54	178–185
70	92	472–477	60	83	402–409	48	73	324–331	36	63	248–255	24	53	170–177
69	91	464–471	58	82	394–401	46	72	318–323	34	62	240–247	22	52	162–169
68	90	456–463	57	81	386–393	45	71	310–317	33	61	232–239	21	51	158–161
			56	80	378–385	44	70	302–309	32	60	224–231	20	50	150–157
												19		142–149
												18		134–141
												17		126–133

women was .61 for beginners and .85 for intermediate skill ability. Reliability for both groups was .80.

1. *Wallboard Volley Tests.* A restraining line is drawn on the floor or ground 27½ feet (8.38 m) from a wall at least 10 feet (3.04 m) high. A net line 3 inches (7.62 cm) wide is painted on the wall 3 feet (0.914 m) above and horizontal to the floor. The volleying area is about 20 feet (6.09 m) wide. A supply of extra balls in a box is located in a back corner—the right corner for right-handed players, the left corner for left-handed players. On the signal "Go" the player drops a ball behind the restraining line, lets it hit the floor once, and then starts rallying it against the wall. The student continues to volley the ball until the signal to stop. Three 30-second trials are allowed. Each time a ball strikes above the net line one point is awarded. The player may cross the restrain-

ing line to retrieve a ball, but all strokes are to be taken from behind the restraining line. Everytime a new ball is put into play, it must be allowed to bounce once. Any tennis stroke may be used. After hitting the wall, the ball may bounce any number of times or it can be returned without a bounce from behind the restraining line.

2. *Forehand–Backhand Drive Test.* One regulation tennis court is marked off as in Figure 8.27. Two lines are drawn across the court 10 feet (3.04 m) inside the service line and 9 feet (2.74 m) outside the service line and parallel to it. Two lines are drawn across the court 5 feet (1.52 m) and 10 feet (3.04 m) respectively outside the baseline and parallel to it. Numbers are placed in the center of each area to indicate that area's scoring value. A rope is stretched 4 feet (1.21 m) above the top of the net. The player being tested stands behind the baseline, bounces

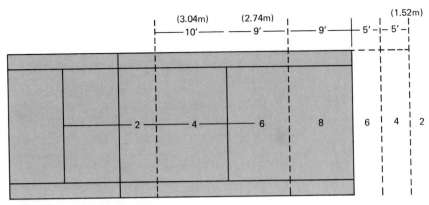

Fig. 8.27   Court Markings for
Forehand-Backhand Drive Tennis Test

the ball, hits it between the top of the net and the rope, and attempts to place it in the back 9 feet (2.74 m) of the opposite court. Each player is allowed fourteen trials on the forehand and fourteen trials on the backhand. Balls that go over the rope score one-half the value of the area in which they land. Missed balls count as a trial. Let balls are taken over. The total score is the sum of the points for all twenty-eight trials.

volleyball

The AAHPER Volleyball Test consists of four items: volleying, serving, passing, and set-ups.[31] Content validity is claimed, as are minimum reliabilities of .80 for events scored on the basis of distance and .70 for events scored on the basis of accuracy and form. Percentile rank norms for boys and girls ages 10 through 18 are presented in Tables 8.40 to 8.43.

1. Volleying. A solid smooth wall is needed with a 1-inch (2.54 cm) line marked on it that is 5 feet (1.52 m) long and 11 feet (3.35 m) above and parallel to the floor. Vertical lines that are 3 feet (0.914 m) or 4 feet (1.21 m) long extend upward from each end of the line. The player with a volleyball stands facing the wall. On the signal "Go" the ball

is tossed against the wall into the area bounded by the lines. On the rebound, the ball is volleyed into the marked area constantly for one minute. The tossed ball and each volley must strike the wall above the 11-foot (3.35 m) line and between the two vertical lines. Scoring is the total number of legal volleys executed within one minute. Tosses do not count in the score.

2. Serving. The server (X) stands opposite the marked court, as in Figure 8.28, in the proper serving position. The server may use any legal serve in hitting the ball over the net into the opposite court. For children below the age of 12, the serving line should be located 20 feet (6.09 m) from the net. The server is given ten trials. Net balls that do or do not go over count as a trial, but no points are awarded. The score is the total number of points made, as determined by where the ball lands in the opposite court. Line balls are awarded the higher score of the areas concerned.

3. Passing. The passer (X), who is the person being tested, stands in the center back position on the court, receives a high

31. American Association for Health, Physical Education and Recreation, *Skills Test Manual: Volleyball for Boys and Girls,* David K. Brace, Consultant (Washington, D.C.: AAHPER, 1969).

Table 8.40   AAHPER Volleyball Test Norms

	Volleying Test (Boys) Percentile Scores Based on Age / Test Scores in Points							Volleying Test (Girls) Percentile Scores Based on Age / Test Scores in Points							
Percentile	10–11	12	13	14	15	16	17–18	10–11	12	13	14	15	16	17–18	Percentile
100	40	42	44	50	50	50	50	47	49	49	50	50	50	50	100
95	24	31	35	39	42	44	45	21	29	31	32	37	40	40	95
90	19	28	30	36	40	41	42	13	24	25	26	31	36	38	90
85	17	24	28	33	36	38	42	10	19	20	21	24	28	31	85
80	15	22	26	31	34	36	41	8	16	17	19	21	25	27	80
75	13	19	24	29	32	34	40	6	13	15	17	18	22	23	75
70	12	18	22	27	30	33	39	5	11	13	14	16	20	20	70
65	11	17	21	26	29	32	37	4	10	11	13	15	18	18	65
60	9	16	19	24	28	30	36	3	8	10	12	13	16	16	60
55	8	15	18	23	27	28	34	3	7	9	11	12	14	14	55
50	7	13	17	21	25	26	32	2	6	8	10	11	12	12	50
45	6	12	15	19	24	25	29	2	5	7	9	10	11	11	45
40	5	11	14	18	22	23	27	1	4	6	8	9	9	9	40
35	4	9	12	17	20	21	24	1	3	5	7	8	8	8	35
30	3	8	11	15	18	19	23	1	2	4	6	7	7	7	30
25	3	7	9	13	17	18	20	0	2	3	5	6	6	6	25
20	2	6	8	11	15	16	19	0	1	1	4	5	5	5	20
15	1	4	7	9	13	15	17	0	1	1	3	4	4	4	15
10	0	3	5	7	10	12	14	0	0	0	1	2	3	3	10
5	0	2	3	5	6	11	11	0	0	0	0	1	2	2	5
0	0	0	0	0	0	0	0	0	0	0	0	0	0	0	0

Table 8.41   AAHPER Volleyball Test Norms

	Serving Test (Boys) Percentile Scores Based on Age / Test Scores in Points							Serving Test (Girls) Percentile Scores Based on Age / Test Scores in Points							
Percentile	10–11	12	13	14	15	16	17–18	10–11	12	13	14	15	16	17–18	Percentile
100	39	40	40	40	40	40	40	36	38	40	40	40	40	40	100
95	29	31	32	34	36	37	37	24	26	26	28	30	31	32	95
90	27	28	29	31	33	33	33	20	22	23	26	26	26	26	90

Table 8.41—*Continued*

Percentile	(Boys) 10–11	12	13	14	15	16	17–18	(Girls) 10–11	12	13	14	15	16	17–18	Percentile
85	25	26	27	29	32	32	32	18	20	20	23	23	24	24	85
80	23	24	26	27	30	30	31	16	18	18	21	21	22	23	80
75	22	23	24	25	28	29	30	15	16	17	20	20	21	21	75
70	21	21	23	24	28	29	30	14	15	15	18	19	20	20	70
65	20	20	22	23	27	28	29	13	14	14	17	17	19	19	65
60	18	19	21	22	25	27	27	12	13	13	15	16	18	18	60
55	17	18	20	21	24	25	26	11	12	12	14	15	17	17	55
50	16	16	19	20	22	23	24	10	11	11	13	14	16	16	50
45	15	15	18	19	21	22	22	9	10	10	11	13	15	15	45
40	14	14	17	18	20	21	21	8	9	9	10	12	14	14	40
35	13	13	16	17	19	19	20	7	8	8	9	11	13	14	35
30	12	12	15	16	18	19	19	6	6	7	8	10	13	13	30
25	11	11	13	15	16	17	17	5	5	5	7	9	11	11	25
20	9	10	12	14	15	15	16	4	4	4	6	8	10	10	20
15	8	9	10	12	12	13	14	2	3	3	5	6	8	9	15
10	7	8	8	10	11	12	12	1	1	1	3	4	7	7	10
5	4	5	5	8	9	10	11	0	0	0	1	2	4	4	5
0	0	3	3	5	6	6	7	0	0	0	0	0	0	0	0

Table 8.42   AAHPER Volleyball Test Norms

Percentile	Passing Test (Boys) *Percentile Scores Based on Age / Test Scores in Points* 10–11	12	13	14	15	16	17–18	Passing Test (Girls) *Percentile Scores Based on Age / Test Scores in Points* 10–11	12	13	14	15	16	17–18	Percentile
100	19	19	19	20	20	20	20	19	19	20	20	20	20	20	100
95	12	14	16	17	17	17	17	10	12	12	13	13	14	15	95
90	10	13	14	16	16	16	16	8	10	10	11	11	12	13	90
85	9	12	13	15	15	15	15	7	8	9	10	10	11	12	85
80	8	11	12	14	14	14	14	6	7	8	9	9	10	11	80
75	7	10	12	13	13	13	13	5	6	7	8	8	8	9	75
70	6	9	11	12	12	12	13	4	6	6	7	7	8	9	70
65	5	8	10	12	12	12	13	3	5	5	6	6	8	8	65
60	4	8	9	11	11	12	12	3	4	4	6	6	7	8	60

Table 8.42—*Continued*

	(Boys)							(Girls)							
Percentile	10–11	12	13	14	15	16	17–18	10–11	12	13	14	15	16	17–18	Percentile
55	4	7	9	10	10	12	12	2	4	4	5	5	6	7	55
50	3	6	8	10	10	11	11	2	3	4	5	5	6	6	50
45	3	5	7	9	9	10	10	1	3	3	4	4	5	6	45
40	2	4	7	8	8	9	9	1	2	3	4	4	4	5	40
35	2	4	6	8	8	9	9	0	2	2	3	3	4	4	35
30	1	3	5	7	7	8	8	0	1	2	3	3	3	4	30
25	1	2	4	6	6	7	8	0	1	1	2	2	3	3	25
20	0	2	4	5	5	6	7	0	0	1	1	2	2	3	20
15	0	1	3	4	4	5	6	0	0	0	1	1	2	2	15
10	0	0	2	3	3	4	4	0	0	0	0	1	1	1	10
5	0	0	1	2	2	2	2	0	0	0	0	0	0	0	5
0	0	0	0	0	0	0	0	0	0	0	0	0	0	0	0

throw from thrower (T), and executes a pass so that it goes over an 8-foot (2.43 m) high rope and onto one of the marked shaded areas in Figure 8.29. The passer is allowed twenty trials performed alternately to the right and to the left. The trial counts, but no points are awarded if the ball touches the rope or net, or does not fall in the target area. One point is awarded for each pass going over the rope and landing on any part of the target area.

4. Set-up. The set-up man (S) stands in mid-court position within the 6-by-5-feet (1.82-by-1.52-m) area, as shown in Figure

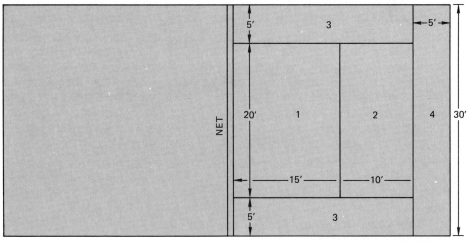

Figure 8.28 AAHPER Volleyball Serving Test

Table 8.43 AAHPER Volleyball Test Norms

Percentile	Set-up Test (Boys) Percentile Scores Based on Age / Test Scores in Points							Set-up Test (Girls) Percentile Scores Based on Age / Test Scores in Points							Percentile
	10–11	12	13	14	15	16	17–18	10–11	12	13	14	15	16	17–18	
100	16	18	20	20	20	20	20	19	20	20	20	20	20	20	100
95	10	14	16	16	16	17	17	11	13	14	14	14	15	15	95
90	9	12	14	15	15	15	15	9	11	11	12	12	12	14	90
85	8	11	13	13	13	14	15	7	9	10	10	11	11	12	85
80	7	10	12	12	12	13	14	6	8	9	10	10	10	11	80
75	6	9	11	11	11	12	13	5	7	8	9	9	9	10	75
70	6	8	10	10	10	10	11	5	6	7	8	8	8	8	70
65	5	8	9	9	9	9	11	4	6	7	7	7	7	7	65
60	5	7	8	8	8	9	10	4	5	6	6	6	7	7	60
55	4	7	7	8	8	8	10	3	5	5	6	6	6	6	55
50	4	6	7	7	7	7	9	3	4	5	5	5	6	6	50
45	3	6	6	6	6	6	9	2	4	4	4	4	5	5	45
40	3	5	6	6	6	6	8	2	3	4	4	4	5	5	40
35	3	5	5	5	5	5	7	2	3	3	3	3	4	4	35
30	2	4	4	5	5	5	7	1	2	3	3	3	3	4	30
25	2	4	4	4	4	4	6	1	2	2	2	2	3	3	25
20	2	3	3	4	4	4	6	1	2	2	2	2	2	3	20
15	1	3	3	3	3	3	5	0	1	1	1	1	2	2	15
10	0	1	1	2	2	2	2	0	0	1	1	1	1	1	10
5	0	1	1	1	1	1	2	0	0	0	0	0	1	1	5
0	0	0	0	0	0	0	1	0	0	0	0	0	0	0	0

8.30. The set-up person receives a high throw from thrower (T), and executes a set-up so that it goes over a rope 30 feet (9.14 m) long and onto the target area. The rope is 10 feet (3.04 m) high for boys and 9 feet (2.74 m) high for girls. Two pupils may be tested simultaneously, one setting the ball to the right and the other to the left. Throws from T that do not fall into the set-up position area are to be repeated. The set-up person has ten trials to the right and ten to the left. The trial counts but no points are recorded if the ball touches the rope or net, or does not fall into the target area. One point is scored for each set-up that goes over the rope and lands on any part of the target area including lines.

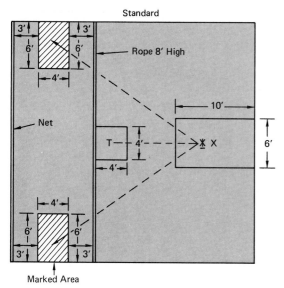

Figure 8.29   AAHPER Volleyball Passing Test

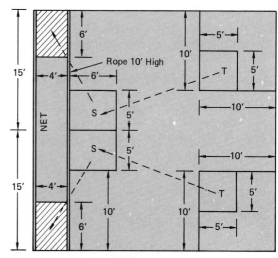

Figure 8.30   AAHPER Volleyball Set-up Test (Two Stations for Right and Left)

brief bibliography of sport skill tests

archery

American Association for Health, Physical Education, and Recreation. *Skills Test Manual: Archery.* David K. Brace, Consultant. Washington, D.C.: AAHPER, 1967.

Hyde, Edith I. "An Achievement Scale in Archery." *Research Quarterly* 8 (1937): 109.

badminton

Davis, Phillis R. "The Development of a Combined Short and Long Badminton Service Skill Test." Master's thesis, University of Tennessee, 1968.

Hicks, Joanna V. "The Construction and Evaluation of a Battery of Five Badminton Skill Tests." Doctoral dissertation, Texas Woman's University, 1967.

Lockhart, Aileene, and McPherson, Frances. "Development of a Test of Badminton Playing Ability." *Research Quarterly* 20 (1949):402–405.

Miller, Frances A. "A Badminton Wall Volley Test." *Research Quarterly* 22 (1951):208–213.

Scott, M. Gladys; Carpenter, Aileen; French, Esther; and Kuhl, Louise. "Achievement Examinations in Badminton." *Research Quarterly* 12, no. 2 (1941):242–253.

basketball

American Association for Health, Physical Education, and Recreation. *Skills Test Manual: Basketball for Boys.* David K. Brace, Consultant. Washington, D.C.: AAHPER, 1966.

American Association for Health, Physical Education, and Recreation. *Skills Test Manual: Basketball for Girls:* David K. Brace, Consultant. Washington, D.C.: AAHPER, 1966.

Barrow, Harold M. "Basketball Skill Test." *Physical Educator* 16 (1959):26–27.

Edgren, H. D. "An Experiment in the Testing of Ability and Progress in Basketball." *Research Quarterly* 3 (1932):159–171.

Johnson, L. W. "Objective Test in Basketball for High School Boys." Master's thesis, State University of Iowa, 1934.

Knox, Robert D. "Basketball Ability Test." *Scholastic Coach* 17 (1947):45.

Leilich, Avis. "The Primary Components of Selected Basketball Tests for College Women." Doctoral dissertation, Indiana University, 1952.

Mortimer, Elizabeth M. "Basketball Shooting." *Research Quarterly* 22 (1951):234–243.

Voltmer, E. F., and Watts, Ted. "A Rating Scale for Player Performance in Basketball." *Journal of Health and Physical Education* 2 (1947): 94–95.

bowling

Martin, Joan L. "A Way to Measure Bowling Success." *Research Quarterly* 31 (1960): 113–116.

Martin, Joan, and Keogh, Jack. "Bowling Norms for College Students in Elective Physical Education Classes." *Research Quarterly* 35 (1964): 325–327.

Olson, Janice, and Liba, Marie R. "A Device for Evaluating Spot Bowling Ability." *Research Quarterly* 38 (1967): 193–201.

Phillips, Marjorie, and Summers, Dean. "Bowling Norms and Learning Curves for College Women." *Research Quarterly* 21 (1950):377–385.

fencing

Cooper, C. K. "The Development of a Fencing Skill Test for Measuring Achievement of Beginning Collegiate Women Fencers in Using the Advance, Beat, and Lunge." Master's thesis, Western Illinois University, 1968.

Safrit, M. J. "Construction of a Skill Test for Beginning Fencers." Master's thesis, University of Wisconsin, 1962.

field hockey

Friedel, J. W. "The Development of a Field Hockey Skill Test for High School Girls." Master's thesis, Illinois State Normal University, 1956.

Schmithals, M., and French, E. "Achievement Tests in Field Hockey for College Women." *Research Quarterly* 11, no. 3 (1940): pp. 83–92.

football

American Association for Health, Physical Education, and Recreation. *Skills Test Manual: Football.* David K. Brace, Consultant. Washington, D.C.: AAHPER, 1965.

Cowell, C. C., and Ismail, A. H. "Validity of a Football Rating Scale and Its Relationship to Social Integration and Academic Ability." *Research Quarterly* 32, no. 4 (1961):461–467.

Lee, Robert C. "A Battery of Tests to Predict Football Potential." Master's thesis, University of Utah, 1965.

golf

Bowen, Robert T. "Putting Errors of Beginning Golfers Using Different Points of Aim." *Research Quarterly* 39 (1968): 31–35.

McKee, Mary E. "A Test for the Full-Swing Shot in Golf." *Research Quarterly* 21 (1950):40–46.

West, Charlotte, and Thorpe, Jo Anne. "Construction and Validation of an Eight-Iron Approach Test." *Research Quarterly* 39 (1968):1115–1120.

gymnastics

Amateur Athletic Union (AAU). *Gymnastics Guide.* AAU, 231 W. 58th St., New York. (Publication updated regularly.)

American Association for Health, Physical Education, and Recreation, Division of Girls' and Women's Sports (DGWS). *Gymnastic Guide.* Washington, D.C.: AAHPER. (Publication updated regularly.)

Harris, J. Patrick. "A Design for a Proposed Skill Proficiency Test in Tumbling and Apparatus for Male Physical Education Majors at the University of North Dakota." Master's thesis, University of North Dakota, 1966.

Johnson, Barry L. "A Screening Test for Pole Vaulting and Selected Gymnastic Events." *Journal of Health, Physical Education, and Recreation* 44 (1973): 71–72.

United States Gymnastic Federation (USGF). *Age Group Workbook.* USGF, P.O. Box 4699, Tucson, Arizona. (Publication updated regularly.)

handball

Cornish, Clayton. "A Study of Measurement of Ability in Handball." *Research Quarterly* 20 (1949):215–222.

Montoye, H. J., and Brotzman, J. "An Investigation of the Validity of Using the Results of a Doubles Tournament as a Measure of Handball Ability." *Research Quarterly* 22 (1951):214–218.

Pennington, G. Gary; Day, James A. P.; Drowatsky, John N.; and Hanson, John. "A Measure of Handball Ability." *Research Quarterly* 38 (1967):247–253.

lacrosse

Lutze, M. C. "Achievement Tests in Beginning Lacrosse for Women." Master's thesis, State University of Iowa, 1963.

Wilke, B. J. "Achievement Tests for Selected Lacrosse Skills of College Women." Master's thesis, University of North Carolina, 1967.

soccer and speedball

Buchanan, Ruth E. "A Study of Achievement Tests in Speedball for High School Girls." Master's thesis, State University of Iowa, 1942.

MacKenzie, John. "The Evaluation of a Battery of Soccer Skill Test as an Aid to Classification of General Soccer Ability." Master's thesis, University of Massachusetts, 1968.

Schaufele, Evelyn F. "The Establishment of Objective Tests for Girls of the Ninth and Tenth Grades to Determine Soccer Ability." Master's thesis, State University of Iowa, 1940.

softball and baseball

American Association for Health, Physical Education, and Recreation. *Skills Test Manual: Softball for Boys.* David K. Brace, Consultant. Washington, D.C.: AAHPER, 1966.

American Association for Health, Physical Education, and Recreation. *Skills Test Manual: Softball for Girls.* David K. Brace, Consultant. Washington, D.C.: AAHPER, 1966.

Everett, Peter W. "The Prediction of Baseball Ability." *Research Quarterly* 23 (1952): 15–19.

Finger, Margaret N. "A Battery of Softball Skill Tests for Senior High School Girls." Master's thesis, University of Michigan, 1961.

Fox, Margaret G., and Young, Olive G. "A Test of Softball Batting Ability." *Research Quarterly* 25 (1954):26–27.

Kelson, Robert E. "Baseball Classification Plan for Boys." *Research Quarterly* 24 (1953):304–309.

Shick, Jacqueline. "Battery of Defensive Softball Skills Tests for College Women." *Research Quarterly* 41 (1970):82–87.

swimming and diving

Arrasmith, Jean L. "Swimming Classification Test for College Women." Doctoral dissertation, University of Oregon, 1967.

Bennett, LaVerne M. "A Test of Diving for Use in Beginning Classes." *Research Quarterly* 13 (1942):109–115.

Durrant, Sue M. "An Analytical Method of Rating Synchronized Swimming Stunts." *Research Quarterly* 35 (1964):126–134.

Fox, Margaret G. "Swimming Power Test." *Research Quarterly* 28 (1957):233–237.

Hewitt, Jack E. "Achievement Scale Scores for High School Swimming." *Research Quarterly* 20 (1949):170–179.

Hewitt, Jack E. "Swimming Achievement Scale Scores for College Men." *Research Quarterly* 12 (1948):282–289.

Rosentsweig, Joel. "A Revision of the Power Swimming Test." *Research Quarterly* 39 (1968):818–819.

table tennis

Mott, J.A., and Lockhart, A. "Table Tennis Backboard Test." *Journal of Health and Physical Education* 17 (1946):550–552.

tennis

Broer, Marian R., and Miller, Donna Mae. "Achievement Tests for Beginning and Intermediate Tennis." *Research Quarterly* 21 (October 1950):303–321.

Cotten, Doyice J., and Nixon, Jane. "A Comparison of Two Methods of Teaching the Tennis Serve." *Research Quarterly* 39 (1968):929–931.

DiGennaro, Joseph. "Construction of Forehand Drive, Backhand Drive, and Serve Tennis Tests." *Research Quarterly* 40 (1969): 496–501.

Dyer, Joanna T. "Revision of the Backboard Test of Tennis Ability." *Research Quarterly* 9 (1938):25–31.

Hewitt, Jack E. "Classification Tests in Tennis." *Research Quarterly* 39 (1968):552–555.

Kemp, Joann, and Vincent, Marilyn F. "Kemp-Vincent Rally Test of Tennis Skill." *Research Quarterly* 29 (1964): 1000–1004.

Timmer, Karen L. "A Tennis Test to Determine Accuracy in Playing Ability." Master's thesis, Springfield College, 1965.

volleyball

American Association for Health, Physical Education, and Recreation, *Skills Test Manual: Volleyball for Boys and Girls.* Clayton Shay, Consultant. Washington, D.C.: AAHPER, 1969.

Brady, George F. "Preliminary Investigations of Volleyball Playing Ability." *Research Quarterly* 16 (1946):14–17.

Clifton, Marguerite A. "Single Hit Volley Test for Women's Volleyball." *Research Quarterly* 33 (1962):208–211.

Crogan, Corrine. "A Simple Volleyball Classification Test for High School Girls." *Physical Educator* 4 (1943):34–37.

Cunningham, Phyllis, and Garrison, Joan. "High Wall Volley Test for Women's Volleyball." *Research Quarterly* 8, no. 2 (1937).

French, Ester L., and Cooper, Bernice I. "Achievement Tests in Volleyball for High School Girls." *Research Quarterly* 8, no. 2 (1937).

Kronqvist, Robert A., and Brumbach, Wayne. "A Modification of the Brady Volleyball Skill Test for High School Boys." *Research Quarterly* 39 (1968):116–120.

Lamp, Nancy A. "Volleyball Skills for Junior High School Students as a Function of Physical Size and Maturity." *Research Quarterly* 25 (1954):189–200.

Liba, Marie R., and Stauff, Marilyn R. "A Test for the Volleyball Pass." *Research Quarterly* 34 (1963):56–63.

Mohr, Dorothy R., and Haverstick, Martha V. "Repeated Volleys Test for Women's Volleyball." *Research Quarterly* 26 (1955):179–184.

Russel, Naomi, and Lange, Elizabeth. "Achievement Tests in Volleyball for Junior High School Girls." *Research Quarterly* 11 (1940):33–41.

wrestling

Yetter, H. "A Test of Wrestling Aptitude." Master's thesis, University of Wisconsin, 1963.

general motor measures

For almost a half century physical educators have clung to the belief that performance in a variety of select motor tasks gives an indication of a child's general motor ability. Information from such testing is thought to enable teachers and coaches to identify quickly the successful athlete, to predict which pupils will do well in a physical education class, or to classify pupils into different ability groups in order to enhance instruction. Before investigating the credibility of this traditional belief, we should first make a distinction between ability and skill as used by specialists in motor learning.[32]

Motor ability is thought to be a general quality that can facilitate more specific fu-

ture performances. That is, motor ability is viewed as an underlying contributor to future success in more specific motor tasks. From birth through early childhood, the individual learns to grasp, to manipulate, and to throw an object. Gradually, the child develops the necessary strength, flexibility, and coordination of appropriate muscle groups to throw a ball a certain distance. We observe the child and indicate that the child possesses throwing ability to some degree. A number of children may exhibit the same motor pattern of throwing. Later these children become interested in different sports. One becomes a catcher in baseball and must develop a new throwing pattern—a specific throwing skill for a specific sport. Another pupil trains to throw the javelin, and another becomes a quarterback in football and learns to pass the ball. Thus, different sports and games require unique throwing patterns or skills; at the same time, they also require unique combinations of strength, flexibility, coordination, balance, speed, timing, and so on.

general motor ability and educability tests

Many general motor ability (GMA) and general motor educability (GME) tests have been proposed that authorities in the past have claimed measure those fundamental general motor qualities thought to be important for successful participation in sports and games. These fundamental general motor abilities are thought to be determined by both genetic and early environmental stimulation. The concepts of *GMA* and *GME* have been presented to physical educators as the Intelligence Quotient (IQ) has been presented to

32. Stallings, *Motor Skills: Development and Learning*, p. 7; Schmidt, *Motor Skills*, p. 120.

psychologists. Both the GME and IQ tests are thought to assess those components basic to future success in motor and cognitive skills. The logic involved is: If a child cannot play a game well, she has not yet developed her general motor abilities. A psychologist may claim that a boy who is doing poorly in reading and arithmetic has an IQ score below normal. To some extent, one cannot fault this logic, especially when it is applied in an individualized diagnostic setting.

General motor ability tests are thought to assess the motor abilities of speed, muscular strength and endurance, power, kinesthesis, eye-hand coordination, eye-foot coordination, agility, flexibility, timing, and sensory motor rhythm. A test item is developed to estimate each component. A composite score is computed for all test items. This composite score becomes the criterion for test validity. Through the data reduction technique of multiple correlation, a relationship is determined between the composite score and a subset of three to five items. Two example tests of GMA are the Scott test for high school and college women and the Barrow test for high school and college men. These and other tests of GMA and GME can be found in the Barrow and McGee, Clarke, Carleton Meyers and T. Erwin Blesh, and Donald Mathews measurement texts.[33] The test items for the Scott and Barrow tests are as follows:

Scott GMA Test	*Barrow GMA Test*
obstacle race	standing broad jump
basketball throw	softball throw
standing broad jump	zigzag run
wall pass	wall pass
4-second dash	medicine ball put
	60-yard dash

Tests of *general motor educability* are proposed as devices that disclose the rapidity with which a child learns motor skills.

The test items are supposed to be unfamiliar motor tasks that the child performs. If a child performs these strange tasks correctly, it is thought that he will experience little difficulty in learning future motor skills. These tests can also be termed motor aptitude tests or tests of motor learning potential. A number of motor educability tests have been developed and, as mentioned, are reviewed in the texts just cited. The twenty-one items comprising the Iowa Brace Motor Educability Test are listed as follows:

1. From side leaning rest position on the right side, raise left arm and leg and hold for 5 seconds.
2. Hold a one-knee balance on the floor for 5 seconds with arms sideward at shoulder level.
3. From balance position in 2, touch head to floor and recover.
4. Standing on one foot, eyes closed, take 5 hops backward, maintaining position.
5. Three push-ups.
6. Jump, swing legs forward and touch toes with hand, not bending knees more than 45 degrees.
7. Full left turn.
8. Double heel click.
9. Move arms in a circle 1 foot in diameter with arms horizontally to the side while bouncing up and down from a full squat position for 10 seconds.
10. Loop jump.
11. Standing on the left foot, jump and make a half-left turn.
12. Swing left leg to the side, jump up with

33. Barrow and McGee, *A Practical Approach to Measurement in Physical Education,* pp. 157–190; H. Harrison Clarke, *Application of Measurement to Health and Physical Education,* 5th ed. (Englewood Cliffs, N.J.: Prentice Hall, 1976), pp. 227–246; Carlton R. Meyers and T. Erwin Blesh, *Measurement in Physical Education* (New York: Ronald Press Co., 1962), pp. 298–332; Donald K. Mathews, *Measurement in Physical Education,* 5th ed. (Philadelphia: W. B. Saunders Co., 1978), pp. 177–224.

right leg, clap feet and land with feet apart.
13. Foot-touch-head.
14. Grapevine.
15. Full right turn.
16. Kneeling jump.
17. Crossed leg sit.
18. Stork stand.
19. Do a Russian dance step by alternately raising legs forward, twice on each side; heel of extended leg may touch the floor.
20. From a sitting position, with lower legs flexed and on the floor, arms under knees, and hands grasping ankles, roll as a top onto right knee, right shoulder, back, left shoulder and knee and recover. Do twice to complete circle.
21. While squatting on either foot, hands on hips, raise other leg forward and hold for 5 seconds.

critique

Tests of general motor ability and general educability are usually proposed to achieve the purposes of predicting learning potential and athletic ability, selecting athletes from a large number of team candidates, and classifying pupils into different groups for physical education instruction. During the past twenty years, much research has been conducted into the effectiveness of general motor measures to achieve these purposes. This research has been well reviewed in the motor learning texts of Stallings, Schmidt, Robert Singer, and John Lawther, to mention a few.[34] A brief summary of these readings reveals the following:

1. General motor ability test scores usually do not correlate well enough with bowling, tennis, basketball, and track and field scores to justify use of these tests to predict future performance. The same can be said for tests of general motor educability. These failed to correlate sufficiently with tests of athletic ability, as well as with learning water skills, tennis, volleyball, field hockey, and wrestling.

2. If one were to use a general test to classify pupils into discrete ability groups at the beginning of a unit of instruction, the classification would soon be of little value. This is because the performance variability (differences) within each group increases as instruction progresses, indicating that differences increase in the rate and amount of pupil learning over time.

3. Motor skills used at the beginning of instruction change in terms of complexity and pattern of execution at more advanced stages of learning. This, plus the information in point 2, partly explains the generally low relationships found between initial and final skill test scores.

4. Frances Cumbee and Chester Harris reveal that use of the composite score as a criterion is a poor technique for test validation since you are essentially correlating the GMA test score with one component.[35] In addition, these multiple correlations are generally inflated because the same items appear in both the test and the composite score.

In summary, the use of general motor measures to classify for instruction, or to predict athletic ability or rate of learning is a questionable practice since the evidence does not seem to warrant such use. Indeed, some question the existence of general motor ability. However, learning of any type is always based on a foundation of prior

34. Stallings, *Motor Skills: Development and Learning,* pp. 103–118; Schmidt, *Motor Skills,* pp. 117–129; Robert N. Singer, *Motor Learning and Human Performance* (New York: Macmillan, 1968), pp. 106–115; John D. Lawther, *The Learning and Performance of Physical Skills,* 2d ed. (Englewood Cliffs, N.J.: Prentice-Hall, 1977), pp. 198–230.
35. Frances Z. Cumbee and Chester W. Harris, "The Composite Criterion and Its Relation to Factor Analysis," *Research Quarterly* 24 (May 1953):127–134.

experiences. As one gets older and progresses through the many motor tasks of childhood, physical activities and skills become more and more specific. Specificity of skills is seen in the low relationship between initial and final score studies. Teaching is more of an art than a science. If you want to classify for instruction, select a test that simulates the particular sport or activity to be learned. But remember, you may have to continuously reclassify some pupils into different ability groups as instruction progresses and you observe various rates of improvement taking place. Make changes when so indicated. Do not "pigeonhole" or "type" a person into a category for a long time because of a preinstruction test score. This action may keep a student in the wrong group and result in low achievement levels; it could also have unfavorable emotional repercussions on the pupil.

One should not get the impression that the general motor measures are of little value to practitioners. On the contrary, they may be of great value at the right age and grade level. Many of the test items can be used in a motor diagnostic clinic to help discover the deficiencies that may be at the root of a child's lack of motor development.

classification methods

Classification is usually defined as the placement of pupils into a homogeneous (similar ability) group or a heterogeneous (differing ability) group based on some common trait or ability. In the first case, pupils are grouped into one of three discrete groups such as beginning, intermediate, or advanced swimming ability. In the second case, pupils are placed on teams in such a way that the teams are equal in strength—this leads to a better competitive atmosphere. Although pupil abilities within a team differ, the goal—

developing teams of equal strength—is accomplished.

The general purposes for using a classification technique may be listed as follows:
1. To create a more effective teaching atmosphere. Teachers need to prepare for only one general ability level within a class. Pupils feel more comfortable knowing that their classmates have similar abilities.
2. Classification produces an atmosphere conducive to motivating pupil participation and performance.
3. Classification makes activities more adaptable to students' interests, needs, and abilities.
4. Classification provides a better basis for evaluating the individual and group performance. Pupils recognize that their performance is being compared to other pupils similar to them in terms of body size and other relevant qualities.
5. A better competitive atmosphere is developed with teams of equal skill and strength.
6. Classification increases the safety factor in competitive sports. This is why we have weight categories in boxing, wrestling, and football.

In reviewing the literature one finds the following methods recommended for classifying people. Teachers must decide which method best suits their instructional goals.

1. *Medical Examination.* This is recommended as the first basis of classification the physical educator should employ. Based on the results of an examination by a physician, a pupil is placed into one of three categories—unlimited participation in all physical education and athletic programs, somewhat restricted activity, and restricted activity. The last two categories require close cooperation among appropriate medical, school, and physical edu-

cation experts in order to diagnose and prescribe appropriate adapted physical education activities.

2. *Sex.* Even taking into consideration the recent proper trend toward coeducational instruction in physical education, there are still some activities such as tackle football and wrestling that should not be offered on a coed basis. Achievement scales, too, such as the archery scales in this chapter, should provide for sex differences.

3. *Interest.* Students classify themselves or select activities of interest to them in elective programs in physical education classes and in intramural and varsity athletic programs.

4. *Age or Grade.* This seems to be the most common technique employed as it is administratively convenient for school authorities to schedule people into classes based on age or grade. When employed in physical education, however, it tells the teacher nothing about the motor abilities of pupils.

5. *Functional Ability.* This is the most specific and logical technique to employ after the medical examination. If a teacher is involved in swimming instruction, a swimming skill test can identify the beginning, intermediate, and advanced swimmers. Note that age or grade cannot provide the teacher with information about swimming ability.

6. *Physical Maturity.* In the 1920s Neilson and Cozens found that two general factors account for successful motor performance, namely, a "body size" factor and a "participation" (skill) factor. This finding substantiated the notion that "structure permits function." As a result, easy-to-use age and height and weight indices were developed by Neilson and Cozens and McCloy. These are to be taken as indicators of physical maturity.

Directions for using the devices appear in Meyers and Blesh, Clarke, and Mathews.[36] As recently as 1961, A. H. Ismail and C. C. Cowell also identified a growth and maturity factor as the most important factor in the motor performance of preadolescent boys.[37] They also found that the boys' standing height was the most influential of the three variables— age, height, and weight—in naming this factor. Height, weight, and age correlated .92, .84, and .75 respectively with the McCloy Classification Index. The classification indices are as follows:

Neilson-Cozens Classification Index for High School Boys
(20 × age) + 5.55 (Height) + (Weight)

McCloy Classification Index I for High School Boys
(20 × age) + (6 × Height) + (Weight)

McCloy Index II for College Men
(6 × Height) + (Weight)

McCloy Index III for Elementary School Boys
(10 × age) + (Height)

A correlation of .98 between the McCloy Index I and the Neilson-Cozens Index is reported in the references previously cited. Thus, the teacher can use either scheme in her class. McCloy reports that a correlation of .82 exists between Index I and success in track and field events.[38] Indeed, the indices

36. Meyers and Blesh, *Measurement in Physical Education,* pp. 312–315; Clarke, *Application of Measurement to Health and Physical Education,* pp. 245–246, 407; Mathews, *Measurement in Physical Education,* pp. 182–184.

37. A. H. Ismail and C. C. Cowell, "Factor Analysis of Motor Aptitude of Preadolescent Boys," *Research Quarterly* 32 (December 1961):507–513.

38. Charles H. McCloy and Norma D. Young, *Tests and Measurements in Health and Physical Education,* 3d ed. (New York: Appleton-Century-Crofts, 1954), p. 62.

seem to be very useful for classifying boys and girls into groups of different body size for instruction and participation in events that are heavily dependent on muscular strength, endurance, speed, and power.

Physical maturity and body structure should also be considered when constructing norm charts. Thus, a boy or girl can compare their performances against those of children with similar body size. The AAHPER norm charts using percentile ranks for each age, which appear in chapter 10, illustrate this principle. In these charts, age is the only differentiating variable in growth and development. This is due to the fact that Anna Espenschade, in studying the motor performances of over 7,600 boys and girls age 10 through 18, found that height and weight added very little additional information to the relationship between age and motor performance.[39] Thus, age is recommended as a quick classifier of physical maturity of children. It is *not* incorrect to use age, height, and weight in combination, but it does save time to use age alone, and using age does secure essentially the same results. Of course, maturity and body structure will vary within the same age group. Certainly we expect children of 12 years and 11 months old to be taller and heavier than children who are 12 years and 1 day old. Also, there is a negative relationship between body weight and some muscular performance items such as pull-ups and dips. This relationship is not taken into account in contemporary norm charts. There is more discussion of this point in chapter 10. Researchers are currently seeking a solution that will take this variability into account when developing norms. This is important because when using norm charts as references in September and June, the current age norms do not permit us to determine if improvements are due to growth or to the effect of our programs.

In summary, classifying by physical maturity for instructional purposes means only that pupils in a given class will be of similar size. You may still have to use a functional skill test to determine ability groupings within a class.

choosing teams in physical education classes and for intramural competition

1. *Choosing by Secret Ballot*

One rather unusual method of selecting teams starts with the election of captains. By secret ballot, each pupil in the class is asked to nominate two class members whom they believe will make the best captains. These votes are then tabulated and the four individuals receiving the largest number of votes become the captains.

To start team selection, each captain is allowed to pick one person to be co-captain. Usually, these selections are made from the class roster before school or during a conference period.

After this, it is the duty of the captains (with the aid of the teacher) to divide the rest of the class into four teams of equal strength. Captains do not know which team will be theirs until every class member has been assigned. The teams are then assigned to the captains and co-captains by means of a drawing.

Since none of the captains knows which team will be assigned to him eventually, he does his best to make sure that all teams are equally good. When the teams have been equalized to the greatest degree possible, and all four captains agree that they would

39. Anna S. Espenschade, "Restudy of Relationships Between Physical Performance of School Children and Age, Height, and Weight," *Research Quarterly* 34, no. 2 (1963):144–153.

be satisfied with any one team, the drawing is made.

No class member may act as a captain twice within the same semester, and since new teams may be selected every six weeks or so, many pupils receive leadership experience through being a captain.

2. *Choosing by Height*

Another way of selecting teams is to line the class up according to height and have it count off by fours. All number 1s become a team; and all number 2s, number 3s, and number 4s become other teams. Each selects its own captain and co-captain. On rare occasions, one team may be much superior to any of the others and some adjustment may have to be made by the teacher.

3. *Skill Test Scores (Functional Basis)*

A third way to select teams is to administer a skill test to all. Rank people on the basis of their test scores and assign them to teams. For example, to get thirty players into five basketball, teams, divide the players as follows:

	Team A	Team B	Team C	Team D	Team E
Players' ranks	1	2	3	4	5
	10	9	8	7	6
	11	12	13	14	15
	20	19	18	17	16
	21	22	23	24	25
	30	29	28	27	26

Compute the mean and standard deviation for each group and, if all are the same, we have teams of equal strength based on the skill test scores. We can also have the various teams or squads (shown vertically) compete in actual play, and have horizontal squads work on skills and drilling.

the psychomotor domain

Chapters 7 and 13, which deal with test construction and measurement in the affective domain, each open with an example of the cognitive domain and the affective domain as applied to physical education. This approach was not used in this chapter on motor skills testing since there is little agreement in the professional literature as to the content of a psychomotor domain. Indeed, John Gilchrist and Joseph Gruber have shown that by 1980 at least twelve separate and distinct taxonomies of the psychomotor domain had been presented.[40] There appears to be as much overlap as specificity among the various taxonomies. Obviously, if physical educators feel it important to identify the elements in the psychomotor domain, some sort of study protocol will have to be adopted so the most pertinent domain content that meets professional needs may be identified.

summary review questions

1. What are the steps in constructing a test of motor performance? (*answer on p. 132*)

2. What are discrete and serial performances and open and closed performance environments? (*answer on p. 133*)

3. Why is it more appropriate to test beginners on *discrete skills* in a *closed performance environment* and intermediate or advanced students on *serial skills* in an *open performance environment*? (*answer on p. 133*)

40. John R. Gilchrist and Joseph J. Gruber, "The Psychomotor Domain," in *Encyclopedia of Physical Education*, vol. 5 (Reading, Mass.: Addison-Wesley, in press [1980]).

4. Evaluation involves testing, measuring, and, above all, professional judgment in making decisions. In what ways can the measurement results from discrete skill testing in a closed performance environment and serial skill testing in an open performance environment help the practicing physical education teacher in formative and summative evaluation? (*answer on pp. 133–135*)

5. What is a motor ability? (*answer on p. 213*)

6. What is a GMA test supposed to measure? (*answer on p. 213*)

7. What are the components of a motor skill? (*answer on p. 213*)

8. What is a general motor educability test supposed to measure? (*answer on p. 214*)

9. Explain why the decision-making model, presented in chapter 1, helps the physical education teacher classify students for instruction. (*answer on p. 216*)

10. What are the methods listed in this chapter for classification of students? (*answer on p. 216*)

bibliography

American Association for Health, Physical Education and Recreation. *Skills Test Manual: Archery.* David K. Brace, Consultant. Washington, D.C.: AAHPER, 1967.

———. *Skills Test Manual: Football.* David K. Brace, Consultant, Washington, D.C.: AAHPER, 1965.

———. *Skills Test Manual: Softball for Boys.* David K. Brace, Consultant. Washington, D.C.: AAHPER, 1966.

———. *Skills Test Manual: Softball for Girls.* David K. Brace, Consultant. Washington, D.C.: AAHPER, 1966.

———. *Skills Test Manual: Volleyball for Boys and Girls.* David K. Brace, Consultant. Washington, D.C.: AAHPER, 1969.

American National Red Cross. *Manual for the Basic Swimming Instructor.* Washington, D.C.: The American National Red Cross, 1974.

Barrett, Jean. *Archery.* Pacific Palisades, Calif.: Goodyear Publishing, 1969.

Barrow, Harold, and McGee, Rosemary. *A Practical Approach to Measurement in Physical Education.* 2d ed. Philadelphia: Lea and Febiger, 1971.

Baumgartner, Ted, and Jackson, Andrew. *Measurement for Evaluation in Physical Education.* Boston: Houghton Mifflin, 1975.

Broer, Marion, and Miller, Donna Mae. "Achievement Test for Beginning and Intermediate Tennis," *Research Quarterly* 21 (October 1950):303–321.

Cowell, C. C., and Ismail, A. H. "Validity of a Football Rating Scale and Its Relationship to Social Integration and Academic Ability." *Research Quarterly* 32, no. 4 (1961):461–467.

Cumbee, Frances, and Harris, Chester. "The Composite Criterion and Its Relation to Factor Analysis," *Research Quarterly* 24 (May 1953):127–134.

Espenschade, Anna. "Restudy of Relationships Between Physical Performance of School Children and Age, Height, and Weight." *Research Quarterly* 34, no. 2 (1963):144–153.

Faulkner, John, and Luttgens, Kathryn. "Introduction to Sports Skill Testing." In *An Introduction to Measurement in Physical Education,* edited by Henry J. Montoye. Boston: Allyn and Bacon, 1978.

Gilchrist, John, and Gruber, Joseph. "The Psychomotor Domain." In *Encyclopedia of Physical Education.* vol. 5. Reading, Mass.: Addison Wesley, 1980.

Haskins, Mary Jane. *Evaluation in Physical Education.* Dubuque, Iowa: Wm. C. Brown, 1971.

Ismail, A. H., and Cowell, C. C. "Factor Analysis of Motor Aptitude of Preadolescent Boys," *Research Quarterly* 32, no. 4 (1961):507–513.

Johnson, Barry, and Nelson, Jack. *Practical Measurements for Evaluation in Physical Education.* 3d ed. Minneapolis: Burgess, 1979.

Kerr, Beth, and Smoll, Frank. "Variability in Individual Student Performance: Implications for Teachers." *Motor Skills: Theory into Practice* 1, no. 2 (1977): 75–86.

Lawther, John. *The Learning and Performance of Physical Skills.* 2d ed. Englewood Cliffs, N.J.: Prentice-Hall, 1977.

McCloy, Charles, and Young, Norma. *Tests and Measurements in Health and Physical Education.* 3d ed. New York: Appleton-Century-Crofts, 1954.

Mathews, Donald. *Measurement in Physical Education.* 5th ed. Philadelphia: W. B. Saunders, 1978.

Meyers, Carlton, and Blesh, T. Erwin. *Measurement in Physical Education.* New York: The Ronald Press, 1962.

Miller, Frances. "A Badminton Wall Volley Test." *Research Quarterly* 22, no. 2 (1951):208–213.

Miller, Wilma. "Achievement Levels in Basketball Skills for Women Physical Education Majors." *Research Quarterly* 25, no. 4 (1954):450–455.

Montoye, Henry. *An Introduction to Measurement in Physical Education.* Boston: Allyn and Bacon, 1978.

Safrit, Margaret. *Evaluation in Physical Education: Assessing Motor Behavior.* Englewood Cliffs, N.J.: Prentice-Hall, 1973.

Schmidt, Richard. *Motor Skills.* New York: Harper and Row, 1975.

Schmithals, Margaret, and French, Esther. "Achievement Tests in Field Hockey for College Women." *Research Quarterly* 11, no. 3 (1940):83–92.

Scott, M. Gladys et al. "Achievement Examinations in Badminton." *Research Quarterly* 12, no. 2 (1941): 242–253.

Scott, M. Gladys, and French, Esther. *Measurement and Evaluation in Physical Education.* Dubuque, Iowa: Wm. C. Brown, 1959.

Singer, Robert. *Motor Learning and Human Performance.* New York: Macmillan, 1968.

Stallings, Loretta. *Motor Skills: Development and Learning.* Dubuque, Iowa: Wm. C. Brown, 1973.

Stroup, Francis. "Game Results as Criterion for Validating Basketball Skill Test." *Research Quarterly* 26, no. 3 (1955):353–357.

Torney, John, and Clayton, Robert. *Aquatic Instruction: Coaching and Management.* Minneapolis: Burgess, 1970.

Vanderhoff, Ellen. "Beginning Golf Achievement Tests." Masters thesis, State University of Iowa, 1956.

exercises

1. The following 12-year-old male students had a calculated composite score on the AAHPER Archery Test: S1 = 87, S2 = 67, S3 = 98, S4 = 93, S5 = 54, S6 = 38, S7 = 81, S8 = 74, S9 = 60, S10 = 47. What is the percentile rank of each from the national norm table (Table 8.1)?

   Answer:
   (S1 = 55%, S2 = 40%, S3 = 65%, S4 = 60%, S5 = 30%, S6 = 20%, S7 = 50%, S8 = 45%, S9 = 35%, S10 = 25%)

2. The following 12-year-old female students had a calculated composite score on the AAHPER Archery Test: S1 = 42, S2 = 55, S3 = 38, S4 = 50, S5 = 46, S6 = 35, S7 = 60, S8 = 64, S9 = 69, S10 = 32. What is the percentile rank of each from the national norm table?

3. Calculate a mean and standard deviation for the scores in problem 1.

   Answer:
   (X = 6.99   σ = 19.1)

4. Calculate a mean and standard deviation for the scores in problem 2.

5. Calculate a Z-score for each student in problem 1.

   Answer:
   (Z1 = .90, Z2 = −.15, Z3 = 1.47, Z4 = 1.21, Z5 = −.83, Z6 = −1.67, Z7 = .58, Z8 = .21, Z9 = −.52, Z10 = −1.20)

6. Calculate a Z-score for each student in problem 2.

7. Calculate a T-score and 6-σ score for each student in problem 1.

Answer:

Student	T-score	6-σ score	Student	T-score	6-σ score
S1	59	65.0	S6	33.3	22.2
S2	48.5	47.5	S7	55.8	59.7
S3	64.7	74.5	S8	52.1	53.5
S4	62.1	70.2	S9	44.8	41.3
S5	41.7	36.2	S10	38.0	30.0

8. Calculate a T-score and 6-σ score for each student in problem 2.

9. Calculate a mean T-score for the boys in problem 1 and the girls in problem 2. Which distribution has the higher mean T-score?

Answer:
boys $\overline{X}$T-score $= 50$; girls $\overline{X}$T-score $= 50$
Neither distribution has the higher $\overline{X}$T-score. Each T-score has an $\overline{X}$ of 50 and $\sigma = 10$.

10. a. Assign a rank for each of the ten male students in problem 1 on the AAHPER Archery Test. Each student was measured for shoulder and arm muscular endurance by recording the number of full length chins each could accomplish, with the following results:

Student	No. of Chins	Student	No. of Chins
S1	10	S6	3
S2	12	S7	13
S3	20	S8	11
S4	21	S9	5
S5	8	S10	9

   b. Assign a rank for each of the ten male students for shoulder and arm muscular endurance.
   c. Calculate a rank order correlation coefficient *rho*.
   d. Calculate the amount of shared variance.
   e. Does muscular endurance of the shoulders and arms seem to affect the accuracy of shooting in archery? Explain your answer to this question.

11. a. Assign a rank for each of the ten female students in problem 2 on the AAHPER Archery Test. Each student was measured for shoulder and arm muscular endurance by recording the length of time, in seconds, each could hold a flexed-arm hang with her chin above a chinning bar with the following results:

Student	Time (sec.) held flexed-arm hang	Student	Time (sec.) held flexed-arm hang
S1	25	S6	15
S2	20	S7	19
S3	23	S8	40
S4	28	S9	38
S5	35	S10	12

b. Assign a rank for each of the ten female students for shoulder and arm muscular endurance.
c. Calculate a rank order correlation coefficient *rho*.
d. Calculate the amount of shared variance.
e. Does muscular endurance of the shoulders and arms seem to affect the accuracy of shooting in archery? Explain your answer to this question.

Answer:

a. and b.

Student	Archery Rank	Hanging Time Rank
S1	7	5
S2	4	7
S3	8	6
S4	5	4
S5	6	3
S6	9	9
S7	3	8
S8	2	1
S9	1	2
S10	10	10

c. .67

d. 45%

e. There is a positive correlation between muscular endurance and archery skill with a shared variance of 45 percent. It appears from the results that muscular endurance mildly affects archery skill or archery skill mildly affects muscular endurance of the shoulders and arms of 12-year-old females.

components of motor performance

Most coaches and physical education teachers would agree that the fundamental motor components or abilities necessary for an effective performance in sports and games include muscular strength, muscular endurance, muscular power, cardiovascular endurance, balance, flexibility, agility, speed, kinesthesis, eye-foot coordination, arm-eye coordination, and whole body coordination. Some of these components comprise what we call motor fitness, physical fitness, and general motor ability. H. Harrison Clarke has developed a chart of physical components that demonstrates the relationship between the fitness and general motor ability concepts (see Figure 9.1.).[1] Additional elements, identified by Charles McCloy and Norma Young, are thought to be cognitive abilities involved in learning and executing motor acts, visual factors, timing, sensory rhythm, and concentration.[2] Of course, not all sports and games require the same components for an effective performance nor does each component exist by itself in a motor performance. Rather, each sport or activity requires a unique interplay of various components. An individual, for example, will not score well on an agility test if his balance and coordination are poor. Tests of motor fitness, physical fitness, and general motor ability have been covered in the chapters dealing with these topics. This chapter deals with those test items that are thought to measure the more important components or abilities listed in Figure 9.1. Emphasis is also placed on presenting tests that do not require expensive equipment.

1. H. Harrison Clarke, *Application of Measurement to Health and Physical Education,* 5th ed. (Englewood Cliffs, N.J.: Prentice-Hall, 1976), pp. 173–174.
2. Charles H. McCloy and Norma D. Young, *Tests and Measurements in Health and Physical Education,* 3d ed. (New York: Appleton-Century-Crofts, 1954), pp. 3–11.

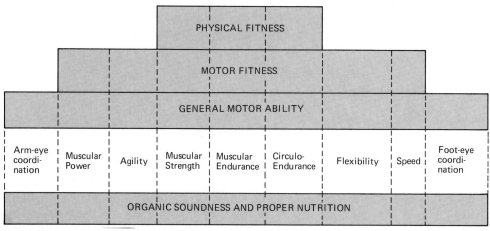

Figure 9.1   Chart of Physical Elements

purposes of testing

The main purposes for testing for the degree of presence of the components or basic abilities underlying motor performances are as follows:

1. To diagnose the pupil's strengths and weaknesses in the components so that remedial activities may be prescribed. Here, developmental needs are identified, individual pupil objectives are established, and a realistic program is designed that can help build an atmosphere of success.

2. To classify pupils into instructional groups, especially in those activities that depend heavily on strength, speed, power, and endurance.

3. To motivate pupils to improve their physical condition and abilities.

4. To serve as a basis for self-testing activities that can occur as a form of circuit training.

5. To demonstrate the effectiveness of the prescribed program.

6. To prepare the pupil for future instruction in motor activities since basic abilities lead to the more complicated motor patterns in sports and games. In addition,

strength development helps prepare the student for future participation in activities that require increased levels of muscular strength and endurance.

Each of the fundamental components or motor abilities can be tested in many different ways. Indeed, both Robert Singer and George Sage[3] provide evidence that the relationships among various tests of balance, tests of kinesthesis, speed of reaction tests, movement time tests, strength tests, and tests of flexibility are generally low, indicating that different types of each ability are being measured by various tests. In addition, these tests do not correlate well with success in sports and games. However, when the ability to be measured is expressed and tested the way it would be used in a specific sport such as baseball, the correlations increase substantially. This evidence again supports the concept of specificity of skill. That is, the existence and/or importance of "general" speed,

3. Robert N. Singer, *Motor Learning and Human Performance,* 2d ed. (New York: Macmillan, 1975), pp. 219–249; George H. Sage, *Introduction to Motor Behavior, A Neuropsychological Approach,* 2d ed. (Reading, Mass.: Addison-Wesley, 1977), pp. 252–255, 300–302.

balance, kinesthesis, and so on is doubtful. Each activity requires a unique type and amount of each motor ability to effect a skillful performance. Thus, the teacher should select or develop a test of the ability that closely resembles the manner in which it would be used in actual game or physical education class situations. Develop your own tests. Most coaches do this when they create situation-specific drills to develop the motor skills of their athletes.

In this text, since no motor ability exists by itself in physical education and athletic activity, the authors of this text present the abilities in terms of a complex of abilities that, in our opinion, seem to go together when employed in sports and games. Thus, sample tests are presented that may be used to estimate a muscular strength–endurance ability, a muscular strength–power ability, an agility–coordination ability, and a flexibility–balance ability.

strength–endurance

The muscles of the body generate the energy required to apply the force of muscular contraction needed to hold the body in a particular position, to move the body from one place to another, and to push or pull objects away from or toward the body. In essence, sufficient general muscular strength and endurance is required to enable us to complete our daily tasks. The intensity and type of strength developed will, by necessity, be specifically related to the nature of the task. Thus, the specific strength requirements of a shot putter will be quite different from the requirements of an office worker, although both individuals need sufficient general bodily strength and endurance to protect them against muscular-skeletal problems that may be reflected in low back pain, abdominal ptosis, and other orthopedic prob-

lems. Thus, general strength is viewed as an important element of health and fitness.

Sufficient muscular strength and endurance readies the individual to participate in future activities requiring strength and endurance for an effective performance. The authors have noted on a number of occasions that a number of preadolescent boys are unable to support their bodies properly with their arms and shoulders as they try to learn simple tumbling stunts such as the forward or backward roll. Testing these children has revealed that they cannot perform one pull-up. Strength conditioning of the upper body has been required to enable these boys to learn simple tumbling stunts effectively.

Strength development is a fundamental prerequisite for success in sports and games. McCloy and Young found a correlation of .91 between Athletic Strength Index Scores and a battery of six track and field events.[4] A further extensive review of the logical and empirical validity of strength tests, either singly or when combined into a battery known as a Strength Index or a Physical Fitness Index, is presented by Clarke.[5]

If you were to review the many measurement texts on the market today, as well as the various manuals concerned with strength testing, you might become confused with all the different types of strength that are measurable. Additional confusion can arise when, in some cases, you see the same test item supposedly measuring different types of strength. We should remember first that any measurement score obtained is only an indirect and rather crude estimate of the type of strength assessed. This is due to the fact that a score reflects only a certain mechanical efficiency of the muscle groups involved.

4. McCloy and Young, *Tests and Measurements in Health and Physical Education*, p. 142.
5. Clarke, *Application of Measurement to Health and Physical Education*, p. 7.

In other words, the maximum tension or contractile force that a muscle can exert is rarely transferred completely into useful work. This maximum tension is rarely tested since the tension against the resistance is not the same tension that occurs in the muscle group. Indeed, Herbert deVries indicates that for any given strength of a muscle there are three practical considerations for teachers and coaches to think about when estimating the external force produced by the muscle: (1) angle of pull of the muscle, (2) length of the muscle at any given time, and (3) velocity of muscle shortening.[6] These conditions will vary continuously as muscles are used to do work of any kind. In other words, the number we record from a test score is relative to a particular situation and does not represent the absolute strength of the muscle groups involved. Nor does the strength score represent an ability of the pupil to use the "tested strength" effectively in a particular activity. Strength application is specific to an activity. The pole vaulter and baseball pitcher may have the same strength test score, but they will apply their strength in different ways. In fact, many physical education and athletic activities do not require a maximal contraction but rather call for repeated submaximal contractions of the muscle groups involved.

strength–endurance definitions

To eliminate some of the confusion over terminology in the literature and to put us all in the same frame of reference, W. D. Van Huss and W. W. Heusner provide us with definitions of strength and endurance that are relevant for testing.[7]

Static strength: the maximum effective force that can be applied only once to a fixed object by a person in a standardized immobile position. The object cannot be moved through a range of motion. The force applied to a leg-lift dynamometer is an example of static strength. This is also referred to as a static contraction or an isometric contraction.

Dynamic strength: the maximum load that can be moved once through a specific joint range of motion, with the body in a particular position. The military press in weight lifting is an example of dynamic strength. This is also referred to as a dynamic contraction or isotonic contraction.

Static muscular endurance: the length of time a given intensity of contraction can be maintained. The flexed-arm hang for time is an example of static muscular endurance.

Dynamic muscular endurance: represents a continuum of activity ranging from moving a heavy resistance through a range of motion at least twice, to moving a light resistance through a range of motion for many repetitions. Dynamic muscular endurance may be divided into three aspects which can be called: (1) *dynamic muscular endurance: short* (short duration, high intensity work for up to 30 seconds—chins, dips, push-ups); (2) *dynamic muscular endurance: medium* (medium duration, moderate intensity work that can last up to 4 minutes—440- and 880-yard (402.44 m and 804.88 m) dashes; and (3) *dynamic muscular endurance: long* (long duration, low intensity work—distance running, cycling, and swimming).

6. Herbert A. deVries, *Physiology of Exercise for Physical Education and Athletics* (Dubuque, Iowa: Wm. C. Brown, 1966), p. 25.
7. W. D. Van Huss and W. W. Heusner, "Strength, Power, and Muscular Endurance," in *An Introduction to Measurement in Physical Education,* vol. 4, *Physical Fitness,* ed. Henry J. Montoye (Indianapolis: Phi Epsilon Kappa Fraternity, 1970), pp. 4–6.

Power: the amount of work that can be done per unit of time. Strength and speed are involved in projecting a body at a maximum rate of movement. In physical education and athletics, explosive movements such as shot putting, 50-yard dash, vertical jump, standing broad jump, and the lineman's charge in football are viewed as power movements.

muscular strength and endurance test batteries

General bodily strength and endurance should not be estimated from one measurement in a single muscle group. Per-Olof Åstrand and Kaare Rodahl report that the correlations between strength measures from different parts of the body are a rather low .40 or less.[8] Hence, a battery of tests should be selected that will measure the strength of the major muscle groups of the body. Since the correlation between dynamic and isometric strength of the same muscles is a rather high .80 in muscles not previously conditioned by either method,[9] dynamic strength testing is recommended when possible because it is easier to administer and the equipment involved costs less.

strength index and the physical fitness index

This is a battery of test items of which some estimate static strength and other items estimate dynamic muscular endurance: short. Even though there is a short form of the test, expensive equipment must be purchased and the test is administered on an individual basis. The Strength Index (SI) score is the sum of five strength tests, plus lung capacity. The strength items are: right grip strength, left grip strength, back strength, leg strength, and arm strength. Arm strength is determined by the formula:

$$(\text{pull-ups} + \text{push-ups}) \left(\frac{\text{weight}}{10} + \text{height} - 60 \right).$$

To administer the test, your school must purchase a spirometer to measure lung capacity, a hand dynamometer, and a back leg lift dynamometer. The Physical Fitness Index (PFI) is derived by comparing the Strength Index score with a norm based on the individual's sex, weight, and age, multiplied by 100 to eliminate the decimal point. The scoring system for the arm strength score unduly punishes the short boy and rewards the tall boy. Also, no rationale is given for dividing the weight by 10 or for multiplying the endurance performance by physical stature. Short forms of this test, which compensate for some of these criticisms, have been developed. The entire test battery, modifications of the test, and directions for administering and scoring it appear in Clarke.[10]

cable-tension strength test batteries

A battery of twenty-five cable-tension static strength test items are described in the H. Harrison Clarke and Richard Munroe test manual.[11] These items are designed to measure the strength of individual muscle groups in boys and girls that may have been weakened due to some disability. Smaller test batteries of three items were developed to predict a person's score on all twenty-five items. The batteries can be administered in upper elementary, junior high school, senior high school, and college. A tensiometer and cable must be purchased, and a padded strength

8. Per-Olof Åstrand and Kaare Rodahl, *Textbook of Work Physiology: Physiological Bases of Exercise,* 2d ed. (New York: McGraw-Hill, 1977), p. 106.

9. *Ibid.,* p. 107.

10. Clarke, *Application of Measurement to Health and Physical Education,* pp. 126–145.

11. H. Harrison Clarke and Richard A. Munroe, *Oregon Cable-Tension Strength Test Batteries for Boys and Girls from Fourth Grade through College* (Eugene: University of Oregon, Microcard Publications in Health, Physical Education and Recreation, 1970).

Figure 9.2   **Bench Press**
Strength Test

test table constructed so that the subject can be placed into the proper position and immobilized if necessary when tested. Only the particular muscle group of interest in each test item is allowed freedom of movement to pull on a cable attached to the tensiometer. Since the effects of corrective exercises for specific muscle groups may be demonstrated, this battery of cable-tension tests is well suited for adapted physical education programs. Only one person at a time can be tested, but this should not be a drawback in an individually prescribed corrective exercise program.

weight-lifting strength testing

If your school has a well-equipped weight-lifting room, a number of dynamic strength tests can be administered. Barry Johnson

and Jack Nelson indicate that some student familiarization with test items needs to be done to determine the maximum weight that can be lifted.[12] The bench press, standing vertical arm press, half-squat, and curls are some suggested strength testing positions (see Figures 9.2 and 9.3). One may also attach a spring scale to a bar and push or pull on the bar to determine the force of contraction. This type of testing may be dangerous, so close supervision and the use of spotters is necessary.

Two problems confound the weight-lifting test score. The first arises when the pupil must do a few lifts to determine when

12. Barry L. Johnson and Jack K. Nelson, *Practical Measurements for Evaluation in Physical Education*, 3d ed. (Minneapolis: Burgess, 1979), p. 95.

Figure 9.3 **Weight Lifting**
Strength Test

he is approaching a maximal effort point. In doing this, some muscle fatigue will occur and the actual test score may underestimate the correct value. The second problem involves the contribution to the test score of learning how to lift weights. In weight-lifting classes, there is usually a rapid gain in the amount of weight that can be lifted. Much of this "strength" gain is probably due to learning to lift correctly rather than to an actual strength gain. However, after learning has occurred and the pupil has been lifting for some time, these weight-lifting tests can give us good estimates of dynamic strength.

aahper fitness test

The items on this test estimate the strength, endurance, and power of the major muscle groups. The items and ability assessed are as follows.

Item	Estimating
Pull-ups	—Dynamic muscular endurance: short
Flexed-arm hang	—Static muscular endurance
50-yard dash (45.73 m)	—Speed or power
Sit-ups (1 minute)	—Dynamic muscular endurance: medium

Standing broad —Power
 jump
600-yd. (548.78m)—Dynamic muscular
 run-walk   endurance: medium
Shuttle run —Dynamic muscular
              endurance: short—
              combined with speed
              and agility

Directions for administering and scoring these items can be found in chapter 10.

dynamic muscular endurance test: short
Michael Yuhasz has proposed a Five-Minute Muscular Endurance Test as a simple and economical measure of the endurance of the major muscle groups, using the body as the restive force.[13] The test is easy to explain and administer individually or in a group setting. One-half of the class can perform the test while the other half counts production and records the score. The test requires no equipment other than a pencil, scorecard, and gym floor. It is applicable to both sexes and almost all ages. The test items may also be used as the core items of a muscular endurance workout, with the children keeping track of weekly progress on their own record forms.

The teacher should determine local test-retest reliability for each test item, and in time can construct norms for the various ages of children. When testing elementary school children the teacher may wish to experiment with reducing the amount of time required to do each item from 60 to 40 seconds for boys and from 30 to 20 seconds for girls *only* if the younger children cannot do the items in the regular time span. Remember, with some conditioning activity most young children may be able to perform the items without a time modification.

measurement technique

For high school boys and men, a minimum

60-second time limit is imposed for four of the six exercises and 30 seconds for the chest raise and the double backward leg raise. With younger boys, girls, and women each exercise is performed for 30 seconds only, except the side leg raise, which is performed for 30 seconds on each side. A 10-second break is allowed between the exercises in order to score the results. The performer attempts to repeat each exercise as frequently as possible within the time limit but may perform them at his own pace and rest whenever he wishes.

The items are illustrated in Figures 9.4 through 9.8.

description of test items

1. Push-ups. (Boys—60 seconds; girls—30 seconds) Record number completed. A front-lying position is taken with the hands at the sides of the chest. The body is raised by extending the arms completely, while keeping the body in a straight line. The principal muscles involved are the pectorals and the triceps.

2. Sit-ups. (Boys—60 seconds; girls—30 seconds) Record number completed. The knees are flexed at 90° with the feet held flat on the floor. The hands are placed behind the head. From the back-lying position the performer sits up and touches both elbows to both knees. Principal muscle involved is the rectus abdominis. (See chapter 10.)

3. Side leg raise. (Boys and girls—30 seconds, each side) Record number completed. A side-leaning rest position is taken with the right side down. The weight of the body is balanced on the right arm and the extended right leg. The left leg is lifted laterally to the horizontal and lowered. At the end of 30 seconds the movement is per-

13. Michael Yuhasz, "The Five-Minute Muscular Endurance Test," University of Western Ontario (personal communication, 1976), test directions and norms used with permission of Dr. Yuhasz.

Figure 9.4   Push-up

formed with the left side down. The pectorals, deltoids, trapezius, and rhomboid muscles fix the balancing arm and shoulder. The sartorius, glutei, vastas lateralis, and tensor fasciae latae are involved in the leg raise.

4. Chest raise. (Boys and girls—30 seconds) Record number completed. A front-lying position is taken with the hands behind the head. The legs are held. The performer raises the chin as high as he can from the floor and then lowers his chest to the floor. Muscles of the neck and shoulder are involved as well as the erector spinae, sacrospinalis, glutei, and hamstrings.

5. Double backward leg raise. (Boys and girls—30 seconds) Record number completed. A front-lying position is taken with the arms along the sides, palms facing downward. The chest is held down. Both legs are lifted upward with the legs held straight to clear the thighs from the floor. The muscles

used are the erector spinea, sacrospinalis, and the gluteus maximus.

6. Sitting tucks. (Boys—60 seconds; girls—30 seconds) Record number completed. A long sitting position is taken with the arms placed palms down behind the hips. The heels are lifted 6 inches off the floor. Both legs are flexed to bring the knees to the chest, heels together, and then the legs are straightened, keeping the heels off the floor. The muscles involved in flexing the leg are the psoas and iliacus, and in extending the legs, the quadriceps and the rectus femoris.

Strength testing data may be recorded on the score sheet illustrated in Figure 9.9. Norms for the Yuhasz Muscular Endurance Test developed on college physical education men and women, as well as on secondary school boys, are presented in Tables 9.1 through 9.5.

Figure 9.5   Side Leg Raise

Figure 9.6   Chest Raise

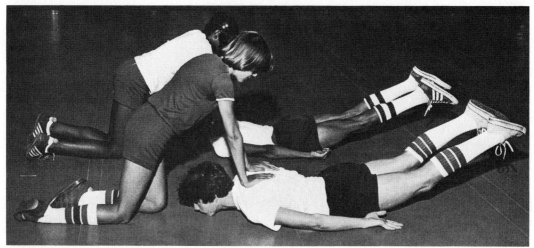

Figure 9.7   Double Backward Leg Raise

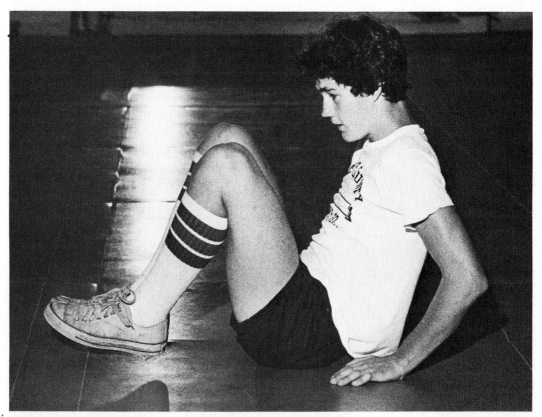

Figure 9.8   Sitting Tucks

Name _____ Age_____ Date of Birth _____

School _____ Height Nearest Inch (cm)_____

Grade_____ Weight Nearest Pound (kg) _____

Test Data _____	Date of Test _____		Date of Test _____		Date of Test _____		Date of Test _____	
	Age Yrs.__ Mos. __		Age Yrs.__ Mos.__		Age Yrs.__ Mos.___		Age Yrs. __Mos.___	
	Raw Score	Centile Rank	Raw Score	Centile Rank	Raw Score	Centile Rank	Raw Score	Centile Rank
5-Minute Muscular Endurance								
1. Push-ups								
2. Sit-ups								
3. Side leg raise								
4. Chest raise								
5. Double backward leg raise								
6. Sitting tucks								

Figure 9.9   Muscular Strength and Endurance Score Sheet

Table 9.1   Yuhasz 5-Minute Muscular Endurance Test Norms Physical Education College Men

Classification	S.S.	Push-ups (60 sec)	Sit-ups (60 sec)	Chest raises (30 sec)	Double leg raises (30 sec)	Side leg raises (60 sec)	Sitting tucks (60 sec)	S.S.
	100	66	59	69	69	131	137	100
Excellent	95	64	57	67	67	129	133	95
	90	63	56	65	66	127	129	90
	85	61	54	63	64	125	125	85
Very Good	80	60	53	62	62	122	121	80
	75	58	51	60	60	120	117	75

Table 9.1—_Continued_

Classification	S.S.	Push-ups (60 sec)	Sit-ups (60 sec)	Chest raises (30 sec)	Double leg raises (30 sec)	Side leg raises (60 sec)	Sitting tucks (60 sec)	S.S.
	70	57	50	58	58	118	113	70
Above Average	65	55	48	56	57	116	109	65
	60	54	47	54	55	114	105	60
	55	52	45	53	53	112	100	55
Average	50	50	44	51	51	110	97	50
	45	49	42	49	49	108	93	45
	40	47	41	47	48	106	89	40
Below Average	35	46	39	45	46	104	85	35
	30	44	38	44	44	101	81	30
	25	43	36	42	42	99	77	25
Poor	20	41	35	40	40	97	73	20
	15	39	33	38	39	95	69	15
	10	38	32	36	37	93	65	10
Very Poor	5	36	30	35	35	91	61	5
	0	35	29	33	33	89	57	0

Date

Table 9.2   Yuhasz 3½-Minute Muscular Endurance Test Norms Physical Education College Women

Classification	S.S.	Push-ups (30 sec)	Sit-ups (30 sec)	Chest raises (30 sec)	Double leg raises (30 sec)	Side leg raises (60 sec)	Sitting tucks (30 sec)	S.S.
	100	33	32	50	68	145	75	100
Excellent	95	32	30	48	66	140	72	95
	90	30	29	46	64	134	68	90
	85	28	28	45	62	129	65	85
Very Good	80	26	27	43	60	123	62	80
	75	25	26	42	58	118	59	75
	70	23	25	41	56	112	56	70
Above Average	65	21	24	39	54	107	53	65
	60	20	22	38	52	101	50	60

Table 9.2—*Continued*

Classification	S.S.	Push-ups (30 sec)	Sit-ups (30 sec)	Chest raises (30 sec)	Double leg raises (30 sec)	Side leg raises (60 sec)	Sitting tucks (30 sec)	S.S.
Average	55	18	21	36	50	96	47	55
	50	16	20	35	48	90	44	50
	45	15	19	34	46	85	41	45
Below Average	40	13	18	32	44	79	37	40
	35	11	17	31	42	74	34	35
	30	9	16	29	40	68	31	30
Poor	25	8	15	28	38	63	28	25
	20	6	14	27	36	57	25	20
	15	4	13	25	34	52	22	15
Very Poor	10	3	11	24	32	46	19	10
	5	1	10	22	30	41	16	5
	0	0	9	21	28	35	13	0

Date

Table 9.3 **Yuhasz 5-Minute Muscular Endurance Test Norms for 17- and 18-year-old Secondary School Boys**

Classification	S.S.	Push-ups (60 sec)	Sit-ups (60 sec)	Chest raises (30 sec)	Double leg raises (30 sec)	Side leg raises (60 sec)	Sitting tucks (60 sec)	S.S.
Excellent	100	61	63	67	69	128	115	100
	95	58	60	65	66	122	110	95
	90	55	58	62	63	116	105	90
Very Good	85	52	55	59	60	110	100	85
	80	49	53	56	57	104	95	80
	75	46	50	54	54	98	90	75
Above Average	70	43	48	51	51	92	85	70
	65	40	45	48	48	86	80	65
	60	37	43	46	45	80	75	60
Average	55	34	40	43	42	74	70	55
	50	31	38	40	39	68	65	50
	45	28	36	37	36	62	60	45

Table 9.3—*Continued*

Classification	S.S.	Push-ups (60 sec)	Sit-ups (60 sec)	Chest raises (30 sec)	Double leg raises (30 sec)	Side leg raises (60 sec)	Sitting tucks (60 sec)	S.S.
Below Average	40	26	33	35	33	56	55	40
	35	23	31	32	30	50	50	35
	30	20	28	29	27	44	45	30
Poor	25	17	26	27	24	38	40	25
	20	14	23	24	21	32	35	20
	15	11	21	21	18	26	30	15
Very Poor	10	8	18	19	15	20	25	10
	5	6	16	16	12	14	20	5
	0	3	13	13	9	8	15	0

Table 9.4   **Yuhasz 5-Minute Muscular Endurance Test Norms for 15- and 16-year-old Secondary School Boys**

Classification	S.S.	Push-ups (60 sec)	Sit-ups (60 sec)	Chest raises (30 sec)	Double leg raises (30 sec)	Side leg raises (60 sec)	Sitting tucks (60 sec)	S.S.
Excellent	100	61	63	65	68	121	115	100
	95	58	60	62	65	115	110	95
	90	54	57	59	62	109	104	90
Very Good	85	51	55	56	59	103	99	85
	80	48	52	53	56	97	93	80
	75	45	50	50	52	91	88	75
Above Average	70	42	47	47	49	85	82	70
	65	39	44	44	46	79	77	65
	60	36	41	41	43	73	71	60
Average	55	32	39	39	40	67	65	55
	50	29	36	36	37	61	60	50
	45	26	34	34	34	55	55	45

Table 9.4—Continued

Classification	S.S.	Push-ups (60 sec)	Sit-ups (60 sec)	Chest raises (30 sec)	Double leg raises (30 sec)	Side leg raises (60 sec)	Sitting tucks (60 sec)	S.S.
	40	23	31	31	31	49	49	40
Below Average	35	20	28	28	28	43	44	35
	30	17	26	25	25	37	38	30
	25	14	23	22	22	31	33	25
Poor	20	11	20	19	19	25	27	20
	15	7	18	16	16	19	22	15
	10	4	15	13	13	13	16	10
Very Poor	5	1	12	10	10	7	11	5
	0	0	10	7	7	1	5	0

Table 9.5   Yuhasz 5-Minute Muscular Endurance Test Norms for 13- and 14-year-old Secondary School Boys

Classification	S.S.	Push-ups (60 sec)	Sit-ups (30 sec)	Chest raises (30 sec)	Double leg raises (30 sec)	Side leg raises (60 sec)	Sitting tucks (60 sec)	S.S.
	100	56	63	63	67	109	100	100
Excellent	95	53	60	60	63	103	95	95
	90	50	57	57	60	98	90	90
	85	46	53	53	56	92	85	85
Very Good	80	43	50	50	53	87	80	80
	75	40	47	47	49	81	75	75
	70	37	44	44	46	76	70	70
Above Average	65	34	41	41	42	70	65	65
	60	31	38	38	39	65	60	60
	55	28	35	35	35	59	55	55
Average	50	25	32	32	32	54	50	50
	45	22	30	30	29	49	45	45

Table 9.5—*Continued*

Classification	S.S.	Push-ups (60 sec)	Sit-ups (30 sec)	Chest raises (30 sec)	Double leg raises (30 sec)	Side leg raises (60 sec)	Sitting tucks (60 sec)	S.S.
	40	20	27	27	25	43	40	40
Below Average	35	17	24	24	22	38	35	35
	30	14	21	21	18	32	30	30
	25	9	18	18	15	27	25	25
Poor	20	6	15	15	11	21	20	20
	15	3	12	12	8	16	15	15
	10	1	10	10	5	10	10	10
Very Poor	5	0	7	7	2	5	5	5
	0	0	4	4	0	0	0	0

power

Power is defined as the work output per unit of time. Chemical energy developed as a result of metabolic processes is transferred into the mechanical process of external work. Work is done when contracting muscles move an object through a distance or space. When the force of muscular contractions moves an object such as a book from one desk to another desk, work has been performed. Power may be calculated using the following formula:

$$\text{power} = \frac{\text{force} \times \text{distance}}{\text{time}},$$

or

$$\text{power} = \frac{\text{work}}{\text{time}},$$

where work = force × distance.

It also follows that since distance/time = velocity, then power = force × velocity.

Coaches often refer to the "explosive power" required to perform certain events such as the lineman's charge in football and the power thrust of the leg for the high jumper. Here maximum force of contraction is accompanied by a maximum speed of contraction. This one contraction or application of force theoretically moves the athlete a maximum distance. In physical education and athletic activities we are not just concerned with how much work is done in a given time span, but rather with the maximum work that can be done per unit of time. Thus a speed event such as the 50-yard (45.73 m) dash qualifies as an estimate of power.

vertical jump

Measuring the distance between a person's standing reach and the maximum height he can jump and touch has been proposed as a test of leg power. If the person's body weight and the speed in performing the jump are not a part of the measurement, however, one cannot regard this test as a true estimate of leg power. It follows that a 170-pound (77.27 kg) boy who jumps vertically 2 feet (60.96 cm) produces less power than a 180-pound (81.81 kg) boy who vertically jumps the same distance. Donald Mathews and Edward Fox have in their text a nomogram that takes into consideration body weight when performing the vertical jump and reach test.[14] The nomogram in Figure 9.10 may be used as follows for a 180-pound (81.81 kg) boy who jumps and reaches 24 inches (60.96 cm): Lay a ruler across the nomogram connecting 180 pounds (right column) and 24 inches (left column). Read from the center column, foot-pounds per second (ft.-lb./sec.) as the power output. Note that the measurements may be in either English or metric units. In the latter units the power output would be 142 kilogram-meter/second (kg-m/sec). Directions for administration of the vertical jump and reach tests are as follows:

> Record the performer's weight in stocking feet. Have the individual assume a standing position facing sideways to the jump board with the hand away from the board placed behind the back at the belt line. The arm nearest the board is raised vertically with the hand turned outward and fingers extended. The fingers should be chalked. The performer stands as tall as possible on his toes and touches the board as high up as he can reach with the middle finger. The performer then adopts a full squat position and, maintaining good balance, jumps as high as possible, touching the board at the maximum extension of the arms at the height of the jump. Three trials are allowed. Record the best score, which is the one showing the greatest distance between the two chalk marks (see Figure 9.11).

The standing broad jump and the 50-yard (45.73 m) dash are also proposed as tests of leg power in the literature. They approach a test of power when body weight is taken into consideration. Nomograms have to be developed.

margaria-kalaman power test

Directions for the administering and scoring the Margaria test, as modified by Kalaman, are given in Mathews and Fox:[15]

> The student stands 6 meters (19.68 ft.) in front of a staircase. He or she approaches and runs up the stairs as rapidly as possible, taking three at a time. A switchmat is placed on the third and ninth stair. (An average stair is 6.84 inches or 174 mm high.) A clock starts as the person steps on the first switchmat (on the third step) and stops as he or she steps on the second mat (on the ninth step). Time is recorded to a hundredth of a second. Three trials are allowed, and the best score is recorded. Power output is computed using the formula:

$$P = \frac{W \times D}{t}$$

where P = Power

W = Weight of person

D = Vertical height between the two switchmats (third and ninth stair)

t = time from first to second switchmat

The test is scored as in the following example: $W = 75$ kg, $D = 1.05$ meters, $t = .49$ sec., hence,

$$P = \frac{75 \times 1.05}{0.49} = 161 \text{ kg-meters per sec.}$$

14. Donald K. Mathews and Edward L. Fox, *The Physiological Basis of Physical Education and Athletics*, 2d ed. (Philadelphia: W. B. Saunders, 1976), pp. 498–503.

15. *Ibid.*

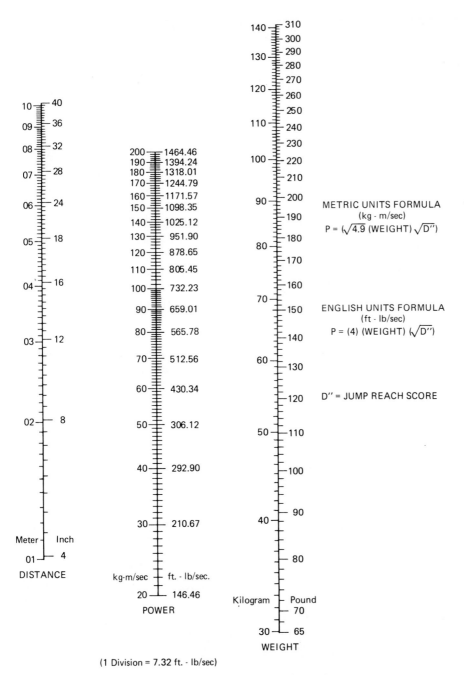

METRIC UNITS FORMULA
(kg - m/sec)
$$P = (\sqrt{4.9} \ (WEIGHT) \ \sqrt{D''})$$

ENGLISH UNITS FORMULA
(ft - lb/sec)
$$P = (4) \ (WEIGHT) \ (\sqrt{D''})$$

D'' = JUMP REACH SCORE

DISTANCE

POWER

WEIGHT

(1 Division = 7.32 ft. - lb/sec)

Figure 9.10 The Lewis Nomogram for Determining Anaerobic Power from Jump-Reach Score and Body Weight

Figure 9.11   Vertical Jump

Norms for this test appear in Mathews and Fox and are reproduced in Table 9.6. Teachers may wish to experiment with this test by using stopwatches if switchmats are unavailable. Also, if the height of the stair is different, the norms in Table 9.6 should not be used.

fifty-yard dash (45.73 m)

In reviewing a study by Kalamen, Mathews and Fox found that a correlation of .974 was obtained between the 50-yard (45.73 m) dash time with a 15-yard (13.72 m) running start and the Margaria-Kalaman Power Test.[16] This correlation indicates that one can substitute the 50-yard (45.73 m) dash and get similar results, while at the same time eliminating expensive equipment. It is also reported that Kalaman obtained an insignificant relationship between the 50-yard (45.73 m) dash and the vertical jump and reach test when body weight was not taken into consideration. If timing equipment and a staircase are available, the Margaria-Kalaman Power Test is superior; if not, the 50-yard (45.73 m) dash may be substituted.

agility–coordination

Coordination may be defined as the harmonious interplay of muscle groups during a motor performance that provides us with some indication of skill. *Agility* is defined as the ability to change direction of the body or parts of the body rapidly. To be agile one must also be well coordinated. Thus, it is difficult to speak of or test for agility and coordination separately. The tests presented here then include both abilities. To score well on tests of agility–coordination ability, one must also possess sufficient strength, endurance, balance, and flexibility.

Two tests of *whole body agility–coordination* that do not involve running are the *squat thrust* as described by McCloy and

16. *Ibid.*

Table 9.6 Guidelines for the Margaria-Kalamen Test (Expressed in kilogram-meters per second)

Classifi-cation	MEN Age Groups (years)				
	15–20	*20–30*	*30–40*	*40–50*	*Over 50*
Poor	Under 113*	Under 106*	Under 85*	Under 65*	Under 50*
Fair	113–149	106–139	85–111	65–84	50–65
Average	150–187	140–175	112–140	85–105	66–82
Good	188–224	176–210	141–168	106–125	83–98
Excellent	Over 224	Over 210	Over 168	Over 125	Over 98

Classifi-cation	WOMEN Age Groups (years)				
	15–20	*20–30*	*30–40*	*40–50*	*Over 50*
Poor	Under 92*	Under 85*	Under 65*	Under 50*	Under 38*
Fair	92–120	85–111	65–84	50–65	38–48
Average	121–151	112–140	85–105	66–82	49–61
Good	152–182	141–168	106–125	83–98	62–75
Excellent	Over 182	Over 168	Over 125	Over 98	Over 75

*kg-m/sec

Young and the modified *Edgren side step.*[17] Directions for the administering and scoring these tests are as follows:

1. *Squat Thrust.* From an erect standing position, lower the body to a squat-rest position, leaning forward and placing the hands on the floor in front of the feet. Thrust the legs backward as far as they will go to a front leaning-rest position with arms fully extended. Return to the squat-rest position and then to the standing position. The test is scored in terms of the number of performances completed in 10 seconds. A complete performance is scored as 1. Scores for a partial performance are one-fourth for touching hands to the floor, one-half for thrusting the legs backward, and three-fourths for returning to a squat-rest position.

2. *Edgren Side Step.* Three parallel lines are drawn on the floor 4 feet (1.22 m) apart. The student stands astride the middle line. On the signal "Go" the pupil *sidesteps* to the right (using any variation of the side step without crossing the feet) until the right foot touches across the line to his right. The student then sidesteps to the left until the left foot has touched across the outside left line, repeating this movement to the right and left between the outside lines as rapidly as possible for 30 seconds. Each trip from the center line to an outside line and back to the center line counts 1 point. Each complete round trip counts 2 points. Three trials are allowed. Circle the best score (see Figure 9.12).

17. McCloy and Young, *Tests and Measurements in Health and Physical Education,* p. 75; Harry D. Edgren, "An Experiment in the Testing of Ability and Progress in Basketball," *Research Quarterly* 3 (March 1932):159–171.

Figure 9.12   **Edgren Side Step**

A few tests of whole body agility–coordination that involve running are the AAHPER shuttle run item on the fitness test, the right-boomerang run, the dodging run, and the auto-tire test. Directions for administering and scoring the last three tests appear in McCloy and Young.[18] These tests are reproduced here.

1. *AAHPER Shuttle Run.* Directions can be found in chapter 10.

2. *Right-Boomerang Run.* A cone marker is place 17 feet (5.18 m) from a starting line; another marker is placed 15 feet (4.57 m) beyond the first marker. Additional cone markers are placed 15 feet (4.57 m) on each side of the first marker (that is, 17 feet or 5.18 m) from the starting line. The performer follows the course indicated in Figure 9.13.

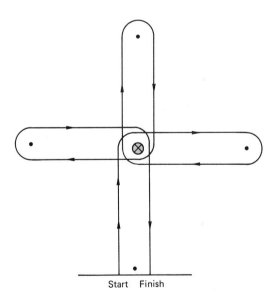

Start   Finish

Figure 9.13   Right-Boomerang Run Test: Floor Markings

18. McCloy and Young, *Tests and Measurements in Health and Physical Education*, pp. 78–81.

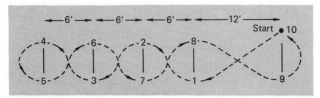

Figure 9.14 Dodging-run Test: Floor Markings

The student makes quarter right turns at the middle marker and half turns at the corner markers. The pupil's score is the time required to complete the course.

3. *Dodging Run.* A starting line 6 feet (1.83 m) long is drawn on the floor. One hurdle is placed 12 feet (3.66 m) in front of the starting line; a second hurdle is placed 6 feet (1.83 m) beyond the first; a third hurdle is placed 6 feet (1.83 m) beyond the second; and a fourth hurdle is placed 6 feet (1.83 m) beyond the third. The performer follows the course indicated in Figure 9.14. The score is the time required to run the complete course.

4. *Auto-tire Test.* A starting line 6 feet (1.83 m) long is drawn on the floor. Five auto tires, with their centers 6 feet (1.83 m) apart are placed in each of two columns, which are 4 feet (1.22 m) apart. The center of the first tire in the column at the left is 6 feet (1.83 m) from the starting line, and the center of the first tire in the column at the right is 3 feet (0.91 m) from the starting line. The performer begins behind the starting line, steps with his right foot into the first tire in the right column, then with his left foot into the first tire in the left row, and continues like this until he has stepped into all the tires. He then turns to the left and returns in the same way to the starting line. (See Figure 9.15.) The score is the time required to make the round trip.

Eye-hand coordination–agility can be estimated by using the *softball repeated throws* test. *Eye-foot coordination–agility* can be estimated by using the *soccer wall volley* and/or the *soccer dribble test.* All three of these test items involve movement of the total body. Directions for administering and scoring these tests are as follows:[19]

1. *Softball Repeated Throws.* This test purports to measure eye-hand whole body coordination and agility. On a flat wall space, mark a target area 5½ feet (1.69 m) wide and at least 10 feet (3.05 m) high, at a distance of 6 inches (15.24 cm) from the floor. A throwing area, 5½ feet (1.69 m) square is

19. Joseph J. Gruber, "Tests and Measurements Laboratory Manual" (Purdue University, 1964).

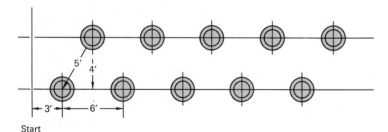

Start

Figure 9.15 Auto-tire Test: Floor Markings

marked on the floor at a distance of 10 feet (3.05 m) from the target and parallel to it. The student stands anyplace she chooses inside the throwing area. At the command "Go" she throws a 12-inch (30.48 cm) softball at the target area using an overhand throw. She continues successive throws until the signal "Stop" is given. The balls may be received from the target either on the bounce or on the fly. The pupil must recover without assistance any balls that get out of control. A 10-second practice trial is allowed. Two 15-second trials are given for the test. Each good hit is worth 1 point. The total number of points is recorded for each trial. Line hits do not count. Circle the best trial score as the pupil's score. (*Note:* This

test can be made more difficult for older children by increasing the distance from the wall and/or placing a 2-foot (0.61 m) square centered inside the larger target area. Award 2 points for a hit in the smaller area.)

2. *Soccer Wall Volley.* This item is proposed as an estimate of eye-foot whole body coordination and agility. A target area 8 feet (2.44 m) long and 4 feet (1.22 m) high from the floor is drawn on the gym wall. An area 12 × 14 feet (3.65 × 4.23 m) is marked on the floor in front of the target area. A restraining line is placed between the baseline and the base of the wall (6 feet or 1.83 m). The ball is set on the restraining line and the subject stands back of it ready to kick on the command "Go." The pupil continues to kick as

Figure 9.16   Soccer Wall Volley

many times as possible, with either foot, by immediately kicking the ball or blocking and steadying it, soccer style, before rekicking. Use of the hands at *any* time is prohibited and 1 point is deducted from the pupil's score for each infraction. Three 20-second trials are taken. The pupil's score is the best of the three trial scores. A student's score is determined by the number of times within the 20-second limit that he successfully propels the ball against the wall. The ball must be directed by the foot, knee, or leg *only*. The pupil must remain behind the restraining line at *all* times. If the pupil kicks in front of the line, falls forward, or steps over the restraining line during the follow-through, that kick does not count (see Figure 9.16).

3. *Soccer Dribble Test.* This is another item that can estimate eye-foot whole body coordination and agility. The pupil starts to dribble the soccer ball with the feet from behind the starting line in and out of the markers as illustrated in Figure 9.17. The examiner times the pupil from the moment she is given the signal "Go" until she returns to the starting line. No practice trials are allowed. Three trials are allowed for the test. The student must finish with the ball in her control. The score for the best trial is recorded in seconds and tenths of a second.

flexibility–balance

The ability of the body and its parts to take various positions, either stationary or moving, requires varying degrees of flexibility and balance responses. The amount and type of flexibility and balance response required is task-related. The specific flexibility and balance responses required by a gymnast performing on a balance beam differ from those needed by an individual with cerebral palsy walking up a flight of stairs. Both individuals need to learn well-defined neuromuscular responses that result in sufficient flexibility and balance to protect them against injury. Flexibility and balance are important commodities of motor performance.

flexibility and balance definitions

Most measurement texts on the market today are in fair agreement about the definitions of flexibility and balance. Barrow and McGee define *flexibility* as "the range of movement in a joint."[20]

20. Harold M. Barrow and Rosemary McGee, *A Practical Approach to Measurement in Physical Education,* 2d ed. (Philadelphia: Lea and Febiger, 1971), p. 577.

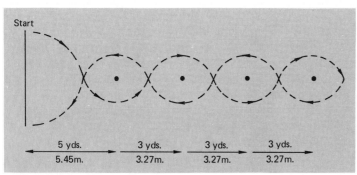

Figure 9.17 Diagram of Soccer Dribble

Baumgartner and Jackson also define *flexibility* as "the range of movement about a joint."[21]

From a scientific viewpoint, testing of flexibility is a long and tedious process. Only one person at a time may be tested. Special restraining gear must be used to hold one part stationary while the angular range of movement of the adjoining part is measured in the various permissible planes. Special equipment for measuring angles must be used.

From a practical viewpoint, we test flexibility by observing and recording the stretching ability of muscles. In other words, most tests of flexibility involve some form of muscle stretching, reaching or bending the segments of the body, and the recording of a distance.

When we speak of flexibility it should be emphasized that the contacting contours and ligaments crossing at joints, along with the protective reflex muscular actions, make a stretching movement distinctive in each individual. Since each individual may differ in his or her stretching ability, unnecessary strain to the muscle attachments and joints should be avoided in testing.

Franks and Deutsch define *balance* as "the ability to maintain equilibrium at rest and during a series of prescribed movements."[22]

Barrow and McGee define *balance* as "the ability of the individual to maintain his neuromuscular system in a static condition for an efficient response or to control it in a specific efficient posture while it is moving."[23]

Balance is a complex phenomenon involving the vestibular system in the inner ears, eyesight, tactile sensations, and proprioceptors, along with the brain-mind complex interpretations, resulting in various motor responses to a given physical situation.

From a scientific viewpoint, testing of balance is a complex process. To test and measure the various responses of the vestibular system to both angular and linear acceleration requires very special equipment. To test and measure conflicting stimulation of the visual, vestibular, tactile, and proprioceptive systems also requires very special equipment. In other words, the scientific testing and measuring of balance is beyond the scope of the practicing physical education teacher.

From a practical viewpoint, we test balance by observing the various responses of an individual to a given physical situation. More often than not we apply two physical situations to test balance. One situation involves the ability of an individual to hold a stationary position, called "static balance," while the other involves the ability of an individual to maintain balance during movement, called "dynamic balance." Most tests applied by the physical education practitioner to test balance involve the motor responses necessary to hold a stationary position or to maintain balance during movement, and the recording of a time element and/or number of errors.

flexibility and balance tests

The tests presented in this section are practical, may be administered to a large number of students in a relatively short period of time, and do not require expensive equipment. The results of these should be used as guides and not absolutes in establishing realistic objectives for program planning. The

21. Ted A. Baumgartner and Andrew S. Jackson, *Measurement for Evaluation in Physical Education* (Boston: Houghton Mifflin, 1975), p. 163.
22. B. Don Franks and Helga Deutsch, *Evaluating Performance in Physical Education* (New York: Academic Press, 1973), p. 125.
23. Barrow and McGee, *A Practical Approach to Measurement in Physical Education,* p. 573.

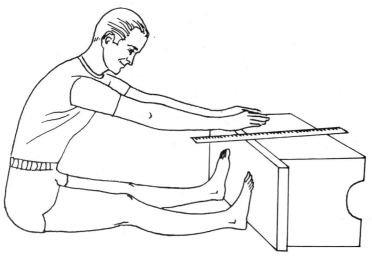

Figure 9.18   Trunk Flexibility Test. Note: The meterstick or ruler or yardstick extends 15 inches (38.1 cm.) over the end of the bench nearest the student.

following tests of flexibility and balance with norms will help the practicing physical education teacher establish these objectives and plan physical activities to meet them.

test 1: trunk flexibility

This particular test is designed to test the stretching ability of the hamstring and lower back muscles.[24] The student sits on the floor with the knees together and the feet flat against a bench turned on its side. With a partner holding the knees straight, the student reaches forward with the arms fully extended. The distance the fingertips reach on the meter or yardstick fixed to the bench is measured and recorded. See Figure 9.18. Face validity is assumed and no reliability coefficients were given. The mean value for males is 45.1 centimeters (17.75 inches) with a standard deviation of 9.7 centimeters (3.81 inches). The mean value for females is 45.85 centimeters (18.05 inches) with a standard deviation of 9.99 centimeters

(3.93 inches). The norms presented in Table 9.7 represent over 3000 subjects with a range in age from 17.6 to 19.5 years.

test no. 2: the stork stand

This test is designed to test the static balance of a student. The student stands on the foot of the dominant leg. He or she places the toes of the subdominant leg against the knee of the dominant leg and places the hands on the hips. Upon command the student raises the heel of the dominant foot from the floor and attempts to maintain balance as long as possible without the heel touching the floor or the ball of the foot moving from its original position or removing the hands from the hips. The best time of three attempts is recorded in seconds. See Figure 9.19.

24. Charles Corbin, Linus Dowell, Ruth Lindsey, and Homer Tolson, *Concepts in Physical Education with Laboratories and Experiments,* 3rd ed. (Dubuque, Iowa: Wm. C. Brown, 1978), p. 173.

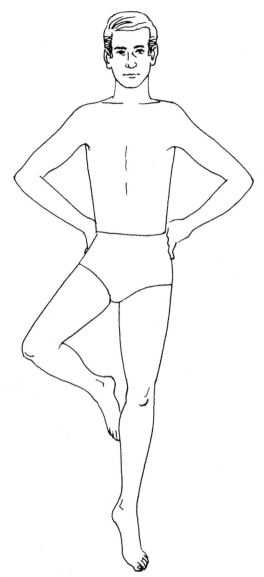

Figure 9.19   Stork Stand for Testing Static Balance

test no. 3: modified bass test of dynamic balance

This test is designed to test the dynamic balance of a student. The student stands on the right foot at the starting point, then hops to the first tape mark on the left foot, and attempts to hold a static position for 5 seconds. After this, the student hops to the second tape mark on the right foot and attempts to hold a static position for 5 seconds. He or she continues to alternate feet, hopping and holding a static position for 5 seconds, until the course is completed. The ball of the student's foot must completely cover each tape mark so that it cannot be seen. A successful try consists of covering each tape with the ball of the foot, not touching the heel or any other part of the body to the floor, and holding a static position on each tape for 5 seconds, keeping the tape mark covered. Five points is earned for landing and covering a tape mark successfully, and an additional 5 points may be earned for each second the student can hold a static balance position. A student can earn a maximum of 10 points on each tape mark or a total of 100 points for the complete course. Each 5-second balance attempt should be counted aloud, with 1 point allowed for each second and a score recorded for each tape marker. (The student is allowed to reposition himself or herself for the 5-second balance attempt after landing unsuccessfully.) The equipment and materials needed are a stopwatch or watch with a second-hand movement, eleven 1 × ¾-inch (2.54 × 1.9 cm) pieces of marking tape, and a tape measure, meterstick, or yardstick. See Figure 9.20 for the proper placement of each tape marker.

A reliability correlation coefficient of .87 was reported in a test-retest situation.[25] Face validity is assumed. The norms presented in Table 9.8 represent 99 male subjects and 114 female subjects of college age.[26]

25. Barry Johnson and Jack Nelson, *Practical Measurements for Evaluation in Physical Education*, 3d ed. (Minneapolis: Burgess, 1979), p. 127.
26. *Ibid.*, p. 233–235.

Table 9.7 Norms for the Trunk Flexibility Test

Percentile	Trunk Flexibility Females		Trunk Flexibility Males	
	cm	in.	cm	in.
100	63.5	25.0	61.0	24.0
90	56.4	22.2	54.9	21.6
80	53.1	20.9	51.8	20.4
70	50.5	19.9	49.8	19.6
60	48.3	19.0	47.5	18.7
50	46.5	18.3	45.2	17.8
40	44.4	17.5	43.4	17.1
30	41.4	16.2	40.1	15.8
20	37.6	14.8	36.3	14.3
10	30.5	12.0	29.7	11.7
0	10.2	4.0	15.2	6.0

Source: William Zuti and Charles Corbin, "Physical Fitness Norms for College Freshmen," *Research Quarterly* 48 (May 1977): 499.

Table 9.8 Norms for the Stork Stand

College Men				College Women			
T-Score	Raw Score (sec)	T-Score	Raw Score (sec)	T-Score	Raw Score (sec)	T-Score	Raw Score (sec)
80	73	57	36	90	62	63	30
79	71	56	34	89	61	62	29
78	70	55	32	88	60	61	28
77	68	54	31	87	59	60	27
76	66	53	29	86	57	59	25
75	65	52	28	85	56	58	24
74	63	51	26	84	55	57	23
73	61	50	24	83	54	56	22
72	60	49	23	82	53	55	21
71	58	48	21	81	52	54	20
70	57	47	20	80	50	53	18
69	55	46	18	79	49	52	17
68	53	45	16	78	48	51	16
67	52	44	15	77	47	50	15

Table 9.8—_Continued_

College Men				College Women			
T-Score	Raw Score (sec)	T-Score	Raw Score (sec)	T-Score	Raw Score (sec)	T-Score	Raw Score (sec)
66	50	43	13	76	46	49	14
65	49	42	12	75	44	48	12
64	47	41	10	74	43	47	11
63	45	40	8	73	42	46	10
62	44	39	7	72	41	45	9
61	42	38	5	71	40	44	8
60	41	37	4	70	38	43	6
59	39	36	2	69	37	42	5
58	37	35	1	68	36	41	4
				67	35	40	3
				66	34	39	2
				65	33	38	1
				64	31		

Source: Barry Johnson and Jack Nelson, _Practical Measurements for Evaluation in Physical Education,_ 2d ed., (Minneapolis: Burgess, 1974), p. 198.

Table 9.9   Norms for the Modified Bass Test for Dynamic Balance

T-Scores	Raw Scores	T-Scores	Raw Scores	T-Scores	Raw Scores	T-Scores	Raw Scores
67	100	40	60	53	79	27	41
66	98	39	59	52	78	26	39
65	97	38	57	51	76	25	38
64	95	37	56	50	75	24	36
63	94	36	54	49	73	23	35
62	93	35	53	48	72	22	34
60	91	34	51	47	70	20	32
59	90	33	50	46	69	19	30
58	88	32	48	45	67	18	29
57	85	31	47	44	66	17	27
56	84	30	45	43	64	16	26
55	82	29	44	42	63	15	24
54	81	28	42	41	62	14	23

Source: Barry Johnson and Jack Nelson, _Practical Measurements for Evaluation in Physical Education,_ 2d ed. (Minneapolis: Burgess, 1974), p. 206.

A test-retest reliability coefficient of .75 and a validity correlation coefficient of .46 were found when compared to the complete Bass Test of Dynamic Balance. The norms presented in Table 9.9 are based on the scores recorded on 100 college women.

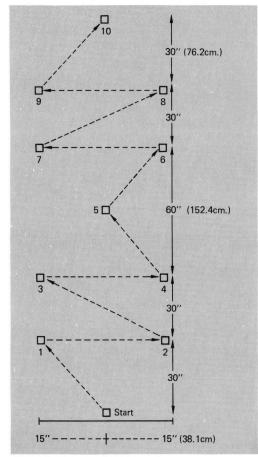

Figure 9.20 Diagram of Modified Bass Test of Dynamic Balance

summary review questions

1. When you run a test for flexibility–balance ability, do you also involve elements of the other motor components such as strength–endurance? Explain your answer. (*answer on p. 224*)

2. List the components of motor performance. (*answer on p. 226*)

3. Relationships between various tests of motor performance are generally low. In addition, these tests usually do not correlate well with success in sports and games. What does this indicate? (*answer on p. 225*)

4. The intensity and type of motor components developed will be task-related. Explain what this means. (*answer on p. 226*)

5. In the testing of strength, the test score we obtain is only an indirect and rather crude estimate of a student's strength. Why? (*answer on p. 226*)

6. Give the various strength and endurance definitions listed in this chapter. What is the basic difference between testing for strength and testing for endurance? (*answer on p. 227*)

7. Why are the tests for power performed by a student only a crude indicator of the student's power? (*answer on p. 241*)

8. From a scientific viewpoint, why is it impossible for a practicing physical education teacher to measure flexibility and balance? (*answer on p. 249*)

9. From a practical viewpoint, when we test a student's flexibility and balance, what do we observe and record? (*answer on p. 249*)

10. Why would tests of coordination–agility be considered the high order of testing of motor components? (*answer on p. 243*)

bibliography

Åstrand, Per-Olof, and Rodahl, Kaare. *Textbook of Work Physiology: Physiological Bases of Exercise.* 2d ed. New York: McGraw-Hill, 1977.

Barrow, Harold, and McGee, Rosemary. *A Practical Approach to Measurement in Physical Education.* 2d ed. Philadelphia: Lea and Febiger, 1971.

Baumgartner, Ted, and Jackson, Andrew. *Measurement for Evaluation in Physical Education.* Boston: Houghton Mifflin, 1975.

Clarke, H. Harrison. *Application of Measurement to Health and Physical Education.* 5th ed. Englewood Cliffs, N.J.: Prentice-Hall, 1976.

Clarke, H. Harrison, and Munroe, Richard. *Oregon Cable-Tension Strength Test Batteries for Boys and Girls from Fourth Grade through College.* Eugene: University of Oregon, Microcard Publications in Health, Physical Education and Recreation, 1970.

Corbin, Charles et al. *Concepts in Physical Education with Laboratories and Experiments.* 3d ed. Dubuque, Iowa: Wm. C. Brown, 1978.

deVries, Herbert. *Physiology of Exercise for Physical Education and Athletics.* Dubuque, Iowa: Wm. C. Brown, 1966.

Edgren, Harry. "An Experiment in the Testing of Ability and Progress in Basketball." *Research Quarterly* 3 (March 1932):159–171.

Franks, B. Don, and Deutsch, Helga. *Evaluating Performance in Physical Education.* New York: Academic Press, 1973.

Gruber, Joseph. "Tests and Measurements Laboratory Manual." West Lafayette, Ind.: Purdue University, Department of Physical Education for Men, 1964.

Johnson, Barry, and Nelson, Jack. *Practical Measurements for Evaluation in Physical Education.* 3d ed. Minneapolis: Burgess, 1979.

McCloy, Charles, and Young, Norma. *Tests and Measurements in Health and Physical Education.* 3d ed. New York: Appleton-Century-Crofts, 1954.

Mathews, Donald, and Fox, Edward. *The Physiological Basis of Physical Education and Athletics.* 2d ed. Philadelphia: W. B. Saunders, 1976.

Sage, George. *Introduction to Motor Behavior: A Neuropsychological Approach.* 2d ed. Reading, Mass.: Addison-Wesley, 1977.

Singer, Robert N. *Motor Learning and Human Performance.* 2d ed. New York: Macmillan, 1975.

Van Huss, W. D., and Herrsner, W. W. "Strength, Power, and Muscular Endurance." In *An Introduction to Measurement in Physical Education,* edited by Henry J. Montoye. Indianapolis: Phi Epsilon Kappa Fraternity, 1970.

exercises

1. The following 25 females performed the Yuhasz 3½-minute endurance test:

	Push-ups 30 sec	Sit-ups 30 sec	Chest raises 30 sec	Double leg raises 30 sec	Side leg raises 30 sec	Sitting tucks 30 sec
S1	18	18	37	50	112	57
S2	8	18	31	37	79	31
S3	12	21	38	54	94	62
S4	31	27	46	63	130	67
S5	7	16	30	35	79	28
S6	13	23	33	53	112	47
S7	3	12	23	36	52	16
S8	23	27	40	57	108	62
S9	16	21	34	48	96	41
S10	32	30	46	68	134	74
S11	4	15	26	39	51	25
S12	17	22	41	55	90	52

	Push-ups 30 sec	Sit-ups 30 sec	Chest raises 30 sec	Double leg raises 30 sec	Side leg raises 30 sec	Sitting tucks 30 sec
S13	18	19	37	52	85	41
S14	21	27	40	53	100	52
S15	9	18	35	46	89	44
S16	21	22	40	51	100	59
S17	15	21	39	46	90	44
S18	28	26	43	62	118	68
S19	3	8	14	31	34	25
S20	17	20	37	46	79	37
S21	16	21	36	48	90	43
S22	14	19	32	45	87	40
S23	30	28	48	62	125	69
S24	16	21	37	49	95	46
S25	10	19	32	43	70	36

a. Determine the approximate percentile rank of each student in each event, and calculate a mean percentile rank for each student over all events.

b. Calculate a $\overline{X}$ and σ for each event.

c. Calculate a Z- and T-score for each student in each event.

Answers:

a.

	Percentile rank: Push-ups	Percentile rank: Sit-ups	Percentile rank: Chest raises	Percentile rank: Double leg raises	Percentile rank: Side leg raises	Percentile rank: Sitting tucks	$\overline{X}$
S1	55	40	60	55	70	70	58.3
S2	25	40	35	25	40	30	32.5
S3	40	55	60	65	55	80	59.2
S4	95	80	90	90	85	90	88.3
S5	25	30	35	20	40	25	29.2
S6	40	60	45	65	70	55	55.8
S7	10	40	65	55	60	5	39.2
S8	70	80	70	75	65	80	73.3
S9	50	55	45	50	55	45	50.0
S10	95	95	90	100	90	100	95.0
S11	15	25	20	30	15	20	20.8
S12	55	60	70	70	50	65	61.7
S13	55	45	60	60	45	45	51.7
S14	65	80	70	65	60	65	67.5
S15	30	40	50	45	50	50	44.2
S16	65	60	70	60	60	75	65.0
S17	45	55	65	45	50	50	51.7
S18	85	80	80	85	75	90	82.5

	Percentile rank: Push-ups	Percentile rank: Sit-ups	Percentile rank: Chest raises	Percentile rank: Double leg raises	Percentile rank: Side leg raises	Percentile rank: Sitting tucks	$\overline{X}$
S19	5	25	0	10	0	20	10.0
S20	55	50	60	45	40	40	48.3
S21	50	55	55	50	50	50	51.7
S22	45	45	40	45	45	45	44.2
S23	90	85	95	85	80	90	87.5
S24	50	55	60	55	55	55	55.0
S25	35	45	40	40	30	40	38.3

b.

Push-ups		Sit-ups		Chest raises		Double leg raises		Side leg raises		Sitting tucks	
$\overline{X}$	σ	$\overline{X}$	σ	$\overline{X}$	σ	$\overline{X}$	σ	$\overline{X}$	σ	$\overline{X}$	σ
16.08	8.78	20.76	4.79	35.8	7.33	49.16	13.24	91.96	23.59	46.64	15.12

c.

	Push-ups		Sit-ups		Chest raises		Double leg raises		Side leg raises		Sitting tucks	
	Z	T	Z	T	Z	T	Z	T	Z	T	Z	T
S1	.21	52.2	−.58	44.2	.16	51.6	.06	50.6	.85	58.5	.69	56.9
S2	−.92	40.8	−.58	44.2	−.65	43.5	−.92	40.8	−.55	44.5	−1.02	39.8
S3	−.46	45.4	.05	50.5	.30	53.0	.37	53.7	.09	50.9	1.02	60.2
S4	1.70	70.0	1.30	63.0	1.39	63.9	1.05	60.5	1.61	66.1	1.35	63.5
S5	−1.03	39.7	−.99	40.1	−.79	42.1	−1.07	39.3	−.55	45.5	−1.23	37.7
S6	−.35	46.5	.47	54.7	−.38	46.2	.29	52.9	.85	58.5	.02	50.2
S7	−1.49	35.1	−1.80	32.0	−1.75	32.5	−.99	40.1	−1.69	33.1	−2.03	29.7
S8	.79	57.9	1.30	63.0	.57	55.7	.59	55.9	.68	56.8	1.02	60.2
S9	−.01	49.9	.05	50.5	−.25	47.5	−.09	49.1	.17	51.7	−.37	46.3
S10	1.81	68.1	1.90	69.0	1.39	63.9	1.42	64.2	1.78	67.8	1.81	68.1
S11	−1.38	36.2	−1.20	38.0	−1.33	36.7	.77	42.3	−1.74	32.6	−1.43	35.7
S12	.10	51.0	.26	52.6	.71	57.1	.44	54.4	−.08	49.2	.35	53.5
S13	.22	52.2	−.37	46.3	.16	51.6	.21	52.1	−.30	47.0	−.37	46.3
S14	.56	55.6	1.30	63.0	.57	55.7	.29	52.9	.34	53.4	.35	53.5
S15	−.81	41.9	−.58	44.2	−.19	48.1	−.24	47.6	−.13	48.7	−.17	48.3
S16	.56	55.6	.26	52.6	.57	55.7	.14	51.4	.34	53.4	.82	58.2
S17	−.12	48.8	.05	50.5	.44	54.4	.24	52.4	−.08	49.2	−.17	48.3
S18	1.36	63.6	1.09	60.9	.98	59.8	.97	59.7	1.10	61.0	1.41	64.1
S19	−1.49	35.1	−2.66	23.4	−2.97	20.3	−1.37	36.3	−2.46	25.4	−1.43	35.7
S20	.10	51.0	−.16	48.4	.16	51.6	−.24	47.6	−.55	44.5	−.64	43.6
S21	−.01	49.9	.05	50.5	.03	50.3	−.09	49.1	−.08	49.2	−.24	47.6
S22	−.24	47.6	−.37	46.3	−.52	44.8	−.31	46.9	−.21	47.9	−.44	45.6
S23	1.59	65.9	1.51	65.1	1.66	66.6	.97	59.7	1.40	64.0	1.48	64.8
S24	−.01	49.9	.05	50.5	.16	51.6	−.01	49.9	.13	51.3	−.04	49.6
S25	−.69	43.1	−.38	46.3	−.52	44.8	−.47	45.3	−.93	40.7	−.70	43.0

2. Twenty male students in a kinesiology class ran a flight of stairs and were timed by a stop-watch. The vertical height of the run was 10 feet:
   a. Calculate the power in ft.-lbs./sec. for each student.
   b. Calculate the power in kg wt-m/sec. for each student.
   c. Calculate a $\overline{X}$ and σ in both systems for the class.
   d. Develop a percentile ranking for the class in both systems.

	Wt. (in lbs.)	Time (in sec.)	Vertical height = 10 ft.
S1	160	1.9	
S2	185	2.2	
S3	160	1.8	
S4	162	1.9	
S5	170	1.8	
S6	175	1.8	
S7	168	2.0	
S8	143	1.6	
S9	210	2.3	
S10	173	2.0	
S11	156	1.6	
S12	162	1.7	
S13	174	1.9	
S14	201	2.0	
S15	193	2.0	
S16	184	1.9	
S17	156	1.8	
S18	144	1.7	
S19	162	2.1	
S20	170	2.2	

3. Thirty female students in their senior year of high school performed the Trunk Flexibility Test with the following results:

Student	Trunk flex in cm	Student	Trunk flex in cm
S1	51.2	S16	44.3
S2	47.0	S17	43.0
S3	42.2	S18	49.2
S4	46.0	S19	46.8
S5	38.5	S20	55.5
S6	56.0	S21	37.2
S7	47.8	S22	45.8
S8	53.0	S23	46.5
S9	41.2	S24	53.2
S10	37.5	S25	43.0
S11	46.0	S26	50.6
S12	44.8	S27	57.0

Student	Trunk flex in cm	Student	Trunk flex in cm
S13	51.2	S28	45.6
S14	53.0	S29	41.0
S15	46.4	S30	47.4

a. Determine the approximate percentile rank of each student.
b. Calculate the $\overline{X}$ and σ for the whole group.
c. Examine the $\overline{X}$ and σ for the college freshmen presented in Table 9.7. Does the $\overline{X}$ for college freshmen plus or minus the σ capture the mean for the high school seniors?

Answers:

a. Student	Approximate percentile rank	Student	Approximate percentile rank
S1	70	S16	40
S2	50	S17	40
S3	40	S18	70
S4	50	S19	50
S5	20	S20	90
S6	90	S21	20
S7	60	S22	50
S8	80	S23	50
S9	30	S24	80
S10	20	S25	40
S11	50	S26	70
S12	40	S27	90
S13	70	S28	50
S14	80	S29	30
S15	50	S30	60

b. $\overline{X} = 46.93$ cm $\sigma = 5.3$ cm
c. Yes, it does capture the $\overline{X}$ for the high school seniors.

4. A physical education teacher wanted to test the static balance ability of her beginning gymnastics class. The twenty girls were in the ninth grade; they secured the following times for the Stork Stand test.

	Time (sec)		Time (sec)
S1	12	S11	12
S2	8	S12	21
S3	10	S13	11
S4	6	S14	8
S5	18	S15	7
S6	5	S16	4
S7	14	S17	13
S8	12	S18	3
S9	9	S19	12
S10	6	S20	12

a. Calculate a percentile rank and graph the results.
b. Calculate an $\overline{X}$ and σ for the group.
c. Calculate a T-Score for each student. Compare the ninth-grade girls' T-Scores with the T-Score norm raw scores (Table 9.7) in seconds for College Women.

5. A high school physical education teacher decided to run a test-retest reliability correlation coefficient on the Modified Bass Test of Dynamic Balance. She tested twenty tenth-grade girls on one day and waited a week, then tested them once again, with the following results:

	Score 1	Score 2
S1	66	69
S2	75	66
S3	67	63
S4	82	79
S5	74	81
S6	57	53
S7	84	88
S8	81	76
S9	53	60
S10	76	78
S11	70	64
S12	72	81
S13	60	57
S14	62	70
S15	75	76
S16	88	79
S17	64	60
S18	58	60
S19	73	75
S20	66	68

Calculate a product-moment correlation coefficient using the ungrouped data.

Answer: (.84)

6. A Junior high school coach wanted to test the agility of his gym class. He decided to use the Right-Boomerang Run. He ran 40 seventh and eighth graders through the test with the following results:

	Time (sec)		Time (sec)
S1	13.5	S21	15.1
S2	13.7	S22	14.8
S3	13.8	S23	14.6
S4	13.4	S24	13.7
S5	13.3	S25	13.6
S6	13.9	S26	13.6
S7	14.0	S27	14.2
S8	14.0	S28	12.0

	Time (sec)		Time (sec)
S9	14.1	S29	11.2
S10	13.2	S30	15.6
S11	13.1	S31	14.2
S12	14.2	S32	13.6
S13	13.1	S33	13.4
S14	14.3	S34	13.9
S15	13.0	S35	13.8
S16	12.4	S36	15.5
S17	14.9	S37	11.1
S18	14.8	S38	13.0
S19	12.1	S39	14.0
S20	12.9	S40	13.7

a. Calculate an $\overline{X}$ and σ for the group.

b. Establish local T-Score norms for the seventh- and eighth-grade boys.

10

motor and physical fitness testing

Improvement in the level of human physical functioning has long been one of the primary goals of physical education programs. When programs have primarily addressed themselves to increasing the participants' muscular strength, endurance, and cardiovascular efficiency and to the reduction of adipose tissue of the body, they have been called conditioning programs, fitness programs, or physical training programs. Some practitioners have adopted more exotic names for their programs such as slimnastics, figure improvement, and body styling, in an effort to attract participants who feel a need to improve their physical appearance and stamina; and, in doing so, add a dimension to the quality of their lives. In an effort to demonstrate program effects, many tests have been proposed by physical educators, exercise physiologists, and physicians through the years. These tests have generally been labeled motor fitness tests, physical fitness tests, and cardiovascular tests. When examining a few of the more popular measurements texts on the market today such as Donald Mathews, H. Harrison Clarke, and Harold Barrow and Rosemary McGee, as well as a 1975 issue of the *Physical Fitness Research Digest,* one notes that many tests and test items are proposed to estimate motor fitness or physical fitness and in some cases both.[1] State departments of physical education, as well as many colleges and universities, have developed tests. The practitioner can easily become confused when reading about all the physical and motor fitness tests. In many cases the same items seem to appear on both motor and physical fitness

1. Donald K. Mathews, *Measurement in Physical Education,* 5th ed. (Philadelphia: W. B. Saunders, 1978), Chapter 5; H. Harrison Clarke, *Application of Measurement to Health and Physical Education,* 5th ed. (Englewood Cliffs, N.J.: Prentice-Hall, 1976), Chapter 9; Harold A. Barrow and Rosemary McGee, *A Practical Approach to Measurement in Physical Education,* 2d ed. (Philadelphia: Lea and Febiger, 1971), Chapter 8; H. Harrison Clarke, ed., "Physical Fitness Testing in Schools," *Physical Fitness Research Digest,* series 5, no. 1 (Washington, D.C.: President's Council on Physical Fitness and Sports, 1975).

tests. Is there a difference between motor and physical fitness? Are the dimensions of fitness equally relevant to all people of all ages? Is the specific importance and meaning of fitness taken into account when tests of motor and/or physical fitness are developed? Obviously, the nature of fitness—what it means to the participant, the type of fitness activities selected, the intensity and duration of exercising—will vary among school children, young adults, the middle-aged, and senior citizens. In other words, fitness too is specific. This is reflected in the long-asked question "Fitness for what?"

definitions of motor and physical fitness

Mathews indicates that the term *motor fitness* became popular during World War II as the military services developed tests to evaluate the capacity of their personnel for vigorous work.[2] Motor fitness is thought to be a limited phase of general motor ability. Elements of motor fitness appear to be endurance, strength, power, flexibility, balance, speed, and agility. These elements are usually reflected in motor performances such as running, jumping, dodging, climbing, swimming, lifting weights, and carrying loads for a prolonged period of time. The President's Council on Physical Fitness and Sports defines *physical fitness* as "the ability to carry out daily tasks with vigor and alertness, without undue fatigue, with ample energy to enjoy leisure time pursuits, and to meet unforeseen emergencies."[3] Implicit in this definition is the ability to bear up, to withstand the stress of life, and to persevere under difficult circumstances. The President's Council identifies the primary components of physical fitness as muscular strength, muscular endurance, and cardio-

respiratory endurance.[4] Other components are identified as muscular power, agility, speed, flexibility, and balance. Apparently, when cardiovascular endurance items are added to motor fitness test items the test becomes known as a *physical fitness test*— a test that attempts to measure the efficiency of both the muscular and cardiovascular systems.

The importance of an optimal level of physical fitness as a reflection of certain aspects of health is demonstrated by Hans Kraus and Wilhelm Raab in *Hypokinetic Diseases,* or diseases directly related to a lack of exercise.[5] These physicians identify low back pain, foot problems, abdominal ptosis, obesity, hypertension, and degenerative cardiovascular diseases as conditions produced by sedentary living in our tension-producing, affluent society. Physical fitness then does convey a meaning of healthy living. Since heart disease, stroke, and circulatory difficulties are still primary causes of death in the affluent nations, the cardiovascular component of physical fitness becomes relevant for all people. Thus, attaining a desirable level of physical fitness is seen as practicing good preventative medicine since physical inactivity seems to be related to coronary heart disease. In other words, sedentary persons have a higher incidence of coronary heart disease than active persons.[6]

2. Mathews, *Measurement in Physical Education,* p. 122.

3. H. Harrison Clarke, ed. "Basic Understanding of Physical Fitness," *Physical Fitness Research Digest,* series 1, no. 1 (Washington, D.C.: President's Council on Physical Fitness and Sports, July 1971), p. 1.

4. *Ibid.,* p. 2.

5. Hans Kraus and Wilhelm Raab, *Hypokinetic Diseases* (Springfield, Ill.: Charles C Thomas, 1961).

6. J. N. Morris et al., "Vigorous Exercise in Leisure Time and the Incidence of Coronary Heart Disease," *Lancet* 1 (1973):333–339; R. S. Paffenbarger and W. E. Hale, "Work Activity and Coronary Heart Mortality," *New England Journal of Medicine* 292 (1975):545–550.

research identification of fitness components

Several researchers have applied the correlational research technique of factor analysis to the many fitness test items proposed by authorities in medicine, physical education, and physiology, in an attempt to eliminate some of the confusion. The idea is to identify basic components found in many of these items, identify the items that contribute most to identifying each component, and, in doing so, eliminating the unimportant items from the measurement scheme. Once the important items for each factor are identified, the researcher attaches a name to the factor based on his judgment of the physiological performances inherent in the test items. The research of Edwin Fleishman, H. B. Falls et al., and A. H. Ismail et al. has made a significant contribution to our understanding of physical fitness.[7] The factors and relevant items named by these scholars are summarized as follows.

7. Edwin A. Fleishman, *The Structure and Measurement of Physical Fitness* (Englewood Cliffs, N.J.: Prentice-Hall, 1964), pp. 127–131; H. B. Falls et al., "Development of Physical Fitness Test Batteries by Factor Analysis Results," *The Journal of Sports Medicine and Physical Fitness* 5 (December 1965): 185–197; A. H. Ismail et al., "Development of a Criterion for Physical Fitness Tests from Factor Analysis Results," *Journal of Applied Physiology* 20 (September 1965):991–999.

Fleishman's Analysis: Nine factors identified with relevant items.

Factors	Items
1. Extent flexibility	—twist and touch, abdominal stretch, toe touching
2. Dynamic flexibility	—lateral bend, one foot tapping, bend-twist and touch for time
3. Explosive strength	—shuttle run, 50-yd. (45.73-m) dash, standing broad jump
4. Static strength	—hand grip strength, medicine ball put, arm pull dynamometer
5. Dynamic strength	—pull-ups, bent-arm hang
6. Trunk strength	—leg lift, half-hold sit-ups
7. Gross body equilibrium	—stand on a stick with preferred foot for time
8. Gross body coordination	—jump through a rope without tripping, falling, or releasing the rope
9. Stamina (cardiovascular endurance)	—600-yard (548.78-m) run-walk for time

Fall's Analysis: Nine factors identified with relevant items.

Factors	Items
1. Athletic fitness	—percent lean body mass, 50-yard (45.73-m) dash, standing broad jump, pull-ups, shuttle run
2. Maximum metabolic rate	—maximum O_2 uptake/kg lean body mass, maximum O_2 uptake, maximum minute volume ventilation
3. Respiratory capacity	—submaximal minute volume ventilation/kg body weight, submaximal minute volume ventilation

4. Basic height of blood pressure   —recovery diastolic blood pressure, resting diastolic blood pressure

5. Heartbeat rate response to exertion   —exercise increase in pulse, maximum heartbeat rate

6. Expiratory capacity   —forced vital capacity

7. Pulse pressure   —post-exercise pulse pressure, resting pulse pressure

8. Force efficiency (balance)   —force platform: vertical score, force platform: frontal score

9. Resting heartbeat rate   —standing heartbeat rate, resting heartbeat rate

The items analyzed by Fleishman include flexibility measures as well as a good number of strength items; those analyzed by Fall include many that physicians and exercise physiologists use to tap the pulmonary and cardiovascular components of physical fitness. These differences illustrate the point that one gets out of a factor analysis only the components that went into it. Ismail's development of a criterion for evaluating physical fitness tests primarily includes these items: percent lean body mass, exercise pulse rate, maximum oxygen intake (ml) per kg lean body mass, and submaximal minute volume ventilation per kg body weight.[8] Most of these items measure the efficiency of the oxygen transport and utilization system of the individual while the individual is performing progressively more difficult work when pedaling a bicycle ergometer or running on a treadmill to exhaustion. Hence, we believe that we are measuring the aerobic work capacity of the individual. Indeed, Kenneth Cooper has derived aerobic exercise programs utilizing the physical activities of jogging, cycling, swimming, and so on to increase the participants' aerobic work capacity.[9]

A more recent factor analysis conducted on both men and women by Marvin Zuidema and Ted Baumgartner identified four factors common to both sexes.[10]

8. Ismail, "Development of a Criterion for Physical Fitness Tests from Factor Analysis Results," 991–999.
9. Kenneth H. Cooper, *The New Aerobics* (New York: Bantam Books, 1970).
10. Marvin A. Zuidema and Ted Baumgartner, "Second Factor Analysis of Physical Fitness Tests," *Research Quarterly* 45 (October 1974):247–256.

The factors and relevant items are:

Factors	Men—Items	Women—Items
1. Upper body strength and endurance	—chins, pull-ups, push-ups	modified push-ups, overhand straight arm hang, modified chin-ups
2. Trunk strength and endurance	—half-hold sit-ups, leg raisers	bent knee sit-ups, half-hold sit-ups
3. Leg explosive strength and endurance	—standing broad jump, jump and reach	standing broad jump, jump and reach, 50-yard (45.73-m) dash

Factors	Men—Items	Women—Items
4. Cardiorespiratory endurance	—12-minute run, 880-yard (804.88-m) run	12-minute run

Components of physical fitness identified by factor analysis agree, in general, with those presented by the President's Council on Physical Fitness and Sports, which were mentioned on page 263. These factors and test items involve elements of motor performance (fitness) and cardiovascular endurance.

purposes of fitness testing

Physical fitness tests can be used by the teacher for one or more of the following reasons:

1. *CLASSIFICATION*—to place pupils into similar groups on the basis of the physical fitness score. All those who have an initially high test score can be put into a class that begins at a high level of exercise intensity. Those who have a low test score may be placed in a class or program that begins at a low level of exercise intensity.
2. *DIAGNOSIS*—to determine the strengths and weaknesses of major muscle groups, as well as cardiovascular efficiency. On the basis of these data, the teacher can prescribe an appropriate conditioning program suited to individual needs.
3. *ACHIEVEMENT*—to show the effects of a fitness program to the participant with initial and periodic testing during the program.
4. *MOTIVATION*—to stimulate participants to improve their level of fitness.
5. *PROGRAM EVALUATION*—to permit teachers to demonstrate the effects of their school physical fitness program to the students, parents, and school ad-

ministrators. Teachers can also compare the mean scores of children from their school against those of children of the same age in other schools in the county, state, region, or nation.

6. *NORM DEVELOPMENT*—to develop average scores for each item collected on a large number of pupils so local norms can be established. A child's performance can then be compared with the performances of other children in the same school.

physical examination

The first test administered to any individual, irrespective of age, should be a thorough examination by a licensed physician. Specific health problems identified by the physician that are contraindications for vigorous physical exercise should be recorded on an appropriate school or agency health appraisal form (Figure 10.1). Based on the medical examination the physician should classify the individual into one of the following categories:

1. Unrestricted activity—Individuals in this category are capable of tolerating the stress of vigorous physical activity in the agency physical education and/or competitive athletic program.
2. Moderate activity—Individuals in this category can perform activities that are submaximal in terms of exercise stress intensity. These individuals, due to minor problems such as asthma, mild heart, or lung disease, can take some exercises but will require frequent rest periods.
3. Restricted activity—These individuals,

SCHOOL _____ BIRTH DATE _____ SEX _____

NAME _____ PARENTS NAME _____

ADDRESS _____ PHONE _____

CODE: 1 = EXCELLENT,   2 = MILD PROBLEM,   3 - RATHER SEVERE

GRADE					Genitalia					
DATE					Nervous System					
Nutrition					Bones and Joints					
Height					Muscle Tone					
Weight					Posture					
Skin and Hair					Type of Inoculation (Date)					
Eyes					Type of Vaccinations (Date)					
Vision Test										
Ears										
Hearing Test										
Nose and Throat					Physician's Remarks and Recommendations:					
Teeth and Gums										
Thyroid Gland										
Lymph Nodes										
Heart and Lungs										
Abdomen										

PHYSICAL EDUCATION AND ATHLETIC PARTICIPATION RECOMMENDATION

1. Unrestricted activity- All vigorous P.E. and competitive athletic programs					
2. Moderate activity- Frequent rest periods; Badminton, Jogging, Volleyball, Tennis					
3. Restricted - Serious health problems - Archery, Golf, Table Tennis, Walking, Bowling					

PHYSICIANS SIGNATURE _____

Figure 10.1 Health Appraisal by Physician

due to serious health problems, are limited to mild forms of exercise such as walking, table tennis, or archery.

Only those individuals in category 1, unrestricted physical activity, should perform all the items on motor and physical fitness tests, since the child is asked to do his or her best or give as maximal a performance as possible on each test item.

aahper youth fitness test

In 1958, the AAHPER Youth Fitness Test Battery was presented to the professional field by Paul Hunsicker, on behalf of a physical fitness research committee, which developed the test to be used nationwide.[11] The committee developed the test as a result of a need to upgrade and assess the fitness status of the youth of our nation, which Hans Kraus and Ruth Hirschland pointed out was below the level of European school children.[12] Over a period of years, extensive test data were collected, and national norms were revised and published in a 1965 test manual.[13] The test included such items as pull-ups for boys, flexed-arm hang for girls, sit-ups to a maximum of 50 for girls and 100 for boys, shuttle run, standing broad jump,

50-yard (45.73-m) dash, softball throw for distance, and the 600-yard (548.73-m) run-walk. The AAHPER Youth Fitness Test was revised again in 1976, with the softball throw for distance being eliminated and the straight leg sit-up being changed to the number of bent-knee sit-ups done in 60 seconds.[14] In addition, the 9- and 12-minute run-walk or the 1-mile (1609.76-m) or 1½-mile (2414.64-m) run for time is proposed as an alternate to the 600-yard run-walk.

Ted Baumgartner and Andrew Jackson[15] summarize the evidence that indicates that, up to a point, the longer the run, the greater the correlation with maximum oxygen uptake.

Current AAHPER test items and factors that appear to be inherent in the items are:

11. Paul Hunsicker, "AAHPER Physical Fitness Test Battery," *Journal of Health, Physical Education and Recreation* 29 (September 1958):24–25.
12. Hans Kraus and Ruth Hirschland, "Minimum Muscular Fitness Tests in School Children," *Research Quarterly* 25 (May 1954):178–188.
13. American Association for Health, Physical Education and Recreation, *Youth Fitness Test Manual*, rev. ed. (Washington, D.C.: AAHPER, 1965).
14. American Alliance for Health, Physical Education and Recreation, *Youth Fitness Test Manual*, rev. 3d ed. (Washington, D.C.: AAHPER, 1976).
15. Ted Baumgartner and Andrew Jackson, *Measurement for Evaluation in Physical Education* (Boston: Houghton Mifflin, 1975), p. 206.

Factors

1. Dynamic strength and endurance of arms and shoulders

2. Trunk strength and endurance

3. Speed and change of direction

4. Explosive strength of legs

5. Explosive strength of legs and speed of lower extremities

6. Cardiorespiratory endurance

Items

—pull-ups or flexed-arm hang

—sit-ups

—shuttle run

—standing broad jump

—50-yard (45.73-m) dash

—600-yard (548.78-m) run-walk;
9- or 12-minute run-walk for distance;
1-mile (1609.76-m) or 1½-mile (2414.64-m) run for time

The AAHPER Youth Fitness Test is easily administered by the teacher with very little equipment required. An additional feature is the extensive national norms presented in the test manual. It is recommended that testing be conducted over a two-day period with pull-ups or flexed-arm hang, sit-ups, and the shuttle run being administered the first day; and the standing broad jump, 50-yard (45.73-m) dash, and 600-yard (548.78-m) run-walk or the 9-minute run-walk or the 1-mile (1609.76-m) run for time being completed on the second day.

testing procedures[16]

1. Pull-up (boys)

Equipment: A metal or wooden bar approximately 1½ inches (3.81 cm) in diameter. A doorway gym bar can be used, and, if no regular equipment is available, a piece of pipe or even the rungs of a ladder can also serve the purpose. (Figure 10.2)

Description: The bar should be high enough so the pupil can hang with his arms and legs fully extended and his feet free of the floor. He should use an overhand grasp, palms facing away from his body. From the hanging position, the pupil raises his body by his arms until his chin can be placed over the bar and then lowers his body to a full hang, as in the starting position. The exercise is repeated as many times as possible.

Rules:
1. Allow one trial unless it is obvious that the pupil has not had a fair chance.
2. The body must not swing during the execution of the movement. The pull must in no way be a snap movement. If the pupil starts swinging, check

Figure 10.2   Pull-ups

this by holding your extended arm across the front of the thighs.
3. The knees must not be raised, and kicking the legs is not permitted.

Scoring: Record the number of completed pull-ups to the nearest whole number.

1. Flexed-arm Hang (girls)

Equipment: A horizontal bar approximately 1½ inches (3.81 cm) in diameter is preferred. A doorway gym bar can be used; if no regular equipment is available, a piece of pipe can serve the purpose. A stopwatch is needed.

Description: The height of the bar should be adjusted so it is approximately equal to the pupil's standing height. The pupil should use an overhand grasp. With the assistance of two spotters, one in front and one in back of pupil, the pupil raises her body off the floor to a position where the chin is above

16. American Association for Health, Physical Education and Recreation, *Youth Fitness Test Manual,* rev. 3d ed. (Washington, D.C.: AAHPER, 1976). Used by permission of the AAHPER.

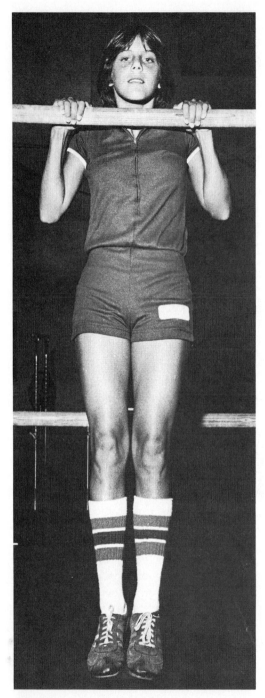

Figure 10-3　Flexed-arm Hang

the bar, the elbows are flexed, and the chest is close to the bar. The pupil holds this position as long as possible. (Figure 10.3)

Rules:
1. The stopwatch is started as soon as the subject takes the hanging position.
2. The watch is stopped when (a) pupil's chin touches the bar, (b) pupil's head tilts backwards to keep chin above the bar, (c) pupil's chin falls below the level of the bar.

Scoring: Record in seconds to the nearest second the length of time the subject holds the hanging position.

2. **Sit-up (flexed-leg) (boys and girls)**

Equipment: Clean floor, mat, or dry turf, and stopwatch.

Description: The pupil lies on his back with his knees bent, feet on the floor and heels not more than 12 inches (30.48 cm) from the buttocks. The angle at the knees should be less than 90 degrees. The pupil puts his hands on the back of his neck with fingers clasped and places his elbows squarely on the mat, floor, or turf. His feet are held by his partner to keep them in touch with the surface. The pupil tightens his abdominal muscles and brings his head and elbows forward as he curls up, finally touching elbows to knees. This action constitutes one sit-up. The pupil returns to the starting position with his elbows on the surface before he sits up again. The timer gives the signal "Ready? Go!" and the sit-up performance is started on "Go." Performance is stopped on the command "Stop." The number of correctly executed sit-ups performed in 60 seconds shall be the score. (Figure 10.4)

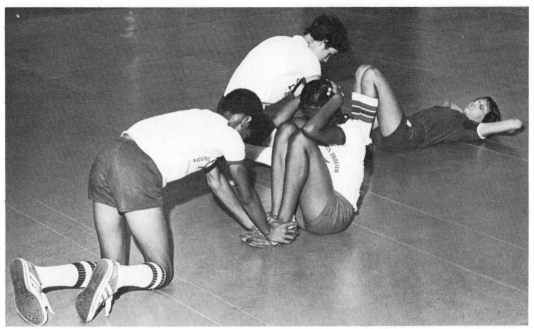

Figure 10.4   Sit-up (Flexed Leg)

Rules:
1. Only one trial shall be allowed unless the teacher believes the pupil has not had a fair opportunity to perform.
2. No resting between sit-ups is permitted.
3. No sit-ups shall be counted in which the pupil does not (a) keep the fingers clasped behind the neck, (b) bring both elbows forward in starting to sit up without pushing off the floor with the elbow, or (c) return to starting position, with elbows flat on the surface, before sitting up again.

Scoring: Record the number of correctly executed sit-ups the pupil is able to do in 60 seconds. A foul nullifies the count for that sit-up. The watch is started on "Go" and stopped on "Stop."

3. Shuttle Run (boys and girls)

Equipment: Two blocks of wood, 2 × 2 × 4 inches (5.08 × 5.08 × 10.16 cm), and stopwatch. Pupils should wear sneakers or run barefooted.

Description: Two parallel lines are marked on the floor 30 feet (9.14 m) apart. The width of a regulation volleyball court serves as a suitable area. Place the blocks of wood behind one of the lines as indicated in Figure 10.5. The pupil starts from behind the other line. On the signal "Ready? Go!" the pupil runs to the blocks, picks up one, runs back to the starting line, and places the block behind the line; she then runs back, picks up the second block, and carries it back across the starting line. If the scorer has two stopwatches or one with a split-second timer, it is preferable to have two pupils running at the same

Figure 10.5   Shuttle Run

time. To eliminate the necessity of returning the blocks after each race, start the races alternately, first from behind one line and then from behind the other. (Figure 10.5)

Rules:

Allow two trials with some rest between.

Scoring: Record the time of the better of the two trials to the nearest tenth of a second.

4. Standing Long Jump (boys and girls)

Equipment: Mat, floor, or outdoor jumping pit, and a metric or English tape measure.

Description: Pupil stands as indicated in Figure 10.6, with the feet several inches apart and the toes just behind the take-off line. Preparatory to jumping, the pupil swings the arms backward and bends the knees. The jump is accomplished by simultaneously extending the knees and swinging the arms forward.

Rules:

1. Allow three trials.
2. Measure from the take-off line to the

heel or other part of the body that touches the floor nearest the take-off line.

3. When the test is given indoors, it is convenient to tape the tape measure to the floor at right angles to the take-off line and have the pupils jump along the tape. The scorer stands to the side and observes the mark to the nearest inch.

Scoring: Record the best of the three trials in feet and inches to the nearest inch (meter to nearest cm).

5. 50-yard (45.73-m) Dash (boys and girls)

Equipment: Two stopwatches or one with a split-second timer.

Description: It is preferable to administer this test to two pupils at a time. Have both take positions behind the starting line. The starter will use the commands "Are you ready?" and "Go!" The latter will be accompanied by a downward sweep of the starter's arm to give a visual signal to the timer, who stands at the finish line. (Figure 10.7)

Rules:

The score is the amount of time between the starter's signal and the instant the pupil crosses the finish line.

Scoring: Record in seconds to the nearest tenth of a second.

6. 600-yard (548.78-m) Run-walk (boys and girls)

Equipment: Track or area marked according to Figure 10.8 and stopwatch.

Description: Pupil uses a standing start. At the signal "Ready? Go!" the pupil starts running the 600-yard (548.78-m) distance. The running may be interspersed with walking. It is possible to have a dozen pupils run at one time by having the pupils pair off before the start of the event. Then each pupil listens for and remembers his partner's time as the latter crosses the finish. The

Figure 10.6   Standing Long Jump

Figure 10.7   50-yard Dash
(Start)

timer merely calls out the times as the pupils cross the finish line. (Figure 10.8)

Rules:

Walking is permitted, but the object is to cover the distance in the shortest possible time.

Scoring: Record in minutes and seconds.

7. 9-minute Run or 1-mile (1609.76-m) Run for Time

Equipment: Track area marked off in known distance segments in yards or meters; stopwatch; score sheets and pencil.

Description: a. At the signal "Ready? Go!" the pupil runs the mile distance in as short a time as possible. Group test as in the 600-yard (548.78-m) run.

b. At the signal "Ready? Go!" the pupil covers as much distance as possible in 9 minutes. If the track or running area is marked off every 200 yards (182.88 m), the runner's partner can keep count of the number of laps completed and additional markers passed. Convert total distance covered to yards or meters.

Rules:

Encourage pupils to run the entire distance, discourage walking.

Norms for the various items on the AAHPER Test are presented on a percentile rank basis for each age and appear in Tables 10.1 through 10.20. A cumulative fitness scoring record is illustrated in Figure 10.9.

Figure 10.8   Distance Run
Finish

Table 10.1   Flexed-arm Hang for Girls

Percentile Scores Based on Age / Test Scores in Seconds

| Percentile | Age | | | | | | | | Percentile |
	9–10	11	12	13	14	15	16	17+	
100th	78	68	84	68	65	83	69	73	100th
95th	42	39	33	34	35	36	31	34	95th
90th	29	30	27	25	29	28	24	28	90th
85th	24	24	23	21	26	25	20	22	85th
80th	21	21	21	20	23	21	17	19	80th
75th	18	20	18	16	21	18	15	17	75th
70th	16	17	15	14	18	15	12	14	70th
65th	14	15	13	13	15	14	11	12	65th
60th	12	13	12	11	13	12	10	10	60th

Table 10.1—*Continued*

Percentile	9–10	11	12	13	14	15	16	17+	Percentile
55th	10	11	10	9	11	10	8	9	55th
50th	9	10	9	8	9	9	7	8	50th
45th	7	8	8	7	8	8	6	7	45th
40th	6	7	6	6	7	7	5	6	40th
35th	5	6	5	5	5	5	4	5	35th
30th	4	5	4	4	5	4	3	4	30th
25th	3	3	3	3	3	4	3	3	25th
20th	2	3	2	2	3	3	2	2	20th
15th	1	2	1	1	2	2	1	2	15th
10th	0	0	1	0	1	1	1	1	10th
5th	0	0	0	0	0	0	0	0	5th
0	0	0	0	0	0	0	0	0	0

Table 10.2   Sit-ups for Girls (Flexed Leg)

Percentile Scores Based on Age / Test Scores in Number of Sit-ups Performed in 60 Seconds

Percentile	Age								Percentile
	9–10	11	12	13	14	15	16	17+	
100th	56	60	55	57	52	58	75	66	100th
95th	45	43	44	45	45	45	43	45	95th
90th	40	40	40	41	43	42	40	41	90th
85th	38	38	38	40	41	40	38	40	85th
80th	35	36	37	38	39	38	36	38	80th
75th	34	35	36	36	37	36	35	35	75th
70th	33	33	35	35	35	35	34	34	70th
65th	31	32	33	33	35	34	33	33	65th
60th	30	31	32	32	33	33	32	32	60th
55th	29	30	30	31	32	32	31	31	55th
50th	27	29	29	30	30	31	30	30	50th
45th	25	28	28	29	30	30	28	30	45th
40th	24	26	27	27	29	29	27	28	40th
35th	23	25	26	26	27	28	26	27	35th
30th	22	24	25	25	25	26	25	26	30th

Table 10.2—_Continued_

Percentile	9–10	11	12	13	14	15	16	17+	Percentile
25th	21	22	24	23	24	25	24	25	25th
20th	20	20	22	22	22	23	22	22	20th
15th	17	18	20	20	20	22	20	20	15th
10th	14	15	17	18	18	20	18	18	10th
5th	10	9	13	15	16	15	15	14	5th
0	0	0	0	0	2	2	0	1	0

Table 10.3   Shuttle Run for Girls

Percentile Scores Based on Age / Test Scores in Seconds and Tenths

Percentile	Age								Percentile
	9–10	11	12	13	14	15	16	17+	
100th	8.0	8.4	8.5	7.0	7.8	7.4	7.8	8.2	100th
95th	10.2	10.0	9.9	9.9	9.7	9.9	10.0	9.6	95th
90th	10.5	10.3	10.2	10.0	10.0	10.0	10.2	10.0	90th
85th	10.9	10.5	10.5	10.2	10.1	10.2	10.4	10.1	85th
80th	11.0	10.7	10.6	10.4	10.2	10.3	10.5	10.3	80th
75th	11.1	10.8	10.8	10.5	10.3	10.4	10.6	10.4	75th
70th	11.2	11.0	10.9	10.6	10.5	10.5	10.8	10.5	70th
65th	11.4	11.0	11.0	10.8	10.6	10.6	10.9	10.7	65th
60th	11.5	11.1	11.1	11.0	10.7	10.9	11.0	10.9	60th
55th	11.6	11.3	11.2	11.0	10.9	11.0	11.1	11.0	55th
50th	11.8	11.5	11.4	11.2	11.0	11.0	11.2	11.1	50th
45th	11.9	11.6	11.5	11.3	11.2	11.1	11.4	11.3	45th
40th	12.0	11.7	11.5	11.5	11.4	11.3	11.5	11.5	40th
35th	12.0	11.9	11.7	11.6	11.5	11.4	11.7	11.6	35th
30th	12.3	12.0	11.8	11.9	11.7	11.6	11.9	11.9	30th
25th	12.5	12.1	12.0	12.0	12.0	11.8	12.0	12.0	25th
20th	12.8	12.3	12.1	12.2	12.1	12.0	12.1	12.2	20th
15th	13.0	12.6	12.5	12.6	12.3	12.2	12.5	12.5	15th
10th	13.8	13.0	13.0	12.8	12.8	12.6	12.8	13.0	10th
5th	14.3	14.0	13.3	13.2	13.1	13.3	13.7	14.0	5th
0	18.0	20.0	15.3	16.5	19.2	18.5	24.9	17.0	0

Table 10.4   Standing Long Jump for Girls

Percentile Scores Based on Age / Test Scores in Feet and Inches

Percentile	9–10	11	12	13	14	15	16	17+	Percentile
				Age					
100th	7'11"	7' 0"	7' 0"	8' 0"	7' 5"	8' 0"	7' 7"	7' 6"	100th
95th	5'10"	6' 0"	6' 2"	6' 5"	6' 8"	6' 7"	6' 6"	6' 9"	95th
90th	5' 8"	5' 9"	6' 0"	6' 2"	6' 5"	6' 3"	6' 3"	6' 6"	90th
85th	5' 5"	5' 7"	5' 9"	6' 0"	6' 3"	6' 1"	6' 0"	6' 3"	85th
80th	5' 2"	5' 5"	5' 8"	5'10"	6' 0"	6' 0"	5'11"	6' 2"	80th
75th	5' 2"	5' 4"	5' 6"	5' 9"	5'11"	5'10"	5' 9"	6' 0"	75th
70th	5' 0"	5' 3"	5' 5"	5' 7"	5'10"	5' 9"	5' 8"	5'11"	70th
65th	5' 0"	5' 2"	5' 4"	5' 6"	5' 8"	5' 8"	5' 6"	5'10"	65th
60th	4'10"	5' 1"	5' 2"	5' 5"	5' 7"	5' 6"	5' 6"	5' 9"	60th
55th	4' 9"	5' 0"	5' 1"	5' 4"	5' 6"	5' 6"	5' 4"	5' 7"	55th
50th	4' 8"	4'11"	5' 0"	5' 3"	5' 4"	5' 5"	5' 3"	5' 5"	50th
45th	4' 7"	4'10"	4'11"	5' 2"	5' 3"	5' 3"	5' 2"	5' 4"	45th
40th	4' 6"	4' 8"	4'10"	5' 1"	5' 2"	5' 2"	5' 1"	5' 3"	40th
35th	4' 5"	4' 7"	4' 9"	5' 0"	5' 1"	5' 1"	5' 0"	5' 2"	35th
30th	4' 3"	4' 6"	4' 8"	4'10"	4'11"	5' 0"	4'10"	5' 0"	30th
25th	4' 1"	4' 4"	4' 6"	4' 9"	4'10"	4'11"	4' 9"	4'11"	25th
20th	4' 0"	4' 3"	4' 5"	4' 8"	4' 9"	4' 9"	4' 7"	4' 9"	20th
15th	3'11"	4' 2"	4' 3"	4' 6"	4' 6"	4' 7"	4' 6"	4' 7"	15th
10th	3' 8"	4' 0"	4' 2"	4' 3"	4' 4"	4' 5"	4' 4"	4' 4"	10th
5th	3' 5"	3' 8"	3'10"	4' 0"	4' 0"	4' 2"	4' 0"	4' 1"	5th
0	1' 8"	2'10"	3' 0"	3' 2"	3' 0"	3' 0"	2' 8"	3' 3"	0

Table 10.5   Standing Long Jump for Girls

AAHPER Percentile Scores Based on Age / Test Scores in Meters

Percentile Rank	9–10	11	12	13	14	15	16	17+	Percentile Rank
				Age					
				Meters					
100	2.41*	2.13	2.13	2.43	2.26	2.43	2.31	2.28	100
95	1.77	1.93	1.87	1.95	2.03	2.00	1.98	2.05	95
90	1.72	1.90	1.82	1.87	1.95	1.90	1.90	1.98	90

Table 10.5—*Continued*

Percentile Rank	9–10	11	12	13	14	15	16	17+	Percentile Rank
					Meters				
85	1.65	1.75	1.75	1.82	1.90	1.85	1.82	1.90	85
80	1.57	1.72	1.72	1.77	1.82	1.82	1.80	1.87	80
75	1.57	1.67	1.67	1.75	1.80	1.77	1.75	1.82	75
70	1.52	1.65	1.65	1.70	1.77	1.75	1.76	1.80	70
65	1.52	1.62	1.62	1.67	1.72	1.72	1.67	1.77	65
60	1.47	1.57	1.57	1.65	1.70	1.67	1.67	1.75	60
55	1.44	1.54	1.54	1.62	1.67	1.67	1.62	1.70	55
50	1.42	1.52	1.52	1.60	1.62	1.65	1.60	1.65	50
45	1.39	1.49	1.49	1.51	1.60	1.60	1.57	1.62	45
40	1.37	1.47	1.47	1.54	1.57	1.57	1.54	1.60	40
35	1.34	1.44	1.44	1.52	1.54	1.54	1.52	1.57	35
30	1.29	1.42	1.42	1.47	1.49	1.52	1.47	1.54	30
25	1.24	1.37	1.37	1.44	1.47	1.49	1.44	1.49	25
20	1.21	1.34	1.34	1.42	1.44	1.44	1.39	1.44	20
15	1.19	1.29	1.29	1.37	1.37	1.39	1.37	1.39	15
10	1.11	1.26	1.26	1.29	1.32	1.34	1.32	1.32	10
5	1.04	1.16	1.16	1.21	1.21	1.21	1.21	1.24	5
0	.50	.91	.86	.96	.91	.99	.81	.99	0

* To convert to centimeters, move the decimal point two places to the right (2.41 meters = 241 centimeters)

Table 10.6   50-yard (45.73-meters) Dash for Girls

Percentile Scores Based on Age / Test Scores in Seconds and Tenths

Percentile	9–10	11	12	13	14	15	16	17+	Percentile
				Age					
100th	7.0	6.9	6.0	6.0	6.0	6.0	5.6	6.4	100th
95th	7.4	7.3	7.0	6.9	6.8	6.9	7.0	6.8	95th
90th	7.5	7.5	7.2	7.0	7.0	7.0	7.1	7.0	90th
85th	7.8	7.5	7.4	7.2	7.1	7.1	7.3	7.1	85th
80th	8.0	7.8	7.5	7.3	7.2	7.2	7.4	7.3	80th
75th	8.0	7.9	7.6	7.4	7.3	7.4	7.5	7.4	75th

Table 10.6—*Continued*

Percentile	9–10	11	12	13	14	15	16	17+	Percentile
70th	8.1	7.9	7.7	7.5	7.4	7.5	7.5	7.5	70th
65th	8.3	8.0	7.9	7.6	7.5	7.5	7.6	7.5	65th
60th	8.4	8.1	8.0	7.7	7.6	7.6	7.7	7.6	60th
55th	8.5	8.2	8.0	7.9	7.6	7.7	7.8	7.7	55th
50th	8.6	8.3	8.1	8.0	7.8	7.8	7.9	7.9	50th
45th	8.8	8.4	8.2	8.0	7.9	7.9	8.0	8.0	45th
40th	8.9	8.5	8.3	8.1	8.0	8.0	8.0	8.0	40th
35th	9.0	8.6	8.4	8.2	8.0	8.0	8.1	8.1	35th
30th	9.0	8.8	8.5	8.3	8.2	8.1	8.2	8.2	30th
25th	9.1	9.0	8.7	8.5	8.3	8.2	8.3	8.4	25th
20th	9.4	9.1	8.9	8.7	8.5	8.4	8.5	8.5	20th
15th	9.6	9.3	9.1	8.9	8.8	8.6	8.5	8.8	15th
10th	9.9	9.6	9.4	9.2	9.0	8.8	8.8	9.0	10th
5th	10.3	10.0	10.0	10.0	9.6	9.2	9.3	9.5	5th
0	13.5	12.9	14.9	14.2	11.0	15.6	15.6	15.0	0

Table 10.7 **600-yard (548.78-meters) Run for Girls**

Percentile Scores Based on Age / Test Scores in Minutes and Seconds

Percentile	Age								Percentile
	9–10	11	12	13	14	15	16	17+	
100th	2′ 7″	1′52″	1′40″	1′43″	1′33″	1′41″	1′45″	1′39″	100th
95th	2′20″	2′14″	2′ 6″	2′ 4″	2′ 2″	2′ 0″	2′ 8″	2′ 2″	95th
90th	2′26″	2′21″	2′14″	2′12″	2′ 7″	2′10″	2′15″	2′10″	90th
85th	2′30″	2′25″	2′21″	2′16″	2′11″	2′14″	2′19″	2′14″	85th
80th	2′33″	2′30″	2′23″	2′20″	2′15″	2′18″	2′21″	2′20″	80th
75th	2′39″	2′35″	2′26″	2′23″	2′19″	2′22″	2′26″	2′24″	75th
70th	2′41″	2′39″	2′31″	2′27″	2′24″	2′25″	2′29″	2′26″	70th
65th	2′45″	2′42″	2′35″	2′30″	2′29″	2′28″	2′32″	2′30″	65th
60th	2′48″	2′45″	2′39″	2′34″	2′32″	2′30″	2′36″	2′35″	60th
55th	2′51″	2′48″	2′43″	2′37″	2′36″	2′34″	2′39″	2′38″	55th
50th	2′56″	2′53″	2′47″	2′41″	2′40″	2′37″	2′43″	2′41″	50th
45th	2′59″	2′55″	2′51″	2′45″	2′44″	2′40″	2′47″	2′45″	45th

Table 10.7—Continued

Percentile	9–10	11	12	13	14	15	16	17+	Percentile
40th	3' 1"	2'59"	2'56"	2'49"	2'47"	2'45"	2'49"	2'48"	40th
35th	3' 8"	3' 4"	3' 0"	2'55"	2'51"	2'50"	2'54"	2'53"	35th
30th	3'11"	3'11"	3' 6"	2'59"	2'56"	2'55"	2'58"	2'56"	30th
25th	3'15"	3'16"	3'13"	3' 6"	3' 1"	3' 0"	3' 3"	3' 2"	25th
20th	3'21"	3'24"	3'19"	3'12"	3' 8"	3' 5"	3' 9"	3' 9"	20th
15th	3'25"	3'30"	3'27"	3'20"	3'16"	3'12"	3'18"	3'19"	15th
10th	3'38"	3'44"	3'36"	3'30"	3'27"	3'26"	3'30"	3'30"	10th
5th	4' 0"	4'15"	3'59"	3'49"	3'49"	3'28"	3'49"	3'45"	5th
0	5'48"	5'10"	6' 2"	5'10"	5' 0"	5'58"	5' 5"	6'40"	0

Table 10.8   9-minute/1-mile (1609.76-meters) Run for Girls*

Percentile Scores Based on Age / Test Scores in Yards / Time

Percentile	9-minute Run Girls Age			1-mile Run Girls (1609.76 m) Age			Percentile
	10	11	12	10	11	12	
	Yards			Time			
100th	2157	2180	2203	6:13	5:42	5:08	100th
95th	1969	1992	2015	7:28	6:57	6:23	95th
90th	1867	1890	1913	8:09	7:38	7:04	90th
85th	1801	1824	1847	8:33	8:02	7:28	85th
80th	1746	1769	1792	8:57	8:26	7:52	80th
75th	1702	1725	1748	9:16	8:45	8:11	75th
70th	1658	1681	1704	9:31	9:00	8:26	70th
65th	1622	1645	1668	9:51	9:20	8:46	65th
60th	1583	1606	1629	10:02	9:31	8:57	60th
55th	1550	1573	1596	10:15	9:44	9:10	55th
50th	1514	1537	1560	10:29	9:58	9:24	50th
45th	1478	1501	1524	10:43	10:12	9:38	45th
40th	1445	1468	1491	10:56	10:25	9:51	40th
35th	1406	1429	1452	11:07	10:36	10:12	35th
30th	1370	1393	1416	11:27	10:56	10:22	30th
25th	1326	1349	1372	11:42	11:11	10:37	25th
20th	1282	1305	1328	12:01	11:30	10:56	20th
15th	1227	1250	1273	12:25	11:54	11:30	15th

Table 10.8—Continued

Percentile	9-minute Run Girls Age			1-mile Run Girls (1609.76 m) Age			Percentile
	10	11	12	10	11	12	
	Yards			Time			
10th	1161	1184	1207	12:49	12:18	11:44	10th
5th	1059	1082	1105	13:30	12:59	12:24	5th
0	871	894	917	14:45	14:14	13:40	0

* From Texas Physical Fitness — Motor Ability Test.

Table 10.9   12-minute/1½-mile (2414.64-meters) Run for Girls, Age 13 and Older*

Percentile Scores Based on Age / Test Scores in Yards/Time

Percentile	12-minute Run Yards	1.5-mile Run (2414.64 m) Time	Percentile
100th	2693	10:20	100th
95th	2448	12:17	95th
90th	2318	13:19	90th
85th	2232	14:00	85th
80th	2161	14:34	80th
75th	2100	15:03	75th
70th	2050	15:26	70th
65th	2000	15:50	65th
60th	1950	16:14	60th
55th	1908	16:34	55th
50th	1861	16:57	50th
45th	1815	17:19	45th
40th	1772	17:39	40th
35th	1722	18:03	35th
30th	1672	18:27	30th
25th	1622	18:50	25th
20th	1561	19:19	20th
15th	1490	19:53	15th
10th	1404	20:34	10th
5th	1274	21:36	5th
0	1030	23:33	0

* From Texas Physical Fitness — Motor Ability Test.

Table 10.10   9-minute and 12-minute Run for Girls

AAHPER Percentile Scores Based on Age / Test Scores in Meters

Percentile Rank	9-minute Run Age			12-minute Run Age	Percentile Rank
	10	11	12	13 and up	
	Meters			Meters	
100	1972.3	1993.3	2014.4	2462.4	100
95	1800.4	1821.4	1842.5	2238.4	95
90	1707.1	1728.2	1749.2	2119.5	90
85	1646.8	1667.8	1688.9	2040.9	85
80	1596.5	1617.5	1638.6	1975.9	80
75	1556.3	1577.3	1598.3	1920.2	75
70	1516.0	1537.1	1558.1	1874.5	70
65	1483.1	1504.1	1525.2	1828.8	65
60	1447.4	1468.5	1489.5	1783.0	60
55	1417.3	1438.3	1459.3	1744.6	55
50	1384.4	1405.4	1426.4	1701.7	50
45	1361.4	1372.5	1393.5	1659.6	45
40	1321.3	1342.3	1363.3	1620.3	40
35	1285.6	1306.6	1327.7	1574.6	35
30	1252.7	1273.7	1294.7	1528.8	30
25	1212.4	1233.5	1254.5	1483.1	25
20	1172.2	1193.2	1214.3	1427.3	20
15	1121.9	1143.0	1164.0	1362.4	15
10	1061.6	1082.6	1103.6	1283.8	10
5	968.3	989.3	1010.4	1140.2	5
0	796.4	817.4	838.5	941.8	0

Table 10.11   Pull-ups for Boys

Percentile Scores Based on Age / Test Scores in Number of Pull-ups

Percentile	Age								Percentile
	9–10	11	12	13	14	15	16	17+	
100th	19	16	18	17	27	20	26	23	100th
95th	9	8	9	10	12	15	14	15	95th
90th	7	6	7	9	10	12	12	13	90th

Table 10.11—*Continued*

Percentile	9–10	11	12	13	14	15	16	17+	Percentile
85th	5	5	6	7	9	11	11	12	85th
80th	4	5	5	6	8	10	10	11	80th
75th	3	4	4	5	7	9	10	10	75th
70th	3	4	4	5	7	9	9	10	70th
65th	2	3	3	4	6	8	8	9	65th
60th	2	3	3	4	5	7	8	8	60th
55th	1	2	2	3	5	7	7	7	55th
50th	1	2	2	3	4	6	7	7	50th
45th	1	1	1	2	4	5	6	6	45th
40th	1	1	1	2	3	5	6	6	40th
35th	1	1	1	2	3	4	5	5	35th
30th	0	1	0	1	2	4	5	5	30th
25th	0	0	0	1	2	3	4	4	25th
20th	0	0	0	0	1	2	3	3	20th
15th	0	0	0	0	1	1	3	2	15th
10th	0	0	0	0	0	1	2	1	10th
5th	0	0	0	0	0	0	1	0	5th
0	0	0	0	0	0	0	0	0	0

Table 10.12   Sit-ups for Boys (Flexed Leg)

Percentile Scores Based on Age / Test Scores in Number of Sit-ups Performed in 60 Seconds

Percentile	Age								Percentile
	9–10	11	12	13	14	15	16	17+	
100th	70	60	62	60	73	72	76	66	100th
95th	47	48	50	53	55	57	55	54	95th
90th	44	45	48	50	52	52	52	51	90th
85th	42	43	45	48	50	50	50	49	85th
80th	40	41	43	47	48	49	49	47	80th
75th	38	40	42	45	47	48	47	46	75th
70th	36	39	40	43	45	46	45	45	70th
65th	36	38	39	42	44	45	44	43	65th
60th	35	37	38	41	43	44	43	42	60th

Table 10.12—_Continued_

Percentile	9–10	11	12	13	14	15	16	17+	Percentile
55th	33	35	37	40	41	43	42	42	55th
50th	31	34	35	38	41	42	41	41	50th
45th	30	33	34	37	40	41	40	40	45th
40th	29	31	33	35	38	40	40	39	40th
35th	28	30	32	34	37	39	38	38	35th
30th	27	28	30	32	35	38	37	37	30th
25th	25	26	30	30	34	37	35	35	25th
20th	23	24	28	29	32	35	34	34	20th
15th	21	22	26	27	21	34	32	32	15th
10th	19	19	23	24	27	30	30	30	10th
5th	13	15	18	20	24	28	28	26	5th
0	2	0	0	2	6	4	12	1	0

Table 10.13   Shuttle Run for Boys

Percentile Scores Based on Age / Test Scores in Seconds and Tenths

Percentile	Age								Percentile
	9–10	11	12	13	14	15	16	17+	
100th	9.2	8.7	6.8	7.0	7.0	7.0	7.3	7.0	100th
95th	10.0	9.7	9.6	9.3	8.9	8.9	8.6	8.6	95th
90th	10.2	9.9	9.8	9.5	9.2	9.1	8.9	8.9	90th
85th	10.4	10.1	10.0	9.7	9.3	9.2	9.1	9.0	85th
80th	10.5	10.2	10.0	9.8	9.5	9.3	9.2	9.1	80th
75th	10.6	10.4	10.2	10.0	9.6	9.4	9.3	9.2	75th
70th	10.7	10.5	10.3	10.0	9.8	9.5	9.4	9.3	70th
65th	10.8	10.5	10.4	10.1	9.8	9.6	9.5	9.4	65th
60th	11.0	10.6	10.5	10.2	10.0	9.7	9.6	9.5	60th
55th	11.0	10.8	10.6	10.3	10.0	9.8	9.7	9.6	55th
50th	11.2	10.9	10.7	10.4	10.1	9.9	9.9	9.8	50th
45th	11.5	11.0	10.8	10.5	10.1	10.0	10.0	9.9	45th
40th	11.5	11.1	11.0	10.6	10.2	10.0	10.0	10.0	40th
35th	11.7	11.2	11.1	10.8	10.4	10.1	10.1	10.1	35th
30th	11.9	11.4	11.3	11.0	10.6	10.2	10.3	10.2	30th

Table 10.13—*Continued*

Percentile	9–10	11	12	13	14	15	16	17+	Percentile
25th	12.0	11.5	11.4	11.0	10.7	10.4	10.5	10.4	25th
20th	12.2	11.8	11.6	11.3	10.9	10.5	10.6	10.5	20th
15th	12.5	12.0	11.8	11.5	11.0	10.8	10.9	10.7	15th
10th	13.0	12.2	12.0	11.8	11.3	11.1	11.1	11.0	10th
5th	13.1	12.9	12.4	12.4	11.9	11.7	11.9	11.7	5th
0	17.0	20.0	22.0	16.0	18.6	14.7	15.0	15.7	0

Table 10.14   Standing Long Jump for Boys

Percentile Scores Based on Age / Test Scores in Feet and Inches

Percentile	Age								Percentile
	9–10	11	12	13	14	15	16	17+	
100th	6' 5"	8' 5"	7' 5"	8' 6"	9' 0"	9' 0"	9' 2"	9'10"	100th
95th	6' 0"	6' 2"	6' 6"	7' 1"	7' 6"	8' 0"	8' 2"	8' 5"	95th
90th	5'10"	6' 0"	6' 3"	6'10"	7' 2"	7' 7"	7'11"	8' 2"	90th
85th	5' 8"	5'10"	6' 1"	6' 8"	6'11"	7' 5"	7' 9"	8' 0"	85th
80th	5' 6"	5' 9"	6' 0"	6' 5"	6'10"	7' 3"	7' 6"	7'10"	80th
75th	5' 4"	5' 7"	5'11"	6' 3"	6' 8"	7' 2"	7' 6"	7' 9"	75th
70th	5' 3"	5' 6"	5' 9"	6' 2"	6' 6"	7' 0"	7' 4"	7' 7"	70th
65th	5' 1"	5' 6"	5' 8"	6' 0"	6' 6"	6'11"	7' 3"	7' 6"	65th
60th	5' 1"	5' 5"	5' 7"	6' 0"	6' 4"	6'10"	7' 2"	7' 5"	60th
55th	5' 0"	5' 4"	5' 6"	5'10"	6' 3"	6' 9"	7' 1"	7' 3"	55th
50th	4'11"	5' 2"	5' 5"	5' 9"	6' 2"	6' 8"	7' 0"	7' 2"	50th
45th	4'10"	5' 2"	5' 4"	5' 7"	6' 1"	6' 6"	6'11"	7' 1"	45th
40th	4' 9"	5' 0"	5' 3"	5' 6"	5'11"	6' 5"	6' 9"	7' 0"	40th
35th	4' 8"	4'11"	5' 2"	5' 5"	5'10"	6' 4"	6' 8"	6'10"	35th
30th	4' 7"	4'10"	5' 1"	5' 3"	5' 8"	6' 3"	6' 7"	6' 8"	30th
25th	4' 6"	4' 8"	5' 0"	5' 2"	5' 6"	6' 1"	6' 6"	6' 6"	25th
20th	4' 5"	4' 7"	4'10"	5' 0"	5' 4"	5'11"	6' 4"	6' 4"	20th
15th	4' 2"	4' 5"	4' 9"	4'10"	5' 2"	5' 9"	6' 2"	6' 2"	15th
10th	4' 0"	4' 3"	4' 6"	4' 7"	5' 0"	5' 6"	5'11"	5'10"	10th
5th	3'10"	4' 0"	4' 2"	4' 4"	4' 8"	5' 2"	5' 5"	5' 3"	5th
0	3' 1"	3' 0"	3' 2"	3' 3"	2' 0"	2' 0"	3' 4"	3' 0"	0

Table 10.15   Standing Long Jump for Boys

AAHPER Percentile Scores Based on Age / Test Scores in Meters

Percentile Rank	9–10	11	12	13	14	15	16	17+	Percentile Rank
				Age					
				Meters					
100th	1.95*	2.56	2.26	2.59	2.74	2.74	2.79	2.99	100th
95th	1.82	1.87	1.98	2.15	2.28	2.43	2.48	2.56	95th
90th	1.77	1.82	1.90	2.08	2.18	2.31	2.41	2.48	90th
85th	1.72	1.77	1.85	2.03	2.10	2.26	2.36	2.43	85th
80th	1.67	1.75	1.82	1.95	2.08	2.20	2.28	2.38	80th
75th	1.62	1.70	1.80	1.90	2.03	2.18	2.28	2.36	75th
70th	1.60	1.67	1.75	1.87	1.98	2.13	2.23	2.31	70th
65th	1.54	1.67	1.72	1.82	1.98	2.10	2.20	2.28	65th
60th	1.54	1.65	1.70	1.82	1.93	2.08	2.18	2.26	60th
55th	1.52	1.62	1.67	1.77	1.90	2.05	2.15	2.20	55th
50th	1.49	1.57	1.65	1.75	1.88	2.03	2.13	2.18	50th
45th	1.47	1.57	1.62	1.70	1.85	1.98	2.10	2.15	45th
40th	1.44	1.52	1.60	1.67	1.80	1.95	2.05	2.13	40th
35th	1.42	1.49	1.57	1.65	1.77	1.93	2.03	2.08	35th
30th	1.39	1.47	1.54	1.60	1.72	1.90	2.00	2.03	30th
25th	1.37	1.42	1.52	1.57	1.67	1.85	1.98	1.98	25th
20th	1.34	1.39	1.47	1.52	1.62	1.80	1.93	1.93	20th
15th	1.26	1.34	1.44	1.47	1.57	1.75	1.87	1.87	15th
10th	1.21	1.29	1.37	1.39	1.52	1.67	1.80	1.77	10th
5th	1.16	1.21	1.26	1.32	1.42	1.57	1.65	1.60	5th
0	.93	.91	.96	.99	.60	.60	1.01	.91	0

* To convert to centimeters, move the decimal point two places to the right (1.95 meters = 195 centimeters)

Table 10.16   50-yard (45.73-meters) Dash for Boys

Percentile Scores Based on Age / Test Scores in Seconds and Tenths

Percentile	9–10	11	12	13	14	15	16	17+	Percentile
				Age					
100th	7.0	6.3	6.3	5.8	5.9	5.5	5.5	5.4	100th
95th	7.3	7.1	6.8	6.5	6.2	6.0	6.0	5.9	95th
90th	7.5	7.2	7.0	6.7	6.4	6.2	6.2	6.0	90th

Table 10.16—*Continued*

Percentile	9–10	11	12	13	14	15	16	17+	Percentile
85th	7.7	7.4	7.1	6.9	6.5	6.3	6.3	6.1	85th
80th	7.8	7.5	7.3	7.0	6.6	6.4	6.4	6.3	80th
75th	7.8	7.6	7.4	7.0	6.8	6.5	6.5	6.3	75th
70th	7.9	7.7	7.5	7.1	6.9	6.6	6.5	6.4	70th
65th	8.0	7.9	7.5	7.2	7.0	6.6	6.6	6.5	65th
60th	8.0	7.9	7.6	7.3	7.0	6.8	6.6	6.5	60th
55th	8.1	8.0	7.7	7.4	7.1	6.8	6.7	6.6	55th
50th	8.2	8.0	7.8	7.5	7.2	6.9	6.7	6.6	50th
45th	8.4	8.2	7.9	7.5	7.3	6.9	6.8	6.7	45th
40th	8.6	8.3	8.0	7.6	7.4	7.0	6.8	6.8	40th
35th	8.7	8.4	8.1	7.7	7.5	7.1	6.9	6.9	35th
30th	8.8	8.5	8.2	7.9	7.6	7.2	7.0	7.0	30th
25th	8.9	8.6	8.3	8.0	7.7	7.3	7.0	7.0	25th
20th	9.0	8.7	8.5	8.1	7.9	7.4	7.1	7.1	20th
15th	9.2	9.0	8.6	8.3	8.0	7.5	7.2	7.3	15th
10th	9.5	9.1	9.0	8.7	8.2	7.6	7.4	7.5	10th
5th	9.9	9.5	9.5	9.0	8.8	8.0	7.7	7.9	5th
0	11.0	11.5	11.3	15.0	11.1	11.0	9.9	12.0	0

Table 10.17   600-yard (548.78-meters) Run for Boys

Percentile Scores Based on Age / Test Scores in Minutes and Seconds

Percentile	Age								Percentile
	9–10	11	12	13	14	15	16	17+	
100th	1'52"	1'47"	1'38"	1'26"	1'27"	1'20"	1'21"	1'20"	100th
95th	2' 5"	2' 2"	1'52"	1'45"	1'39"	1'36"	1'34"	1'32"	95th
90th	2' 9"	2' 6"	1'57"	1'50"	1'44"	1'40"	1'38"	1'35"	90th
85th	2'11"	2' 9"	2' 0"	1'54"	1'47"	1'42"	1'40"	1'38"	85th
80th	2'15"	2'12"	2' 4"	1'57"	1'50"	1'45"	1'42"	1'41"	80th
75th	2'17"	2'15"	2' 6"	1'59"	1'52"	1'46"	1'44"	1'43"	75th
70th	2'20"	2'17"	2' 9"	2' 1"	1'55"	1'48"	1'46"	1'45"	70th
65th	2'27"	2'19"	2'11"	2' 3"	1'57"	1'50"	1'48"	1'47"	65th
60th	2'30"	2'22"	2'14"	2' 5"	1'58"	1'52"	1'49"	1'49"	60th

Table 10.17—*Continued*

Percentile	9–10	11	12	13	14	15	16	17+	Percentile
55th	2'31"	2'25"	2'16"	2' 7"	2' 0"	1'54"	1'50"	1'50"	55th
50th	2'33"	2'27"	2'19"	2'10"	2' 3"	1'56"	1'52"	1'52"	50th
45th	2'35"	2'30"	2'22"	2'13"	2' 5"	1'57"	1'54"	1'53"	45th
40th	2'40"	2'34"	2'24"	2'15"	2' 7"	1'59"	1'56"	1'56"	40th
35th	2'42"	2'37"	2'28"	2'20"	2'10"	2' 1"	1'58"	1'57"	35th
30th	2'49"	2'41"	2'32"	2'24"	2'12"	2' 5"	1'59"	1'59"	30th
25th	2'53"	2'47"	2'37"	2'27"	2'16"	2' 8"	2' 1"	2' 2"	25th
20th	2'59"	2'54"	2'42"	2'32"	2'22"	2'11"	2' 4"	2' 6"	20th
15th	3' 7"	3' 2"	2'48"	2'37"	2'30"	2'15"	2' 9"	2'12"	15th
10th	3'14"	3'14"	2'54"	2'45"	2'37"	2'23"	2'17"	2'22"	10th
5th	3'22"	3'29"	3' 6"	3' 0"	2'51"	2'30"	2'31"	2'38"	5th
0	4'48"	6'20"	4'10"	4' 0"	6' 0"	4'39"	4'11"	5'10"	0

Table 10.18   9-minute/1-mile (1609.76-meters) Run for Boys*

Percentile Scores Based on Age / Test Scores in Yards/Time

Percentile	9-minute Run Boys Age			1-mile Run Boys (1609.76 m) Age			Percentile
	10	11	12	10	11	12	
	Yards			Time			
100th	2532	2535	2578	5:07	4:44	4:21	100th
95th	2294	2356	2418	5:55	5:32	5:09	95th
90th	2166	2228	2290	6:38	6:15	5:52	90th
85th	2081	2143	2205	7:06	6:43	6:20	85th
80th	2011	2073	2135	7:29	7:03	6:40	80th
75th	1952	2014	2076	7:49	7:26	7:03	75th
70th	1902	1964	2026	8:05	7:42	7:19	70th
65th	1853	1915	1977	8:22	7:59	7:36	65th
60th	1804	1866	1928	8:38	8:15	7:52	60th
55th	1762	1824	1886	8:52	8:29	8:06	55th
50th	1717	1779	1841	9:07	8:44	8:21	50th
45th	1672	1734	1796	9:22	8:59	8:36	45th

Table 10.18—*Continued*

Percentile	9-minute Run Boys Age			1-mile Run Boys (1609.76 m) Age			Percentile
	10	11	12	10	11	12	
	Yards			Time			
40th	1630	1692	1754	9:32	9:13	8:50	40th
35th	1581	1643	1705	9:52	9:29	9:06	35th
30th	1532	1594	1656	10:09	9:46	9:23	30th
25th	1482	1544	1606	10:25	10:02	9:39	25th
20th	1423	1485	1547	10:35	10:22	9:59	20th
15th	1353	1415	1477	11:08	10:45	10:22	15th
10th	1268	1330	1392	11:36	11:13	10:50	10th
5th	1140	1202	1264	12:19	11:56	11:33	5th
0	901	924	927	14:07	13:44	13:21	0

* From Texas Physical Fitness—Motor Ability Test.

Table 10.19   12-minute/1½-mile (2414.64-meters) Run for Boys, Age 13 and Older*

Percentile Scores Based on Age / Test Scores in Yards/Time

Percentile	12-minute Run Yards	1.5-mile Run (2414.64 m) Time	Percentile
100th	3590	7:26	100th
95th	3297	8:37	95th
90th	3140	9:15	90th
85th	3037	9:40	85th
80th	2952	10:01	80th
75th	2879	10:19	75th
70th	2819	10:34	70th
65th	2759	10:48	65th
60th	2699	11:02	60th
55th	2648	11:15	55th
50th	2592	11:29	50th
45th	2536	11:42	45th
40th	2485	11:55	40th
35th	2425	12:10	35th
30th	2365	12:24	30th

Table 10.19—*Continued*

Percentile	12-minute Run Yards	1.5-mile Run (2414.64 m) Time	Percentile
25th	2305	12:39	25th
20th	2232	12:56	20th
15th	2147	13:17	15th
10th	2044	13:42	10th
5th	1888	14:20	5th
0	1594	15:32	0

* From Texas Physical Fitness—Motor Ability Test.

Table 10.20   9-minute and 12-minute Run for Boys

AAHPER Percentile Scores Based on Age / Test Scores in Meters

Percentile Rank	9-minute Run Age			12-minute Run Age	Percentile Rank
	10 Meters	11	12	13 and up Meters	
100	2315.2	2318.0	2357.3	3282.7	100
95	2097.6	2154.3	2211.0	3014.7	95
90	1980.6	2037.2	2093.8	2871.2	90
85	1902.8	1959.5	2016.2	2777.0	85
80	1838.8	1895.5	1952.2	2699.3	80
75	1784.9	1841.6	1898.3	2632.5	75
70	1739.1	1795.8	1852.5	2577.7	70
65	1694.3	1751.0	1807.7	2522.8	65
60	1649.5	1706.2	1762.9	2467.9	60
55	1611.1	1667.8	1724.5	2421.3	55
50	1570.0	1626.7	1683.4	2370.1	50
45	1528.8	1585.5	1642.2	2318.9	45
40	1490.4	1547.1	1603.8	2272.2	40
35	1445.6	1502.3	1559.0	2217.4	35
30	1400.8	1457.5	1514.2	2162.5	30
25	1355.1	1411.8	1468.5	2107.6	25
20	1301.2	1357.8	1414.5	2040.9	20
15	1237.1	1293.8	1350.5	1963.2	15
10	1159.4	1216.1	1272.8	1869.0	10
5	1042.4	1099.1	1155.8	1726.3	5
0	823.8	844.9	847.6	1457.5	0

Name _____ Date of Birth _____

School _____ Medical Clearance for Testing Date _____

Grade _____ Sex _____

TEST ITEMS	Date of Test _____ Age Yrs. ___ Mos. ___		Date of Test _____ Age Yrs. ___ Mos. ___		Date of Test _____ Age Yrs. ___ Mos. ___		Date of Test _____ Age Yrs. ___ Mos. ___	
	Raw Score	Centile Rank	Raw Score	Centile Rank	Raw Score	Centile Rank	Raw Score	Centile Rank
Height								
Weight								
Pull-up (Boys)								
Flexed-arm Hang (Girls)								
Sit-ups in 60 sec.								
Shuttle run								
Standing Broad Jump								
50-yd. dash (45.73m)								
600-yd. run (548.78m)								
9-minute run or 1-mile run (1609.76m)								
Step Test								
Percent Body Fat								
Body Density								

Figure 10.9   Cumulative Scoring Record for AAHPER and Other Fitness Items

critique of the aahper test

validity

A comparison of the test items on the AAHPER test with the items that measure the various factors of motor and/or physical fitness described in an earlier section of this chapter reveals that the AAHPER test provides estimates for a number of the factors. One may conclude, therefore, that the AAHPER test possesses factorial validity. This type of validity identifies the more important test content underlying certain fitness constructs (factors). Not all fitness factors are included in the items on the AAHPER test. Indeed, if the practitioner desires to measure flexibility or balance, specific flexibility and balance items should be used.

A. H. Ismail, D. F. McLeod, and H. B. Falls[17] studied the relationship between the composite scores on the AAHPER test and composite scores on other fitness tests such as the Purdue Motor Fitness Test, the JCR test, Larson Muscular Strength Test, California Physical Efficiency Test, United States Air Force Test, Southern Methodist Test, and the Indiana Motor Fitness Tests. The correlations between the AAHPER test and the other tests ranged from .63 to .98. This is not too surprising since similar items are found on most of these tests. The longest run on any of the tests was 600 yards (548.78 m). In another study Ismail et al. report correlations ranging between .51 and .59 among the AAHPER composite score and scores on physical fitness criterion test batteries.[18] The criterion batteries are primarily composed of percentage of lean body mass, maximum oxygen uptake/kg lean body mass, exercise pulse rate, pulmonary ventilation, and blood pressure items. Based on these data it is reasonable to conclude that the AAHPER test with the 600-yard (548.78-m) run primarily measures motor fitness and is only moderately related to physical fitness as defined by the criterion test batteries. Margaret Safrit presents correlations obtained in a number of studies on males and females, ages 11 years to middle-age, between the 600-yard (548.78-m) run and maximum oxygen uptake of −.27, −.53, −.62, −.64, −.66, −.68, and −.71.[19] Baumgartner and Jackson summarize the evidence that indicates the longer the run, the higher the correlation with maximum oxygen uptake.[20] The most recent research by Andrew Jackson and A. Eugene Coleman on elementary school boys and girls and by Edmund Burke on male college students supports this contention.[21] They found that the 9-minute run for elementary children and the 12-minute run for college men were the most valid measures of aerobic power (maximal oxygen uptake) when compared to the shorter 600-yard (548.78-m) run. They report validity coefficients of .82 for elementary boys, .71 for elementary girls, and .90 for college men. In the elementary school study increasing the time from a 9- to 12-minute run did not increase the validity of the test. Since the 1976 revision of the AAHPER test includes

17. A. H. Ismail, D. F. McLeod, H. B. Falls, "Evaluation of Selected Tests of Motor and/or Physical Fitness," West Lafayette, Ind.: Purdue University, Department of Physical Education for Men, 1964.

18. Ismail et al., "Development of a Criterion for Physical Fitness Tests from Factor Analysis Results," 991–999.

19. Margaret J. Safrit, *Evaluation in Physical Education: Assessing Motor Behavior* (Englewood Cliffs, N. J.: Prentice-Hall, 1973), p. 230.

20. Baumgartner and Jackson, *Measurement for Evaluation in Physical Education.*

21. Andrew S. Jackson and A. Eugene Coleman, "Validation of Distance Run Tests for Elementary School Children," *Research Quarterly* 47 (March 1976):86–94; Edmund J. Burke, "Validity of Selected Laboratory and Field Tests of Physical Working Capacity," *Research Quarterly* 47 (March 1976):95–104.

runs longer than 600 yards (548.78 m), the teacher will come closer to estimating physical fitness with the longer run and will be estimating aspects of motor fitness primarily with the remaining items.

reliability of aahper test items

Quite a few reliability studies of the AAHPER test are reported in the literature. Safrit summarizes these studies conducted primarily on elementary and secondary pupils.[22] The range of reliability coefficients for the various items presented by her are as follows:

Pull-ups	.82 to .89
Flexed-arm hang	.74
Standing broad jump	.83 to .98
50-yard (45.78-m) dash	.83 to .94
Softball throw	.90 to .93
Sit-ups to maximum	.57 to .68
Shuttle run	.68 to .75
600-yard (548.78-m) run-walk	.65 to .92

In addition, Baumgartner and Jackson report a reliability coefficient as high as .98 for students tested on separate days in either the 12- or 9-minute run-walk.[23]

A convenient cumulative score record for fitness testing appears in Figure 10.9 and a profile sheet is illustrated in Figure 10.10. One may use a different colored line for different testing dates to indicate changes in fitness profile.

recommendations for revision of aahper youth fitness test

In 1975 a joint committee composed of members representing the Measurement and Evaluation, Physical Fitness and Research Councils of the Association for Research, Administration, Professional Councils and Societies of AAHPER, studied the need for revision of the AAHPER Youth Fitness Tests.

Based on their work, a position paper was developed and presented to the AAHPER membership at the national convention in Milwaukee, Wisconsin, in 1976.[24] The committee made the following recomendations:

I-1. That a battery be developed to measure the component of physical fitness as identified and defined by the joint committee. Such a physical fitness test should meet the following criteria:

    a. That it measure components that extend from severely limited dysfunction to high levels of functional capacity.

    b. That it be improved with appropriate physical activity.

    c. That its changes in functional capacity be accurately reflected by changes in test scores.

The first criterion links physical fitness directly to health. The committee then identified the areas of health that are of national concern and that appear to meet the first criterion, such as cardiovascular endurance, obesity, and musculoskeletal dysfunction, particularly low back pain and tension.

I-2. That a separate battery be developed consisting of motor performance items that have historically been included in physical fitness batteries.

22. Safrit, *Evaluation in Physical Education: Assessing Motor Behavior*, pp. 227, 232.

23. Ted A. Baumgartner and Andrew S. Jackson, *Measurement for Evaluation in Physical Education: Review and Resource Manual* (Boston: Houghton Mifflin, 1975), p. 113.

24. Andrew S. Jackson et al., *Revision of the AAHPER Youth Fitness Tests*, a position paper presented at the Measurement and Evaluation, Physical Fitness and Research meetings, National Convention of the American Alliance for Health, Physical Education and Recreation, Milwaukee, Wisconsin, 1976.

PHYSICAL FITNESS: SEMESTER PROFILE FOR _____

Rank In Group	INDEX	Letter Grade	T Score	AAHPER Test Items						Alternate Items			Knowledge	Ratings
				Pull-Up Or Flexed Arm Hang	Stand. Broad Jump	50-Yd. Dash (45.73m)	No. of Sit-Ups In 60 Seconds	Shuttle Run	600-Yd. Run (548.78m)	1-Mile Run Or 9 Min. Run	Step Test	Vertical Jump	Physical Fitness Knowledge Test Score	
99			80											
			78											Excellent
	6.5	A+	76											
98	6.0	A	74											
			72											
95			70											
	5.7	A-	68											Very Good
90	5.3	B+	66											
			64											
80	5.0	B	62											
75			60											Above Average
70	4.7	B-	58											
60	4.3	C+	56											
			54											
50	4.0	C	52											Average
			50											
40			48											
30			46											Below Average
25	3.7	C-	44											
20	3.3	D+	42											
			40											
10	3.0	D	38											Poor
			36											
5	2.7	D-	34											
			32											
2	2.0	F	30											Very Poor
			28											
			26											
			24											
1			22											
			20											

RECREATIONAL SPORT SKILLS ACQUIRED THIS SEMESTER_____

COMMENTS:_____

Figure 10.10 Physical Fitness Profile Sheet

physical fitness battery

II-1. That distance run tests be used as field tests of cardiovascular endurance. The recommended test is:
   a. 1-mile (1609.76-m) run-walk for time; or
   b. 9-minute run-walk for distance.
II-2. That a national study be conducted to estimate the body composition of American boys and girls by the use of appropriate statistical procedures and that these results be used to establish desirable levels of body fat.
II-3. That the maximum number of flexed leg sit-ups achieved in one minute be the test to measure abdominal strength. This test is currently part of the 1976 revision of the AAHPER Youth Fitness Test.

motor performance

III-1. That the present AAHPER tests: pull-ups (boys) and flexed-arm hang (girls) be retained, with the change that the reverse grip rather than the forward grip be used.
III-2. That the present 50-yard (45.73-m) dash test be retained.
III-3. That the present shuttle run be retained and, in addition, optional tests that require more turning be considered as an alternate test.
III-4. That the present standing broad jump be retained and, as an option, include the vertical jump test, which is more relevant for sports such as basketball and volleyball.

1979 revision of the aahper youth fitness test

In 1977 a task force was established to consider the recommendations of the 1976 Committee report that was presented at the Milwaukee AAHPER Convention. The task force is comprised of members of the Measurement and Evaluation Council and the Physical Fitness Council of AAHPER. After two years of work the Task Force on Fitness reported at the AAHPER National Convention in March, 1979, in New Orleans. The report specified the rationale for the 1979 revision of the test as the AAHPER Physical Fitness Test. The Task Force on Fitness in cooperation with AAHPER is in the process of developing a test manual, which should be available during the summer of 1980.

The new 1979 test emphasizes a shift from sport and motor fitness performance to a primary focus on the health aspects of fitness. The task force recommends that current motor and sport performance items be examined and revisions made taking into consideration the elements they are supposed to measure. In the meantime, teachers can continue to use the sport and motor fitness items if they wish to test for those components. The new test manual will include norms for the following four items that will focus on the health aspects of fitness: (a) cardio-respiratory fitness—the distance run; (b) body composition—percent body fat; (c) musculo-skeletal function in the low back and hamstring muscle areas of the body—timed, flexed-knee sit-ups and a sit-and-reach test.

Validity of the musculo-skeletal function tests has been established by clinical observations of physicians, logic, and electro-myographical tracings. Validity of the distance run has already been discussed and the skinfold tests correlate with values of body composition obtained by the underwater weighing method. Body composition measures will be discussed more fully in a later section of this chapter. The reliability of the four tests is well established with coefficients ranging from .68–.98.

aahper physical fitness test procedures—1979 proposed revision

A. *The Distance Run*

Purpose

The purpose is to measure the maximal function and endurance of the cardiorespiratory system.

Test Description

Standardized procedures and norms are provided for two optional distance run tests: the mile run (1609.76 m) for time and the nine minute run for distance. The decision as to which of the two tests to administer should be based on facilities, equipment, time limitations and personal preference of the teacher.

1. *Mile Run* (1609.76 m)—Students are instructed to run one mile (1609.76 m) in the fastest possible time. The students begin on the signal, "ready go!" As they cross the finish line, elapsed time should be called to the participants (or to their partners). Walking is permitted, but the object is to cover the distance in the shortest possible time.

2. *Nine Minute Run*—Students are instructed to run as far as possible in nine minutes. The students begin on the signal, "ready go!" Participants continue to run until a whistle is blown at nine minutes. Walking is permitted, but the object is to cover as much distance as possible during the nine minutes.

Optional Distance Runs for Older Students

For students 13 years of age and older, the 1.5 mile run (2414.64 m) for time or the twelve minute run for distance may be utilized as the distance run item. Administrative procedures for these tests are the same as for the mile and nine minute runs.

Equipment and Facilities

Either of the distance run tests can be administered on a 440 yard track (402.34 m) or on a flat, measured area. Examples of appropriate measured areas are the 110 yard (100.58 m) straightaway or other outside field or indoor court.

Scoring

The mile run (1609.76 m) is scored to the nearest second. Nine minute run is scored to the nearest ten yards. Performances should be recorded on a score card.

Administrative Suggestions

In order to obtain valid results, students must be adequately prepared for the test. First, the school nurse should be consulted to identify children with medical problems which would indicate abstention from the test.

Secondly, students should be allowed to practice distance running with emphasis placed on the concept of pace. Most uninstructed children will run too fast early in the test and then be forced to walk during the latter stages. Results are usually better if the child can maintain a constant pace during most of the race, walking for short periods of time only if necessary, and perhaps using a strong closing effort.

Thirdly, students should be properly motivated. This test, like many other physical education tests, is only as good as the effort provided by the participant.

Warm-up and taper down activities such as slow stretching, walking, and jogging should be encouraged prior to and following the run.

B. *Sum of Skinfolds (Triceps and Subscapular)*

Purpose

The purpose is to evaluate the level of fatness in school-aged boys and girls.

Test Description

In a number of regions of the body, the subcutaneous adipose tissue may be lifted with the fingers to form a skinfold. The skinfold consists of a double layer of subcutaneous fat and skin whose thickness may be measured with a skinfold caliper. Two skinfold sites (triceps and subscapular) have been chosen for this test because they are easily measured and are highly correlated with total body fat.

The triceps skinfold is measured over the triceps muscle of the right arm halfway between the elbow and the acromial process of the scapula with the skinfold parallel to the longitudinal axis of the upper arm. The subscapular site (right side of body) is 1 cm below the inferior angle of the scapula in line with the natural cleavage lines of the skin.

The recommended testing procedure is:

1. Firmly grasp the skinfold between the left thumb and forefinger and lift up.

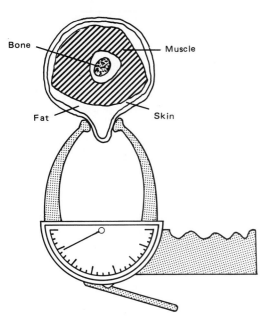

Bone

Muscle

Fat

Skin

the sum of the two skinfolds; however, if it is feasible to secure just one skinfold, the triceps should be selected.

Administrative Suggestions

For testers who have not used these calipers before, we advise that each tester practice locating the sites and measuring them on several children. When a reproducibility of less than 2 mm is consistently achieved, then the

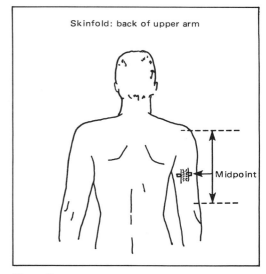

Figure 2.

2. Place the contact surfaces of the caliper 1 cm above finger.
3. Slowly release the grip on calipers enabling calipers to exert their full tension on skinfolds.
4. Read skinfold to nearest millimeter after needle stops (1 to 2 seconds after releasing grip on caliper).

Equipment

Data from a large sample of children in the United States were obtained using the Lange Caliper (Cambridge Scientific Industries, Maryland). Characteristics of this skinfold caliper include accurate calibration capability and a constant pressure of 10 gm/mm² throughout the range of skinfold thicknesses. Care needs to be taken to insure that the instrument is properly calibrated and when in the closed position that the caliper registers zero.

Scoring

The skinfold measurement is registered on the dial of the caliper. Each measurement should be taken three consecutive times with the final score being the mean of the three scores. Each reading should be recorded to the nearest 0.5 mm. Norms are provided to interpret the sum of the scapula and triceps, and only the triceps. The recommended procedure is to use

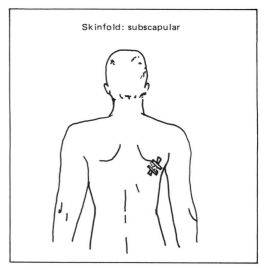

Figure 3.

tester can begin evaluating skinfolds for school children. On occasion, consecutive measurements will differ by more than 2 mm especially in obese children even with experienced testers. If this is the case, we recommend an additional set of three measurements be taken and averaged with the first set of data.

Skinfold fat measures should be conducted separately for each child without comment or display. Each child has the right to share or withhold the results of this test. In all cases, interpretation of the measures should be individually given.

For location of the triceps site, it is essential to locate the measurement at the midpoint of the back of the upper arm and avoid measuring above, below or to either side of the midpoint as described.

Whenever possible, it is recommended that the same tester administer the skinfold fat test on the same persons on subsequent testing periods. Inter-tester error is common and may make the interpretation or serial results confusing and misleading.

C. *Sit-ups*

Purpose

The purpose is to test abdominal strength and endurance.

Test Description

The pupil lies on his back with knees flexed, feet on floor, with the heels between twelve (30.48 cm) and eighteen inches (45.72 cm) from buttocks. The pupil crosses arms on chest placing hands on the opposite shoulder. His feet are held by his partner to keep them in touch with the testing surface. The pupil, by tightening his abdominal muscles, curls to the sitting position. Arm contact with the chest must be maintained. The sit-up is completed when elbows touch the thighs. The pupil returns to the down position until the midback makes contact with the testing surface.

The timer gives the signal "ready go," and the sit-up performance is started on the word "go." Performance is stopped on the word "stop." The number of correctly executed sit-ups performed in sixty seconds shall be the score. Rest between sit-ups is allowed, and the pupil should be aware of this before initiating the test.

Equipment

Mat or other comfortable surface and a stop watch.

Scoring

Record the number of correctly executed sit-ups that the pupil is able to do in sixty seconds.

Administrative Suggestions

1. Because of the importance of the heel placement in relation to the buttocks, the teacher may wish to use a yard stick or precut measured yarn to determine this distance.
2. The supervising tester acts as the timer.
3. Partners will count and record each other's score. The supervising tester must carefully observe to assure that the sit-ups are being done correctly.
4. The partner is to keep the feet in contact with the testing surface. The partner may hold the feet, the ankles or the calves.
5. The pupil should remain in the curled position for each repetition.
6. The teacher can improve the validity and reliability of individual scores by providing sufficient instruction and practice in the correct sit-up technique prior to collection of any test data.

D. *Sit and Reach*

Purpose

The purpose is to test the flexibility of the low back and posterior thigh.

Test Description

The pupil removes his shoes and assumes the sitting position with the knees fully extended and the feet against the apparatus shoulder width apart. The arms are extended forward with the hands placed one on top of the other. The pupil reaches directly forward, palms down, along the measuring scale. In this position, the pupil slowly stretches forward four times and holds the position of maximum reach on the fourth count. The position of maximum reach must be held for one second with knees in full extension while the feet are in contact with the apparatus. The pupil receives one four count trial.

The standard test apparatus shall consist of a bench or box with a measuring scale where 23 cm is at the level of the feet. The testing apparatus should be placed against a wall or other firm vertical surface.

Scoring

The score is the maximum distance reached measured to the nearest cm.

Administrative Suggestions

1. The teacher can improve the validity and reliability of individual scores by providing sufficient time and instruction for warm-up. Slow sustained static stretching of the low back and posterior thighs preceding the test is suggested.
2. If the hands reach out unevenly, the test trial must be repeated.
3. If the knees become flexed, the trial must be repeated. The tester can monitor this by placing his hand lightly across the pupil's knees.*

field estimates of cardiovascular efficiency

distance running

The 1-mile (1609.76-m) run-walk for time or the 9-minute run-walk for distance covered is recommended for upper elementary and secondary school boys and girls. Information concerning validity, reliability, norms, and directions for administering and scoring this test have already been presented. Due to problems encountered in motivating young children, Hugh Welch recommends that the 600-yard (548.78-m) run-walk be used in the lower elementary grades.[25]

Cooper proposes a 12-minute running test or a 1½-mile run as a field estimate of aerobic power and presents age-adjusted standards in Table 10.21 that permit adult men to determine their fitness category.[26] Based on the category, an individual is placed into an appropriate intensity level aerobic program. Cooper strongly recom-

mends that medical clearance be secured and that sedentary men over 30 complete a basic walking/running program for 6 weeks before they take the test. Cooper reports a validity coefficient of .90 between the run and a laboratory assessment of maximum oxygen consumption. Safrit summarized the validity and reliability of the 12-minute run, and presents validity coefficients of .65, .90, and .89 from three different studies.[27] The criterion was maximum oxygen uptake. Reliability coefficients from four studies ranged from .82 to .94.

Mildred Cooper and Kenneth Cooper have developed optional fitness tests for women.[28] They are: women's optional 12-minute running test, women's optional 12-minute swimming test, women's optional 12-minute cycling test, and the women's optional 3-mile (4829.28-m) walking (no running) test. Age-adjusted standards for determining fitness category are presented in Table 10.22. Again, a medical examination and clearance should be secured before testing.

The field tests of running are easy to administer and do not require expensive and elaborate laboratory equipment such as treadmills, bicycle ergometers, and apparatus for determining concentrations of oxygen and carbon dioxide in expired air. Rather, only a stopwatch, whistle, and a running area marked off in distance segments is required. The running field tests can be ad-

* Proposed revision: Paper distributed at AAHPER annual meeting, New Orleans, La., 1979.

25. Hugh G. Welch, "Endurance," in *An Introduction to Measurement in Physical Education,* ed. Henry J. Montoye (Boston: Allyn and Bacon, 1978), p. 88.

26. Cooper, *The New Aerobics,* pp. 29–31.

27. Safrit, *Evaluation in Physical Education: Assessing Motor Behavior,* p. 232.

28. Mildred Cooper and Kenneth H. Cooper, *Aerobics for Women* (New York: Bantam Books, 1972), pp. 51–54.

Table 10.21   Fitness Categories by Age for the Cooper Running Tests for Men

12-MINUTE TEST FOR MEN*
(Distance in Miles Covered in 12 Minutes)

	Age (years)			
Fitness Category	*under 30*	*30–39*	*40–49*	*50+*
I. Very poor	$<$ 1.0	$<$ .95	$<$ .85	$<$ .80
II. Poor	1.0 — 1.24	.95 — 1.14	.85 — 1.04	.80 — .99
III. Fair	1.25 — 1.49	1.15 — 1.39	1.05 — 1.29	1.0 — 1.24
IV. Good	1.50 — 1.74	1.40 — 1.64	1.30 — 1.54	1.25 — 1.49
V. Excellent	1.75 +	1.65 +	1.55 +	1.50 +

1.5-MILE RUN TEST FOR MEN*
(Running Time in Minutes for 1.5-Mile Distance)

	Age			
Fitness Category	*under 30*	*30–39*	*40–49*	*50+*
I. Very poor	16:30 +	17:30 +	18:30 +	19:00 +
II. Poor	16:30 — 14:31	17:30 — 15:31	18:30 — 16:31	19:00 — 17:01
III. Fair	14:30 — 12:01	15:30 — 13:01	16:30 — 14:01	17:00 — 14:31
IV. Good	12:00 — 10:16	13:00 — 11:01	14:00 — 11:39	14:30 — 12:01
V. Excellent	$<$ 10:15	$<$ 11:00	$<$ 11:38	$<$ 12:00

$<$ means "less than."

 * From THE NEW AEROBICS by Kenneth H. Cooper, M.D., M.P.H. Copyright © 1970 by Kenneth H. Cooper. Reprinted by permission of the publisher, M. Evans and Company, Inc., New York, N.Y. 10017.

Table 10.22   Fitness Categories by Age for the Women's Optional Tests

WOMEN'S OPTIONAL 12-MINUTE RUNNING TEST*
(Distance in Miles Walked and Run in 12 Minutes)

	Age (years)				
Fitness Category	*under 30*	*30–39*	*40–49*	*50–59*	*60+*
I. Very poor	$<$ .95	$<$ .85	$<$ .75	$<$ .65	
II. Poor	.95 — 1.14	.85 — 1.04	.75 — .94	.65 — .84	
III. Fair	1.15 — 1.34	1.05 — 1.24	.95 — 1.14	.85 — 1.04	
IV. Good	1.35 — 1.64	1.25 — 1.54	1.15 — 1.44	1.05 — 1.34	
V. Excellent	1.65 +	1.55 +	1.45 +	1.35 +	

Table 10.22—*Continued*

WOMEN'S OPTIONAL 12-MINUTE SWIMMING TEST
(Distance in Yards Swum in 12 Minutes)

Fitness Category	Age (years)				
	under 30	30–39	40–49	50–59	60+
I. Very poor	< 300	< 250	< 200	< 150	< 150
II. Poor	300 — 399	250 — 349	200 — 299	150 — 249	150 — 199
III. Fair	400 — 499	350 — 449	300 — 399	250 — 349	200 — 299
IV. Good	500 — 599	450 — 549	400 — 499	350 — 449	300 — 399
V. Excellent	600 +	550 +	500 +	450 +	400 +

WOMEN'S OPTIONAL 12-MINUTE CYCLING TEST
(3-Speed or Less)
(Distance in Miles Cycled in 12 Minutes)

Fitness Category	Age (years)				
	under 30	30–39	40–49	50–59	60+
I. Very poor	< 1.5	< 1.25	< 1.0	< 0.75	< 0.75
II. Poor	1.5 — 2.49	1.25 — 2.24	1.0 — 1.99	0.75 — 1.49	0.75 — 1.24
III. Fair	2.5 — 3.49	2.25 — 3.24	2.0 — 2.99	1.50 — 2.49	1.25 — 1.99
IV. Good	3.5 — 4.49	3.25 — 4.24	3.0 — 3.99	2.50 — 3.49	2.0 — 2.99
V. Excellent	4.5 +	4.25 +	4.0 +	3.5 +	3.0 +

WOMEN'S OPTIONAL 3-MILE WALKING TEST (NO RUNNING)
(Time in Minutes Required to Walk 3 Miles)

Fitness Category	Age (years)				
	under 30	30–39	40–49	50–59	60+
I. Very poor	48:00 +	51:00 +	54:00 +	57:00 +	63:00 +
II. Poor	48:00 — 44:01	51:00 — 46:31	54:00 — 49:01	57:00 — 52:01	63:00 — 57:01
III. Fair	44:00 — 40:31	46:30 — 42:01	49:00 — 44:01	52:00 — 47:01	57:00 — 51:01
IV. Good	40:30 — 36:00	42:00 — 37:30	44:00 — 39:00	47:00 — 42:00	51:00 — 45:00
V. Excellent	< 36:00	< 37:30	< 39:00	< 42:00	< 45:00

< means "less than."

ministered on a group basis. The school teacher should be cautioned against using the norms determined on adults. It is recommended that local teachers compute their own norms for each age level.

step tests

The Harvard Step Test was developed by Lucian Brouha and proposed as an estimate of the capacity of the body to adjust to and recover from hard muscular work.[29] The test was originally developed on 2200 college men, and it does discriminate between those who are in good and in poor physical condition such as trained athletes and nonathletes. The test consists of stepping up and down a 20-inch (50.8-cm) high bench, thirty times a minute for 5 minutes. The test directions are as follows:

Equipment needed: Stopwatch and a 20-inch (50.8-cm) high bench or stool.

Description: The student steps up and down on a bench thirty times a minute for 5 minutes or until he can no longer perform. He steps up with the left foot and brings the right foot alongside the left foot on the bench. The student then steps down with the left foot and follows with the right foot to the floor. The timer may use a metronome or the sweep secondhand of a watch to count the cadence—every other second say "Up." The lead foot may be changed during the exercise. Immediately after completing the exercise, the student being tested sits down and prepares for the pulse counts.

Scoring: The pulse is counted three times for 30 seconds beginning 1 minute after exercise, 2 minutes after exercise, and 3 minutes after exercise. The pulse may be counted at the carotid or radial artery. The Physical Efficiency Index is calculated as follows:

$$PEI = \frac{\text{duration of exercise in seconds} \times 100}{2 \times \text{sum of pulse counts in recovery}}$$

The class must be trained in taking and recording the pulse before the test begins. Do not begin testing until all students can take pulse counts accurately. If several benches are available, one-half of the class can take the test while the other half steadies the bench, spots for the person exercising, and counts the pulse. The teacher may keep time and count the cadence.

The PEI score is interpreted according to the following standards:

below 55—poor physical condition
55–64—low average
65–79—high average
80–89—good
above 90—excellent

The following scoring scheme should be used for those failing to complete the 5-minute test and for whom no pulse counts were taken:

Duration of Exercise	PEI score
less than 2 minutes—	25
2 to 3 minutes—	38
3 to 3½ minutes—	48
3½ to 4 minutes—	52
4 to 4½ minutes—	55
4½ to 5 minutes—	59

A short form of the Harvard Step Test is reviewed by Peter Karpovich and Wayne Sinning.[30] The short form involves counting the pulse only once from 1 to 1½ minutes after

29. Lucian Brouha, "The Step Test: A Simple Method of Measuring Physical Fitness for Muscular Work in Young Men," *Research Quarterly* 14 (March 1943): 31–36.

30. Peter V. Karpovich and Wayne E. Sinning, *Physiology of Muscular Activity,* 7th ed. (Philadelphia: W. B. Saunders, 1971), pp. 289–292.

exercise. The short form is scored and interpreted as follows:

$$PEI = \frac{\text{duration of exercise in seconds} \times 100}{5.5 \text{ (pulse count)}}$$

below 50—poor
50–80—average
above 80—good

Both the long and short form pulse scores were correlated with counting the pulse continuously for 10 minutes after exercise. The correlations between the 10-minute pulse count and the three pulse counts was .98 and between the 10-minute pulse count and the one pulse count of the short form was .92. Test-retest reliability was .83 and .89 for the three and one pulse count, respectively. Thus, the short form seems to be as effective a test as the long form.

modifications of harvard step test

A number of modifications of the Harvard Step Test have occurred so that it may be used on both sexes at various ages.[31] Most of the changes involve bench height, ca-

dence, duration of exercise, and scoring scheme. They are summarized in Table 10.23. Again, information in the references indicates that modified step tests discriminate between individuals in good and in poor physical condition. Test-retest reliabilities of .825 for trained testers and .820 for untrained testers are reported by Vera Skubic and Jean Hodgkins.[32] The PEI classifications for high school boys, ages 12 to 18 years is as follows:

50 or less—very poor
51 to 60—poor
61 to 70—fair

31. J. Roswell Gallagher and Lucian Brouha, "A Simple Method of Testing the Physical Fitness of Boys," *Research Quarterly* 14 (March 1943):24–30; Vera Skubic and Jean Hodgkins, "A Cardiovascular Efficiency Test for Girls and Women," *Research Quarterly* 34 (May 1963):191–198, "Cardiovascular Efficiency Test Scores for College Women in the United States," *Research Quarterly* 34 (December 1963):454–461, and "Cardiovascular Efficiency Test Scores for Junior and Senior High School Girls in the United States," *Research Quarterly* 35 (May 1964):184–192; and Carleton R. Meyers and T. Erwin Blesh, *Measurement in Physical Education* (New York: Ronald Press, 1962), p. 242.

32. Skubic and Hodgkins, "A Cardiovascular Efficiency Test for Girls and Women," p. 197.

Table 10.23   Variation in Testing Procedures for the Harvard Step Test According to Age and Sex

Ages	Bench Height	Steps Per Minute	Exercise Time	Scoring Formula
College Men—Older	20″ (50.8 cm)	30	5 Minutes	Duration of Exercise in Seconds X 100 / 2 X Sum of Pulse Counts
High School Boys 12 to 18 yrs. of age	18″ (45.7 cm)	30	4 Minutes	Same as College Men
College Women	18″ (45.7 cm)	24	3 Minutes	Duration of Exercise in Seconds X 100 / Pulse Count (5.6)
High School Girls	18″ (45.7 cm)	24	3 Minutes	Same as College Women
Junior High Girls	18″ (45.7 cm)	24	3 Minutes	Same as College Women
Elementary School Boys and Girls 8–12 yrs. of age	14″ (35.6 cm)	30	3 Minutes	Same as College Men
Under 7 yrs.	14″ (35.6 cm)	30	2 Minutes	Same as College Men

Table 10.24   **Ratings Corresponding to Cardiovascular Efficiency Test Scores on the Step Test for Girls and Women**

Rating	Junior High Girls N = 686		Senior High Girls N = 1332		College Women N = 2360	
	Cardiovascular Efficiency Score	*30-Second Recovery Pulse*	*Cardiovascular Efficiency Score*	*30-Second Recovery Pulse*	*Cardiovascular Efficiency Score*	*30-Second Recovery Pulse*
Excellent	72–100	44 or less	71–100	45 or less	71–100	45 or less
Very good	62–71	45–52	60–70	46–54	60–70	46–54
Good	51–61	53–63	49–59	55–66	49–59	55–66
Fair	41–50	64–79	40–48	67–80	39–48	67–83
Poor	31–40	80–92	31–39	81–96	28–38	84–116
Very poor	0–30	93 and over	0–30	96 and above	0–27	117–120

71 to 80—good
81 to 90—excellent
91 or more—superior

Cardiovascular efficiency scores and ratings for junior high school girls, senior high school girls, and college women are presented in Table 10.24. The pulse is counted only once, from 1 to 1½ minutes after exercise for these girls and women. The PEI score for elementary school boys and girls is categorized according to the following standards:

Age	Average Score	No. of Children Studied
7 and under	40	225
7 to 10 years	57	725
10 to 12 years	61	650

Scores above average are considered good, below average scores are considered poor.

evaluation of the harvard step test

One of the most extensive reviews of the Harvard Step Test and its modifications was conducted by Henry Montoye.[33] His findings may be summarized as follows:

1. In general, maximum work capacity or endurance performance on the treadmill and in various distance runs including cross country is not highly correlated with heart rate response in the step test. Nor is the relationship high between maximum oxygen uptake and the step test score. Thus, the step test score does not give a very precise estimate of aerobic work capacity.

2. The step test scores discriminate between people who are in good or poor physical condition. In addition, the effects of a vigorous conditioning program lowers the pulse count in both trained and untrained subjects.

3. Reliability of administering and scoring the step test is more than adequate, especially with trained testers.

4. In over ten studies on children and young adults, it was revealed that there is almost

33. Henry J. Montoye, "Circulatory-Respiratory Fitness," in *An Introduction to Measurement in Physical Education*, pp. 55–63.

no correlation of the step test scores with height, weight, body surface area, or lower extremity length. In general, obese people do poorly.

5. The correlation between the sum of the three heart rates after recovery (long form) and the heart rate taken once (short form) is almost perfect; thus it is wasteful to take the last two pulse counts.

Apparently, the most beneficial use of the Harvard Step Test or its modifications would be in demonstrating the effects of a conditioning or fitness program to the participants. Also, it could be used to classify participants into groups that begin conditioning programs at various levels of exercise stress. For individuals at above average levels of physical fitness, the Harvard Step Test should not be used as an indicator of aerobic work capacity.

cotton group cardiovascular step test

Doyice Cotton has developed a modified step test for group cardiovascular testing on college men.[34] The test is felt to be quite applicable to school situations since one-half of the class may be tested at one time by stepping up and down the bottom step of the gymnasium bleachers (approximately 17 inches ([43.18 cm] high). Test-retest reliability of the modified step test was .95 in college men and .75 in high school boys. Training high school pupils in taking the pulse count should increase the reliability coefficient. A validity coefficient of .84 was obtained between the step test score and the time it took the heart rate to reach 180 (near exhaustion) on the Balke Treadmill Test.

description of the test:
The test consists of 18 consecutive innings of stepping on a 17-inch (43.18-cm) bleacher step. Each inning consists of 30 seconds of

work and 20 seconds of rest with no pause between innings. There is a total testing time of 15 minutes. During the 20-second rest period, the subject's pulse is taken for 10 seconds beginning with second "5" and stopping at second "15." A buddy system is used, with one partner exercising and the other partner counting the pulse.

An increased workload is provided by the three phases of the test.

Phases I, II, and III are continuous. Each phase consists of 6 innings—Phase I: 24 steps/minute cadence; Phase II: 30 steps/minute cadence; and Phase III: 36 steps/minute cadence.

An individual has completed the test when his heartbeat rate reaches 150 beats per minute (25 beats in the 10-second counting period), or when he completes 18 innings. The score is the inning in which the heartbeat rate reaches 150. If he completes 18 innings, he is assigned a score of 19.

equipment needed:
1. Bleacher step 17 inches (43.18 cm) high.
2. The test directions and cadences prerecorded on tape, and a tape recorder.
3. A score sheet for each pupil, listing innings 1–18.

test instruction:
To ensure correct timing and cadences, the commands and cadences for all 18 innings should be prerecorded on tape. Before starting the tape, the teacher gives the following instructions: "At the command, you will step up and down in cadence with the step. You will stop at a given command and your partner will count your pulse and record it. To acquaint you with the procedure, a complete inning will be demonstrated. Be aware of

34. Doyice J. Cotton, "A Modified Step Test for Group Cardiovascular Testing," *Research Quarterly* 42 (March 1971):91–95.

the cadence and instructions as to the exact moment your partner is to begin counting your pulse and the point at which he is to stop. When your pulse count reaches 25 for the 10-second period, the test will be terminated. The inning in which this occurs will be your score."

rules for test administration

1. Prerecord commands and cadences for 18 innings. Provide a reminder prior to inning 7 and 13 that the pace is increasing.
2. On the day of the test, no vigorous exercise should precede the test period.
3. Divide the class into pairs.
4. Have the exercising member of each pair sit on the bottom bleacher step and his partner sit behind him on the second row.
5. A 15-minute rest period should precede the test. During this time, instructions should be given and a complete inning demonstrated. Have each person practice finding and counting their partner's pulse.
6. After the rest-practice period, the subjects on the bottom row stand and face the bleachers. The instructor says "Prepare to exercise," and starts the tape.

Norms are unavailable for college men or high school boys. Local teachers should develop their own school norms. There is no reason why this test cannot be used for high school girls or college women.

percent body fat and body density

The point was made earlier that physical fitness includes not only motor and cardiovascular fitness, but in a sense reflects a degree to which an individual is free of disease or of symptoms that may indicate a pending health problem. One such problem reaching serious levels in our affluent sedentary society is obesity. Jean Mayer[35] reveals that an increased level of obesity is positively related to mortality rates and is one of the underlying conditions of most aspects of heart disease—hypertension, atherosclerosis, and hypercholesterolemia. Thus, it is important that physical educators be able to estimate level of obesity so pupils may be counseled into taking remedial action.

Height-weight tables in many cases do not provide us with an accurate estimate of obesity—being over the weight given in the table does not mean that one is obese. Football players and lumberjacks generally are much taller and heavier than the "average" values found on age-height-weight tables, yet they are not obese; in fact, in most cases they are quite lean. They possess a very desirable body composition reflected in a high lean-to-fat ratio. Putting it another way, a small percentage of their body weight is fat. Hence, it is more accurate and appropriate to estimate percent body fat and use it as an indicator of degree of obesity. Percent body fat and lean body weight are calculated after we estimate the body density or specific gravity of the individual. Two people of the same age, height, weight, and sex can have quite different body densities. The first person can have larger bone development and/or muscle tissue on his or her body. The second person may have smaller bones, less muscle, and a good deal of body fat. Bone and muscle tissue is denser than fat since 1 cubic centimeter of bone or muscle weighs more than 1 cubic centimeter of fat. Thus, the first person has a higher body density or specific gravity than the second. When asked to float in a swimming pool, the first person will tend to sink while the second person will find it easier to float.

The terms *specific gravity, specific weight,* and *specific density* all have the same

35. Jean Mayer, *Overweight—Causes, Cost, and Control* (Englewood Cliffs, N.J.: Prentice-Hall, 1968), pp. 100–115.

meaning in physics, namely, the ratio of the density of one substance to that of another substance. Water is the standard against which the densities of all solids and liquids are compared.[36] In physics the term *specific* is used to imply a ratio. Hence, the weight of a substance compared to the weight of an equal volume of the standard (water) is called its *specific weight*. In estimating the specific gravity or body density of a human being, we apply Archimedes' principle as follows: (1) Weigh the person to find his or her weight in air; (2) find the weight of an equal volume of water by discovering how much weight the body loses when submerged in water; and (3) divide the weight of the body in air by the weight of the same volume of water. Since the specific gravity of water is 1.0, a body will float (because it is less dense) when it has a specific gravity of less than 1.0. A body will sink (because it is denser) when it has a specific gravity of more than 1.0 or when the weight of the body in air is greater than the weight of the volume of water that the body displaces.

A number of laboratory methods for determining lean body weight and percent body fat have been proposed. They include weighing tissue resulting from cadaver dissection, radiography, measuring total body water, measuring total body potassium, helium dilution, and body density (specific gravity as described above). Virtually all of these methods are beyond the scope of practitioners in physical education. However, we can make a few estimated predictions of percent body fat and lean body weight. Jack Wilmore and Albert Behnke have developed a number of prediction equations for lean body weight and body density using anthropometric measurements such as height, weight, diameters of certain bony areas of the body, circumference of certain body parts, and skinfold measurements.[37] The equation that can be used most feasibly by teachers in the field to predict lean body weight in young adult males is as follows (see Figure 10.11):

lean body weight in kg (LBW kg) = 44.646 + (1.0817 × body weight in kg) − (0.7396 × abdominal circumference in centimeters)

The correlation between predictions from this equation and actual estimates of lean body weight arrived at by the underwater weighing method is $r = .938$. The standard error of estimate is 2.815 kg. Abdominal circumference is measured at the level of the umbilicus using a cloth tape. Percent body fat is then estimated from the following equation:

$$\text{percent fat} = 100 - 100 \times \frac{\text{LBW}}{\text{body weight}}$$

The following is an example of how the technique is applied in a young man.

NAME: *Bill Smith:* body weight = *89 kg;* abdominal circumference = *88 cm.*

$$\text{LBW} = 44.646 + (1.0817 \times 89)$$
$$- (0.7396 \times 88)$$
$$= 44.646 + 96.2713 - 65.0848$$
$$\text{LBW} = 75.8225 \text{ kg}$$

$$\text{percent fat} = 100 - \left(100 \times \frac{75.8225}{89}\right)$$
$$= 100 - (100 \times .8519)$$
$$= 100 - 85.19$$

percent fat = 14.81 or 15%

For a young adult female the Prediction equation becomes:

lean body weight in kg (LBW kg) = 8.987 + 0.732 (weight in kg) + 3.786 (wrist diameter in cm.) − 0.157 (maximum abdominal circum-

36. Charles E. Dull, H. Clark Metcalfe, and William O. Brooks, *Modern Physics*, rev. ed. (New York: Henry Holt, 1949), pp. 42–44.
37. Jack H. Wilmore and Albert R. Behnke, "An Anthropometric Estimation of Body Density and Lean Body Weight in Young Men," *Journal of Applied Physiology* 27 (July 1969):25–31.

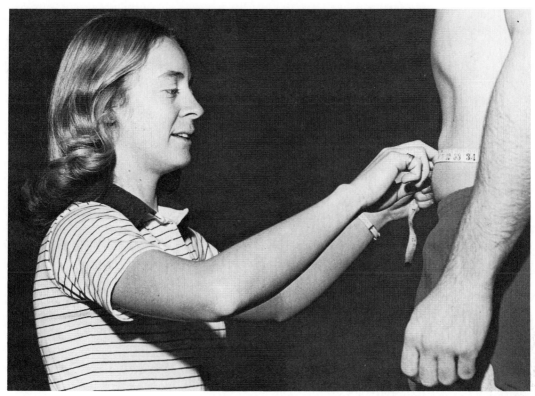

Figure 10.11   Abdominal
Circumference

ference in cm.) − 0.249 (hip circumference
in cm.) + 0.434 (forearm circumference in
cm.)

The correlation between predictions
from this equation and estimates of lean body
weight by the underwater weighing method
is $r = .922$. Wrist diameter is the distance
between the styloid process of the radius and
ulna; abdominal circumference is measured
at the level of the umbilicus; hip circumference is measured at the maximum protrusion
of the gluteal muscles; and forearm circumference is the maximal girth with the elbow
extended and the hand supinated.[38]

Another simple equation for predicting
body density and total body fat using two
skinfold measurements in young adult men

and women with an accompanying nomogram has been developed by A. W. Sloan and
J. B. de V. Weir.[39]

In young men (aged 18–26 years), the
best prediction was found to be made from a
vertical skinfold in the anterior midline of the
thigh, halfway between the inguinal ligament
and the top of the patella, and a subscapular
skinfold running downward and laterally in
the natural fold of the skin from the inferior
angle of the scapula. The body density pre-

38. Albert H. Behnke and Jack H. Wilmore, *Evalua-
    tion and Regulation of Body Build and Composi-
    tion* (Englewood Cliffs, N.J., Prentice-Hall, 1974)
    pp. 41–47, 66–67.
39. A. W. Sloan and J. B. de V. Weir, "Nomograms for
    Prediction of Body Density and Total Body Fat from
    Skinfold Measurements," *Journal of Applied Phys-
    iology* 28 (February 1970):221–222.

diction equation for young men is as follows (see Figures 10.12 and 10.13).

density (gm/ml) = 1.1043 − (0.00133 × thigh skinfold in millimeters) − (0.00131 × subscapular skinfold in millimeters)

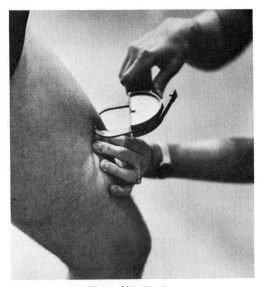

Figure 10.12   Thigh Skin Fold

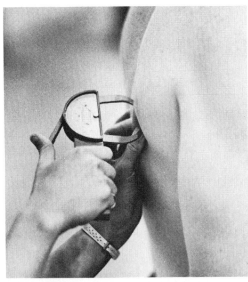

Figure 10.13   Subscapular Skin Fold

$$\text{percent fat} = 100 \left(\frac{4.570}{d} - 4.142 \right)$$

In young women (aged 17–25 years), the best prediction was found to be made from a vertical skinfold over the iliac crest in the mid-axillary line, and from a vertical skinfold on the back of the arm (triceps) halfway between the acromion and olcranon processes with the elbow extended as in Figures 10.14 and 10.15. The body density prediction equation for young women is as follows:

density (gm/ml) = 1.0764 − (0.00081 × suprailiac skinfold in millimeters) − (0.00088 × arm skinfold in millimeters)

$$\text{percent fat} = 100 \left(\frac{4.570}{d} - 4.142 \right)$$

The following example of a prediction of percent body fat for a young woman illustrates the technique.

NAME: *Suzi Smith:* suprailiac skinfold = *18 mm;* arm skinfold = *16 mm.*

d gm/ml = 1.0764 − (0.00081 × 18) − (0.00088 × 16)

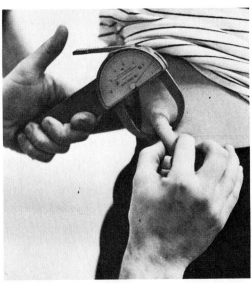

Figure 10.14   Suprailiac Skin Fold

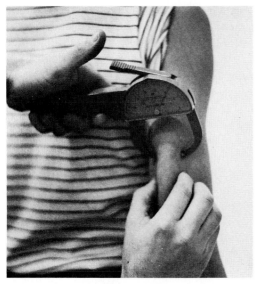

Figure 10.15 Arm Skin

$$= 1.0764 - 0.0146 - 0.0141$$

$$\text{density} = 1.0477$$

$$\text{percent fat} = 100 \left(\frac{4.570}{1.0477} - 4.142 \right)$$

$$= 100 \, (4.3619 - 4.142)$$

$$= 100 \, (.2199)$$

$$\text{percent fat} = 21.99 \text{ or } 22\%$$

To simplify computation, one can get body density and percentage of fat for adult men and women directly from the nomograms in Figures 10.16 and 10.17. You must purchase a caliper to measure thickness of skinfolds. Two of the more popular calipers are the Lange skinfold caliper and the Harpenden caliper.* Reliability of skinfold measurements can be a problem unless the measurement is taken at exactly the same site, the same way, and at the same time of day.

The above equations are used to predict the percent body fat and body density that would otherwise have been obtained by the underwater weighing method—itself a relative approximation of the values. Hence,

these prediction equations provide for approximations of percent body fat and body density.

Practitioners should not use these equations on children younger than 17 years of age. Prediction equations and norms have to be developed for elementary and secondary school boys and girls. The sites to be measured and the degree of importance of each site measured in the prediction of body density and percent fat in boys and girls may vary among different body types for various age groups of each race.

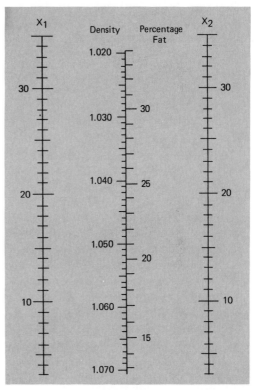

Figure 10.16 Young Women. $X_1 =$ suprailiac skinfold thickness (mm) and $X_2 =$ back of arm skinfold thickness (mm).

* The Lange calipers are sold by Cambridge Scientific Industries, 527 Poplar Street, Cambridge, Maryland. Harpenden calipers are sold by the H. E. Morse Co., 455 Douglas Ave., Holland, Michigan 49423.

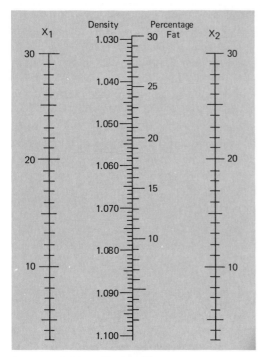

Figure 10.17   Young Men.
X_1 = thigh skinfold thickness (mm) and X_2 = subscapular skinfold thickness (mm).

Since obesity is defined by Mayer as the presence of excessive body fat, the problem is to determine the cutoff point for obesity in individuals of different body types at various ages.[40] If we estimate percent body fat for college-age men and women, we arrive at average and perhaps "desirable" values of 19–25 percent fat for women and 13–17 percent for men. These values vary depending on occupational or athletic activity participation. The 1974 University of Western Kentucky Cross-Country runners had an average predicted value of 5 percent body fat.[41] Athletes and manual laborers generally have values

less than "average." Behnke and Wilmore indicate that the nature and intensity of physical training may alter body composition.[42]

When a person's triceps skinfold measurement is more than one standard deviation above the mean for his age, Mayer maintains that the individual is obese.[43] The values for the various age groups appear presented by Mayer in Table 10.25.

In the absence of prediction equations, we may subjectively estimate "fatness" using one of the following procedures proposed by Mayer.[44]

The mirror test: While naked, look at yourself in the mirror. If you look fat, you probably are fat.

The pinch test: In people under 50 it is estimated that at least one-half of the body fat is found directly under the skin. At many locations of the body such as the back of the upper arm, the side of the lower chest, the back just below the shoulder blade, the back of the calf, or the abdomen, a fold of skin may be lifted free, between the thumb and the forefinger, from the underlying soft tissue and bone. In general, the layer beneath the skin should be between one-fourth and one-half inch; since the skinfold is a double thickness it should therefore be one-half to 1 inch. A skinfold from the back of the upper arm thicker than 1 inch indicates excessive body fatness; one less than one-half inch, abnormal thinness.

40. Mayer, *Overweight—Causes, Cost, and Control*, p. 26.
41. Thad R. Crews and Jay T. Kearney, "A Physiological Profile of Selected Members of the 1974 Western Kentucky Cross Country Team," *Kentucky Association of Health, Physical Education and Recreation Journal* 13 (November 1976):15–17.
42. Behnke and Wilmore, *Evaluation and Regulation of Body Build and Composition*, chap. 9.
43. Mayer, *Overweight—Causes, Cost, and Control*, p. 34. Used by permission of Prentice-Hall, Inc.
44. *Ibid.*, pp. 29–30. Used by permission of Prentice-Hall, Inc.

Table 10.25   Obesity Standards in Caucasian Americans

Age (years)	Minimum Triceps Skinfold Thickness Indicating Obesity (millimeters)	
	Males	*Females*
5	12	14
6	12	15
7	13	16
8	14	17
9	15	18
10	16	20
11	17	21
12	18	22
13	18	23
14	17	23
15	16	24
16	15	25
17	14	26
18	15	27
19	15	27
20	16	28
21	17	28
22	18	28
23	18	28
24	19	28
25	20	29
26	20	29
27	21	29
28	22	29
29	22	29
30–50	23	30

From: C.C. Seltzer and J. Mayer, "A Simplified Criterion of Obesity," *Postgraduate Medicine* 38, no. 2 (1965):A–101.

The ruler test: This has to do with the slope of the abdomen when an individual is lying on his back. If he or she is not too fat, the surface of the abdomen between the flare of the ribs and the front of the pelvis is normally flat or slightly concave and a ruler placed on the abdomen along the midline of the body should touch both the ribs and the pelvic area. Pregnancy and certain pathological conditions can interfere with this test.

The belt-line test: In men, the circumference of the chest at the level of the nipples should exceed that of the abdomen at the level of the navel. If the latter is greater, it usually means excessive abdominal fat.

REMEMBER: IF YOU ARE FIT YOU ARE
NOT FAT; AND IF YOU ARE
FAT YOU ARE NOT FIT!

body size and muscular performance

Taller and/or heavier people perform more poorly than lighter individuals on certain muscular performance items and better than shorter or lighter people on other types of items. Fleishman provides us with direct evidence that there is a significant negative correlation between one's body weight and performance on muscular endurance items such as pull-ups, flexed-arm hang, and dips; thus, lighter people have an advantage and tend to score higher on these items.[45] Power tests that involve moving the total body weight quickly such as the vertical jump, rope climb for time, and the 50-yard dash are also negatively related to body weight. Thus, we should not expect people of different body weight to perform equally well on such items. However, there is a positive relationship between body weight and static strength measures such as the dynamometer press, a dynamometer arm push or pull, and the medicine ball put. Correlations are high enough to justify developing norms for some of the items based on age, sex, and body weight. Unfortunately, most norm charts in use today do not take body weight into account. An excellent theoretical discussion explaining the correlations reported by Fleishman can be found in Per-Olof Astrand and Kaare Rodahl.[46]

Other arguments and examples are offered by Benjamin Ricci, who suggests that not only should norms be developed taking body type into account, but also that one can look at scoring pull-ups from a biomechanical point of view.[47] Here, one would consider body weight and displacement of the body as a pull-up is performed, and calculate the amount of work accomplished in kilogram-meters.

It is important that teachers take care in using normative data. If we use norms to classify people for instructional purposes, we probably do not have to worry much about the relationship between body weight and performance. However, if we use norms when making critical decisions such as predicting success, when selecting students, or when grading, then we must take into consideration the factor (body weight) known to influence performance.

The following practical example illustrates how one can take into consideration the influence of body weight when scoring a strength test. This assumes that the muscular strength component of fitness is relative to the individual pupil's fitness level. Two pupils perform one maximal repetition of a dynamic strength chinning test with weights attached to their waist and achieve the same score of 200 pounds. Pupil A weighs 175 pounds and pupil B weighs 150 pounds. The strength to weight ratio for pupil A = 200/175 = 1.14 and for pupil B = 200/150 = 1.33. Clearly, pupil B has a greater strength to weight ratio.

summary review questions

1. What is a physical fitness program? (*answer on p. 262*)

2. What is a physical fitness test? (*answer on p. 263*)

45. Fleishman, *The Structure and Measurement of Physical Fitness*, pp. 60–61.
46. Per-Olof Åstrand and Kaare Rodahl, *Textbook of Work Physiology: Physiological Bases of Exercise*, 2d ed. (New York: McGraw-Hill, 1977), pp. 369–388.
47. Benjamin Ricci, "Fitness Testing," chapter in *Issues in Physical Education and Sport*, George H. McGlynn, ed. (Palo Alto, Calif., National Press Books, 1974) pp. 73–80.

3. What are the components of physical fitness according to the President's Council on Physical Fitness and Sports? (*answer on p. 263*)

4. What are the four physical fitness factors common to both men and women according to Zuidema and Baumgartner? What test items are indicators of the four factors for men and women? (*answer on p. 265*)

5. For what purposes can one use physical fitness test results? (*answer on p. 266*)

6. What examination should always precede a test or program for physical fitness? (*answer on p. 266*)

7. What are the items on the revised AAHPER Youth Fitness Test? What factors does each item indicate? (*answer on p. 296*)

8. Why should the practicing physical education teacher use the AAHPER Youth Fitness Test? (*answer on p. 266*)

9. What did Montoye's investigation concerning step tests reveal? (*answer on p. 305*)

10. What two methods are presented in this chapter for estimating percentage of body fat? (*answer on p. 308*)

bibliography

American Association for Health, Physical Education and Recreation. *Youth Fitness Test Manual.* Rev. ed. Washington, D.C.: AAHPER, 1965.

American Association for Health, Physical Education and Recreation. *Youth Fitness Test Manual.* Rev. 3d ed. Washington, D.C.: AAHPER, 1976.

Åstrand, Per-Olof, and Rodahl, Kaare. *Textbook of Work Physiology: Physiological Bases of Exercise.* 2d ed. New York: McGraw-Hill, 1977.

Barrow, Harold, and McGee, Rosemary. *A Practical Approach to Measurement in Physical Education.* 2d ed. Philadelphia: Lea and Febiger, 1971.

Baumgartner, Ted, and Jackson, Andrew. *Measurement for Evaluation in Physical Education.* Boston: Houghton Mifflin, 1975.

Behnke, Arthur, and Wilmore, Jack. *Evaluation and Regulation of Body Build and Composition.* Englewood Cliffs, N.J.: Prentice-Hall, 1974.

Brouha, Lucian. "The Step Test: A Simple Method of Measuring Physical Fitness for Muscular Work in Young Men." *Research Quarterly* 14 (March 1943): 31–36.

Burke, Edmund. "Validity of Selected Laboratory and Field Tests of Physical Working Capacity." *Research Quarterly* 47 (March 1976):95–104.

Clarke, H. Harrison. *Application of Measurement to Health and Physical Education.* 5th ed. Englewood Cliffs, N.J.: Prentice-Hall, 1976.

Clarke, H. Harrison, ed. "Basic Understanding of Physical Fitness." *Physical Fitness Research Digest,* series 1, no. 1. Washington, D.C.: President's Council on Physical Fitness and Sports, 1971.

Clarke, H. Harrison, ed. "Physical Fitness Testing in Schools." *Physical Fitness Research Digest,* series 5, no. 1. Washington, D.C.: President's Council on Physical Fitness and Sports, 1975.

Cooper, Kenneth. *The New Aerobics.* New York: Bantam Books, 1970.

Cooper, Mildred, and Cooper, Kenneth. *Aerobics for Women.* New York: Bantam Books, 1972.

Cotton, Doyice. "A Modified Step Test for Group Cardiovascular Testing." *Research Quarterly* 42 (March 1971):91–95.

Crews, Thad, and Kearney, Jay. "A Physiological Profile of Selected Members of the 1974 Western Kentucky Cross Country Team." *Kentucky Association of Health, Physical Education and Recreation Journal* 13, no. 1 (1976):15–17.

Dull, Charles; Metcalfe, H. Clark; and Brooks, William. *Modern Physics.* Rev. ed. New York: Henry Holt, 1949.

Falls, H. B. et al. "Development of Physical Fitness Test Batteries by Factor Analysis Results." *The Journal of Sports Medicine and Physical Fitness* 5 (December 1965):185–197.

Falls, H. B. "Task Force on Youth Fitness" in *Research Consortium Newsletter,* Bruce Noble, editor, vol. 4, no. 1, Washington, D.C., American Alliance for Health, Physical Education, and Recreation, 1979.

Fleishman, Edwin. *The Structure and Measurement of Physical Fitness*. Englewood Cliffs, N.J.: Prentice-Hall, 1964.

Gallagher, J. Roswell, and Brouha, Lucian. "A Simple Method of Testing the Physical Fitness of Boys." *Research Quarterly* 14 (March 1943):24–30.

Hodgkins, Jean, and Skubic, Vera. "Cardiovascular Efficiency Test Scores for College Women in the United States." *Research Quarterly* 34, no. 4 (1963):454–461.

Hunsicker, Paul. "AAHPER Physical Fitness Test Battery." *Journal of Health, Physical Education and Recreation* 29 (September 1958):24–25.

Ismail, A. H. et al. "Development of a Criterion for Physical Fitness Tests from Factor Analysis Results." *Journal of Applied Physiology* 20 (September, 1965):991–999.

Ismail, A. H. et al. "Evaluation of Selected Tests of Motor and/or Physical Fitness." West Lafayette, Ind.: Purdue University, Department of Physical Education for Men, 1964.

Jackson, Andrew, and Coleman, A. Eugene. "Validation of Distance Run Tests for Elementary School Children." *Research Quarterly* 47 (March 1976):86–94.

Jackson, Andrew et al. *Revision of the AAHPER Youth Fitness Tests.* Position paper presented at the Measurement and Evaluation, Physical Fitness and Research meetings, National Convention of the American Alliance for Health, Physical Education and Recreation, Milwaukee, Wisconsin, 1976.

Johnson, Barry L., and Nelson, Jack K. *Practical Measurements for Evaluation in Physical Education,* 3d edition. Minneapolis: Burgess, 1979.

Karpovich, Peter, and Sinning, Wayne. *Physiology of Muscular Activity.* 7th ed. Philadelphia: W. B. Saunders, 1971.

Kraus, Hans, and Hirschland, Ruth. "Minimum Muscular Fitness Tests in School Children." *Research Quarterly* 25 (May 1954):178–188.

Kraus, Hans, and Raab, Wilhelm. *Hypokinetic Diseases.* Springfield, Ill.: Charles C. Thomas, 1961.

Mathews, Donald. *Measurement in Physical Education.* 5th ed. Philadelphia: W. B. Saunders, 1978.

Mayer, Jean. *Overweight—Causes, Cost and Control.* Englewood Cliffs, N.J.: Prentice-Hall, 1968.

Meyers, Carleton, and Blesh, T. Erwin. *Measurement in Physical Education.* New York: Ronald Press, 1962.

Montoye, Henry. "Circulatory-Respiratory Fitness." In *An Introduction to Measurement in Physical Education.* Vol. 4, *Physical Fitness.* Edited by Henry J. Montoye. Indianapolis: Phi Epsilon Kappa Fraternity, 1970.

Montoye, Henry. *An Introduction to Measurement and Evaluation.* Boston: Allyn and Bacon, 1978.

Morris, J. N. et al. "Vigorous Exercise in Leisure Time and the Incidence of Coronary Heart Disease." *Lancet* 1 (1973):333–339.

Paffenbarger, R. S., and Hale, W. E. "Work Activity and Coronary Heart Mortality." *New England Journal of Medicine* 292 (1975):545–550.

Ricci, Benjamin. "Fitness Testing." In *Issues in Physical Education and Sport.* Edited by George H. McGlynn. Palo Alto, Calif.: National Press Books, 1974.

Safrit, Margaret. *Evaluation in Physical Education: Assessing Motor Behavior.* Englewood Cliffs, N.J.: Prentice-Hall, 1973.

Skubic, Vera, and Hodgkins, Jean. "A Caridovascular Efficiency Test for Girls and Women." *Research Quarterly* 34 (May 1963):191–198.

Skubic, Vera, and Hodgkins, Jean. "Cardiovascular Efficiency Test Scores for Junior and Senior High School Girls in the United States." *Research Quarterly* 35 (May 1964):184–192.

Sloan, A. W., and de V. Weir, J. B. "Nomograms for Prediction of Body Density and Total Body Fat from Skinfold Measurements." *Journal of Applied Physiology* 28 (February 1970):221–222.

Welch, Hugh G. "Endurance." In *An Introduction to Measurement in Physical Education.* Edited by Henry J. Montoye. Boston: Allyn and Bacon, 1978.

Wilmore, Jack, and Behnke, Albert. "An Anthropometric Estimation of Body Density and Lean Body Weight in Young Men." *Journal of Applied Physiology* 27, no. 1 (1969):25–31.

Zuidema, Marvin, and Baumgartner, Ted. "Second Factor Analysis of Physical Fitness Tests." *Research Quarterly* 45 (October 1974):247–256.

exercises

1. A physical education teacher used the AAHPER Youth Fitness Test to estimate the physical fitness of her fifth-grade class. She applied the test and got the following measurements:

Student	Sex	Age	Sit-up	Shuttle Run	Long Jump	50-yd. Dash	9-min. Run	Flexed-arm Hang	Pull-up
S1	M	11	35	10.6	5– 5	7.9	1824		3
S2	F	11	30	11.3	4–10	8.2	1537	10	
S3	F	10	29	11.8	4– 8	8.6	1478	9	
S4	F	11	29	11.5	5– 0	8.3	1501	11	
S5	M	11	33	10.9	5– 2	8.0	1734		1
S6	M	12	39	10.5	5– 8	7.5	1886		4
S7	F	11	30	11.3	5– 0	8.2	1573	10	
S8	M	11	34	11.1	5– 0	8.0	1734		1
S9	F	11	22	11.7	4–11	8.4	1573	8	
S10	F	12	24	12.0	4– 8	8.5	1491	2	
S11	M	11	37	10.8	5– 2	8.0	1779		3
S12	M	11	31	10.9	4–11	8.3	1594		0
S13	F	10	33	11.2	5– 0	8.3	1583	18	
S14	M	11	38	10.5	5– 6	7.7	1915		2
S15	F	11	32	11.3	5– 1	8.2	1573	15	
S16	M	11	30	11.4	4– 8	8.5	1544		0
S17	F	11	33	11.0	5– 3	8.1	1645	15	
S18	F	11	29	11.5	4– 8	8.4	1468	11	
S19	F	11	30	11.9	4– 7	8.5	1393	7	
S20	F	12	28	11.4	4–11	8.0	1560	10	
S21	M	11	33	11.1	4–10	8.3	1779		1
S22	F	11	35	11.0	5– 1	8.0	1645	20	
S23	F	11	29	11.7	4–11	8.3	1537	11	
S24	M	11	37	10.6	5– 6	7.9	1824		3
S25	F	11	28	11.7	4– 8	8.4	1501	7	

From the national norm tables find the percentile rank for each student in each event.

Answer:

Student	Sit-up	Shuttle Run	Long Jump	50-yd. Dash	9-min. Run	Flexed-arm Hang	Pull-up
S1	55	60	60	60–65	55		60–65
S2	55	55	45	55	50	50	
S3	55	50	50	50	45	50	

Student	Sit-up	Shuttle Run	Long Jump	50-yd. Dash	9-min. Run	Flexed-arm Hang	Pull-up
S4	50	50	55	50	45	55	
S5	45	50	50	50–55	45		30–45
S6	65	60	65	70	55		70–75
S7	55	55	55	55	55	50	
S8	50	40	40	50–55	45		30–45
S9	25	40	50	45	55	45	
S10	25	25	30	30	40	20	
S11	60	55	45–50	50–55	50		60–65
S12	40	50	35	40	30		0–25
S13	85	70	70	65	60	75	
S14	65	65–70	65–70	70	65		50–55
S15	65	55	60	55	55	65	
S16	35	30	25	30	25		0–25
S17	70	65–70	70	60	65	65	
S18	50	50	40	45	40	55	
S19	55	35	35	40	30	40	
S20	45	50	45	55	50	50	
S21	45	40	30	40	50		30–45
S22	75	65–70	60	65	65	75	
S23	50	40	50	50	50	55	
S24	60	60	65–70	60–65	55		60–65
S25	45	40	40	45	45	40	

2. Calculate a class $\overline{X}$ and σ for each event in problem 1.

3. Calculate an $\overline{X}$ and σ for each event from the results produced by the girls in problem 1.

   Answer:

	Sit-ups	Shuttle Run	Long Jump	50-yd. dash	9-min. run	Flexed-arm hang
$\overline{X}$	29.4	11.5	4–8.6	8.3	1,537.2	10.9
σ	3.3	.3	2.4 in.	.2	67.4	4.6

4. Calculate an $\overline{X}$ and σ for each event from the results produced by the boys in problem 1.

5. Calculate a Pearsonian correlation coefficient between the results of the shuttle run and the 50-yard dash in problem 1. *Caution*—do not use rounded values.

   Answer:
   ($r = .86$)

6. Convert the $\overline{X}$ values for the long jump and 9-min. run in problem 3 to meters.

7. A high school student in the tenth grade performed the Harvard Step Test and completed the full test. His pulse was counted three times 1 minute after exercise, 2 minutes after

exercise, and 3 minutes after exercise, with the following results: 1 min. = 72 beats, 2 min. = 55 beats, 3 min. = 40 beats. What is his PEI? How does he rate in physical conditioning?

Answer:

[PEI = 90 (excellent)]

8. Use the value of the heartbeat after the 1-minute rest in problem 7 to calculate the student's PEI using the short form of the Harvard Step Test. What is his PEI? How does he rate in physical conditioning using the short form?

9. Estimate the lean body mass of a student who weighs 72.7 kg wt and has an abdominal circumference of 81.3 cm. What is the estimated percentage of body fat of the student?

Answer:

(LBW = 63.16 kg wt percent fat = 12.5)

10. A 19-year-old young woman was measured in a physiology of exercise class with the following results: suprailiac skinfold = 15 mm, arm skinfold = 12 mm. What is her estimated body density in gm/ml? What is her estimated percentage of body fat?

testing preschool and early elementary school children

Teachers who work with preschool and early elementary school children should be concerned with basic motor development. Early identification, through testing, of preschool and early elementary school children who may have difficulties with movement situations will enable us to ready these children for a good elementary physical education program. Without this identification and the correction of basic physical difficulties, the child will fall further and further behind his or her peers as they grow older and progress through more difficult play skills. A basic developmental program in either preschool or early elementary school is of value to the success of a physical education program. The following tests will help the teacher evaluate children.

evaluation of perceptual-motor movement patterns

This test is designed to help the teacher intensify his or her powers of observation concerning movement of preschool and early elementary school children. It focuses the attention of the tester (teacher) toward finger-hand dexterity, eye movements, and gross motor movements. The fingers, hands, eyes, and gross motor movements of preschool and early elementary school children are those areas where permanent or temporary physical disabilities could adversely affect the child's present and future physical performance.

The purpose of this subjective evaluation is to observe children as they perform various physical activities during the school day and to make decisions concerning their need for help. We observe and evaluate small motor movements that require hand and finger dexterity and eye movement. We observe and evaluate gross (large) motor movements where the child performs various physical activities that require movement of the arms, legs, and whole body.

Children who receive a rating of "inadequate" or "can't do" in any item under Finger-Hand Dexterity, Eye Movement, or Gross Motor Movement should be considered in need of help for that particular item. Once a need has been established, the teacher can more realistically establish objectives, design a program of activities for improvement, apply the program, and then reevaluate the results after a period of time to see if the objectives are being accomplished. If a child continues to have a problem in performing a particular item, the teacher might decide to have that child evaluated by a specialist, such as an ophthalmologist, neurologist, or orthopedist.

procedures

No special material or equipment is needed. Observe two or three children each day as they perform various physical activities in the classroom, recess, or physical activity class. Subjectively evaluate each child and place a check mark in the appropriate column for each activity (see Figure 11.1).

diagnostic motor ability test

The Arnheim and Sinclair Basic Motor Ability Test (BMAT) is designed to help the practitioner evaluate motor response to a battery of nine tests, seven of which are presented in this chapter.[1] The practitioner can apply each test and, from the results, make an evaluation of eye-hand coordination, large-muscle control, static balance, agility, and flexibility.

According to Daniel Arnheim and William Sinclair, a child can be tested in approximately 12 to 15 minutes. They point out that norms were established by testing 1065 children from various ethnic, cultural, social, and economic groups. The retest reliability for the entire test was found to be .89. Face validity was assumed.

procedures

subtest 1: target throwing (figure 11.2)

Children from 4 to 5 years of age stand behind a restraining line 7 feet (2.1 m) from the target; those from 6 to 7 years of age stand behind a restraining line 10 feet (3.1 m) from the target. The difference in throwing distance is made to minimize the adverse effects of the lack of arm strength in younger children. The tester demonstrates by throwing two bags at the target, while explaining that the small square has a value of 3 points, the middle square a value of 2 points, and the large square a value of 1 point. The child is then told to score as many points as possible in fifteen throws. The total score is determined by adding the points earned in the fifteen throws. If a bean bag lands on a line between two squares, the larger score is awarded. This is a test for eye-hand coordination.

The equipment and materials needed for this subtest are:

1. A target consisting of three concentric squares measuring 5 inches (12.7 cm) square, 11 inches (27.9 cm) square, and 18 inches (45.7 cm) square attached to a wall, with the bottom edge of the 11-inch square located 4 feet (122 cm) from the floor
2. Fifteen 4 × 5-inch (10.2 × 12.7-cm) bean bags

subtest 2: back and hamstring stretch (figure 11.3)

The child sits on the floor with legs fully extended and heels approximately 6 inches

---

1. Daniel Arnheim and William Sinclair, *The Clumsy Child* (St. Louis: C. V. Mosby, 1975).

Name _____ Age _____ Sex _____

School _____ Teacher _____ Date _____

Finger/Hand Dexterity	Adequate	Inadequate	Can't Do
1. Finger to palm — Both hands. Palmer grasp (i.e. picking up objects such as eraser, pencil, book, etc.)			
2. Fingers to thumb — Both hands, Pincer grasp (i.e. picking up objects such as eraser, pencil, book, etc.)			
3. Turns single pages of a book — Both hands.			
4. Catches rolling ball with palms.			
5. Catches rolling ball with fingers.			
6. Catches bouncing ball with palms.			
7. Catches bouncing ball with fingers.			
8. Catches thrown air-borne ball with palms.			
9. Catches thrown air-borne ball with fingers.			

Eye Movement			
1. Focusing — Both eyes contraction			
2. Fixation — Both eyes together on a target.			
3. Release — Both eyes together from a target.			
4. Occular pursuit — Following a target with both eyes.			
5. Accommodation — Seeing near and far target.			
6. Peripheral — Seeing out of corner of eyes a target.			

Gross Motor Movement	Adequate	Inadequate	Can't Do
1. Crawling (Prone-on stomach)			
a. Homologous (Arms move together—legs move together.)			

Figure 11.1. Perceptual-Motor Movement Pattern Check Sheet

b. Homolateral (Arms and leg of same side move together.)	
c. Cross-pattern (Arms and leg of opposite sides move together.)	
2. Creeping (Hands and knees on all fours.)	
a. Homologous (Hands move together—knees move together.)	
b. Homolateral (Hand and knee of same side move together.)	
c. Cross-pattern (Hand and knee of opposite sides move together.)	
3. Walking	
a. Homologous (Body falls forward as a whole.)	
b. Homolateral (Hand and knee of same side move together, "toddler.")	
c. Cross-pattern (Hand and knee of opposite sides move together.)	
4. Running	
a. Homolateral (Hand and knee of same side move together "awkward.")	
b. Out-of-sync (Hand and knee of opposite sides not in good cross-pattern "uncoordinated.")	
c. Cross-pattern (Hand and knee of opposite sides move together "coordinated.")	

Figure   11.1.   *Continued*

(15.2 cm) apart. A meter- or yardstick is placed between the child's legs with the 20-inch or 30-cm mark even with his or her heels. Keeping the knees straight, the child bends forward, reaching down the measuring stick as far as possible without bouncing. Three attempts are allowed. Record the farthest point reached by the child's fingertips in the three attempts. Measure to the nearest centimeter or eighth of an inch. This is a test for flexibility of back and hamstring muscles.

The equipment and materials needed for this subtest are a meter- or yardstick.

subtest 3: standing long jump (figure 11.4)

First the tester demonstrates and explains the proper way to jump. The test is executed by swinging the arms back and bending the knees. Then the arms are swung forward and the legs are extended at the moment of take-off. A maximum of three trials is allowed. The longest jump of the three trials is recorded in centimeters or inches. This is a

Figure 11.4   Standing Long Jump

Figure 11.2   Target Throwing

test for strength and power in the thigh and lower leg muscles.

The equipment and materials needed for this subtest are:

1. A meter- or yardstick
2. Nonslippery surface for taking off and landing

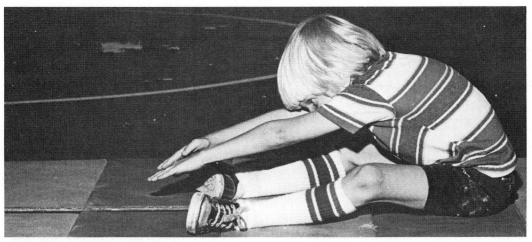

Figure 11.3   Back and Hamstring Stretch

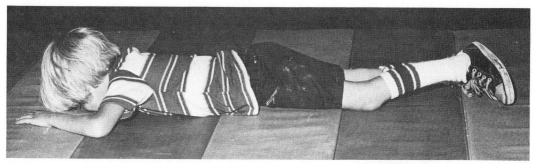

Figure 11.5　Face Down to Standing

subtest 4: face down to standing (figure 11.5)

The tester demonstrates twice while explaining that the child is to start on his or her stomach with the forehead touching the mat. On the command "Go," he or she rises to an erect standing position with the knees straight. The child repeats this cycle as many times as possible without bouncing. Record the number of times the child is able to get to the standing position within 25 seconds. This is a test for speed and agility in changing from a prone to a standing position.

The equipment and materials needed for this subtest are:

1. A mat or carpeted surface
2. Stopwatch

subtest 5: chair push-ups (figure 11.6)

The examiner demonstrates twice while explaining to the child that a front-leaning rest position should be assumed with the legs to-

gether, feet against the wall, arms fully extended, and the body forming a straight line from head to feet. Record the number of correct push-ups completed in 20 seconds. This is a test for arm and shoulder girdle strength.

The equipment and materials needed for this subtest are:

1. Stopwatch
2. A chair or bench whose seat is 14 to 18 inches (35.6 to 45.7 cm) above the floor.

subtest 6: static balance (figure 11.7)

The tester demonstrates on each balance board, explaining that either foot may be used but that the hands must be kept on the hips with the nonsupporting foot behind the other knee. First, the child is given one trial on each board with the eyes open; then the trial is repeated with the eyes closed or blindfolded. If the child refuses the blindfold or is unable to keep the eyes closed, the test

Figure 11.6   Chair Push-ups

should be considered incomplete. Record the total number of seconds the child can maintain a balanced position, up to 10 seconds maximum for each trial: with eyes open on the 2-inch board, then on the 1-inch board, and with eyes closed on the 2-inch board, then on the 1-inch board. Criteria for discontinuing a trial are touching the foot to the floor, removing either hand from the hips, or opening the eyes. This is a test for static

Figure 11.7   Static Balance

Figure 11.8   Agility Run

subtest 7: agility run (figure 11.8)

Cones (or chairs) are placed 5 feet (1.5 m) apart in a straight line. The examiner demonstrates the test and explains that on the command "Go," the child is to run as fast as possible in a zigzag pattern around the cones, starting on the right side of the first cone. Scoring is based on the total number of cones passed in 20 seconds. For a complete run down and back, the child receives a total of 8 points. This is a test of the ability to move the body rapidly and alter direction.

The equipment and materials needed for this subtest are:
1. Four marker cones
2. Stopwatch

balance, first with eyes open and then with eyes closed.

The equipment and materials needed for this subtest are:
1. Stopwatch
2. Two balance boards, one 2 inches (5.1 cm) wide and the other 1 inch (2.5 cm) wide

Norms: Arnheim and Sinclair
(BMAT)[2]

Table 11.1   Arnheim and Sinclair Basic Motor Ability Test for 4-Year-Old Girls

Per-centiles	Target throwing	Back and hamstring stretch		Standing long jump		Face down to standing	Static balance	Chair push-ups	Agility run
		(cm)	(in.)	(cm)	(in.)				
90+	22	52	28¾	129	50¾	10	17	8	20
75	17	47	26¾	99	39	8	15	6	18
50	11	36	22⅜	89	35	6	11	5	16
25	3	28	19¼	60	23⅝	4	8	2	12
1	1	19	15¾	30	11¾	2	2	0	6

From Daniel D. Arnheim and William A. Sinclair, *The Clumsy Child* (St. Louis: C. V. Mosby, 1975).

Table 11.2   Arnheim and Sinclair Basic Motor Ability Test for 4-Year-Old Boys

Per-centiles	Target throwing	Back and hamstring stretch		Standing long jump		Face down to standing	Static balance	Chair push-ups	Agility run
		(cm)	(in.)	(cm)	(in.)				
90+	22	52	28¾	130	51¼	10	18	9	20
75	16	45	25⅞	100	39⅜	8	15	7	18
50	10	36	22⅜	89	35	6	10	5	16
25	3	27	18¾	60	23⅝	4	7	2	12
1	1	18	15¼	30	11¾	2	3	0	7

From Daniel D. Arnheim and William A. Sinclair, *The Clumsy Child* (St. Louis: C. V. Mosby, 1975).

Table 11.3   Arnheim and Sinclair Basic Motor Ability Test for 5-Year-Old Girls

Per-centiles	Target throwing	Back and hamstring stretch		Standing long jump		Face down to standing	Static balance	Chair push-ups	Agility run
		(cm)	(in.)	(cm)	(in.)				
90+	22	50	27⅞	135	53⅛	10	21	15	21
75	18	43	22½	108	42½	9	19	10	20
50	14	32	20¾	95	37⅜	7	13	8	17
25	7	27	18¾	67	26⅜	5	9	7	11
1	4	15	14⅛	35	13¾	2	5	4	8

From Daniel D. Arnheim and William A. Sinclair, *The Clumsy Child* (St. Louis: C. V. Mosby, 1975).

2. *Ibid.*

Table 11.4   Arnheim and Sinclair Basic Motor Ability Test for 5-Year-Old Boys

Per-centiles	Target throwing	Back and hamstring stretch (cm)	(in.)	Standing long jump (cm)	(in.)	Face down to standing	Static balance	Chair push-ups	Agility run
90+	22	52	28¾	139	54¾	11	22	15	22
75	19	44	25½	110	43¼	10	17	10	20
50	15	33	21¼	97	38¼	7	11	8	18
25	8	25	18	70	27⅝	5	8	7	11
1	5	15	14⅛	40	15¾	3	3	4	9

From Daniel D. Arnheim and William A. Sinclair, *The Clumsy Child* (St. Louis: C. V. Mosby, 1975).

Table 11.5   Arnheim and Sinclair Basic Motor Ability Test for 6-Year-Old Girls

Per-centiles	Target throwing	Back and hamstring stretch (cm)	(in.)	Standing long jump (cm)	(in.)	Face down to standing	Static balance	Chair push-ups	Agility run
90+	16	54	29⅜	145	57⅛	16	28	16	28
75	11	46	26¼	125	49¼	13	22	14	24
50	6	35	22	100	39⅜	10	17	8	22
25	1	24	17⅝	74	29⅛	7	8	4	17
1	—	13	13	49	19¼	3	3	1	11

From Daniel D. Arnheim and William A. Sinclair, *The Clumsy Child* (St. Louis: C. V. Mosby, 1975).

Table 11.6   Arnheim and Sinclair Basic Motor Ability Test for 6-Year-Old Boys

Per-centiles	Target throwing	Back and hamstring stretch (cm)	(in.)	Standing long jump (cm)	(in.)	Face down to standing	Static balance	Chair push-ups	Agility run
90+	23	50	27⅞	156	61⅜	15	27	18	28
75	17	42	24¾	133	52⅜	13	20	14	24
50	9	32	20¾	104	40⅞	10	16	9	22
25	1	22	16⅞	75	29½	7	8	4	17
1	0	13	13¼	49	19¼	5	3	1	11

From Daniel D. Arnheim and William A. Sinclair, *The Clumsy Child* (St. Louis: C. V. Mosby, 1975).

Table 11.7 Arnheim and Sinclair Basic Motor Ability Test for 7-Year-Old Girls

Per-centiles	Target throwing	Back and hamstring stretch		Standing long jump		Face down to standing	Static balance	Chair push-ups	Agility run
		(cm)	(in.)	(cm)	(in.)				
90+	15	48	27⅛	166	65⅜	16	31	16	33
75	11	41	24¼	141	55½	13	24	12	31
50	6	32	20¾	111	43¾	10	14	7	27
25	1	23	17¼	80	31½	7	8	3	20
1	—	14	13¾	49	19¼	4	3	—	16

From Daniel D. Arnheim and William A. Sinclair, *The Clumsy Child* (St. Louis: C. V. Mosby, 1975).

Table 11.8 Arnheim and Sinclair Basic Motor Ability Test for 7-Year-Old Boys

Per-centiles	Target throwing	Back and hamstring stretch		Standing long jump		Face down to standing	Static balance	Chair push-ups	Agility run
		(cm)	(in.)	(cm)	(in.)				
90+	28	47	26¾	171	67¼	16	28	19	35
75	21	39	23½	146	57⅜	14	18	15	30
50	12	29	19⅝	115	45¼	11	16	10	28
25	3	19	15¾	83	32¾	8	9	5	21
1	1	10	12⅛	52	20½	4	4	1	17

From Daniel D. Arnheim and William A. Sinclair, *The Clumsy Child* (St. Louis: C. V. Mosby, 1975).

aahper youth fitness test and physical fitness profile

The administration and scoring procedures for the AAHPER test are given in chapter 10. For younger children it is recommended that two days be used for testing.

Day 1 test for:
Flexed-arm hang
Sit-ups
Shuttle run
Standing broad jump

Day 2 test for:
40-yd. (36.6-m) dash
Softball throw
400-yd. (365.8-m) run-walk

Table 11.9   **AAHPER Youth Fitness Test (Standards for AAHPER Youth Fitness Test and Physical Fitness Profile*)**

	Boys or girls, flexed-arm hang in seconds Age				
Percentile	5	6	7	8	9
100	80	95	105	113	122
95	37	40	43	45	49
90	29	32	35	38	42
85	24	27	29	32	34
80	20	22	24	26	28
75	18	20	21	23	24
70	16	18	19	21	22
65	14	16	17	19	20
60	12	13	14	16	17
55	10	11	12	14	15
50	8	9	10	11	12
45	7	8	9	10	11
40	6	7	8	9	10
35	5	6	7	8	9
30	4	5	6	7	8
25	3	4	5	6	7
20	2	3	4	5	6
15	1	2	3	4	5
10	1	1	2	2	3
5	1	1	1	1	1
0	0	0	0	0	0

* Standards for ages 5 through 9 modified from Educational Research Council of America Physical Education Program. Gabriel J. D. Santis and Lester V. Smith. Cards 1357–1367. Copyright 1969 by Educational Research Council of America. Published by Charles E. Merrill Publishing Company, Columbus, Ohio. Standards for ages 10 through 14 from American Association for Health, Physical Education, and Recreation, Washington, D.C.

Table 11.10   **AAHPER Physical Fitness Profile**

	Boys or girls, sit-ups Age				
Percentile	5	6	7	8	9
100	50	50	50	50	50
95	50	50	50	50	50
90	50	50	50	50	50

Table 11.10—*Continued*

Percentile	5	6	7	8	9
85	50	50	50	50	50
80	45	50	50	50	50
75	39	40	50	50	50
70	33	34	45	50	50
65	30	31	40	47	50
60	27	28	36	45	49
55	23	25	30	40	44
50	21	23	28	36	39
45	20	22	25	33	35
40	18	20	22	30	31
35	16	19	20	27	29
30	14	17	18	24	26
25	11	14	16	21	24
20	9	12	14	19	22
15	6	8	12	16	19
10	4	6	10	13	16
5	1	3	5	7	9
0	0	0	0	0	1

Table 11.11 **AAHPER Physical Fitness Profile**

| | Boys or girls, shuttle run in seconds | | | | |
| | Age | | | | |
Percentile	5	6	7	8	9
100	11.1	10.9	10.3	10.1	9.9
95	11.6	11.1	10.5	10.3	10.1
90	12.5	12.2	11.6	11.2	10.8
85	12.7	12.5	11.8	11.5	11.0
80	12.9	12.6	12.0	11.7	11.2
75	13.1	12.8	12.2	11.9	11.4
70	13.2	12.9	12.3	12.0	11.5
65	13.4	13.2	12.5	12.2	11.7
60	13.5	13.3	12.7	12.3	11.8
55	13.7	13.5	12.9	12.5	12.0
50	13.9	13.7	13.0	12.6	12.1
45	14.1	13.9	13.2	12.8	12.2
40	14.3	14.1	13.3	13.0	12.3

Table 11.11—*Continued*

Percentile	5	6	7	8	9
35	14.4	14.2	13.4	13.1	12.4
30	14.5	14.3	13.5	13.2	12.5
25	14.7	14.5	13.7	13.4	12.7
20	14.8	14.6	13.8	13.5	12.8
15	15.2	15.0	14.3	13.8	13.1
10	15.5	15.3	14.6	14.1	13.4
5	16.5	16.1	15.5	14.8	14.2
0	17.5	17.1	16.3	15.6	14.9

Table 11.12   AAHPER Physical Fitness Profile

	Boys or girls, standing broad jump in feet and inches and in meters									
	Age									
	5		**6**		**7**		**8**		**9**	
Percentile	ft./in.	meters	ft./in.	meters	ft./in.	meters	ft./in.	meters	ft./in.	meters
100	4'2"	1.27	4'8"	1.42	5'5"	1.65	5'11"	1.80	6'6"	1.98
95	3'10"	1.17	4'1"	1.25	4'8"	1.42	5'1"	1.55	5'6"	1.68
90	3'9"	1.14	4'	1.22	4'5"	1.35	4'10"	1.47	5'3"	1.60
85	3'8"	1.12	3'11"	1.19	4'3"	1.30	4'8"	1.42	5'	1.52
80	3'7"	1.09	3'10"	1.17	4'2"	1.27	4'6"	1.37	4'11"	1.50
75	3'6"	1.07	3'9"	1.14	4'0"	1.22	4'5"	1.35	4'10"	1.47
70	3'5"	1.04	3'8"	1.12	3'11"	1.19	4'3"	1.30	4'9"	1.45
65	3'4"	1.02	3'7"	1.09	3'10"	1.17	4'2"	1.27	4'8"	1.42
60	3'3"	.99	3'6"	1.07	3'9"	1.14	4'1"	1.25	4'7"	1.40
55	3'2"	.97	3'5"	1.04	3'8"	1.12	4'	1.22	4'6"	1.37
50	3'1"	.94	3'4"	1.02	3'7"	1.09	3'11"	1.19	4'5"	1.35
45	3'	.91	3'3"	.99	3'6"	1.07	3'10"	1.17	4'4"	1.32
40	2'11"	.89	3'2"	.97	3'5"	1.04	3'9"	1.14	4'3"	1.30
35	2'10"	.86	3'1"	.94	3'4"	1.02	3'8"	1.12	4'2"	1.27
30	2'	.61	3'	.91	3'3"	.99	3'7"	1.09	4'	1.22
25	1'8"	.51	2'11"	.89	3'2"	.97	3'6"	1.07	3'10"	1.17
20	1'7"	.48	2'10"	.86	3'1"	.94	3'5"	1.04	3'9"	1.14
15	1'6"	.46	2'9"	.84	3'	.91	3'4"	1.02	3'7"	1.09
10	1'5"	.43	2'8"	.81	2'11"	.89	3'3"	.99	3'6"	1.07
5	1'2"	.36	2'5"	.74	2'8"	.81	3'	.91	3'4"	1.02
0	1'	.31	2'2"	.66	2'4"	.71	2'6"	.76	2'8"	.81

Table 11.13   AAHPER Physical Fitness Profile

Percentile	Boys or girls, 40-yard (36.6-m) dash in seconds Age				
	5	6	7	8	9
100	6.7	6.6	6.3	5.8	5.6
95	7.2	7.1	6.8	6.2	6.1
90	7.6	7.5	7.2	6.7	6.6
85	7.7	7.6	7.4	6.9	6.7
80	7.8	7.7	7.6	7	6.8
75	7.9	7.8	7.7	7.2	6.9
70	8	7.9	7.8	7.3	7
65	8.1	8	7.9	7.5	7.1
60	8.2	8.1	8	7.6	7.2
55	8.3	8.2	8.1	7.7	7.3
50	8.4	8.3	8.2	7.8	7.4
45	8.5	8.4	8.3	7.9	7.5
40	8.6	8.5	8.4	8	7.6
35	8.8	8.7	8.6	8.2	7.7
30	8.9	8.8	8.7	8.3	7.8
25	9.1	9	8.9	8.4	8
20	9.2	9.2	9	8.5	8.1
15	9.4	9.2	9.1	8.8	8.3
10	9.5	9.4	9.3	9.1	8.4
5	9.7	9.5	9.4	9.2	8.9
0	11.8	11.5	11	10.5	9.8

Table 11.14   AAHPER Physical Fitness Profile

Percentile	Boys or girls, softball throw in feet and in meters Age									
	5		6		7		8		9	
	feet	meters	feet	meters	feet	meters	feet	meters	feet	meters
100	64	19.5	78	23.8	95	30.0	120	36.5	142	43.3
95	47	14.3	58	17.7	75	22.9	88	26.8	104	31.7
90	42	12.8	47	14.3	62	18.9	76	23.2	96	29.3
85	39	11.9	43	13.1	57	17.4	72	22.0	88	26.8
80	37	11.2	40	12.2	53	16.2	68	20.7	81	24.7
75	35	10.7	37	11.3	49	14.9	63	19.2	78	23.8
70	31	9.5	34	10.4	46	14.0	60	18.3	74	22.6
65	28	8.5	30	9.1	44	13.4	55	16.8	69	21.0
60	26	7.9	28	8.5	42	12.8	51	15.5	65	19.8
55	25	7.6	27	8.2	39	11.9	48	14.6	60	18.3

Table 11.14—*Continued*

Percentile	5		6		7		8		9	
	feet	meters	feet	meters	feet	meters	feet	meters	feet	meters
50	24	7.3	26	7.9	36	11.0	45	13.7	56	17.1
45	22	6.7	24	7.3	33	10.1	42	12.8	52	15.9
40	20	6.1	22	6.7	31	9.5	40	12.2	49	14.9
35	18	5.5	20	6.1	28	8.5	37	11.3	45	13.7
30	16	4.9	18	5.5	26	7.9	35	10.7	42	12.8
25	15	4.6	17	5.2	24	7.3	32	9.8	39	11.9
20	14	4.3	16	4.9	22	6.7	29	8.8	37	11.3
15	12	3.7	14	4.3	20	6.1	26	7.9	33	10.1
10	11	3.4	13	4.0	19	5.8	24	7.3	30	9.1
5	8	2.4	10	3.1	13	4.0	19	5.8	25	7.6
0	5	1.5	8	2.4	9	2.7	10	3.1	17	5.2

Table 11.15   AAHPER Physical Fitness Profile

Percentile	Boys or girls, 400-yard (365.8-m) run-walk in minutes and seconds Age				
	5	6	7	8	9
100	1'49"	1'42"	1'35"	1'28"	1'22"
95	1'52"	1'45"	1'38"	1'33"	1'28"
90	1'55"	1'48"	1'43"	1'38"	1'31"
85	1'58"	1'53"	1'48"	1'41"	1'32"
80	2'	1'55"	1'49"	1'43"	1'34"
75	2'2"	1'56"	1'50"	1'45"	1'37"
70	2'3"	1'57"	1'52"	1'47"	1'38"
65	2'4"	1'59"	1'54"	1'48"	1'40"
60	2'6"	2'1"	1'55"	1'50"	1'41"
55	2'11"	2'5"	2'	1'51"	1'42"
50	2'15"	2'10"	2'1"	1'52"	1'44"
45	2'20"	2'11"	2'2"	1'54"	1'46"
40	2'21"	2'12"	2'4"	1'57"	1'49"
35	2'22"	2'14"	2'7"	1'59"	1'50"
30	2'24"	2'17"	2'9"	2'1"	1'54"
25	2'30"	2'19"	2'12"	2'3"	1'58"
20	2'32"	2'25"	2'16"	2'10"	2'8"
15	2'38"	2'29"	2'23"	2'19"	2'15"
10	2'42"	2'36"	2'32"	2'24"	2'19"
5	2'49"	2'45"	2'37"	2'30"	2'21"
0	3'5"	2'56"	2'48"	2'39"	2'30"

sources of additional preschool and early elementary school children tests

The need for a movement specialist when working with preschool and early elementary school children has been acknowledged by teachers, supervisors, and administrators. However, due to both the lack of trained movement specialists and budget priorities, most nursery and early elementary schools still depend on the classroom teacher to organize a physical education program for the children. Regardless of who has the responsibility of organizing a physical movement program, however, it is imperative that the physical activities presented serve the purpose of improving the current physical functioning level of each child. It has been stressed throughout this book that current physical functioning level may be determined through testing and evaluation. The selected tests that follow are by no means a comprehensive list; they were selected to help teachers determine the current physical functioning level of the children under their supervision.

1. Movement Pattern Checklist
   a. May be used to evaluate basic movement patterns.
   b. May be used by trained or untrained persons.
   c. Materials and equipment are held to a minimum.
   d. For information write:
      Department of Physical Education
      University of Illinois
      Urbana, Illinois 61801
2. Purdue Perceptual-Motor Survey
   a. May be used to evaluate perceptual motor patterns.
   b. Clear and precise instructions for administering and scoring.

c. Some special equipment must be used.
   d. For information write:
      Charles E. Merrill Publishing Company
      1300 Alum Creek Drive
      Columbus, Ohio 43216
3. Physical Ability Rating Scale
   a. May be used to evaluate basic physical functioning.
   b. May be used by trained or untrained persons.
   c. Some special materials and equipment must be used.
   d. Norms are available.
   e. For information write:
      University Hospital School
      Iowa City, Iowa 52240
4. Hughes Basic Gross Motor Assessment
   a. May be used to evaluate gross motor ability.
   b. May be used by trained or untrained persons.
   c. Some special inexpensive material must be used.
   d. For information write:
      Office of Special Education
      Denver Public Schools
      Denver, Colorado 80203

Most of the tests presented in chapter 12 may be used with preschool and early elementary school children.

summary review questions

1. What is the purpose of the Arnheim and Sinclair Basic Motor Ability Test (BMAT)? (*answer on p. 321*)

2. What is (a) pincer grasp and (b) palmer grasp? (*answer on p. 323*)

3. What does (a) homologus, (b) homolateral, and (c) cross-pattern movement mean? (*answer on p. 323*)

4. What do ocular (a) fixation, (b) release, (c) pursuit, (d) accommodation, and (e) peripheral mean? (*answer on p. 323*)

5. Why should we be concerned with basic motor development in preschool and early elementary school children? *(answer on p. 320)*

6. Of what value are the normative data on the AAHPER Youth Fitness Test and Physical Fitness Profile? (*answer on p. 321*)

bibliography

American Association for Health, Physical Education and Recreation. *Foundations and Practices in Perceptual Motor Learning: A Quest for Understanding.* Washington, D.C.: AAHPER, 1971.

Anderson, Marian; Elliot, Margaret; and Laberge, Jeanne. *Play with a Purpose.* New York: Harper and Row, 1966.

Arnheim, Daniel, and Pestolesi, Robert. *Developing Motor Behavior in Children.* St. Louis: C. V. Mosby, 1973.

Arnheim, Daniel, and Sinclair, William. *The Clumsy Child.* St. Louis: C. V. Mosby, 1975.

Barsch, Ray. *Achieving Perceptual Motor Efficiency.* Vol. 1. Seattle: Special Child Publication, 1967.

Burton, Elsie. *The New Physical Education for Elementary School Children.* Boston: Houghton Mifflin, 1977.

Corbin, Charles. *Becoming Physically Educated in the Elementary School.* 2d ed. Philadelphia: Lea and Febiger, 1976.

Cratty, Bryant. *Perceptual Motor and Educational Processes.* Springfield, Ill.: Charles C. Thomas, 1969.

Dauer, Victor, and Pangrazi, Robert. *Dynamic Physical Education for Elementary School Children.* 5th ed. Minneapolis: Burgess, 1975.

Espenschade, Anna, and Eckert, Helen. *Motor Development.* Columbus, Ohio: Charles E. Merrill, 1967.

Fait, Hollis. *Physical Education for the Elementary School Child.* 2d ed. Philadelphia: W. B. Saunders, 1971.

Frostig, Marianne. *Movement Education: Theory and Practice.* Chicago: Follett Publishing, 1970.

Gallahue, David; Werner, Peter; and Luedke, George. *A Conceptual Approach to Moving and Learning.* New York: John Wiley and Son, 1975.

Kirchner, Glenn. *Physical Education for Elementary School Children.* 2d ed. Dubuque, Iowa: William C. Brown, 1970.

Kirchner, Glenn et al. *Introduction to Movement Education.* Dubuque, Iowa: William C. Brown, 1970.

Kruger, Hayes, and Kruger, Jane. *Movement Education in Physical Education: A Guide to Teaching and Planning.* Dubuque, Iowa: William C. Brown, 1977.

Mosston, Muska. *Teaching Physical Education.* Columbus, Ohio: Charles E. Merrill, 1966.

O'Quinn, Garland. *Gymnastics for Elementary School Children.* Dubuque, Iowa: William C. Brown, 1967.

Piaget, Jean. *The Development of the Concept of Space in the Child.* New York: International University Press Publishers, 1970.

Schurr, Evelyn. *Movement Experiences for Children.* Des Moines, Iowa: Meredith, 1967.

exercises

1. A 4-year-old female student was given the Arnheim and Sinclair BMAT. The following results were obtained:

   Subtest 1: Target throwing ___17___

   Subtest 2: Back and hamstring stretch ___26¾___ in.

   Subtest 3: Standing long jump ___35___ in.

   Subtest 4: Face down to standing ___4___

   Subtest 5: Static balance ___11___

   Subtest 6: Chair push-ups ___2___

   Subtest 7: Agility run ___16___

What is the (a) percentile ranking of the child for each subtest and (b) mean percentile ranking over all the subtests?

Answers:

a. 75, 75, 50, 25, 50, 25, 50
b. 50

2. A 4-year-old male student was given the Arnheim and Sinclair BMAT. The following results were obtained:

Subtest 1. Target throwing ___10___
Subtest 2: Back and hamstring stretch ___25⅞___ in.
Subtest 3: Standing long jump ___51¼___ in.
Subtest 4: Face down to standing ___8___
Subtest 5: Static balance ___10___
Subtest 6: Chair push-ups ___7___
Subtest 7: Agility run ___18___

What is the (a) percentile ranking of the child for each subtest and (b) mean percentile ranking over all the subtests?

3. A 6-year-old male student was given the Arnheim and Sinclair BMAT. The following results were obtained:

Subtest 1: Target throwing ___20___
Subtest 2: Back and hamstring stretch ___46___ cm
Subtest 3: Standing long jump ___136___ cm
Subtest 4: Face down to standing ___17___
Subtest 5: Static balance ___26___
Subtest 6: Chair push-ups ___16___
Subtest 7: Agility run ___25___

What is the approximate percentile ranking of the child for each subtest?

Answer:

Approximately 82.5, 82.5, 76.95, 90+, 87.85, 82.5, 78.75

4. A 5-year-old female was given the Arnheim and Sinclair BMAT. The following results were obtained:

Subtest 1: Target throwing ___13___
Subtest 2: Back and hamstring stretch ___44___ cm
Subtest 3: Standing long jump ___85___ cm
Subtest 4: Face down to standing ___12___
Subtest 5: Static balance ___18___
Subtest 6: Chair push-ups ___10___
Subtest 7: Agility run ___19___

What is the approximate percentile ranking of the child on each subtest?

5. The following ten 4-year-old preschool children were tested using the Arnheim and Sinclair BMAT.

Raw Scores on Ten 4-Year-Old Children (BMAT)

Subject	Sex	Target throwing	Back and hamstring stretch	Standing long jump	Face down to standing	Static balance	Chair push-ups	Agility run
S_1	F	17	43 cm	96 cm	7	14	5	17
S_2	F	20	46 cm	120 cm	11	17	10	22
S_3	F	9	26 cm	75 cm	3	10	5	12
S_4	F	12	38 cm	90 cm	6	12	6	15
S_5	F	17	48 cm	103 cm	7	11	6	18
S_6	M	14	38 cm	97 cm	5	13	6	15
S_7	M	8	35 cm	92 cm	5	12	5	16
S_8	M	24	55 cm	130 cm	9	18	7	19
S_9	M	12	47 cm	93 cm	8	14	6	15
S_{10}	M	11	38 cm	60 cm	5	10	1	10

a. Determine a percentile rank for each subject in each factor.

Answer:

Subject	Sex	Percentile target throwing	Percentile back and hamstring stretch	Percentile standing long jump	Percentile face down to standing	Percentile static balance	Percentile chair push-ups	Percentile agility run
S_1	F	75	69.44	67.5	62.5	68.75	50	62.5
S_2	F	84	72.72	85.5	90+	90+	90+	90+
S_3	F	43.75	19.66	37.93	13	41.66	50	25
S_4	F	54.16	54.54	52.5	50	56.25	75	43.75
S_5	F	75	78	77	62.5	50	75	75
S_6	M	66.66	55.55	68.18	37.5	65	62.5	43.75
S_7	M	42.85	47.22	56.81	37.5	60	50	50
S_8	M	90+	90+	90+	82.5	90+	75	82.5
S_9	M	58.33	79.28	59.09	75	70	62.5	43.75
S_{10}	M	54.16	55.55	25	37.5	50	13	15.4

b. Calculate a $\overline{X}$ and σ for each subtest (each column).

Answer:

	Target throwing	Back and hamstring stretch	Standing long jump	Face down to standing	Static balance	Chair push-ups	Agility run
$\overline{X}$	14.4	41.4	95.6	6.6	13.1	5.7	15.9
σ	11.8	7.72	18.91	2.2	2.58	2.1	3.23

c. Calculate a Z- and T-score for each subject in each subtest.

Answer:

Student		Target throwing	Back and hamstring stretch	Standing long jump	Face down to standing	Static balance	Chair push-ups	Agility run
S_1	Z	.54	.21	.02	.18	.35	−.33	.34
	T	55.4	52.1	50.2	51.8	53.5	46.7	53.4
S_2	Z	1.17	.60	1.29	2.0	1.51	2.05	1.89
	T	61.7	56.0	62.9	70	65.1	70.5	68.9
S_3	Z	−1.13	−1.99	−1.09	−1.64	−1.20	−.33	−1.21
	T	38.7	30.1	39.1	33.6	38.0	46.7	37.9
S_4	Z	−.50	−.44	−.30	−.27	−.43	.14	−.28
	T	45.0	45.6	47.0	47.3	45.7	51.4	47.2
S_5	Z	.54	.85	.39	.18	−.81	.14	.65
	T	55.4	58.5	53.9	51.8	41.9	51.4	56.5
S_6	Z	−.08	−.44	.07	−.73	−.04	.14	−.28
	T	49.2	45.6	50.7	42.7	49.6	51.4	47.2
S_7	Z	−1.33	−.83	−.19	−.73	−.43	−.33	.03
	T	36.7	41.7	48.1	42.7	45.7	46.7	50.3
S_8	Z	2.00	1.76	1.82	1.09	1.90	.62	.96
	T	70.0	67.6	68.2	60.9	69.0	56.2	59.6
S_9	Z	−.50	.73	−.14	.67	.35	.14	−.28
	T	45.0	57.3	48.6	56.7	53.5	51.4	47.2
S_{10}	Z	−.71	−.44	−1.88	−.73	−1.20	−2.24	−1.83
	T	42.9	45.6	31.2	42.7	38.0	27.6	31.7

d. Calculate a $\bar{X}$ T-score for each subject, then rank the students in descending order.

Answer:

S1 = 51.8;   S2 = 65.0;   S3 = 37.7;   S4 = 47.0
S5 = 52.8;   S6 = 48.1;   S7 = 44.6;   S8 = 64.5;
S9 = 51.4; S10 = 37.1

Rank	Student	Rank	Student
1	S2	6	S6
2	S8	7	S4
3	S5	8	S7
4	S1	9	S3
5	S9	10	S10

6. The following ten 6-year-old first-grade children were tested using the AAHPER Youth Fitness Test.

Raw Scores on Ten 6-Year-Old Children (AAHPER Youth Fitness Test)

Student	Sex	Flexed-arm hang	Sit-ups	Shuttle run	Standing broad jump	40-yd. dash	Softball throw	400-yd. run-walk
S_1	F	5	17	14.5	2'11"	8.7	17	2'29"
S_2	F	18	34	12.8	3'10"	7.6	47	1'53"
S_3	F	40	50	12.2	4'1"	6.6	78	1'40"
S_4	F	16	31	12.9	3'9"	7.9	37	1'55"
S_5	F	8	22	13.7	3'5"	8.1	26	2'5"
S_6	M	27	50	11.1	4'9"	6.5	58	1'42"
S_7	M	16	28	13.2	3'8"	7.9	40	1'56"
S_8	M	4	12	15	2'8"	9.2	14	3'12"
S_9	M	8	25	13.7	3'3"	8.3	26	2'5"
S_{10}	M	20	40	12.6	3'11"	7.6	47	1'45"

   a. Determine a percentile rank for each student in each factor.
   b. Calculate a $\overline{X}$ and σ for each subtest (each column).
   c. Calculate a Z- and T-score for each student in each subtest.
   d. Calculate a $\overline{X}$ T-score for each student, then rank the subjects in descending order.
   e. Calculate a rank order correlation coefficient between the 40-yard dash and the 400-yard run-walk.

7. Calculate the distance that student 2 in problem 6 jumped in the standing broad jump in (a) centimeters and (b) meters.

   Answer:
   a. 117 cm
   b. 1.17 m

8. Calculate the distance that student 8 in problem 6 jumped in the standing broad jump in (a) centimeters and (b) meters.

9. Calculate the distance the 6-year-old male jumped in the standing long jump in problem 3 in (a) inches and (b) feet.

   Answer:
   a. 53.5 in.
   b. 4.46 ft. or 4 ft. 5.5 in.

10. Calculate the distance the 5-year-old female jumped in the standing long jump in problem 4 in (a) inches and (b) feet.

12 tests and measurements for adapted physical education

Adapted physical education teachers often forget that one of the primary objectives of a physical education program is to improve the present physical functioning level of the participants in the program. They go to textbooks that have programs already developed for the age level, specific impairments, and resulting disabilities of the participants with which they work; they consider carefully the information presented in the books and spend many hours trying to determine the best sequence to use in presenting the indicated areas of physical education that should be stressed. They outline a semester or year-long program using the sequence chosen, along with the approximate date each will be presented to the participants and then go back to the textbooks and search long and hard for specific physical activities that will fit nicely under each area. When the school year starts, they apply the program to the participants. The participants enter, take part in varying degrees, then exit the program. Regardless of how teachers evaluate each participant, they still do not know whether each has improved, maintained the same level, or decreased the physical functioning level from that with which each entered the program simply because, more likely than not, they did not evaluate each participant's entry physical functioning level.

In adapted physical education it is essential that the present physical functioning level of each participant be evaluated before a program of physical activities is applied. This is necessary because the adapted physical education teacher must:

1. Determine the various physical limitations imposed by an impairment and the resulting disability.
2. Understand the limitations imposed and establish objectives.
3. Use the established objectives and develop a program of physical activities that will challenge but not frustrate.
4. Determine, after applying the developed program of physical

activities over a period of time, whether progress, leveling, or regression is occurring for each participant—that is, determine whether the impairment and resulting disability are becoming less of a handicap, staying the same, or becoming more of a handicap.

Although the terms *impaired, disabled,* and *handicapped* are frequently used interchangeably, each does have a specific and different meaning. Some individuals with impairments resulting in specific disabilities do not consider themselves handicapped.

decision making in program planning

Knowledgeable practitioners working in the field of adapted physical education approach the problem of program planning with a definite decision-making pattern. First, they try to determine the present physical functioning level of the participants. This requires decisions about what to test, what tests to employ, and how to use the information derived from the tests. This information should help the practitioner establish the priorities and objectives for each participant. Once the objectives have been set, the next step is to choose activities for the program that should achieve the objectives. Periodically retesting the participants on the same tests established to determine the entry physical functioning level will enable practitioners to decide if present physical functioning level has improved, stayed the same, or regressed. Based on the results of such test comparisons, a cycle of continuous modification to improve the program and/or objectives for each participant can be established.

This planning process is participant-focused and a dynamic interrelation of tests, measurements, and evaluations. It is designed to detect and then take into consideration the fact that the physical functioning level of certain participants will improve more rapidly than that of others, while some will regress even after the application of a program over a period of time. The planning process is also designed to allow for continuous modification of the program and/or objectives when deemed necessary.

before initial testing

Most likely the decision maker will be the adapted physical education teacher. The adapted physical education teacher has a number of crucial decisions to make, namely:

1. What rules and regulations has the institution established toward testing?
2. How many participants are to be tested?
3. What, concerning the participants, should be observed and subjectively evaluated?
4. Are there past records on each participant?
5. What physical factors should be tested?
6. What tests are available to test the physical factors selected?
7. What equipment is necessary to use each test?
8. How much money does it cost to use each test?
9. Is there enough money available to use each test?
10. How much time is needed to perform each test?
11. What space is needed for each test?
12. Is there enough space for each test?
13. What is the most efficient method for employing each test?
14. What is the most appropriate method for recording test results?
15. How many people are necessary to employ each test?
16. Must other people be trained to give a certain test?

17. What is the best method for training people on how to give a certain test?
18. Which tests are to be administered?
19. On what dates will the selected tests be administered?

after initial testing

After testing, the adapted physical education teacher must evaluate the results and make decisions concerning the following:

1. What is the strength and weakness of each participant?
2. What is the present physical functioning level of each participant?
3. What objectives should be established for each participant?
4. What physical activities should be used to help improve the physical functioning level of each participant?
5. Will grouping of certain participants help in the efficient application of the program?
6. Will the present structure of the institutional system allow for such groupings?
7. Will volunteers be necessary to assist in applying the program?
8. What is the best method for training volunteers so that they may be effective?
9. Where do the volunteers come from?
10. How much money is necessary for purchasing new equipment to be used in the program?
11. How much money is available for purchasing new equipment or building improvised equipment?
12. What is the equipment priority list?

after retesting

After a period of time has elapsed, the adapted physical education teacher retests the participants, evaluates the results, and makes decisions concerning the following:

1. Has the physical functioning level of each participant improved, leveled, or regressed?
2. What is the present physical functioning level of each participant?
3. Must the objectives be modified for each participant?
4. Must the program of physical activities be modified for each participant?

The adapted physical education teacher has numerous vital decisions to make. The program design should have an element of success for the participant. At the same time it should be a challenge; it should not frustrate the participant by being too easy or too difficult. The testing, measuring, and evaluating process built into the planning model found in chapter 1 gives the adapted physical education teacher some solid objective results from which to design such a program.

What physical factors to test should be decided by the adapted physical education teacher. Since there are numerous different impairments, disabilities, and handicaps, it would be virtually impossible to list in this chapter all the physical factors that could or should be tested. The adapted physical education teacher is the best judge of this. There is, however, a hierarchy of components of physical functioning that should be considered when testing for the present physical functioning level of the participant, namely:

I. Basic Areas
  A. Strength
  B. Endurance, muscular and cardiovascular
  C. Range of motion
  D. Balance
II. Intermediate Areas
  A. Body awareness
  B. Body sides awareness
  C. Space awareness
  D. Timing awareness

III. Advanced Areas
  A. Coordination
  B. Agility

The basic area, which comprises four factors in definite sequence—strength, endurance, flexibility, and balance—should be the first consideration of the adapted physical education teacher. The *strength factor* is the primary essential in human movement; without it, no movement can be made. A participant might easily be diagnosed as lacking balance, for example, but the lack of balance might be due to a lack of strength. Once the teacher has determined that the strength factor is sufficient, he or she should focus attention on the *endurance factor*. The endurance factor too is essential to human movement; without it, sustained movement progressively decreases. If the endurance factor is sufficient, the adapted physical education teacher should next determine the *range of motion* of the segments of the body. If this is found sufficient to perform the test activities, the teacher should consider *balance* the next priority for testing and evaluating.

If the adapted physical education teacher is satisfied that the participant has no fundamental weakness in these basic areas of physical functioning, then he or she should test and evaluate the participant in the intermediate areas of functioning.

The *intermediate area* comprises four factors in definite sequence—body, body sides, space, and timing awareness. One of the major obstacles a participant has in developing body or body segment coordination is not understanding the body and its relationship to space and movement time.

The body is point zero, the beginning point, for physical movement. More specifically, the trunk is the segment around which the other body segments operate. Testing will help the adapted physical education teacher evaluate and decide whether the participant has this *body awareness*.

Next, the teacher should test and determine whether the participant understands his or her *body sides*. The body and its segments have a top and bottom, a front and back, and a right and left. Mastery of body awareness and segment sides is the beginning for oral directions for physical movement.

Orientation of the body and its segments in *space,* through an awareness of the body and body sides, is the beginning point for understanding three-dimensional space and its relationship to the body (zero point). Three-dimensional space, and objects within that space, have top and bottom sides, front and back sides, and right and left sides. All sports and recreational games have rules that use boundaries (up-down, back-forward, right-left, and so on). Furthermore, many sports and some recreational games use an object (or objects) that is three-dimensional and must be manipulated by the body and body segment sides. Some activities even require the manipulation of an object with an object. The fact that an individual defends the goal behind him or her, or that there is an "out of bounds" where play stops, or that one must hit the ball over the net with the front part of the gut section of a racquet and keep it in bounds, and so on requires an understanding of space and its relationship to body and the body sides.

The last factor to be considered in the intermediate area is that of *time:* reaction time within the segments of the body, response time of the segments as they go through a given movement, and total body movement time in space.

The *advanced area* of physical functioning includes coordination and agility, in that order. *Coordination* is a delicately balanced interplay of strength, endurance, range of motion, balance, body, body sides, space, and time. *Agility* is the ability to change whole body directions and body segment directions (up-down, back-forward, right-left, and so on) quickly and accurately in a co-ordinated manner. The ability to perform with agility in sports or recreational activities is the highest level of physical functioning.

selected tests

Once the adapted physical education teacher has decided what factors to test he or she must decide what tests to use. This should be the teacher's decision because he or she knows the system and is intimately involved with the participants in that system.

The tests presented below in outline form are not all the tests that could or should be used in testing for the factors involved in physical functioning level, but they do include some that may be used to make decisions concerning the hierarchy of components of physical functioning presented in the previous section.

I. Basic Area Tests
  A. Strength: Moving the weight of the body segment(s) against gravity.
    1. Purpose: The primary purpose is to determine if an impaired, disabled, or handicapped participant has enough strength to move the weight of the various body segments through a reasonable range of motion against the pull of gravity. The secondary purpose is to secure a better insight into the possible areas of weakness concerning the anteroposterior and lateral-medial antigravity musculature for balance response and physical movement disabilities imposed by impairments.
    The body segments are:

a. Head/neck	f. Trunk
b. Upper arm	g. Upper leg
c. Lower arm	h. Lower leg
d. Hand	i. Foot
e. Whole arm (b-d inclusive)	j. Whole leg (g-i inclusive)

    2. Equipment and materials: a relatively hard gym mat.
    3. Procedure: Score one point if motion is completed and zero if not completed. Space for comments (such as, can't innervate muscles, or amputation of segment, or lacks mental capacity to understand) is provided after each item.
    a. Have participant lie on back with both arms at sides.

      (1) Move right hand up and down. _____

        Comments:

      (2) Move left hand up and down. _____

        Comments:

(3) Move right lower arm up and down. _____

Comments:

(4) Move left lower arm up and down. _____

Comments:

(5) Move right arm at least 45° off mat. Keep the wrist and elbow joints locked so that the hand, lower arm, and upper arm form a straight line. Return.
_____

Comments:

(6) Move left arm up at least 45° off mat. Keep the wrist and elbow joints locked so that the hand, lower arm, and upper arm form a straight line. Return. _____

Comments:

(7) Lift head up and down. _____

Comments:

(8) Fold arms across chest; lift trunk at least 45° off mat (another individual must hold both legs firmly down against mat). Return. _____

Comments:

(9) Fold arms across chest; move right leg at least 45° off mat. Keep the knee joint locked so that the lower leg and upper leg form a straight line. Return.
_____

Comments:

(10) Fold arms across chest; move left leg up at least 45° off mat. Keep the knee joint locked so that the lower leg and upper leg form a straight line. Return.
_____

Comments:

(11) Fold arms across chest: move both legs at least 45° off mat. Keep the knee joint locked so that the lower leg and upper leg of each whole leg form a

straight line. Keep both legs together. Return. _____

Comments:

(12) Point the toes downward and bring them back (legs extended along mat).

_____

Comments:

Maximum points 12. Points obtained by participant = _____

$$\text{Percent of attainment of participant} = \frac{\text{points obtained by participant}}{\text{maximum points}} \times 100$$

Percent attainment = _____

b. Have participant lie on stomach, arms at sides.

(1) Lift head up and down. _____

Comments:

(2) Move right arm up at 45° off mat. Keep the wrist and elbow joints locked so that the hand, lower arm, and upper arm form a straight line. Return.

_____

Comments:

(3) Move left arm up at least 45° off mat. Keep the wrist and elbow joints locked so that the hand, lower arm, and upper arm form a straight line. Return.

_____

Comments:

(4) Place hands in small of back and lift trunk at least 10° off mat (another individual must hold both legs firmly down against mat). Return. _____

Comments:

(5) Place hands in small of back and lift right leg at least 45° off mat. Keep the knee joint locked so that the lower leg and upper leg form a straight line.

Return. _____

Comments:

(6) Place hands in small of back and lift left leg at least 45° off mat. Keep the knee joint locked so that the lower leg and upper leg form a straight line. Return. _____

Comments:

(7) Place hands in small of back and lift both legs at least 10° off mat (another individual must hold the trunk firmly down against mat). Keep the knee joint locked so that the lower leg and upper leg form a straight line. Keep legs together. Return. _____

Comments:

(8) Place hands in small of back and lift right lower leg at least 45° off mat. Return. _____

Comments:

(9) Place hands in small of back and lift left lower leg at least 45° off mat. Return. _____

Comments:

Maximum points 9. Points obtained by participant = _____

Percent of attainment by participant $= \dfrac{\text{points obtained by participant}}{\text{maximum points}} \times 100$

Percent attainment = _____

c. Have participant lie on right side, arms folded across chest, and left leg resting on right leg.
   (1) Lift head up to the left and return. _____

   Comments:

   (2) Lift left arm up at least 45° off body. Keep the wrist and elbow joints locked so that the hand, lower arm, and upper arm form a straight line. Return to folded position across chest. _____

   Comments:

(3) Lift trunk up to left at least 10° off mat (another individual must hold both legs firmly down against mat). Return. _____

Comments:

(4) Lift left leg up at least 45° off right leg. Keep the knee joint locked so that the lower leg and upper leg form a straight line. Return. _____

Comments:

(5) Lift both legs up at least 10° off mat (another individual must hold the trunk firmly down against mat). Keep the knee joint locked so that the lower leg and upper leg form a straight line. Keep the legs together. Return. _____

Comments:

Maximum points 5. Points obtained by participant = _____

Percent of attainment by participant $= \dfrac{\text{points obtained by participant}}{\text{maximum points}} \times 100$

Percent attainment = _____

d. Have the participant lie on left side, arms folded across chest, and right leg resting on left leg.
   (1) Lift head up to right and return. _____

Comments:

(2) Lift right arm up at least 45° off body. Keep the wrist and elbow joints locked so that the hand, lower arm, and upper arm form a straight line. Return to folded position across chest. _____

Comments:

(3) Lift trunk up to right at least 10° off mat (another individual must hold both legs firmly down against mat). Return. _____

Comments:

(4) Lift right leg up at least 45° off left leg. Keep the knee joint locked so that the lower leg and upper leg form a straight line. Return. _____

Comments:

Figure 12.1   Strength—Lifting right leg up to 45°

(5) Lift both legs up at least 10° off mat (another individual must hold the trunk firmly down against the mat). Keep the knee joint locked so that the lower leg and upper leg form a straight line. Keep both legs together. Return. _____

Comments:

Maximum points 5. Points obtained by participant = _____

Percent of attainment by participant = $\dfrac{\text{points obtained by participant}}{\text{maximum points}} \times 100$

Percent attainment = _____

Maximum total points 31. Total points obtained by participant = _____

Total percent of attainment of participant =
$$\dfrac{\text{total points obtained by participant}}{\text{maximum total points}} \times 100$$

Total percent attainment = _____

Name _____ Sex _____

Date Test Taken _____

Age _____

B. Endurance
1. Purpose: The primary purpose is to secure an indication of the muscular endurance and cardiorespiratory endurance of a participant. The secondary purpose is to acquire a better insight into possible areas of weakness and subsequent corrective measures concerning the anteroposterior and lateral-medial antigravity musculature for balance response, especially as it relates to muscular endurance.
2. Equipment and materials: a relatively hard gym mat, a soft pillow, a hand-held stopwatch, and an adjustable horizontal bar.
3. Procedure: Secure and record the amount of time in seconds it takes a participant to complete each physical act.
   a. Muscular endurance
      (1) Have the participant lie on back, arms folded across chest. Place pillow under head. Have participant form bridge. Record the length of time participant

      can hold back bridge. No. of sec. _____
      (2) Have participant lie on stomach and place both hands at small of back. Place pillow under head. Have the participant form bridge. Record the length of time

      participant can hold front bridge. No. of sec. _____
      (3) Adjust a horizontal bar to approximately the standing height of the participant. May use chair or lift participant to a position where he can grasp the

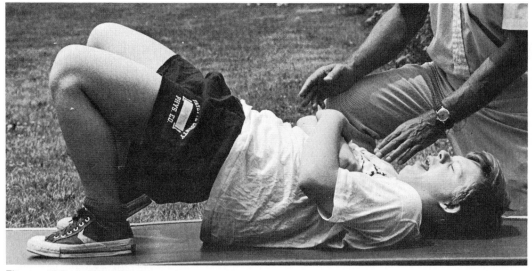

Figure 12.2 Muscular endurance—Student attempting back bridge unsuccessfully

bar with an overhand grasp with chin above bar. Record the length of time participant can hold chin above bar unaided. No. of sec. _____

(4) Record length of time participant can hold trunk up at 45° with arms folded across chest while lying on back. Another individual must hold both whole legs firmly down against mat. No. of sec. _____

(5) Record length of time participant can hold both legs about 25 centimeters off mat with arms folded across chest while lying on back. Must keep both legs together and straight. No. of sec. _____

(6) Record length of time participant can hold trunk up at least 10° with hands placed in small of back while lying on stomach. Another individual must hold both legs firmly against mat. No. of sec. _____

(7) Record length of time participant can hold both legs about 25 centimeters off mat with hands placed in small of back while lying on stomach. Another individual must hold trunk firmly against mat. No. of sec. _____

(8) Record length of time participant can hold trunk at least 10° up to the left while lying on right side with arms folded across chest. Another individual must hold both legs firmly against mat. No. of sec. _____

(9) Record length of time participant can hold both legs about 25 centimeters off mat, up to the left, while lying on right side with arms folded across chest. Keep both legs together and straight. Another individual must hold trunk firmly against mat. No. of sec. _____

(10) Record length of time participant can hold trunk at least 10° up to right while lying on left side with arms folded across chest. Another individual must hold both legs firmly against mat. No. of sec. _____

(11) Record length of time participant can hold both legs about 25 centimeters off mat, up to the right, while lying on left side with arms folded across chest. Keep legs together and straight. Another individual must hold trunk firmly against mat. No. of sec. _____

b. Cardiorespiratory endurance

(1) Record length of time it takes a participant to cover a 400-meter run-walk. No. of sec. _____

[It should be noted that in item b(1) under cardiorespiratory endurance, a shorter time indicates a better result, while in each item a(1) through a(11) under muscular endurance, a longer time indicates a better result. It is recommended that if a participant can't complete the 400-meter run-walk that the approximate distance and time be recorded. If a participant can't perform a given item a(1) through a(11), a zero time is recorded.]

Name _____ Sex _____

Date Test Taken _____

Age _____

C. Range of motion
1. Purpose: The purpose is to determine whether a participant has a reasonable range of motion of various selected body segments.
2. Equipment and materials: a relatively hard gym mat.
3. Procedure: Score one point if motion is completed and zero if not completed. Space for comment is provided after each item.
   a. Have participant lie on back with both arms at sides.

   (1) Raise head and look at toes. _____

   Comment:

   (2) Touch point of chin to right shoulder. _____

   Comment:

   (3) Touch point of chin to left shoulder. _____

   Comment:

   (4) Touch right shoulder with right hand. _____

   Comment:

   (5) Touch left shoulder with left hand. _____

   Comment:

   (6) Bring both arms, in a locked straight position, up off mat, and touch mat over head with backs of hands. Return. _____

   Comment:

   (7) Slide both arms, in a locked straight position, along mat until hands touch above head. Return. _____

   Comment:

(8) Touch any part of right upper leg to stomach region. Must bend lower leg to accomplish. Return. _____

Comment:

(9) Touch any part of left upper leg to stomach region. Must bend lower leg to accomplish. Return. _____

Comment:

(10) Place both arms, in a locked straight position, about 45° out from trunk with palms of hands on floor. Lift extended both legs and touch floor beyond head. Return. _____

Figure 12.3 Range of motion of student placing both legs behind head

Comment:

(11) Sitting on floor, touch toes with both hands, keeping legs straight. _____

Comment:

(12) Sit with soles of feet together and the feet pulled back as close to the body as possible. Curl forward at the waist and reach as far in front as possible with both hands and touch the mat. See if the point of the chin is beyond or above

the feet. _____

Comment:

(13) Sit with both legs together and extended. Twist the trunk right and look backward. See if left shoulder has rotated above or past the left upper leg. Return.

_____

Comment:

(14) Sit with both legs together and extended. Twist the trunk left and look backward. See if the right shoulder has rotated above or past the right upper

leg. Return. _____

Comment:

(15) Lie on stomach both legs together and extended. Bend the right lower leg

up and touch any part of the right upper leg. Return leg. _____

Comment:

(16) Lie on stomach both legs together and extended. Bend the left lower leg

up and touch any part of the left upper leg. Return leg. _____

Comment:

Maximum total points 16. Total points obtained by participants = _____

$$\text{Total percent of attainment} = \frac{\text{total points obtained by participant}}{\text{maximum points}} \times 100$$

Total percent attainment = _____

Name _____ Sex _____

Date Test Taken _____

Age _____

D. Balance Response
  1. Purpose: The primary purpose is to secure an indication of a participant's response to two basic balancing situations, namely:
     a. Static medium—static individual
     b. Static medium—dynamic individual
     The secondary purpose is to acquire an insight into possible problem areas and subsequent corrective measures concerning body positioning and dynamic body movement when a participant takes part in physically active games and sports activities that require various responses to balancing situations.
  2. Equipment and materials: a relatively hard gym mat, masking tape, and a hand-held stopwatch.
  3. Procedure: Score one point if the physical act is completed and zero if not completed.
     a. Static medium—static individual. Have the participant get on hands and knees (creeping position on all fours) on mat.
        (1) Extend right leg until it is parallel with the mat. Hold leg extended for 10 seconds. Return. _____

           Comment:

        (2) Extend right arm until it is parallel with the mat. Hold for 10 seconds. Return.
           _____
        (3) Extend left leg until it is parallel with the mat. Hold for 10 seconds. Return.
           _____
        (4) Extend left arm until it is parallel with the mat. Hold for 10 seconds. Return
           _____
        (5) Extend right leg and left arm until each are parallel with the mat. Hold for 10 seconds. Return. _____
        (6) Extend left leg and right arm until each are parallel with the mat. Hold for 10 seconds. Return. _____
        (7) Extend right leg and right arm until each are parallel with the mat. Hold for 10 seconds. Return. _____
        (8) Extend left leg and left arm until each are parallel with the mat. Hold for 10 seconds. Return. _____
        (9) Have the participant kneel on both knees, feet touching mat. Hold for 10 seconds. _____

Figure 12.4   Balance—Static   dent attempting to extend right
medium–Static individual stu-   leg and left arm.

(10) Have the participant kneel on one knee, opposite foot on mat. Hold for 10
     seconds. _____

(11) Have the participant stand upright, both feet on mat. Hold for 10 seconds.
     _____

(12) Have the participant stand on right foot, left foot not touching mat. Hold
     10 seconds. Return. _____

(13) Have the participant stand on left foot, right foot not touching mat. Hold
     for 10 seconds. Return. _____

(14) Have the participant stand on right foot, left leg extended in front of body
     with the left foot at least 10 inches off mat. Hold for 10 seconds. Return.
     _____

(15) Have the participant stand on left foot, right leg extended in front of body
     with the right foot at least 10 inches off mat. Hold for 10 seconds. Return.
     _____

(16) Have the participant stand on right foot, left leg extended and abducted to
     the left side with left foot at least 10 inches off mat. Hold for 10 seconds.
     Return. _____

(17) Have the participant stand on left foot, right leg extended and abducted to

the right side with right foot at least 10 inches off mat. Hold for 10 seconds. Return. _____

(18) Have the participant stand on right foot, left leg extended in back of body with left foot at least 10 inches off mat. Hold for 10 seconds. Return. _____

(19) Have participant stand on left foot, right leg extended in back of body with right foot at least 10 inches off mat. Hold for 10 seconds. Return. _____

(20) Have participant stand on right foot, left foot not touching mat, with eyes closed. Hold for 10 seconds. Return. _____

(21) Have participant stand on left foot, right foot not touching mat, with eyes closed. Hold for 10 seconds. Return. _____

Maximum total points 21. Points attained by participant = _____

$$\text{Percent of attainment} = \frac{\text{points attained by participant}}{\text{maximum total points}} \times 100$$

Percent attainment = _____

b. Static medium—dynamic individual. Have the participant standing with both feet on the floor.

(1) Rock the trunk forward and backward in the sagittal plane at least three times. _____

(2) Rock the trunk right and left in the frontal plane at least three times. _____

(3) Stand on the right foot, extend left leg forward, sideward, backward, without touching the floor with the left foot, then down. _____

(4) Stand on the left foot, extend right leg forward, sideward, backward, without touching the floor with the right foot, then down. _____

(5) Stand on the right foot, left foot off floor, bend trunk forward and backward in sagittal plane at least three times. Down. _____

(6) Stand on the left foot, right foot off floor, bend trunk forward and backward in sagittal plane at least three times. Down. _____

(7) Stand on the right foot, left foot off floor, bend trunk right and left in the frontal plane at least three times. _____

(8) Stand on the left foot, right foot off floor, bend trunk right and left in the frontal plane at least three times. _____

Using masking tape, tape two parallel lines 8 meters in length on the floor. The inner edges of the two lines should be 16 centimeters apart. During the execution of the following activities, touching either line or outside the line constitutes a no-pass situation.

(9) Walk forward from one end to the other end. _____

(10) Walk backward from one end to the other end. _____

(11) Turn the right side of the body and cross the left foot over the right foot (cross step right over left) from one end to the other. _____

(12) Turn the left side of the body and cross the right foot over the left foot (cross step left over right) from one end to the other. _____

(13) Walk forward to the center, turn around (180°) to the right and walk backward to the other end. _____

(14) Walk forward to the center, turn around (180°) to the left and walk backward to the other end. _____

(15) Walk backward to the center, turn around (180°) to the right and walk forward to the other end. _____

(16) Walk backward to the center, turn around (180°) to the left and walk forward to the other end. _____

(17) Walk forward to the center, turn 90° to the right (clockwise) and cross step the right foot over the left foot to the other end. _____

(18) Walk forward to the center, turn 90° to the left (counterclockwise) and cross step the left foot over the right foot to the other end. _____

(19) Hop on the right foot from one end to the other. _____

(20) Hop on the left foot from one end to the other. _____

Maximum total points 20. Points attained by participant = _____

Percent of attainment = $\dfrac{\text{points attained by participant}}{\text{maximum total points}} \times 100$

Percent attainment = _____

II. Intermediate Area Tests
   A. Body Segment and Body Part Awareness
      1. Purpose: The primary purpose is to see whether the participant has knowledge about the location of various body segments and body parts. The secondary purpose is to acquire a better insight into the possible areas of weakness and subsequent corrective measures concerning physical movement involving direction, coordination, and agility.
      2. Equipment and materials: no special equipment needed.

3. Procedure: Score one point if act is completed and zero if not completed. Give no visual clues to participant. Have the participant:

(1) Shake head. _____ (10) Touch wrists. _____
(2) Touch ears. _____ (11) Shake hands. _____
(3) Touch nose. _____ (12) Touch stomach. _____
(4) Touch eyes. _____ (13) Touch back. _____
(5) Touch chin. _____ (14) Shake legs. _____
(6) Touch neck. _____ (15) Touch knees. _____
(7) Touch chest. _____ (16) Touch ankles. _____
(8) Shake arms. _____ (17) Shake feet. _____
(9) Touch elbows. _____

Comments:

Maximum total points 17. Total points obtained by participant = _____

$$\text{Total percent of attainment} = \frac{\text{total points obtained by participant}}{\text{maximum total points}} \times 100$$

Total percent of attainment = _____

Name _____ Sex _____

Date Test Taken _____

Age _____

B. Body Segment and Body Part Side Awareness
1. Purpose: The primary purpose is to see if the participant has knowledge about the sidedness of the various body segments and body parts. The secondary purpose is to acquire a better insight into the possible areas of weakness and subsequent corrective measures concerning orientation in three-dimensional space, coordination, and agility.
2. Equipment and materials: no special equipment needed.
3. Procedure: Score one point if act is completed and zero if not completed. Give no visual clues to participant. Have the participant:

(1) Touch the top, right side, left side, and back of head. _____

(2) Touch the right ear, then the left ear. _____

(3) Touch the right eye, then the left eye. _____

(4) Touch the left shoulder, then the right shoulder. _____

(5) Touch the left, then the right arm. _____

(6) Touch the right elbow, then the left elbow. _____

(7) Touch the left wrist, then the right wrist. _____

Figure 12.5 **Body segment** and body part awareness—student touching left ear.

(8) Shake the right hand, then left hand. _____

(9) Take the left hand and touch the back, front, right side, and left side of the right hand. _____

(10) Take the right hand and touch the back, front, right side, and left side of the left hand. _____

(11) Take the right hand and touch the left side and front of the trunk. _____

(12) Take the left hand and touch the right side and back of the trunk. _____

(13) Take both hands and touch the front, back, right, and left side of the right upper leg. _____

(14) Take both hands and touch the left, back, right, and front side of the left lower leg. _____

(15) Take the left hand and touch the front, back, right, and left side of the left knee. _____

(16) Take the right hand and touch the right, left, front, and back side of the right ankle. _____

(17) Take both hands and touch the top, bottom, right, left, front, and back side of the right foot. _____

(18) Take both hands and touch the top, bottom, right, left, front, and back of the whole body. _____

Comments:

Maximum total points 18. Total points obtained by participant = _____

$$\text{Total percent of attainment} = \frac{\text{total points obtained by participant}}{\text{maximum total points}} \times 100$$

Total percent of attainment = _____

Name _____ Sex _____

Date Test Taken _____

Age _____

C. Space Awareness
  1. Purpose: The primary purpose is to see whether the participant can project his or her knowledge of body and body side awareness into three-dimensional space awareness. This is a crucial awareness because without it the participant will have great difficulty in orientating his or her body in three-dimensional space. Without this ability the participant will have difficulties with physical activities that require coordination and agility. Therefore, the secondary purpose is to acquire a better insight into the possible areas of weakness and subsequent corrective measures concerning coordination and agility.
  2. Equipment and materials: a room, a basketball or playground ball, and another person (besides participant).
  3. Procedure: Score one point if act is completed and zero if not completed. Give no visual clues to participant. Have the participant:
     (1) Stand in middle of a room and point to the front, back, right, left, top, and bottom sides of room. _____
     (2) Stand and face in another direction in the middle of the room and point to the front, back, right, left, top, and bottom sides of room. _____
     (3) Hold a ball and touch the top, bottom, front, back, left, and right sides of the ball. _____

Have the participant stand face to face with another individual. Have the participant touch:

     (4) the top of own head, then top of head of other. _____

**Figure 12.6   Space aware-
ness**—student touching head
of self then other.

    (5) right side of own head, then other. _____

    (6) left side of own head, then other. _____

    (7) back of own head, then other. _____

    (8) own left ear, then other. _____

    (9) own right ear, then other. _____

  (10) own right eye, then other. _____

  (11) own left eye, then other. _____

  (12) own left shoulder, then other. _____

  (13) own right shoulder, then other. _____

  (14) own left arm, then other. _____

  (15) own right arm, then other. _____

  (16) own left hand, then other. _____

  (17) own right hand, then other. _____

(18) own left leg, then other. _____

(19) own right leg, then other. _____

(20) own right knee, then other. _____

(21) own left knee, then other. _____

(22) own right ankle, then other. _____

(23) own left ankle, then other. _____

(24) own right foot, then other. _____

(25) own left foot, then other. _____

Have the participant stand at head of another individual lying face up (supine) on the floor. Have the participant touch:

(26) the top of own head, then other. _____

(27) right side of own head, then other. _____

(28) left side of own head, then other. _____

(29) back of own head, then other. _____

(30) own left ear, then other. _____

(31) own right ear, then other. _____

(32) own right eye, then other. _____

(33) own left eye, then other. _____

(34) own left shoulder, then other. _____

(35) own right shoulder, then other. _____

(36) own left arm, then other. _____

(37) own right arm, then other. _____

(38) own left hand, then other. _____

(39) own right hand, then other. _____

(40) own left leg, then other. _____

(41) own right leg, then other. _____

(42) own right knee, then other. _____

(43) own left knee, then other. _____

(44) own right ankle, then other. _____

(45) own left ankle, then other. _____

(46) own left foot, then other. _____

(47) own right foot, then other. _____

Comments:

Maximum total points 47. Total points obtained by participant = _____

$$\text{Total percent of attainment} = \frac{\text{total points obtained by participant}}{\text{maximum total points}} \times 100$$

Total percent attainment = _____

Name _____ Sex _____

Date Test Taken _____

Age _____

D. Response Time
1. Purpose: The primary purpose is to secure the right- and left-hand response time and the right- and left-foot response time. The secondary purpose is to acquire a better insight into the possible areas of weakness and subsequent corrective measures concerning response time in physical movement, especially of the hands and feet.
2. Equipment and materials: a glass marble, a ruler marked in centimeters, and a table.
3. Procedure: Hold the ruler in an upright position on a table, the bottom part of the marble placed at the 22-centimeter position. The participant stands upright and, with the palm of the hand up, places the back of the hand flat on the table. Place the midpoint of the side of the palm opposite the thumb, against the ruler. Have the participant watch the marble and remove the hand before the marble hits the hand after it has been released. Move the marble up or down 1 centimeter at a time until the participant cannot remove the hand on three consecutive hits at a given height. Subtract the height of the hand at the touch point from the height of the drop point of the marble to secure the true distance the marble dropped upon hitting the hand three consecutive times. Secure the true distance for both the right and left hands.

Place the ruler in an upright position on the floor, the bottom part of the marble at the 22-centimeter position. Shoes and socks removed, the participant places the back part of the little toe against the ruler. Have the participant stand upright and watch the marble, and then, as the marble is released, remove the foot before the marble hits the foot. Move the marble up or down 1 centimeter at a time until the participant cannot remove the foot on three consecutive hits at a given height. Subtract the height of the foot at the touch point from the height of the drop point of the marble to secure the true distance the marble dropped upon hitting the foot three consecutive times. Secure the true distance for both the right and left feet. To secure the response time, use the formula:

$$t = \sqrt{\frac{2s}{g}}$$

where t = time in seconds (calculated)

   s = true distance in centimeters (measured)

   $g = 980 \, cm/sec.^2$ (acceleration due to gravity a constant)

(1) Right hand

   $s =$ _____ cm

   $t =$ _____ sec.

(2) Left hand

   $s =$ _____ cm

   $t =$ _____ sec.

(3) Right foot

   $s =$ _____ cm

   $t =$ _____ sec.

(4) Left foot

   $s =$ _____ cm

   $t =$ _____ sec.

Comments:

III. Advanced Area Tests

A. Coordination

1. Purpose: The purpose is to secure an indication of a participant's ability to move the arm and leg segments in a coordinated manner, particularly in the lateral-medial and anteroposterior directions.

2. Equipment and materials: masking tape, a metronome, and a meterstick or metric tape.

3. Procedure: Tape two 30-centimeter squares on the floor 1 meter apart. The tester demonstrates each set of coordinated moves at one square, followed by the participant attempting to copy the same moves at the other square. Score one point for *each set* of coordinated moves completed without error and zero if not completed. Adjust the metronome to a steady 1-second beat.

   The tester sits outside the square, with the participant facing in the same direction. The tester places both hands inside the square and moves them to each beat of the metronome, in the following manner (see Figures 12.7 and 12.8). The participant follows.

   In sets 9 through 12 the tester and participant *stand* in their respective squares. Sets 9, 10, 11, and 12 are done in the same manner as sets 1, 2, 3, and 4, except that the feet are moved instead of the hands.

   Score _____ set 9   Score _____ set 11

   Score _____ set 10   Score _____ set 12

   Start with set 9 and move continuously through sets 9, 10, 11, and 12 (16 beats of the metronome, using the feet). Score one point for each set completed successfully and zero for each set not completed successfully. Score _____ (0, 1, 2, 3, 4 points possible)

   In sets 13 through 16 the tester and participant *stand* in their respective squares. Sets 13, 14, 15, and 16 are done in the same manner as sets 5, 6, 7, and 8, except that the feet are moved instead of the hands.

   Score _____ set 13   Score _____ set 15

   Score _____ set 14   Score _____ set 16

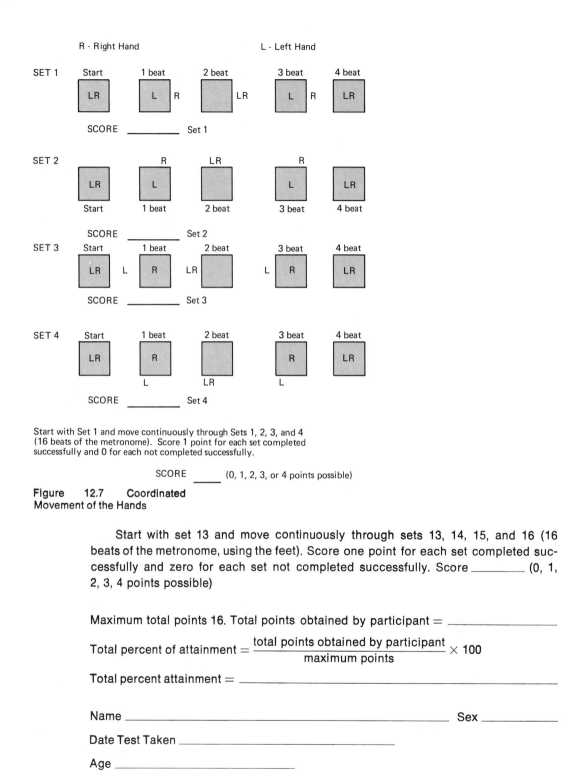

Figure 12.7 Coordinated Movement of the Hands

Start with set 13 and move continuously through sets 13, 14, 15, and 16 (16 beats of the metronome, using the feet). Score one point for each set completed successfully and zero for each set not completed successfully. Score _____ (0, 1, 2, 3, 4 points possible)

Maximum total points 16. Total points obtained by participant = _____

$$\text{Total percent of attainment} = \frac{\text{total points obtained by participant}}{\text{maximum points}} \times 100$$

Total percent attainment = _____

Name _____ Sex _____

Date Test Taken _____

Age _____

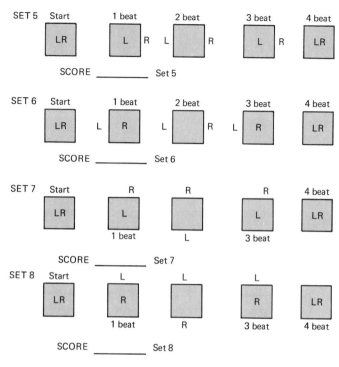

Start with Set 5 and move continuously through sets 5, 6, 7, and 8 (16 beats of the metronome). Score 1 point for each set completed successfully and 0 for each not completed successfully.

SCORE _____ (0, 1, 2, 3, or 4 points possible)

Figure 12.8 Coordinated Movement of Hands in Opposite Pattern

B. Agility
1. Purpose: The purpose is to secure an indication of a participant's whole body agility in the sagittal and frontal planes.
2. Equipment and materials: masking tape, a hand-held stopwatch, and a meterstick or metric tape.
3. Procedure: Using the masking tape, tape a 30-centimeter square on the floor. Four meters from the midpoint of each of two sides of the 30-centimeter square, tape two 1-meter squares. The midpoint of each near side of each 1-meter square should form a right angle with a line drawn perpendicular from the midpoint of each of the two sides of the 30-centimeter square. (See Figure 12.9)

The participant stands in the 30-centimeter square facing one of the two 1-meter squares. The participant starts by moving as fast as possible to the square he or she is facing and places both feet inside that square, then moves as fast as possible backwards, without turning around, to the 1-meter square directly behind him or her. The tester may have to demonstrate the moves. The tester starts the stopwatch

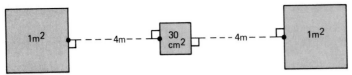

Figure 12.9 Placement of Squares for Whole Body Agility Test

upon the initial move of the participant, and counts the number of times the participant gets both feet inside a 1-meter square within 30 seconds in the sagittal plane (forward and backward movement). Record the number of times the participant successfully completes the physical act. Sagittal Plane: No. of Times _____

The participant stands in the 30-centimeter square with the 1-meter squares to the right and left and moves as fast as possible to the 1-meter square to the right, then to the left. The participant may slide-step or cross-step but not turn and run to the squares in the frontal plane (right and left). The tester may have to demonstrate a slide-step or cross-step for the participant. The tester starts the stopwatch upon the initial move of the participant, and counts the number of times the participant gets both feet inside a 1-meter square within 30 seconds in the frontal plane (right and left movement). Record the number of times the participant successfully completes the physical act. Frontal Plane: No. of Times _____

Name _____ Sex _____

Date Test Taken _____

Age _____

summary review questions

1. What should be the major objective of an adapted physical education program? (*answer on p. 342*)

2. An individual may have an impairment and a resulting disability but not consider himself or herself handicapped. Explain. (*answer on p. 343*)

3. Why should you test and evaluate the entering physical functioning level of a participant? (*answer on p. 342*)

4. Why should you periodically retest? (*answer on p. 343*)

5. Sketch from memory the planning model for the decision-making process presented in chapter 1.

6. What decisions are necessary:
   a. before initial testing?
   b. after initial testing?

c. after retesting?

(*answer on pp. 343–344*)

7. What is the hierarchy of components of physical functioning, presented in this chapter, that should be considered when testing for the present physical functioning level of a participant? (*answer on p. 344*)

8. Who should decide what to test and what test to employ? (*answer on p. 346*)

9. How does one know if the physical functioning level of an impaired or disabled or handicapped participant has progressed, leveled, or regressed? (*answer on p. 343*)

bibliography

Adams, Ronald. *Games, Sports, and Exercises for the Physically Handicapped.* Philadelphia: Lea and Febiger, 1972.

American National Red Cross. *Adapted Aquatics.* Garden City, N.Y.: Doubleday, 1977.

Arnheim, Daniel; Auxter, David; and Crowe, Walter. *Principles and Methods of Adapted Physical Education.* 3d ed. St. Louis: C. V. Mosby, 1977.

Bilensky, Robert. *A Swimming Program for Blind Children.* New York: American Foundation for the Blind, 1955.

Churchill, Don; Alpern, Gerald; and DeMyer, Marian. *Infantile Autism.* Springfield, Ill.: Charles C. Thomas, 1971.

Conner, James. *Classroom Activities for Helping Hyperactive Children.* New York: The Center for Applied Research in Education, 1974.

Cratty, Bryant. *Developmental Games for Physically Handicapped Children.* Palo Alto, Calif.: Peek Publications, 1969.

Cunningham, Susanne, and Reagan, Cora Lee. *Handbook of Visual Perceptual Training.* Springfield, Ill.: Charles C. Thomas, 1972.

Daniels, Lucille, and Worthingham, Catherine. *Muscle Testing Techniques of Manual Examination.* 3d ed. Philadelphia: W. B. Saunders, 1972.

Dauer, Victor. *Essential Movement Experiences for Preschool and Primary Children.* Minneapolis: Burgess, 1972.

Doman, Glen. *What To Do About Your Brain-Injured Child.* Garden City, N.Y.: Doubleday, 1974.

Fait, Hollis. *Special Physical Education.* Philadelphia: W. B. Saunders, 1972.

Garret, James, and Levine, Edna. *Rehabilitation Practices with the Physically Disabled.* New York: Columbia University Press, 1973.

Hayden, Frank. *Physical Fitness for the Retarded.* Toronto: Metropolitan Toronto Association for Retarded Children, 1964.

Institute for Physical Education. *The Handbook of Physical Education and Activities for Exceptional Children.* Old Saybrook, Conn.: Institute for Physical Education, 1975.

Johnson, Barry. *A Beginner's Book of Gymnastics.* New York: Appleton-Century-Crofts, 1966.

Kephart, Newell. *The Slow Learner in the Classroom.* Columbus, Ohio: Charles E. Merrill, 1960.

Krusen, F. H. *Handbook of Physical Medicine and Rehabilitation.* Philadelphia: W. B. Saunders, 1965.

Logan, Gene. *Adapted Physical Education.* Dubuque, Iowa: William C. Brown, 1972.

Montessori, Maria. *The Montessori Method.* Cambridge, Mass.: Bentley Company, 1964.

Newman, Judy. *Swimming for Children with Physical and Sensory Impairments.* Springfield, Ill.: Charles C. Thomas, 1976.

Piaget, Jean. *The Development of the Concept of Space in the Child.* New York: International University Press Publishers, 1970.

Reynolds, Grace, ed. *A Swimming Program for the Handicapped.* New York: Association Press Publishers, 1973.

Robins, Terris, and Robins, Janet. *Educational Rhythms in Mentally and Physically Handicapped Children.* New York: Association Press Publishers, 1970.

Sherrill, Claudine. *Adapted Physical Education and Recreation.* Dubuque, Iowa: Wm. C. Brown, 1976.

Wallace, Gerald, and McLaughlin, James. *Learning Disabilities.* Columbus, Ohio: Charles E. Merrill, 1975.

Valett, Robert. *The Remediation of Learning Disabilities.* Belmont, Calif.: Fearon Publishers, 1967.

exercises

1. Twenty learning disability children 8 to 10 years of age were tested using the battery of tests presented in this chapter. Each column in Table 12.1 represents a test, and each row represents the score obtained by each participant on each test. The total raw scores are presented in Table 12.1 on page 373.

   a. Calculate an $\overline{X}$ and σ for each physical functioning factor (each column 3 through 18).
   b. Calculate a Z- and T-score for each participant in each factor (each column 3 through 18). *Note:* In a column where a smaller time indicates a better effort (columns 5, 12, 13, 14, and 15), change the sign of the Z-score so that you may compare it with other Z-scores and T-scores. Calculate a mean T-score for each participant.
   c. Calculate a Pearsonian correlation coefficient for strength (column 3) and muscular endurance (column 4). Develop a predictive equation for estimating muscular endurance from strength.
   d. Calculate a Pearsonian correlation coefficient for body sides (column 10) and space awareness (column 11). Develop a predictive equation for estimating space awareness from body sides.
   e. Calculate a Pearsonian correlation coefficient for right foot response time (column 14) and agility sagittal (column 17). Develop a predictive equation for estimating agility sagittal from right-foot response time.
   f. Calculate a Pearsonian correlation coefficient for right-foot response time (column 14) and agility frontal (column 18). Develop a predictive equation for estimating agility frontal from right-foot response time.
   g. Calculate a Pearsonian correlation coefficient for left-foot response time (column 15) and agility sagittal (column 17). Develop a predictive equation for estimating agility sagittal from left-foot response time.
   h. Calculate a Pearsonian correlation coefficient for left-foot response time (column 15) and agility frontal (column 18). Develop a predictive equation for estimating agility frontal from left-foot response time.
   i. Calculate a Pearsonian correlation coefficient for right-foot response time (column 14) and left-foot response time (column 15). Develop a predicitive equation for estimating left-foot response time from right-foot response time.
   j. Calculate a Pearsonian correlation coefficient for agility sagittal (column 17) and agility frontal (column 18). Develop a predictive equation.
   k. Calculate a Pearsonian correlation coefficient for any two factors that interest you.

Table 12.1   **Raw Scores on Twenty Learning Disability Children**

1. Student	2. Age in years	3. Strength	4. Muscular endurance time sec.	5. Cardiorespiratory endurance sec. 400-meter run walk	6. Range of motion	7. Balance response Static medium—static individual	8. Balance response Static medium—dynamic individual	9. Knowledge of body segments—parts	10. Knowledge of body and body segment—part sides	11. Knowledge of space	12. Response time, right hand in seconds	13. Response time, left hand in seconds	14. Response time, right foot in seconds	15. Response time, left foot in seconds	16. Coordination	17. Agility, sagittal	18. Agility, frontal	19. Sex
S₁	9	21	55	118	15	17	15	17	7	3	.26	.29	.39	.37	12	8	4	M
S₂	8	18	43	150	12	17	16	15	8	6	.30	.34	.38	.38	10	6	4	F
S₃	10	19	58	136	16	18	18	14	10	5	.27	.30	.33	.34	24	8	6	M
S₄	8	15	34	180	10	15	12	14	3	0	.60	.80	.80	.90	2	1	1	M
S₅	9	23	72	120	16	21	20	17	12	23	.28	.29	.34	.34	23	10	9	M
S₆	8	16	43	135	16	19	15	17	5	2	.33	.34	.39	.40	8	5	4	F
S₇	10	25	84	110	16	21	20	17	12	30	.18	.18	.19	.19	30	12	10	F
S₈	10	20	71	115	16	21	20	17	13	26	.20	.23	.30	.26	26	9	8	F
S₉	9	18	54	145	15	18	19	16	8	6	.21	.23	.32	.28	24	9	6	F
S₁₀	8	19	49	148	16	20	19	16	9	6	.31	.36	.37	.38	20	8	4	F
S₁₁	10	19	56	150	15	21	20	17	14	36	.25	.29	.31	.30	22	10	8	M
S₁₂	8	15	41	170	16	16	15	16	7	5	.34	.40	.40	.42	8	6	6	M
S₁₃	8	15	43	165	15	17	14	16	6	6	.31	.38	.39	.39	10	5	4	F
S₁₄	10	25	86	104	16	21	20	17	14	33	.16	.16	.18	.18	30	12	11	F
S₁₅	8	14	38	161	12	16	14	17	6	5	.32	.33	.36	.38	12	6	4	M
S₁₆	9	20	60	122	16	21	20	17	8	6	.28	.26	.34	.30	23	9	6	F
S₁₇	9	19	56	138	16	19	20	16	7	6	.24	.23	.36	.34	12	9	6	M
S₁₈	10	21	76	112	16	21	20	17	12	28	.18	.19	.19	.19	32	12	14	F
S₁₉	8	17	40	168	15	19	14	16	7	6	.36	.38	.40	.42	9	6	3	M
S₂₀	9	19	64	160	14	17	14	14	6	3	.36	.40	.43	.44	4	4	2	M

Answer:

a.

	Col. 3	4	5	6	7	8	9	10
$\overline{X}$	18.9	56.14	140.35	14.95	18.75	17.25	16.15	8.7
σ	3.04	14.99	22.24	1.65	1.99	2.77	1.06	3.08

	Col. 11	12	13	14	15	16	17	18
$\overline{x}$	12.05	.287	.319	.358	.360	17.05	7.75	6.0
σ	11.65	.09	.13	.12	.14	9.05	2.80	3.13

b.

		Col. 3	4	5	6	7	8	9	10
S1	Z	.69	−.08	1.00	.03	−.88	−.81	.80	−.55
	T	56.9	49.2	60.0	50.3	41.2	41.9	58.0	44.5
S2	Z	−.30	−.88	−.43	−1.79	−.88	−.45	−1.08	−.23
	T	47.0	41.2	45.7	32.1	41.2	45.5	39.2	47.7
S3	Z	.03	.12	.19	.64	−.38	.27	−2.03	.42
	T	50.3	51.2	51.9	56.4	46.2	52.7	29.7	54.2
S4	Z	−1.28	−1.48	−1.78	−3.00	−1.88	−1.90	−2.03	−1.85
	T	37.2	35.2	32.2	20.0	31.2	31.0	29.7	31.5
S5	Z	1.35	1.06	.91	.64	1.13	.99	.80	1.07
	T	63.5	60.6	59.1	56.4	61.3	59.9	58.0	60.7
S6	Z	−.95	−.88	.24	.64	.13	−.81	.80	−1.20
	T	40.5	41.2	52.4	56.4	51.3	41.9	58.0	38.0
S7	Z	2.00	1.86	1.36	.64	1.13	.99	.80	1.07
	T	70.0	68.6	63.6	56.4	61.3	59.9	58.0	60.7
S8	Z	.36	.99	1.14	.64	1.13	.99	.80	1.40
	T	53.6	59.9	61.4	56.4	61.3	59.9	58.0	64.0
S9	Z	.30	−.14	−.21	.03	−.38	.63	−.14	−.23
	T	47.0	48.6	47.9	49.7	46.2	56.3	48.6	47.7
S10	Z	.03	−.48	−.34	.64	.63	.63	−.14	.10
	T	50.3	45.2	46.6	56.4	56.3	56.3	48.6	51.0
S11	Z	.03	−.01	−.43	.03	1.13	.99	.80	1.72
	T	50.3	49.9	45.7	50.3	61.3	59.9	58.0	67.2
S12	Z	−1.28	−1.01	−1.33	.64	−1.38	−.81	−.14	−.55
	T	37.2	39.9	36.7	56.4	36.2	41.9	48.6	44.5
S13	Z	−1.28	−.88	−1.11	.03	−.88	−1.17	−.14	−.88
	T	37.2	41.2	38.9	50.3	41.2	38.3	48.6	41.2
S14	Z	2.00	1.99	1.63	.64	1.13	.99	.80	1.72
	T	70.0	69.9	66.3	56.4	61.3	59.9	58.0	67.2
S15	Z	−1.61	−1.21	−.93	−1.79	−1.38	−1.17	.80	−.88
	T	33.9	37.9	40.7	32.1	36.2	38.3	58.0	41.2
S16	Z	.36	.26	.83	.64	1.13	.99	.80	−.23
	T	53.6	52.6	58.3	56.4	61.3	59.9	58.0	47.7
S17	Z	.03	−.01	.11	.64	.13	.99	−.14	−.55
	T	50.3	49.9	51.1	56.4	51.3	59.9	48.6	44.5
S18	Z	.69	1.32	1.27	.64	1.13	.99	.80	1.07
	T	56.9	63.2	62.7	56.4	61.3	59.9	58.0	60.7
S19	Z	−.59	−1.08	−1.24	.03	.13	−1.17	−.14	−.55
	T	44.1	39.2	37.6	50.3	51.3	38.3	48.6	44.5
S20	Z	.03	.52	−.88	−.58	−.88	−1.17	−2.03	−.88
	T	50.3	55.2	41.2	44.2	41.2	38.3	29.7	41.2

11	12	13	14	15	16	17	18	$\overline{X}$ T-score
−.78	.30	.22	−.27	−.07	−.56	.09	−.64	
42.2	53.0	52.2	47.3	49.3	44.4	50.9	43.6	49.1
−.52	−.14	−.16	−.18	−.14	−.78	−.63	−.64	
44.8	48.6	48.4	48.2	48.6	42.2	43.7	43.6	44.2
−.61	.19	.15	.23	.14	.78	.09	0.0	
43.9	51.9	51.5	52.3	51.4	57.8	50.9	50.0	50.1
−1.03	−3.47	−3.68	−3.68	−3.86	−1.66	−2.41	−1.60	
39.7	15.2	13.2	13.2	11.4	33.4	25.9	34.0	27.1
.94	.08	.22	.15	.14	.65	.80	.96	
59.4	50.8	52.2	51.5	51.4	56.4	58.0	59.6	57.4
−.86	−.48	−.16	−.27	−.29	−1.00	−.98	−.64	
41.4	45.2	48.4	47.3	47.1	40.0	40.2	43.6	45.8
1.54	1.19	1.07	1.40	1.21	1.43	1.52	1.28	
65.4	61.9	60.7	64.0	62.1	64.3	65.2	62.8	62.8
1.20	.97	.68	.48	.71	.99	.45	.64	
62.0	59.7	56.8	54.8	57.1	59.9	54.5	56.4	58.5
−.52	.86	.68	.32	.57	.78	.45	0.0	
44.8	58.6	56.8	53.2	55.7	57.8	54.5	50.0	51.5
−.52	−.26	−.32	−.10	−.14	.33	.09	−.64	
44.8	47.4	46.8	49.0	48.6	53.3	50.9	43.6	49.7
2.06	.41	.22	.40	.43	.55	.80	.64	
70.6	54.1	52.2	54.0	54.3	55.5	58.0	56.4	56.1
−.61	−.59	−.62	−.35	−.43	−1.00	−.63	0.0	
43.9	44.1	43.8	46.5	45.7	40.0	43.7	50.0	43.7
−.52	−.26	−.47	−.27	−.21	−.78	−.98	−.64	
44.8	47.4	45.3	47.3	47.9	42.2	40.2	43.6	43.5
1.80	1.41	1.22	1.48	1.29	1.43	1.52	1.60	
68.0	64.1	62.2	64.8	62.9	64.3	65.2	66.0	64.2
−.61	−.37	−.08	−.02	−.14	−.56	−.63	−.64	
43.9	46.3	49.2	49.8	48.6	44.4	43.7	43.6	43.0
−.52	.08	.45	.15	.43	.66	.45	0.0	
44.8	50.8	54.5	51.5	54.3	56.6	54.5	50.0	54.1
−.52	.52	.68	−.02	.14	−.56	.45	0.0	
44.8	55.2	56.8	49.8	51.4	44.6	54.5	50.0	51.2
1.37	1.19	.99	1.40	1.21	1.65	1.52	2.56	
63.7	61.9	59.9	64.0	62.1	66.5	65.2	75.6	62.4
−.52	−.81	−.47	−.35	−.43	−.89	−.63	−.96	
44.8	41.9	45.3	46.5	45.7	41.1	43.7	40.4	44.0
−.78	−.81	−.62	−.60	−.57	−1.44	−1.34	−1.28	
42.2	41.9	43.8	44.0	44.3	35.6	36.6	37.2	41.7

c. Between strength and muscular endurance: $r_{xy} = .92$, $\hat{y} = -29.8 + 4.55 \times$
d. Between body sides and space awareness: $r_{xy} = .91$, $\hat{y} = -18.1 + 3.48 \times$
e. Between right-foot response time and agility sagittal:
   $r_{xy} = -.88$, $\hat{y} = 14.9 + (-19.99) \times$
f. Between right-foot response time and agility frontal:
   $r_{xy} = -.78$, $\hat{y} = 13.1 + (-19.9) \times$
g. Between left-foot response time and agility sagittal:
   $r_{xy} = -.87$, $\hat{y} = 13.8 + (-16.8) \times$

Table 12.2   Raw Scores on Twenty Educable Retarded Children

1. Student	2. Age in years	3. Strength	4. Muscular endurance time sec.	5. Cardiorespiratory endurance 400-meter run-walk sec.	6. Range of motion	7. Balance response Static medium—static individual	8. Balance response Static medium—dynamic individual	9. Knowledge of body segments—parts	10. Knowledge of body and body segments—part sides	11. Knowledge of space	12. Response time, right hand in seconds	13. Response time, left hand in seconds	14. Response time, right foot in seconds	15. Response time, left foot in seconds	16. Coordination	17. Agility, sagittal	18. Agility, frontal	19. Sex
S_1	10	28	133	88	16	21	20	17	15	30	.18	.19	.21	.23	26	12	10	F
S_2	8	25	77	122	16	18	19	15	12	25	.19	.17	.26	.23	12	8	6	F
S_3	9	27	115	93	15	20	20	15	11	30	.16	.18	.25	.26	18	9	8	M
S_4	9	28	120	92	16	19	20	17	14	34	.18	.18	.23	.25	20	10	6	F
S_5	8	24	78	130	16	19	18	14	10	16	.21	.20	.25	.23	10	6	5	M
S_6	10	30	138	94	16	21	20	17	18	34	.17	.19	.20	.22	24	10	8	F
S_7	8	25	82	118	15	17	14	12	11	22	.21	.22	.24	.24	14	8	5	F
S_8	9	26	123	96	15	18	16	17	14	28	.17	.16	.19	.18	22	6	10	M
S_9	10	29	136	88	16	21	20	17	18	42	.19	.19	.21	.23	24	12	8	M
S_{10}	8	24	76	123	16	19	16	15	11	24	.23	.20	.26	.23	12	10	5	M
S_{11}	8	24	79	120	16	18	16	16	12	20	.18	.19	.25	.26	16	12	10	F
S_{12}	10	29	132	85	16	21	20	17	18	40	.16	.17	.19	.21	32	16	15	M
S_{13}	10	28	130	86	16	21	20	17	14	35	.18	.19	.20	.22	26	14	10	F
S_{14}	10	31	156	82	15	20	20	17	16	38	.18	.20	.22	.25	24	14	10	M
S_{15}	9	28	125	95	14	19	18	16	15	34	.21	.23	.26	.26	15	10	6	F
S_{16}	9	29	126	92	16	19	17	14	16	36	.18	.20	.23	.25	20	12	8	F
S_{17}	8	25	84	126	16	17	18	15	12	28	.20	.23	.28	.24	14	6	4	F
S_{18}	9	28	119	94	16	19	19	20	16	40	.16	.18	.20	.22	22	12	11	M
S_{19}	8	25	80	122	16	17	15	13	9	16	.21	.22	.25	.27	16	6	5	F
S_{20}	8	24	79	128	16	18	17	14	10	20	.19	.19	.23	.22	10	8	8	M

h. Between left-foot response time and agility frontal:
$r_{xy} = -.75$, $y = 11.8 + (-16.0) \times$
i. Between right-foot response time and left-foot response time:
$r_{xy} = .99$, $y = -.058 + (1.167) \times$
j. Between agility sagittal and agility frontal:
$r_{xy} = .89$, $y = -1.71 + .995 \times$
k. Depends on your choice.

2. Twenty educable mentally retarded children 8 to 10 years of age were tested through the battery of tests presented in this chapter. The total raw scores are presented in Table 12.2 on page 375.

a. Calculate an $\overline{X}$ and σ for each physical functioning factor (each column 3 through 18).
b. Calculate a Z- and T-score for each participant in each factor (each column 3 through 18). *Note:* In a column where a smaller time indicates a better effort (columns 5, 12, 13, 14, and 15), change the sign of the Z-score so that you may compare it with other Z-scores and T-scores. Calculate a mean T-score for each participant.
c. Calculate a Pearsonian correlation coefficient for strength (column 3) and muscular endurance (column 4). Develop a predictive equation for strength (X) and muscular endurance (Y).
d. Calculate a Pearsonian correlation coefficient for body sides (column 10) and space awareness (column 11). Develop a predictive equation for body sides (X) and space awareness (Y).
e. Calculate a Pearsonian correlation coefficient for any two factors that interest you.

measurement in the affective domain

The affective domain of development is concerned with the values, appreciations, attitudes, and interests of people, and the personal-social behavior related to them. Indeed, Charles Bucher and James Baley and David Field[1] report that personal-social development has long been one of the general objectives of physical education. Quite often, affective goals are presented as concomitant learnings, those things Robert Ebel claims are difficult to teach for, but yet occur, as instruction in more tangible elements takes place.[2] The affective goals linger on and become part of our personality; in the future, they will probably influence us to behave in a certain way. We have all listened to coaches and sportswriters who proclaim that the "character" and "sportsmanship" developed on the playing fields will help steer us through life's future journey. Don Kirkendall tells us that, unfortunately, affective objectives are rarely developed and learning outcomes rarely evaluated in school physical education and athletic programs.[3] In spite of a lack of formalized teaching strategies designed to develop affective learnings, nearly all fitness and psychomotor objectives have an affective component involved. If a child is taught physical fitness activities, but participates only if forced to do so, an important affective goal was not achieved.

1. Charles A. Bucher, *Foundations of Physical Education,* 7th ed. (St. Louis: C. V. Mosby, 1975); James A. Baley and David A. Field, *Physical Education and the Physical Educator: An Introduction* (Boston: Allyn and Bacon, Inc., 1970).
2. Robert L. Ebel, "What Are Schools For?" *Phi Delta Kappan* 54 (1972):3–7.
3. Don R. Kirkendall, "Physical Education Effects in the Affective Domain," *75th Proceedings, National College Physical Education Association for Men,* 1972, pp. 147–151.

example taxonomy of the affective domain

A taxonomy of educational objectives dealing with the affective domain was developed by David Krathwohl et al.[4] The domain is ordered on a continuum from a base level, where an individual is aware of a value construct, up to a persuasive outlook that influences a person's actions. Kirkendall provides us with the following example of how the taxonomy can be applied to physical education, where the teacher is interested in developing a sense of "fair play" in students.[5]

1.0 Receiving
- 1.1 *Awareness*—develops an awareness that there is such a thing as fair play in sport.
- 1.2 *Willingness to Receive*—appreciates observing activities where honesty is demonstrated by others.
- 1.3 *Controlled or Selected Attention*—student begins looking for situations where respect for others and fair play occur.

2.0 Responding
- 2.1 *Acquiescence in Responding*—at the request or threat of the teacher, the pupil observes all the rules in the game.
- 2.2 *Willingness to Respond*—sometimes the student calls rule violations on himself, but mainly to please the teacher.
- 2.3 *Satisfaction in Response*—becomes emotionally involved and begins to get some personal pleasure out of being honest.

3.0 Valuing
- 3.1 *Acceptance of a Value*—accepts that honesty and fair play in sports is a good thing.
- 3.2 *Preference for a Value*—calls rule violations on himself without any prompting because he strongly feels this is the right thing to do.
- 3.3 *Commitment* (conviction)—now clearly holds this value of "fair play." He not only demonstrates this by his own actions, but tries to convince others this is the way to enjoy the game.

4.0 Organization
- 4.1 *Conceptualization of a Value*—sees how the concept of honesty and fair play can be used in other aspects of life.
- 4.2 *Organization of a Value System*—places the sense of "fairness" into his life's total value system.

5.0 Characterization by a Value or Value Complex
- 5.1 *Generalized Set*—becomes consistent in all aspects of his life in the display of "honesty."

This hierarchy of a developing value construct can be applied to many of the other desirable affective behaviors we claim are inherent in physical education, sports, and games. Once we recognize their existence, define them, and plan and teach for student acquisition and display of the behaviors, we are in a position to determine how well the pupils have acquired and used the values taught.

classification of instruments

Many instruments have been constructed to measure certain aspects of personal-social behavior, attitudes, and adjustment in physical education. We can subjectively classify

4. David R. Krathwohl et al., *Taxonomy of Educational Objectives, The Classification of Educational Goals, Handbook II: Affective Domain* (New York: David McKay, 1964).
5. Kirkendall, "Physical Education, Effects in the Affective Domain," pp. 147–151.

these measuring instruments into the following general categories.

Interest inventories: usually a self-report inventory in which the individual expresses her likes and dislikes for certain activities, situations, or programs. Quite often interest inventories are used as the basis for establishing programs and program content in recreational settings. Students generally participate in intramural sports or elect a particular activity from the physical education offerings, based on their liking for a particular sport. One's interest in a particular activity may be developed by past experience, peer pressure, teacher or parent stimulation, and other cultural factors. An expressed interest may reflect one's attitude toward certain forms of activity. A person who values physical activity from an aesthetic point of view will probably express a preference for dance as opposed to football.

Attitude inventories: usually a self-report inventory in which the pupil is asked to reveal his state of mind or feelings about specific objects, events, people, activities, social institutions, and so on. One's attitude or basic feeling about physical activity is thought to be a prime motivating force in the degree of future participation in a selected physical activity.

Sportsmanship: a self-report or a report by others concerning the degree to which one abides by the rules, accepts victory or defeat graciously, and is willing to make personal sacrifices for the good of the group. Quite often this trait is viewed as "character" being displayed in game situations.

Leadership: a report made by members of a group in which they are asked to identify individuals in the group who would make or are the class leaders. This is a difficult identification to make unless all group members are given an equal opportunity to function as a leader.

Social development: instruments designed to measure aspects of social development; these may take the form of self-reports, ratings by teachers, and ratings by the peer group. One type of instrument attempts to assess the degree to which a pupil has adjusted to the social environment of the class and school. Other instruments can give an indication of the degree of acceptance by one's peers (peer status or popularity).

Behavior ratings: these ratings are made by the teacher after having observed the child over a period of time. Ratings are usually confined to the content of a particular instrument. Traits that are found on a number of instruments include: acting-out, withdrawal, disturbed peer relations, immaturity, loyalty, self-control, leadership, sociability, and conforming to class procedures and cooperation, to mention a few. The validity, reliability, and objectivity of behavior ratings are open to question. Quite often the child's rating is a function of the "halo effect" or the tendency of a teacher to give students he likes a high rating and students he dislikes a low rating. In addition, not all students have an equal opportunity to display in similar situations the behavior being rated.

Personality inventories: these inventories are largely paper-and-pencil self-report inventories in which the respondent is presented with a series of questions describing typical behavioral patterns. One's score consists of the number of questions answered in a direction supposedly displaying the behavioral trait. Some personality inventories are designed to measure only one trait, such as anxiety. Other inventories attempt to measure as many as sixteen personality factors. The study and evaluation of human personality is an exceedingly complex phenomenon beyond the scope of the typical physical educator's professional training. Hence, it is strongly recommended that the assessment and interpretation of personality traits be left to qualified school psychologists.

types of measurements

Information in the affective domain is usually collected in one of three ways, namely, teacher ratings of observed pupil behavior, pupil self-ratings or self-report, and pupil ratings of other pupils in the group. The same instrument can be used by teachers and pupils. In this way, information concerning a particular mode of behavior can be secured from three different points of view. Indeed, it is imperative that when crucial decisions about pupils are made, information be secured from a variety of sources. The relevancy of this tactic is vividly illustrated by the findings of a number of studies. W. P. Jackson and H. M. Lahaderne found that teachers were poor predictors of the affective responses of their students.[6] In the area of social adjustments, Charles Cowell found that the relationship between teacher ratings of social adjustment and pupil ratings of other pupils was only .50.[7] This may indicate that either different behavior was being recorded, or that the behavior was being interpretated differently by the teachers and pupils. More recently, Melody Noland and Joseph Gruber demonstrated that the scores obtained by two different sets of teachers on a problem identification checklist were independent.[8] That is, the objectivity or between-scorer reliability was quite low. This occurred in a school setting in which the teachers had constant supervision over the children for more than a month before the ratings were made. The general problem then becomes one of pooling information from a variety of sources when planning educational programs. It is imperative that self-report data be reliable so that one can place confidence in them. Gruber reports that the reliabilities of

personality trait inventory scores on a highly refined instrument (self-report) were low in three different samples of students.[9] Thus, pupils are inconsistent in reporting their own responses to questions on a personality inventory. Certainly repeated observations must be made to ensure some consistency in reporting behavior. The crucial question then still remains: Which data are more influential in decision making, the teachers' or pupils', and why?

Many problems encountered in securing affective measurements may underlie the lack of relevancy and consistency of affective data. These problems are discussed later in this chapter.

types of scales

Data representing aspects of the affective domain can be secured from various types of scales. Two scales, namely the Thurstone equal appearing interval scale[10] and the Gutmann scaling procedures[11] are seldom used in physical education. Both require a large pool of items to start with and demand

6. W. P. Jackson and H. M. Lahaderne, "Scholastic Success and Attitude Toward School in a Population of Sixth Graders," *Journal of Educational Psychology* 58, no. 1 (1967):15–18.

7. Charles C. Cowell, "Validating an Index of Social Adjustment for High School Use," *Research Quarterly* 29 (March 1958):7–18.

8. Melody Noland and Joseph J. Gruber, "Self-Perception, Personality and Behavior in Emotionally Disturbed School Children," *Behavioral Disorders*, 4, no. 1 (Nov., 1978):6–12.

9. Joseph J. Gruber, "Comments on the Reliability of a Personality Questionnaire Used in Physical Education and Sport Research," *International Journal of Sport Psychology*, 9, no. 2 (1978):111–118.

10. L. L. Thurstone, *The Measurement of Values* (Chicago: University of Chicago Press, 1959).

11. L. Guttman, "The Cornell Technique for Scale and Intensity Analysis," *Educational and Psychological Measurement* 7 (1947):247–279.

rigorous procedures in their construction, along with extremely high item reliability. Other procedures such as Likert scales, the semantic differential, rating scales, and questionnaires appear to be used with greater frequency in physical education and sport. Hence, we briefly describe each technique and present a few sample items for each.

likert scales

One of the most widely used techniques for attitude measurement is the Likert scale in which a statement usually is followed by a five-response continuum on which the respondent is to indicate the degree of affect or intensity of feeling about the statement. A typical positive attitude item could be:

> "The best way to become more socially desirable is to participate in group physical activities."

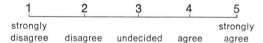

1	2	3	4	5
strongly disagree	disagree	undecided	agree	strongly agree

The subject selects the category that best describes her reaction to the statement. At times, attitude scales present both positively and negatively worded statements. The following is an example of a negatively worded statement:

> "There are better ways of getting to know people than through games and sports."

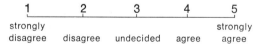

1	2	3	4	5
strongly disagree	disagree	undecided	agree	strongly agree

Care must be taken when scoring that the point value for the negative statement scale is reversed, that is, subtracted from the total number of categories plus 1. After the negatively worded scores have been converted, the total scale or subscale score can be totaled.

Fewer or more than five categories can be used. With younger children, two categories such as yes–no; like–dislike; like me–not like me; or present–absent are often found as two-dimensional choice responses. J. P. Guilford demonstrated that reliability increases as the number of response choices increases, with the greatest reliability found at around seven categories.[12]

semantic differential

A technique that may become increasingly useful in physical education attitude measurement is the semantic differential developed by C. Osgood.[13] Concepts such as exercise or physical fitness are measured and portrayed in three dimensions of meaning that Osgood calls "semantic space." These dimensions or factors are: evaluation (good-bad), potency (strong-weak), and activity (fast-slow). Each dimension or factor has a series of bipolar adjective pairs that the respondent considers. A minimum of three adjective pairs is needed for each factor, nine pairs to measure all three factors. Care must be taken that vocabulary and concepts are suitable to the age level, reading comprehension, and culture of the people responding. It is most important that the concepts presented are valid in the educational world of the child, and that adjective pairs are developed that will permit a projection of actual feelings held by people. Some concepts that can be projected in physical education are: exercise, team sports, swimming, playmates, physical education class, the coach, athletics, and so on. Remember, concepts are selected in order to provide meaningful feedback to the teacher about the instructional atmosphere and possible problems in modifying pupil be-

12. J. P. Guilford, *Psychometric Methods,* 2d ed. (N.Y.: McGraw-Hill, 1954), pp. 392–393.
13. C. Osgood et al., *The Measurement of Meaning* (Urbana, Ill.: University of Illinois Press, 1957).

pleasant	unpleasant	(Evaluation)
relaxed	tense	(Activity)
passive	active	(Activity)
unsuccessful	successful	(Evaluation)
delicate	rugged	(Potency)
fast	slow	(Activity)
good	bad	(Evaluation)
weak	strong	(Potency)
lazy	busy	(Activity)
masculine	feminine	(Potency)
heavy	light	(Potency)
unfair	fair	(Evaluation)

* Reprinted from MEASUREMENT FOR EVALUATION IN PHYSICAL EDUCATION by Ted A. Baumgartner and Andrew S. Jackson. Copyright © 1975 by Houghton Mifflin Company. Used by permission.

Figure 13.1 Example of a Semantic Differential Scale

havior. A good example of a semantic differential applied in physical education is provided by Ted Baumgartner and Andrew Jackson and illustrated in Figure 13.1.[14]

A response to the first adjective pair (pleasant–unpleasant) in Figure 13.1 can be checked at one of seven points. Hence, this scale provides for seven categories. Again, in order to arrive at a total score for all twelve adjective pairs, the score must be reversed as previously indicated for the adjective pair in which the least desirable adjective appears on the left. Responses to the scale depicted in Figure 13.1 are likely to vary from class to class, especially if one class is taking archery and another aerobics. Differences in teaching methods, teacher personality, teaching materials, and atmo-sphere can all cause different responses to concepts presented. Therein lies one of the chief values of this type assessment.

rating scales

Rating scales differ from Likert scales only in the fact that instead of using a standard set of response categories for each statement presented, rating scales use descriptive terms for each category of the statement. The following example items dealing with affective traits illustrate how a rating scale is presented. The value of a separate descriptive term for each category lies in focusing on specific behavior boundaries when

14. Ted A. Baumgartner and Andrew S. Jackson, *Measurement for Evaluation in Physical Education* (Boston: Houghton Mifflin, 1975), p. 270.

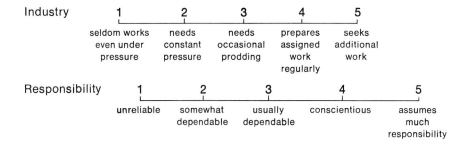

making a rating. Also, this should increase the reliability and objectivity of the scale since all raters will hopefully be rating the same dimensions of behavior.

questionnaires

The questionnaire format involves presenting a set of self-report questions either through the mail, to a captive audience such as the students in our classes, or through interviews by a trained interviewer, who asks questions of most individuals in a particular locale. The questions usually begin with background data such as date of birth, sex, number of years of school completed, marital status, race, mode of residence, and so on. The next set of questions will be germane to the information needed and to how the investigator intends to use the information. Questions may ask for factual information, an expression of opinion, a survey of interests, or an expression of values and their clarification. Responses can be projected in a variety of ways, including a one-word response, a brief statement, or an indication of appropriate category on a rating scale. Quite often we use questionnaires in physical education and recreation to survey student interests and needs in order to provide more effective instructional and recreational programs.

Questionnaires suffer from many of the usual limitations of self-report inventories. Inadequate sampling procedures or inadequate number of responses to the questionnaire can inject a bias into any generalizations made of the data. Under what conditions and at what time of day did the respondent fill out the questionnaire? Did all respondents take the same care and thought in responding to the questions? Some respondents may send back unusable or illegible answer sheets. If the topic being surveyed is a particularly sensitive one, such as sex attitudes and behavior, anonymity of respondent must be guaranteed if one wants to minimize distortion of responses. In any event, the validity of data depends on adequate sampling, careful directions to respondents as to when and how to make responses, anonymity, and effective follow-up procedures. Follow-up is an essential step in order to increase the number of respondents needed to fulfill sampling requirements.

considerations in affective measurements

There are a number of considerations and problems involved in measuring aspects of the affective domain, irrespective of the manner in which we collect data, that are discussed by Julian Stanley and Kenneth Hopkins and summarized below.[15] First, a

15. Julian C. Stanley and Kenneth D. Hopkins, *Educational and Psychological Measurement and Evaluation* (Englewood Cliffs, N.J.: Prentice-Hall, 1972), pp. 282–301. (By permission of Prentice-Hall, Inc., Englewood Cliffs, New Jersey.)

fundamental difference exists between a physical fitness, psychomotor, and cognitive item score as contrasted with an affective item score. In the former we are usually interested in a person's maximal performance or what the person can do on the test item; in the latter we are interested in the person's typical response or what the person does or feels under ordinary circumstances. Obviously one of the uses of an affective device is to discover the person who deviates markedly from the typical or norm.

Second, the correct response to an affective statement depends on the person being questioned, while the correct response to a cognitive question is the same for all pupils. In other words, two different pupils can differ in their appreciation of distance running but the same two people must know that a field goal in basketball is worth two points in order to receive credit for a correct response. There is rarely, if ever, a "correct" response or a "right-wrong" answer to an affective statement.

Third, the situational factors of the examiner and the assessment environment may play a role in the results of the measurement. If the respondent perceives that the examiner is in a position to make crucial decisions about her or him, and if the respondent does not understand the use to be made of the data, we have a situation that may produce invalid results.

Fourth, the cultural background of the pupil shapes a response as well as acceptance of what constitutes the appropriate display of behavior.

Fifth, we all have a tendency to put our best foot forward when we know we are being rated. As a result, teachers likely are not getting the respondent's typical score.

And sixth, almost all affective measures are unstable. This is probably due to diurnal variation as well as the instability of what is being measured.

The most serious problems encountered in affective measurements tend to deal with: (a) fakeability, (b) self-deception, (c) semantics, and (d) criterion inadequacy. Since affective measures usually do not lend themselves to intrinsic right–wrong responses, it is quite easy for the respondent to fake a response. Quite often one is motivated to project what one perceives to be the socially acceptable answer instead of a true feeling. A number of self-report inventories have been constructed to include a distortion scale so that individuals with a tendency to fake their responses can be identified. However, affective measures can still be falsified, no matter how well they are constructed. Faked scores lack validity, and the purpose in administering the instrument cannot be achieved. In order to increase the validity of affective measures some type of anonymity should be provided the respondent. In this way one can reduce the incentive to be untruthful.

Another problem with affective measures lies in the tendency of the respondent to indulge in self-deception, or to want to like what we see when engaging in introspection. If you really believe you are a great athlete when in fact you are not, your responses to particular items will convey this distortion, and your projected behavior when at play will probably be influenced by this belief. Self-deception and its related manifestations are usually indicative of some personality problem. Students who exhibit aspects of self-deception should be referred to appropriate school psychologists.

Semantics is also a problem in affective measurements. Usually responses convey a difference in degree such as "often," "seldom," "frequently," "most of the time," and so on. Unfortunately, there is considerable variation in the meaning various people attach to these words. "Often" may mean most of the time for one person and about one-third of the time for another person. The meaning attached to terms such as *acceptable–unacceptable* with respect to a particular situation varies from age group to age group and culture to culture. What do we really mean when we use terms such as *interesting* or *easily*? How interesting is "interesting"? How easy is "easily"? The validity of affective measures is reduced to the extent that we do not have uniform meaning across respondents. Uniform meaning can be increased when constructing instruments by carefully defining a meaning for each descriptive category and exhorting the respondent to use a particular category in such a way that the category definition corresponds to the actual feeling, belief, or practice of the respondent.

Criterion inadequacy is another serious problem in affective measurement. It is extremely difficult to identify and obtain a criterion measure to correlate with scores on an affective measuring device. This fact coupled with an incentive to fake responses on emotionally sensitive questions makes instrument validation extremely difficult. One can, however, use techniques to develop internal validity by identifying the traits or constructs that are being measured by the items on the measuring instrument. Factor analysis is the correlational research tool that identifies the factors being estimated by certain items. Once identified, the factor is given a psychological name, such as *anxiety* or *dependence*. The name is also referred to as a "construct." Thus, construct validity of an instrument can be developed through factor analysis. We then know what dimension of an affective instrument, such as an attitude scale, is being measured by each item. An excellent example of factor analysis being applied to the multidimensional area of values in physical activity is provided by Gerald Kenyon who identified six constructs in his model.[16] The second validity step is the identification of an external criterion measure. As stated previously, this is a difficult process. However, the problem must be solved before we use scores in any predictive fashion. Due to the many problems, we must use extreme caution in interpreting scores obtained on affective measuring devices. Certainly information from a variety of sources, as well as repeated measures should be obtained before crucial decisions are made about a pupil.

purposes of affective measurements

The general purposes or reasons why teachers collect information with affective measuring instruments may be summarized as follows. (1) When affective goals are planned for and when certain pupil behavioral patterns are expected by teachers as part of the learning process, it is logical to use affective information as part of the grading scheme. In some schools a separate grade may be given for the area of "personal-social" development and another grade given for motor skills. The authors of this text recommend that when program objectives are established, a separate grade be allocated to each objective area. (2) Periodic appraisal of affective behaviors can help the teacher identify pupils with problems that inhibit pupil achievement or that interfere with the achievement of other pupils in class. If necessary, *referral* of the pupil to appropriate specialists may help alleviate the problem. In other cases, *placement* of the pupil into a more appropriate physical education setting may eliminate or modify adverse behavior. (3) Appropriate instruments can help identify the socially rejected or unpopular

16. Gerald S. Kenyon, "A Conceptual Model for Characterizing Physical Activity," *Research Quarterly* 39 (March 1968) pp. 96–105.

child. Some children are rejected because they lack adequate play skills. Placement into a remedial skills program may provide them with the game skills valued by their peers. The teacher may also use information from sociometric measures to structure squad memberships in such a way that integration into a social group may be fostered. (4) The discovery of basic student interests or preferences for certain physical education activities helps us schedule classes in which pupils voluntarily enroll. In this way, we can assist future participation in those physical activities that are appealing to our pupils. (5) A physical education course, the teacher, and teaching methods can be evaluated by using data from an appropriate instrument. (6) The teacher can help in data collection for needed research in the school so we can better understand why people play or compete in athletics. In addition, coaches can identify the rationale for certain psychological strategies employed in preparing athletes for competition.

types of affective instruments

A large number of instruments and techniques have been developed to collect information relative to the many aspects of the affective domain. Only a few examples of interest to physical educators will be presented in this chapter. Information concerning additional data collection techniques can be found in the brief bibliography at the end of this chapter.

anecdotal record

The anecdotal record is defined as a written statement of the various types of behavior exhibited by a pupil. Usually, the teacher describes the behavior that deviates markedly from the norm for the pupil. The purpose of the anecdotal record is to record information that cannot be obtained using other instruments. The teacher records what is actually seen or heard, being careful to give an interpretation of behavior that is not

---

Name _____

Directions

   In the space provided, record observations that bear on the individual's physical, mental, and social development under the respective headings of technical, associated, and concomitant learnings. <u>Do not evaluate, but describe.</u> Avoid vague words such as good, strong, shy, etc. Enter statements of what happened or what you saw, as "Did three push-ups and couldn't do any more" or "cried and started fighting when he was called out." <u>Date and sign each entry</u>.

                               Date   Signature

Technical Learning:

Associated Learning:

Concomitant Learning:

Figure 13.2 Anecdotal Record for Physical Education

influenced by "halo effect." To use anecdotal records effectively one should (1) observe conduct, (2) record observation, (3) analyze and interpret anecdotes, and (4) use the information. The most important element is using the information. Based on the type of information recorded, the pupil may be referred to a specialist for further diagnosis. The anecdotal records are also fruitful as input into case conferences with other teachers or when discussing a child's progress with parents. Anecdotal records should be obtained periodically and, when made part of the cumulative record of the pupil, they permit one to note changes in behavior over time. An example of an anecdotal record that can be used in physical education is presented by Carlton Meyers and T. Erwin Blesh and illustrated in Figure 13.2.[17]

class behavior checklist

Genevie Dexter has developed a class behavior checklist that is filled out by the pupil.[18] It is a self-appraisal of behavior in a physical education class that was developed for high school girls. It can be very easily adapted for use by boys. Also, the teacher can use the same checklist. In this way class behavior can be scrutinized from the point of view of both the teacher and student. When used in this way, both the differences and agreed deviations from acceptable practice can form the basis for counseling. Validity and reliability of the checklist, illustrated in Figure 13.3, have not been determined. Teachers can run their own reliability check. Teachers should also be encouraged to define the class behaviors they expect from their pupils. Once this is accomplished, the teacher can make up her own checklist. The checklist provides us

with an opportunity to record behavior periodically.

sport and behavior

A number of the learning outcomes that at times are presented under the rubric of "sportsmanship" or "character education," which is supposed to develop as one participates in physical education and athletics, are the basis for the *Cowell Outcomes of Sports Check-Sheet* that is illustrated in Figure 13.4.[19] The Check-Sheet is intended for use by high school boys. It can also be used with girls. This device provides for a self-analysis of the extent to which a pupil has attained certain behavioral goals. No data are available relative to the validity or reliability of the instrument.

sportsmanship attitude scale

Marion Johnson has devised a *Sportsmanship Attitude Scale* for use by both junior high school boys and girls.[20] Alternate form reliability is reported as .856; and test-retest reliability for forms A and B, respectively, is .812 and .863. The content for the instrument is based on football, basketball, and baseball situations. The scale presented below is designed to detect attitudes, changes in attitudes, and to be used as material for class discussion.

17. Carlton R. Meyers and T. Erwin Blesh, *Measurement in Physical Education* (New York: The Ronald Press, 1962), p. 417.
18. Genevie Dexter, *Teachers' Guide to Physical Education for Girls in High School* (Sacramento, Calif.: State Department of Education, 1957), p. 318.
19. Charles C. Cowell, "Our Function Is Still Education!" *The Physical Educator* 14 (March 1957):6–7.
20. Marion L. Johnson, "Construction of a Sportsmanship Attitude Scale," *Research Quarterly* 40 (May 1969):312–316.

The Checklist

Name _____   Date _____

Directions: Read each statement and think how it will describe your behavior. Put a check in the column that tells most nearly what statement is correct for you.

Always	Often	Seldom	Never	

Self-Direction

1. I work diligently even though I am not supervised.

2. I practice to improve the skills I use with least success.

3. I follow carefully directions that have been given me.

4. I willingly accept constructive criticism and try to correct faults.

5. I play games as cheerfully as I can.

6. I appraise my progress in each of my endeavors to learn.

Social Adjustment

1. I am considerate of the rights of others.

2. I am courteous.

3. I am cooperative in group activities.

4. I accept gladly responsibility assigned me by a squad leader.

5. I accept disappointment without being unnecessarily disturbed.

6. I expect from the members of my group only the consideration to which I am entitled.

Always	Often	Seldom	Never	

Participation

1. I am prompt in reporting for each class.

2. I dislike being absent from class.

3. I ask to be excused from an activity only when it is necessary.

4. I do the best I can regardless of the activity in which I am participating.

5. I give full attention to all instructions that are given in class.

6. I encourage others with whom I am participating in an activity.

Figure 13.3 Class Behavior Checklist

Measurement in the Affective Domain   389

Care of Equipment and Facilities

_____ 1. I use equipment as I am supposed to use it.

_____ 2. I return each piece of equipment to its proper place after using it.

_____ 3. I avoid making my dressing area untidy.

_____ 4. I arrange my clothes neatly in my locker.

Personal Attractiveness

_____ 1. I am particular about my personal appearance.

_____ 2. I take a shower after I have participated in any vigorous activity.

_____ 3. I wear clean clothes in physical education class.

_____ 4. I dress appropriately for each activity.

_____ 5. I bathe regularly.

Figure 13.3 *Continued*

To What Extent Did I Learn:	(5) A very Great Deal	(4) A Great Deal	(3) Somewhat	(2) Very Little	(1) Not at All
1. To sacrifice my own personal "whims" or desires for the good of the group or team?					
2. To test myself-to see if I could "take it," endure hardship and "keep trying" to do my best even under adversity?					
3. To overcome awkwardness and self-consciousness?					
4. To recognize that the group can achieve where the individual alone cannot?					
5. That each team member has a unique or special contribution to make in the position he plays?					
6. To share difficult undertakings with my "buddies" (teammates) because of struggling together for a goal?					

Figure 13.4 Cowell Social Outcomes of Sports: An Evaluation Check-Sheet

To What Extent Did I Learn:	(5) A very Great Deal	(4) A Great Deal	(3) Somewhat	(2) Very Little	(1) Not at All
7. To respect the skill and ability of my opponents and be tolerant of their success?					
8. To make friendships with boys from other schools and to maintain good guest/host relationships in interschool games?					
9. To feel that the school team helped break up "cliques" and factions in the school by developing common loyalty and community of interests?					
10. To consider and practice correct health and training routine, such as proper eating, sleeping, avoidance of tobacco, etc?					
11. To "take turns" and to "share"?					
12. To develop physical strength, endurance, and a better looking body?					
13. To be loyal and not "let my buddy, the coach, team, or school down"?					
14. To give more than I get-not for myself but for an ideal or for one's school, town, or country?					
15. To develop a sense of humor and even to be able to laugh at myself occasionally?					
16. To think and act "on the spot" in the heat of a game?					
17. To understand the strategy —the "why" of the best methods of attack and defense in games?					
18. To understand and appreciate the possibilities and limitations of the human body with respect to skill, speed, endurance, and quickness of reactions?					
19. That in sports there is no discrimination against talent? It is performance and conduct and not the color of one's skin or social standing that matters.					
20. That nothing worthwhile is accomplished without hard work, application, and the "will to succeed"?					

Directions: This booklet contains several statements describing events that happen in sports and games. Read each statement carefully and decide whether you approve or disapprove of the action taken by the person. Circle the ONE response category that tells the way you feel. PLEASE COMPLETE EVERY ITEM.

Example: A pitcher in a baseball game threw a fast ball at the batter to scare him.

Strongly Approve   Approve   Disapprove   **Strongly Disapprove**

(If you strongly approve of this action by the pitcher, you circle the first response category as shown.)

The four responses can appear either after each item or an answer sheet can be used.

Form A

1. After a basketball player was called by the official for traveling, he slammed the basketball onto the floor.
2. A baseball player was called out as he slid into home plate. He jumped up and down on the plate and screamed at the official.
3. After a personal foul was called against a basketball player, he shook his fist in the official's face.
4. A basketball coach talked very loudly in order to annoy an opponent who was attempting to make a very important free throw shot.
5. After a baseball game, the coach of the losing team went up to the umpire and demanded to know how much money had been paid to "throw" the game.
6. A basketball coach led the spectators in jeering at the official who made calls against his team.

7. After two men were put out on a double play attempt, a baseball coach told the players in his dugout to boo the umpire's decision.
8. As the basketball coach left the gymnasium after the game, he shouted at the officials, "You lost me the game; I never saw such lousy officiating in my life."
9. A basketball coach put sand on the gym floor to force the opponents into traveling penalties.
10. A football coach left the bench to change the position of a marker dropped by an official to indicate where the ball went out of bounds.
11. During the first half of a football game a touchdown was called back. At halftime the football coach went into the official's dressing room and cursed the officials.
12. A football player was taken out of the game for unsportsmanlike conduct. The player changed jerseys and the coach sent him back into the game.
13. Following a closely played basketball game, the coach of the losing team cursed his boys for not winning.
14. After a basketball game the losing team's coach yelled at spectators to "Go get the Ump!"
15. A baseball coach permitted players to use profanity loud enough for the entire park to hear when the players did not like a decision.
16. The basketball coach drank alcoholic beverages while supervising his basketball team on a trip.
17. A college football player was disqualified for misconduct. While on the way to the sideline, the player attacked the official.
18. During a time-out in a basketball game, the clock was accidentally left running. The coach whose team was behind ran over to the scoring table and struck the timekeeper.

19. After a basketball player was knocked into a wall, his coach rushed onto the court and hit the player who had fouled.

20. After a baseball player had been removed from the game, the coach met him at the sidelines and hit him.

21. After a runner was called out at first base, the baseball coach went onto the field and wrestled the umpire down to the ground.

Form B

1. During a basketball game the B team coach sat on the bench and called loudly to the officials telling them who to watch for fouls.

2. Repeated complaints and griping came from the football players on the bench toward the officials when fouls were called on their team, and the coach did nothing to stop this action.

3. After a basketball game the hometown coach made fun of the visiting team's playing ability.

4. A football coach took time out and came onto the playing field and accused referees of cheating his team.

5. During a football game a player made an error that resulted in a touchdown for the opponents. The coach ran onto the field and bawled out the player in front of the fans.

6. After a questionable foul was called against a football player, his coach went onto the field and refused to leave when the referee told him to do so.

7. During a basketball game the coach of the losing team yelled that the officials had been "paid off" by the opposing team.

8. A baseball coach acted as referee for an important game and called in favor of his team.

9. A basketball coach installed a light to blind the opponents when they were shooting at a goal.

10. After a third baseman caught a ball which put a player out, the opposing coach cursed the third baseman.

11. A football coach used profane language during workouts and in conversation with the boys.

12. A baseball coach cursed loudly after a runner was called out on first base.

13. After a football game a player attacked the official who had taken him out of the game. The coach covered up for the player and said the player had not done such a thing.

leadership

The development of leadership traits is thought to be one of the goals of sports participation. Leadership can only be defined by the items that appear on an appraisal instrument. Leadership assessment should not be attempted until all pupils have interacted with one another in the group for a long period of time. The time span must be long enough to allow each pupil an opportunity to perform in a leadership role. The teacher should assign leaders to squads within a class on a rotating basis. In the final analysis, the teacher should define those qualities of leadership that one strives to develop in a physical education class and then devise a situation-specific rating scale for each quality. One example of a leadership scale developed to identify athletic leaders among boys and girls in junior high through college appears in the Barry Johnson and Jack Nelson text, and is illustrated in Figure 13.5.[21] Students write the names of their choices in the blanks labeled A and B on the questionnaire.

21. Barry L. Johnson and Jack K. Nelson, *Practical Measurements for Evaluation in Physical Education*, 2d ed. (Minneapolis: Burgess, 1974), p. 396–397.

A. _____ B. _____	1. If you were on a trip and had a choice of the players you would share the hotel room with, who would they be?
A. _____ B. _____	2. Who are the most popular members of the team?
A. _____ B. _____	3. Who are the best scholars on the team?
A. _____ B. _____	4. Which players know the most about the sport, in terms of strategy, rules, etc?
A. _____ B. _____	5. If the coach were not present for a workout, which athletes would be the most likely to take charge of the practice?
A. _____ B. _____	6. Which players would you listen to first if the team appeared to be disorganized during a crucial game?
A. _____ B. _____	7. When the team is behind in a close match and there is still a chance to win, who is the most likely teammate to score the winning points?
A. _____ B. _____	8. Of all of your teammates, who exhibits the most poise during crucial parts of the match?
A. _____ B. _____	9. Who are the most valuable players on the team?
A. _____ B. _____	10. Who are the players who play "most for the team"?
A. _____ B. _____	11. Who are the most consistent point makers for the team?
A. _____ B. _____	12. Who are the most respected performers on the team?
A. _____ B. _____	13. Which teammates have the most overall ability?
A. _____ B. _____	14. Which teammates train the hardest to improve their performance off season?
A. _____ B. _____	15. Who are the most likeable players on the team?
A. _____ B. _____	16. Which players have most favorably influenced you?
A. _____ B. _____	17. Which players have actually helped you the most?
A. _____ B. _____	18. Which teammates do you think would make the best coaches?
A. _____ B. _____	19. Which teammates do you most often look to for leadership?
A. _____ B. _____	20. Who are the hardest workers during regular practice hours?

Figure 13.5 Modified Nelson Sports Leadership Questionnaire

These authors report reliability coefficients of .96 for ninth-grade football players and .78 for college basketball players.

social adjustment

Social development has long been claimed as one of the goals of a physical education program. As pupils interact and exhibit play skills to one another they are, at the same time, exhibiting the extent to which they have adapted to the behavioral standards of the school, class, and peer group. Selected aspects of behavior in a social group are usually presented in the form of a rating scale that is completed by teachers and pupils or both. A few rating scales have been developed specifically in junior and senior high school physical education class settings. Three such devices are the *Cowell Social Behavior Trend Index,* which is completed by teachers; the *Cowell Personal Distance Ballot;* and a *Who's Who in My Group.*[22] The latter two devices are measures of what we usually refer to as peer status, degree of group integration, social acceptance, or popularity within the group.

The *Cowell Social Behavior Trend Index* presents ten behavioral trends from a positive (Form A) and negative (Form B) point of view. Three teachers who have been observing the children for some time complete Form A in Figure 13.6 and then three weeks later complete Form B, which appears in Figure 13.7. The pupil's score is the algebraic sum of the score from both forms. Cowell reports a validity coefficient of .824 with teachers ratings of the "best" and "worst" socially adjusted boys.[23] The alternate form reliability is .82.

The *Cowell Personal Distance Ballot* in Figure 13.8 is a simple, quick way of determining the extent of belonging to or being accepted as a member of one's own social group. Validity of the ballot is indicated by a correlation of .90 with Guidance Office Ratings and .844 with the *Who's Who in My Group* score. Reliability coefficients of .91, .88, and .93 are also reported by Cowell.[24]

In another article, Cowell and A. H. Ismail summarize the research into the relationships between social and physical factors.[25] They conclude that boys who score high on physical measures are likely to have leadership potential, to be quite popular with their peers, and to be socially well adjusted. In addition, those participating in team sports are likely to be better accepted in the group than those engaged in individual physical activities.

attitude scales

Attitude usually reflects the degree of one's feeling, appreciation, or concern about a particular concept. One's attitude toward participating in physical activities is thought to be an underlying dimension of motivation. That is, it is believed that if one enjoys exercising and values exercise for a particular purpose, such a person will participate in a physical activity program in the future. Quite a few attitude scales developed for use in physical education appear in the literature. Most consider attitude towards physical activity to be unidimensional. Some are situation-specific such as "the gym class," "athletic participation," "physical fitness," and "sportsmanship." Sources for locating these attitude inventories appear at the end of this chapter.

Kenyon has employed factor analysis to a large number of items thought to measure hypothesized attitude dimensions.[26] The results of the factor analysis confirmed that six different constructs were being measured. Thus, Kenyon developed a multidimensional

22. Cowell, "Validating an Index of Social Adjustment for High School Use."
23. *Ibid.,* pp. 8, 11.
24. *Ibid.,* pp. 9–10.
25. Charles C. Cowell and A. H. Ismail, "Relationships Between Selected Social and Physical Factors," *Research Quarterly* 33 (March 1962):40–43.
26. Kenyon, "A Conceptual Model for Characterizing Physical Activity," *Research Quarterly* 39 (March 1968):96–105 and "Six Scales for Assessing Attitude Toward Physical Activity," *Research Quarterly* 39 (October 1968):566–574.

Behavior Trends	Descriptive of the Student			
	Markedly (+3)	Somewhat (+2)	Only Slightly (+1)	Not at All (+0)
1. Enters heartily and with enjoyment into the spirit of social intercourse				
2. Frank; talkative and sociable, does not stand on ceremony				
3. Self-confident and self-reliant, tends to take success for granted, strong initiative, prefers to lead				
4. Quick and decisive in movement, pronounced or excessive energy output				
5. Prefers group activities, work or play; not easily satisfied with individual projects.				
6. Adaptable to new situations, makes adjustments readily, welcomes change				
7. Is self-composed, seldom shows signs of embarrassment				
8. Tends to elation of spirits, seldom gloomy or moody				
9. Seeks a broad range of friendships, not selective or exclusive in games and the like				
10. Hearty and cordial, even to strangers, forms acquaintanceships very easily				

Date: _____ Grade: _____

Describer: _____
Last Name   First Name

School: _____ Age: _____

INSTRUCTION: Think carefully of the student's behavior in group situations and check each behavior trend according to its degree of descriptiveness.

Figure 13.6 Cowell Social Behavior Trend Index (Form A)

Behavior Trends	Descriptive of the Student			
	Markedly (-3)	Somewhat (-2)	Only Slightly (-1)	Not at all (-0)
1. Somewhat prudish, awkward, easily embarrassed in his social contacts.		. . . .	. . . .	. . . .
2. Secretive, seclusive, not inclined to talk unless spoken to		. . . .	. . . .	. . . .
3. Lacking in self-confidence and initiative, a follower		. . . .	. . . .	. . . .
4. Slow in movement, deliberative or perhaps indecisive. Energy output moderate or deficient		. . . .	. . . .	. . . .
5. Prefers to work and play alone, tends to avoid group activities		. . . .	. . . .	. . . .
6. Shrinks from making new adjustments, prefers the habitual to the stress of reorganization required by the new.		. . . .	. . . .	. . . .
7. Is self-conscious, easily embarrassed, timid or "bashful"		. . . .	. . . .	. . . .
8. Tends to depression, frequently gloomy or moody		. . . .	. . . .	. . . .
9. Shows preference for a narrow range of intimate friends and tends to exclude others from his association.		. . . .	. . . .	. . . .
10. Reserved and distant except to intimate friends, does not form acquaintanceships readily		. . . .	. . . .	. . . .

Date: _____   Grade: _____

_____

Last Name   First Name

Describer: _____   School: _____   Age: _____

INSTRUCTION: Think carefully of the student's behavior in group situations and check *each behavior trend* according to its degree of descriptiveness.

Figure 13.7 Cowell Social Behavior Trend Index (Form B)

What To Do!		I would be willing to accept him:					
If you had full power to treat each student in this squad as you feel, just how would you consider him? Every student should be checked in some *one* column. Circle your own name and be sure you check every student in *one* column only.	Into my family as a brother	As a very close "pal" or "chum"	As a member of my "gang" or club	On my street as a "next-door neighbor"	Into my class at university	Into my University	Into my City
	1	2	3	4	5	6	7
1.							
2.							
3.							
4.							
5.							
6.							
7.							
8.							
9.							
10.							
11.							
12.							
13.							
14.							
15.							
16.							
17.							
18.							
19.							

Figure 13.8 Confidential Personal Distance Ballot

scale for college men and one for college women. The men's scale consists of fifty-nine items and the women's scale has fifty-four items. Scoring is on a seven point Likert-type scale ranging from "very strongly disagree" to "very strongly agree."

Construct validity for Kenyon's scale has been demonstrated. The six constructs or attitude dimensions with their reported reliabilities are as follows: (1) Social Experience: .70–.72 for men, .68–.72 for women; (2) Health and Fitness: .79 for men, .83 for women; (3) Pursuit of Vertigo: .88–.89 for men, .89 for women; (4) Aesthetic Experience: .82 for men, .87 for women; (5) Catharsis: .77 for men, .79 for women; (6) Ascetic Experience: .81 for men, .74–.78 for women.

The first four items for each dimension of the men's and women's scale appear below. The complete scale with directions for administration and scoring can be obtained from Dr. Gerald S. Kenyon.[27]

Dimension 1: physical activity as a social experience. Physical educators maintain that physical activity meets certain social needs of individuals. Individuals who score high on this factor would value physical activities "whose primary purpose is to provide a medium for social intercourse, i.e., to meet new people and to perpetrate existing relationships."

MEN

It is important that everyone belong to at least one group that plays games together.

I like to engage in socially oriented physical activities.

College should sponsor many more physical activities of a social nature.

I enjoy sports mostly because they give me a chance to meet new people.

WOMEN

The best way to become more socially desirable is to participate in group physical activities.

I like to engage in socially oriented physical activities.

Colleges should sponsor many more physical activities of a social nature.

I enjoy sports mostly because they give me a chance to meet new people.

Dimension 2: physical activity for health and fitness. The importance of physical activity for maintaining health and fitness is generally recognized. Individuals who score high on this factor would value physical activity for its "contribution to the improvement of one's health and fitness."

MEN

Of all physical activities, those whose purpose is primarily to develop physical fitness would not be my first choice.

I would usually choose strenuous physical activity over light physical activity, if given the choice.

A large part of our daily lives must be committed to vigorous exercise.

Being strong and highly fit is not the most important thing in my life.

WOMEN

Physical education programs should stress vigorous exercise since it contributes most to physical fitness.

The need for much higher levels of physical fitness has been established beyond all doubt.

Of all physical activities, those whose

27. Dr. Gerald S. Kenyon, Faculty of Human Kinetics and Leisure Studies, University of Waterloo, Waterloo, Ontario, Canada, N2L 3G1.

purpose is primarily to develop physical fitness would not be my first choice.

If given a choice, I sometimes would choose strenuous rather than light physical activity.

Dimension 3: physical activity as the pursuit of vertigo. The pursuit of vertigo is considered to be "those physical experiences providing, at some risk to the participant, an element of thrill through the medium of speed, acceleration, sudden change of direction, or exposure to dangerous situations, with the participant usually remaining in control."

MEN

I would prefer quiet activities like swimming or tossing a ball around rather than such activities as automobile or speedboat racing.

The risk of injury would be well worth it when you consider the thrills that come from engaging in such activities as mountain climbing and bobsledding.

Among the best physical activities are those which represent a personal challenge, such as skiing, mountain climbing, or heavy-weather sailing.

Frequent participation in dangerous sports and physical activities is alright for other people but ordinarily they are not for me.

WOMEN

I would prefer quiet activities like swimming or golf, rather than such activities as water skiing or sailboat racing.

Among the best physical activities are those which represent a personal challenge, such as skiing, mountain climbing, or heavy-weather sailing.

Frequent participation in dangerous sports and physical activities is alright

for other people but ordinarily they are not for me.

The least desirable physical activities are those providing a sense of danger and risk of injury such as skiing on steep slopes, mountain climbing, or parachute jumping.

Dimension 4: physical activity as an aesthetic experience. Many people believe that some forms of physical activity are generally pleasing to view. People that score high on this factor perceive physical activity as having "aesthetic value" for the individual—that is, activities are conceived as possessing beauty or certain artistic qualities.

MEN

Among desirable forms of physical activity are those that show the beauty and form of human movement, such as modern dance and water ballet.

The degree of beauty and grace of movement found in sports is sometimes less than claimed.

Physical education programs should place a little more emphasis upon the beauty found in human motion.

I am not in the least interested in those physical activities whose sole purpose is to depict human motion as something beautiful.

WOMEN

The most important value of physical activity is the beauty found in skilled movement.

Among the most desirable forms of physical activity are those which present the beauty of human movement such as modern dance and water ballet.

I am not particularly interested in those physical activities whose sole purpose is to depict human motion as something beautiful.

Physical education programs should place much more emphasis upon the beauty found in human motion.

Dimension 5: physical activity as catharsis. It is commonly believed that physical activity can provide a release from frustration created by pressures of modern living. Catharsis involves "physical activity perceived as providing a release of tension precipitated by frustration through some vicarious means." The validity of the catharsis factor has not been fully established. A negative relationship was reported between catharsis scores and preference for "physical activity for recreation and relaxation."

MEN

A happy life does not require regular participation in physical activity.

Almost the only satisfactory way to relieve severe emotional strain is through some form of physical activity.

There are better ways of relieving the pressures of today's living than having to engage in or watch physical activity.

For a healthy mind in a healthy body the only place to begin is through participation in sports and physical activities every day.

WOMEN

Almost the only satisfactory way to relieve severe emotional strain is through some form of physical activity.

There are better ways of relieving the pressures of today's living than having to engage in or watch physical activity.

For a healthy mind in a healthy body the only place to begin is through par-

ticipation in sports and physical activities every day.

Practically the only way to relieve frustrations and pent-up emotions is through some form of physical activity.

Dimension 6: physical activity as an ascetic experience. Individuals who score high on this scale value the type of dedication involved for championship level performance. Such physical activity involves long strenuous and often painful training and stiff competition demanding a deferment of many gratifications.

MEN

I would gladly put in the necessary years of daily hard training for the chance to try out for the U.S. Olympic Team.

I prefer those sports which require very hard training and involve intense competition such as interscholastic and intercollegiate athletics.

I would get by far the most satisfaction from games requiring long and careful preparation and involving stiff competition against a strong opposition.

A sport is sometimes spoiled if allowed to become too highly organized and keenly competitive.

WOMEN

I would gladly put up with the necessary hard training for the chance to try out for the U.S. Olympic Team.

The years of strenuous daily training necessary to prepare for today's international competition is asking a lot of today's young women.

I would get by far the most satisfaction from games requiring long and careful preparation and involving stiff competition against a strong opposition.

A sport is sometimes spoiled if allowed to become too highly organized and keenly competitive.

Kenyon has also provided a scale for use in secondary schools.[28] In addition, Julie Simon and Frank Smoll have modified Kenyon's secondary school scale for use on fourth-, fifth-, and sixth-grade children.[29]

self-perception

Measures of self-perception usually attempt to secure information about the self-concept or how one views one's self. Devices have been developed to measure body image; body cathexis or the amount of psychological energy attached to the body; and a more global self-esteem. Self-perception is a constant force in everyday living since it is felt that the value one places on one's self may be the prime determiner of one's behavior. Changes in body weight, fitness, strength, stature, skill, and ability can affect the body image element of self-concept.[30] In her book, *Involvement in Sport,* Dorothy Harris also provides the reader with two excellent chapters summarizing the literature dealing with self-concept, body image, and physical attributes.[31]

A simple, easy to score instrument that is available for use in elementary and junior high school is the Coopersmith Self-Esteem Inventory.[32] The modified version entitled "How I See Myself" appears in Figure 13.9. Coopersmith reports a test-retest reliability following a five-week interval of .88.[33] In addition, Noland and Gruber found a test-retest reliability over a two-week period of .74 and a validity coefficient of —.70 with the anxiety second-order factor of the Children's Personality Questionnaire.[34] This indicates that children who view themselves more favorably tend to have lower anxiety feelings.

trends in affective measurements

When one reviews the completed research in sport personology, it becomes clear that much confusion exists due to contradictory study findings. Differences in the results of these studies can be due to different or inappropriate measuring instruments being employed, different study procedures, or to the use of inappropriate statistical methods. After describing methodological problems involved in sport personality assessment, both Leon Smith and Walter Kroll indicate there is a need to counter the traditional ways of applying psychological theories to problems in physical education and sport.[35] One approach proposes that stable trait characteristics of a person interact with specific situations and each can influence the other. Thus, momentary environmental situations play a role in influencing observed behavior. This seems to call for the development of situation specific measuring instruments—

28. Gerald S. Kenyon, *Values Held for Physical Activity by Selected Urban Secondary School Students in Canada, Australia, England, and the United States* (Washington, D.C.: United States Office of Education, 1968).

29. Julie A. Simon and Frank L. Smoll, "An Instrument for Assessing Children's Attitudes Toward Physical Activity," *Research Quarterly* 45 (December 1974):407–415.

30. Dorothy V. Harris, *Involvement in Sport: A Somatopsychic Rationale for Physical Activity* (Philadelphia: Lea and Febiger, 1973), p. 163.

31. *Ibid.*

32. Stanley Coopersmith, *The Antecedents of Self-Esteem* (San Francisco: W. H. Freeman, 1967), pp. 265–266.

33. *Ibid.,* p. 5.

34. Noland and Gruber, "Self-Perception, Personality and Behavior in Emotionally Disturbed Children."

35. Leon E. Smith, "Personality and Performance Research," *Quest* 13 (1970): 74–83 and Walter Kroll, "Current Strategies and Problems in Personality Assessment of Athletes," in *Psychology of Motor Learning,* ed. L. E. Smith (Chicago: The Athletic Institute, 1970).

Name: _____ No: _____

School: _____

Please mark each statement in the following way:

    If the statement describes how you usually feel, put a check (✓) in the column "Yes."

    If the statement does not describe how you usually feel, put a check (✓) in the column "No."

There are no right or wrong answers.

		Yes	No
1.	Do you spend a lot of time daydreaming?		
2.	Do you feel pretty good about what you say and do?		
3.	Do you often wish you were someone else?		
4.	Are you easy to like?		
5.	Do you and your parents have a lot of fun together?		
6.	Do you wish you were younger?		
7.	Can you make up your mind without too much trouble?		
8.	Do you get upset easily at home?		
9.	Are you proud of your school work?		
10.	Do you always have to be told what to do?		
11.	Does it take you a long time to get used to anything new?		
12.	Are you often sorry for the things you do?		
13.	Do kids your own age like you?		
14.	Do your parents care about how you feel?		
15.	Do you usually let others have their way?		
16.	Can you usually take care of yourself?		
17.	Would you rather play with children younger than yourself?		
18.	Do your parents think you can do better than you do?		
19.	Do you like to be called on in class?		
20.	Do you understand yourself?		

Figure 13.9 How I See Myself

	Yes	No
21. Is it pretty tough to be you?		
22. Do kids usually follow your ideas?		
23. Do you get enough attention at home?		
24. Would you say you are doing as well in school as you would like to?		
25. Can you make up your mind and stick to it?		
26. Do you feel bad about yourself?		
27. Do you like to be with other people?		
28. Are there many times when you would like to leave home?		
29. Do you often feel upset in school?		
30. Do you often feel ashamed of yourself?		
31. Would you say you're as nice looking as most people?		
32. If you have something to say, do you usually say it?		
33. Do your parents understand you?		
34. Does your teacher make you feel you're not good enough?		
35. Do you get upset easily when you're fussed at for doing something wrong?		
36. Are most people better liked than you are?		
37. Do you usually feel as if your parents are pushing you?		
38. Do you ever feel like giving up in school?		
39. Do things usually bother you?		
40. Can you be depended upon?		

an approach that appears particularly suitable to an athletic situation. Brent Rushall maintains this is the most viable and effective approach, since these inventories would take into account the conceptual structure underlying assessing a person's behavior in a specific environment.[36] A few early attempts at sport specific measuring instruments have been presented earlier in this chapter, namely, the Cowell *Social Outcome of Sports Check-Sheet;* the Johnson *Sportsmanship Attitude Scale* for the football, basketball, and baseball situations; the Kenyon attitude

36. Brent S. Rushall, "Environment Specific Behavior Inventories: Developmental Procedures," *International Journal of Sport Psychology,* vol. 9, no. 2 (1978):97–110.

scales; and the *Nelson Sports Leadership Questionnaire.*

Another recent trend is the differentiation between *trait* and *state* measures and the construction and validation of *trait* and *state* inventories for the specific sport environment. Trait and state anxiety inventories are an example. *Trait* anxiety is a relatively stable, general personality trait that predisposes an individual to perceive certain situations as threatening and to respond with varying levels of *state* anxiety. State anxiety, then, is how one feels at that point in time when a perception of threat or danger is experienced in a specific situation; such as prior to an athletic contest when the athlete's reputation is at stake and the outcome of the contest is uncertain. In an extensive series of sequential studies, Rainer Martens has constructed the *Sport Competition Anxiety Test* to assess competitive trait anxiety.[37] This instrument, possessing both construct and concurrent validity, is a better predictor of state anxiety than a general trait anxiety inventory, and as the time to compete nears the *Sport Competition Anxiety Tests'* ability to predict anxiety states improves. Two forms of the fifteen-item *Sport Competition Anxiety Test* exist, namely, Form A for adults fifteen years and older and Form C for children ages ten–fourteen years. Example items from Form A to which the respondent indicates degree of affect on a Likert-type scale are as follows:

1. Competing against others is socially enjoyable.

2. Before I compete I feel uneasy.

3. Before I compete I worry about not performing well.

4. I am a good sportsman when I compete.

5. When I compete I worry about making mistakes.

To fill the need for a competitive state anxiety inventory, Martens proposed a ten-item instrument possessing construct validity.[38] Joseph Gruber and Diane Beauchamp have found this *Competitive State Anxiety Inventory* to be quite relevant for detecting changes in anxiety states of university women varsity basketball players.[39] They noted that the changes in anxiety states were a function of winning or losing the game and the importance of the contest to the women. Sample items from the *Competitive State Anxiety Inventory* to which the respondent indicates intensity of feeling at that particular moment on a Likert-type scale are:

I feel at ease.
I feel nervous.
I feel comfortable.
I am tense.
I feel secure.

Thus, it appears that development of sport situation specific measuring instruments is a step toward increasing the validity of measurement in the affective domain.

bibliography of affective measures

general test reviews

The following sources contain reviews of the many intelligence tests, interest inventories, personality measures, sociometric tests, aptitude inventories, attitude inventories, and sensory-motor tests that are on the market today.

Buros, Oscar K., ed. *The Seventh Mental Measurements Yearbook.* Vol. I and Vol. II. Highland Park, N.J.: The Gryphon Press, 1972.

37. Rainer Martens, *Sport Competition Anxiety Test* (Champaign, Ill.: Human Kinetics, 1977).
38. *Ibid.*, pp.108–116.
39. Joseph J. Gruber and Diane Beauchamp, "Relevancy of the Competitive State Anxiety Inventory in a Sport Environment," *Research Quarterly,* vol. 50, no. 2 (May 1979):207–214.

Buros, Oscar K., ed. *Tests in Print II*. Highland Park, N.J.: The Gryphon Press, 1974.

class behavior

Blanchard, B.E. "A Behavior Frequency Rating Scale for the Measurement of Character and Personality Traits in Physical Education Situations." *Research Quarterly* 7 (May 1936):56–66.

Cassidy, Rosalind. "The Cassidy Class Experience Check List." In *Counseling in the Physical Education Program*. New York: Appleton-Century-Crofts, 1959), pp. 89–91.

Hamalainen, Arthur E. *An Appraisal of Anecdotal Records*. Contributions to Education, No. 891. New York: Teachers College, Columbia University, 1943.

Traxler, Arthur E. *The Nature and Use of Anecdotal Records*. Educational Records Bureau Supplementary Bulletin D, Revised. New York: Educational Records Bureau, 1949.

Van Alstyne, Dorothy. "A New Scale for Rating School Behavior and Attitudes in the Elementary School." *Journal of Educational Psychology* 27 (December 1936):677.

sportsmanship

*Bovyer, George: "Children's Concepts of Sportsmanship in the Fourth, Fifth, and Sixth Grades." *Research Quarterly* 34 (October 1963):282–287.

Haskins, Mary Jane. "Problem-Solving Test of Sportsmanship." *Research Quarterly* 31 (December 1960):601–606.

Johnson, Marion L. "Construction of Sportsmanship Attitude Scales." *Research Quarterly* 40 (May 1969):312–316.

Lakie, William L. "Expressed Attitudes of Various Groups of Athletes Toward Athletic Competition." *Research Quarterly* 35 (December 1964):497–503.

McAfee, Robert A. "Sportsmanship Attitudes of Sixth, Seventh, and Eighth Grade Boys." *Research Quarterly* 26 (March 1955):120.

social adjustment

Breck, Sabina June. "A Sociometric Measurement of Status in Physical Education Classes." *Research Quarterly* 21 (May 1950):75–82.

Cowell, Charles C., and Ismail, A.H. "Validity of a Football Rating Scale and Its Relationship to Social Integration and Academic Ability." *Research Quarterly* 32 (December 1961):461–467.

Hale, Patricia W. "Proposed Method for Analyzing Sociometric Data." *Research Quarterly* 27 (May 1956):152–161.

McCraw, L.W., and Tabert, J.W., "Sociometric Status and Athletic Ability of Junior High School Boys." *Research Quarterly* 24 (March 1953):72–78.

Nelson, Jack K., and Johnson, Barry L. "Effects of Varied Techniques in Organizing Class Competition Upon Changes in Sociometric Status." *Research Quarterly* 39 (October 1968):634–639.

Ondrus, Joseph. "A Sociometric Analysis of Group Structure and the Effect of Football Activities on Inter-Personal Relationships." Doctoral dissertation, New York University, 1953.

Peterson, Beverly A. "A Comparision of the Social Efficiency of Selected Groups of Tenth and Twelfth-Grade Girls." Master's thesis, San Diego State College, 1965.

Skubic, Elvera. "A Study of Acquaintanceship and Social Status in Physical Education Classes." *Research Quarterly* 20 (March 1947):80–87.

Todd, Frances. "Sociometry in Physical Education." *Journal of Health, Physical Education and Recreation* 24 (May 1953):23–24.

Trapp, William G. "A Study of Social Integration in a College Football Squad." In *56th Annual Proceedings*. College Physical Education Association, 1953.

Walters, C. Etta. "A Sociometric Study of Motivated and Nonmotivated Bowling Groups." *Research Quarterly* 26 (March 1955):107–112.

Yarnell, C. Douglas. "Relationships of Physical Fitness to Selected Measures of Popularity." *Research Quarterly* 37 (May 1966):286–288.

attitudes

Adams, R.S. "Two Scales for Measuring Attitudes Toward Physical Education." *Research Quarterly* 34 (March 1963):91–94.

Carr, Martha G. "The Relationship Between Success in Physical Education and Selected Attitudes Expressed in High School Freshman Girls." *Research Quarterly* 16 (October 1945):176–191.

Drinkwater, Barbara L. "Development of an Attitude Inventory to Measure the Attitudes of High School Girls Toward Physical Education as a Career for Women." *Research Quarterly* 31 (December 1960): 575–580.

Edgington, Charles W. "Development of an Attitude Scale to Measure Attitudes of High School Freshman Boys Toward Physical Education." Ed.D. dissertation, Colorado State College, Greeley, 1965.

Johnson, Marion L. "Construction of Sportsmanship Attitude Scales." *Research Quarterly* 40 (May 1969): 312–316.

Kappes, Evalina A. "Inventory to Determine Attitudes of College Women Toward Physical Education and Student Services of the Physical Education Department." *Research Quarterly* 25 (December 1954):429–438.

Kneer, Marian E. "The Adaptation of Wear's Physical Education Attitude Inventory for Use with High School Girls." Master's thesis, Illinois State University, Normal, 1956.

Lakie, William L. "Expressed Attitudes of Various Groups of Athletes Toward Athletic Competition." *Research Quarterly* 35 (December 1964):497–503.

McCue, Betty F. "Constructing an Instrument for Evaluating Attitudes Toward Intensive Competition in Team Games." *Research Quarterly* 24 (May 1953): 205–210.

McGee, Rosemary. "Comparison of Attitudes Toward Intensive Competition for High School Girls." *Research Quarterly* 27 (March 1956):60–73.

McPherson, B.D., and Yuhasz, M.S. "An Inventory for Assessing Men's Attitudes Toward Exercise and Physical Activity." *Research Quarterly* 39 (March 1968):218–219.

Mercer, Emily-Louise. "An Adaptation and Revision of the Galloway Attitude Inventory for Evaluating the Attitudes of High School Girls Toward Psychological, Moral-Spiritual, and Sociological Values in Physical Education Experiences." Master's thesis, The Woman's College of the University of North Carolina, 1961.

Penman, Mary M. "An Adaptation of Wear's Physical Education Attitude Inventory for Inner-City Junior High School Girls." Master's thesis, Wayne State University, 1967.

Richardson, Charles E. "Thurstone Scale for Measuring Attitudes of College Students Toward Physical Fitness and Exercise." *Research Quarterly* 31 (December 1960):638–643.

Scott, Phebe M. "Attitudes Toward Athletic Competition in Elementary School." *Research Quarterly* 24 (October 1953):352–361.

Seaman, Janet A. "Attitudes of Physically Handicapped Children Toward Physical Education." *Research Quarterly* 41 (October 1970):439–445.

Simon, Julie A., and Smoll, Frank L. "An Instrument for Assessing Children's Attitudes Toward Physical Education." *Research Quarterly* 45 (December 1974):407–415.

Wear, Carlos B. "Construction of Equivalent Forms of an Attitude Scale." *Research Quarterly* 26 (March 1955):113–119.

self-perception

Doudlah, Anna May. "Doudlah Movement-Concept Statements" and "Doudlah Body Image Statements." In *A Practical Approach to Measurement in Physical Education*. Edited by Harold R. Barrow and Rosemary McGee. Philadelphia: Lea and Febiger, 1971, pp. 466–471.

Gordon, Ira J. "How I See Myself Scale." In *A Practical Approach to Measurement in Physical Education*.

Edited by Harold R. Barrow and Rosemary McGee. Philadelphia: Lea and Febiger, 1971, pp. 457–464

Martinek, Thomas J., and Zaichkowsky, Leonard D. *"Development and Validation of the Martinek-Zaichkowsky Self-Concept Scale for Children."* Paper presented at the Research Section of the American Alliance for Health, Physical Education and Recreation, Milwaukee, Wisconsin, April 1976.

Nelson, Sara M. "Nelson Self-Concept Statements." In *A Practical Approach to Measurement in Physical Education*. Edited by Harold R. Barrow and Rosemary McGee. Philadelphia: Lea and Febiger, 1971, pp. 461–466.

Reynolds, Robert N. "Adjective Check List for Physical Education." In *A Practical Approach to Measurement in Physical Education*. Edited by Harold R. Barrow and Rosemary McGee. Philadelphia: Lea and Febiger, 1971, pp. 454–456.

Secord, Paul F., and Jourard, Sidney N. "The Appraisal of Body Cathexis: Body Cathexis and the Self." *Journal of Consulting Psychology* 17 (October 1953): 343–347.

summary review questions

1. What are the areas of concern in the affective domain? (*answer on p. 378*)

2. What is Kirkendall's hierarchy of a developing value construct for fair play? (*answer on p. 379*)

3. What are the general categories of instruments in the affective domain constructed to measure? (*answer on p. 380*)

4. What three ways is information usually collected in the affective domain? (*answer on p. 381*)

5. What are the types of rating scales? (*answer on p. 382*)

6. What are the problems and considerations involved in measuring aspects of the affective domain? (*answer on p. 384*)

7. What are the general purposes or reasons why teachers collect information in the affective domain? (*answer on p. 386*)

8. What types of affective instruments are listed in this chapter? (*answer on p. 387*)

bibliography

Baley, James, and Field, David. *Physical Education and the Physical Educator.* 2d ed. Boston: Allyn and Bacon, 1976.

Baumgartner, Ted, and Jackson, Andrew. *Measurement for Evaluation in Physical Education.* Boston: Houghton Mifflin, 1975.

Bucher, Charles. *Foundations of Physical Education.* 7th ed. St. Louis: C. V. Mosby, 1975.

Coopersmith, Stanley. *The Antecedents of Self-Esteem.* San Francisco: W. H. Freeman, 1967.

Cowell, Charles. "Our Function Is Still Education." *The Physical Educator* 14 (March 1957):6–7.

Cowell, Charles. "Validating an Index of Social Adjustment for High School Use." *Research Quarterly* 29 (March 1958):7–18.

Cowell, Charles, and Ismail, A. H. "Relationships Between Selected Social and Physical Factors." *Research Quarterly* 33 (March 1962):40–43.

Dexter, Genevie. *Teachers' Guide to Physical Education for Girls in High School.* Sacramento, Calif.: State Department of Education, 1957.

Ebel, Robert. "What Are Schools For?" *Phi Delta Kappan* 54 (1972):3–7.

Gruber, Joseph J. "Comments on the Reliability of a Personality Questionnaire Used in Physical Education and Sport Research." *International Journal of Sport Psychology* 9 (1978):111–118.

Gruber, Joseph J. and Beauchamp, Diane. "Relevancy of the Competitive State Anxiety Inventory in a Sport Environment." *Research Quarterly,* vol. 50, no. 2 (May 1979):207–214.

Guilford, J. P. *Psychometric Methods.* 2d ed. New York: McGraw-Hill, 1954.

Guttman, L. "The Cornell Technique for Scale and Intensity Analysis." *Educational and Psychological Measurement* 7 (1947):247–279.

Harris, Dorothy V. *Involvement in Sport: A Somatopsychic Rationale for Physical Activity.* Philadelphia: Lea and Febiger, 1973.

Jackson, W. P., and Lahaderne, H. M. "Scholastic Success and Attitude Toward School in a Population of Sixth Graders." *Journal of Educational Psychology* 58, no. 1 (1967):15–18.

Johnson, Barry, and Nelson, Jack. *Practical Measurements for Evaluation in Physical Education.* 2d ed. Minneapolis: Burgess, 1974.

Johnson, Marion. "Construction of a Sportsmanship Attitude Scale." *Research Quarterly* 40 (May 1969): 312–316.

Kenyon, Gerald. "A Conceptual Model for Characterizing Physical Activity." *Research Quarterly* 39 (March 1968):96–105.

Kenyon, Gerald, "Six Scales for Assessing Attitude Toward Physical Activity." *Research Quarterly* 39 (October 1968):566–574.

Kenyon, Gerald. *Values Held for Physical Activity by Selected Urban Secondary School Students in Canada, Australia, England and the United States.* Washington, D.C.: United States Office of Education, 1968.

Kirkendall, Don. "Physical Education Effects in the Affective Domain." In *Seventy-fifth Proceedings, National College Physical Education Association for Men,* 1972, pp. 147–151.

Krathwohl, David et al. *Taxonomy of Educational Objectives, The Classification of Educational Goals, Handbook II: Affective Domain.* New York: David McKay, 1964.

Kroll, Walter. "Current Strategies and Problems in Personality Assessment of Athletes." In *Psychology of Motor Learning,* edited by L. E. Smith. Chicago: The Athletic Institute, 1970.

Martens, Rainer. *Sport Competition Anxiety Test.* Champaign, Ill.: Human Kinetics, 1977.

Meyers, Carlton, and Blesh, T. Erwin. *Measurement in Physical Education.* New York: The Ronald Press, 1962.

Noland, Melody, and Gruber, Joseph. "Self-Perception, Personality, and Behavior in Emotionally Disturbed School Children." *Behavioral Disorders* 4, no. 1 (November 1978):6–12.

Osgood, C. et al. *The Measurement of Meaning.* Urbana, Ill.: University of Illinois Press, 1957.

Rushall, Brent S. "Environment Specific Behavior Inventories: Developmental Procedures." *International Journal of Sport Psychology* 9 (1978):97–110.

Simon, Julie, and Smoll, Frank. "An Instrument for Assessing Children's Attitudes Toward Physical Activity." *Research Quarterly* 45 (December 1974): 407–415.

Smith, Leon E. "Personality and Performance Research." *Quest* 13 (1970):74–83.

Stanley, Julian, and Hopkins, Kenneth. *Educational and Psychological Measurement and Evaluation.* Englewood Cliffs, N.J.: Prentice-Hall, 1972.

Thurstone, L. L. *The Measurement of Values.* Chicago: University of Chicago Press, 1959.

Following are two examples of outlines of measurement and evaluation programs. One is given for the secondary level and one for elementary school.

measurement and evaluation program for high school ninth-grade coeducational physical education

It will be assumed that the school year consists of thirty-two weeks of instruction. Physical education meets for three 50-minute periods per week. The following activities will be taught for the durations indicated.

Archery (4 weeks)	Badminton (5 weeks)
Gymnastics (6 weeks)	Basketball (4 weeks)
Swimming (6 weeks)	Golf (6 weeks)

Before the start of the year, students will be required to have a health appraisal by a physician in order to identify those students needing special programs, as well as providing the teacher with protection in a possible law suit. Necessary adaptations will be made for those students with special needs.

During the first week of school, the AAHPER Youth Fitness Test will be administered to all students. The 9-minute run-walk will be used as the cardiorespiratory endurance test in place of the 600-yard run-walk. Based on the results of this test, an individual fitness program will be planned for each student. For example, students who score low on upper body strength and endurance will be given a program designed to improve the same. Ten minutes at the beginning of each class period will be spent on fitness. It is during this time that roll can be taken. Testing of weak areas will be repeated every six weeks, and students' fitness programs will be adjusted according to the results. Each student will keep his/her own profile chart. Copies of these will also be kept by the teacher.

The results of the fitness tests will also be used in identifying students who will need special attention in the activities planned for the year. For example, the student who cannot do a single chin will need to use a very lightweight bow in archery.

For purposes of grading, students will be classified according to sex and a pretest for each activity. There will be three initial ability categories for each sex in each activity. In some activities there may be additional classification on body weight since in some activities body weight is negatively related to performance (see chapter 10). Grades will be determined solely on the basis of physical performance and written tests. The weight of each will be indicated later for each activity. An anecdotal record on each student will be kept in order to identify students who may be having special problems. These records will not be used in the determination of student grades. In general, the following distribution of grades will be used for each of the six units.

A—10%   C—45%   F—5%
B—25%   D—15%

Anytime a grade is assigned, consideration will be given for an individual student's circumstances.

The following is an outline of the tests to be used.

A. Archery
1. Pretest. AAHPER Archery Skills Test (chapter 8) will be administered in order to classify students into three groups for each sex and to identify the problems of individual students. This test will be repeated at least once every third class period.
2. Posttest. Same as pretest. It will count for 50 percent of student's grade.
3. Written test. A test on rules, safety, and technique will be given. It will

count for 50 percent of student's grade.

B. Badminton
1. Pretest. A rating scale similar to the one described on page 157 will be used while observing students playing during the first week of instruction. Students will be classified into three groups within each sex for instruction. The test results will be used to identify specific individual problems.
2. Posttest. A round robin tournament will be played within each group, and during that time the same rating scales will be applied. The rating scale score will count for 60 percent of the student's grade.
3. Written test. A test on rules, strategy, and technique will be given. It will count for 40 percent of the student's grade.

C. Gymnastics
1. Pretest. On the basis of the fitness test, students who are identified as lacking sufficient strength will be placed in appropriate activities. For each apparatus or tumbling item, students will perform progressive stunts until they reach a point in the progression where they cannot perform. This point will be determined subjectively by the teacher. This progression testing will be continuously applied throughout the unit.
2. Posttest. Each student will put together a routine consisting of three to five stunts for at least three apparatus or exercise items. Performance will be judged much the same as a gymnastics meet. However, difficulty will count in relation to where the student started the instructional unit. This will count as 70 percent of the student's grade.
3. Written test. A test on spotting and performance technique and on judging

rules will be given. This will count for 30 percent of the student's grade.

D. Basketball
1. Pretest. During initial drills, students will be rated on the skills of dribbling, passing, defense, and shooting. This will provide the direction of instruction for individuals throughout the remainder of the unit.
2. Posttest. Ratings will again be done during game playing conditions. These ratings will be compared to the initial ratings and a grade assigned by the teacher. This will constitute 40 percent of the grade.
3. Written test. A test on the various offenses and defenses, technique, and rules will be given for the other 60 percent of the grade.

E. Swimming
1. Pretest. Since swimming is available in this school, students will be classified into the Red Cross categories from Nonswimmer to Lifesaving. Programs for each category will be planned. Rating sheets such as the one given in chapter 8 will be completed for each stroke.
2. Posttest. An achievement test for high school swimming will be given within each classification group. This will constitute 60 percent of the grade.
3. Written test. A test on water safety and skill technique will be given for 40 percent of the grade.

F. Golf
1. Pretest. Students will be required to play nine holes of golf and turn in a verified score. Also, the golf rating scale presented in chapter 8 will be applied to each student.
2. Posttest. Students will again be required to play nine holes and the rating scale will again be applied. For 60 percent of the student's grade, im-

provement on the rating scale will be used with the improvement in the nine hole score being used for those "borderline" cases.
3. Written test. A test on club selection, rules, and etiquette will be given for the remaining 40 percent of the grade.

measurement and evaluation in the development of a fitness program for 8-year-old elementary school children

I. Proceed with Testing

Based on results of medical examinations on all pupils, proceed with testing for those ready for it.

II. Identify Testable Components

One of the major decisions that the physical education teacher has to make is what factors to test. Those factors chosen should be basic to human movement. In our example we have decided to test the following factors:
A. Strength-endurance complex
B. Speed-power complex
C. Agility-coordination complex

III. Choose Tests to Employ

Once the physical education teacher has decided what factors to test, he or she must decide what tests to employ. The tests chosen should measure those factors recognized by the physical education teacher as being important. The tests must be valid and reliable, should have normative data, and be economical and easy to administer. In our example, we have decided to use the AAHPER Youth Fitness Test.
A. Apply the AAHPER Youth Fitness Test.
1. Day one test items
a. Flexed-arm hang (measures

grip, arm, and shoulder girdle strength and endurance)
  b. Sit-ups (abdominal strength and endurance)
  c. Shuttle run (whole body agility)
  d. Standing broad jump (strength and power)
  2. Day two test items
    a. 40-yard (36.6-m) dash (speed)
    b. Softball throw (coordination)
    c. 400-yard (365.8-m) run-walk (cardiorespiratory endurance) Older children can run a longer distance.
B. Record results for each student for each event.
  1. Compare results to national norms. Record a percentile rank for each student.
  2. Calculate and record a mean for each event.
  3. Record the fiftieth percentile (P_{50}) score for each event from the national norm tables.
  4. Post national, regional, or local norms in the gym. The student can then find out how well he or she did.

IV. Make Decisions Based on Testing
    Examination of the recorded results will help the elementary physical education teacher determine areas of strength and weakness for the class as well as for each student. In our example, after appraising the recorded results, it was our decision to:
A. Compare the national normative P_{50} score for each event with that of the corresponding mean values for each event.
  1. Consider those mean values that fall below the normative P_{50} score as weak areas.
  2. Consider those mean values that

are at or above the normative P_{50} score as strength areas.
B. Examine each student's percentile rank in each event. Consider those students at or below the 20th percentile rank in any event as having serious problems needing special attention in those factors that the event indicates.

V. Establish Objectives
    The data we have recorded and appraised will allow us to establish realistic objectives. These objectives should be challenging but not frustrating. The establishment of measurable objectives will determine the physical activities we choose to use in our class program and for individual students. In our example, it was decided to establish the following objectives:
A. Group objective 1: When the mean value in an event falls below the P_{50} score from the national norms (weak areas), improve those mean values to at least the P_{50} score.
B. Group objective 2: When the mean value for an event is at or above the P_{50} score from the national norms (strength area), improve those mean values.
C. Individual objective 1: Have each student improve his percentile rank in each event.
D. Individual objective 2: Have each student whose percentile rank is 20 or below improve at least 15 percentile rank points.

VI. Design a Program Based on Objectives
    Establishing objectives allows the physical education teacher to decide what physical activities should be applied and with what intensity in order to improve those factors that have been evaluated as weak areas. Likewise, he or she can decide what activities should

be applied and with what intensity for strength areas. In other words, the physical education teacher now has an indication of the present functioning level of his class and each individual in it. He or she now has direction for choosing those physical activities that he hopes will improve the present level and not allow regression to occur in any of the basic factors.

In our example we have decided to present the results of testing twenty-five third-grade (8-year-old) children for each event. Table 14.2 presents the raw score for each child in each event with a calculated $\overline{X}$ score at the bottom of each event. Comparing the P_{50} score from Table 14.1 to the $\overline{X}$ value in Table 14.2 for each event, we find that our third-grade students as a whole have *weak areas* in the flexed-arm hang ($P_{50} = 11$, $\overline{X} = 10.16$), the sit-ups ($P_{50} = 36$, $\overline{X} = 34.04$), the softball throw ($P_{50} = 45'$, $\overline{X} = 42'$), and the 400-yard run-walk ($P_{50} = 1:52$, $\overline{X} = 1:56$).

Likewise, as a whole our third-grade class has *strength areas* in the shuttle run ($P_{50} = 12.6$, $\overline{X} = 12.62$), standing broad jump ($P_{50} = 3'11''$, $\overline{X} = 3'11''$), and the 40-yard dash ($P_{50} = 7.8$, $\overline{X} = 7.8$).

From the comparison of the norm P_{50} score and group $\overline{X}$'s we found this third-grade class lacking most in cardiorespiratory endurance. We decided to start each class session with 10 to 15 minutes of continuous movement to music. It was felt that this continuous movement could act as a warm-up before regular activity, and at the same time begin to correct the lack of cardiorespiratory endurance. We further decided to build a program of activities that would attack a weak area, then a strong area, in alternating order. An outline of our program follows:

A. Coordination (ball handling skills)
    1. Continuous movement music (10–15 minutes)
    2. Ball skills
        a. Basic
        b. Intermediate
        c. Advanced
B. Jumping and standing
    1. Continuous movement music (10–15 minutes)
    2. Jumping activities
        a. In place
        b. On the move
        c. Over apparatus

Table 14.1 P_{50} Score from Norm Tables AAHPER Fitness Test

Event	P_{50} Score for 8-Year-Olds (3rd Grade)
Flexed-arm hang in seconds	11
Sit-ups	36
Shuttle run in seconds	12.6
Standing broad jump in ft. or m	3'11" or 1.19 m
40-yard dash in seconds	7.8
Softball throw in ft. or m	45' or 13.7 m
400-yard run-walk in minutes and seconds	1 min. 52 sec.

From chapter 11, Testing Preschool and Early Elementary School Children, Tables 11.9 through 11.15.

Table 14.2   Raw Scores on Twenty-Five 8-Year-Old Third-Grade Children AAHPER Youth Fitness Test

Student	Flexed-arm hang (sec.)	Sit-ups (no.)	Shuttle run (sec.)	Standing broad jump (ft. and in.)	40-yd. dash (sec.)	Softball throw (ft.)	400-yd. run-walk (min. and sec.)
S1	9	34	12.5	3'11"	7.7	40'	1'57"
S2	7	30	12.6	3'10"	7.8	42'	1'58"
S3	11	39	12.6	4'	7.7	41'	1'57"
S4	11	38	12.3	4' 1"	7.6	45'	1'59"
S5	9	33	12.9	3'10"	7.8	40'	1'52"
S6	5	18	13.3	3' 6"	8.4	26'	2'11"
S7	12	40	12.6	4'	7.7	40'	1'51"
S8	8	24	13.2	3' 9"	7.7	38'	1'59"
S9	9	35	12.5	3'11"	7.6	41'	1'54"
S10	14	43	12.0	4' 1"	7.5	55'	1'50"
S11	13	44	12.2	4' 1"	7.6	49'	1'50"
S12	2	12	14.8	3' 3"	9.2	26'	2'42"
S13	8	24	12.7	3' 8"	8.0	43'	1'53"
S14	15	44	11.9	4' 3"	7.3	52'	1'47"
S15	10	37	12.6	3'11"	7.8	42'	1'52"
S16	10	35	12.6	3'10"	7.8	41'	1'54"
S17	14	45	12.3	4' 1"	7.5	52'	1'50"
S18	8	29	12.5	4'	7.9	38'	1'59"
S19	7	24	13.0	3' 6"	8.0	35'	2'
S20	9	35	12.5	3' 9"	7.8	41'	1'57"
S21	10	36	12.5	4' 1"	7.7	43'	1'57"
S22	14	40	12.4	4' 3"	7.5	46'	1'50"
S23	13	33	12.3	4' 3"	7.6	48'	1'52"
S24	15	45	12.2	4' 4"	7.5	50'	1'46"
S25	11	34	12.5	3'10"	7.9	40'	1'54"
	$\Sigma x = 254$	$\Sigma x = 851$	$\Sigma x = 315.5$	$\Sigma x = 98'$	$\Sigma x = 194.6$	$\Sigma x = 1054$	$\Sigma x = 48.5'$
	$\overline{X} = 10.16$	$\overline{X} = 34.04$	$\overline{X} = 12.62$	$\overline{X} = 3'11"$	$\overline{X} = 7.8$	$\overline{X} = 42'$	$\overline{X} = 1'56"$
	45th Percentile Rank	45th Percentile Rank	50th Percentile Rank	50th Percentile Rank	50th Percentile Rank	45th Percentile Rank	30th Percentile Rank

C. Developing muscular strength
1. Continuous movement music (10–15 minutes)
2. Basic gymnastics
  a. Mat and floor activities
    (1) Basic body positions
    (2) Stunts
      (a) Inchworm
      (b) Bear walk, etc.
  b. Tumbling
    (1) Rolls
    (2) Stands

(3) Balance
(4) Low vaulting box
c. Scooter board activities
(1) Prone activities
(2) Kneeling activities
(3) Races and scooter soccer
D. Speed and fun
1. Continuous movement music (10–15 minutes)
2. Group games
a. Speed games
b. Agility games
3. Novelty relays
E. Developing muscular endurance
1. Continuous movement music (10–15 minutes)
2. Bench
3. Ropes
4. Chinning bars
F. Rhythmic activities
1. Introductory activities
a. Scatter formation
b. Partner formations
c. Basic ways of moving
2. Mimetics in rhythms
a. Walking
b. Running
c. Galloping
3. Phrasing
a. Time
b. Weight
c. Space
d. Flow
G. Primary play days
Play days are different from the annual field day. In a play day the children in the class *participate in teams* rather than as individuals. Emphasis is upon participation rather than achievement of a few. Items to be included are:
1. Obstacle course team time
2. Standing broad jump team distance
3. High jump team height
4. Sit-ups team number
5. 400-yard run-walk team time
6. Softball throw for distance-team
7. Flexed-arm hang team time
8. 40-yard dash team time
9. Shuttle run team time
We will use the results of the play days as our first retest situation.
H. Identifying students who need special help
Table 14.3 presents the percentile rank for each student in each event compared to the national norms. Those students who scored in the 20 percentile rank or below were considered special problems who needed special attention. For example, student 12 (S12) needs special help in all the basic factors tested, namely: strength-endurance, speed-power, and agility-coordination. Student 6 (S6), on the other hand, needs special help in: strength-endurance and co-ordination.

As we go through the program, these students will be given special help by adapting the activities so they may be challenged to improve but not be frustrated. They will take part in the regular program but receive special attention from the teacher when necessary.
I. Retest (mid-year) all grade levels
1. Record the results of the play days
a. For each student
b. For each event
2. Compare results to national norms
a. Record a percentile rank for each student
b. Rank in descending order each student in each event
3. Calculate and record a mean for each event
J. Decisions about the program of activities
1. Compare the results of the present tests to the past tests
a. Are the group's objectives being attained? As a whole, has each grade level:

Table 14.3   Percentile Rank for Each Student in Each Event AAHPER Youth Fitness Test

Student	Flexed-arm hang	Sit-ups	Shuttle run	Standing broad jump	40-yd. dash	Softball throw	400-yd. run-walk
S1	40	45	55	50	55	40	25
S2	30	40	50	45	50	45	25
S3	50	55	50	55	55	40	25
S4	50	50	60	60	60	50	25
S5	40	45	40	45	50	40	30
S6	20*	20*	25	25	25	15*	20*
S7	50	55	50	55	55	40	35
S8	35	30	30	40	55	35	25
S9	40	50	55	50	60	40	30
S10	55	60	70	60	65	65	35
S11	55	60	65	60	60	55	35
S12	10*	10*	5*	10*	5*	15*	0*
S13	35	30	45	35	40	45	30
S14	60	60	75	70	70	60	45
S15	45	50	50	50	50	45	30
S16	45	50	50	45	50	40	30
S17	55	60	60	60	65	60	35
S18	35	40	55	55	45	35	25
S19	30	30	40	25	40	30	25
S20	40	50	55	40	50	40	25
S21	45	50	55	60	55	45	25
S22	55	55	55	70	65	50	35
S23	55	45	60	70	60	55	30
S24	60	60	65	70	65	60	70
S25	50	45	55	45	45	40	45

* Need special attention

(1) Improved in each event?
(2) Leveled in each event?
(3) Regressed in each event?
b. Are the individual objectives being attained? Has each individual:
(1) Improved in each event?
(2) Leveled in each event?
(3) Regressed in each event?

The present test results indicate the present level of each group and individual. Comparing the present test results to the past test results allows us to see if we are attaining the objectives and if necessary, we will redesign the program to meet the needs of the students. A series of cycles that serve for continuous modification of program and/or objectives will be established to improve the level of each participant.

appendix

application of analysis of variance in determining an intraclass correlation coefficient

As presented in chapter 5, the variability among any group of scores may be characterized as $\sigma_{os}^2 = \sigma_t^2 + \sigma_e^2$

where

σ_{os}^2 = total variance for observed scores

σ_t^2 = true score variance

σ_e^2 = error score variance

It was further stated in that chapter that

$$\text{reliability} = \frac{\sigma_t^2}{\sigma_{os}^2} = \frac{\sigma_{os}^2 - \sigma_e^2}{\sigma_{os}^2}$$

or that reliability is the relative proportion of total variance that is true score variance. The Pearson product-moment correlation coefficient was presented as one means of estimating this reliability. However, we saw the inadequacy of this technique when more than two trials of a test are administered, which is frequently the case in motor performance tests. In order to determine an appropriate reliability coefficient for multitrialed tests, an estimate of the variance components indicated above must be found. They are found by analysis of variance techniques, which allow the determination of an intraclass correlation coefficient.

For demonstrating the techniques desired, a simple example problem is presented here. Assume that four students performed the maximum number of chins that they could on three different occasions. The hypothetical results are presented in Table A.1.

Table A.1 Three Trials of Chins for Four Students

Student	Trial 1 Score	Trial 2 Score	Trial 3 Score	Student Total Score	Student Mean Score
A	9	8	9	26	8.67
B	1	2	3	6	2.00
C	3	2	2	7	2.33
D	5	5	3	13	4.33
Trial totals	18	17	17	52	
Trial means	4.5	4.25	4.25	4.33	

From chapter 4, we know that the variance for the entire group of twelve scores will be $\sigma_x^2 = \Sigma(X - \bar{X})^2/N$. However, since the use of analysis of variance requires the assumption of inference, we use

$$s_x^2 = \Sigma(X - \bar{X})^2/N - 1.$$

Further, we first wish to determine the total amount of *variation* present among scores, not the average variation or variance. Therefore, we find $\Sigma(X - \bar{X})^2$, which is the total sum of squares, denoted by SST. Thus, SST $= \Sigma(X - \bar{X})^2 = \Sigma X^2 - (\Sigma X)^2/N$, which for our example,

$$SST = 316 - (52^2/12) = 316 - \frac{2704}{12}$$
$$= 316 - 225.33 = 90.67$$

Now, our problem is to find the sum of squares for the true scores and the sum of squares for the error scores. If our scores were perfectly reliable, there would be no variation from trial to trial for each student. To determine the amount of trial-to-trial variation for each student, we find the sum of the squared differences between each trial score for a student and his mean score.

For example, student B's variation would be $(1 - 2)^2 + (2 - 2)^2 + (3 - 2)^2 = 1 + 0 + 1 = 2$. Symbolically, we can write this as

$$\Sigma(X_B - \bar{X}_B)^2 = \Sigma X_B^2 - T_B^2/n = (1^2 + 2^2 + 3^2) -$$
$$(6)^2/3 = (1 + 4 + 9) - \frac{36}{3} = 14 - 12 = 2$$

where $T_B = $ total score for student B and $n = $ number of trials.

For student A, we would have

$$\Sigma(X_A - \bar{X}_A)^2 = \Sigma X_A^2 - T_A^2/n = (81 + 64 + 81)$$
$$- (26)^2/3 = 226 - 676/3 = 226 - 225.33 = .67$$

Similarly, for student C we would have

$$\Sigma X_C^2 - T_C^2/n = 17 - \frac{49}{3} = 17 - 6.33 = .67$$

and for student D,

$$\Sigma X_D^2 - T_D^2/n = 59 - 169/3$$
$$= 59 - 56.33 = 2.67$$

Therefore, the total error variation, called the "sum of squares error (SSE)," is equal to the sum of the individual variations. In our example,

$$SSE = 2 + .67 + .67 + 2.67 = 6.01$$

This procedure condensed results in a general formula for finding SSE, which is much easier to use than separately finding the variation for each student. The condensed formula is: SSE $= \sum X^2 - \sum_{i}^{k} T_i^2 / n$

where

$T_i =$ the total score for student i

$k =$ number of students, and

$n =$ number of trials

To see that this works the same way for our example, if we use this condensed formula we find

$$\text{SSE} = \sum X^2 - \sum_{i}^{k} T_i^2 / n$$
$$= 316 - (676 + 36 + 49 + 169)/3$$
$$= 316 - 930/3 = 316 - 310 = 6$$

which, within rounding, is the same as before.

We would expect students, on the average, to differ in how well they perform. An estimate of this among student variation is defined as:

$$\text{SSA} = n \sum_{j=1}^{P} (\overline{X}_j - \overline{X})^2$$

where

$\overline{X}$ represents the overall mean or the mean of all scores

$\overline{X}_j$ represents the mean score for a particular student

p represents the number of students, and

n represents the number of trials

For our example:

$$\text{SSA} = 3[(8.67 - 4.33)^2 + (2 - 4.33)^2 +$$
$$(2.33 - 4.33)^2 + (4.33 - 4.33)^2]$$
$$= 3 (18.84 + 5.43 + 4 + 0) = 3(28.27)$$
$$= 84.81$$

A simpler formula to use for SSA is:

$$\text{SSA} = \sum_{i}^{k} T_i^2 / n - (\sum X)^2 / nk$$

where the symbols represent the same as before. Using this formula for the example problem, we find

$$\text{SSA} = 930/3 - 2704/(3 \times 4) = 310 - 225.33$$
$$= 84.67$$

which is the same, within rounding, as before. Notice that for our example, we have found:

SST $= 90.67$

SSE $= 6$, and

SSA $= 84.67$

In fact, SST $=$ SSA $+$ SSE.

In order to determine intraclass correlation, we must use variances instead of variations. These variance estimates are called "mean squares." In order to find the variance among the students scores (MSA) we divide the sum of squares among (SSA) by one less than the number of students, or $k - 1$. Thus, MSA $=$ SSA$/(k - 1)$.

For the error score, we divide the error sum of squares (SSE) by one less than the number of trials, or $n - 1$. Thus, MSE $=$ SSE$/(n - 1)$. In statistics, these divisors are called the *degrees of freedom* for each variation component and denoted as *df*. For our example, MSA $=$ SSA$/(k - 1) = 84.67/(4 - 1) = 84.67/3 = 28.22$ and MSE $=$ SSE$/(n - 1) = 6/(3 - 1) = 6/2 = 3.00$.

At first glance, we might think that MSA would be a likely candidate for estimating true score variance. However, MSA cannot actually be used as an estimate of true score variance since it in fact contains measurement error. This is so because in the calculation of SSA, the actual observed scores are used; these contain measurement error as well as the true score. So MSA is considered to be the total or obtained score variance in which we are interested. To find an actual estimate of the true score variance we must subtract the error score variance estimate from the among student variance estimates.

In other words,

estimated $\sigma_t{}^2 = \text{MSA} - \text{MSE}$

Since MSA is considered to be the total or obtained score variance in which we are interested, and reliability is defined as $\sigma_t{}^2/\sigma_{os}{}^2 = (\sigma_{os}{}^2 - \sigma_t{}^2)/\sigma_{os}{}^2$, our reliability estimate, called "intraclass correlation" and symbolized by R is defined as:

$$R = \frac{\text{MSA} - \text{MSE}}{\text{MSA}}$$

In our example:

$$R = \frac{28.22 - 3.00}{28.22} = \frac{25.22}{28.22} = .89$$

It should be noted that this coefficient is the estimated reliability for total scores. If one wishes to determine the reliability of some other number of trials, then the appropriate formula to use is:

$$R = \frac{\text{MSA} - \text{MSE}}{\text{MSA} + \left(\frac{n}{n'} - 1\right)\text{MSE}}$$

where n' is the desired number of trials for which a reliability estimate is needed.

In our example, if we wished to determine the reliability for a single trial, then $n' = 1$ and

$$R = \frac{25.22}{28.22 + \left(\frac{3}{1} - 1\right)3} = \frac{25.22}{28.22 + 6} = \frac{25.22}{34.22}$$

$$= .74$$

We can see that our original formula given for total score is a special case of this present formula, since in the original case $n = n'$ and $(n/n' - 1) = 0$. All of the procedures introduced thus far are summarized in Table A.2.

Table A.2 Analysis of Variance and Intraclass Correlation

Sources of Variation	Sum of Squares	Degree of Freedom	Mean Squares
Among students	SSA	$k - 1$	$\text{MSA} = \dfrac{SSA}{k - 1}$
Error	SSE	$n - 1$	$\text{MSE} = \dfrac{MSA}{n - 1}$

$$SSA = \sum^{k} T_i^2/n - \left(\sum X\right)^2/nk$$

$$SSE = \sum X^2 - \sum^{k} T_i^2/n$$

where

n = number of trials

k = number of students

T_i = total score for student i

Intraclass correlation $R = \dfrac{\text{MSA} - \text{MSE}}{\text{MSA} + \left(\dfrac{n}{n'} - 1\right)\text{MSE}}$

It must be emphasized that the procedures described above have assumed that no trend exists across trials. More specifically, it has been assumed that there is not a significant difference among trial means. For our example, we saw that the trial means were: $\overline{X}_1 = 4.5$, $\overline{X}_2 = 4.25$, and $\overline{X}_3 = 4.25$, which subjectively would indicate that no trial-to-trial trend exists.

The technique for objectively determining the existence of trend requires the application of an inferential statistical procedure called "two-way analysis of variance." This method will not be presented here. Rather, it is suggested that at this point in your studies you always determine the means of each trial, and if there subjectively appears to be trend present, use the trials where stability appears to be present in the determination of intraclass correlation and the subsequent use of the test.